THE LIFE AND MYTH OF

CHARMIAN
CLIFT

THE LIFE AND MYTH OF

CHARMIAN CLIFT

Nadia Wheatley

flamingo
An imprint of HarperCollins*Publishers*

The writing of this project was assisted by the Commonwealth Government through the Australia Council, its arts funding and advisory body.

Flamingo
An imprint of HarperCollins*Publishers*, Australia

First published in Australia in 2001
by HarperCollins*Publishers* Pty Limited
ABN 36 009 913 517
A member of the HarperCollins*Publishers* (Australia) Pty Limited Group
http://www.harpercollins.com.au

HarperCollins*Publishers*
25 Ryde Road, Pymble, Sydney, NSW 2073, Australia
31 View Road, Glenfield, Auckland 10, New Zealand
77–85 Fulham Palace Road, London, W6 8JB, United Kingdom
Hazelton Lanes, 55 Avenue Road, Suite 2900, Toronto, Ontario M5R 3L2
and 1995 Markham Road, Scarborough, Ontario M1B 5M8, Canada
10 East 53rd Street, New York NY 10022, USA

National Library of Australia Cataloguing-in-Publication data:

Wheatley, Nadia, 1949– .
The life and myth of Charmian Clift
Bibliography.
Includes index.
ISBN 0 7322 6885 0.
1. Clift, Charmian, 1923–1969. 2. Women authors, Australian – 20th century – Biography.
3. Authors, Australian – 20th century – Biography.
4. Johnston, George, 1912–1970. I. Title.
A828.309

Cover design by Katie Mitchell, HarperCollins Design Studio
Map: The Telltale Art – Trudi Canavan
Typeset by HarperCollins in 10.5/14 Minion
Printed and bound in Australia by Griffin Press on 70gsm Ensobelle

5 4 3 2 1   01 02 03 04

If the fixture of Momus's glass in the human breast, according to the proposed emendation of that arch-critic, had taken place, [...] nothing more would have been wanting, in order to have taken a man's character, but to have taken a chair and gone softly, as you would to a dioptrical bee-hive, and looked in, — viewed the soul stark naked; — observed all her motions, — her machinations; — traced all her maggots from their first engendering to their crawling forth; — watched her loose in her frisks, her gambols, her capricios; and after some notice of her more solemn deportment, consequent upon such frisks, &c— then taken your pen and ink and set down nothing but what you have seen, and could have sworn to: — But this is an advantage not to be had by the biographer in this planet.

Laurence Sterne, *The Life and Opinions of Tristram Shandy*[1]

CONTENTS

PART III

THE PROMISED LAND

PART IV

RETURN TO ITHACA

AUTHOR'S NOTE

'This story is fiction. The characters do not exist, nor did the incidents occur, excepting in my imagination'. Thus Charmian Clift, in the Author's Note for her novel *Honour's Mimic,* distanced herself from any obligation to defend the truth of her tale. Her husband George Johnston, in the note to his autobiographical novel *My Brother Jack,* took a somewhat different stance by way of quoting the French writer André Gide: 'Fiction there is — and history. Certain critics of no little discernment have considered that fiction is history which *might* have taken place, and history fiction which *has* taken place'. In regard to the work at hand, it would be amusing to follow Clift's line that 'This story is fiction', but maybe more true to paraphrase Gide: in the case of Charmian Clift and George Johnston, biography is 'fiction which *has* taken place'.

Where, then, lies the truth?

In this book I try to keep myself off the page. I never met Charmian Clift or George Johnston, and I was not present during any of the incidents that take place in this account. Everything I know comes from interviews; from written texts ranging from letters to fiction (published and unpublished) to secondary sources; and — I have to admit it — from my imagination. Like any historian, I am sometimes forced to make deductions in order to fill in the spaces that lie between the available sources. As obviously all the opinion in this book is mine, it seemed unnecessary to state this at every point. Of course, this technique of the invisible narrator is an artifice: the writer is still, in fact, present on every page. However, as I am not overtly there for the reader to interrogate, it seems only fair that I start by declaring my hand, in regard both to my relationship with the subject of this book, and to my historiographical approach. This is particularly the case because, while my viewpoint on the events is mainly that of an outsider, at times I had, willy-nilly, a bit of an inside view. To explain this, I have to begin with something of my own story.

In my second year at Sydney University, in 1967, I found myself in a weekly English Honours seminar in which — among the fifteen or twenty other students — there was a very tall and very thin young man with long dark hair and long white hands. He always wore black skivvies and black trousers and he sat beneath the arched Gothic window of the seminar room and incessantly smoked black Sobranies. It seemed as if the tutor spent the whole session eliciting this particular student's opinions on the required reading for the week, and this young man would answer in a light, precise voice, and these answers would be pedantically erudite, and once he gave them, none of the other students would ever dare disagree. At the end of each seminar, as I was leaving, I would hear the tutor talking to this young man about some latest thing that his parents had written, or perhaps some thing which had been written about his parents.

I could not help but be aware that this student's father had published a highly acclaimed novel called *My Brother Jack,* which I hadn't got around to reading. I'd somehow also missed the television serial of the same name, which had gone to air on Saturday nights towards the end of 1965; perhaps, like many other young Australians, I had been watching the *Mavis Bramston Show,* which was on at the same time. Although I didn't know that this student's mother had written the script for the TV show, I did know that she wrote a weekly column in the *Sydney Morning Herald.* So infuriated was I, however, by something about the young man that I did not read his mother's column. If I wouldn't read things *by* these writers, I also wasn't going to read *about* them; and so, over the next few years, although I was generally aware of the lives and then the deaths of Charmian Clift and George Johnston, I did my best to avoid information about this family. Somehow, the whole media thing really annoyed me; it was (I realise now) the Clift/Johnston myth that I loathed.

Over these years, the student himself abandoned university, and became initially a journalist and later a scrounging freelancer, in order to support his habit of writing poetry. Meanwhile, I also escaped the English Department, and majored in Australian history. By the winter of 1972, I was enrolled in a masters degree when my circle of pub friends came to include a number of chess players, and through this I found myself sometimes sitting at the same table as Martin Johnston. I guess it helped that he was always totally absorbed in moving pieces around a board, for he didn't seem nearly as pretentious as the young man from the English Honours seminars. It probably also helped that he had changed from Sobranies to Alpine, although he still marked his individuality by having a dash of cloves in his beer. And as I was on a Commonwealth postgraduate scholarship and he was totally broke, I sometimes bought him a beer (with a dash of cloves), and he always thanked me in a way that was almost excessively polite. By the time summer came, we were living together.

Of course, something else happened in Australia in 1972, something even more momentous than a love affair. I mean, of course, the election of the Labor Government, which put an end to the conservative rule which seemed to have held the nation in thrall for two decades. Indeed, looking now at this story from the outside, and with the benefit of hindsight, I find a curious symmetry to the fact that it was in this year that marked the end of a political era that I came to know Martin and (by repute) his parents, for it was in direct response to the beginning of the Menzies period that Charmian Clift and George Johnston had left Australia and begun their expatriate life.

More immediately, for Martin, the election of the Whitlam Government offered the possibility of a year's reprieve from the grinding poverty and drudgery of a freelance writer's life. In 1973 the Literature Board of the Australia Council received increased funding, and a greatly enlarged program of grants was advertised. As just about everyone who had ever published a poem was going to apply, Martin decided that he would have a greater chance of success if he put himself forward in a different genre. Turning to the subject matter which was closest at hand, he volunteered to write a kind of memoir of his parents. I remember him talking about Edmund Gosse's *Father and Son* as the sort of literary model which he had in mind. That is, his work would be a personal view from inside the family circle. At the time, I did not see as significant the fact that he chose a model which examines the relationship between two generations of men. This was quickly irrelevant, anyway, for when Martin actually received what seemed like the extraordinary sum of $5000, he embarked upon an experimental novel entitled *Cicada Gambit*.

During these early years of living with Martin, I read most of the books that Charmian Clift and George Johnston had published, and naturally I absorbed bits and pieces of information about Martin's parents. In conversation, Martin would frequently refer to something which 'Mum always said' or which 'Dad used to say', and I developed a fairly strong idea of what his parents had believed about life, literature, politics, and so on. At the same time, there were little details such as the fact that 'Dad used to make a really good egg and bacon pie' or 'When my mother was a little girl, she used to starbake on the beach at night, in the belief that she would turn silver'. There were other contributors to my impression of Martin's family life, because we would also sometimes see people who had been friends of his parents, as well as occasionally having a meal with his sister Shane or his brother Jason. All of this built up a picture, in the same way that I no doubt created a picture for Martin of my dead mother and my long-absent father. But we didn't ever sit down and consciously talk about our parents: we were young, and much more interested in ourselves.

Martin's novel was rejected, my postgraduate work in history was completed, and life went on. As the Greek Junta fell in 1974 and the Whitlam Government suffered a coup in 1975, Martin and I switched countries. At the same time, I switched to writing fiction. During the next two and a half years, while we lived in Greece, I sometimes met former friends and acquaintances of the Johnstons, such as George's great friend Grace Edwards, and other people who had been part of the Hydra scene. Apart from Grace, however, Martin usually tried to avoid these contacts and, in this whole Greek sojourn, we spent only one night on Hydra.

Perhaps the most significant thing that I learned about Charmian Clift and George Johnston, through Martin, was their commitment to writing on a regular basis. In this period, Martin would sit at the typewriter for up to eight hours a day, six days a week, for ten months of the year. Stuck in a village or small town with no one to talk to in English apart from Martin himself — what could I do but follow his example, which he in turn had acquired from his parents? Although the regular practice of writing every day — come hell or high hangover — was a great legacy which Martin bequeathed to me, as I became more and more committed to my own writing, and as the prospect of returning to Australia loomed in 1978, I found myself wondering whether there was room in a relationship for two writers. If Martin were to tell the story of why our partnership ended, it would no doubt be different. However, I know that he would agree that the friendship, and in particular our interest in talking to each other about books and writing, remained.

* * *

In 1979, when we were back in Sydney but no longer living together, Martin again received Literature Board support to research a biography of his parents. This particular grant funded travel to Greece, where Martin talked to Grace Edwards and other associates of his parents, and even spent a couple of nights on Hydra, staying in a hotel which had once been a house where a family friend had hanged himself. A sonnet entitled 'Biography', written at this time, reveals something of Martin's distaste for the project he had undertaken:

> Back past the sold houses in the lost domains
> down in the midden-humus
> glows the rotting trelliswork of 'family',
> odd slug-coloured tubers wince at the touch
> with feigned unanthropomorphic shyness,
> naked pink tendrils explore holes.

By the time Martin returned to Australia in March 1980, he was very apprehensive about the personal pain which would be involved in writing about his parents. However, he still felt himself to be committed to the project. One Literature Board grant could be shrugged aside; it was harder to ignore two.

Meanwhile, I had completed a novel, which nobody seemed to want to publish. Although I had received some funding for a film script, I had been living on the dole for most of the previous eighteen months and I was wondering if I would ever survive as a writer of fiction. That was my problem, the day that Martin arrived for lunch and started talking about the problems he was having, writing a biography of his parents. As we discussed his situation, it emerged that he felt that his particular area of difficulty was in dealing with the half of the story which would be about Charmian Clift. This was partly because of unresolved pain and confusion connected with his mother's death. Martin also talked about the fact that, as a man, he did not feel that he would be able to enter imaginatively into the experience of a woman, in the way which would be necessary in order to write her biography. On top of that, he complained, the thing which he hated about the biography was all the time that he would have to spend in libraries. This was made particularly difficult by the fact that you couldn't smoke in libraries, and Martin couldn't concentrate without a cigarette.

At what stage of that afternoon did we get the crazy notion that we could both solve our work problems by combining them? All I know is that, by the time Martin left, we had a piece of paper on which we had a plan for a collaborative biography of Charmian Clift and George Johnston

The idea was, we would together write a study of two writers who were collaborators. According to our one-page outline, Martin would be responsible for the chapters dealing with Johnston, and I would be responsible for the chapters dealing with Clift. While we proposed to share our work back and forth as we wrote, the plan was that there would be two distinct voices — one male and one female — running through the text, as we respectively discussed the male and female subjects. There were also to be 'interludes' in which our two voices would discuss the ideas which could not be parcelled off into the two separate areas.

It is clear from this that the text was to approach Clift and Johnston primarily as writers, and through their written work. In particular, it was the idea of collaboration in which we were most interested. We planned to focus our study on the writing partnership, particularly the cross-fertilisation and sharing of ideas from one writer to another. In a situation where the two collaborators were the kind of writers who draw directly from personal experience and autobiographical material, any study of the literary partnership would naturally raise questions about the use of material, the ownership of joint experience, and the way the mind plays an editorial role in the selecting and shaping of memory. This in turn raised issues to do with the nature of fiction, and the whole process of the literary imagination.

As far as Martin was concerned, the immediate benefit which he would get from our collaboration would be that I would do most of the research. Although I also disliked working in libraries, I was fairly accustomed to spending weeks wading through newspaper files, making slabs of notes, organising material, keeping footnotes and sources in order. I also had experience in preparing and conducting oral history interviews and transcribing audiotapes. (Martin's interviews so far had been conducted without tape recorder or even notepad.)

For me, the project seemed a way that I could maybe use some of my training and experience. While I hadn't really thought much about the historiography of biography, I imagined that it was positioned somewhere between history and fiction. That is, I thought it would require the analytical approach of a historian, combined with a novelist's ability to enter into the mind of a character. Naively, I thought that being a bit of a historian and a bit of a fiction writer might suit me for this hybrid genre.

Fairly soon after we agreed on the deal I went to Canberra and began some preliminary research in the National Library, where the papers of Charmian Clift and George Johnston are stored. In July of that year, Martin got a job subtitling Greek movies for the fledgling Special Broadcasting Service. I also had other things happening in my life, including at last the acceptance of my first novel. There was no real urgency about the biography, but I kept sporadically doing research.

I guess it was in 1982 that Martin told me that he had been approached by an academic who wanted to do a PhD about George Johnston's writing. A bit later, Martin told me that this academic's thesis was now to be a biography, intended for publication. There wasn't room in the market for two books on George Johnston, Martin declared, and so he was pulling out of his half of our project. However, he insisted that he had told Garry Kinnane that I was 'doing' the Clift half of the story.

I didn't want to write a biography, under those terms. I couldn't see how the material could be divided into a 'Johnston' book and a 'Clift' book. It wasn't fair on Garry Kinnane, or on me, or on Charmian Clift, or on George Johnston. I told Martin that I wanted to abandon the work. By now I was living in Melbourne, and planning to move to a remote area of the Victorian countryside. My first book was published. I had finished my second novel, and was at work on my third. Why would I want to write a biography?

Martin was adamant, however, that I should write a book about his mother. Over the next few years, every time I tried to winkle out of it, he would say, 'Oh, but Nard ...' And I would give in.

So, in a half-hearted fashion, I started to build up my research material, both from interviews and from primary and secondary written sources, in between doing what I wanted to do — which was to write fiction. Meanwhile, Martin withdrew so completely from the project that he would only consent twice to be interviewed by me — once at the ABC studios, for a radio program which I did in collaboration with Garry Kinnane, and once at dinner in a restaurant, on condition that I didn't have a tape recorder.

I say this in order to make it clear that, while my first impressions of the domestic and professional lives of Charmian Clift and George Johnston had been unconsciously gleaned during the seven years when Martin and I were living together, Martin had no hand in the development of this text, and indeed he did not read any of the work-in-progress. I should also say that there were no guidelines for the project. Just as Martin had stressed in his

Literature Board application in 1979 that his solo work would neither be hagiographic nor 'Official/Authorised', Martin simply said that he didn't want me to write a hagiography. There was no notion that my work would have some sort of seal of family authorisation or approval. As a historian, I could not have agreed to work under any conditions about content or interpretation.

At the same time, although I knew Charmian and George's younger son, Jason, and saw him quite often through all these years, I believed that he had no interest in what I would write. And as I also mistakenly thought that he, like Martin, did not want to talk about his family, I did not ask for his version of events until I had completed a draft of the whole story. I wish that I had consulted him earlier. However, my involvement in this project has often caused me to feel as if I were walking on eggshells.

Overall, it sometimes seemed as if I had the worst of both worlds, in regard to being both inside and outside the circle of family and friendship. While I felt I was too far 'in' to be told some things, I was too far 'out' to be told other things. There were quite a few people whom I knew socially, through the Johnston connection, who did not wish to be formally interviewed, but who nevertheless talked to me about Charmian and George. The result of this was that I sometimes ended up with information which I could not include. Particularly problematic was an affectionate relationship which developed with Charmian's sister, Margaret Backhouse (whom I had not known when I was living with Martin). After a while I started to visit her in order to see *her*, and not to talk about her sister.

There was also the whole business of deciding what sort of historiographical approach I would take. Even with Martin out of the project, my main interest was still with Clift as a writer. As Clift happened to be a female writer, I was also interested in how her gender affected her career. This would have come into play no matter what occupation her husband had followed. But as her partner was a male writer, his career provided a convenient point of comparison.

To this degree, the theoretical framework of my study could be categorised as feminist. And after all, the politics of feminism were bound up in the reason that Martin wanted me to take part in the project in the first place. As well as this, it seemed to me that a feminist approach was relevant to this subject, whose writing and life had foreshadowed some of the preoccupations of second wave feminism which were starting to float around at the time of her death.

This brings me to my next area of concern. Essentially, I am a social historian before I am a biographer. I was interested in writing about a life which raised certain social and political issues of the watershed period from the 1920s to the 1960s. Of course, Charmian Clift was not a 'typical' woman of her time. But that is the point. By seeing how and why this particular square peg did not fit into the round hole which society had fashioned for her, we can gain some insight into the lives and expectations of other women and wives and mothers who seemed to fit more neatly into their economic, domestic and social roles, and yet who instantly identified with the attitudes expressed in Clift's newspaper column.

A final historiographic matter needs to be raised. As well as avoiding the personal pronoun, I choose to present the material here as a chronological narrative. It is true that fracturing and fragmenting a biographical narrative is a way of highlighting interesting juxtapositions. However, such a method can tend to increase the problem of distortion which is already inherent in the act of writing — and reading — biography.

In her novel *According to Mark*, the British author Penelope Lively has her biographer hero Mark realise that he 'contemplates [his subject] all the time with the wisdom of foresight'. That is, as Mark researches his subject's early life, he does it in the light of knowledge which his subject did not have, about how the life would turn out, and even end. While this 'wisdom of foresight' means that the biographer has a tendency to shape the material so that it seems to reveal its significance in terms of subsequent events, it is also the case that the reader usually approaches the story of the subject's life with a similar pre-existing knowledge. It is, after all, part of the nature of reading a biography that, when we start, we tend to know the broad details of the subject's life, in a way we do not know the plot of a novel before we read it. Thus we read the life knowing what the subject did not know: which was how the tale would end.

This is especially difficult if, as in Charmian Clift's case, the story ends in suicide. While, by its taboo nature, this form of death seems to create a particular type of curiosity, many people seem so determined to find a 'cause' for it that anything — or everything — in the life is seen as leading to the death. If I had any single historiographic aim, it was to try to present the life as Charmian herself lived it, not knowing what the next day would bring. In other words, I wanted to *not* write a life which seemed to lead inevitably to a death.

There was also another reason why an old-fashioned combination of chronological method and third-person narrator seemed to me the right one for the book. This was because, in various tellings of the story of Charmian Clift, there had already been a considerable blurring of the boundaries between fact, fiction and myth. The confusion in people's perceptions of Clift's life had been furthered by the deliberate fragmentation and rearrangement of chronology which had occurred in George Johnston's second autobiographical novel, *Clean Straw for Nothing*. In response to this, I felt that the sober accumulation of information — alleviated by occasional dashes of imagination — was the only way to separate the life from the legend. And yet, while I have tried to be factual, this study does not pretend to be the full truth, or indeed the final word.

Nadia Wheatley, 2001

ACKNOWLEDGEMENTS

My first thanks go to the Johnston Estate — Jason Johnston, Roseanne Bonney and Rebecca O'Connor — for permission to quote from letters and drafts as well as the published writing of Charmian Clift and George Johnston. Additional thanks go to Jason, for agreeing to be interviewed for this book and for allowing me to reproduce photographs from his family collection. In thanking Jason, I should stress that his assistance does not mean that this is in any way an authorised biography. While the book could not have been completed without his co-operation, he may not agree with my interpretation.

This book could also not have been written without the time and help given to me by many friends and colleagues of Charmian Clift and George Johnston, in the form of interviews, letters, and telephone conversations. Although I took so long to write the book that many of the people involved are not able to read it, I would still like to record my gratitude to Mary Andrews, Allan Ashbolt, Margaret Backhouse, Toni Burgess, James Calomeras, June Crooke, Anne Deveson, Hume Dow, Maisie Drysdale, Joan Flanagan, Cedric Flower, Bet Hall, Rodney Hall, Edward Heffernan, Greeba Jamison, Barbara Jefferis, Bruce Kneale, Patricia Lovell, Mungo MacCallum, Tessa Mallos, Jo Meyer, John Douglas Pringle, Ray Taylor, Margaret Vaile, Storry Walton, Nona Wood.

My thanks also go to the Kiama people who talked to me about their memories of Charmian and her family during the 1920s and 1930s: Jean Brown, Mrs Davies, Maisie James, Mavis Keavis, Joan King, Cecily Leatham, Roy Phillis, Mrs Richardson, Neil Simmons, Cliff Sweet, Marg Weston.

Thanks also to people who provided additional mementoes or memories, especially Douglas Barrie, Joan Fraser, Clifford Meredith, Harry Pike, Jean Skea, Mrs Telfer, Graham Tucker, Albie Thoms.

I am grateful to Suzanne Chick for permission to quote from *Searching for Charmian*, to Garry Kinnane for permission to quote from *George Johnston: A Biography* and to Rodney Hall, for permission to quote from his Introduction to *The World of Charmian Clift*.

I am also indebted to the following libraries and research facilities: Mitchell Library, State Library of New South Wales (for the Angus & Robertson Collection); National Library of Australia (for the Charmian Clift Collection and the George Johnston Collection); Australian Archives (for the Commonwealth Literary Fund Records); Harry Ransom Humanities Research Center, The University of Texas at Austin (for the David Higham Archives); Manuscripts Department, Lilly Library, Indiana University (for the Bobbs-Merrill Collection).

To thank all of those who have provided personal support during the last twenty one years would require another volume. I will therefore simply thank Jenny Pausacker and Ken Searle. In addition, many people have provided professional assistance, but I will limit my thanks to the book's freelance editor, Jo Jarrah, and my editor in-house at HarperCollins, Vanessa Radnidge.

Finally, I wish also to thank the Literature Fund of the Australia Council and its supporters, the Australian taxpayers. It is extraordinarily expensive for anyone not employed by a tertiary institution to engage in a lengthy non fiction project. Without Australia Council assistance, I could not have afforded to write this book.

PROLOGUE

Where does it start? Where does it end? Is there any true line of demarcation between what is veritable and what is not?[1]

We cannot overcome the tendency to shape ourselves in the image other people have of us. People we meet cast us in a role, and we play it whether we will or not. It is not so much the example of others we imitate as the reflection of ourselves in their eyes.[2]

This is the story of three women — a real woman, called Charmian Clift, a fictional woman, best known as Cressida Morley, and a third woman, who has become more famous than either of these. This third figure is the mythical Charmian — partly the product of the inventions of Clift herself and her husband George Johnston, but even more the creation of a collaboration between the Australian media and the Australian public. While the biographies of these three women are of considerable interest in themselves, this book is also concerned with mapping the invisible boundaries that lie between the territories known as 'real life', 'fiction' and 'myth'.

To some extent, we all fabricate at least something of our biographical stories. Even Sigmund Freud is supposed to have said: 'We don't remember our childhood. We remember our memories of our childhood'. And yet while most people live their lives twice — once when the events occur, and another time in the selective and partly imagined memory of those events — the difference with Charmian Clift is a matter of purpose and of degree. Like many authors, Clift set out to write her account of her early life for publication as an autobiographical novel. But she didn't do this once, and get it over with. She did it again and again, through three decades of abandoned typescripts.

It seems that even in childhood, Charmian was already imagining a kind of parallel version of her life, featuring a young girl who was similar to her, but far happier and more successful. When she began writing seriously, in her late teens or early twenties, her subject was herself and her home town landscape. By the beginning of her professional career, in the late 1940s or early 1950s, Charmian Clift was naming her alter ego 'Christine Morley' in various drafts of an autobiographical novel entitled *Greener Grows the Grass*. In 1962 Charmian Clift renamed this character 'Cressida Morley' when she started the novel again, with the title *The End of the Morning*.[3]

While neither of these texts was completed and none of Clift's writing about the Morley family was ever published, the author's husband George Johnston, working sometimes alone and sometimes in collaboration with his wife, also used aspects of the character and experience of Charmian Clift to develop a fictional female character who went under a couple of different names and who adopted slightly different guises. In particular, as Clift in the Greek winter of 1962–63 put aside her work on *The End of the Morning* so that she could assist her sick husband with *his* autobiographical novel, her fictional alter ego slipped from one text to the other. Thus the reading public first became acquainted with Cressida Morley when George Johnston's novel *My Brother Jack* was published in 1964. While Cressida makes only a cameo appearance in that work, the character of the green-eyed gunner with sand between her toes is so vivid that she immediately took an unforgettable place in contemporary Australian fiction. This place would be confirmed when Cressida reappeared in the second book of Johnston's trilogy in the guise of a beautiful but unfaithful wife.

While the development — the biography — of Cressida Morley is problematic, the difficulties compound when Charmian Clift in 'real life' seems to follow patterns foreshadowed in the fictions, growing into Cressida Morley or her other alter egos in the same way that the early autobiographical characters grew out of Charmian Clift.

As the process of writing and rewriting — of creating role after role and alter ego after alter ego — went on, the story of the past went through a series of changes. It would be simple to say that, as these texts were purporting to be fiction, then all versions are 'true'. However, as fictional details started to feel like memories, these 'memories' were also incorporated into the overtly non-fictional record of Clift's newspaper column, and they further appeared in interviews which the author gave. In this way, the writer's fiction began to turn into myth.

As time went on, Clift increasingly blurred the boundaries between public and private, between fiction and non-fiction, and between her work and her life. The ultimate manifestation of this is the alter ego persona that Charmian Clift adopted, under her own name, for the weekly newspaper column which she published between 1964 and 1969. Sometimes the writer dropped into this column whole slabs of the 'fiction' narrated by Cressida Morley.

While this biography sets out to explore the way in which a writer (or, in this case, *two* writers) draw upon life in order to create fiction, the story of Charmian Clift also reveals the way in which fiction can start to influence and even direct life — causing new 'real' events which in turn influence or direct the next development in the 'fiction'. When experience immediately becomes grist to the writer's mill, it is sometimes only a small step to the creation or provocation of events in order to improve the plot or move the story along. Thus to a great degree Charmian Clift could be seen as an autobiographical writer who self-consciously lived out her text, with herself as both hero and narrator. This life/novel crosses between the genres of autobiography, fiction and non-fiction in a distinctly postmodern fashion.

It can be dangerous, of course, to cross boundaries. While George Johnston's self-assurance grew as he charted the development of his alter ego David Meredith, Charmian Clift privately became less and less secure as she increasingly found herself publicly revealed, either in her own creations or in those of her husband. Perhaps the problem lies in the fact that the Cressida Morley story was a collaborative novel. As the model for the character increasingly lost her 'real' identity, it became more and more difficult for her to keep control of the plot.

Overall, Charmian Clift's published literary output was relatively small, consisting as it does of three novels written in partnership with her husband, two travel books, two solo novels, and 225 essays. Of her two decade career as a published writer, she spent only eight of these twenty-one years in her homeland. Yet her effect on Australian society was far greater than these statistics suggest. In every generation there are certain writers who function as national weather vanes, recording change in the social and political climate. Charmian Clift was one of these. Yet as well as recording political change in the volatile years of the 1960s, she was also instrumental in helping Australian society discard many of the narrow and xenophobic values which it had held through the Cold War period.

Outside the covers of their various texts, the lives of Charmian Clift and George Johnston encapsulated certain archetypal elements of the twentieth century Australian experience. George Johnston's autobiographical novel *My Brother Jack* was both a popular and a literary success because it told the story that a generation of Australians had lived, through the period between the wars. Clift's story — published in snippets through her column — picked up the tale of a Depression childhood and presented a liberated woman's view of life on the suburban home front. While Charmian Clift and George Johnston did not consciously set out to shape Australian identity and history, they are nevertheless significant transformational figures. Again and again we find them expressing ideas that would not become current for years or even decades. More significantly, we find them not just thinking but acting on and living out these ideas. For example, finding life in post-war Australia politically and socially claustrophobic, they voted against Menzies by living in exile. Returning to their homeland after thirteen years, they immediately engaged with challenges such as Australia's role in Asia and the increasingly multicultural nature of Australian society. If these were some of the political themes of the Great Australian Novel which these two writers collaboratively presented to their compatriots, the tale could be subtitled 'The Story of a Modern Marriage'.

To a great degree Charmian Clift and George Johnston played out in their own relationship in the 1950s and 1960s the conflict of the realignment of gender roles which would be the subject of feminist theory and debate in the 1970s. Not only did they tackle issues of freedom and control within relationships at a time when most post-war marriages were placidly following the pre-war model, but they confronted these issues in a particularly head-on way. Just as Charmian Clift was passionately committed to a belief in her inalienable right to personal freedom, George Johnston — born half a generation earlier — was at heart a traditional husband. Yet because of his generally liberal views, he would question his own position and try to understand what he could not endorse. Naturally, in the manner of revolutionary vanguardists, these two discovered that omelettes cannot be made without the breaking of eggs.

It is because Clift and Johnston were forerunners and extremists that the story of their lives and their relationship has become important to many Australian people — even to those who have barely read a word they wrote.

They were archetypes; ourselves writ large; experimenters who could test and try things for us; legendary figures through whom we could live vicariously. So important were they as cultural figures that their story is still current, three decades after their deaths. Through their lives they may have written the Great Australian Novel, but since their deaths they have developed into mythical figures.

Of course, while myth has no real beginning or end, it also does not bother itself with cause and effect. Nor does it worry about contradictions. Parallel tellings are vital to the fabric. Truth is an irrelevance. In life, however, and in biography, there are no such luxuries. If there is trouble when the boundary between fact and fiction is breached, it is also the case that every action holds within itself every past action, while simultaneously contributing to the shape of the future.

So how did it happen that Charmian Clift defied society's limitations? Why did she aspire, like Icarus, to reach the sun? And how did there develop around her a myth so strong that she herself would become lost in it — a myth so necessary to the Australian public that they would continue to seek it and feed it long after her death?

Even to begin to answer these questions it is necessary to *place* Charmian Clift — not at a Sydney party of the 1960s, among a crowd of actors and anti-Vietnam activists; not in Greece of the 1950s, at a waterfront table where international jet-setters mingle with artists of every nationality; and not in the heady scene of wartime Melbourne, where any number of brass hats are keen to buy a drink for a beautiful young lieutenant. The key to Charmian Clift can be found in a small, dull country town in the period between the wars.

PART I

SMALL TOWN GIRL

1

THE CENTRE OF
THE WORLD

The centre of the world was the last house of five identical wooden
cottages at the bottom of the hill, just before the new concrete bridge
that spanned the creek [...]
It was obviously the end, rather than the beginning of somewhere.[1]

Kiama is a dot on the New South Wales coastline, twenty-five kilometres
from the industrial city of Wollongong and a hundred kilometres south
of Sydney.

Ringed by the hazy blue bulk of the Illawarra escarpment, a series of
steep hills spill down to a narrow coastal strip, where jutting promontories
of purplish black rock are intersected by ragged inlets, or sweeps of silver
sand. During the long time of Aboriginal history, these inlets provided
fishing grounds rich in blackfish, flathead and bream, while from the rock
platforms around the headlands there could be gathered an abundance of
shellfish, crabs and small octopus, or sometimes even the crayfish that
lurked on the shelves beneath the water.

One of these rock platforms was special. Here a shift in the earth's crust
had created a large cone-shaped hole that opened into an underwater cavern.
As the surf frothed and boiled inside this funnel, there was a constant hiss
and thundering, as if a mighty creature were trapped below; it spouted like a
whale when the seas pounded hard from the southeast. For the local people,
this blowhole provided a landmark, a meeting spot, probably a sacred place:
translations of the Aboriginal name 'Kiaramaa' include the meanings 'where

the sea makes a noise' and 'a mysterious spirit' as well as the equally apt description of 'plenty of food; good fishing ground'.[2]

This food included the small animals as well as the fruits and vegetables to be found in the subtropical rainforest which covered the ridges and valleys that ran back to the escarpment. With the area's high rainfall there was also plenty of fresh water, and rivers and creeks spilled down the gorges before collecting into wide-mouthed lagoons that ran sluggishly out to sea. In the forest itself, ferns and vines sheltered under a canopy that included the trees which would later acquire the European name of cedar.

It was for the cedar trees that the white men came in the 1820s, logging the forest giants and shipping them out from the small bay that was protected by the promontory where the blowhole provided a convenient marker to boats coming in. As a tribute to the abundance of cedar, some of the early loggers dubbed this little harbour 'Lebanon Bay'; long after the last evidence of the forest was gone, this name would be incorporated into the mythology of the place, and Charmian Clift would use it as the fictional name for the township in her novel *Walk to the Paradise Gardens*.[3] In the area just behind the bay a site for a town was reserved as early as 1826, although the first allotments were not sold until 1840. When laying out the grid of streets on paper, the Sydney surveyors made no allowance for the terrain: many of the streets shoot straight up and over the hills, skewing the perspectives and testing the fitness of pedestrians.

Once the loggers had cleared the trees, it was easy for squatters to move in with their herds of livestock. By the 1830s, tracts of the coastal hinterland were being granted for the grazing of beef cattle, and the original inhabitants were forced off their hunting grounds, back to the thin coastal strip. Treated as pariahs in the small developing township, a number of Koori families made a base for themselves on a massive promontory situated a couple of kilometres to the north of 'Kiaramaa'. The people had their own name for this headland area, too; when the white men heard it, they would write it down as 'Bombo'. There was good fishing here, in the deep chasms of the rock platform, and good shelter around a small enclosed bay on the northern side.

Meanwhile, in the rolling grasslands, the graziers could hardly believe how lush the pastures were. It seemed a waste to use this land for beef cattle, and so by the middle of the nineteenth century the farmers changed over to dairy. While this change resulted in small family farms rather than large landholdings, it would also affect the social climate of the area.

As dairy cows have to be milked morning and night, dairying families lead lives of restricted movement and rigid timetables. This causes a kind of fettered mindset, which in turn produces a particular type of rural conservatism. As the market centre for the cluster of little settlements around the area, Kiama developed as a typical dairying town, where the solid citizens and their wives seemed at times as slow and complacent as the local livestock.

Yet the location of Kiama at least allowed a sea breeze to blow upon the inhabitants of the respectable white-painted residences that clambered prettily up the amphitheatre of hills rising back from the sea. The location was also a drawcard for visiting holiday-makers; by the 1860s and 1870s tourists were already catching the steamer down from Sydney in order to see the extraordinary blowhole on the point, or to paddle at the edge of the safe beaches to the south of the town. (Swimming in the surf would not be legal in Kiama until 1908.[4])

While the volcanic soil provided excellent pastures, the land was also rich in basalt. In the 1870s the newcomers started opening up quarries in the heart of Kiama and in the nearby hills and headlands. Now the town began to echo with the boom of gelignite and the hoot of the steam whistle blowing for smoko or knock-off — or sometimes, unexpectedly and terribly, to announce an accident. By 1883 the volume of blasting and crushing was so great that 400 tons of stone a day were being shipped out of Kiama harbour by sail and by steam, in order to provide blue metal for the roads and tram tracks and railway lines of the developing colony.[5]

Around this time the commissioners in charge of the New South Wales Railways established their own quarry on the headland known as Bombo, and built their own jetty in the little bay on the northern side, which was dubbed 'the Boneyard'.

It was time-consuming, however, to load the gravel into ships, and so in 1893 the railway line was brought down from Sydney to service both the Commissioners' Quarry and the quarries around the township. After cutting deep through Bombo hill, the trains ran along the dunes, crossed a trestle over a reedy creek, threaded their way through another tunnel beneath Pheasant Point, and finally crossed the town to the siding where the gravel was loaded. Twenty years later, the quiet of Kiama was shattered even more irrevocably when a set of tracks was laid along the two main thoroughfares, and steam trams began to rattle back and forth, taking gravel to the railway siding or to the huge hoppers built on the edge of the harbour basin.

Of course, the growth of the quarry industry brought a radical change to the social composition of the town. Now, alongside the population of shopkeepers and service providers, dairy farmers and wheat growers, there was a large workforce of stone crushers and spawlers as well as a smaller number of skilled quarry workers. Morning and night the hilly streets resounded with the tramp-tramp of hobnailed boots as men in loose-crotched working trousers and flannel undershirts and peaked caps marched back and forth with their crib-tins. Single men with dirty faces jammed the hotels and boarding houses, to the dismay of those landladies hoping for a nice clientele of family holiday-makers, and the respectable menfolk of the town became concerned lest their daughters and sisters should meet — or even marry! — such rabble. As a result of community pressure, the quarry proprietors started to build terraces of small weatherboard cottages which could be rented to long-term employees; the aim was to attract a stable core of married workers.

Out at Bombo, the little Koori settlement had been swelled by a shanty town of itinerant stone crushers who lived around the edges of the quarry in shacks built of scavenged tin and hessian bags. It was a kilometre or so back along the highway towards town that the railway commissioners built their string of worker cottages on the flat land that adjoined the reedy creek, alongside the Kiama cemetery. Though tactfully given the name of North Kiama, this small huddle of poky dwellings that squatted in salty gardens beside the dusty road was regarded by the townsfolk as the backblocks — the sticks — the farthest outpost of civilisation. It was here, where the creek formed a stagnant pool beneath the road bridge, that a sign announced the end of the Kiama municipality.

And it was in the very last house out of town, the one next to the creek, overlooking the graveyard, that Charmian Clift was born on 30 August 1923.

> The centre of the world was the last house of five identical wooden cottages at the bottom of the hill, just before the new concrete bridge that spanned the creek.
>
> It was the last house of the town in fact, because on the other side of the bridge you were in a different municipality, and there was no other settlement until you came to the small village of Bombo, a mile or so away over the hills — unless you counted the white settlement of the dead in which my mother gratefully took refuge from Boles's cows, and at which she looked with loathing from the security of her kitchen window.

The creek looped around the five cottages, separated from their front picket fences by the width of the highway, then trickled through the tall striding silvery legs of the railway bridge and spread out on the beach beyond in a wide brackish bowl which we children dignified with the name of lagoon; all of us had to learn to swim in it first, before our father permitted us the lovely dangerous pleasures of the surf.

The house was permeated by the smell of this creek, a richly rotten smell of hot mud and decaying seaweed [...] and invaded by drifts of fine yellow sand. Only the retaining wall of the railway embankment kept the beach in its place, you felt. But for that the sand would long ago have reclaimed highway, creek and houses too. You could never forget how close the sea was. Once, after a heavy storm, there had been seaweed draped on the front fence in the morning.

My mother had done what she could with the front of the house, screening the verandah with a jungle of plants: there were asparagus ferns, fat hydrangea bushes with huge heads the colour of litmus paper, climbing geraniums of red and pink and white, sweet peas in season, and a marvellous fuchsia bush hung with brilliant satiny bells. But nothing could disguise the shabbiness of the cottage, nor really distinguish it materially from its neighbours. It remained a square wooden box, bisected laterally by a narrow hall, and vertically by thin weatherboard walls which divided it into four compartments of equal size. There was a small room tacked on behind to serve for a kitchen, a tin shed for washing, and up at the end of the yard a high narrow dunny which discreetly faced the paling fence and was partly hidden by sunflowers or staked dahlias according to the season.

Apart from this terrace of quarry cottages there was not more than a score or so of houses at this end of the town, all variations on the same architectural butterbox theme, their faded corrugated iron roofs straggling down beside the plunging swoop of the gunmetal highway.

It was obviously the end, rather than the beginning of somewhere.

Lebanon Bay proper lay over the hump of Pheasant Point and through the Cutting. It was a pretty place of solid brick bungalows and older, more graceful houses of stone and wood with wide verandahs held by slim cedar posts, set down in pleasant gardens on vertiginous hills and laced together about two wide shopping streets and a small hoop of harbour with the dark stiff serried verticles of Norfolk pines.[6]

This picture of her birthplace which Charmian Clift gives in the unfinished autobiographical novel *The End of the Morning* shows her photographic sense of recall.[7] In regard to the real landscape, its small and perfect self-containment cannot be overemphasised. Here, in a valley that could be seen in a glance, was everything in the young child's world: the quarry where the father worked, the home where the mother worked, enclosed on all sides by sea and hills. There was also a shop, a railway station, a graveyard, and a road running straight through the middle. If a child were building a landscape in a sandpit, this is the sort of microcosm that she would make. But for this particular child, the microcosm was all the world.

When Charmian was born, her brother was aged only fourteen months, and her sister was not yet at school. Their mother cannot often have braved the walk to town: it would have been near impossible for her to push two babies in a pram up the terrible hill over Pheasant Point, or to take the other way, through the Cutting. As the young Charmian began to crawl, to walk, she would only have gone as far as the yard and the beach. And as she looked towards the horizons of the sea and the hilltops, it must have seemed as if that was all there was. So that when Clift described her house as 'the centre of the world', she was speaking quite literally. To a child toddling towards the gate of that cottage, looking up and around, the feeling was of being at the earth's hub. And in the mornings, as the heat haze rose, the valley seemed to lie under a spell ...

Morning then was a long time, or even, if you came to think about it, a round time — symmetrical anyway, and contained under a thin, radiant, dome-shaped cover that was perhaps the celestial pattern for all the dome-shaped covers which in those days still preserved such sentimental mementos as bridal wreaths, cake decorations from weddings and christenings, funeral ribbons, army biscuits carved with camels, sphinxes modelled from matchsticks, golden keys presented at twenty-firsts, babies' shoes, and small bullet-dented Bibles that had been worn over soldiers' hearts.[8]

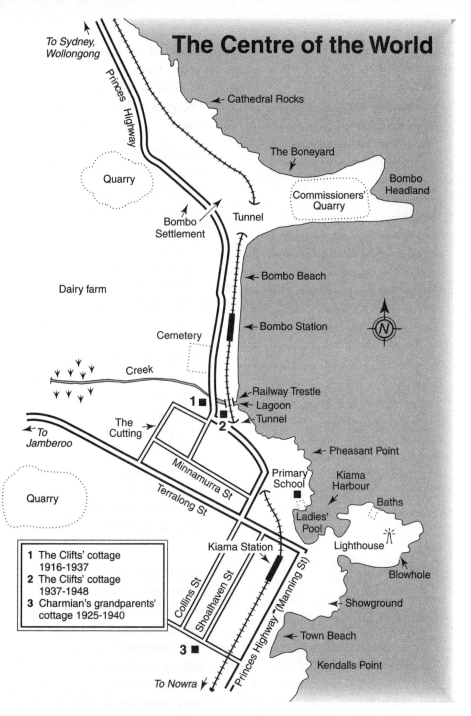

The Centre of the World

To Sydney, Wollongong

Princes Highway

Quarry

Cathedral Rocks

The Boneyard

Bombo Headland

Commissioners' Quarry

Tunnel

Bombo Settlement

Dairy farm

Bombo Beach

Cemetery

Bombo Station

Creek

N

Railway Trestle

Lagoon

The Cutting

1 ■

2 ■

Tunnel

To Jamberoo

Pheasant Point

Quarry

Minnamurra St

Terralong St

Primary School

Kiama Harbour

Baths

Ladies' Pool

Kiama Station

Collins St

Shoalhaven St

Lighthouse

Blowhole

Princes Highway (Manning St)

Showground

1 The Clifts' cottage
  1916–1937
2 The Clifts' cottage
  1937–1948
3 Charmian's grandparents'
  cottage 1925–1940

3 ■

Town Beach

Kendalls Point

To Nowra

Simplified representation of North Kiama, Bombo and Kiama, as they were from the 1920s to 1940s.

In this description, which is part of the opening passage of *The End of the Morning*, Clift uses the conceit of the glass dome to run through a list which includes the main aspects of human life on earth — from birth to death, from peace to war, through the rituals of baptism and wedding and funeral, and with reference to pagan as well as Christian ritual. The mementos themselves are the sort which could be found inside the glass domes which normal families — such as George Johnston's semi-fictionalised Meredith family — gave 'place of honour on top of the pianola'.[9] Charmian's family, however, (for here the novel can be read as non-fiction) was above such mundane and mortal things.

> We Morleys, having neither wreath, ribbon, nor army biscuit (my mother […] had been married sensibly in a coat and skirt; my father […] had curtly refused to go and fight for bloody England; not one of us three children had been christened; and the thought of death in connection with any of us was absurd), laughed contemptuously at the dusty relics that other people preserved. We were an arrogant lot and all inclined by temperament to prefer celestial domes anyway.

In this 'celestial dome', we see the world that the child Charmian saw as she lifted her eyes to the horizons of her bowl-shaped valley:

> The morning dome was a beautiful one, pure, and of a size adequate to encompass the far blue bulk of Jamberoo and the Saddleback; a hundred or so round hills […] and even the sea itself — so vast, so silky dark, so brilliantly glittering, advancing unhurriedly in measured ranks of terrible power that curled out slow white banners as they neared the beach.
> The sound of the sea filled the mornings. It was like living inside a shell. The soothing monotonous surf music beat and beat back from the hills, crump and swoosh, crump and swoosh, over and over and over.[10]

Yet if Charmian's childhood world was complete, it was not a completeness which reduced itself to a single tone. While the landscape acquainted the child with the frenzy of the elements,[11] this same landscape also made her feel secure. This feeling is captured when Julia, in *Walk to the Paradise Gardens*, returns to Lebanon Bay.

Wherever she had walked in her childhood Julia had been conscious of those miles of ocean advancing; and conscious, too, of the security of great blue basalt columns beneath her feet, supporting paddocks and houses and towns and farms.

And now again there returned to her the old childish feeling of security and certainty, the old unthinking chant that had always risen in her in the presence of majesty: the earth is strong: the sea is big.[12]

This sense of the earth as 'majesty' expresses the pantheism that was the unconscious religion of Charmian's childhood: she worshipped her own place, and all that was in it.

It is indicative of Charmian Clift's obsession with her birthplace that she would frequently return to it in her fiction. On at least four separate occasions she wrote 'arrival scenes' — scenes in which the reader is invited, through the eyes of different protagonists, to see the place for the first time. These arrivals always go beyond mere descriptions of setting, for they represent epiphanies; not for nothing is the earliest of these accounts entitled 'The Awakening'.

In the novel *Walk to the Paradise Gardens*, the writer's alter ego appears in the guise of the urban sophisticate Julia, who is somewhat reluctantly visiting her home town of Lebanon Bay in the company of her wealthy architect husband Charles, who has never been to the area before. The author brings the couple into town from the south and positions them on the crown of Pheasant Point, where 'suddenly, magically' they 'discover Lebanon Bay'. Through the eyes of Charles and Julia, we are able to get both an outside and an inside viewpoint. On his first sight of the valley and beach, Charles exclaims not just at the view, but at his wife's secret possession of it:

'What right did you have to withhold all this from your lawful husband? For that matter, how could you? You must have had it there in your head, all the time, all these years. How *could* you carry it about with you for so long? All those funny round hills bumping about under your hats ... that enormous quantity of sea battering endlessly behind your eyes!'

Indeed, Julia has so internalised the landscape that the sight of it is almost painful:

It had been in her head, all of it, for all these years. Even the sea itself, so vast, so silky dark, so brilliantly glittering, brushed with moving acres of silver where the swell breathed against the sun, and with a ship as big as a matchstick held motionless on the far curved line of the horizon [...]

She felt that her eyes were bulging with the enormous pressure of the sea behind them. As if, literally, the neat, small, durable casing of her skull had expanded to contain all that was Lebanon Bay, perfectly preserved under its thin, radiant, dome-shaped cover of sky.[13]

With this extraordinary image of her own skull expanding to encase the dome of sky which in turn is the transparent lid which preserves her childhood universe, Clift allows us to enter her body for a moment and experience the beating of the sea inside her brain. At the same time, we sense the fragility of the thin shell of bone and flesh that has to hold all this.

As Julia turns to her husband to 'offer to him what she had unwittingly but so perfectly preserved', she finds that the moment to share her secret possession is over: Charles is reversing the Jaguar, going back into the town of Lebanon Bay that lies on the other side of the hill. It is the town that makes Julia reluctant to return; the town and its people.

While landscape is the first key to Charmian Clift, it is not just the geography of the small valley at North Kiama, but also the social landscape of the town that clung to its carefully graded structures as tightly as it clung to the rugged coastline on which it was perched. Kiama in the period between the wars was a place where the open wildness of nature was in stark contrast to the restrictions of the social scene.

As well as residents of the township, the social network of Kiama stretched to include the farming families of the district and the inhabitants of the outlying hamlets. Local newspapers of the time give a picture of the residents as hardworking country folk, not much interested in national — let alone international — events, and somewhat suspicious and resentful about goings-on in distant places such as Sydney and 'the southern state'. It was the rural part of the local economy which was privileged in the Kiama media: the majority of news items during the 1920s and 1930s revolved around matters such as milk and butter prices, stock sales and agricultural shows, the eradication of rabbits, the value of silage, or the meetings of organisations such as the Kiama Pastures Protection Board, the Southern Branch of the Illawarra Milking Shorthorn Association or the Agricultural Societies of Kiama itself and nearby towns such as Dapto, Albion Park and Berry. Despite the fact that the town relied heavily on its industrial base, there were only occasional articles referring to quarrying, or even to the developing coastal tourist industry.

Like most local rags, however, the *Kiama Independent* (which came out on Saturdays) and the *Kiama Reporter* (the Wednesday paper)[14] mainly existed in order to advertise and report on the social functions of the various clubs and societies. These included daytime activities such as flower shows and fetes, picnic sports days and sales of work, while at night there were concerts and dances, euchre parties and balls; in any week there would be a dozen events going on. These were usually 'benefits' — fundraising 'dos' organised by the various churches or by secular organisations such as the Oddfellows or the Loyal Star of the South Lodge, the Kiama Ambulance and Hospital, the football clubs or surf clubs, the Rover Scouts, the Parents and Citizens, the Women's Guild, the Red Cross, the Rifle Club, or the Kiama Municipal Band.[15] There was also a range of sporting competitions — for men, at least — including golf and bowls and tennis as well as rifle shooting, football, cricket and surfing. The ladies could watch.

As for culture, that was safely governed by the School of Arts Association. In most of the south coast hamlets, as well as in Kiama itself, there was a School of Arts hall, where occasional lectures were held as well as balls and meetings; and there was always a shelf or two of dusty volumes tucked out of the way of the tea urn. The town of Kiama even boasted its own library, stocked with British classics and popular romances. Meanwhile, the Kiama cinema provided an increasingly popular form of narrative escape, and opened a window onto the world of glamour and romance.

Glancing through the yellowing copies of these old local newspapers, it is easy to get the impression that the residents of Kiama and the surrounding district were a 'clubbable' folk, revelling in every possible variety of harmless fun. On any given day or night there seems to have been a range of social activities in which any citizen could have chosen to participate. This was not in fact the case. Reading between the lines, there is evident a rigid social code which would have signalled itself to the Kiama cognoscenti. No left-footer, for instance, would have attended the Annual Dance of the Loyal Star of the South Lodge, just as the members of the audience for the Grand

Concert with minstrels in aid of the Jamberoo Methodist Church would not have considered attending the Convent Euchre Party and Dance at Shellharbour.

As well as differing religious loyalties, there were other divisions just as clear. Although the Australian rhetoric of democracy would not openly acknowledge the existence of a class system, everybody knew which prominent local families were in 'the silvertail set',[16] and which were not. It was, of course, the older rural families who comprised this Kiama upper crust, together with certain families in which the breadwinner owned an established business or worked in a professional or managerial capacity. Beneath this there was the 'respectable' working class — the skilled workers and tradesmen, some of whom even owned their own houses. And at the bottom of the social pyramid there were the unskilled quarry workers and their families, whose position was openly signalled by the fact that they lived in the strings of identical tiny weatherboard cottages which were owned by the quarry companies.

In Charmian Clift's very early unfinished novel *Greener Grows the Grass*, there is a sort of rehearsal for Julia and Charles's discovery of Lebanon Bay. Here the author's alter ego, Christine Morley, is still young and unsophisticated; she has escaped from her home town but has not completed her climb up the class scale. The text opens as this young woman brings her older and decidedly cosmopolitan lover Justin to the town where she grew up, and where her parents still reside. Like Charles, Justin stops the car on a bluff overlooking the landscape; like Charles, he feels left out, and oddly embarrassed to be there: 'It was her moment, not his. He couldn't share it with her'. Christine herself is so overwhelmed that she weeps. 'I didn't think it would be as important as this, coming home', she tells her lover. And later she warns him: 'It gets you, you know, this place. Wait a while darling, and it'll get you too. Wherever you are it will get you and drag you back'.

Although Christine at this moment is happy to be returning, her mood shifts on the next page as the couple drive through the town and she starts to remember her past there. Some of these memories reflect the class distinctions of the place where the writer grew up. Christine, giving directions to her parents' house, tells Justin to go: 'Up the hill and over. Then we're on the wrong side of the hill. I suppose it still is the wrong side of the hill. It always has been'. She concludes with a promise to herself: 'I'll show the bastards on the right side'.

As Justin follows the directions, we get the full sense of the social as well as the physical landscape — as seen through the unsentimental eyes of Christine Morley's upper-class lover:

> The houses had thinned out now, and they were not the solid, comfortable houses of the town. Weatherboard instead of brick. No trees. Not many gardens. Shabby. A haze quivering on red tin roofs. The brakes yelped when he pulled up the car.
>
> He felt embarrassed again. He felt somehow flat, too. The house wasn't what he had expected, though he didn't know quite what he had expected. Putty-coloured weatherboard, red tin roof. Some roses growing in the yard or two of ground behind the white picket fence. A small house. A narrow, uninteresting house. Not right for her. He couldn't fit her into it.[17]

As we shall see, the author, like her alter ego, did not 'fit in', either to the little hamlet of North Kiama/Bombo, or to the township of Kiama proper, over the hill. Because of certain peculiarities of her family's background and aspirations, Charmian would occupy an ambiguous position in regard to the local class structure. This would result in her feeling excluded from the social framework. The memories of this social isolation would drag her back — wherever she was. At the same time, a great deal of her life would be spent in an attempt to 'show the bastards on the right side' of the hill.

Freedom/restriction. Wildness/security. Beauty/ugliness. Pull/push ...

Throughout her life, Charmian Clift had a relationship with her home town which combined love and loathing in about equal degrees. Although as a child she thought it was paradise, as a young woman she found it a trap from which she couldn't get out quickly enough. The dreams of escape which Charmian harboured during her adolescence were to become a dangerous habit, causing her to feel throughout most of her adult life that the grass would be greener just a little bit over the hill. All she had to do to get out of the trap was cut and run, make a fresh start ... Yet if Charmian Clift's escape route took her further and further afield, she was only ever comfortable in landscapes that reminded her of her birthplace; and she could never live happily away from the sea. To the painter Cedric Flower, who knew Charmian from her early twenties to the end of her life, she was always 'just the girl from Kiama'.[18] And that part of the fictional Cressida

Morley which was depicted as the girl with sand between her toes was — with a little poetic licence — drawn from life.

Yet while the geography of Kiama became almost part of Charmian Clift's body, the social scenery imprinted itself firmly onto her soul. The sensible and sympathetic general practitioner who was Charmian's family doctor in Sydney in the 1960s commented, 'Of course, she was always just a small town girl at heart'.[19] This doctor saw through the sophisticate in his surgery to the woman who lacked self-assurance to an extraordinary degree; he caught a glimpse of the girl who had grown up on the wrong side of town, in a position of social isolation and ambiguity, and who always felt that she had to act somehow bigger, better, brighter, bolder in order to make up for it.

2

LIARS AND EMBROIDERERS

All my family were tremendous liars and inventors and embroiderers
[...] It didn't seem like lying exactly, but just rearranging and
augmenting a little to get a richer or more dramatic or more unusual
effect. Maybe a lot of it was actually true.[1]

Charmian Clift would spend her whole writing career going back again
and again not just to her birthplace but to the story of what had
happened before she was born. Like the narrator of her favourite book, *The
Life and Opinions of Tristram Shandy*, Charmian was fascinated by the
question of how the accident of her birth had happened. Probably rightly,
she seemed to feel that her mother's story held some vital clue.

Amy Lila Currie was born in the New South Wales township of Inverell
on 16 December 1886, the first child of James Archibald Currie, a twenty-
three year old coachbuilder, and Sarah Currie née Carson, aged twenty. In
describing her mother's background, Clift notes that Amy was descended
from 'a Scottish father with a dash of French in his blood, and a mother
who was a beautiful Irish Jewess'.[2] In regard to Amy's fictional counterpart,
Grace Morley née Carson, Clift refers to Grace's 'mixed ancestry (Scotch,
Irish and French as well as Jewish)', then goes on to stress the Jewish
component as Grace's 'dominant race strain'.[3] Later in *The End of the
Morning*, Clift identifies herself through Cressida with this maternal side,
declaring that she and her beloved brother 'reflected [their] mother's mixed
ancestry (Scotch and Irish as well as Jewish)'.[4]

It is typical of Charmian Clift that she would be inordinately proud of
her Jewish ancestry, for she liked to identify herself with a race of outsiders

and wanderers who had suffered centuries of exile and oppression. And so again and again, in fictional and non-fictional accounts, she describes her maternal grandmother, Sarah Carson, the 'Irish Jewess'. However, Charmian never realised that her little blonde paternal grandmother was also Jewish.

Overall, Sarah was the most important figure in the family legend, in spite — or perhaps because — of the fact that she was the only grandparent whom the Clift children never met. And if Charmian Clift chose to identify with Sarah in her fiction — bestowing her first name upon one of her earliest alter egos and giving her surname to Cressida Morley's mother — this too was appropriate, for the young Charmian had a great deal in common with this vivacious grandmother.

Sarah Jane Carson was born in January 1866 in Muswellbrook, New South Wales. Her father, Samuel Carson, was a thirty-two year old storekeeper who had been born in Ireland. Her twenty-one year old mother, Caroline Day, was from a hamlet near the township of Singleton.[5] The couple had married three years previously, and already had a son. By the time Sarah was a young woman, the family had moved to Inverell, where again the parents had a general store. From all accounts, Samuel and Caroline were mean and unkindly. Sarah was the opposite. On more than one occasion Clift refers to

> A story my mother used to tell of my grandmother, Sara [sic]
> Carson, who, according to family legend, was a tragically beautiful
> Irish-Jewess with a hand so small that she could put it inside a
> lamp chimney to clean it, and who won waltzing competitions in
> a rose taffeta dress with a glass of water balanced on her lovely
> head and eggshells on the heels of her dancing slippers.[6]

Appropriately, in a family of embroiderers and yarn spinners, she made lace to sell.[7]

While Sarah formed an exquisite little figure in Amy's stories, the sad fact — which Amy almost certainly did not know — was that Sarah became pregnant out of wedlock at the age of twenty. It is easy to imagine the misery of this in a small country town, where Sarah's parents were prominent business people. There may have been resistance to marriage by Sarah's lover or his family, for the couple were wed only fourteen weeks before Amy Lila was born.

Amy's father, James Currie, came of Scottish farming stock. His father John Currie was 'fiery' according to family tales,[8] while his mother Anne (née Moir) appears to have been a kind and hardworking countrywoman.[9] James was born in 1863 at Mungle Creek, New South Wales, but soon his parents moved to Queensland, where more children were born. By the 1880s the family had returned to New South Wales and bought a dairy farm at Inverell, where there was a sizeable and clannish Scottish community. Indeed, James had a slight Scottish accent, and throughout his life (his granddaughter Margaret related) he 'emphasised the Scottish thing'. In appearance he was 'rather a square sort of man, not terribly tall, but very strong. Sandy, in the Scottish manner'.[10] By nature he would seem to have been a dour, perhaps even harsh man.

Though Sarah had suffered small town scandal and the disapproval of her parents and parents-in-law, she dearly loved her daughter Amy, sewing her garments and dressing her up in pretty frocks. For the first four years of her life, Amy was the sole object of her mother's petting and attention, but in 1890 Sarah gave birth to another child. This second baby was a boy, named Albert, and over the next eight years, another four sons were born. In later years Amy would frequently tell her own daughters how, after Sarah's fifth child was born, the doctor told James that if his wife became pregnant again, nothing would save her.[11] In a first draft passage of *The End of the Morning* Clift puts the anger which Amy used to express against her father, and by extension all men and male sexuality, into the dialogue of Cressida's mother, Grace: 'Men are swine. Brutes. Vandals! Goths! Scythians! [...] He knew that another baby would kill her. He was told that. By the doctor. And yet. Oh the bestial lust of men. He killed her. She was so beautiful'.[12] Following on from her mother's account Clift, in a non-fiction version of this story, notes that Sarah 'died of the sixth [child], not putting aside until the last moment of agony the lace she was making to trim [Amy's] petticoat for market day'.[13]

It is probably true that when dainty little Sarah died in 1899, at the age of thirty-three, it was due to the exhaustion of bearing and nursing baby after baby. However, she did not die in labour, but of heart disease, a year or so after the sixth child was born.[14] That Amy — who was twelve at the time — should remember this death as occurring in childbirth reveals how strongly she resented her father, and also probably her little brothers, who one after another kept on taking the mother's attention away from the first-born. This would have a marked effect on the way in which Amy would treat her own first-born.

Sarah's death scarred the young Amy for life. From now on, she would carry a burden of grief and resentment, and would withdraw into herself, finding no need for friends and little use for affection. She would also develop a feeling of repugnance towards sexuality, which would extend into a prudishness about all bodily functions. Yet her mother's death would also ultimately strengthen Amy and make her independent.

In the aftermath of the tragedy, the children were farmed out to different relatives, and it was Amy's 'misfortune to be allotted to her Jewish grandparents', Charmian later wrote.

> They immediately took my mother from school, sacked the maid
> and put my mother to work. This grieved and angered a young
> girl mad about learning but she bided her time, read books at
> night by a candle, and saved every penny she could.[15]

Possibly Caroline and Samuel were afraid that if they weren't strict with this young girl, she might 'stray' as Sarah had. They needn't have worried. While Amy Lila had the ardent nature of her mother, she was earnest and intellectual, and expressed her individuality not by dancing and frivolity but through her ambition to cultivate her mind. A photograph of her at this time shows her in a serge sailor suit, looking — Charmian would remark — like Beth in *Little Women*.[16] Her looks belied her nature, for there was nothing meek about her. Indeed, if she was like any of the March girls it was her namesake that she most resembled, for Amy Currie, like Amy March, was determined to do well for herself; this included making a good marriage.

In other ways she was more like Jo, and she would scratch away at her writing and lose herself in the world of fiction. Even leaving aside the meanness of her foster home, a country town was no place for a young bluestocking such as this. And so when Amy was about seventeen or eighteen — around 1904 or 1905 — she saved the fare to Sydney and a pound or two extra, and enlisted the help of her favourite brother Albert.

> One night she let a sheet down from her window in approved
> fashion and slid right into the buggy which her brother had
> standing there, and in a mad midnight dash across the
> countryside held up the train for Sydney at a siding and set out
> for adventure [...] She skivvied again in a boarding house in
> Kings Cross, graduated to selling lingerie, and all the time
> worked at night at shorthand typing until she was accomplished
> enough to apply for a job. She became a Gallery Girl, she went to

concerts and theatres, she wrote romantic verse in secret notebooks, and locked them up in her tin trunk.[17]

'She must have blossomed in those years', Charmian Clift concludes this telling of the tale. Yet in another essay Clift makes a grimmer and probably more accurate guess as to the reality behind Amy's heroic story:

> My mother used to say that the best time of her life was the period that followed her arrival in Sydney [...] She used to tell of it with a wicked glee and an overweening pride in her own audacity. But the facts, the indisputable facts, are that for a year at least she scrubbed floors, emptied slop buckets, waited on tables [...], was snubbed and derided and neglected, and lay down to sleep at night in a bed where the bugs lurked.
>
> Surely even the brave glow of audacity must sometimes have been dimmed by sheer sordidness, loneliness, doubt, terror? Panic in the night?[18]

But whether afraid at times or not, Amy had managed to escape. Over the next nine or ten years she cultivated her cultural ambitions and improved her education and social position, eventually becoming the receptionist at the Berlitz School of Languages.[19] Meanwhile, in the proper manner of any tale of romance, the life of a man named Sydney Clift was moving him inexorably towards the selfsame boarding house where Amy Currie resided.

To Charmian, growing up with the story of her maternal origins, it seemed that grandmother Sarah had the aura of a beautiful and tragic princess. As the young girl came to learn about her father's background, she naturally again sought an exotic element. This was provided by a backdrop of the Mysterious East. Charmian's paternal grandfather, William Clift, was born on 21 June 1865 at Benares in India, where his father Charles Clift was a sergeant in Her Majesty's 7th Division Grenadiers.[20] Of his mother, Mary Clift née Mason, nothing is known except that she was said to have borne ten sons, all of whom grew to be over six feet tall. Most excitingly, as a baby William was bitten on the head by a sacred monkey when his cradle floated off down the flooding Ganges; sixty years later he would delight in showing his grandchildren the scar. And Will's father, the sergeant, after retiring to cold England, set his beard alight to keep his chest warm rather than drink mutton broth.[21] Meanwhile, somewhere further back, there was allegedly an ancestor hanged at Tyburn tree for highway robbery.[22]

After the monkey, Will's life appears to have been pretty unexceptional, and it is likely that he was only a child when his parents returned to England, where they settled in Chester. Though Will's brothers all went off to serve in the army, William himself became a railway clerk; by now his father had become a station master. In September 1886 — the very month when James Currie married Sarah Carson in the Presbyterian church at Inverell — William Clift, aged twenty-one, married a twenty-four year old schoolmistress named Emma Sharman in the Anglican church in the parish of March in Cambridgeshire.[23]

Born in the town of March in February 1862, Emma was the daughter of Henry Levi Sharman, at that time a groom and later a baker, and Susannah Sharman, née Crech or possibly Crick.[24] Like Sarah Carson, Emma Sharman was short and dainty; in every other way, Charmian's two grandmothers were chalk and cheese. Thus while Sarah danced through the night with eggshells on her heels, Emma channelled her musical talents into singing contralto in an amateur operetta society. While Sarah sewed lace for her party frocks, Emma dabbled at watercolour landscapes. And while flighty Sarah was obviously quite charming and delightful, Emma was a tartar and a tyrant, and the worst sort of petit-bourgeois snob.

It goes without saying that Emma Sharman would not get pregnant before the wedding ceremony, and so it was in August 1887 — a decent eleven months after her marriage to Will — that she gave birth to Sydney Clift in New Town in the county of Huntingdon.[25] She subsequently had another son, whom she named Frank.

Syd's childhood was not miserable in the way of Amy's, but nor was it happy. According to the stories that he would later tell his own children, his father Will 'had beaten him quite savagely and often in boyhood', for Emma's motto was 'Spare the rod and spoil the child'.[26] This former schoolteacher exerted her own punishments by nagging and by purse-lipped disapproval, and the whole atmosphere of the home was empty of joy and love. Duty and order were the cornerstones of this domestic edifice: everyone should know his or her place, and stay in it. The worst sin was to presume to ape one's betters. Syd would rebel in his individual fashion, by pretending to copy what he believed to be the manners of his 'worsers'.

Perhaps to escape from his restrictive family life, the young Syd took up a variety of sports. Though not as tall as his father and uncles, he did inherit some of the relevant genes from the paternal line of Grenadiers. Indeed, he gave the impression of height, for his upper half was muscular, with arms strengthened from swimming, but the lower part of his body didn't quite match. 'He should have been tall and slim and taut', Charmian would note of his fictional counterpart. 'Not that he was short, exactly, but he was bulky, muscular, slightly bow-legged'.[27] In regard to Syd's sporting triumphs, Charmian believed her father to have been a county cricketer, and also a water polo star.[28] Syd's elder daughter Margaret added that he had excelled at soccer and marathon swimming, as well as winning cups for skating. In any sporting field, she concluded, 'It didn't matter what he attempted to do, he could do it'.[29] Although Syd's daughters exaggerated their father's achievements, it is true that he was an exceptional natural athlete, with great powers of endurance.

As to Syd's educational achievements, there are no records. However, he was highly intelligent, with a quick perception and a thirst for knowledge about every possible thing under the sun. In *The End of the Morning* Grace declares that her husband Tom Morley could easily have got a scholarship to Cambridge but his mother apprenticed him to a trade because that was more fitting to his station in life. However, it is more likely that Syd himself preferred to join the practical, 'manly' world of physical work rather than enter the cloisters of academe, and he would not have wished to follow in his father's footsteps and spend his life working at a desk. Certainly, there was never any suggestion from Syd Clift himself that he was anything but delighted with his chosen trade of engineer, although he would also do fitters' work and electricians' work and labourers' work and anything else he felt like putting his hand to.

It was around the turn of the century when Syd Clift was signed over to the Haslam Foundry and Engineering Company in Derby. As an apprentice he worked an eleven-hour day for seven years, but there was still time for swimming in the Derwent, playing cricket at dinner time with the other lads, going to the YMCA for chess lessons and — a fact which he kept secret from his children — singing in the Anglican church choir.[30]

Despite these bucolic pleasures, Syd hated the country and people of his birth, later railing against 'bloody Pommies' and commenting that living in England was like residing in the heart of a lettuce.[31] The day he finally got his trade papers — in 1909 — twenty-two year old Syd found himself a job on a refrigeration ship to Australia, and swore never to return.[32] Once here, he met another lad from the Haslam Company, and 'after all sorts of jobs they landed up in the canefields at Mackay'.[33] A bit later, Syd moved on to Glen Davis, an isolated shale oil mining town to the west of Lithgow in New South Wales.

Meanwhile, as Syd worked in this wild and remote valley, an archduke was assassinated in far-off Europe, and the Australian Prime Minister, Andrew Fisher, declared that in defence of the Home Country, Australia would go to war 'down to its last man and its last shilling'.[34] That last man wasn't going to be Syd Clift. If he wouldn't live in England, he certainly wasn't going to die for the place. But although he was determined not to enlist, he left Glen Davis towards the end of 1914 and went to Sydney for a month or two.

During this sojourn in the city, he happened to stay at a boarding house where the landlady had three unmarried daughters. By now aged twenty-seven, Syd Clift was an extremely handsome man whose face was composed of strong flat planes, 'finely if coldly chiselled'.[35] Apart from his looks, a skilled tradesman such as Sydney Clift was a great catch, especially as more and more of the country's eligible bachelors were leaving for the trenches. While Syd found it easy to attract women, he was still determined not to settle down. The landlady's three unmarried daughters were just as determined to change his mind. Amongst the permanent lodgers there was another spinster. She could not be called beautiful, and indeed was probably getting a little beyond the marriageable age, but she possessed a pair of dark eyes which seemed to shine with passion and intelligence. He privately christened her 'Hermia', because she was small and fierce.[36]

If Syd was thinking in terms of Shakespeare, in Amy's telling of this bit of the tale she casts herself as Cinderella. When Charmian rewrote this as Grace's story, she bestowed Amy's own name on one of the ugly sisters; however, we can be certain that the following version was pretty much as Charmian's mother told it — and retold it.

> 'Tell us about that, Mum,' we would wheedle [...]
> 'Oh, you don't want to hear that old story again.'
> 'Yes! We do. We do. Go on, Mum. You were a shorthand-typist ...'
> 'The very first lady shorthand-typist in Sydney.'
> 'And you were living in the boarding house [...]'

'With the three fat girls.'

'Florrie and Lily and Amy ...'

'...And the new boarder was Dad.'

'Go *on*,' she said. 'You know the story better than I do.'

But, 'Tell!' we pleaded, and (as always) she told.

'Your father had just come down from Glen Davis, where he had been installing the machinery for the shale oil experiment. He was the handsomest man any of us girls had ever seen, and Florrie and Lily and Amy were all determined to get him [...]

'They were very high-coloured and had masses of blonde hair, and I was so little and dark and insignificant. And of course they had their mother to help them with their angling and I didn't have anybody at all [...]

'Well, Florrie and Lily and Amy all made new dresses, cut very low in the front. And every evening after supper [...] their mother would call them over to the piano and ask them to sing [...] Of course they knew all the songs off by heart. So did I, but I couldn't sing [...]

'So while they were warbling and rolling their eyes and sticking their fronts out, I sat in a corner and talked to your father about books. And I would deliberately disagree with him and make him argue and he would become so heated that half the time he didn't know the girls were there at all. They were furious,' said my mother complacently [...]

'So he took the girls out, one after another in their new dresses, and at night in the bedroom they discussed what he had said and which one of them had the better chances, and they quarrelled among themselves as to who should have him. But every time he asked me out I refused or made an excuse. Then one evening he asked me if I could play chess, because he would love a game and had nobody to play with. And when I said I couldn't, he offered to teach me.'[37]

And so, lacking a fairy godmother as well as a real mother, the little orphan-girl used her brains and her bookishness to win the prince. Now she secretly enrolled in chess classes with a professional, and studied chess manuals, so that a couple of weeks later when Syd renewed his offer of lessons, he declared 'he had never met a more intelligent pupil in his life'.[38]

He was so impressed that he stopped taking out the three bosomy sisters, and hung around the parlour at night to see if this clever woman wanted to play chess or borrow a book.

Decoding this fable, we find a number of messages which this unusual mother was passing on to her daughters:

(1) The way to a man's heart is through his head. So cultivate your brains, increase your knowledge.

(2) In this world, it is every woman for herself. There is no place for sisterhood with rivals, for even blood sisters have no loyalty to each other.

(3) It is permissible — indeed advisable — to cheat and lie and use every ruse and stratagem in order to get the right husband.

The only justification needed was success. '*Anyway, it worked!*' Amy used to boast at the end of this tale. Indeed it did. When Amy's birthday came around, in December 1914, Syd presented her with a leather-bound copy of Ruskin's *Sesame and Lilies*.

After this informal token of engagement, off Syd Clift wandered again, but Amy wasn't worried. And sure enough, back he came two years later to marry her at the Anglican Christ Church St Lawrence on 2 October 1916. It is surprising that they got married in a church, for both were agnostic, perhaps even atheist. Anyway, it was more like a civil service than a church wedding, for there were only the witnesses present. Typically, Amy would make a virtue of the fact that she had no family to provide her with a trousseau or a wedding party, and it would become one of her boasts that she had been married 'sensibly in a coat and skirt and chiffon blouse'. Although both bride and groom were twenty-nine, the former moved her age down two years on the certificate, and the latter bumped his up to thirty.[39]

The truth is an elusive concept with people such as this. After all, in one of her essays Charmian Clift herself boasts: 'All my family were terrible liars and inventors and embroiderers'.[40] And in *The End of the Morning*, she tells the reader that

> All the Morleys were tremendous embroiderers, which I felt but didn't quite understand, like so many other things. It didn't seem like lying exactly, but just rearranging and augmenting a little to get a richer or more dramatic effect. Maybe a lot of it was actually true.[41]

Of course, in the creation of the 'history' of a family, memory plays an editorial role, as Clift herself was well aware. In retelling the story of her paternal ancestry in one of her essays, the writer confesses:

> One grows up on this sort of family thing, stories and legends, and what is true and what is false I haven't the faintest idea […] My grandfather Will used to tell such things, and he was a truthful man, but then he was old too, and memory is a tricky thing, forever discarding, rejecting, or embroidering what is retained, making transformations, building up the small and ordinary into the grand and exceptional.[42]

For any child, even immediate ancestors such as parents and grandparents are to some extent fictional characters, for everything that occurred before the child herself entered the story must always be in the realm of rumour, hearsay, gossip, myth. In family fables, moments of tragedy and comedy are highlighted; scandals and skeletons are usually omitted; dates and timespans are hazy and variable. And as children plead for the same stories over and over, characters are streamlined into a few memorable attributes of good or evil, while even the wording develops its patterns, its repetitions, its Homeric epithets.

In any family, the methodology of all this is closer to fairytale than it is to oral history — let alone to historiography of the more documented kind. The difference with the Clift family was in the skill of the tale-tellers: it was as if the children were hearing the stories straight from the mouths of Monsieur Perrault and Mother Goose.

While it is necessary in a work of this kind to peg these accounts to dates and verifiable information where possible, the yarn must still be allowed to spin out free and bright: for these fables were the facts of Charmian's childhood. This was the history that she inherited, the history that she believed, the history that shaped her; it was also the history that she bestowed upon Cressida and the Morley family.

Important as these stories were in themselves, one of the richest gifts Charmian Clift inherited from her ancestry was the family tradition of embroidering and editing a story until it rang with the kind of felt truth which may have nothing to do with facts. Years later, when news of her publishing success became known in Kiama, there was no surprise among the locals. As one of her contemporaries commented: 'We always said that she'd have to be a writer, because her father was the biggest liar this side of the Black Stump!'[43] Although it was Syd who astonished the neighbours with his skills as a storyteller, Amy also had a knack of teasing out the best of a tale — as the story of her courtship shows.

Other traits also revealed Charmian's inheritance of the strong brew of Carson and Currie, Sharman and Clift, which came directly to her through Amy and Syd. In all of this, nurture no doubt played as large a role as nature, but it is certainly the case that Charmian grew up with two parents whose opposite qualities were evenly balanced.

As a way of summing up the different temperaments of Amy and Syd, it is illuminating to apply a sort of test which the adult Charmian and her friends on Hydra used to try out on new acquaintances. The opening gambit was to ask people to categorise themselves according to whether they thought Daedalus or Icarus more deserving of admiration:

> Daedalus being the engineering genius who designed the wings for himself and his son to escape Crete, and Icarus the reckless fool who became so intoxicated with flight that despite all his father's warnings he flew higher and higher until he flew so close to the sun that the wax fixing his wings melted and he plummeted to death from the blue to the blue.[44]

This game became a way of dividing the world into two sorts of people — cautious types and reckless types, pessimists and optimists, nay-sayers and yea-sayers, craftspersons and artists ... Charmian herself had no doubt about which side she would take:

> While I dips me lid to Daedalus — most wholeheartedly too — it is really Icarus with whom I feel an affinity. Quite possibly there is some desperation in my nature that causes me (sometimes) to be defiant of limitations. I have always loved high-diving for this reason.

If Charmian was a spirit of air and water, an embodiment of the boy who disobeyed his father's warning and flew too close to the sun, her mother Amy was also an Icarus character. Indeed, in *The End of the Morning* the author describes the mother figure as a 'poor Icarus'[45] (poor because confined to a tiny patch of earth). Syd, of course, was a Daedalus; he was even — like the mythical maze-maker — an engineer. While Charmian's mother was the spirit that sought to fly, we should not underestimate how much this daughter inherited from Syd the craftsman — nor how much of the Daedalus side was manifest in Charmian. At times it was as if these oppositional forces waged war inside her.

Yet there were also certain elements which Amy and Syd had in common, and which were passed directly to Charmian. One was intelligence, although there were differences in the form that this would take. From both parents there came a quick mind and a love of learning, but it was from Syd that Charmian derived her curiosity and her strange habit of amassing information: she would describe her father as having 'more useless information on a greater variety of subjects' than anybody else she had ever known.[46] And it was from Syd that Charmian inherited a strenuous, questioning mind which loved to argue with itself and others in order to tease out strands of thought. This particular type of intelligence would reveal itself in the argument of Charmian Clift's essays. At the same time, Amy's legacy would be evident in the lyricism which prevented the essayist's voice from sounding strident or didactic. It was from this maternal side that Charmian's passion came, her 'romantic' qualities. It was also Amy who would provide the initial impetus for Charmian's writing — whether by genetic input or practical example, it doesn't really matter.

Another quality which Charmian inherited from both her parents was a strength of character, which revealed itself under various guises — independence, wilfulness, restlessness, a headstrong and tempestuous nature. When Amy couldn't bear life in a country town, she climbed out the window, fled to the city, and fended for herself. Meanwhile Syd travelled halfway across the world in order to escape his origins. In the same way Charmian would favour bold action; she would have a predilection for cutting and running, for making her escape.

In Syd this wilful temperament would also manifest itself in a social and political stance that bucked against any form of authority. Describing him as a 'born rebel', his elder daughter would add that Charmian took after him.[47] Compared with Syd's defiance, Amy's way of rebellion was less ostentatious, but she too would spend her life swimming against the stream. Where Syd confronted, Amy subverted; Charmian would display both tactics in her essays.

From both sides of the family, Charmian received a legacy of good looks. Indeed, it was the mix of Amy's broad cheekbones and upward-tilting eyes with Syd's strong facial planes that would give Charmian her distinctive features. It was purely from the Clifts, however, that Charmian inherited her height and her strong body frame, her wide shoulders and superb physique.

There was something Grenadier-like in her extraordinarily straight back and the proud carriage of her head, which so many people would remark upon as being exceptional. Together with these characteristics went litheness and speed plus a level of physical coordination which would allow her as a young woman to excel — like Syd — at any sport she attempted.

In this pursuit of excellence we see yet another quality which Syd and Amy shared, for in both Charmian's parents there was a quality of pride or superiority which would not be satisfied with anything less than first prize. In their own lives, circumstances had thwarted their chances, and they had relinquished any personal hope of reaching a great goal. Yet they held a firm belief that a great talent lay within the family. Charmian would grow up with this sense of being part of a chosen elite.

3

RATHER AN ALIEN FAMILY

> I could go on for a long time about […] the sort of family we were,
> […] and the fact of being rather an alien family in this small town […]
> In a sense that has stayed with me. I think I have always been on the
> outside looking in a little bit.[1]

If Charmian's talent for embroidering a story was inherited or learned from her family, she also used it to extraordinary effect when she was portraying her family. The picture of her background familiar to most people — whether her own children, her friends, or her reading public — was of an unusual but happy family, with loving parents whose marriage was very solid. While she had probably managed to convince herself of this version of the situation, Charmian had not always seen things this way. Certainly, during her childhood, Charmian believed (or chose to believe) that she had a happy family. By the time of her adolescence, however, she knew that there was a rift in her parents' relationship, and a deep unhappiness in the North Kiama cottage. In some of her early fiction, Charmian Clift would try to depict this (maybe in an attempt to make sense of it for herself) through the first-person narratives of a character called Alma Morley, drawn from Amy Clift. However, she was always unable to carry this version of events very far — perhaps because any conclusion would have been too painful either for the author, or for the model.

As time went on, Clift's way of writing about — and indeed remembering — her parents and family would again change radically, and an increasingly idealised version would be incorporated into the Charmian Clift myth. As the writer's own marriage became more and more difficult, her sense of security would seem to become vested in a belief in the happiness and stability of her parents' marriage. Yet even in the most glowing descriptions of this 'wonderful family', there are hints that things were really not as rosy as Charmian would have liked to believe.

A similar pattern of revision and further revision occurred in the author's portrayal of the position which her family occupied in society. When Charmian was a young woman, she shared her mother's aspiration to escape from her origins by moving up the social scale; the key to such mobility was seen to be partly through personal development and education, but more importantly through connecting with the 'right' sort of people and making a 'good' marriage. Through her adolescence and early twenties Charmian liked to give the impression that her background was rather more elevated than was in fact the case. This sort of aspiration is revealed in the writer's earlier texts, such as *Greener Grows the Grass*.

Ironically, however, the successful husband whom Charmian ended up winning was someone who came from pretty much the same class as herself, and who also had aspired upwards. Moreover, through their careers in the arts, the couple became part of a small subgroup of the middle class that flouted conservative values and social conventions. In the democratic circle in which Charmian moved, a working class origin was nothing to be ashamed of; indeed, it could be regarded as a badge of honour. And so Charmian Clift would not only disavow her mother's attitude of social climbing, but she would start to copy her father's habit of aspiring downwards.

By at least the 1960s, Charmian's portrayal of her family's working class origins was an important part of the picture she liked to give. In essays and interviews the author would frequently describe herself as being part of 'the Depression generation', and again and again she depicted her family as being poor in material things, but rich in matters of culture and the spirit, of physical health and laughter and love. 'We were very poor, but we never felt poor because we had the beach', Clift declared in her 1965 interview for the National Library, and in a 1968 synopsis of what she termed her 'semi-autobiographical' novel, *The End of the Morning*, she described Cressida Morley's 'eccentric family' as being 'poverty-stricken (although not one of the children realise, until adolescence, that they are poor: they've always felt themselves to be rich)'.[2]

And yet, while the change in Charmian Clift's way of writing about her family's origins reflects the change that occurred in her own attitude, it is also the case that, when Charmian was growing up, she suffered a real confusion about what her family's position was, because the Clifts occupied a decidedly ambiguous place in Kiama society. In this matter of ambivalence, the house where the family lived assumes a very important role. As we have seen in the text describing Christine Morley's return to her birthplace, the small and ugly quarry cottage becomes the objective correlative of the 'place' which the Morleys occupy in society. It literally signifies their position — at the very end of town, at the very lowest level of the class scale, in a neighbourhood of unskilled labourers and their families. And of course this was true in fact. However, the Clifts were 'out of place' in this place. So how did they come to be there?

Since emigrating to Australia in 1909 or so, Syd Clift had not looked for a permanent job, for with his skills he could get work anywhere. Shortly before his wedding in 1916, he had found employment as resident engineer at the Railway Commissioners' Quarry at North Kiama. He didn't see this as a career for the rest of his life, but as a temporary job in a delightful place, where he would stay until deciding the next port of call. Although he was employed at the quarry in a senior capacity, he took a lease on one of the rough little cottages built for the quarry labourers. While this accommodation was convenient, the choice also expressed Syd's ongoing rebellion against his background. Perhaps he was afraid that his new position of authority would cause him to lead the sort of life his parents had led. Determined to keep working 'hands on' with his machines, he was also set on looking and living like an unskilled labourer. As a kind of insurance policy against the possibility of purchasing a house in the township and settling down permanently, he spent most of his own and his new wife's savings on a sailing boat. With what was left over, Amy bought lace tablecloths and a Spode dinner service instead of pots and pans.[3] And so this pair of romantics set off into married life as if it were to be an elegant seaside holiday. As far as Amy's future was concerned, nothing could have been further from the truth.

After their unostentatious wedding ceremony at Christ Church St Lawrence, Syd and Amy were able to walk around the corner to Central Railway Station and set off on their new life. It was all unfamiliar territory to Amy, as the train took her south through little coal towns to the industrial city of Wollongong/Port Kembla, and then on through a scattering of sidings and one-horse hamlets until they reached a most peculiar platform situated halfway down a long deserted stretch of sand dunes. The sign said BOMBO; it looked like the middle of nowhere. And Syd announced that this was their destination!

Drawing from tales her mother told her, Charmian Clift wrote a variety of accounts of the lives of Amy and Syd Clift over the first few years of their marriage. The tale of their arrival at the quarry settlement appears in one of the early fragments of *Greener Grows the Grass*. In this, Amy's own point of view is expressed as a first-person narrator named Alma Morley looks back from the vantage point of middle age to remember her arrival at the little quarry settlement:

> I was happy. Excitement knotted around me in tight bands. Excitement and pride. The clunketing of the train wheels kept saying over and over 'Alma Morley. Alma Morley. Alma Morley.' I liked the sound of it. I liked being Alma Morley. I liked belonging to Tom Morley. Just the thought of that — really belonging to someone — made a fog of sheer happiness blanket down around me warmly [...] 'You're going home. You're going home. You're going home,' the train said. Home at last. A real home. Home with Tom.[4]

It is easy to imagine that this was how Amy Clift really felt, for she had not lived in a home of her own since the age of twelve, when her mother died. Nor had she had anyone to belong to since that day. However, there is also a touch here of Charmian's own sense of the need to belong — to a person, and a place — that would preoccupy her from a very early age.

In this account, Alma and Tom arrive at the little station on the dunes, and Alma is at first sight delighted by the 'peacock sea' and the 'rhythm' of the hills folding down. But as the couple cross the bridge that spans 'a sluggish creek', Alma begins to smell something 'sweetly-rotten' in this tiny kingdom, and when she gazes expectantly upwards at a nice white house on the hill, Tom tells her that the 'awful dingy cottage' in front of her is where they are going to live.

> I do not know whether its dirty buff colour is paint or only the dust from the road. Tin cans and bottles are stacked untidily in front of it. It looks back at me with a sort of furtive, unkempt look. My nostrils and my clothes are permeated with the stench of rotting seaweed. I am home. I dam the rush of hysterical tears

gathering behind my eyes. Two small black faces peering through the slewed picket fence of the next cottage split suddenly into whiteness and shrill giggles quiver in my ears even when they rush inside and return with a young gin who smiles at me shyly between the creaking verandah posts. There seem to be people on all the other verandahs too. Slatternly looking women and ragged kids. All smiling at me. Welcoming me.

It is fascinating that, in order to emphasise how far 'out' or 'down' this area is, the author has invented a family of Aboriginal neighbours. In fact, although Kooris continued to live in the settlement up on Bombo hill and would frequently be seen walking along the road to town, none actually lived in the quarry cottages at North Kiama.[5]

As this text continues, Alma does not respond to her neighbours' welcome, but retreats inside to 'pea-green walls and poky dog-box rooms'. When Alma's husband, puzzled by his bride's reaction, points out the benefits of the place, the writer borrows the dialogue directly from her father Syd: 'It's just what we want. See, it's close to the quarry for my work, and there's the beach right in front, under the railway bridge. I don't have to walk miles for my fishing'.[6]

And so Alma 'pull[s] down a shutter over the image of that white house', resolving that she can make a garden and cover the cottage with vines, and that she can do 'anything so long as Tom is happy. I'll get used to the smell of the creek. I won't be a snob'. With this last comment, the author acknowledges that the issue of class is absolutely central to the whole business of Amy's attitude to the neighbourhood. Amy continues to plan how she will deal with the situation:

I'll make nice friends in town and they'll be glad to come out here. And after a while I can look round for the sort of place I'd like and gradually I'll get Tom to see that he has a social position to keep up. After all it doesn't matter now. We're together. We can be happy in any shack. I have all the years ahead to plan and scheme. Just now Tom's mouth is on mine, and the smell of the creek is all mixed up with the dry clean smell of his skin and his hair.[7]

At this point the writer added — and subsequently crossed out — 'And I am blooming. Burning'.

It is here that the narrative abruptly breaks off. Although this passage is very short, it introduces two themes which recur through Charmian Clift's fiction. Firstly, this is a portrayal of a marriage which fails from the very beginning, partly because the two protagonists have different expectations of life, but essentially because there is no communication or comprehension between them. Secondly, the swooning embrace is for the woman a Judas kiss: passion betrays her by befuddling her brain and preventing her from seeing that she should bail out while she can.

In regard to the relationship of the real Syd and Amy, there would remain throughout the marriage a terrible division caused by Amy's desire to move into town and Syd's determination to stay in the quarry settlement. By the time Clift wrote *The End of the Morning* she would present this simply as 'common family knowledge', and would treat it as some sort of bygone whim of Grace Morley (as Alma/Amy is now called). However, in her earlier work the wife is depicted as very much the victim of the marriage, and the feud over where the family lived is presented as a matter of ongoing conflict.[8]

The short story 'The Awakening' was published as early as 1946. In this text, written before the author had secured her own social position, the balance of sympathy clearly lies with the Amy-character, who is here named Hannah Grey. The story opens with this woman plodding wearily back from town 'along the simmering bitumen road that swung like a strap over the shoulder of the hill'. As she looks down towards 'the little quarrying settlement, huddled parched and gasping in the heat', she acknowledges 'that the hill would always stand a parched merciless barrier between her and the dignity of pearl earrings and afternoon teasets'. This knowledge brings 'a sort of resignation, tinged with the bitterness that comes when dreams are dead'.[9]

When Hannah's husband Charlie comes home, we can recognise Syd Clift, although the writer's attempt at transcribing a working class accent feels false and self-conscious — no doubt because it wasn't true to life. This is the only occasion on which the author puts her father's point of view on the subject of her mother's social aspirations:

> 'Wot's the matter, ole girl? Not still dreamin' of a mansion over the 'ill, are ya?'
>
> There was something of fear in his voice, and bewilderment, for he had never understood Hannah's desperate yearning for something better than the life they led. You never heard Bill Dooley's wife whingeing for carpets and teasets and the like

[. . .] If she wanted to give tea parties, why wasn't she a bit more friendly with her neighbours, instead of getting herself talked about and called 'Lady Muck'.

In this story, Hannah and Charlie are childless. A fragment of another story (probably written shortly before the *Greener Grows the Grass* passage already quoted) leads up to the conception of the couple's first child. Again the tale is narrated by Alma; it opens this time on a night of storm and high wind — wind that 'puts the madness' into the narrator. It is still the first year of Alma's marriage, but for six months the wind has been saying to her: 'Fool! You've been cheated. Cheated. Cheated. Why don't you get out while you can? Pack your bags. Go on. Get out. You'll never change him. You're a fool fool fool'.[10] Alma's husband Tom gets out of bed to battle around to the harbour basin to tie up his fishing launch, the *Alma*, muttering that the boat is 'more trouble than it's worth' and he has 'a mind to sell it'. Alma mentally agrees that he should have put the money into a house, as she'd wished, but says nothing because she has already learned that 'his anger was equal to [her] own — and most violent when he was in the wrong'.

As the woman lies alone in bed she thinks again of how she longs to move into town, and how she is 'exasperated' by her husband's 'complete lack of ambition and his preference for the bawdy, tangy company of fishermen and labourers'. He has been so 'consistently rude to any nice woman from the town who came out to visit' that none would come any more, and he calls her a snob for not mixing with the local women — although he is secretly snobbish enough himself not to want her getting fat and dropping her aitches and gossiping over the fence.

Now the surf joins with the wind to tell Alma, 'Get out. Get out. Tomorrow. Tomorrow', and this time the narrator is 'receptive to the rhythm'. But Tom's 'icy flesh' slides into the bed beside her; exulting in the storm, he presses Alma to 'make [him] warm'. Again, the wife submits to the husband's passion and loses her chance for her own life:

> Somewhere far away I heard the surf crashing its entreaty 'Get out. Get out. There's time still. Refuse him. Get out.' But it was dim and distant and unreal and I let my mouth open under his, and my senses sing beneath his sudden weight.[11]

Once again, as soon as the embrace is written, the writer breaks off from the narrative — here even starting a new section with the numeral '2', but not even attempting to write anything beneath it. We can be sure, however, about what was to follow in the plot. One thing was a child, for the trap of marriage is not fully sprung for a woman until a baby is born. Another thing was to be the loss of the boat.

This boat incident is also related a number of times through the drafts of *Greener Grows the Grass* and *The End of the Morning*. A supposedly non-fictional telling of this story also appeared in the essay 'A Portrait of My Mother'. Here, having skimmed through the story of the courtship (complete with bogus chess lessons), Charmian Clift moves into the Kiama bit of the tale:

> They moved romantically from the city to the coastal town [...]
> and for years it must have been a golden idyll [...] My father
> bought for her pleasure as well as his own a second-hand
> schooner which they refurbished at the weekends. And she
> planted vines and shrubs to hide the little cottage, which was
> only temporary of course. Next year, if they could sell the
> schooner for a decent profit, they would have a good scout
> around for something roomier, where she could display her
> pretty linen and lace and china, and scrap the old deal furniture
> they had only bought to Make Do.
>
> I wonder how long it took her to realise she was stuck. She
> didn't have children for six years, and in the meantime life was
> pleasant enough, although she [...] found herself spending her
> weekends entertaining the wives of my father's fishermen friends.
> And then my father heard of a better schooner and sailed his up
> to Port Jackson to get it, and was in such a hurry to get home to
> show it off that he forgot to insure it, and they were caught in a
> terrible storm and the schooner sank. And now there was no
> money any more for houses.[12]

In regard to the 'golden idyll' of the first years of her mother's marriage, the writer was closer to the truth in her early fiction. Clearly for Amy the rot set in the minute she walked across the smelly creek. Also, it was only two years after Syd and Amy's marriage that their first child, Margaret, was born. It was a couple of years after this that Syd traded in his boat for another and better vessel, which was christened the *Peggy* in Margaret's honour.[13] This was the boat that sank, uninsured, as Syd (alone) sailed it home. As this vessel represented the couple's entire savings, there sank with it Amy's last hope of buying a house in town and moving up the social scale. Now she was well and truly stuck in the little valley. From this time on, Amy Clift would find her only outlet in her children.

Syd and Amy would attempt to raise their offspring in line with certain principles put forward in John Ruskin's *Sesame and Lilies*. As this was also the doctrine that underpinned the marriage, it is worth taking a moment to consider this curious text.

Originally published in 1871, *Sesame and Lilies* is comprised of two of Ruskin's lectures.[14] 'Sesame' deals with the books that one should read and how one should read them. 'Lilies' is concerned with a woman's role in life, the relationship between men and women in marriage, and the way in which girls should be educated. In regard to the relationship between the sexes, Ruskin's main argument is that 'equal but separate spheres' benefit both men and women. Home should be a place of peace and shelter, with Man protecting the outside and Woman caring for what is within. Ruskin elaborates: 'Man's power is active, progressive, defensive. He is eminently the doer, the creator, the discoverer, the defender [...] The woman's power is for rule [...] for sweet ordering, arrangement and decision [...] Her great function is Praise'.

Old-fashioned though such categorisation now seems, Ruskin's stress on equality in marriage was progressive for his time. Even more radical were Ruskin's opinions on the education of young women. He stressed the importance of physical training and exercise, and referred to the necessity for 'freedom of the wild outdoors'. In general he noted that 'a girl's education should be nearly, in its course and material of study, the same as a boy's; but quite differently directed'. Of the two, 'the girl should be earlier led, as her intellect ripens faster, into deep and serious subjects'. Further, 'her range of literature should be, not more, but less frivolous', and — very radically — Ruskin advised that there should be no restrictions on a girl's reading. Here, as in all Ruskin's strictures on the upbringing of a girl, the important thing was her freedom:

> Turn her loose into the old library every wet day, and let her
> alone. She will find what is good for her; you cannot; for there is
> just this difference between the making of a girl's character and a
> boy's — you may chisel a boy into shape, as you would a rock, or
> hammer him into it, if he be of a better kind, as you would a

piece of bronze. But you cannot hammer a girl into anything. She grows as a flower does — she will wither without sun; she will decay in her sheath, as a narcissus will, if you do not give her air enough; she may fall, and defile her head in dust, if you leave her without help at some moments of her life; but you cannot fetter her.

Syd and Amy's application of this educational theory was to be liberating for the Clift girls, who were allowed to grow like the wild morning glory that spilled over the nearby hillside. The Clift boy on the other hand — like the local basalt — suffered the effect of the chisel and the hammer.

Margaret was born on 21 November 1918, just after the declaration of peace in Europe. She was a beautiful baby — fair-skinned, rosy-cheeked, and with the strong limbs and blooming health which she had inherited from her father's family. Photographs of her as a toddler show a chubby, winsome child. By the time she was five or six she was extremely pretty in the style that was fashionable for little girls in that era. Even at a young age it was clear that Margaret was very intelligent, with an artistic streak that revealed itself in her early crayon scribbles. She would amuse herself for hours, playing with petals and shells, arranging them in pretty patterns. She did not like dolls; to her doting parents, this seemed further evidence of her superiority to other children.[15]

In order to make any sense of the relationships which would develop between the siblings in this family, it must be understood that this first-born child was the apple of her parents' eye. As to the extent of the mother's love, this lonely woman was — perhaps unconsciously — recreating her own mother Sarah's love for her young self through the devotion she showered upon Margaret; if Amy was living out the role of Sarah, Margaret was (in her mother's eyes) Amy writ large. It had always been a source of grief to Amy that (as the relatives had repeatedly told the orphan-girl) she was not nearly as beautiful as her mother.[16] For Amy, it was sheer joy therefore to look into the mirror of her daughter and discover a prettier self.

While Margaret was the recipient of all the love that Amy had been storing up since her own mother's death, she provided for her father an opportunity to ease the pain of *his* childhood memories of beatings and mean-spiritedness by lavishing attention on this child. Sixty years later, she commented:

I think possibly because I was the oldest, because he had no *thing* about the fact that I was a girl, or anything else, he treated me like the son — his child.

I was taught to fish, I went out in the boat with him, and things like that. Did all the things that an elder son would do. And he'd take me down on the beach, we'd fish at night, he'd discuss the planets and the stars and the tides, which was all grist to my mill.[17]

If Margaret was a surrogate son to Syd, a real son was born in 1922. By now it was six years since Amy had moved into the supposedly temporary dwelling of the quarry cottage beside the creek. The boat had sunk. All the savings were gone. Amy's despair had set in. Another child meant more work and less time to lavish upon the prodigious Margaret. Yet Amy was pleased to bear a son for her husband — not least because this allowed her to feel that her childbearing (and perhaps even sexual) duties were over.

Syd too was delighted to have a son, with whom he could play cricket and football and other manly games. But this son wasn't the sporty sort of boy that Syd wanted. Perhaps the trouble started with calling the infant 'Barré'; a name with an accent didn't go down at all well in Kiama, and though it was quickly changed by the locals to 'Barry' (and by the family to 'Badge'), there would remain an association of foreignness and femininity. More likely, however, it was the rheumatic fever which the boy suffered during early childhood that gave him the softness and sweetness which Charmian would later describe in an essay:

> He was a peculiarly gentle boy, more-than-average good at everything if he had a chance to work on it laboriously and in secret, but excelling in nothing except his instinct for what was kind and generous and brave and true. He was sick with apprehension before any competition, and when he came first it was by virtue of will and endurance and to please us, who valued such things [...]
>
> He had too what is rare in a child — acceptance. Whether it was a cut with a tomahawk that sliced off the end of his finger [...] or a belting with the razor-strop for some particularly dangerous piece of devilment I had led him into and left him to take the blame for, he accepted it without fuss. When he cried or raged it was always alone.

So he was at his happiest and most relaxed with animals and smaller children, who always recognised him instinctively and didn't care about first prizes any more than he did.[18]

In his gentleness, his sensitivity, and his non-competitiveness, Barré was everything his father was not. In addition, Syd had no patience for sickness, and found it somehow tainted and sissy. These inadequacies — from Syd Clift's point of view — served to deepen the father's love for Margaret, and to increase the way in which he allowed her to share his manly world.

It was only a few months after the birth of Barré that Amy found herself pregnant again. In the cruel fashion of family 'jokes', it was to be openly acknowledged that this third conception was 'a Mistake'; and indeed by the time she was a young woman, Charmian was to know that Amy had considered an abortion.[19] Perhaps it wasn't so much that the infant was unwanted, as unnecessary: the parents already had a daughter and a son, and the quarry cottage was small. It is quite likely that some of Amy's concern was on medical grounds: given that she believed that her own mother had died of childbirth, it cannot have been a pleasant surprise to find herself pregnant again so soon.

Once this second daughter was born, Syd and Amy certainly loved her. It was just that they continued to love the first daughter more. Within the family, Charmian's role was that of the Afterthought: the wearer of hand-me-downs, the one who is more or less expected to bring herself up in the wake of the others because the novelty of parenting has worn off.

At one point in *The End of the Morning* the child-character Cressida looks back to a time of ultimate happiness that existed — and ended — before the time of her own birth. This reflection occurs when Cress sees her father at the doorway of the machine shop of the quarry; the image blurs with another image 'familiar from the family photograph album' of her father in this exact place but holding a small dog in his arms. The child finds the sepia photo 'mysterious beyond telling, for it belonged to the inconceivable time before I, Cressida, was born'.

> And that had been my father and yet not my father because I was unborn ... Ah, how could that be?... When and what was that time? Passionately I loved that unknown sepia man with the dear little unknown sepia dog. He would never have shouted 'bloody fool!' at me nor have preferred Cordelia. Oh, that still brown world of before when everything had happened! Everything! [...] There

had been boats, flat and elegant and the colour of weak milk coffee — the *Grace*, the *Kestrel*, the *Valkyrie*, the *Cordelia*. (Cordelia, of course, had existed in that misty brown world; I did not question this, being accustomed to Cordelia getting the first and best of everything.)[20]

With this we hit the chord of sibling rivalry which reverberates through all of Clift's autobiographical fiction. Yet in her account of the evidence for the richness of the world before she was born, Charmian wasn't exaggerating. Margaret herself noted: 'I have a photograph album full of the family, where there was only me'.[21] And while this passage reflects the feeling — fairly common to the youngest in a family — of being left out of everything, there is also a sense of something deeper working: self-blame, perhaps, or even guilt.

> How rich and mysterious that lost brown world seemed. When things had *happened*. Why was it all over before I was born? ... or perhaps ... it was an uneasy thought and seldom admissable ... it was myself being born that had done it, for I was, I knew from a bellowed, inexplicably amused remark of my father's, a Mistake. Perhaps, in some dreadful, incomprehensible way, I was responsible for the *Cordelia* being sunk and the Spode being broken and the disappearance of the lace tablecloths, for certainly nothing had happened since I was born, nothing at all, as though my mother and father had known, the very day of my birth, that it was all up now and nothing *could* happen any more until they got Cordelia ready for whatever marvellous thing it was that was certainly going to happen to her.[22]

This passage is written so lightly, yet its poignancy is none the less for that. Did Charmian — like her beloved Tristram Shandy — see her conception as setting in motion a series of family catastrophes?

These two things — feeling unwanted, and feeling that she played second fiddle to Margaret — would establish a rhythm during Charmian's childhood that would beat through the rest of her life.

By the time Charmian was born, Syd — now aged thirty-six — had well and truly settled into the role that he would play in his small community. Decades later, when Kiama people spoke of him, a certain phrase recurred: 'Syd was a character ... Yes, Syddie was a *real* character'.

'Real characters', of course, are people whose characteristics are so exaggerated or so eccentric that they are fabulous — unbelievable — more like figures from fiction than human beings from real life. Syd Clift was certainly that. Indeed, it is almost impossible to get him down on paper in a non-fiction account; for Syd Clift, the novel is the right genre (as Charmian well knew). This is not surprising, for Charmian's father spent most of his time acting a role which he had written for himself — some elements of which were cribbed from a couple of his favourite fictional characters. Yet perhaps the primary part of this persona was the manifestation of the downward mobility which has already been mentioned: Syd would set out to convey the impression of being a fair dinkum Australian working class bloke, insofar as he understood what that entailed.

First of all, he put on (or took off) the costume: 'Mr Clift was a man that I never ever seen dressed up', declared a woman neighbour. 'You know, he was casual, always in the bare feet.'[23] And a workmate added that 'He was always a man who'd get around in a pair of shorts and no singlet on — *you* know. He was a man who liked to show his muscles and what-have-you'.[24]

Syd made his supremely masculine presence strongly felt in the physical world — working up at the quarry until he dropped, fishing from the rocks or the beach, playing cricket in the local team, yarning and chewing over politics at the 'Corner Parliament' outside Davies' shop where the men 'regularly amalgamated for a bit of a night-time session'.[25] Even when Syd was lying at home reading, he signalled his existence to those outside by the stream of tobacco juice that spurted out the window and splashed down the wall, or the pipe-smoke that pulled the next-door kids across to hear a tale of all the bream he'd caught that morning simply by tying a string to his bare toe and hauling the fish all the way from the beach through the window to his couch.[26]

Another story he sometimes told concerned an incident which supposedly happened during one of the marathon swims he would make, way beyond the last line of breakers. On this particular occasion, the swimmer was so far out to sea that the crew of a passing ocean liner thought he was shipwrecked! The vessel pulled alongside him, a rope was thrown down and the 'shipwrecked mariner' was pulled aboard. Syd had a cup of tea and a bit of a yarn with the captain and crew as the ocean liner made its way up the coast. Eventually at Five Islands, off the coast at Port Kembla, he'd finished his cuppa, and so he just dived over the side again and swam ashore. As his North Kiama audience would shake their heads in wonder, Syd would reach his punchline: 'It wasn't the swim that beat me', he used to declare. 'It was the bloody walk back home from Port Kembla!'[27]

As part of his persona of the physical, knockabout bloke, Syd clearly felt it was necessary to act and speak in a manner that would shame the proverbial bullocky. Oddly, however, the fictional model for this part of his act was based on Rabelais. Syd Clift incorporated into his speech the French novelist's explicit but archaic bawdry, and he set out to appear 'as self-indulgent in the motions of his body as Gargantua' — publicly farting, belching, chewing tobacco, spitting, picking his nose and scratching his crotch, to the shame of his wife and daughters.[28] While obviously Syd thought such roughness added authenticity to his image, in fact his coarse language and behaviour shocked the North Kiama neighbours, who decades later would complain that Syd's swearing 'would make your hair stand up'. His booming voice and his rich Derbyshire accent made his expletives all the more noticeable. And to everyone's profound shock, 'he swore in front of his daughters'. But that wasn't all. One of the local men declared: 'They tell me he used to get around in the house in the nuddy, among the girls and that. I never seen it, but I would believe it'.[29]

This story must surely be baseless gossip, for Amy was extremely prudish, even by the standards of the time: while it was her 'curious boast' that her husband had never seen her naked, she would also go to elaborate lengths of tacking her way down the back yard in order to disguise her visits to the dunny, and would not even display her underclothes on the washing line. ('Where and when she washed them, how she dried them, or indeed if she possessed such articles, nobody knew'.[30]) Yet Syd's frankness of speech and his displays of bare flesh could easily give rise to rumours like this in a community unaccustomed to such things. Indeed, 'His nickname was Chidley', a couple of his workmates remembered. 'Yes, Chidley Clift. That was his name'.[31] The real Chidley was an eccentric social reformer who, in the 1920s and '30s, used to wander about Kings Cross and the Domain dressed in a kind of loincloth and distributing pamphlets he had written about sex and physical culture. It is easy to see how, in North Kiama, Sydney became Chidley.

Yet if Syd's expletives and mannerisms were borrowed from Rabelais, his opinions were frequently those of Laurence Sterne's character Mr Shandy, with whom Charmian's father shared a deep affinity. Each was 'something of a moral philosopher' as well as 'a good natural philosopher'; each was a 'born orator', 'proud of his eloquence'; each was self-taught, or '*theodidaktos*', taught by God rather than by a university; each was obstinate; on the physical side, each was short; but most importantly, each had a mind so singular, so ingenious, that he 'would see nothing in the light in which others placed it; — he placed things in his own light'.[32]

A character composed of such disparate elements would appear strange, no matter what the circumstances. The particular problem with Syd Clift was that this hugely energetic and idiosyncratic person was stuck in a valley so small that he did not encounter in his daily life enough new things and new people to challenge his brain. Without sufficient outlets for his physical, intellectual and emotional needs, he resorted to bullying and petty tyrannising. Like a lion in a cage, unable to work off its energy hunting for large prey, he would ease his boredom by batting at the mice and cockroaches that scurried around the floor.

Like a lion, and also (his wife used to say) like a big frog in a tiny puddle. And yet, of course, the cage or the puddle was entirely of his own choosing. Why?

'Because he's indolent', Alma Morley explains to her daughter Christine in *Greener Grows the Grass*. 'And because it's much easier to be a big frog in a little puddle than to be a little frog in a big puddle'.[33] In *The End of the Morning* Tom Morley's wife tells her children that their father 'is totally lacking in ambition'.[34]

It was not really that Syd Clift lacked ambition but that he saw ambition as part of the middle class aspirations that he had officially renounced. Besides, he adored fishing and pottering in his shed and reading and yarning: it is appropriate that Clift titled one of her essays about him 'The Pleasure of Leisure'.[35] At the same time, however, Syd was highly competitive, totally elitist, and he possessed a great sense of his own superiority. Indeed, his elitism and competitiveness were so strong that they led him to the belief that 'nothing was worthwhile doing if you didn't do it better than anybody else'.

> My mother had wanted once to have Cordelia taught the piano
> [...] But my father had said there was no point learning the
> piano unless you were going to be Paderewski, and he had
> bought a mouth organ and given it to Cordelia. When, after
> two weeks, not one of us could play a tune on it, he was
> triumphant. Obviously, there was no musical genius among us.
> Therefore, why piano lessons?[36]

Overall, the level of excellence which a member of the *Clift* family would have to reach was so high that it would be impossible to achieve. So why try anything? While this sort of attitude stems from a deep-seated fear of failure, it also assumes the role of a self-fulfilling prophecy. It would prove a dangerous outlook, when passed on to the three Clift children.

Syd's paradoxical temperament and ambiguous class position were also manifest in his politics. Indeed, the ambivalence of Syd's political stance was such that his daughter would describe his beliefs in very different ways. In one essay Charmian recalls that

> At the time of the Spanish Civil War my father used to pace around the house at night, restless, bitter, impotent of action. It was all so far away, he was no longer young, there was nothing he could do. He was a liberal humanist, his passion for justice was intense, his rages against persecution and oppression were monumental, his condemnations absolute and unalterable. We were conscious through all our childhood of vast forces working for good and evil and that such forces directly concerned us: at the time of Munich my father wept.[37]

Yet in *The End of the Morning* Cressida Morley's father is described not as a liberal humanist but as a 'theoretical Marxist' who 'had a passionate faith in the Great Russian Experiment' and who 'voted Labor, but would have voted Communist if there had been a Communist to vote for'.[38] In fact, on the south coast of New South Wales in the Depression years there was ample scope for a Communist to practise what he preached, for the Communist Party of Australia was active in the Port Kembla union movement, and was also busy organising the unemployed in the shanty towns and dole camps: the South Coast Dole Riots of 1931 are among the most famous protests of the period.[39] Syd Clift made no effort, however, to take part in any such political action.

Another of Syd's pet hobbyhorses was Major Douglas's theory of Social Credit.[40] Because Charmian herself did not know what this economic philosophy was, she did not realise that it was very much at odds with the leftist views which she believed her father to have held. In fact this theory, developed during the 1920s by a Scottish engineer, was put forward as an alternative to socialism. As the historian of the Social Credit movement, C B MacPherson, has noted: 'No doctrine could have been better designed to appeal to the middle class'. Yet it was most particularly the 'insecure sections of society [...] whose economic position may be defined as *petit-bourgeois*' which MacPherson pinpointed as taking up the major's nostrums.[41] While the social aspect of Douglas's theory centred on self-help individualism, the economic solution included bypassing democratic government and appointing technical experts who would fix the price of products and issue the population with social credits — rather along the lines of the economic policy which the One Nation Party would promulgate in the 1998 federal election.[42]

If Syd the engineer and descendant of a family of professional soldiers included this Scottish military engineer among his role models, this was also a matter of rhetoric rather than action. Although Charmian did not understand her father's politics, she was fairly close to the mark when she noted in another essay:

> Actually, my father was only militant in conversation, being a hedonist by nature and finding fishing more to his liking than union meetings, but he paid his dues regularly and had Strong Opinions, upon which he discoursed lengthily and passionately. (I was wrong to use the word 'conversation'. He probably never had a conversation in his life: at least I never heard anybody else get a word in.)[43]

And as she says of Tom Morley, it didn't matter if he neglected to attend a union meeting, because 'he could always tell them what they should have said or done or resolved after'. If Syd's sloth was at odds with his activism, his sense of superiority added an autocratic element to his support for the working class. After political conversations with his workmates he often stormed home in fury: ' "What's the flaming use?" he demanded of my mother. "Even if they vote the right way they don't know why. Don't even *want* to know why. Silly buggers won't be *told*! You can't *tell* them!" '[44] This fits with the part of Syd Clift that revelled in Wagner, that thought fair people naturally superior to dark people, and that was 'intolerant of anything else than physical perfection and intellectual excellence'.[45] This was the part of Syd that caused him to stuff his judgements and his tastes down everyone's throat, that caused him to make Amy live in a place that she hated, and that caused Charmian to refer to him on one occasion as 'the terrible tyrant'.[46]

Tyrant — monster — and yet there was still something attractive about this preposterous man; and something liberating, despite his authoritarianism. It was as if you couldn't be near him without being swept up into his wildness, his strength. Whatever his faults, he blew like a breath of ocean air:

> True Shandeism, think what you will against it, opens the heart and lungs, and like all those affections which partake of its nature, it forces the blood and other vital fluids of the body to run freely through its channels, and makes the wheels of life run long and cheerfully round.[47]

As one of the neighbours declared: 'The old chap, he was friendly, he'd roar like a bull. He was tops, you know, as far as that went'.[48] Unlike the rest of the Clifts, Syd was liked in the little settlement — not least because, as the Depression set in, he was pretty well responsible for the livelihood of the whole community. The story goes that when the Railway Commissioners decided to close down the Bombo quarry because they couldn't afford to pay for maintenance on the equipment, Syd Clift made a deal with them that if he could keep the machines running for nothing, no men would be laid off. According to his daughters, he kept 'the Meccano set' (as he called it) going 'with hairpins and bits of wire and string', and 'although half the male population of the town was on the dole, no man in the quarry lost his job'.[49] A bit of embroidery may have been done upon this tale, but certainly it is true that, although the men of the local community suffered the standard Depression wage cuts, the Commissioners' Quarry stayed open.

Yet while people respected Syd's position and rather enjoyed the colourfulness which this character brought to the dull little settlement, no one pretended to understand him. Of course the working class act did not fool the North Kiama residents, for everyone knew that Syd's salary was considerably higher than that of the other men.[50] The thing no one could work out was: why would a highly skilled man want to pretend to live like a labourer? Indeed, why would anyone live in that place, if they could afford not to? It was all a mystery, like so many things about the Clift family. And while Syd's yarning cronies satisfied his need for male company, they were just an audience for his tales and his physical prowess. He was happy to play to this crowd, but he did not take this companionship to the level of exchanging home visits. The class line was drawn at the front fence.

During the three decades that Syd and Amy Clift lived in the tiny and closely knit community of North Kiama, they did not invite their adult neighbours into the house. Nor did they visit the homes of their neighbours.

> *Roy:* They were a family that always kept to themselves.
> *Cliff:* I don't think they ever had any visitors, like.
> *Roy:* Oh, no, no.
> *Cliff:* Not any neighbours like, or anything like that.
> *Roy:* Oh, no no.
> *Cliff:* Not that I can ever remember. Never. No, they kept to themselves. Always. I mean, they weren't like other people around here.
> *Roy:* Oh no! Different altogether!
> *Cliff:* I mean, neighbours here, they come now and again and visit you, like. Or you go down to them. But they never done that.
> *Roy:* No.
> *Cliff:* I think they were a funny family.
> *Roy:* Oh yes, they were a funny family.[51]

Roy Phillis and Cliff Sweet lived all their lives in the tiny North Kiama settlement and worked for years with Syd at the quarry, but decades later they still expressed a sense of great puzzlement as they talked about the Clifts.

Another neighbour, Mrs Richardson, who lived next door to the family for about fifteen years, also remarked upon the way the Clift family had kept to itself:

> Well, see — in these places you sort of know everybody, and you're more or less one big family and friendly. But they'd never ask you to come in, and they'd never ask you to go anywhere or anything like that, you know. Whereas we would.[52]

Yet if the family in general kept itself remote, this aloofness was taken to an extreme by Amy.

> *Cliff:* She never had much to do with anybody, did she?
> *Roy:* No, she was a person who always kept to herself.
> *Cliff:* Yes! Always to herself!

On the subject of Amy's aloofness, Mrs Richardson added:

> Very few people knew anything about Mrs Clift. She was a real lady [...] I always found her very nice whenever I did speak to her [...] But even though we lived beside Mrs Clift, you

wouldn't say that Mrs Clift would say, 'Come in and have a cup of tea.' And I couldn't say to Mrs Clift, 'Would you come in?'

While Syd took up a large space in the social canvas of the valley, Amy appeared to the locals as a small and often invisible presence. Given the amount of stickybeaking and gossip that clearly went on in the tiny community, it is easy to understand her closed door policy — although, if the neighbours had occasionally been invited in, they wouldn't have been so keen to know what went on inside the mysterious Clift cottage. While mention has already been made of the story of Syd walking around 'in the nuddy', another piece of gossip seems more credible, and — if true — more significant. According to one woman neighbour, Amy was a 'wardrobe drinker', while Syd was 'a heavy drinker'; a couple of the local men also remember Syd having a drink after work.[53]

This is completely at odds with the picture which Charmian Clift conveys in *The End of the Morning*, where the mother is so saintly that it is unnecessary to mention her sobriety, and where the author makes a point of differentiating between Tom Morley's abstemious behaviour and that of the other quarry men: 'My father neither drank nor gambled [...] For a self-indulgent man he was capable of great self-discipline. He loved drink as much as he loved tobacco, and deprived himself of it for [our mother's] sake, I think, and for us'.[54]

In regard to these apparently conflicting pictures, it is possible that they derive from differing periods. Charmian is, after all, describing characters based on her parents as she knew them while she was growing up. Perhaps Syd allowed himself to spend some of his wages on beer when he was no longer responsible for his children's upkeep. And perhaps Amy also started having an occasional drink at this time. It does have to be said that, at the very least, this picture is not out of character, either with Syd's 'self-indulgence', or with Amy's habits of concealment.

Certainly, Amy was a recluse. Moreover, she set out to avoid people noticing her. The diminutive impression of herself which she gave belied both her strength of character and the physical energy which she put into every day's work. In both fictional and non-fictional portraits, Charmian Clift has described her mother's 'small broad face, sagging with tiredness and neglect, seamed with worry lines', her wide and full-lipped mouth, her short nose, her 'honey-coloured' eyes, tilted slightly above the 'heroic cheekbones' which bore 'curious dark indentations like bruises or the stains of tears'.

> A kindly, ageing little woman you would think, noticing the dignity and strength of the crumpled face, the premature silver of the wispy hair, and perhaps missing the entirely youthful recklessness of the ardent golden eyes. A woman who would lie uncomplainingly in the bed she had made, mind her own business, and keep her own counsel.[55]

If Syd's whole persona was a public performance, it is just as clear that Amy was an intensely private person. Charmian notes in an essay that her mother 'nurtured an unrequited passion for privacy [and] used to wish with a fervent hopelessness for a ten foot wall around our weatherboard cottage'.[56] This privacy of Amy's had probably developed during the miserable time after her mother died: the time when the young woman seems to have closed everything in around herself, like a sea anemone retracting its slender tentacles. Yet it is possible that Amy might have been a loner, whatever the circumstances. Certainly, Charmian saw herself as sharing her mother's lone-ness and her passion for privacy, and declared that she had 'always been a loner by nature'.[57]

This passion cannot, however, fully account for Amy's complete isolation from her neighbours. Part of the problem was that Amy and the other women of North Kiama did not share the same interests. The only person who does claim to have talked with her from time to time was Mrs Davies, who ran the little store at North Kiama — and was therefore a little up the class and educational scale from the housewives in the quarry cottages. Amy would sometimes exchange library books with the shopkeeper, who remembered Mrs Clift making one of her rare expeditions out of the valley, to see Dobell's notorious portrait of Joshua Smith when it was displayed in Wollongong.[58] It is also important to note that Amy did not include children in her social ban. Joan King (née McAuliffe) lived next door to the Clifts as a child, and remembered running in and out of their house. She stated unequivocally: 'I loved Charmian's mother'.[59] And although Amy could not do things *with* her adult neighbours, she would do things *for* them. Mrs Richardson remembered: 'If she could do you a good turn, she would. I was very ill and I had to go to hospital and I had three little children and Mrs Clift was very good and she'd cook something and send it in'.[60]

Charmian hit upon the main cause of her mother's social isolation in her early fiction when she portrayed the snobbery of the woman who went under the name of Alma Morley, or Hannah Grey — the woman who wanted to have afternoon tea parties with the wives of the gentry in the township proper over the hill, and who saw the quarry wives as being beneath her. As time went on, however, the writer found it increasingly difficult to come to terms with this aspect of her mother, and so in *The End of the Morning* Mrs Morley's social aspirations are played right down, and it is even claimed that 'oddly' the neighbours 'never seemed to resent her aloofness'.[61] Yet even in this text, as in the short story 'The Awakening', the mother figure wins the local nickname of Lady Muck — and indeed is quite proud of it.[62]

Living in such isolation from the outside world, it is no surprise that Amy Clift's life revolved around the family, and the home. Indeed, Ruskin could have had Syd and Amy as his model when he was elaborating his polarity of the Husband as the ruler of the outside sphere and the Wife as the one caring for the peace and shelter within. Despite this balance of qualities, and despite Ruskin's policy, this marriage was not a relationship of two equals. Rather than King and Queen, Syd and Amy were in the roles of God and High Priestess, with Amy living out Ruskin's notion of 'untiring service'. It was not only Syd she served, but the children, and also the ideal of service itself.[63] Yet though she was to adopt the role of family servant, this was not the result of any servility in her nature. It was perhaps partly from habit — all those early years of skivvying had made housework second nature — and partly because the skivvying she had done in her youth had made her swear that no child of hers should waste her precious time on chores.

And so she would rise at the crack of dawn, before anyone else, and split the kindling on the woodblock, for neither Syd nor Barré did this for her. After a fight to get the temperamental stove alight, she'd cook porridge and a hot breakfast. Once her husband and children were out of the house, she would make the beds, sweep the floors and scrub the tattered lino. Even on weekends and school holidays, the girls were not expected to lift a finger around the house; nor did they, apart from occasional drying up.[64]

Next Amy would go out into the yard, split more wood for the washing copper, get a load of clothes boiling in the tin wash-house that in summer reverberated the heat like a drum. She scrubbed the grime from Syd's work clothes, hauled the wet weight of sheets and towels through the mangle, doing the whole process alone — unlike the neighbourhood women who often dropped in to help each other with the heavy work. Perhaps it was for this reason that Amy's wash would still tend to look grubby, just as her scrubbed floors would not shine and her darning was obvious, and even the dresses sewn so lovingly for Margaret would have bumps in the seams. Or perhaps it was just that — apart from cooking — Amy somehow lacked the knack of housework.

Struggling outside with the steaming laundry basket, her hair hanging in sweaty strands across her forehead, her clothing drabber and dowdier than anything her neighbours would be seen dead in, Amy Lila would still sometimes be moved to poetry. On one such occasion in the summer holidays, her young daughter (sitting idly in the long grass by the woodblock) observed the scene:

> As she set the basket down by the lines, she stood very still, and with an extraordinary expression, a listening expression, like a child with a seashell.
>
> And I heard it too, what she was hearing: that enormous beating beating beating of the surf, so close, so loud, so familiar that one never did hear it unless one listened.
>
> Then she flung her arms wide and declaimed in a sonorous voice: 'Roll *on* thou *deep* and dark blue *ocean* ... *rolllll!*'
>
> Sometimes, she said later to one or the other of us, you were *driven* to it.[65]

But with the time racing on towards midday, poetry had to be put aside, for Syd's crib-tin must be filled with its 'hot shepherd's pie or cauliflower cheese, its small glass jars of salad and cold butter and creamy rice pudding, packed according to ritual'.[66] Then Amy would trek up the dusty highway, past the cemetery, past the station, under a railway trestle, along a dirt road beside the beach, and finally up the hill to the headland quarry, where she would deliver Syd his dinner. Arriving back home, Amy would only have a few minutes before the children would come trotting over the hill from school, hungry for their lunches.

Another meal, another wash-up. Then out to the yard to see how the clothes were drying. While out there she would hoe and water the vegetable garden, for it took as much time as she could give it: unlike the rich volcanic soil of the township gardens, the earth at North Kiama was salty and arid. This gardening of Amy's was not a hobby or recreation, but more work that had to be done. Syd and Barré would sometimes provide fish or rabbits, but Amy's vegetables were the staple.

By mid-afternoon, as the children arrived home again, it was time for Amy to build up the stove and prepare the evening meal. A range of labour-saving appliances came onto the market in this period between the wars — and indeed these 'mod cons' were used by the neighbourhood women — but Amy did not have them.[67] Nor did she buy time for herself by purchasing bread instead of baking it, or by copying her neighbours' habit of sometimes serving up a meal of pork fritz and some of the tinned goods that were now available. Although this was partly done to save money (especially for a private little nest egg that Amy was putting away), it was also the case that she loved cooking, and she got a sense of pride from turning a scrag end of mutton into a savoury ragout. She got pleasure, too, from presenting her food beautifully upon the dining room table — not least because this drew a clear class line between her family and the others roundabout, who ate in the kitchen off a bare table.

This evening meal was the culmination of the priestess's day: it was a time of ritual and communion, with the food as the sacrament.

> There were always two courses for dinner and in winter usually three, and since she deplored the labour-saving practice of dishing up portions onto individual plates in the kitchen our old dining table always looked opulent with soup tureen and vegetable dishes and meat platter and sauce boat, in spite of the fact that the crockery was the cheapest possible, the cutlery stainless steel, and the tablecloth and napkins worn and washed to rags. The colours and the smells were gorgeous, and there were flowers for a centrepiece — nasturtiums in a stone ginger jar, spikes of stock, asters or crysanthemums, shaster daisies.[68]

Reading on through this account, it becomes clear why the author grew dissatisfied with changing Amy's name merely to Alma in her fictional recreations of family life, and chose instead the mystic name of Grace for her portrait of her mother in *The End of the Morning.*

> There was something ceremonious in our meal, the culmination of the day, the gathering together of all our disparate personalities into the affirmation of family. It was the recurring measure of my mother's creativeness, and although we never said

grace and would have howled with laughter had anybody suggested we ought, I think that we were all closer to being in a state of grace at our dinner table than at most other times.

Reverting to this topic a few pages later, the author is even more explicit:

High Priestess she was then, in drab print shapeless dress and horny toenails and bunion decently covered by sagging lisle stockings and run down court shoes, transmuting [such] ordinary substances as butter and flour and fish heads and vegetables and bloody scrag of meat into another sort of poetry, or communion, or grace.

Of course, a vital part of any sacrament is the sacrifice it requires. After dinner, the priestess began to slave and serve again.

Water was heated now for the washing-up, which Amy did in a tin bowl, perhaps with one of the children drying. Syd meanwhile lay with his feet up on the old brown couch and read — sharing his favourite bits out loud — or maybe listened to opera records on the gramophone which he himself had made (complete with a needle fashioned from the thorn of one of the aloes that grew in the dunes). While the evening wore on, Amy gave advice and encouragement as the children did their homework at the dining table. At the same time, she herself was busy darning linen or mending Syd's work clothes, or designing and sewing new dresses for Margaret. When the children went to bed there would be some talk with Syd about the children, until he went out to the verandah to relieve himself noisily into the fuchsia bush before turning in.

At last it would be Amy's time. She would take down from the mantelpiece the brown tobacco jar with the key pattern, and roll herself a ragged cigarette, and she would scribble away till very late with her scratchy pen, writing poetry which she would eventually scrumple up in frustration and poke into the embers of the dying fire.[69] Then she would sleep, in order to start all over again the next day.

It is little wonder that Amy's dreams were of the glorious escapes which could be made by her children:

So, as we grew, and my mother's imagination bounded and cavorted wantonly into the future, soared on ardent wings closer and closer to the sun — poor Icarus she — her physical world contracted more and more. Tighter and tighter. The quarry, the house, the beach [...]

When she wasn't ranging into the limitless future she was wandering dreamily into the past — the far past, that is — where her beautiful invalid mother — Sarah, the Jew — forever crocheted lace for her little starched petticoats and lovingly tied her waist with a buttercup ribbon [...]

The middle distance was blurry, and apparently of no significance whatever. Excepting that out of it came Cordelia.[70]

In this fictionalisation, Clift captures the intensity of her mother's vicarious aspiration. And this Cordelia — whom both parents believed was going to soar to the very pinnacle of achievement — was not Charmian, but her beautiful and artistic elder sister, Margaret.

Although by the latter part of her life Charmian Clift had almost completely rewritten her memory of her parents' marriage, occasionally she reveals a darker insight. In an essay about reading — written in December 1968 — she had this to say:

A friend of mine told me that she could never have properly or fully understood her own family background if she had not read Henry Handel Richardson's *The Fortunes of Richard Mahony*. Certainly I know that I would not have understood mine without the light shed upon it by D.H. Lawrence's *Sons and Lovers* and all his other stories of the pits and collieries, and lately, with painful recognition, by Christina Stead's *The Man Who Loved Children*.[71]

Through this reference to Lawrence's world of pits and collieries the author makes a link with the Kiama quarries. And yet the connection is far stronger. It is, after all, *family* background that the author is discussing here. It is surely no coincidence that the surname of Clift's fictionalised Morley family so closely mimics Lawrence's autobiographical family, the Morels. In reading *Sons and Lovers* as a young woman, Charmian Clift must have been struck by the similarity between Lawrence's mother-figure, Gertrude Morel, and her own mother — particularly the way in which both women lived vicariously through their aspirations for their children. Certainly, Mr Morel and Syd Clift had less in common, for Morel is a drunkard, an unskilled worker, a man with none of Syd's love of learning and literature. Yet there is a similarity of temperament — Morel is also given to explosive outbursts — and even Morel's dialogue would have evoked for Charmian her father's accent.

Given these parallels, Charmian Clift must also have been able to recognise, through this novel, the situation that existed between her own parents — a situation as terrible in its way as the 'deadlock of passion' which Lawrence describes as existing between the Morels.[72] If this seems unreasonable, given the number of descriptions of the happy Clifts and Morleys, then what are we to make of the 'painful recognition' with which Charmian had read Stead's novel, in which the author's family is transformed into the eccentric Pollit family? While there is not a great deal in common between Henny Pollit and Amy Clift, the similarities between Sam Pollit and Syd Clift are quite uncanny. Both are overblown, tempestuous, expansive characters who act with largesse to the world — but are bullies on the home stage.

Overall, the links with both these novels are so strong that a combination of these two fictional relationships — a marriage between Gertrude Morel and Sam Pollit — would be a pretty good facsimile of the marriage of Amy and Syd Clift. And of course the Pollit marriage — like the Morel marriage — is doomed from the beginning. Both these fictional households live in a state of constant warfare. Although sometimes the battles rage noisily, the worst thing about these two marriages is the enormous silence that seems to hang between husband and wife: there is not a moment of communication between the spouses. The same was surely true of Syd and Amy. They lived their lives in separate spheres — and indeed in all Charmian's accounts of her family, she presents her parents quite separately.

After all the trouble Syd had taken to escape his origins, he found his past catching up with him in about 1925, when his parents Will and Emma emigrated from England and settled in a wooden bungalow in the main residential section of Kiama township. For the former railway clerk, retirement to this sunny land opened up a whole new way of life:

> When my grandfather Will came to Australia he threw away his spats and he took off his bowler hat and hung it upside down on three chains from the veranda ceiling and grew a fern in it. The bowler hat stayed there until it rotted, and meantime Pardie Will went in for broad-brimmed felts, very dashing, and in summer

panamas, as broad-brimmed as the winter felts and rolled a little rakishly at the edges [...]

Anyway, apart from the broad-brimmed hats and the old, comfortable suits of fine cut and cloth, Pardie Will wore button-up boots, very thin and elegant, and a gold seal ring on his finger and a gold watch and a sovereign case with ten sovereigns in it on a gold chain looped across his lean old stomach. His head was bald and sun-browned and shiny and [...] he wore a military-looking moustache with waxed ends. His eyes were very brown and very warm behind gold-rimmed glasses. He smoked Capstan cigarettes from a flat gold case. His pockets were always filled with coins of small denomination which he jingled constantly in readiness for any small child who might be just thinking about an ice-cream or a lemonade or a chocolate bar.[73]

If this sounds a different person from the man who used to beat his young son Syd, the explanation for Will's former harshness — at least as given by Amy — was that his wife Emma had 'put him up to it'. This former schoolmistress was unchanged in her new role as Mardie.

She was such a scrap of a thing, smaller even than our mother, and still so pink and blue and fragile and pretty, with her hair in silver puff curls over her ears and drawn up into a high flat bun at the back. Only her mouth was wide and thin and clamped like a trap and she had a disproportionately long upper lip crackled all over with fine lines, and no eyebrows at all — just pink fleshy folds resting on the tops of her glasses, which were gold-rimmed like Pardie Will's and had worn a deep groove in the bridge of her nose. We admired her, for she was superior in every way to every other grandmother we knew or had heard of, but we loved Pardie Will and she knew it.

Meanwhile, between Mardie and her daughter-in-law 'there was an undeclared state of war', with Amy Clift 'acting meek' and Emma Clift 'ostentatiously not interfering'. If opposites attract, then perhaps there is some law that similar people repel each other. Certainly, Syd had married a woman who in some ways was very like his mother; and as Amy's dark hair would early turn to silver, the two women even looked like a pair of matching book ends.

Despite this mutual enmity, there was a 'formal ritual of visiting' between the two parts of the Clift family, with the grandparents coming to afternoon tea at North Kiama on Wednesdays, and Amy and the children spending the afternoon with the grandparents on Sundays. (Syd himself stayed clear of these occasions.) For these visits to town, Margaret would be 'beautiful in her latest dress — something special that my mother had copied from a magazine' and the two younger children would at least be 'scrubbed in the washing copper, our sores and welts bandaged, our hair combed, our feet constricted in shoes and socks'.

Once there, the elder granddaughter would present some hand-made novelty such as a little painting, or a cigar box decorated with shells, to the grandmother, who would praise the child and take all the credit for her artistic leanings: 'She's a Sharman, right enough. A Sharman through and through [...] Of course I painted myself when I was a girl'. (It goes without saying that Margaret was the favourite of the grandparents too.)

And then Pardie Will would escort the visitors on a tour of inspection of the vegetable garden — for he grew every imaginable vegetable and fruit and berry in his section of the half-acre block, which was separated by a privet hedge from Mardie's garden of English cottage flowers.

If the locals got a lot of pleasure from observing and discussing Syd and Amy, the senior branch of the Clift family also did not go unremarked. The attitude to these older Clifts was ambivalent. To some extent they were held in good regard because (unlike Syd and Amy) they at least conformed to a recognisable type, and observed the social niceties. 'They were a very gentle, distinguished type of couple. Very upright and proper, but gentle and kind', commented Marg Weston, who remembered them from her childhood.[74] On the other hand, this type was not only uncommon in Kiama but it carried a certain stigma. Mrs Richardson summed this up by mimicking a plummy accent: 'The old lady and her husband, they were *aristocrats*, you know [...] They were an English lady and gentleman!'[75] Of course, at 'Home' (which Emma openly pined for) they would have been regarded as lower middle class, but in Kiama their accent and manner gave the impression that they belonged to the upper-class.

In the locals' reaction to the combined nationality and perceived class of the senior Clifts there can be seen a mixture of respect and resentment. While people were in awe of Will and Emma, they also regarded them — quite correctly — as 'Pommy snobs'. This attitude to the grandparents flowed on to other members of the family, so that people would snipe at the 'superior ways' of the Clift girls, and would agree that 'Charmian had a lot of the English in her'.[76]

To be 'English' was, of course, to be foreign. Alien. On one occasion, as Charmian was coming home from school through the Cutting, she was attacked by a 'big bully-girl', who wrenched the little girl's shoulder and tore her dress and scattered her school books and started accusing her in a 'jeering' voice. ' "You're a bloody little Pommy," she [...] hissed with sadistic certainty. "That's all you are. A bloody little Pommy" '. As well as being upset, the victim was mystified by the epithet. The confusion increased when she went home and told her father. Given Syd's loathing for his country of origin, his reaction was predictable:

> My father's rage, unleashed, was always frightening, but this time
> it was catastrophic. His neck swelled. Veins stood out on his
> temples. He shook my poor bewildered childish person until my
> teeth rattled [...]
> 'You are *not*,' he bellowed in his rich Derbyshire accent. 'You are
> *not* a bloody little Pom. Never you forget it. You are not ... *not* ... a
> bloody little Pom. You are ... you are ...' and his huge fist groped
> to heaven for an identity tag. 'You are ... a bloody little *kangaroo!*'[77]

But, of course, it is understandable that the other kids saw Charmian as a Pom, for her father and grandparents were indeed English, and the Clift children spoke with a posh or 'English' accent. They also set themselves apart by using long words and 'correct' grammatical forms. To make things worse, this verbal priggishness was mixed with Syd's Rabelaisian vocabulary, and Amy's habit of throwing snatches of poetry into the conversation. All these things made the Clift kids 'talk funny', in the opinion of the locals.[78] Throughout her life, Charmian's manner of speaking would have the effect of making some people think that she was 'bunging on side'.[79] The unusually low pitch of her voice made her distinctive accent even more noticeable.

Overall, while Charmian felt unloved and left out, even inside her own family, this feeling of isolation was compounded by her sense of alienation from the community around her. As a Clift, she may have taken pride in being different, but she was enough of an ordinary child to wish at times that she was more like the others in her peer group.

Her very name set her apart. Amy may have borrowed it from one of Cleopatra's handmaidens in Shakespeare's *Antony and Cleopatra*, but this cut no ice in Kiama. Charmian would later relate how 'as a small girl in a small country town' she had 'suffered under' her name:

> Among the more orthodox Thellies and Winnies and Gwennies and Bettys [...] my own name had an outlandish quality that my mother, who believed passionately in the potency of names, had obviously never foreseen. Useless for her to drag in Shakespeare, or Plutarch either: everybody in the town *knew* she had made it up.[80]

While Charmian's name made her an oddity, there were a number of other peculiarities that made the child feel different from the people who lived around her. The difference was essentially a matter of class. By the most basic indicators of income, occupation and education, Syd Clift was quite a few notches up the scale from the quarry labourers amongst whom he lived. Decades later, an overwhelming sense of bewilderment rang out as one old North Kiama neighbour talked about this family who 'didn't do things like we do'. She ended up concluding: 'And at the back of it all, you wouldn't know what it was all about, you know?'[81]

This confusion was shared by Charmian herself, and by her sister Margaret. Trying to explain why the family had not fitted in, both would focus on the actual structure of the Clift family unit. Thus in her 1965 interview for the National Library, Charmian Clift makes quite a point of the social effect which the smallness of her family had had upon her.

> We were very separate, quite alien in a way, and I think that has stayed with me all my life, in that we didn't have cousins and grandmothers and all the usual paraphernalia of people who had been born into a community where their ancestors have lived for a long time. In a sense that has always stayed with me. I think I have always been on the outside looking in a little bit.[82]

Some time later in this interview, she returns to this theme. Rather curiously, after saying how 'tremendously happy and tremendously valuable' her childhood was, she continues: 'I could go on for quite a long time about that, about the sort of family we were, and the fact that in this isolation and in those days and the fact of being rather an alien family in this small town, we cultivated our own amusements'.

From here she launches into a description of herself and her siblings reading and writing and drawing and painting — the sort of thing which is part of the standard myth of the happy and clever Clift family — but the words that really ring out in this jumbled passage are 'isolation' and 'alien'. Meanwhile Margaret commented much more succinctly that as a child she 'had a very bad time' because she 'wasn't related to anybody'.[83]

Of course, the size of the Clift family unit was in itself a class indicator. Only posh people had small families. In this rural working class community, there would be up to a dozen children in a family, and at times the networks appeared to extend so far that everybody seemed to be related to everybody else. Within this web of kinship, there was little formality: relatives were always popping in and out of each other's houses, and meals were a matter of stretching whatever was in the pot at the time.

What a contrast this was to the tight and tiny unit of the Clifts. Once or twice, Grandpa Currie came to visit from his farm at Griffith,[84] but this could not make up for the complete absence of aunties and uncles and cousins and babies. Nor could the formal ritual of twice-weekly visiting between the two sections of the Clift family compensate for the frequent informal visiting of all the other families.

While the Clift children missed out on the fun of a big family, they also missed the support which comes from kinship; they missed the sense of deep-rootedness in the community which the long-established families possessed; and — perhaps most important of all — they lacked the opportunities the other kids had for learning how to socialise. Throughout her life, Charmian would seem to some people to be cold and unaffectionate. She did not find it easy to make friends.

As a child, she longed for the kind of social contact that a big family provided. Joan King remembered that whenever her numerous aunts and uncles and cousins arrived, Charmian used to run into their house and revel in the hubbub.[85] It was one of these sorts of occasions that the adult Charmian recalls in the essay 'Other People's Houses', in which she describes visiting a neighbouring cottage one evening when the family was eating in the kitchen:

> The kitchen smelled of cabbage steam, damp baby, and boiled corned beef. It was crowded with unnecessary furniture, cheap and ugly, and family photographs, and simpering religious prints, and inexplicably I wanted to cry, wanted to be part of it,

wanted to eat corned beef off lino and live in that steamy kitchen
for ever and ever.[86]

In this lament of the child, wanting so poignantly to 'be part of it', we
catch a glimpse of a feeling which would be revealed throughout Charmian
Clift's life — the desperate desire to be on the inside, rather than 'outside
looking in'. This was also, of course, a wish to be ordinary, rather than
exceptional. For superior though the Clifts might have been, they were as
alien in their environment as if they had come by spaceship from another
planet.

Throughout her childhood and adolescence, Charmian would resort to
various strategies aimed at passing herself off as one of the insiders —
firstly with the quarry kids, and later with 'the silvertail set' in the town. She
would fail in both regards.

4

A FREE CHILD

My own Australian childhood had been wild and free. And although the
details and even the names of the games we played then were lost to me,
I had never lost the knowledge that was woven into those games —
a free child's certain knowledge of the limitless possibilities of the
human body, the limitless aspirations of the human soul.[1]

In 1929, Charmian was five years old, turning six in August.
This year when she hung around her dad at night as he sat with the
other men up at the Corner Parliament, she found the conversations
turning from fascinating subjects like blackfish weed and cricket scores to
boring things like money and politics. Sometimes when Syd came home
from one of these sessions he seemed worried. 'Jesus, Amy', he'd say. 'There's
a bad time coming'. Over the next few years Charmian would hear more
talk, 'about deflation, retrenchment, Sir Otto-bloody-Niemeyer, and Jacky
Lang. Always Jacky Lang'. There was a song, too, about going in Jacky Lang's
boat. And Syd would explain Douglas Social Credit to the other fathers, and
get angry and shout when they didn't understand. 'Ignorant bloody fools!
They won't be *told*!'[2]

But to the little girl, skipping on the footpath as she eavesdropped, none of
this mattered. In 1929 something happened — something far more
momentous than the growth of Australia's external debt or the election of the
Scullin Labor Government — for it was now that Charmian started school.
Barré was going into first class, and Margaret was about to enter fifth class.

It is significant that, in all the childhood stories told in Clift's essays and
her autobiographical novel drafts, there is not a single anecdote about

primary school; only in a very early short story do we find a school scene. Indeed, of the education of the young Cressida Morley, the only reference to schooling is to deny its role: 'The beach was our nursery, playground — yes, and our school too, for although we went formally to the free state school over the hill in town, the important things we learned we learned on the beach'.[3]

The impression given by this passage is of the children as barefoot ingénues who learn from nature. This impression is reinforced in the essay 'Goodbye Mr Chips', in which the author lightheartedly claims to have received no benefit at all from her schooling:

> The only things I learned at school that proved applicable to my own highly personal life were reading and writing, and since I could read and write before I ever went to school, and nothing and nobody in the world would ever have stopped me reading and writing, I might as well have spent some of those years doing something I really wanted, like joining a circus or a ballet school or a theatrical troupe or a band of gypsies.[4]

In fact Charmian, through her primary school days, was a keen and good scholar. In keeping with her parents' ambitions she and her siblings went not to the one-teacher school up at the Bombo settlement, which many of the North Kiama kids attended, but to the large old stone school on the edge of the harbour. This was called a Superior Public School because secondary as well as primary classes were offered: students stayed on after sixth class until they reached the legal leaving age of fourteen, and it was even possible to do the third year Intermediate Certificate there. As a result, Charmian would go to the same school as her big sister, even during Margaret's secondary years. This encouraged the younger girl to strive in the field of academic achievement, which Margaret found difficult; by doing something better than her big sister, Charmian hoped to win the approval of her parents.

None of this, however, fitted into Charmian's picture of herself, or the picture which she wanted to show to other people. Free spirits do not sit in smelly classrooms, agonising over long division. In one of the earliest drafts of *The End of the Morning*, young Miranda (as the alter ego character was then called) is described as being 'always top of her class at school'.[5] By the next draft of this novel, as Miranda changed to Cressida, any such reference to scholastic achievement was omitted. Even the appearance of Charmian dressed for school is at odds with the image of the little pagan with sand between her toes. In a country town in these Depression years, many students came to school without shoes on their feet or food in their bellies, but the Clift children were well fed and they wore shoes and socks, and their clothes were always clean and ironed — even if Charmian's frocks were Margaret's carefully mended hand-me-downs.

Another piece of the primary school picture also had to be edited out, for while Charmian was happy for people to know that she was a clever child, she didn't like to think of herself as having been good. It is clear, however, that this student was well behaved in class. She was also hardworking: unlike some clever children, she wasn't shy, but was keen to be the first to put her hand up and answer a question. Naturally, her answer was usually right, for she had a wide general knowledge. She did her homework, too — her mother saw to that — and she decorated it prettily with her own drawings, or with pictures cut from magazines. In fact, she liked school so much that she wanted to be a schoolteacher herself when she grew up.[6]

Although she would have hated to admit it, the truth of the matter is that the barefoot little beachcomber had all the qualities of a Teacher's Pet. None of this fitted into the myth-memory which Charmian Clift wanted to create.

While the theme of childhood was almost an obsession in Charmian Clift's unpublished fiction, it also assumed an extraordinary importance in her life. 'Isn't it strange', she asked in one of the essays, 'how your childhood dogs you and tracks you and will not let you be?'[7] And in the National Library interview she stated, 'The older I grow, the more I realise how I draw upon [my childhood] all the time, those very important formative years'.[8]

Well, yes. It goes without saying that childhood is the formative time, upon which we all draw — subconsciously as well as consciously — throughout our adult lives. But as for childhood dogging us and tracking us … Doesn't this usually happen to those whose childhoods have been *unhappy*? Charmian Clift, of course, always maintained that hers had been not just happy but idyllic.

In fact, Charmian's preferred view of her own childhood combines two different mythic notions of Paradise: the Judaeo-Christian ideal of Eden before the Fall is merged with the pagan ideal of the Golden Age. Thus childhood is seen as a time of primordial innocence and bliss, an existence lived in a garden so enclosed, so perfect, that unhappiness is excluded.

Simultaneously, childhood is seen to encompass a wild freedom which looks back to Olympus and beyond. It is, in short, presented as an Australian pastoral: *et ego in Kiama* ...

In the following account, Christine Morley is a young woman in her early twenties, sitting with her lover Justin in a bar, trying to explain how her 'memories of childhood [are] permeated with the smell of the creek':

> I suppose I always think of it because it was the only time in my life I was really happy — without complications. I can't remember being aware of injustices or inequalities, although I suppose I must have been, because I got myself the reputation of being a stormy petrel. But as far as I can remember I thought my father was the cleverest man in the world, and my mother the most understanding mother, I was in perfect accordance with my brother John and I *worshipped* Judith. I used to feel sorry for the kids in town because they couldn't possibly have such a wonderful family as mine, and because they didn't have the creek and the beach. The town kids had to swim at the town surf beach and they had nowhere at all where they could paddle canoes, even if their fathers were clever enough to make them ... God, Jus, the smell of that creek, and the paddles swish-swishing, and the kids screaming and the dogs yelping.[9]

In her first travel book, *Mermaid Singing*, Clift gave as one of her reasons for moving from London to Greece her concern at the restrictions of city life upon her two children, contrasting this with the wonderful childhood which she had experienced.

> My own Australian childhood had been wild and free. And although the details and even the names of the games we played then were lost to me, I had never lost the knowledge that was woven into those games — a free child's certain knowledge of the limitless possibilities of the human body, the limitless aspirations of the human soul.[10]

The writer hadn't actually forgotten the details of the games, but this wasn't the place for a wholesale act of remembering. What is important about these passages is that they contain between them the essence of Charmian Clift's particular myth-memory of childhood. In the first — Christine's account — there is an Eden of perfect contentment. This little girl who is 'really happy — without complications', who adores all her family and thinks she lives in the best bit of the world (or Kiama, which is the same thing), has certainly not tasted the apple of discord. In the second passage Clift, writing in the persona of herself, draws upon the pagan mythology of the Golden Age of childhood in order to evoke a picture of a 'free child' who is surely godlike in her 'limitless' powers.

These two ideals — perfect happiness and freedom without limits — are the two poles upon which the axis of Charmian Clift's world of childhood turns. These were also the poles which Clift used as navigation points throughout her life. But to what extent were the memories of these ideals based upon fact? Was this child completely happy? Did she feel loved?

Certainly, Christine Morley's description of her father as the cleverest father and her mother as the most understanding mother in the world would be repeated with minor variations throughout Clift's writing career. But of course, a clever father is not necessarily a lovable one. This is Cressida's description of the children's relationship with the father, from the earliest extant version of *The End of the Morning*: 'Cordelia placated him, Ben feared him, and I lied to him or defied him'.[11] In the next version of this crucial passage, the author chopped the reference to her alter ego's defiance, and wrote 'and I lied to him for a crumb of approval'. The description continues:

> I don't think that any of us loved him, not in the way we loved our mother at any rate, but we respected him with all the strength of our childish imaginations and would not have exchanged him for a father more human or tender or kind. Our superiority was based on him.[12]

In an even later version, Cordelia is described as wooing as well as placating him, and in brackets the writer adds 'except Cordelia perhaps' to the statement that none of the children loved him.[13] While the subtle changes show how consciously the author was choosing which details she wanted to include or omit in her representation of family life, between them these three texts probably give a fair estimate of the Clift children's attitude to Syd. The necessity to excel was a terrible burden which this father placed upon all three of his offspring, a thing which 'dominated' their lives.[14] While it pushed Charmian initially to show off and boast to her father, and later to develop a pattern of behaviour that swerved between deceit and defiance, it completely undermined the confidence of poor Barré. Margaret's response was to sell her talent short. It is true, however, that the elder daughter loved her father — or perhaps 'worshipped' would be a better term:

> He was possibly the most honourable man I ever knew. There was absolutely nothing about him that was small or mean or petty or nasty. Nothing! And he and Charmian — she used to attack him about things, you know? But I believed everything he said. Quite frankly, I mean I didn't have to worry about religion and God, because I lived with *him*.[15]

It is relevant to point out that when writing *The End of the Morning*, Charmian named her sister for Lear's faithful daughter Cordelia, who gave love and service without questioning; although the fictionalised Syd was named after Tom o'Bedlam, both the fictional character and the model can also be seen as an exiled king, testing his children.

But if Margaret worshipped her father, Syd also assumed an exalted status in Charmian's eyes during the years of early childhood. In *The End of the Morning* the father is described as 'godlike in the number of things he could do better than anyone else',[16] and an extended portrayal of Cress taking the crib-tin to the machine shop 'that was my father's kingdom' is potent with Promethean (and Priapic) imagery. Not only is the room itself 'filled with such a humming and throbbing and whining that all the darknesses, gleams and solidities [are] blurred with waves of vibration' but the father emerges 'goggled and grunting from a rain of blue fire', the only thing to seem 'solid and hard among the shaking waves of noise and shadow'. After bending his cheek for his daughter's 'proffered kiss', he moves to the doorway and stands 'watching the sea with his cold blue eyes'. Cressida, looking back upon this memory of her childhood, exclaims: 'How powerful my father seemed then among the pillars of the earth!'[17] (It is salient here to remember that an earlier name for Cressida was Miranda. If Tom Morley is Prometheus, he is also Prospero.)

But again, none of this was very lovable — or indeed loving, at least by the usual standards of fatherly affection. Thus in *Greener Grows the Grass* the author writes that, although Christine was 'so proud' of her father 'because he was different to [...] the other men who went to work with him', she wished that 'she could get close to him as she did to her mother, but always when she wanted to confide in him she went cold and fluttery inside, for fear his face would wrench up in anger and he would shout "bloody fool" at her'.[18]

Top and below right:
Amy Clift née Currie.

Below: Syd Clift.

Syd and Margaret outside the machine shed at the quarry (c. 1921).

Margaret, aged 6, Charmian, 1, and Barré, 2½ (1924).

Will Clift with his grandchildren on Bombo beach (c. 1926).

Charmian, Margaret and Barré with Emma and Will Clift (c. 1936).

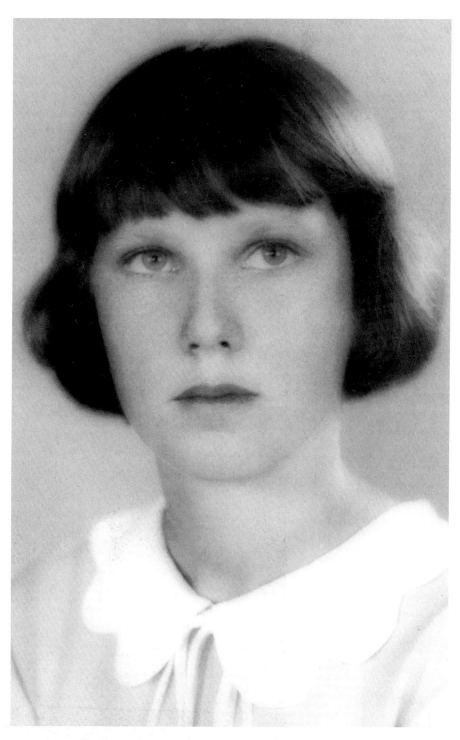

Charmian, aged 8.

Charmian in the back yard
of *Hilldrop* (aged 13–14).

Left: Charmian at *Hilldrop* (aged about 16).

Right: Portrait of Charmian (aged about 14) by Margaret Clift.

Charmian posing
for Margaret's
photography
portfolio (1940–1).

New South Wales title-holder, *Pix* Beach Girl competition, 1941.

While Syd was a far from comfortable father, it also seems that Amy was not a particularly affectionate mother. Despite references, such as the one above, to Christine or Cressida being able to 'get close' to her mother, there is no evidence in the various autobiographical texts of such closeness actually *happening*. Throughout her life, Charmian's need for love, and for the security that love brings, was so extreme that it is hard not to feel that the source of this anxiety was a childhood feeling of unhappiness.

If the idea of the happy and loving family was part of the fiction that Charmian liked or needed to invent, another fabrication was the picture of Charmian as a 'free child', unaware of 'injustices and inequalities', as she played merrily in the creek with a happy little gang of mates. To put this a slightly different way — if she was purely and simply happy, why did she get the reputation of being 'a stormy petrel'?

The other children certainly didn't find her easy. Because the North Kiama valley functioned as an enclosed world, Charmian's playmates in the early years were not from school and the town, but from the crowded quarry cottages. These were the kids to whom she would so often refer in her essays and in her fiction, sometimes running through a roll call of outlandish local nicknames such as the Bawny Crab, Flossie Dog, Pronson, Zulu, Honk, Donk, Geik, Splonge, Googles, Tom Fly, Little Woola and Creeping Jesus.[19]

If these kids were the cast, Charmian was usually in the combined roles of auteur director and dramatic lead. Charmian took these roles because of her quick intelligence, her imagination, and her physical skills at running and swimming and ball games. She also had the ability to throw herself completely into a game, and she was daring enough to perform dangerous feats, and to risk adult trouble by doing things and going to places that were forbidden.

The playing ranged from standard games to special ones inspired by the landscape. Charmian writing in the persona of Cressida remembers:

> Sometimes we played organised games (Ben and I were great organisers) like Rounders or Blind Man's Buff, It, Statues, Cowboys and Indians. Sometimes we fought pitched battles among the marram grass on the hills and in the valleys of the dunes. Sometimes, if the lagoon ponged, we organised labour gangs to dig a trench down to the sea. As the first sluggish trickle became a rush the escaping water gouged wet yellow cliffs out of

the sand, cliffs that split and crumbled and plopped and were wonderful for rolling down. Then, when the rush became a torrent, we would pelt back to the house and drag our tin canoes down through the rushes to the creek and paddle furiously around the loop and under the railway trestle and shoot rapids right down to the surf.

The railway trestle was the centrepiece for our most thrilling game. It was about fifty yards long from the tunnel mouth in the hill to the embankment on the other side of the creek, and supported on its long silvery legs at least thirty feet above the water. The idea was that when a train entered the tunnel on the town side of the hill (and you judged this by the whistle) we would begin walking across the trestle. If our timing was right we just made the safety of the embankment on the other side and slid down through the blue morning glory to the dunes as the train shot out of the tunnel. Nobody was ever killed, and of the very few of us reckless enough to play the game I was the only one who ever had to jump for it. The creek was full at the time and all I suffered was a badly wrenched ankle. But we never played that game again.[20]

Typically, on this occasion all the other kids 'were belted that night with their father's razor strops' (one of the mothers had seen), but Charmian and Barré 'lied [their] way out of it as usual'. Clift adds that she never walked the trestle again because she 'had felt fear for the first time [...], real fear, the kind that maddens or paralyses'. Yet she remained fearless in many other areas.

Bombo beach is notorious on the south coast for its dangerous rips and channels; a number of people have drowned there over the years. In Charmian's time, the local parents wisely restricted their offspring to the shallows, but the Clift children 'had full and free permission from the time [they] were seven and had passed [their] father's tests to swim out as far as [they] liked or could, out through the crash and foam into the marvellous dark exultant blue'. In reminiscing about the pleasures of this, Clift describes not just the sensation of the 'watery wheels' of the waves and the 'exhilarating ride' of surfing, but the joy of landing 'triumphantly on the sand among the timid paddling feet of Little Woola and the Bawny Crab and Tom Fly and the rest'. Mimicking her father, she exclaims: 'Ignorant fools! Ignorant bloody fools! They were beneath even contempt'.[21]

How the other children must often have detested as well as envied the Clifts! To be bodysurfing Bombo beach at the age of seven was extraordinary. And for a girl to be doing this was seen as something completely freakish.[22]

In contrast to these wild and active pleasures, there was the secret joy of cubbies. In an obituary essay for her brother, Clift notes:

> One cubby house was on the beach, just above the dunes and under the shadow of the cliff. It was made of four huge old aloe plants whose fleshy spears, broad-based and thick as paddles, were brushed with bloom and edged with rose-pink thorns. The light was always greenish inside the cubby. It was a still place, an away place, a place made for secrets.[23]

The writer then moves on to a description of other cubbies — in the lantana near Jacob's Ladder, in the bullrushes beside the creek, in the stones of the Bullring and right up the creek under the lilli-pilli tree. However, in *The End of the Morning* the author continues the story of what went on in the aloe cubby:

> Outside the cubby we never spoke of anything that had happened there — neither to each other nor to Creeping Jesus or Flossie Dog or any of the other snot-nosed sniggerers who were permitted to join us — but we kept a sort of record on the leaves, where we carved sets of initials, dates, dirty words, and crude drawings of genitalia. These carvings grew with the growth of the aloe spears, and I know that years later both Ben and I, grown out of such childishness, made separate furtive trips there with our rabbit-skinning knives to hack away the by then glaring evidence of our first explorations into sex.[24]

Another game played by the North Kiama kids involved spying on a strange old woman called Selina, who lived in a humpy up near Bombo quarry. According to local lore, Selina had once had a lover who had been helped over the edge of the quarry by her jealous husband. Charmian, Barré and some of the other kids would lie in the long grass and watch as the woman stood on a rock overlooking the precipice; it seemed as if she were waiting for someone.

The Selina story played such a vivid part in Charmian's imagination that the character of Selina would crop up years later in various narratives about the child alter egos, and the tale would provide a kind of key for the melodramatic element of *Walk to the Paradise Gardens*. In that novel, as Julia tells her husband the Selina story, she suddenly finds herself wondering 'if she *really* knew. Had she ever seen that still figure on the rock, or was she only repeating folklore told and retold until it had become fixed in her mind as reality?' Towards the end of the novel, Julia even wonders whether she had actually heard the story, or 'made it all up'.[25] While there really was a funny old woman among the humpy-dwellers up near the quarry,[26] this comment provides a timely warning about the nexus between hearsay and history, and the care that must be taken before one accepts this author's recycled folklore as fact. Like Julia, she was quite capable of believing her own stories.

As well as all these pastimes and games, there was hunting and gathering to be done. In these Depression years the North Kiama kids had an important role in helping eke out their family's provisions, and although the Clifts may not have been dependent on wild food, Amy was always grateful to save the housekeeping money and have something fresh for the pot. Charmian and Barré would roam the hillsides searching for mushrooms and blackberries in autumn, and often at dusk they would wander through the paddocks with a shotgun, looking for rabbits. A skill of Barré's (which even Charmian didn't seek to emulate) was to dive down beside the rocky reef at the southern end of Bombo beach to pull lobsters barehanded from the crannies.

Some games required props or toys. The Clift children had more of these than the other quarry children, for Syd's love of pottering in his shed meant that he would sometimes make elaborate playthings for his children. His greatest triumph was the canoes which he created, one particular summer, out of sheets of corrugated iron — first a sleek one for Margaret, and then one for Barré, and finally (when he was sick to death of the whole business) a potbellied and unstable tub for Charmian. These canoes crop up frequently in Charmian's accounts of childhood, but while in *Greener Grows the Grass* Tom Morley is portrayed as giving in to the wheedling of the neighbourhood kids and making canoes for quite a number of them as well,[27] this does not seem to have been true. A complaint made years later about the Clift children was that 'they never *shared* their canoes'.[28] Naturally, the comparative abundance of playthings available to the Clifts reinforced the view that they were 'better off'.

This jealousy on the part of the other children was not helped by Margaret's air of superiority, or by Charmian and Barré's tendency to take over the games. The problem with the Clift kids (some locals remembered) was that 'they weren't very good playmates, you know, because they always had other ideas'. They were bossy and impatient, and liked things done *their* way.[29] But as well as that, there was something you couldn't quite put your finger on: Charmian and Barré were the leaders in the games 'because they seemed to *know*, you know?'[30] All in all, Charmian's depiction of herself and her brother as being happy members of a little gang of mates does not fit with the memories of her contemporaries.

Charmian's sister Margaret remembered how she had 'wanted so much to be like the rest of them, but didn't know how to do it'. In return for her ignorance, the kids dubbed her 'the Duchess' and sent her to Coventry. Naturally, she found this experience terribly painful.[31] Charmian also seemed to know everything in the world, except how to be a child just like the others. Luckily, however, her closeness to Barré would spare her the ultimate misery of isolation which Margaret suffered.

Until Charmian was about ten or eleven, her brother was her 'first and best friend', both outside and inside the home. In the obituary essay, she declares:

> Being, as we were, a year apart in age, an inch apart in height, and a class apart in school, we were almost like twins.
> [...] We preferred each other's company to any other in the world. We were an alliance, wordless but unquestioned, against the world of adults and authority. We had, as far as we knew, no limitations whatever.[32]

The paradisiacal nature of the childhood of these two siblings is one of the themes of *The End of the Morning*, with Barré (thinly disguised as Ben) playing a young Adam to Cressida's Eve. In regard to the autobiographical nature of the depiction of Charmian and Barré as Cressida and Ben, it should be mentioned that most of the obituary essay was lifted verbatim from the novel, and Charmian's sister Margaret would speak wistfully about the friendship between her two siblings — 'They were mates. They were really good mates'. North Kiama neighbours would also comment on the closeness between Charmian and Barré as something exceptional.

Yet if the two younger siblings were true friends, the relationship between the sisters was extremely complicated. From Margaret's point of view, it seems barely to have existed: Margaret maintained that she and Charmian hardly knew each other until they both joined the army as grown women, and she was puzzled when told how strongly she featured (as Cordelia) in the drafts of *The End of the Morning*.

'But we led a totally different life!' she protested. 'Charm was just "Little Sister".'[33] (From Charmian's point of view, the dismissiveness of those last three words sums up the whole problem.) And Margaret always referred to the age difference between herself and her sister as being one of seven years, not five.

Although it is clear that from a very early age Charmian felt that she played second fiddle to Margaret, the painfulness of this did not really hit until Charmian began to approach adolescence — and Margaret simultaneously began to enter the adult world. Up to the age of nine or ten, the little sister mostly accepted the status and privileges conferred on Margaret by right of primogeniture; indeed, she claims that she was a more fervent worshipper of her sister than anybody else.[34] Though sometimes hurt by the way her parents and grandparents made such a fuss of Margaret's pretty face and artistic ability, Charmian had at this stage no particular ambitions in these fields so was happy to cultivate her own particular talent. In *Greener Grows the Grass*, the mother tells Chris: 'If Judith is my beauty and John is my only son, you're my brainy one. Judith never won prizes at school like you do, and she can't make up poetry. Being clever is just as important as being beautiful, Chris'.[35] This is echoed in *The End of the Morning* when Cressida overhears her mother comment that Cordelia is 'not clever in the way that Cress is'. The young girl secretly congratulates herself: 'Oh the joy of that! Cress is clever. Cress is clever. Clever Cress'. Overjoyed at her parents' 'approval' of her cleverness, she goes on to vow: 'Oh, I would be clever all right. That was going to be my specialty'.[36]

In a couple of the very early versions of the autobiographical novel, although Ben and Miranda (as the Cress character was then called) are described as 'an alliance against Cordelia', they are also described as having 'too much to do to worry about Cordelia'.[37] This was probably a fair description of how Charmian felt about Margaret most of the time, when she was a young child. As we shall see, it was later, as she reached adolescence, that Charmian began to bear a sense of terrible injustice that she would carry for the rest of her life.

Though Charmian could rely on Barré's loyalty, there were many times when he wasn't around to provide companionship, for he would be off with the other boys, either just roaming about or taking part in organised activities such as Cubs or team sport. Then Charmian would have to rely on the local girls.

In a short story entitled 'The End of the Morning' (written more than a decade before the novel of the same name was begun), the young heroine Sarah Clint is very much the leader of the female gang. The story begins with Sarah sitting alone on the woodblock. Through the paling fence creep the three next-door girls, who stand 'like suppliants' waiting for something to do until Sarah musters them into an expedition to clean up some graves in the cemetery across the creek from her house. The dialogue points up differences of education, as well as sensibility, between Sarah and the others. Here they discuss the grave-digger:

> 'Oh.' Sarah set down her bucket and craned her neck. 'I don't think Mr Bunger is here yet.'
>
> 'Per'aps,' said Doreen, busily scooping white pebbles into the pocket of her pinafore, 'there ain't been nobody died.'[...]
>
> 'Oh silly creatures!' Sarah took a lordly stance with her mop. 'Mr Bunger doesn't just dig graves. He is *entirely* responsible for the tidiness of this *entire* cemetery.'
>
> Phemie snickered. 'Mum says 'e's cracked. Bet 'e is too.'[38]

If Sarah lords it over the other children, she has cause to envy those who come from bigger and more ordinary families, for she has seen their 'small, important figures' in the funeral processions that pass her house: 'Sometimes it seemed to Sarah that no one would *ever* die in her family'. As the three other girls swap graveside reminiscences, Sarah has to take the lead again: 'Grabbing a mushy circle of rotting stalks she crammed it on her head and began to jig: "Look at me! I'm the Queen of Sheba!" '

At the end of the story, Sarah experiences a sort of epiphany about mortality when the girls discover a new grave-digger digging a grave for his predecessor. When the man shouts at the children, Winnie misinterprets Sarah's 'silent, scarlet concentration' and slings an arm around her shoulders. Sarah shrugs off the comfort.

Although the writer clearly intends that the reader should sympathise with Sarah's viewpoint, this is a sad story for quite the wrong reasons. Once again, the author fails to see that Sarah is an outsider to the world of the other girls because of her different social position. While Sarah's speech sets her apart, just as Charmian's way of speaking marked her difference, we also see the isolation of the Clifts in the alter ego character's frustrated feeling that her family is too small even to have a death in it. Overall, Sarah is a lone figure in the tale. At the opening, she sits by herself; at the end, she resists Winnie's overture of friendship and plunges into the private turmoil of her feelings. And in the Queen of Sheba scene, we see how the child's assertion of leadership is a cover for her embarrassing ignorance of ordinary life.

And yet, while it was at times a lonely childhood, this did mean that Charmian learned to develop her own resources, and to enjoy solitary pleasures. It is no surprise that one of these was reading.

Charmian was speaking the truth when she claimed that she could read and write before she went to school; certainly, she couldn't remember learning to do either of these things.[39] Precocious though she was, this early reading was the standard fare of nursery rhymes and children's books. However, when she was about eight years old — when she was in second class or third class — she 'discovered the novel'. On three separate occasions she would describe this momentous occasion:

> The first book I remember reading (I mean after *Henny Penny* and *Chicken Licken*) was *A Yankee at the Court of King Arthur*, and I was [eight] years old and sitting on the woodblock behind the laundry and the sun was beating on the tin behind my back and there was that smell of hot tin and the smell of wood chips and the smell of white stock that grew along the paling fence, heavy and hot and sweet beyond telling, and I still remember how Mark Twain got through to a small girl and I howled with laughter and tears streamed down my face and I suddenly knew what a wonderful thing it was to be able to read and what incomparable treasure there might be in the world of books. World beyond world beyond world.[40]

But Syd Clift wasn't content just to see his daughter reading for pleasure.

> Soon after [this discovery] my father, who believed in excellence in all things, gave me Laurence Sterne and said, 'Read that and you're educated.' I read it and I loved it, although I didn't understand it at all, and that love stayed with me too.[41]

This act of forcing Sterne on Charmian ultimately backfired on Syd:

> By galloping through *Tristram Shandy* at the age of ten I was enabled to recognise that my father was, in fact, actually modelling

himself on Mr Shandy, filching Shandeisms and using them as his own, expounding Shandy philosophies every day of the week with never a word of acknowledgement. This precocious perception of mine subtly altered my relationship with my (to then) infallible parent. I knew he was playacting, and that he playacted as often as I playacted, but the difference was that he didn't know that I knew. In a way it was saddening. It made him vulnerable.[42]

While the tone of this account — written more than three decades after the realisation — is mellow, surely the child was not saddened, but first shocked and then triumphant.[43]

Although — or perhaps because — Charmian's early reading of *The Life and Opinions of Tristram Shandy* caused her father to fall off his pedestal, she was always to claim that it was 'far and away [her] favourite novel',[44] and indeed in her adult life it was to become for her a sort of combination between a philosophy, a talisman and a security blanket.

Laurence Sterne wasn't the only author whom Syd thrust upon his young daughter. In a number of accounts Charmian boasts about the 'required reading' which she was 'force-fed' by her father at an early age:

My father often quoted Rabelais. He quoted Laurence Sterne too, who all in all was probably his favourite author, and he quoted Cervantes and Montaigne (or Laurence Sterne's opinions on Cervantes and Montaigne) and he quoted Gibbon and he quoted Voltaire. *Tristram Shandy, Don Quixote,* and the *Essays* of Montaigne were thrust upon all of us before we had fairly got started on *Tanglewood Tales* or *The Wind in the Willows.* We had Balzac's *Contes Drollatiques* instead of fairy stories and the adventures of Gargantua instead of the adventures of Tarzan.[45]

Other names are sometimes added to the list: Shakespeare, Plutarch, Carlyle, Homer, Johnson, Ruskin.

With this, we are starting to slip again into Charmian Clift's preferred version of events. Despite the breezy tone of these accounts, we should pay attention to words such as 'required reading', 'thrust upon us' and 'force-fed'. Yet if the child didn't enjoy these books, why would she persevere with them? A passage from *Greener Grows the Grass* is probably closer to the truth of the situation than the later fictional and non-fictional accounts.

Here the heroine is aged ten:

> Christine had tried to read Balzac and Plato and *The History of the French Revolution*, so she could talk to [her father], but she couldn't understand it very well and she was really more interested in the illustrations in the Balzac book than the writing, which was full of funny words and descriptions that made her go hot and clammy in turns, even though she couldn't quite grasp what Balzac was trying to convey. When she told her mother about it, Alma Morley clasped the skinny, eager, puzzled little figure and said, 'Don't worry about it, Chris, my darling. You'll understand it all one day. Don't grow up too soon, Chris [...] Dad doesn't expect you to know everything [...]' Christine was still left with the feeling that her father *did* expect them all to know everything, so she kept on trying with Balzac, which was easier than the others, after all, because it had pictures.[46]

Although Syd's reading policy caused the child to feel that she didn't measure up, there is no denying that this early familiarity with the classics was to stand Charmian in good stead throughout her life. Just as important was the breadth of this reading: she would grow up to be a general reader, like her father — enjoying history, biography, philosophy, popular science, and 'bad novels' as well as literary fiction. Yet the genre to move her 'most deeply' was poetry.[47]

Charmian would always attribute her particular love of poetry to Amy. As with the anecdote about discovering the novel, she frequently described how she had been awakened by her mother not just to poetry but to the joy of speaking it out loud. In response to her mother's declaration that 'Sometimes you were driven' to poetry, the author notes: 'I didn't have to be driven. She had impressed me profoundly'.[48]

Yet if poetry was for reciting out loud, it was also for acting. Charmian and Barré used to play at being their favourite literary characters, as well as contemporary heroes such as Amy Johnson and Kingsford Smith. Thus they would take on the role of figures such as Don Quixote, whom they loved for his 'brave innocence'; naming their home-made hobbyhorse Rosinante they would gallop over the backyard paspalum, tilting at windmills and having 'high and splendid adventures'.[49] When Barré wasn't around, Charmian's favourite solo part was to wait on the woodblock 'for tirra lirra (from the creek) and the glint of Lancelot's gemmy bridle'.

In fact I carried out my impersonation of the Lady of Shalott to the lengths of decking my red tin canoe with arum lilies (plucked from the dung heap in the farmer's field opposite) and floating down the creek with my hands piously clasped on my skinny chest, faintly and fervently declaiming.[50]

If one could chant poetry, and act poetry, it followed that one could make the stuff oneself. In the National Library interview, Charmian dated her earliest literary efforts from the same year as her discovery of the novel and poetry:

> I've written ever since I could remember, I think [...] My mother used to write poetry which she always tore up and threw into the fireplace, and so I suppose I get my particular talent (if it is a talent) from her. When I was eight I wrote a book of poetry, an exercise book, and illustrated it myself.[51]

Charmian was very fortunate that, unlike most Australian children, she was brought up to see poetry as part of daily life. Observing her mother writing verse, it was easy to follow suit. But if Amy destroyed her work, Charmian took *her* poems to school.

In 1933 Charmian went into fourth class. She was nine, turning ten in August. This year her teacher was Miss Turner, who instantly recognised that her new pupil was something quite out of the ordinary. Kiama residents remember that 'Miss Turner always had a very high regard for Charmian. She always knew she'd go places. As a kid at school, Charmian always wrote a lot of poems'.[52] A contemporary recalled that 'Miss Turner always used to say that Charmian would never use only one adjective — she'd always use at least two'.[53] And Miss Turner's sister remembered that the teacher was so 'very proud of her pupil Charmian' that she kept 'quite a lot of her work' for many years, and used to show it to friends and colleagues and later pupils.[54]

Only a tiny fragment of Miss Turner's collection remains,[55] but it is enough to provide a fascinating window through which to view the nine year old Charmian Clift. The few pages of juvenilia torn from an exercise book show four drawings, two of which are illustrations to poems. The drawings themselves are technically of a standard which is above average for a child of this age, but — apart from one — they are contrived and not particularly original. Both the subject matter and the competence of the draughtsmanship reveal the influence of Margaret: the images in two of the pictures bring to mind Charmian's descriptions of her sister endlessly drawing shepherdesses. A third picture is rather more unusual. Here a young woman with a cloud of golden curls sits on a bench in front of a bare wall built of blocks of stone. Her pose is coquettish — legs twined together, body half-turned, lips pouted, eyelashes fluttering. She could be a chorus girl — or (given the position of the legs) almost a mermaid.

While these three images of female pulchritude depict girls who are quite a bit older than nine, the fourth drawing is a Portrait of the Artist. It illustrates a poem entitled 'My Little Red Canoe', which opens:

> Now school is over for the day
> The sun is bright, the sky is blue
> This is a happy time to play
> I'll

Obviously 'canoe' was to be the rhyme-word, but at this point the poet ran out of time to copy her draft with pen and ink. The picture shows a girl, aged about nine, with brownish hair in a short bob, paddling a canoe called *Water Baby* beside the high reeds of a creek. Poem and picture both speak from the heart — naturally, spontaneously. It is interesting that here the poet does not feel any need to pile up the adjectives: the language is clear, simple, *felt*.

The other extant poem is a very different case. This shows the author striving desperately for the sort of effect which tends to impress adults. Titled 'In Grandma's Day', we can easily imagine it as something written with one eye on Miss Turner and the other eye on that other schoolteacher, Mardie Emma. If Margaret could give her grandmother pictures of shepherdesses on the Wednesday afternoon visits, Charmian would seek approval with a poem as well — for this verse accompanies an illustration of a girl who could be Little Bo Peep. It goes:

> Little Miss Prue,
> All dressed in blue
> With long frilly pantelettes
> Black latticed shoe.
>
> In her hat is a feather
> That curls right around
> And her dainty frilled crinoline
> Near touches the ground!

She bows and she curtseys
She walks with a swing
Round her neck is a locket
On her finger a ring.

Self-consciously signed 'C Clift' (with a scroll beneath) this piece shows an odd spark (such as the 'latticed shoe') and a sophisticated mastery of rhythm and syntax. There is, however, no sense here of the highly individual writer who would grow out of this child. With its perfect spelling, its carefully rounded handwriting, its archaicising 'poetic' quality, 'In Grandma's Day' induces the opposite emotion to the sense of the free child which permeates the canoe verse. Like the story of Sarah in the graveyard, the overall effect of this fragment of juvenilia is a sad one. Notwithstanding the joy of the canoe poem and illustration, the feeling which comes across from these few pages is one of isolation. In all four drawings, there is a solitary female figure, alone in a landscape.

A terrible sense of loneliness also permeates Charmian's only school story. Entitled 'Even the Thrush Has Wings', this was written in the late 1940s but was not published during the writer's lifetime.[56] The story's heroine, ten year old Tina, is the earliest extant portrait of Charmian Clift's child alter ego. This abbreviation of the name 'Christine' would later expand to its full form, then contract to 'Chris', and finally change into 'Cress(ida)'.

Tina lives out of town in a poor cottage in what is clearly the quarry settlement. Her father, like Syd, has a quick and noisy temper; this seems to induce an almost perpetual state of anxiety in the young girl.[57] The mother character is fat (unlike Amy), but her face shares Amy's expression of 'forbearance'. Despite this, she is frequently impatient with the child, who always takes 'a long time to walk to school'. (The reason will be revealed in the story's punchline.) Another problem with Tina is that she always seems to be in the way; she keeps getting under her parents' feet.

Tina herself looks like the young Charmian — or like Charmian *thought* she looked, for the effect of all the fuss about Margaret's prettiness was to make Little Sister feel like Plain Jane. This particular alter ego is described as having 'a skinny, undersized body', a thin face splotched with freckles, and hair 'of very ordinary and very uninteresting mouse-brown'. Although Tina worries about the freckles on her nose, the kindly local garbage collector says they make her look like 'a little speckled thrush'. Hence the thrush in the title, for here the fable of the Ugly Duckling is transformed into a story about an ugly thrush.

It opens with the surprising information that 'Tina was ten when she learned how to fly'. Then the text moves on to the account of a particular day which '[begins] like any other' but goes from bad to worse. When Tina gets to school (late as usual) 'the day pull[s] at every ink-smelling hour, and it [is] full of historical dates and elementary algebra and the precise punctuation of Miss Appleby's voice'. Although — unlike the author — this child is not 'clever at school' and is passed over by the teacher, some similarity does remain. Tina tries at her work in a way that is reminiscent of Christine Morley's attempt to read difficult books in order to win her father's approval: 'Perhaps if she really studied hard she'd get to be a brilliant scholar and a useful citizen and Mum and Dad would be terribly proud of her and Mum's face wouldn't look crumpled any more'.

After the lunch recess, Miss Appleby tells the children that they will be giving a display of folk dancing at the town Flower Festival. When it comes to choosing 'a little queen of the dance', Tina's heart lurches.

> Please, she whispered inside herself, please, please, *please*! Just
> this once let me have something special. Let Miss Appleby pick
> me for queen. Oh, please. And I'll never ask for anything special
> again. Just this once. Let me have a blue dress and a crown and
> lead the dancers in and make Mum proud of me. Please!

Predictably, Miss Appleby chooses Angela, a crawler of a girl with 'long yellow curls' (the blonde-ringletted shepherdess; or is it Margaret?[58]). When Tina goes home and cries to her parents, they offer neither comfort nor understanding. At last, the child slides into bed and all her misery pours out:

> She wouldn't care so much about dancing and things like that if
> she were pretty like Angela Watts or clever at school or if Mum
> would say just once that she was a help around the house. Oh,
> Tina whispered, I wish I was one of those little insects with lovely
> coloured wings flying round and round in beautiful blue light.
> Flying so lightly, drifting and soaring.

Suddenly the story takes off — quite literally — for without any explanation the writer presents us with an image of Tina 'finding herself suspended, arms outstretched, three feet above the bed'. She falls back to bed, lifts again, starts to get the knack of flying, and now 'it [doesn't] really seem odd that she should be rocking in the air above her bed. It [seems] a familiar thing that she [has done] many times before and [has] only just remembered'. At last, alas, her nose bumps the windowpane and Tina falls. There is 'a blinding pain inside her head' and 'the room [spins] into darkness ... '

The story resumes the next morning, with Tina feeling unaccustomedly happy. It is part of the genre of stories about magical night adventures that the hero always finds something which proves that the remembered event wasn't just a dream. In Tina's case, the talisman is upon her own body. This morning when she looks in the mirror she does not see her freckles or ugliness, but only 'the wide unlovely bruise' (from bumping her nose). Her heart sings at its 'loveliness':

> It was all true — and it was better than dancing or being a brilliant scholar or anything — or anything at all! She had flown! And if she had flown once then she could fly again. Tonight she could fly — *every* night! Out of the window and away over the fields and the farms and up up into the wide bright sky.

The story should have stopped here, but on it goes, with Tina — sluggard no longer — hurrying down the road to school. Mum wonders what on earth has got into the child.

> And then it occurred to her that the bump on the head might have done something the doctors hadn't been able to do. She shrugged away the possibility. Still, funnier things had happened. Certainly Tina was walking straighter on that withered, crippled leg than she could ever remember before.

Despite this novice writer's lapse into sentimentality at the end, the symbolic meaning of this story is undamaged. Tina's physical disability is, of course, the objective correlative of the disability which she suffers through her sense of ugliness, through her feeling of not being appreciated or wanted at home, through her isolation (for reasons not stated) from the other children at school. A standard fictional solution to these problems would be to have the child do something in public which would win her recognition from her family and her peers. The solution given to Tina, however, is completely solitary and private: she does her flying alone, and no one else sees or knows, or even needs to know. The reader realises that the little thrush does indeed have wings — that even a plain child with an unhappy life at home and at school can escape. Whether this is through her imagination or through a real miracle of flight — who cares? Tina has flown and will do so again, at will.

It is in the combination of themes that the autobiographical elements of this story lie, and not in incidental details such as whether Miss Appleby is based on Miss Turner, or whatever. Loneliness. Unhappiness. Being without friends. Being on the outside. Feeling second rate. Feeling as if one is in the way. Feeling ugly. Feeling rejected. Desperately longing for love. All these pains are ranged against a private magic which allows the child to escape and enjoy her solitary state, for she possesses a secret talent that is both unique and thrilling.

If Tina has the escape of flying, the young Charmian also had her magical escape mechanisms. Whether she really was 'a loner by nature' (as she claimed) or whether loneliness was forced upon her as a child, she learned to enjoy being alone. One of the main joys of this, of course, was escaping into the 'world beyond world beyond world' of fiction. This fiction was already her own work — inscribed in her imagination — as well as the stories written down in books by other people.

We can only speculate as to the exact content of the stories which the young Charmian made up, but surely the lead role was played by a little girl who bore a remarkable resemblance to Charmian Clift — a little girl who was sometimes the Lady of Shalott and sometimes Don Quixote, but who also did the sort of things that Charmian did. The difference was, she did them better, and enjoyed them much more. It was as if the Girl in the Red Canoe looked like the Blonde Shepherdess. Whereas many children have an imaginary friend, Charmian's invisible playmate was the alter ego which she began to develop at this early stage. The world of this imaginary character coexisted alongside the real one. Or perhaps it could be said that inside the dome of Charmian's head there was the Paradise landscape of sea and valley, where everything was perfect, whereas outside the child there was another and not-quite-parallel universe.

The effect of all this was that already, over the real events of childhood, Charmian was writing in her mind the Revised and Authorised Version of the Childhood of Charmian Clift. It was now that the myth of contentment was started, the idealised picture of herself as the most perfectly happy child in the world, with the cleverest father and most understanding mother and so on. This private storytelling of the childhood — part escape, part defence mechanism — would become a public storytelling by at least the time Charmian was in her early twenties.

If writing (both on paper and in the mind) and reading were solitary pleasures, another of the child's greatest joys was akin to Tina's flying. This was something which, although she describes it lightly, was clearly both a mystic and a sensual experience. When Charmian went down to the beach at night on fishing expeditions with her father and Barré, she would wander away by herself, take her clothes off and lie in a rockpool. Naked beneath the night sky, the child would 'starbake in the confident expectation of turning silver'. The author went on to describe how, during this starbaking, 'I would look up into blazing majesty and I would sometimes feel that I might fall off the turning earth and into the sky, falling very slowly, falling away into something else entirely'.[59]

This memory of the sensation of starbaking, and particularly the giddying spin of looking into the sky, was something very special which Charmian Clift, throughout her life, would look back upon and talk about as an epiphanic experience.

Whatever Charmian experienced as she lay in the rockpools at night, this ritual expressed the sense of being at one with the universe, which was part of Charmian Clift's own pantheistic religion of childhood; throughout her life she would remain to some extent a spiritual mystic, who worshipped the elements of the landscape around her.

Finally, of course, the descriptions of starbaking, together with the thrush story, provide a link with Icarus — that other youthful flyer. As Charmian approached adolescence, the ability to fly (in her imagination at least) and to enjoy her own solitude were to disappear. Yet these other elements of the Icarus story would come into play: defiance, disobedience, and straining for something just out of reach.

5

THE DRAGGING YEARS OF DEPENDENCE

To me the very air was filled with purpose and high endeavour. The sky
was bigger, bluer, the roll of the Pacific surf more majestic, the broad
highway filled with promise […] And our childhood became a
straining to get it out of the way as quickly as possible, to fling off the
dragging years of dependence and get on with the big adventure.[1]

It was around the end of 1933 that Charmian first started to feel
childhood ending. Despite her precocious leadership of other kids
outside the home, she took her own lead from her older siblings, so it was
when Margaret and Barré underwent rites of passage into growing up that
Charmian began to lose the sense of 'perfect contentment' with her little
Eden. As the Golden Age ended, she also lost the childish sense of limitless
freedom and possibility.

Through the first thirty to forty pages of both texts of *The End of the
Morning*, Cress is nine, Ben is ten, and Cordelia — in her first year of high
school — is thirteen. In fact, when Margaret was at this stage of her
schooling, Charmian was only seven. The changing of these ages is
indicative of the way in which the author regarded the age of nine as a kind
of pivotal or representative year of childhood;[2] imagining the past in this
way also allowed her to shorten the gap between herself and her sister.

In the earlier extant version of this novel, there is a short space in the
typing on the 38th page, and then the narrative resumes with the
observation that 'In her final year of school Cordelia was more remote from

Ben and me than ever'.[3] In the lives of the models for these characters, this makes the time jump to 1933, when Margaret was doing her third or Intermediate year, Barré was in fifth class, and Charmian — now actually nine, and turning ten in August — was in fourth class. This year, Amy's singling out of her first-born daughter became even more noticeable as Margaret blossomed into beauty:

> My mother cut her long brown hair and she was suddenly grown up. She was shaped soft and full, but fragile-boned and slender with it and her waist was so small that all her belts had to be cut down by half. Her wrists and ankles were delicate and her long smooth throat carried her head high and haughty. She walked disdainfully, swinging the newly-cut hair around the oval of her face like a shining bronze bell. My mother couldn't keep her eyes off her. Neither could my father. Sometimes they both looked disbelieving.[4]

As the Intermediate exams approached, Margaret begged to be allowed to leave school, for she knew that her father — with his standard of perfection — would expect her to pass brilliantly, and she 'prudently thought it easier to dodge'. This suited the plans that Amy was secretly hatching, and Margaret was allowed to do as she wished.[5]

Through the long, hot summer that followed the end of her schooling, Margaret was busy going to dances and cricket matches and the cinema and the physical culture club, and one of the local lads came calling formally twice a week.

> There was such an air of *imminence* surrounding [her], as though all the years of grooming, all the shampooing and brushing and massaging, the glasses of senna tea for her complexion, the olive oil smoothed on her brows and lashes to keep them dark and silky, the bay rum on her hair, had brought her to the point of *happening*. But what was to happen?[6]

By day, Charmian hung around the house, watching her mother sew dresses for her big sister, or she ran errands to town for buttons and lining silk; and through 'those summer nights, thick with the smell of stocks and the smell of rotting seaweed in the lagoon, hot mud and sweet peas, and the sound of the sea beating and beating', she would lie in bed and eavesdrop as her mother gently nagged and wheedled her husband into allowing

Margaret to go to Sydney to study art. When Charmian's father objected that there was no money for this scheme, Amy confessed that over the years she had secretly been scrimping on the housekeeping in order to put aside money for this very purpose. (Of course, insofar as the family was 'poor' during these Depression years, Amy's private nest egg was the main reason.) During these eavesdropping sessions, Charmian also overheard her mother explaining that, if the family made the financial sacrifice and sent Margaret to be trained as a commercial artist, she would get a job and earn good money and be able to help the younger two 'when their turn came along'. At the very least, she would make a good marriage.[7]

At last Syd Clift agreed, and in early 1934 Margaret began studying art at East Sydney Technical College. From this time, Charmian's contentment with living in the little valley of North Kiama was at an end.

> To me the very air was filled with purpose and high endeavour. The sky was bigger, bluer, the roll of the Pacific surf more majestic, the broad highway filled with promise. For if Cordelia had gone, then Ben and I would go too. Our turns would come. Our mother had said so. And our childhood became a straining to get it out of the way as quickly as possible, to fling off the dragging years of dependence and get on with the big adventure.
>
> Now all our talk was of what we would be and do. Whatever it was had fame attached to it. Ben favoured Test Cricket, or being Kingsford Smith or Zane Grey. If Ben could be Kingsford Smith then I could be Amy Johnson. Or I would be a ballerina. I would be an actress. But in fact there could be nothing in the world more distinguished than being Cordelia, so I did my best to become her, and practised walking in a haughty way and drew and painted for hours or coloured the Virgil drawings in *Smith's Weekly*. My parents said indifferently that they weren't bad at all.[8]

In this account the two younger siblings still appear as mates together. However, when the school year of 1934 started, Barré started to streak ahead of the little girl: he was now one of the big boys, doing his last year of primary school. At the end of this year he passed his Qualifying Certificate, which meant that he would go up to the senior school in the new year of 1935.

Barré himself was more excited about the fact that he and his mate, the Bawny Crab, graduated from Cubs to Scouts. Through yet another summer holiday,[9] Charmian found herself mooching about alone. This time it was Barré's world that she was left out of, as the two boys 'spent a lot of time practising knots and signals and morse', and going on organised hikes instead of the old rambles around the hillsides.

Then something terrible happened. The Bawny Crab died of lockjaw that he acquired when he got a scratch pinching brown eggs for Charmian through the rusted wire of his mother's fowl run. Although Charmian's rival was gone now, her brother did not resume the old mateship — the twinship — with Charmian.

> Ben went into a quiet time, sad and puzzled and uncommunicative, and he shut himself up in his room a lot, and didn't talk much at meal-times, and sometimes he watched me in a way that made me uncomfortable. I was sorry about the Bawny Crab too, but I couldn't help it about the scratch. The Bawny Crab had been pinching brown eggs for me for all the years I could remember. And I cried for him, briefly but so copiously that my mother rebuked me for my immoderation in that as in all other matters of emotion and said I was doing myself a disservice — in later life, she said — by behaving like a stormy petrel.[10]

Both the younger children had been made restless by Margaret's escape, but for Charmian, left behind in primary school while Barré started senior school, the sense of being stuck in childhood was particularly strong. In her adult life, Charmian Clift would periodically speak of feeling 'trapped' — in particular places, in particular situations. This last dragging year at the end of primary school was her first experience of the feeling. No longer was she content with life under the celestial dome in the little valley where she had been born. The image of the transparent lid enclosing the child and her family within their small landscape promised complete safety: nothing could get in to harm her. At this time, however, the young girl began to realise that lids keep things in, as well as keeping things out. Heavenly though it might be, the dome was nothing other than a very pretty trap. She had to beat her way out from it.

It was at this same unhappy time that the rivalry with Margaret really set in. Naturally the younger sister thought that now that the elder was 'out of the way', her own grooming would start. In fact, 'the house still revolved around' Margaret, who would come home every weekend 'looking a little older, a little more beautiful, a little more sophisticated', and would swan off to town dances in yet another new dress which Amy had sewn. In Charmian's description of this, written thirty years later, the terrible pain of continually being passed over still rings out.

> 'Never mind, Cress,' said my mother, finding me howling miserably and not knowing why. 'Your turn will come.'
> 'But when Cordelia was eleven her turn had come already,' I shouted in a fury. 'It's been Cordelia's turn all the time.'
> And of course I got the bit about jealousy in a family and how ugly it was, and this made me more miserable than ever. Because I didn't understand that I was jealous. I was perhaps a more fervent Cordelia-worshipper than anybody else. But I wanted to *be* Cordelia. Even a second-best Cordelia.[11]

At the end of 1935 Charmian, now aged twelve, did so well in the Qualifying Certificate exams that she won a State Bursary. This meant that she would start the new year at Wollongong High School rather than staying on at the Kiama school like Barré and most of the local kids. Sadly, her parents' approval 'fell rather flat', for they had 'taken it for granted' that their clever third child would win a bursary: wasn't she, after all, going to become a schoolteacher? This section of the novel concludes with a cry from the young girl's heart: 'I would rather have looked like Cordelia than have won all the bursaries in the world'.[12]

It was from this time that Charmian became dissatisfied with herself and started to regard herself as an Ugly Duckling. From now on, she would value beauty (which she thought she did not possess) over the brains which she knew she had.

'All these things happened at the same time', Clift wrote at the beginning of the next section of *The End of the Morning*. 'Cordelia leaving home. Me winning the bursary and moving on to Wollongong High School. Ben and I, the inseparables, separating'.[13] In fact — as we have seen — these events were staggered over two years. However, in this passage — which is very much a first draft — the writer compressed all these things together, for all were signposts indicating the change from one period of life to another.

Starting high school at Wollongong in early 1936 was the first widening of Charmian's boundaries, her first experience of the world beyond Kiama. It was also her first independence — and the first time she was doing something which her elder sister and brother had not done before her.

While this was to bring the final break to the bond between Charmian and Barré, the new life also cut Charmian off from the gang of North Kiama kids, and from home itself. In order to get to school, she had to catch the train at 7.30 a.m., and she didn't return until 5 p.m. In a note to herself for this section of the novel, the author wrote: 'Into this you must get the first feeling of separation from the unit of family. Perhaps through the train, the daily being somewhere else. Half your life lived somewhere else which yet you don't belong to'.[14] If the commuting stopped her from seeing the local kids, it also prevented her from having 'any outside-of-school contact with [her] new friends', and she 'wished passionately' that her family lived in Wollongong. The separation from Barré, however, was intellectual as well as social: it was tied up with the excitement of Charmian's new interests and her sense of specialness as a high school student: 'I felt important to be learning Latin and French and chemistry and physics, and terribly superior to Ben, who [...] was plodding along at his good average rate of progress'.[15]

Despite a bit of bullying by a fifth form girl who 'tortured and tormented' the new girl,[16] Charmian initially adapted to high school with great ease and happiness. The lessons themselves were 'as easy to [her] as they had always been', and to the joy of this stage-struck young girl, she acted for the first time in a play. There were also new games to learn such as hockey and basketball at which, she notes with no exaggeration, she 'excelled'. Already tall for her age, with long legs and strong shoulders, Charmian found in sport an outlet for both her energy and her competitiveness. In one of her essays she declares:

> As for team spirit, as far as I know my school years did not succeed in stirring in me the faintest response to such a concept. I loved playing sport because I was healthy and loved using my body, but I played strictly to win, and I strongly suspect that everybody else really good at sport did too.[17]

At this same time Charmian joined the Kiama Physical Culture Club, which she also loved:

> To dance is for me a great joy [...] and I love my little maroon tunic which shows my legs to mid-thigh [...] I am young and filled with my own hard strength and the first consciousness of beauty. For it is beautiful to move with grace and control. To use my body in this way is as great a joy as swimming or diving.[18]

And so, as she noted in the novel draft, 'all in all it was fun', this first year of high school.

It was in the summer holidays of 1936–37 — the holidays bridging her first and second year of high school — that Charmian, aged thirteen, 'discovered the town'. This represented a new stage of her process of separation from the small world of the North Kiama settlement. It happened at the same time as another signpost of adolescence. In the notes for the part of the novel that deals with this particular summer, Clift told herself to write 'a piece on puberty [...] The step out of childhood that should be marked with a ceremony'. The writer's description of menarche again reveals the contrasting difficulties that she faced with her parents. In *The End of the Morning*, the embarrassed mother fails her daughter 'terribly by her furtiveness and fluster':

> When it actually happened I felt so ashamed that it was hours before I could tell her, and she went dusky with embarrassment and wouldn't look at me and scurried out and brought back a folded rag and a piece of elastic and two pins and said I was to put the rag in the fire when it was used and get another. I felt so dirty and embarrassed I could have died. Cordelia had had boxes of Kotex and proper sanitary belts [...] And I was only worth a bit of old rag. It was years before I got over my shame at menstruating, and I couldn't have walked to the kitchen with the used rag and burn it in the grate. It would have killed me. So I used to stuff them away in an old sewing bag in my bedroom and shove it under the bed [...] And my father said with a bellow of laughter that now my water was beginning to smell a bit. And what with his bawdry on the one side and my mother's prudishness on the other I hated them both and hated my own body worst of all.[19]

In the note prefacing this passage, the author reminded herself: 'Puberty and Thellie go together'. It was in the same fortnight that Charmian made her first friendship:

> You go for a Sunday walk with Winnie Hammond and meet with Muriel Canham and Thellie Brown. Somehow or other you change partners, and from now on Thellie Brown is your dearest friend, the way Cordelia and Ezzie and Gwennie used to be, only

more so, because you two don't need any third. Thellie is sixteen, three years older than you are, and you remember her from school. She left when she was fourteen, of course, and has been working for two years at various domestic jobs [...] She is a beautiful and refined looking girl, very tall and slim and willowy, with the most elegant and slender hands and feet and rich nut-brown hair that waves softly and naturally.[20]

In the beginning of this alliance, the main attraction for Charmian was the chance to associate with someone from a normal sort of family. The Browns were truly and unambiguously working class, without all the confusion associated with the Clifts. Although they were as poor as any working people in this hard economic time, there was always food and drink and home-made music in the Brown household, and there was an atmosphere of ordinary warmth and hospitality that drew Charmian like a wasp to a honeypot. In contrast to the Clift family's strivings to be best at everything, the Browns weren't ambitious for anything more than they had, and 'none of them [had] the slightest yearning to be educated'. Just as the steamy kitchen down the quarry row had once caused envy in the little girl, the whole Brown establishment 'exerted a strange fascination' on this slightly older Charmian. Looking back on this family with the hindsight of more than twenty years, Clift uses the Browns as a way of pointing out one of her own youthful limitations.

> They were my inferiors in education, intelligence, and aspiration, but they had a grip on life — the here and now of it — that I did not have and probably never would have. I wanted more than they did, but they had it within themselves to realise the little they did want.[21]

Charmian also got great joy from having, for the first time in her life, a close girlfriend. Given that her tendency to dominate was one of the things that had previously prevented her from forming a close friendship, it is interesting that she would make an alliance in which she was very much the junior partner. At the beginning, Charmian's relationship with Thellie was a schoolgirl crush — Clift herself referred to her 'infatuation with Thellie', and said she was 'enormously flattered' by Thellie's friendship. Just as Charmian had been infatuated with her big sister, she looked to another older girl as her model now that Margaret was gone. Thellie was (in Charmian's eyes) not only beautiful, but 'refined-looking' and 'very ladylike' — attributes shared by Margaret/Cordelia. At sixteen, and as a cousin of Margaret's two best friends, Thellie could have been in Margaret's gang; in a sense Charmian's precocious friendship was part of her trying to *be* her sister.

Unlike Margaret, however, Thellie returned the friendship. Although (according to Clift's notes) Thellie said she 'felt funny sometimes going about with a kid like me', and urged Charmian to get a perm so she would look older, the two girls called each other Skipper and Buddy and swore that they would be friends until they died. At this early stage of the relationship, Charmian and Thellie were happy just to be with each other. They walked up and down the main street on Friday late-shopping nights, and on Sundays strolled out along the Scenic Point. Saturday afternoons were spent at Thellie's place, 'learning the words of the newest popular songs from the *Boomerang Songster*' as Thellie set Charmian's awful new perm.

> Mostly we talk about boys and sex. We go to the pictures every Saturday night and fall in love with film stars. I say I'm in love with Robert Taylor, but actually I'm in love with Conrad Veidt and this seems so perverse that I don't dare confess to it. We fall in love with Fred MacMurray too, and George Raft.[22]

For a girl in a small country town, the cinema was a window to the world. Although Charmian may have fallen in love with the male stars, it was the female stars who influenced her. In the films of this period between the wars, women trailed across the screen in long elegant gowns, or posed in unnatural positions. While these movies filled the young girl's head with dreams of a life of wealth and glamour, we can also see their influence in the way the adult Charmian would pose herself for the camera. At the same time, the weekly 'flicks' were having another influence on Charmian's subconscious. Even in her earliest novel, there is a strong cinematic feeling which reveals itself in both the broad pictorial sweep and the way in which the scenes are cut to build the tension. Three decades later, the author would be amazed at how easily she would take to writing for television, given that she had barely seen the medium. But of course she had steeped herself at a vulnerable age in the moving pictures on the screen of the Kiama cinema.

When Charmian went back to the environment of the classroom after this summer of freedom, she started again to feel confined — trapped — as she had during the last year of primary school. In her own account, it is just after these three signposts — the beginning of menstruation, the new friendship, and the discovery of the town — that there came the 'shattering' of Charmian's enjoyment of school, the end of 'the simplicity of doing well and being approved'.

Halfway through this second year of high school, Charmian dropped Latin and took art instead, which lowered her from the A to the B class. About this she was 'both ashamed and defiant'.

> There were two reasons I didn't mention in justifying myself. The first was that I had lost all my textbooks on the train and didn't dare to ask for ten and sixpence to hire new ones, so I started my second year without textbooks and couldn't keep up. The second reason was that in my fear of doing badly in the middle year exams I wet myself in the middle of the examination room, and the humiliation was so shattering that I never recovered from it. Children are cruel about those things. And it was something I couldn't tell at home.[23]

While these two events gave Charmian private reasons for moving down a class, this action was also a kind of reprise on Margaret's decision to leave school before the Intermediate Certificate exams: Syd Clift's belief that if you weren't going to be the best you might as well not try was to cause all his children, in different ways, to sell themselves short. The change of subject also reflects a further attempt to follow in Margaret's artistic footsteps. And it marked the beginning of a campaign to thwart Amy's ambition for Charmian to be a schoolteacher. Most importantly, however, it was a symptom of the general moodiness of this adolescent, and of her restless and inchoate yearning to do — exactly what, she didn't know. In her notes to herself for this section, Clift writes:

> Next convey the delinquent phase. Bravado and I don't care. The rowdiest and worst-behaved children as companions. Shop-lifting from Woolworths, playing truant from school, damaging railway property, ruining the teachers' clothes with ink. And behind all this is the Love me Love me plea, Help me someone. Because you sense now that it isn't Latin and chemistry you want to learn — that's not going to help you at all. It is something else entirely, something about living, something that is an ache in you all the time. And you still know that it is easy for you, if you want

to, to do a hard burst of work and catch up and be approved again. But you'd rather be disapproved. You become a moody, lonely child. You haven't any friends at all, and eat your lunch alone under a tree in the playground while everybody else is in groups. They are frightened of you, or troubled by you. You make them uneasy anyway, and you know it and feel it like some unsightliness that you must hide.[24]

The poignancy of this passage is heightened by the fact that it is a raw first draft, addressed to the writer herself. This is probably as close as we will ever get to Charmian Clift's 'true' thoughts.

Love me Love me. Help me someone.

It is the cry that would be Charmian's throughout her life. Yet throughout her life it would be hidden — as it is here — behind a facade of bravado, of rowdy wildness. The ache would remain too — the desperate longing to discover 'something about living' — to find an answer so nebulous that she would never even be able to formulate the question. Also throughout Charmian's life there would remain the terrible sense of loneliness and alienation which runs through this passage. And there would remain the tension between approval and disapproval: having spent her primary school days desperately seeking approbation, she was now as keen to win the opposite.

For the moment, however, the yearning ache of incomprehension — and the pains of loneliness — could be eased by the pursuit of more immediate excitement, and of something that almost felt like affection. It was around the end of this year of 1937, when Charmian was just fourteen, that she entered the next stage of growing up. A new section of the novel, in draft form, begins:

Sunday afternoons were for picking up boys with motor-bikes or cars. Preferably cars [...] They came in hunting packs [...] and cruised up and down the main street where the girls strolled in pairs [...] I walked arm in arm with Thellie Brown, wearing Cordelia's clothes and Thellie's lipstick and looking at least five years older than my age. We eyed the boys carefully as the cars slowed down, but we weren't hurrying about our selection. Usually we walked up and down the street a couple of times, then strolled around under the hoppers to the swimming pool, back again, then up to Blowhole Point. By that time there was usually a car or a couple of motor-bikes trailing us, and the rest was simple. Thellie always had first choice by right of seniority and beauty — 'I'll have the one driving', she'd say, and then, the car now stopped, the young men would make an obvious remark about the day or the weather, or wouldn't you like to come for a drive, and Thellie and I would hesitate, smiling, while we all looked each other over, and Thellie would say in the most ladylike fashion that we didn't mind, only not too far since we had to be back for tea, and then the young men would get out and open doors, Thellie would slip into the front seat and me into the back, and we would tell our names, and they tell theirs — Clive or Alan or Keith or Wally or whatever, and where they came from — and then we'd be off, whizzing through the town and out into the country, to Jamberoo or Gerringong or sometimes as far as Bulli Pass, and in a little while Thellie and I would begin to sing the harmonies we'd been practising the day before. The boys always said we should be on Amateur Hour at least. We stopped at a pub somewhere — bona fide travellers — and had some drinks and told jokes, and if the boys were nice and good spenders we would agree to go out with them again in the evening. Usually it turned out that they were from the Port Kembla steelworks — steelworkers were the only young men around with money for cars — but once we landed a couple of S.P. bookies, and another time a taxi-driver and his friend who was a drummer in a dance band, but Thellie liked the S.P. bookie and I didn't like his friend so much, and I liked the drummer [...] and she didn't like the taxi-driver [...]

Well, then we would go home to Thellie's place or to mine for Sunday tea, having arranged to meet the boys later — I envied Thellie greatly that she could talk about the boys at home where I could not, and there was also the further stricture of having to be home at ten o'clock, which didn't give us much time for parking. Dark cars pulled in on the side of dark roads, cigarettes glowing and fading. Experimenting like mad with Clive or Keith or Wally, only not letting them go too far, of course, because they don't respect you if you do.

'He got that worked up,' Thellie would say later, 'I didn't know what to do. Just as well you were there in the back. How was Clive?'

I would tell how Clive was. 'Passionate,' I'd say. 'He tried to put his hand inside my dress.'

'You ought to wear a brassiere,' Thellie would say.

'Mum won't let me. Anyway, I haven't got that much, and neither have you.'

'I've got more than you,' said Thellie, but she hadn't actually — neither of us had any breasts to speak of.

Still, we got awfully flushed and excited in those cars and were often tempted to let the boys go too far even if they didn't respect us afterwards. Still, we didn't.

We talked about it often and were determined to keep ourselves pure for marriage. But how we wondered what it was like to do it with someone you were crazy about — I had filched *Married Love* one time [from my parents' bottom drawer] so Thellie could read it too. 'Oh I'll die, I'll die,' she said, scarlet in the face and with her eyes glittering wildly — in the bedroom with the brass bedstead, imagining one was in the bed, properly married to Robert Taylor (Conrad Veidt) and he came through the door in silk pyjamas and a beautiful dressing gown and ...

'I wonder if Cordelia has ever let anyone?'

'Oh no,' I said, 'Cordelia *wouldn't*.' [25]

This behaviour of fourteen year old Charmian could easily be misread.[26] It must be borne in mind that, in the 1930s, the streets of Kiama were safe, that the serial killing of hitchhikers was unheard of in Australia, and that — then as now — rape was more likely to be committed by a 'friend' than by a stranger.

Indeed, when trouble did come, it was predictably from someone whom Charmian had reason to trust. Some years after this, when she was in her early twenties, Charmian would confide in a male colleague a very painful anecdote:

As a young girl, she had a traumatic experience. Without details she told me that one day she had accepted a lift from a friend of the family, [was] taken to a lonely spot, and raped. There were scars for I recall she broke down as the story unfolded.[27]

How old the 'young girl' was at the time of the rape isn't clear; perhaps it happened after she had left school, but she was obviously still in her teens.

This male adult friend of the family must have been a friend or associate of Syd's; while this would have increased the girl's sense of betrayal, it would also have made it very difficult for her to tell her parents what had happened. Besides, in the face of her father's ribaldry and her mother's reticence, it was simply impossible to discuss sexual matters. And so the girl kept quiet, and the blame which should have been carried by the rapist was converted into self-blame.

Charmian, like many victims of sexual abuse, would bear throughout her life a terrible burden of guilt and self-castigation — for this and other 'offences'. Eventually, she would see the Sunday car trips as other evidence of her having been a 'bad girl', and she would reproach herself decades later in terms that reveal how deeply she punished herself.[28]

Overall, the strongest impression given by Clift's actual description of the Sunday afternoons is one of naivety. Yet if Charmian was naive, there were those in Kiama who did not find her innocent. She is still remembered by a number of people as having been 'wild', and two women who were her contemporaries remarked that they wouldn't have gone out with her 'for fear of catching her reputation for chasing the boys'. However, as one of the women pointed out, 'For these days she'd just be normal — but *then*!'[29]

Given that 'nice' Kiama girls didn't do what Charmian did — or at least didn't do it openly — why did she do it? What was she seeking?

The car trips to Jamberoo or the Bulli Pass represent the first attempts of the fledgeling to get out of the North Kiama nest, for the family did not have a car and rarely went anywhere. But if Charmian wanted a bit of fun and adventure, there was an even greater need operating. In *Greener Grows the Grass*, when Christine Morley brings her cosmopolitan lover Justin back to her home town and they drive through the main street, she confesses to him:

> 'Once I used to come down here on Friday nights with another little frippet and let myself be picked up by young men in motor cars. I wanted adventure. Do you see?'
> 'Yes, darling, I see,' [he replied]. 'But you're safe now.'
> She said very humbly, 'I wasn't very nice. I'm glad you didn't know me then.'[30]

The lover's reassuring response ('You're safe now') in this passage is odd, for safety is not usually the solution to a quest for adventure. It would be more natural, surely, for Justin to promise that he would take Christine on far better adventures in far more exciting places; this indeed was the promise made by Justin's model, George Johnston. Here again — probably unconsciously — Clift reveals that necking with boys in cars was tied up with her desperate need for security.

As well as security, she wanted romance. Not hands inside her dress, but tirra lirra. Here she was the victim of her mother's poetry, of her own childhood play-acting of the Lady of Shalott. Writing in an essay about this time of early 'practising on men', she notes: 'I had no standards of comparison then, apart from literary ones [...], and current film stars'. The local talent didn't quite match these ideals. Describing the 'loutish, lumpish boys [...] with big soft ears and great mottled hands', she concludes:

> Now I may be quite wrong about this, but I don't think there was a Sir Lancelot in the whole bunch. Or even a potential Sir Lancelot. Tirra lirra never sounded, however muffled, by the rank and reedy creek that flowed sluggishly beneath my splintered window, although I listened for it desperately enough and performed prodigies of imagination in trying to transform coarse country adolescents into parfait gentil knights.[31]

Of course, all this searching for security, for romance, and for sheer affection was part of the *Love me Love me* plea. As an adolescent, Charmian Clift wanted unqualified love — love that would love no matter who she was or what she did. And in order to see if it existed, she pushed love to the limit. Just as she pushed approval. Combined with this plea for love, for approval of herself even if she didn't match her parents' expectations, was the first realisation of the power of shock value: if people would not love, like, or approve her, she would make damned sure that at least they noticed her. If they were going to disapprove, she would really give them something to disapprove of. As a Clift, she had to be best at whatever she did. And so, if she couldn't be best at being good, she would be best at being bad.

As Charmian's world expanded, and as she discovered new standards of measurement, her old world shrank. Although the Great Depression had been at its height during Charmian's primary school years, it was now that she became 'conscious of poverty for the first time'.

Going to a big school in a big town I was meeting children who came from well-to-do households, the daughters and sons of doctors and lawyers and businessmen. Our house seemed smaller and shabbier and meaner, and my father uncouth [...] I wished that he wouldn't spit and fart and belch and I began to watch for the tightening of my mother's mouth and feel my own tightening in sympathy.[32]

It is hardly surprising that, at this time, Charmian began to agree with Amy's aspirations toward the sort of life which the family could have claimed for itself. It was now that Charmian realised that the cottage where she lived would be seen as the most significant indicator of her background. Her father's crude behaviour would reinforce the family's lowly position. Now Charmian took up the cry that her mother had been making for so many years. In a passage from *Greener Grows the Grass*, Alma remembers one of her daughter's outbursts:

I can see Christine, her grasshopper body restless under a hated black tunic, her eyes green fire in the freckled broadness of her face. 'You should be ashamed!' she storms at poor, bewildered Tom. The child's voice is scornful: 'Resident engineer. And you live in a dump. A dump!' Christine, the rebel ...[33]

As both women joined forces, fate played into their hands, for out of the blue the quarry owners 'issued an ultimatum that the tenants either buy the terrace houses or get out'. Syd immediately decided that 'the place [was] a bloody dump'; after 'paying for it ten times over' in rent, he was 'buggered if [he'd] pay for it again'. Instead, he bought a small weatherboard cottage named *Hilldrop*, situated a couple of hundred metres up the hill, on the other side of the highway. The new house was still in the quarry settlement of North Kiama. The front verandah looked out on the dusty main road, while from the back fence there was a view of the railway line and the beach. But at least this place belonged to the family. When she heard of this decision, Charmian was delighted, dropping 'her new tight cloak of self-consciousness' and whooping around the kitchen. The young girl's ecstasy ended, however, when her father decided that they wouldn't get a removal lorry but would shift everything themselves, 'in relays'. How mortifying it was to tramp up and down the highway exposing to the view of the neighbours the old furniture and battered belongings which had been concealed for so long behind the closed doors of the Clift cottage. Of this experience the author notes: 'Christine's existence was almost swamped in humiliation because at this time she was fourteen years old'.[34]

... *Fourteen*. If in her descriptions of her early life Clift uses eight or nine as the archetypal time of childhood, fourteen is the age to which she assigns all the major storms of adolescence. It was while she was fourteen that she dropped down to the B class, that she discovered boys, that she started rebelling against her parents. She was fourteen in 1938, when she went into her third and final year of high school.

With the Intermediate exams looming, it was now that Amy Clift began to worry about the connected problem of her fourteen year old daughter's schoolwork and her socialising. In a passage of *Greener Grows the Grass*, Alma remembers:

> At fourteen my grasshopper Chris was a problem that I knew I could not leave much longer to lie uneasily in my mind's pending basket.
>
> I had never thought of Chris being a problem. She had always been a stormy petrel, sometimes uncomfortably precocious, but fundamentally normal and sound enough. Besides, I had been too preoccupied with Judith's future to give much thought to making plans for the other two. John and Christine were, after all, so much younger [...] I suppose I had taken it for granted that Christine would finish high school in her usual easy brilliance and go on to teachers' college. It never occurred to me that this was wishful thinking.[35]

Meanwhile Alma in this fiction, like Amy in life, was slaving even harder at the cooking and the housework and the garden, going to extraordinary lengths to cut back the family budget because she was secretly sending money each week to the daughter at art school, and slightly less secretly buying material to make new dresses for this daughter when she came home on weekends. And so — as this is related in the fictional version — for a while the mother did not realise that the younger daughter was changing, although 'if she hadn't been so tired she might have seen that respectability would never satisfy Chris'.

Predictably, it is a poor school report that makes Alma realise that her 'family worries [are] only just starting'. Predictably, too, she is concerned because her daughter has 'tagged herself to a town girl very much older than herself'. One night she comes into Christine's bedroom and broaches the subject by suggesting that Chris is 'seeing a bit too much of Enid Small' (as Thellie Brown is called in this version of the tale). Christine leaps 'spitting to the attack', accusing her mother of being a snob and of trying to keep her 'shut up like a prisoner in this old hovel'. But it is when the mother brings up the topic of the girl's falling school marks — reminding her that 'we want you to go on to be a teacher just as you'd planned' — that Christine's resentment is really unleashed:

> 'I don't want to be a damned school marm! I hate school! I hate it! I don't belong there any more! I hate wearing this ugly tunic. I'm sick of being treated as a child. I'm nearly fifteen!' Her stiff resistance crumpled suddenly and she turned in my arm and buried her head in my shoulder, snivelling. 'Mum. Oh Mum. Latin and algebra and sewing samplers aren't the things I want to learn. I don't want to be a schoolteacher any more, Mum. Please let me leave school at the end of the year and learn art like Judith. Miss Crater says my drawing is very good ... Mum?'[36]

This plea to go to art school represents Charmian's own desperate ambition at this time. It is also, of course, the pivot of this scene. Although the mother-character here is allowed to present her version of the story in first-person narrative, all the reader's sympathies are directed to the daughter:

> I stroked the tousled brown head and tried out of the ache in my heart to find words to tell her. 'Darling, I suppose that trying to limit you to the normal life of a fourteen-year-old is like binding a Chinese girl's feet. If you really want to leave school at the end of the year and go out into the world I suppose I'll have to let you, Chris, though Daddy will be very disappointed. But as for art school ... See darling, one of the reasons we were so happy about you being a teacher was that it wouldn't cost us much. We haven't any money left, Chris, to give you and John expensive training. I hoped that by the time you were ready to start out in life Judith would be earning enough to help you. That's partly why we spent so much money on her ... In a few years maybe, darling, she'll be in a fine job. If you could wait till then, maybe you could start art school.'

The whimpering bundle wrenched herself out of my arms and ground clenched fists into her eyes. There was a fiendish hatred in her scream. 'Judith! Judith! Always Judith! Yes, Judith must have the best. Oh, yes, nothing is too good for Judith. No, it doesn't matter who else goes without as long as Judith can have new clothes and expensive training and dancing classes and all the rest. I tell you, I'm damn sick of Judith. I'm tired of having her condescending to me. I'm tired of wearing her cast-off clothes ...' She looked at me and the moment snapped. She hissed, 'I *hate* Judith.'

Sheer hatred would have been easy. In fact, although Charmian did not now 'worship' her big sister as she had (or claimed she had) in childhood, she was completely caught up in the sense of cosmopolitanism and art world glamour and beauty that seemed to emanate from Margaret when she came down to North Kiama to visit. But there is a bit of the writer's artfulness in this too. While all the scenes with Judith or Cordelia are constructed so that the elder sister appears in a bad light, the fact that the younger sister does *not* simply hate the elder pushes the reader into taking up cudgels on behalf of young Chris or Cress.

But was the situation in Charmian's home really as unfair as this account would suggest? The model for the Judith character, Margaret Backhouse née Clift, never saw any of *Greener Grows the Grass*, but after reading in typescript *The End of the Morning* (which is considerably less extreme in its portrayal of the elder sister than this earlier telling of the story), Margaret wept. 'I had no idea', she protested. 'I simply had no idea!' [37] Certainly, as an adult, Margaret was extremely unselfish and tender-hearted. She was also the first one to go in to bat if any public slight were made to Charmian's posthumous reputation. [38]

If blame is to be apportioned, it is not Margaret who deserves it for accepting what she was given. She was unaware of the sacrifices that her mother — and willy-nilly her younger siblings — made on her behalf. It is, of course, Amy and Syd who caused the trouble by always making it so obvious that they favoured the first-born. Even Charmian herself noted, in a draft section of the later novel, *The End of the Morning*:

Cordelia was a nice girl, really, and quite attached to her family, but she had been spoilt from the day she was born and accepted her position as favourite with a naturalness that was graceful because there wasn't an ounce of scheming in it. She called me 'kiddo' and patronised me quite kindly and expected me to pick up her things and polish her shoes and just run off and fetch this or that, but she also showed me how to block out faces and my drawing improved a lot. She did some pencil sketches of me and I was so pleased and proud. (Yes, must remember all the nice things. Like asking me to go hiking. And of course she gave me all her cast-off clothes to be cut down. I hated them really.)[39]

If the domestic incidents of sibling rivalry which Charmian Clift related — two or three decades later — sound trivial, this only underlines how important they had seemed to the slighted fourteen year old. It is, after all, the girl who does *not* get the new dress who remembers every inch of its fabric, while the one who receives the frock soon grows out of it, and forgets it completely.

For Charmian, this feeling of being passed over, of being treated as second rate, of playing second fiddle, which she suffered so terribly during adolescence was to make her extremely vulnerable to the pain — years later — of being regarded as the junior partner in the Johnston/Clift writing team. It was also to make her even more ruthlessly determined to go where she wanted, get what she wanted, by any means available. In her vow to come back and 'show the bastards', it was her family as well as the townsfolk of Kiama whom she wanted to impress.

In fact, she was already 'showing' people. Despite her new interest in clothes, boys and films, Charmian had retained her love of sport, especially swimming. Even here, however, there was a new aspect to the old pastime. In *Greener Grows the Grass*, Alma reflects that 'until the two secret mounds began to bud out of her flat chest', Christine had been quite content to spend her weekends with her brother and the rest of the terrace kids 'romping around the beach'. But now Christine 'with a much-rehearsed imitation of Judith's arrogance [...] renounced such childish occupations'.

Gone was the joy of basking undisturbed on the long lonely beach, with only the seagulls' screams and an occasional surprised hoot from a chattering locomotive to break the sleepy swoosh of the surf. Christine no longer wanted loneliness. She wanted people to see her basking. She wanted people to watch in admiration as she timed a wave and curved her brown body into a sculptured figurehead for the inrushing boil of green and white. So she took her bathing suit and walked the half mile to the crowded town beach where she felt her surfing prowess would be better appreciated.[40]

Charmian also used swimming as a way to assert a kind of protest against local conventions. In Kiama in those days women and girls frequented the Ladies' Pool at Pheasant Point, while men and boys used to swim in the pool near the Blowhole, where the surf washes in over the rocks. Charmian of course swam at the Blowhole, and (one of her female contemporaries remembered) 'If she was in the pool, you'd just stand and watch her!'[41]

In her third year of high school Charmian was junior swimming champion and also girls' sports captain of Keira House; she is named along with three others in the school's official history as being 'among the top sportswomen' of this time.[42] This precocious young woman stood out from the crowd in other ways, too. A fellow pupil remembered that, as well as being 'prominent in sports', Charmian was seen as 'a literary person'. Furthermore, 'sometimes she was driven home by the history teacher [...] in his pale blue single-seater sports car. This was much talked about in an era when even Year 5 [final year] students were still "children" '.[43]

At the end of 1938 Charmian sat for the Intermediate Certificate, gaining As in English and elementary science and Bs in maths I, maths II, history, French and needlework.[44] Obviously she had dropped art. This must have been because of timetable clashes rather than choice, for she continued to draw at home, sometimes with Margaret's guidance. If Charmian's Intermediate pass was respectable, it neither met Syd's standard of excellence nor gave much encouragement to Amy's dream that her youngest child would be a schoolteacher. For these very reasons, it pleased Charmian herself.

And so she left school, 'much against [her] parents' wishes', deciding 'to tackle the world ready or no, rather than submit for another moment to the monumental boredom and frustration of amassing dreary facts towards no foreseeable purpose'.[45] She was at this time fifteen years and three months. Years later, however, in interviews, she would always say that she had been fourteen when she'd left school[46] — partly because this made her seem precocious, but also because fourteen was the age that she gave to these couple of years that seemed to drag on for an eternity.

It is appropriate now to pause for a moment, and try to assess this adolescent Charmian. As to her appearance, one of Margaret's sketches from this period — of Charmian in her physical culture class tunic — shows a tall and rather hefty girl, with broad shoulders and well-developed leg muscles.[47] Perhaps even more striking than the figure itself is the pose: although one foot is pointed, ballet-fashion, the whole stance is one of defiance, strength, challenge. This is someone, we feel, who would take on the world. Two photographs Margaret took in the back yard of *Hilldrop* at this same time show that the drawing did not exaggerate the young girl's physique. In another sketch we can see the beauty which would grow out of Charmian's face, but from the photos we can understand why the fourteen year old thought herself plain. Whereas in later years cameras would bring out the best in Charmian's strong facial planes, her wide mouth and long jawline, at this early age photography merely emphasised the enormous size of everything.

As well as the fact that she had not yet grown into her bone structure, Charmian did not meet contemporary standards of attractiveness. In those days, film stars provided the ideal. Margaret 'was often compared to Gloria Swanson (as she was then; later it was to Dorothy Lamour)' and one of her best friends (a cousin of Thellie Brown's) was compared to Myrna Loy; Thellie herself was seen as having 'rather a Katharine Hepburn look'.[48] But there was no film star who looked like Charmian did at this time. Certainly, she was not locally regarded as a beauty. Although her good figure was remarked upon, people remembered that she'd had very coarse and pimply skin, and that she wasn't at all pretty or good-looking. '*Margaret* was the looker!' the locals insisted.[49] Yet, as Mrs Davies from the shop across the road remarked, 'Charmian had what we used to call "It" in those days'.[50]

If her looks were perceived as ordinary, in some other ways, too, Charmian Clift was a typical adolescent. In her love of sport, in her hatred of school, in her passion for films, in her interest in clothes and boys and romance, and in her rebelliousness against her parents and her home, she was like many Australian girls, of her time or today. Where she differed from the other girls of Kiama was in her twin ambitions to *do* something, and to get out of town:

> I wanted to get out into the big bad world and do — I didn't
> know what I wanted to do, but like most kids with any sort of
> creative ability I wanted it to be big, I wanted it to be enormous,
> I wanted to see the world, I wanted to do something — I didn't
> know what — better than anyone else could do.[51]

In this desire to do some enormous thing — and do it better than anyone else — we see, of course, Syd's compulsion to excel. The form of this 'thing' was still, however, like the eleven year old child's dreams of being an aviator or a ballerina or an actor. Similarly, the fifteen year old Charmian wanted to be an artist; she wanted to be a film star; she wanted to be a dancer; she wanted, with Thellie, to be a nightclub singer. But her 'dearest ambition [...] was to have a long lamé gown, long earrings, and a white car with red upholstery'. Thus everything she thought of (she later reflected) 'was rather in an exhibitionist sort of way'. She added, 'My ambitions, as I said, were very large'.

One of the options she didn't consider, however, was professional writing. Three decades later she would explain that she simply 'never knew that a writer was something one could *be* in the way that one could be a schoolteacher'. (The second part of this comment underlines the fact that teaching really had been a career option.)

> [I was] still writing all the time but only for myself, because no one had ever said, 'You should be a writer', and again, as I say, I didn't know that a writer was a thing one was. Books existed and I loved books but I never thought that authors earned a living. I don't know how I thought they did it — in spare time, perhaps, as I did.

This 'writing all the time' that Charmian did was partly the old habit of writing her idealised autobiography in her imagination, but she was also writing on paper. Indeed it was during her school days that she received the first public recognition of her ability. In 1937 or 1938 the now-defunct *Illawarra Star* newspaper ran a short story competition. A story by Charmian was, according to one judge, far and away the best, and won first prize; it was published in the newspaper, but unfortunately no copies of the old *Star* exist.[52]

As to Charmian's other ambition — to get out of town — she made this crystal clear to everyone. ('She wouldn't let anything stand in her way', a woman from her peer group later remembered. 'She left us all behind'.[53]) If in the desire to be best we see Syd Clift, this wish to flee from Kiama reflects Amy's influence. It would be a couple of years, however, before she would make her escape.

In the new year of 1939 Charmian enrolled at a business school in Wollongong; this was simply 'a way of getting out into the big bad world and taking a job'.[54] Although in an interview she would describe the time at business college as 'six abortive months',[55] learning to type was to prove the most useful thing Charmian Clift would do over the next few years. While this skill later enabled her to get interesting jobs in the army and in journalism, Clift was to use her typing throughout the rest of her life. Indeed, her usual way of writing was to work straight onto the typewriter, and she would often type even the first notes for an essay or a work of fiction.

'Very large' though her ambitions were at this stage, Clift later declared that 'the only thing I could do about them at that time was to become a stenographer in a garage where I kept the books, pumped petrol and so on'.[56] After her secretarial course, Charmian began work at Kiama Motors, owned by one of the prominent local families, the Hindmarshes. Even at this early age she displayed her distinctive and individual fashion style and her habit of dressing for a role: when working in the garage she would wear a man's shirt with cuff links and a tie. This was seen as so odd that a contemporary would remember it, decades later.[57]

By this time, Thellie Brown had acquired a steady boyfriend; she would soon be married. Charmian sorely missed the friendship which had been epitomised by the nicknames Skipper and Buddy. Without her girlfriend to accompany her on double dates, Charmian started socialising alone. Now the men were older, and of a different type to the steelworkers and other lads with whom Charmian and Thellie used to go for country drives. Charmian's new admirers were the commercial travellers whom she would meet at the garage. In one of the versions of *Greener Grows the Grass,* Christine Morley, returning to the town in her early twenties, shamefully reminisces about this time that she spent 'bashing a typewriter and serving petrol and never meeting anyone except the same commercials'.

> All married. All out for their 'bit of fun'. But their 'bit of fun' was snide and dirty. It was furtive, back-room fun. It was gay little dinners — 'Oh don't go home by train, Chris. Come and have dinner at the pub with me and I'll drive you home' — it was wine and food and flattery and the slime creeping over their eyes and then the slime slithering over her body with their pawing hands on the way home. 'Oh Chris, be a sport. You don't know how lonely it is for a man travelling round all the time. It isn't often he meets a good sort like you.' And she had accepted the dinners, because what other entertainment was there for her?

They were nice dinners too, and she felt completely grown-up and sophisticated. Yes, and wanted. Even if it was a furtive wanting, [and] they still had hunger in their eyes. She was important to those commercials. She was desirable. And even if she got no pleasure from the gallery of suffused middle-aged faces, the thinning hair, the wet slippery mouths, bending over her young face in the dark cramped space of a car's front seat, she gave pleasure, and it was so much easier to give pleasure than to hurt them. She could endure their kisses and their groping tremulous middle-aged hands — as long as they didn't go too far — it was better than coming home [...] every night and just sitting down after tea with a book, and listening to her father grunting, and never going anywhere at all. A country town was so dull, unless you were in with the right set, and played tennis and belonged to the golf club [...] And her father had certainly seen to it that they never did get in with the right set. So she endured the commercials, and was oddly grateful to them for letting her have a little slice of glamour and sophistication, even though they made her feel cheap and dirty sometimes.[58]

Although *Greener Grows the Grass* is overtly a work of fiction, this passage is nakedly autobiographical. Of the list of reasons that the writer gives for Christine's behaviour, surely the most poignant is the young girl's need to feel wanted. Here again is the *Love me Love me* plea. If this need for love stemmed partly from the adolescent Charmian's belief that she was continually passed over in favour of Margaret, it surely also links right back to her father's jokes about how her conception had been a mistake. Throughout Charmian Clift's life, this need to feel wanted was to cause her to seek from sexual encounters a sense of security and of belonging. Of course, the likely failure of such a quest was apparent even at this novice stage: the girl's wants and the men's wants were wildly at variance. Perversely, the more men wanted her for her looks and her body, the less secure she felt about the greater asset of her mind, and the value of her whole being. And, with this diminished sense of her innate worth, the more she needed to feel wanted.

Syd, meanwhile, would not take the bait which his daughter was offering him: would not show his love by laying down limits. Indeed, he treated the whole thing as a joke. He would sit with his workmates across the road at the 'Parliament' and draw their attention to Charmian arriving home in different cars with different men. 'Ar well!' he'd declare to his cronies, 'I always say — there's safety in numbers! Eh? Safety in numbers!' He'd slap his thigh and laugh fit to burst at his own wit.[59] The other men, of course, would take this as a licence to show disrespect for Charmian, and soon stories would spread about the young woman's behaviour. And once the stories were going around, Charmian was expected to live up to them.

But if Syd's crudeness was partly responsible for Charmian's reputation, perhaps by her behaviour she was trying to shame him or pay him back. In this passage about Christine going out with the commercials, the author makes it clear that it is the father's fault that the young woman has to 'endure' these slimy men, for his behaviour has put her outside the world of 'the right set'. It was at this time that Charmian Clift really became aware of the class barrier represented by the hill which lay between the quarry settlement and the town.

While the social life of Kiama revolved around the seemingly endless number of parties and dances organised by the many different local organisations, Charmian's problem was that her parents did not belong to any clubs or groups. The Clift family's isolation was compounded by their lack of any extended family network. As Thellie's experience showed, if you didn't have a 'good' family, it was important to have a big one. By these standards, Charmian had nothing and no one.

Some of the North Kiama people — content with their own place in the social hierarchy — remember her as a young woman 'chasing after the silvertail set'.[60] Of course she did. The aspirations which Amy had given her, combined with her own naive notions of glamour, meant that Charmian desperately wanted to be courted by the sons of the wealthy dairying families or of the town's small number of professional families.

It didn't work. It couldn't work. Certainly, such young men might dance with her at the Oddfellows Hall on a Saturday night, or go outside with her for a walk, but they weren't going to take her home to meet their parents. She came from the wrong side of town. These rebuffs and rejections only strengthened the young woman's resolve to get out of Kiama and do something better than anybody else in the world.

6

A COUNTRY GIRL'S SEARCH

I came to Sydney on the search for glamour. This is
a country girl's search. I think country girls always dream of
the big bad city and glamour in that sense.[1]

Despite — or perhaps because of — the 'gay little dinners' with commercial travellers, working at the Kiama garage quickly began to pall. According to Clift's own account:

> [This job] lasted for a year or so until I grew very bored with it,
> because that wasn't getting me any closer to Sydney and the big,
> bad world. So then, again on a large scale [...] I had been reading
> a novel about nurses and glamorous doctors, so I thought I
> would become a nurse.[2]

As well as the novelistic image of herself as a pretty nurse, it is quite possible that Charmian saw herself soothing fevered brows as a form of atonement for her sexual encounters; anyway, the job offered escape from the continual reminders of them.

It was around mid 1940 that Charmian saw an advertisement for trainee nurses at Lithgow Hospital, and applied to join the staff. Situated beyond the Blue Mountains on the western plains of New South Wales, the small coal-mining township of Lithgow was a long way from the bright lights of the city. But it was also a long way from Kiama. In *Greener Grows the Grass*, Christine is thrilled by the thought of 'a new town — miles away over the mountains'. The author originally added: 'where no one knew', and then crossed out this suggestive phrase.[3]

It seems that there was a particular embarrassment which the young woman was fleeing. Decades later, an army roommate of Charmian's remembered one of the rare occasions when Charmian had told a story about her home town:

> There was one episode she talked about — I forget what it was that brought it up — Oh, *pine trees*, because Manly was full of pine trees and I said I loved pine trees, and she said there were some lovely pine trees in a whole strip at her place and that she … She said it was a very narrow-minded town, but there was a very nice assistant clergyman there, and he was friends with a girl and they went for a walk one day, and they thought they'd sit down behind the bridle path and there would be no horses there on a weekday or anything like that, but a riding party came flying over the hurdles and caught them in a rather awkward situation. And because of that, he left the town and transferred to another country town.
> 'Oh dear!' I said. 'What happened to the girl?'
> And she said, 'Oh, she left the town too.'
> She was very angry about that.[4]

If, as it seems, Charmian was the girl caught in a compromising situation near the Norfolk pine trees, it is little wonder that Amy supported her younger daughter's sudden vocation. 'Nurses don't have time to get into much mischief', Alma Morley reflects in *Greener Grows the Grass*, adding: 'You'll have an assured social position anyway'. But the father-figure, Tom Morley, snorts: 'You'll never be a nurse. You don't have the makings of a nurse', and he points out that Lithgow is 'a stinking rotten dirty factory town'.[5]

For once Syd Clift's negative attitude was justified: Charmian's nursing career was short-lived. In interviews given in the 1960s, Clift declared that she 'couldn't stand the discipline' and so after six weeks' probationary training she 'crawled out a window one night and fled'.[6] While the window was probably borrowed from Amy's story of escaping from her grandparents' home to the city, the time spent as a probationer was more like six months than six weeks.[7] And Charmian Clift sold herself short when she simply attributed her dislike of the job to the discipline, for she was to adapt quickly to army discipline.

Something closer to the truth is suggested in *Greener Grows the Grass* when Christine comes back from nursing 'still with the horror and disgust in her, still with the stench of decay in her nostrils, still with the ache in her body, still with the sickness in her heart, and the pity that tore her'. In this fragment of the novel, when seventeen year old Christine returns from nursing she feels that she has 'let them all down'. Moreover, 'she was right back where she started, six months ago. Except that now she was a failure — and six months ago she had known so certainly that she was going to be a success'.[8]

Failure, to a Clift, was anathema, of course. Although Amy received her daughter back 'sweetly and reasonably as ever', Syd was smugly victorious.[9] Meanwhile Margaret pulled a 'dreadful older sister stunt'.

> 'Look Chris,' Judith had said, 'You can't go on all your life starting things and then dropping them [...] Mummy spent a good twenty pounds on your uniforms and you've just thrown that away.'
>
> 'How dare you!' Christine had wanted to scream. 'How dare you! You to talk of money wasted! Mummy spent a good three hundred pounds on your training, and look what you've done with it. Just look at the shining success you are. A colourist in a photography studio. And I did without — I wore your cast-off clothes for that!'[10]

Although some of the portrayal of Judith is highly fictionalised, this account of her sister's attitude appears to have been drawn straight from life. Years later, Margaret's comment on Charmian's nursing episode was still derisory: 'I was a good deal older and I knew damn well she wasn't the right type'.[11] As to this fictional account, the rawness of the description of Christine's pent-up anger against Judith reveals, once again, just how intensely the author had felt the difference in the siblings' opportunities. The fact that in life, as in fiction, Margaret had turned out to have a small flair for art rather than a great talent made the sacrifice seem even worse to her ambitious little sister.

After returning from Lithgow — probably towards the end of 1940 — Charmian stayed home, without a job. The atmosphere in *Hilldrop* was now even more claustrophobic, because Charmian's grandmother had moved in after the death of her husband in June 1940. Emma and Amy were of course too well mannered to argue, but there was a continual state of tension between the women, and Charmian had to put up with her grandmother's tight-lipped disapproval.

On weekends she would still go off to dances at the Oddfellows Hall, but this was mostly a time of loneliness and isolation. For days on end, Charmian escaped by herself to the beach, where she read novels and poetry, and wallowed in her emotions. In the description of this time in *The End of the Morning*, it is clear that the young woman's huge ambitions had not been daunted by the failure of the first attempt at escape.

> I spent all my days surfing or just lying on the dunes, chasing my wrathful or moody thoughts round and round inside my head, or reading the gloomier Russians, to whom I had become addicted. Sometimes I still danced on the hard wet sand where the waves frilled in, but there didn't seem to be much point. It wasn't as though anyone was ever going to see me, and I seemed to have lost the old gift of dancing for the pleasure it gave my body. I was in a bad, hating way, and at the same time in a rage to live, to be, to do what was splendid, unique, and spectacular. To *show* them.[12]

Unable at this time to 'do' anything unique or spectacular, Charmian lived vicariously, through literature. While her taste for 'gloomy Russians' was to remain a lifelong addiction (especially at times of her own unhappiness), it was also now that she developed 'a taste for the sinister and the mysterious' and she 'gorged [herself] intemperately on everything bizarre in the way of reading'. It was during this period that she discovered *The Moonstone*, *The Castle of Otranto*, Edgar Allan Poe, things of that ilk.[13] Naturally, poetry was also part of these emotional and literary binges:

> One had outgrown the necessity for acting out favourite poems, and was more inclined to sneak away to lonely places — sand-dunes and cliff tops and hilltops too — to indulge in private orgies of words and tears (tears being part of all that time too). I remember that I assuaged my sense of dreadful and irremediable loss (and how right I was to feel it all so terribly, because childhood was over then) by falling in love with Browning and Byron and Marvell, whom I would not share with anyone, and only put aside temporarily for the Rubaiyat of Omar Khayyam period [...]
> 'Why fret about it if today be sweet?' lasted me as a publicly and privately declaimed philosophy until the time came for the

exchange of slim vols [...] One learned sonnets then, and the love poetry of John Donne, and Yeats and Yeats and more Yeats, and long roads white in the moon with Housman (not every young man had a car).[14]

All this reading and imagining was working to an unseen end. Clift rightly sums up her description of her girlhood Gothic phase by noting: 'What I was probably doing was becoming a writer, although I didn't know it then'.[15] While we can be sure that Charmian Clift was writing on paper in these years, just as important is the fact that she was still writing all the time inside her head.

Naturally, these solitary preoccupations did not make Charmian cheery company at home. In *Greener Grows the Grass*, Alma at this stage of the story reflects:

> Oh, this strange, unhappy, moody child she had borne. Always restless, always dissatisfied. Eternally groping for something. For what? Alma didn't know. She sometimes wished she had sent Christine to learn art instead of Judith. Christine didn't draw much any more, but she had the right temperament.[16]

Although Charmian's mother may well have shared Alma's concern about her difficult daughter, it is wishful thinking which makes the mother-character regret the training lavished on the elder girl. Anyway, despite Charmian's continuing jealousy over the art course, she would at this time often pose for Margaret, who was trying to build up her photography portfolio. On Margaret's weekend visits home, Charmian would dress up as belle of the ball or ingénue, or even undress to pose as a courtesan, complete with a chain around her ankle.

These photographs show a very different young woman from the lumpy fourteen year old whom Margaret had earlier caught on film. In four years the ugly duckling had become a swan of the finest degree. By this time, Charmian's body had fined down while retaining the grace of the athlete, and the elements of her face had settled into proportion. Although it would still be a few years before she reached her ultimate beauty, she already seemed to shine with some inner quality which sent ripples of light across the mobile features. There is something else as well, which these images capture: that indefinable thing which makes a certain face photogenic. It is clear that the camera loved Charmian — and that the feeling was mutual.

It is also clear that by this time Charmian had worked hard at developing her poses — copied, we can be certain, from movies and magazines, and practised in front of the bedroom mirror. Although there are certain distinctive features — such as the half-turned position of the body — perhaps the most surprising thing is the variety of different images which Charmian could project. This was the product of the years of solitary play-acting: Charmian could transform herself so completely from role to role that it is often hard to believe that it is the same girl posing. Whatever character she was assuming, however, you would never pick her as a teenager from the sticks.

Ironically — given Charmian's feeling that Margaret and her art training had taken away her own chances — it was to be Margaret and her photography that were to provide the younger sister with the way into the next stage of her life. In early 1941, *Pix* magazine ran a Beach Girl competition: readers were invited to send in snapshots of themselves — or their girlfriends — in swimming costumes. Margaret Clift was then going out with Alf Backhouse (whom she would soon marry), and 'as a joke' Alf decided to send in a beach photograph he'd taken of Margaret. Margaret in turn sent in, without her sister's knowledge, a photo she had taken of Charmian posed provocatively against the rocks of Pheasant Point. In Margaret's words, this image showed 'the personality popping out of her'.[17]

In May 1941, *Pix* published the prizewinners: while Miss M Clift of Petersham, Sydney, was featured as one of the entrants, the New South Wales state title-holder and winner of the Wool Board prize was 'Miss C Clift of Bombo-road Kiama'.[18] The prize money of twenty — or maybe even fifty — pounds[19] represented a small fortune for a young woman with no job and no prospects. Given Charmian's sense that she had always been passed over in favour of her sister, this victory was particularly sweet — even if it had been won through Margaret's initiative and Margaret's art training.

The prize operated in a magical sense: just as in a novel some unforeseen stroke of luck puts the hero on the road to fame and fortune, the Beach Girl quest gave Charmian Clift the key to escape from her home town, for with the money she was able to move to Sydney 'on the search for glamour'.[20]

After winning the *Pix* prize, Charmian went up to Sydney and rented a 'broom cupboard' in the Darlinghurst/Kings Cross area, where the young Amy Lila had once resided. But Charmian's dreams were very different from those her mother had dreamed three decades earlier, and she certainly did not skivvy for a living. As a result of the magazine publicity she was able to get some modelling work for the Bjelke Petersen physical culture studios, and she also did some photographic modelling for the studio where Margaret worked.[21] Her main job, however, was working as an usherette at the Minerva Theatre.

When describing this part of her life in the interview for the National Library oral history collection, Charmian Clift declared that her search for glamour was 'a country girl's search'; she went on to say that she thought country girls 'always dream of big bad cities and glamour'. In mid 1941, the ultimate in big bad city life in Australia was Kings Cross. Although the onslaught of American servicemen on the area had not quite begun, it was already a focal point for Australian soldiers and sailors on leave. It was also the long-established centre for artists, musicians and the Bohemian fringe, as well as prostitutes and criminals, the poor and the outcast. At the same time, the area was a gathering point for Sydney's socialite set. The Cross revelled in the juxtaposition of seediness and sophistication.

The latter reached its pinnacle in the Minerva Theatre, situated at the corner of Macleay and Orwell Streets, Potts Point. Under the directorship of the entrepreneur David N Martin, the building had been designed to incorporate the latest technical and architectural innovations. When the theatre opened in mid 1939 the magazine *The Film Weekly* devoted thirty-six pages spread over two issues to its praise — despite the fact that it was presenting live stage plays rather than films.[22] As well as stalls and dress circle seating for nearly a thousand patrons, the theatre boasted an elaborate series of stairways, vestibules, foyers, retiring rooms, even a soundproof 'babies cry-room' with an observation window and speakers. Next door to the theatre itself was the Minerva Building, which housed a cafe, a delicatessen, a French perfumery, and other elegant shops.

David N Martin employed as much fastidious care in the selection of his front-of-house staff as he did in every other detail. According to Martin's chief electrician, Harry Pike, the usherettes were 'high classy — he used to hand-pick them', paying particular attention to their carriage. These usherettes — there would be about ten of them employed at any time — were tall and beautiful and well spoken. They wore long evening gowns and gloves, and the costume was periodically changed.[23] In May 1941, when Charmian Clift was just about to join the Minerva, the theatre's operation was leased by Whitehall Productions (run by actor/director Kathleen Robinson and her author/producer husband, Alec

Coppell); the electrician remembered that Martin's criteria for front-of-house staff were retained.

To the stage-struck girl from Kiama who had dreamed of wearing a long lamé gown, the Minerva job seemed — in the beginning at least — like something out of a fairytale. Surely she would be able to graduate from usheretting to acting? Or mightn't she find herself a glamorous husband from among either the actors or the theatre's rich patrons? In fact, there was little mixing between the actors and the theatre staff, but Charmian Clift did 'hang around backstage, and all that was marvellously exciting'.[24]

Among those who worked backstage was the artist William Constable, who was the scenic designer for Whitehall Productions. After the string of crass, groping commercial travellers, Constable seemed wonderful to the young woman from Kiama: his photograph in the *Mr Smart Guy* program shows a slender, handsome man in his mid-thirties, with a dapper little moustache and a look of mischievous amusement in his eyes. He had gone to London in 1930 to study theatre design; after returning he had become known for his decor and set designs for Borovansky ballets, one of which had been taken to New York.[25] He and Charmian Clift started seeing quite a bit of each other, but alas, he was married. Although the affair had to end, a friendship remained.[26]

Meanwhile, as well as opportunities for romance and the general excitement of the job, there was a whole city to explore. Although at this time Minerva usherettes worked a long evening shift that began around 5 p.m., matinées were only on Wednesdays and Saturdays. This left plenty of time for the Bjelke Petersen modelling job, and simply for shopping and drinking coffee and strolling through the Cross. All in all, Charmian filled in her time very pleasantly. And yet, as the fictional Alma thinks in regard to her restless daughter:

> You couldn't go tearing through life the way Chris did, with that
> eagerness pulsing in your eyes, and that impudent, inviting tilt to
> your breasts, and that yearning for new sensations — any sort of
> new sensations — without getting yourself hurt.[27]

At this point in Charmian Clift's own accounts of her life the narrative suddenly slides or shudders. In a 1969 interview with the journalist Clifford Tolchard for *Walkabout* magazine, for example, she describes coming to

Sydney and getting the job at the Minerva, where she 'worked for a year'. Then the war came, she told Tolchard. 'So I joined the army overnight'.[28] In the interview for the National Library, she talks about the excitement of hanging around backstage at the Minerva; suddenly, she seems to falter: 'Then because of a series of things I went back home for a while, and then, finding that I hadn't made the grade on the stage, I found that there was a war on'.[29]

In this account, too, she immediately joins up. Of course, the war was well and truly 'on' in mid 1941 when Charmian Clift joined the Minerva — although as she was only seventeen at that time, she couldn't have enlisted. In fact she did not join up until April 1943. Accepting her statement that she was at the theatre for a year, this leaves us with the time from about mid 1942 until April 1943 unaccounted for.

The reason for this gap in the record is — sadly, for Charmian — the obvious one. Around late March 1942 the eighteen year old girl became pregnant. Whatever the circumstances of the conception, it was a crushing blow. Within a year of leaving home, all her hopes and dreams and plans were ruined. Marriage wasn't an option; indeed, it appears that the connection with the child's father was so tenuous that Charmian did not inform him of her pregnancy.[30] So there were three courses of action open to her: abortion, adoption or single motherhood. All were terrible choices.

Although abortions were illegal, costly and potentially dangerous, it would have been quite possible for Charmian, with her associations in the theatrical and Kings Cross world, to find an abortionist and to come up with the cash.[31] Given her agnostic upbringing, she can have had no orthodox religious objections. And indeed, twenty-five years later she was to write an impassioned plea for the legalisation of abortion 'not to belittle the value of human life, but to dignify it'. So why didn't Charmian Clift seek an abortion? Maybe at first she simply dithered. In the pro-abortion essay, the author notes that

> More often than not [a pregnant girl] is most dreadfully alone, and in her terror and ignorance lets weeks and even months go by or resorts to quack pills, making the abortion finally more dangerous and painful than it need have been and increasing the risk of serious illness, sterility, and even death.[32]

Perhaps she waited too long: Charmian would have been terrified of an abortion. During her childhood she had heard the local stories of girls 'getting into trouble':

Ruby Riddell (King that was) began swelling up straight after the wedding. My father said that young Frank Riddell was so gormless he always started before the whistle.

Up on the hill Dulcie Dunger died. Of a knitting needle. 'Poor thing,' my mother said. 'Poor silly young thing.'[33]

But what did Amy say when it was her own daughter 'in trouble'? And what did Margaret say? Or did Margaret not know? When questioned about this matter, many years later, Charmian's sister burst out laughing. 'I have never heard anything so ridiculous in all my life!' she declared.[34] And yet she must have known. It is impossible to believe that Amy would not have called on Margaret's support, especially as Margaret was living in Sydney and was available if there should be any emergency. According to Toni Burgess, who became Charmian's closest woman friend some six years after this pregnancy, Charmian had wanted to keep the baby but Amy had made her agree to adopt it out, pointing out that she, Amy, could not afford to support her daughter and grandchild, and that Charmian as a single mother would not be able to manage. Burgess maintained that 'Charmian never forgave her mother for making her give up the child'.[35]

As to the abortion question — perhaps it was now that Amy told Charmian the story of how she herself had considered an abortion on discovering that she was pregnant again only a few months after the birth of Barré. Although Margaret would deny any knowledge of her sister's first child, perhaps this was what she was remembering when she said that 'As a young woman, Charm was always grateful to my mother for having her'.[36]

Was this kind of moral blackmail brought into play? *You can't have an abortion because if I'd had one you wouldn't be here ...* It seems quite possible. As to Charmian's own reason for not seeking an abortion, Toni would attribute this partly to her friend's sense of propriety:

Although many people won't believe this, for all her unconventionality she was inculcated with the correct forms. As a girl in her insular family she learnt the right way to do things — you know: 'this is the way the Clifts do things'. And when she had an illegitimate baby, she did the right thing for the time.

On top of this, there was guilt. When Toni herself had an abortion, for medical reasons, during the time she and her friend were young married women, Charmian was 'horrified'. 'She didn't understand how I could bear the guilt'.[37]

In both these attitudes we see, of course, the background of this small town girl. Charmian's feeling that abortion would lead to guilt must be linked to her sense of the guilt and shame of sexuality in the first place; she had been bad and now she must take her punishment. A city girl could go to an abortionist; this country girl could not.

Nor, of course, could she keep the child: Amy and Margaret would have been quite firm on that. A Clift could not return to Kiama with a baby in a bundle and no prospect of a husband on the horizon. Amy's fierce pride and the standard of superiority which the Clifts had set themselves meant that this family could not accommodate any scandal. Besides, even if Amy could have borne the gossip of the locals, she could not have stood the continual disapproval of her resident mother-in-law.

There was also little possibility of Charmian keeping the baby in Sydney and supporting herself and her offspring at a time when there was no government pension for single mothers. Even if she were to manage to get a job, who would look after the child while she went to work?

In the limited range of Charmian's choices we see again the way in which the small size of the Clift family, together with Amy's grandiose social aspirations, worked against happiness. In larger and less snobbish working class families, there would have been a possibility of keeping the child and leaving its care to other female family members while the young woman worked. But neither Amy nor Margaret wanted the child. Indeed, Margaret was soon to be married to her respectable fiancé Alf Backhouse; she wasn't going to ruin her chances by lumbering herself with an illegitimate baby.

And so there was really no choice for Charmian. Only one option was possible: she would have to give birth to the child, and put it up for adoption.

The misery of all this is hard to imagine. In the abortion essay, Clift notes how 'pitiable is the plight of the unmarried girl, who, having made a "mistake", must at all costs conceal it from her employer, family, friends, teachers, or become an object of pity or scorn'.[38] Here 'pity' is the key word. Charmian Clift could hold her head high against scorn, but accepting pity, as a single and apparently deserted woman, was another matter entirely.

Now the decision had been made, there was the practical problem of where to go. Returning to Kiama for the confinement was clearly not possible. With her tall, strongly boned build and her erect carriage, Charmian was able to conceal her pregnancy for some time. Once it became obvious, however, she would have to disappear, as unmarried mothers did in those days.

Only a step and a jump away from Charmian's Darlinghurst accommodation was Crown Street Women's Hospital. It was well known that the matron of this establishment, Miss Edna Shaw, regarded adoption as her specialty: all an unmarried girl had to do was front up, and Matron would arrange the rest. It was expected that the girl would move into the hospital as soon as she began to 'show', and would work as a domestic — peeling vegetables, preparing food trays — until she came into labour. Then she was provided with a wedding ring, and a polite 'Mrs' was added to her name, before she went into the labour ward alongside the respectably married mothers.[39] Meanwhile, Matron would arrange the adoption, either through the public channels, or privately, for in those days it was possible for someone in Matron Shaw's position to sidestep the standard procedures and regulations, and simply give a baby to someone of her choice. Sometimes it would happen that one of the married women would lose her baby, and the matron would arrange that she took home a child anyway.[40] As to the controversial issue of whether or not a relinquishing mother should be allowed to see or feed her child — Matron Shaw advised the girls against doing so, but she allowed them to nurse their babies for two weeks if they insisted.[41]

It was in the latter months of 1942 that Charmian went for her interview with Matron. Although Edna Shaw saw young women from wealthy families as well as poor ones, Charmian stood out as being a cut above the usual sort of young women in this situation. Perhaps it was her looks and general physical well-being; perhaps it was the educated 'English' accent which impressed the matron. Whatever it was, she discussed the girl with her friend, the hospital secretary, who fifty years later would find herself remembering the conversations.[42] She promised Charmian — as she promised all the relinquishing mothers — that she personally would make sure that the baby went to a good home.

And so Charmian disappeared from the Kings Cross scene and moved into Crown Street. The irony was cruel: only two years previously she had fled from Lithgow Hospital, where she had hated the dreary routine of hospital life, the hard slog of skivvying in the wards, the smell of illness and disinfectant, and — perhaps most of all — the fact of living at close quarters with other people. Now she was back in a hospital again, but this time there was no easy escape. She had to be patient and wait — not Charmian's greatest talent. As her body grew larger and heavier, the Sydney summer began. It was sticky and humid, and she couldn't go outside for a walk, in case someone who knew her from the Cross passed by and recognised her. This was the worst trap she had ever been in.

The final twist of the knife was that it was on Christmas Day that the baby was born. It was a beautiful and healthy girl, whom Charmian named Jennifer.[43] This may seem a rather ordinary choice, but 'Jennifer' was beginning to be a popular name for girls, and perhaps — for once in her life — Charmian wanted to do something conventional.

Did she at this time dither, as many young women did when faced with the reality of adoption? (Matron admitted that 'more often than we'd like' the legal process came unstuck at this stage.[44]) Perhaps Amy and Margaret had to weigh in again with all the arguments against keeping the baby.

Whatever private turmoil went on, in early January 1943 Charmian saw Jennifer for the last time.[45] She would suffer intermittent bouts of anguish over this matter for the rest of her life.

Studies of relinquishing mothers show that, even if the woman has other children, the sense of loss is usually sharp and ongoing. Although it is similar to the loss felt when a baby dies, there is an extra edge to the pain, for there is the continual uncertainty about where the child is, whether the child is happy and healthy. This anguish often manifests itself in recurring periods of depression.[46]

Certainly, Charmian did sometimes seem to shift into a mood of melancholy or darkness, and no doubt there were occasions when wondering or worrying about the fate of Jennifer made her very depressed. However, it is important not to view this one very real reason for sadness as some sort of dominant force, ruling the rest of Charmian's life. The phenomenon that was often described, both in fact and in fiction, of Charmian Clift or Cressida Morley bursting suddenly and for no apparent reason into tears was probably sometimes triggered by a memory of this very deep loss. Similarly, Clift's fey silences, the sense she frequently gave of listening for something just out of earshot, can partly be put down to this source of anxiety.

In his biography of George Johnston, Garry Kinnane notes that: 'Johnston told Grace Edwards that Clift's deep regret over the matter' of the relinquished child 'might have explained her frequent retreats into silence and her often otherwise inexplicable tears'.[47] Certainly it might have, at least on some occasions. Yet there were often other things which caused Charmian to weep. One of these was sheer happiness, for Charmian's emotions were always very close to the surface, and tears would be a frequent release. At the same time, her attitude of quiet listening was not necessarily a manifestation of sadness, but could be a retreat into solitude and daydreaming. And even misery could have its pleasurable moments. In her descriptions of herself as an unhappy adolescent, there always seems to be a certain element of pleasure in the accounts of tearful wallowing in the marram grass. At a later time, Charmian would be interested in the whole business of melancholy, and would enjoy dipping into Robert Burton's *Anatomy* of that subject.[48] Overall, this episode would cause a form of ongoing pain which would sometimes seem to build to a crescendo of anxiety and unhappiness. However, for Charmian as for other relinquishing mothers, life would go on — with its ups and downs, its triumphs and its other causes of pain.

Whatever effect the loss of her first child had upon her emotional state, this experience of illegitimate pregnancy was to have other effects on Charmian Clift's behaviour. We have seen how, from the time of furtive dinners with commercial travellers, the young woman suffered from a sense of shame at her own sexuality. While she didn't give a damn what people thought or said about her, she did care for her opinion of herself. A sizeable body of literature has been written about the burden of guilt carried by Catholic girls, but a sense of moral failure can be just as sharp for those brought up in the belief that it is only themselves that they must honour. From this time, Charmian's feeling that she was a 'bad girl' was confirmed.

This is evident in the way in which the author frequently excoriates her alter ego heroines for their sexual behaviour. In one version of *Greener Grows the Grass*, Christine Morley goes out for a drink with a journalist named Martin Smith (a character clearly based on George Johnston) and their mutual friend, Bill Eaton. Here the charge of immorality is laid again and again both by Eaton and by Christine Morley herself. When first describing Christine to Smith, Eaton tells him: 'She's a bitch. She's the mother of all wantons'. On realising that she is attracted to Smith (who is married), Christine tells herself: 'You're dirty. You're cheap'. And Eaton joins in the chorus of castigation: 'Why try to fight against yourself? You're the mother of all wantons, my dear. Why not admit it? Christine, you're destined to have men in and out of your life like boozers through a swinging door'. Christine momentarily looks 'confused and ridiculously young and somehow frightened', but then the 'varnish of sophistication' smooths over her again. She laughs lightly and replies: 'So what [if] I'm a bitch? I've never denied it, have I?'[49] In the author's two published novels as well, the heroines are punished dreadfully for their sexual passion. In *Honour's Mimic*, Kathy is so much the Scarlet Woman that she is even stoned at the end of the book.

For Charmian Clift, the pregnancy was proof that she wasn't a 'nice girl'. And her nature was such that she would now set out to demonstrate the proof again and again. In some of Clift's later sexual adventures there was a distinct element of self-degradation, as if she sought to punish herself for breaking a code which owed much to the old-fashioned Kiama values which she professed to reject.

Two decades later, in the essay 'On Coming to a Bad End', the author made a powerful case against the sort of narrow-minded small town attitudes that she had grown up with. In this piece, she pointed out that ends such as 'great loneliness, or a souring of the pleasure in living, or self-hatred, or hatred of others' were worse than the bad end that local gossips of her home town had had in mind when they 'equated morality solely with the reproductive functions'.[50] While this was sound wisdom, it came too late for the author herself.

Yet while a link between sex and shame runs through Charmian Clift's work and her life, this matter of the guilt caused by the relinquishment of her first child should — like accounts of the anguish — not be overstated. Perhaps more destructive than the guilt was the way in which the circumstances surrounding the birth of Jennifer set up a pattern of secrecy. Again, the testimonies of other relinquishing mothers show that hiding the past is a terrible burden. Charmian Clift's way of dealing with this was erratic.

For example, fairly soon after the adoption she confided in at least two male friends.[51] At some stage — although the timing of this isn't clear — she would tell George Johnston. In the late 1940s she told her friend Toni Burgess. Years later, she would sometimes confess the matter when she was maudlinly drunk.[52] However, while she would sometimes confide in people to whom she wasn't particularly close, she didn't tell some of her women friends, and she certainly never told her three legitimate children. This made the whole situation terribly complicated, for she lived in the peril that those whom she had told might tell those whom she hadn't. When she became a public figure, the issue became a time bomb waiting to go off: hence the way she handled (or failed to handle) this period of her life in interviews. As the years went on, the pattern of hiding, of secrecy, that began with the pregnancy gradually became habitual. This behaviour connected with Charmian Clift's various forms of role-playing, for acting is of course a way of concealing the truth.

In regard to her fiction writing, this feeling that the experience must not become public knowledge was one of the main reasons why Charmian Clift again and again abandoned the tale of her alter ego character, Christine/Cressida. Although the character Eaton in *Greener Grows the Grass* tells Martin Smith that Christine 'came from somewhere in the backblocks with some unimportant tragedy that seemed very important to her',[53] Clift could not make sense of the character and the story without dealing with this tragedy, and she feared the personal exposure which this would entail.

And in her newspaper column she would never go close to hinting about her first child — for the mother of Jennifer was a different person. Charmian Clift the columnist didn't have an illegitimate daughter.

After leaving Crown Street Women's Hospital in the new year of 1943, Charmian returned to Kiama. She seemed to be replaying the events of two years earlier when she had fled from Lithgow, for once again it was high summer, and once again Charmian spent much of her time alone on the beach, reading and crying in the dunes. The difference was that this time, when she cried for the loss of her childhood, there was another lost child on her mind as well. Then she would plunge into the sea and float in the icy water for hours to try to wash away the past, as Julia in *Walk to the Paradise Gardens* floats 'until her skin [begins] to look plucked and her fingers and toes [turn] white and crumpled and soggy' in order to punish herself and purge herself after a shameful sexual encounter.[54]

In addition to Charmian's immediate source of pain, this was not a happy time at home. After the freedom she had experienced with her own living quarters in Kings Cross, it was hard to be stuck back in that cramped cottage with her irascible father and martyrish mother and the added trial of snobbish, disapproving Mardie. Barré was no company — off working in Wollongong all day. And she could not help but feel that the neighbours were all gloating that here she was, back again with her tail between her legs, this girl who reckoned she'd get out of town and *do* something!

If even the tiny valley seemed to be full of prying eyes, there was at least one place where Charmian could retreat in absolute privacy, and one way in which she could escape the grief and shame. She could move into herself, and write.

Some months later, in Sydney, a friend would happen to mention that she had just heard a recording of Delius's 'Walk to the Paradise Gardens'. Charmian, who was lying flat on her bed at the time, 'sat bolt upright'.

> She said, 'Did you say "Walk to the Paradise Gardens"?'
> I said, 'Yes — why?'
> She said, 'I've written a story called "Walk to the Paradise Gardens".'
> I said, 'Why don't you bring it in? I'd love to read it.'
> She said, 'No — it's all locked away.' She said, 'I've written a book, too.'
> I said, 'A whole book?'
> 'Yes,' she said, 'I've written a whole book, but I can't get the end of it.'[55]

Exactly what this book was about we cannot know, but we can be certain that it was autobiographical. Her subject always was her own story, or that of her family. It is likely that it was now that the author began writing some sort of fictionalised version of the story of her parents' lives during the early years of their marriage — the sort of narrative that we find in the tale of Alma and Tom arriving at the settlement, or the account of the stormy night when the boat was lost, or the epiphany that occurs in 'The Awakening'. Whether this text had already assumed the title *Greener Grows the Grass* cannot be said. It is easy to see, however, how such a title would occur. While it fitted with the sense of longing for a better life which Charmian shared with her mother (and with the female figure in the Alma narratives), it also resonates in a literal sense if we imagine the young author sitting in that trap of a little valley, gazing at the hill which seemed the barrier to the green grass of opportunity which lay on the other side. As to why the author would turn to her mother's story, there are two very good reasons. First, it links back with Charmian's childhood sense that everything important had happened before she was born. Like Tristram Shandy, she felt she could only make sense of her own story by documenting everything that led to the moment of her conception. Secondly, it must have seemed easier to write her mother's story rather than her own, for her autobiography now contained a secret which could not be put onto paper, even in the guise of fiction.

This surely was what the young author was thinking about when she told her friend that she couldn't get the ending of her book. However much she had actually written, surely this book with the ending which the author could not resolve was essentially the same book with which she would struggle all her life. *Greener Grows the Grass — The End of the Morning* — it would have various titles, just as the alter ego would change her name from Sarah to Tina to Christine to Miranda to Cressida, or would sometimes launch into the variations of Kathy, Kate or Julia. The fact that around this time the author had also written a story with the Delius title shows that she was exploring personal material, because in all its reworkings the *Paradise Gardens* novel was concerned with Clift's home landscape.[56]

The reason the ending of the book could not be solved, of course, was because it included the recent events which the author was trying to lock away — as she subsequently locked away the drafts of the novel. For the rest of her life, as Charmian Clift battled with this book, she would remain unable to unlock the ending. In August 1968 when she applied for a Commonwealth Literary Fund fellowship to complete *The End of the Morning*, she stated: 'The morning ends, and that's the end of the book'. The author added: 'I know the last sentence'.[57]

This makes it clear that the novel's conclusion would be connected with the 'end' referred to in the title. But did the author really know the ending? Or did she just think she did? Because, once again, she would be unable to complete the novel. She would keep getting bogged, at the same point at which she had got bogged on all the drafts of *Greener Grows the Grass*. This is the point at which the alter ego moves out from the safety of the dome into the big world, and explores her sexuality. The problem was — the author did not know the end of the story.

The main trauma of the relinquishment of Jennifer was not so much guilt as the anxiety of ignorance. What happened? Did the story end happily ever after — or not? She didn't know, and she would never know, and so she couldn't finish the book.

This would probably be the worst legacy of this whole episode for Charmian Clift, both as an author and as a human being. She needed to write her autobiographical novel about growing up, and get it over and done with, early in her career. She needed to do *her* equivalent of *My Brilliant Career*. Once she had written it, she would have finished with that piece of literary subject matter and she would also have been able to draw a line beneath that part of her life. In both ways — in living and in writing — she would have been able to move on. Her fiction would have been able to take off, to become truly fiction, rather than an endless series of variations on the same autobiographical characters and the same incidents and themes and landscapes. But it couldn't — because she was stuck — and would remain stuck for the rest of her life.

This was an enormous trap from which Charmian Clift would never free herself. She had an extraordinary lyrical talent for handling prose; she had an acute ability to observe the nuances of human character; she had a pantheistic sense of nature and landscape; she had a broad general knowledge and a sharp, questing mind; and she was a natural-born storyteller. Against all this, however, was balanced the fact that, as a writer, she was locked inside the small world of her early experience, and she could not move out. As time went on, the circle of Charmian Clift's writing would become smaller and smaller — until it shrank to the size of a five hundred word personal essay. Perfect, of course. But limited and limiting.

Meanwhile, as Charmian Clift could not write about her life on paper, she would turn her life into her version of the Great Australian Novel. She would live it — she would be it — if she could not write it.

By April 1943, the blue and gold days of the Illawarra summer were starting to fade and Charmian was spending less time on the beach and more time in the small cottage. Although she would retreat for hours into her room and scribble her novel furiously on odd scraps of paper, the atmosphere in the cottage was always claustrophobic and often stormy. While Amy was feeling the strain of having a grown-up daughter to care for as well as her mother-in-law, Syd was experiencing some sort of pain that exacerbated his temper. He and Charmian clashed just as they always had. And beyond the small and stifling world of the family there was the dullness of the town, which was harder to bear now that Charmian had experienced the bright lights of Kings Cross. After meeting cosmopolitan men such as William Constable, even the silvertails of Kiama seemed like hicks and hayseeds.

One of the great attractions of writing fiction is the possibility of putting aside the drafts and messes and mistakes of the past, and starting afresh with a new sheet of blank paper. For Charmian it was already time to start a new chapter. Or maybe even a whole new plot, with new characters and a change of setting. The first attempts to escape hadn't been at all successful. But it must soon be time to set off on the big adventure which she had been dreaming about for so long.

PART II

THE BIG ADVENTURE

7

THE TERMS OF A NOVEL

*This was, in a way, the most wonderful period of my life,
because I was still very young, and I was still young enough to be
seeing all this in the terms of a novel, and of great drama,
myself in character, as it were.*[1]

It was all very well to decide to set off on a new life. But how could a young woman achieve this, with no job and no money and nowhere to live, apart from her parents' cottage? It was Margaret who got Charmian out of the trap of Kiama in April 1943, just as she had opened the way for her little sister's escape to the big city, two years earlier. 'Come on', Margaret urged, 'let's join up'.[2]

The army was the obvious solution: it would provide Charmian with accommodation as well as a demanding occupation which would take her mind off her unhappiness. It would give her a chance to start a new life with new associates in a new place. The only problem with the plan was that it meant that Margaret would have to enlist too, because Charmian didn't want to do it by herself. Still shaken by the trauma of the past months, she wanted Margaret as backstop. For Margaret, enlistment would represent a considerable sacrifice: she had recently married her fiancé, Alf Backhouse, and was living with him in the inner Sydney suburb of Lewisham. That she would leave a new husband and go off to live in barracks indicates the strength of her family loyalty, and perhaps her desperation that something be done to get her sister out of her predicament. And so Charmian Clift and Margaret Backhouse joined the army together on 27 April 1943.[3] Their enlistment occurred at the beginning of the main expansion of the Australian Women's Army Service.[4]

Like many of the men and women who joined the services, Charmian Clift was motivated partly by patriotism, and partly by the allure of action and excitement. When describing her enlistment in her 1965 interview for the National Library, she linked it to her earlier dream of acting. Finding that she 'hadn't made the grade on the stage' and that 'there was a war on', she thought: 'Now that is it — here is my big stage set for adventure'. Later in the same interview she added: 'This was, in a way, the most wonderful period of my life, because I was still very young, and I was still young enough to be seeing all this in the terms of a novel, and of great drama, myself in character, as it were'.[5]

Charmian Clift's choice of words is most revealing. 'Stage' ... 'great drama' ... 'the terms of a novel' ... and — perhaps most significant of all — 'myself in character'. This was Charmian talking about how she acted out in real life the role of her own alter ego. Yet as she acted the part, she was also developing, rehearsing, rewriting the role as she went along. The three years which she spent in the army were crucial in the development of the Charmian Clift character. These years also provided the author/actor with the two vital starting points for the next stage of the plot: by the end of this period she would be confirmed in her vocation, and she would find the love of her life.

For many Australian servicewomen the war years offered great opportunity. 'Ar-wars', as they were called, were given a chance to learn new skills, and to do jobs which had traditionally been reserved for men. Living and working together in difficult conditions, women developed the mateship which was also traditionally seen as the prerogative of men. Though Margaret was to hate the army, Charmian took to service life with enthusiasm and skill, remembering afterwards the 'texture' of that period as being 'young and wild and audacious and adventurous'.

> I don't really think we helped much to win the war, but we won ourselves and our own identities and our own sort of confidence and our own sort of discipline. And whatever it was all about, looking back on it, I wouldn't have missed it for anything in the world.[6]

Again, the reference to winning an identity is revealing: in these three years, the young woman would begin to develop a particular identity which people would see as being the real Charmian Clift.

Along with the other Sydney recruits of that time, Clift did her rookie training at Ingleburn, on the western outskirts of Sydney. During this initial training period, recruits were given an intelligence test and were interviewed to assess their suitability for different branches of the AWAS. It was decided that both Charmian and Margaret would join the 15th Australian Heavy Anti-Aircraft Battery. Requirements for anti-aircraft duties included intelligence (especially computational skills), personality, good eyesight, commonsense and quick reflexes.

In the wake of the successful recruitment drive of April 1943, the army offered fast-track promotion to certain AWAS recruits. It is not surprising that both Clift girls took the opportunity of accelerated advancement. In October 1943 Margaret jumped from the rank of gunner (equivalent to private) to that of lance bombadier (equivalent to lance corporal).[7] Charmian would also quickly become an NCO.

With her steady temperament and capability, combined with her respectability as a married woman, Margaret was soon put in charge of two dozen AWAS gunners who were accommodated in private housing in the Sydney suburb of Drummoyne, adjoining the gun site at Iron Cove, where the harbour runs into the Parramatta River. The NCO was a stickler for propriety; yet as long as the lower ranks behaved, she allowed them to call her 'Meg'. One of the girls in her charge was Gunner Nona Wood, who remembers how one day, not long after the group was formed, she was told to move her gear into a small double room, because someone new was joining them. A couple of days later Gunner Wood walked into the room and found the new girl lying on the spare bed.

> She was like Loretta Young — she really was. At this time her hair was always a light blondey colour and it was almost a pageboy — she used to wear it just curled under. And she had big green eyes — they were a fox-like green with a hazel glint in them — and when she came outside you'd always see these green eyes, even under the brim of her hat, because the light would get behind them.
>
> She was tall and lithe — she was tall at the back — you always knew the back of Charmian. And her walk was something. We had men's boots during the day, and you can't bend your feet very well in a man's boot, but she walked like a ballerina. She'd glide — she had a ballerina's walk — her feet folded over, one over the other, in these boots.[8]

Moving into communal housing represented an abrupt change of lifestyle for this young woman who had never been part of a gang of girlfriends and who guarded her privacy. At first, Charmian found it difficult. There was a bit of 'catfighting' among the other girls 'about the way these two sisters came into the army with stripes', but although some of the other gunners complained, Gunner Wood liked the addition to the group. Soon the two young women would talk 'for long hours into the night about books', and it was to Nona that Charmian confided the fact that she had written a book herself.

At this stage of Charmian's army career there was no time for writing, but she was always observing things and saving things for later use. Even a phrase could be stored away. On one occasion, Gunner Wood came back from leave with a bag of white grapes — a luxury at the time, though these ones had large pips and thick skins.

> I sat on the edge of my bed and I peeled each grape [...] and I turned round and I saw her staring at me. She was reading my copy of Tennyson at the time *and* she was watching, and she was so still.
>
> The Mess signal went, and I said to her, 'There's Mess — are you going to come in?'
>
> And she said, 'No, I don't feel hungry.'
>
> I got down the end of the hall and the voice floated after me: 'Peel me a lotus!'
>
> And I always think that that must have been the birth of that idea — she was reading 'The Lotus Eaters' by Tennyson.

Although she got on with her roommate, Charmian didn't develop friendships with the other girls at Drummoyne. At this time, she tended to rely on her sister. Margaret herself would later say: 'I only really got to know Charm as a person rather than being "Little Sister" when we were in the army together'.[9] To Nona it seemed that the sisters were 'very close' and that Meg protected Charmian; in particular, Nona remembers Charmian suffering from devastating period pain, and Meg looking after her. And the NCO made sure her little sister wasn't overworked: 'Charmian didn't go on Manning every day — there was some sort of talk among the girls that she got out of it a lot'.

There was also a bit of talk about what the new girl's past history might have been, and whom she knew among the male troops. Nona fended off the other gunners' questions, feeling that there was some source of hidden sadness which Charmian was 'upset about'. Sometimes she would 'sulk a little bit' — would clam up and suddenly not say anything — and her roommate wouldn't say anything either. Charmian 'knew [Nona] would never ask'.[10]

Christmas 1943 was a painful time — the first anniversary of Jennifer's birth. On one of her leaves Charmian went back to Crown Street Hospital with some baby clothes which she gave to Matron Shaw, asking her to see that her daughter received the birthday present. Of course, this was something which relinquishing mothers frequently did; Matron would agree to pass on the gift but would send it to some charity. The rules were clear: there could be no contact after adoption.

It must have been terrible for Charmian to return, but this was not the worst of it. When she told this story some years later to her closest woman friend, Charmian went on to say that when she was walking back to town from the hospital, she happened — quite by coincidence — to bump into the child's father, whom she had not seen or contacted throughout the whole episode. When he asked, 'What are you up to?' she replied, 'I have just been to Crown Street to leave a present for our child'. The man exclaimed, 'You bloody liar!' He turned on his heel and — the story concludes — Charmian did not see him again.[11]

Despite the unhappiness of the recent past, and despite the watchful eye of her sister, Charmian would soon start to socialise again. In one of her essays, the author was to express her belief that wars 'hold some sort of clue' to Australian men, for in wartime they are liberated into travel and adventure, and indulge in the 'tirra lirra' that she had always hankered for.

> My great and glorious period of Australian men was in war-time, when it was fairly simple to transform them into romantics. Lancelots abounded, vowing vows and throwing down gages and begging for hair-ribbons to wear over their hearts. Australian men were still lean and slouchy and brown in those days (poor damn Depression kids that they were) and under the emotional stress of partings came up with the occasional poetry of inarticulate men, poignant beyond telling. Tirra lirra rang like a tocsin through those years.[12]

It wasn't just Australian men who wooed the young servicewoman: Charmian 'knew a lot of Americans', Nona remembered from her roommate's conversations. She also frequently talked to Nona about going to the Journalists' Club on her weekly leave.[13] This was a meeting place for people generally involved in the arts, and in the choice of this venue we see where the interests of the young servicewoman lay. Quite often Charmian would return late after leave, for Drummoyne was hard to reach by public transport, and she would complain of the difficulty of getting back. Perhaps she also started to tire of Margaret's supervision. And so — using transport as the reason — she transferred over to the AWAS quarters at Kensington.

Here Charmian really started to enjoy the army, and to make friends. In her new role, she even acquired a new name: it was the Kensington girls — Reevsie and Gerry, Big Red and Little Pat and Jeannie and the rest of the crew — who bestowed upon Charmian the name of 'Cliftie', which she liked so much. In her essay memorialising this time and these friends, she would remark: 'I've always been a loner by nature and those 1110 days of service were the only time I've ever lived communally with other women and in retrospect I was a little surprised at how much I'd really enjoyed it'.[14]

In fact Cliftie would spend only a small amount of her army time actually living with other servicewomen, but her memory of the happiness of this period was genuine. What she really loved was the time that began in the early months of 1944, when the gun sites at both Iron Cove and at Kensington were dismantled, and the girls from both establishments were moved to Moore Park golf course where they camped out in 'igloos' (Quonset huts).

If Clift's life was a novel, this was the period when it was written in the girls' boarding school genre. The male NCOs and officers occupied the role that teachers play in stories of that ilk, and Cliftie was one of the leaders of the naughty girls who teased the authority figures. When a male officer 'barked an order at her' she would 'smirk' — 'she was the same height as he was, and she only had to glare back at him and he would feel a fool'[15] — and she even produced a camp newsletter, with 'drawings [...] of the line-up of male NCOs'.[16]

And as in all boarding school stories there would be hilarious times after lights out. Gunner Wood had ended up in the same igloo as her erstwhile roommate, and vividly remembers a night when the girls played with 'a squeegee board' which they put on the soldier's box that served as a table in the igloo. They turned a glass upside down and watched to see if it would move around the alphabet chart . . .

> We all had a go, and it didn't do anything.
> Then Charmian came in. 'What are you doing?'
> So we explained . . .
> 'Oh let *me* have a go!'
> So Charmian sat down, cross-legged, at this soldier's box. *And the glass wrote!* It just went on and on! It wrote beautifully!

And the Lights Out went and we all went to bed, and Charmian went on with this blooming glass!

She said, 'It says I'm going to live on an island!'

Someone said, 'Shut up, Cliftie.'

'I am! An island — it says "An island south of Budapest". Does anyone know what the island south of Budapest is?'

We didn't have an atlas, and we didn't know.

'Anyway,' she said, 'where's Budapest?'

[...] And she asked, 'Will J be married?'

Then she sang out: 'Yes!'

She was going to have — I forget how many children — but she was quiet and she was thinking for a bit then.

And on she went with this glass. Our lights were out, you know, and she was sitting at this thing, and we could hear this scraping [...]

And that was Charmian — that was really Charmian — sitting there with the glass turned upside down and shouting at it the whole time.[17]

In Clift's own account of this period, the boarding school genre crosses over into girls' own adventure.

We, who handled guns and ammunition and delicate precision instruments, always used to feel ourselves to be an elite. It was rough and tough, and we lived in tin sheds on a golf course and slept on straw palliasses and wore nothing more feminine than battle-dress and boots and we manned the guns at dawn and dusk and stood guard at night with fixed bayonets and studied by torches to get our specialist badges and peeled potatoes and cleaned the grease traps and latrines and fell out at all hours for alarms and mock air-raids and went through rifle drill until our shoulders ached and fell into love too and out of it again at any season at all and got no quarter from the men in the other line of tin huts across the parade ground and all for four and fourpence a day and the privilege of being gunners. We used to turn the height-finder onto the people playing golf beyond our barricades of barbed wire and feel ourselves to be superior.[18]

With its outdoor freedom, combined with the sense of elitism, and the unaccustomed comradeship thrown in, life on the golf course seemed paradise — at least for a while. Throughout the rest of her life, Charmian would remember this period as a vitally important experience, even though it actually only lasted a couple of months.

This experience would also become a significant part of the fictional record. Though George Johnston never met Charmian Clift when she was in anti-aircraft, he drew upon her memories of that time during the writing of *My Brother Jack*, for — as we shall see — Clift had a great deal of input into the writing of that book. Given that George's Great Australian Novel (as the couple both saw *My Brother Jack*) was autobiographical, then Clift's 'novel' experience of the war years was a fitting part of it. All in all, the account of what Cressida Morley was like in this period of her life must be seen as Clift's own 'authorised version' of this segment of her story.

In this bit of the novel it is 1943, and the war correspondent David Meredith is home on leave in Melbourne. The location of Clift's golf course is moved from Sydney to Melbourne[19] in order to set up a scene in which David Meredith can meet a beautiful female gunner when he is taken by a nervous young lieutenant to inspect an anti-aircraft training camp:

> We came to Number 3 gun-pit and surprised five girls cleaning ammunition, and I said to the lieutenant, 'Well, it's nice to see that a woman's place is still with a duster in her hands!' but even as I spoke I was conscious of a pair of marsh-green eyes, cloudy and a little scornful, and of a grubby hand pushing a book surreptitiously between the grass and the sandbags.[20]

As a mock 'action' is suddenly staged and the 'girl with the green eyes' takes up her position at her instruments, David Meredith seizes the opportunity to check the hidden book. Naturally, this is Charmian Clift's own favourite novel — *Tristram Shandy*. The war correspondent wants 'to laugh out loud'. As he watches the girl going through the motions of shooting down the plane, he reflects that she is 'like a child playing soldiers', and that she is 'the youngest thing' he has 'ever seen in [his] life'. After the action finishes, he engages her in conversation.

> 'Well,' I said, taking advantage of my VIP standing, 'that was a very efficient show, Gunner —?'

'Morley, sir,' she returned briskly. 'Instrument specialist.'

'And does Gunner Morley, instrument specialist, also happen to have a first name?' I said, deliberately teasing her.

'Yes, sir,' she said, and her eyes were as cool and deep and clear as the reef seas and her mouth lifted its wide ripply corners, almost tremulously, as if she might really burst into laughter from sheer happiness. 'Cressida, sir,' she said.

As the narrator goes on to muse upon this encounter with the hindsight of two decades or so, it is clear that Cressida Morley is going to play a part of great significance in the life of David Meredith. He refers to possessing 'a snapshot' which 'must have been taken of her around that time', and he uses this as a way in which to dwell again upon the striking physical appearance of the young gunner.

All her features were too big for her, as if she had not really grown into them yet. (She was only a couple of months past eighteen at that time, and in fact she did not realise her full beauty until she was almost thirty.) Her broad, sun-freckled brow looked too wide, her cheekbones too heroic, and she wore her extraordinary mouth and eyes like finery she was not quite sure of and was trying to be nonchalant about. Nor, in those days, was anything quite under control, neither eyes nor mouth, nor the contralto voice that was also too big and with a husky lilt to it, nor the body in that ridiculous stained battle-dress, still with a child's gawkiness about it ... and she seemed to have no breasts at all, but her shoulders were broad and her hips lean, and with the gawkiness she had a certain quick, boyish grace. Boy's hands, too, square and brown and muscular and grubby. And even if nothing of all this was under control then, there was a sense of vital power about her, as if she were practising with everything all at once and on any person available.

After this brief encounter, the war correspondent spends the next two years overseas. Returning to Melbourne for a week's leave in the first half of 1945, he happens to bump into Cressida in a restaurant. Now a twenty year old lieutenant, she is dining with her army boss, Gavin Turley, who is an old journalist mate of Meredith's. As the evening progresses, the narrator falls in love.

Although Charmian Clift spent years developing the fictional character of Cressida Morley through various stages and under different names, this character first appeared in public in *My Brother Jack*. This gun-pit scene is therefore crucial. It takes only two pages — indeed, all the Cressida Morley material amounts to only fifteen pages of a lengthy novel — but it leaves an indelible impression on the mind of the reader. These passages introduce a number of the significant attributes which would run through the subsequent portrayal of the Cressida Morley character. These would also become vital patterns in the Clift myth.

From the moment she appears on stage, she is 'the girl with the green eyes'. Just as important as the colour is the way the eyes evoke images of water — initially marsh water (where cress would grow) or more significantly water 'as cool and deep and clear as the reef seas'. In the gun-pit scene, David Meredith does not actually know that there is any link between Cressida Morley and the sea, but at his subsequent meeting with her the connection is spelled out. Here the light plays 'in the girl's green eyes like seaweed moving in the shoalwater tides', and Gavin Turley informs his mate that 'You have here a savage, David [...] She was born on a barren mile of Pacific beach'. David muses:

> It was perfectly and absolutely *right,* of course! It had to be — that was where her eyes came from, out of the ocean, out of the endless Pacific depths. And that was precisely what she was — a savage, a pagan, an authentic something that was quite different from anything else ... and she was only twenty now, and she would have gone from her long lonely beach to a gun-site and from a gun-site to Gavin Turley, and she would never have known a suburban street in her life, or a garden subdivision, and she wouldn't know an *Antirrhinum* from a *Phlox drummondii* or a mock-orange if one fell on her![21]

Gavin Turley cuts into Meredith's musings with additional information about the 'savage': 'Never wore a pair of shoes until she was thirteen [...] Like Christopher Robin, she still has sand between the toes'.

These elements — the wild pagan quality and the ignorance of suburban mores — would, together with the green eyes, be vital ingredients in the characterisation of Cressida Morley. Of course, these details were basically biographical, but it should be realised that they were also *autobiographical*. This Cressida Morley is a slightly older version of the character of Cressida Morley whom we meet in *The End of the Morning*, and who is in turn a development of Clift's other alter egos, especially Christine Morley. If we were in any doubt of Clift's authorial input into this part of *My Brother Jack,* the 'heroic' cheekbones would be the giveaway: this was the phrase which Clift used again and again when describing Grace Morley and her two lookalike children, Ben and Cressida; it was also the expression Clift used in non-fictional descriptions of her mother, brother and self.

Another part of Clift's Cressida to recur here is the depiction of the character as a freckled grubby tomboy. We are reminded of the young Cressida, who played boys' games with Ben. In *My Brother Jack* the boyishness connects with the youthfulness of the Cressida character — which is a significant part both of the fictional portrait and of the Charmian myth. However, there is something else operating here.

In the gun-pit scene, Cressida has lost two years. As we have seen, when Charmian enlisted in 1943, she was nineteen; by 1944, when she was training on the golf course, she was twenty. In the novel Cressida in 1943 is 'only a couple of months past eighteen'; this is the youngest possible age she could be, if she is to be in the army. Again and again the text reinforces the joint notions of Cressida's youth and boyishness: 'Like a child playing soldiers' she is 'the youngest thing' the narrator has seen. Her body still has 'a child's gawkiness about it'. Indeed, 'she seem[s] to have no breasts at all'. When Meredith meets her again two years later, Cressida still 'seem[s] to have no breasts'. And Gavin Turley refers to her as 'the child Cress'.

But why would George Johnston and/or Charmian Clift wish to reduce the age of the character? After all, if Cress had been twenty when Meredith met her on the golf course, she still would have been young.

The point, of course, is the *particular* two years which are expunged from the record. Cressida went straight 'from her long lonely beach to a gun-site' — thus losing the two years in which the model for the character lived in Kings Cross and gave birth to a child. This careful editing of the personal record is reinforced by the character's appearance: boyish, breastless, there is nothing maternal about Cressida. This woman could not have borne a child: she is herself a child.

If this portrayal of the boyish and exceptionally young Cressida suited Clift, it equally served the interests of Johnston. Seen through the eyes of David Meredith, Cressida's androgynous body is very sexy. The youthfulness also fulfils the common male fantasy of Older Man and Child Bride. This would be a vital part of the fictional portrait of David Meredith and Cressida Morley. It would also become part of the public image of George and Charmian.

Yet from the first there is also a hint that the youth will rebel. Those marsh-green eyes are 'scornful' of the helpless officer put in charge of her, and none of the girl's features is 'quite under control'. As the story develops, it will be more than the character's appearance which is uncontrollable. And so the battle lines will be drawn, between the independence of the pagan savage and David Meredith's will to subdue this 'vital force' which challenges him. Among the many antecedents of this story is the tale of Robinson Crusoe and Man Friday.

In life, however, all this is yet to come. Although this gun-pit scene would draw upon the identity which Charmian Clift was developing on the golf course, no such meeting between her and the model for the Meredith character occurred while Clift was a gunner. In the absence of George Johnston, however, there were plenty of others for her to do her 'practising' on.[22] Yet the vital difference between the Cressida of the gun-pit and Charmian of the gun-pit was the matter of the two years which were written out of the fictional record. Even in the happiness of camping out and playing soldiers, the past continued to haunt the young woman.

Forty years later, a man who had been a subaltern at the Moore Park anti-aircraft battery vividly remembered some 'revelations' which Cliftie had made to him. The ex-subaltern began by noting that of the twenty or so keen young Ar-wars in his charge, Charmian Clift quickly 'separated from the squad. With her intellect and other attributes, her services were called on for administrative purposes, resulting in a close association'. During their 'more intimate moments' Charmian told the subaltern about winning the *Pix* prize, moving to the Cross and usheretting at the Minerva. 'This led to an affair that was never spoken of, but resulted in a child that was foremost in her mind. On numerous occasions at night and on parade tears would be flowing and they were all for Jennifer'.[23] This unhappiness was a good reason to move on again, and get far away from Sydney and the past.

Towards the middle of the year, the friendly subaltern was asked to submit to his superiors the names of women with officer potential; he of course included ('with Charmian's able assistance') a résumé on Clift. It was around this same time that Margaret, realising that her sister was now well and truly able to survive in the army without her, applied for a discharge on compassionate grounds. Poor Meg had always 'hated the army'; with her home-making skills she was keen to get back to her marriage. She left the army in early June 1944.[24]

A couple of weeks later, Charmian began a course at officer school at Darley, near Bacchus Marsh, in the Victorian countryside. In August of that year she was commissioned as a lieutenant, just two weeks before her twenty-first birthday; she was later always proudly to claim that she had been the army's youngest commissioned officer.[25] The fledgeling lieutenant was now sent to Broadmeadows, outside Melbourne, to join a squad of Ar-wars (some of whom were not commissioned) undergoing special training in army administration. A male staff sergeant who was doing a parallel course provided a vivid description of her:

> The 'star' of the AWAS squad was Charmian Clift, who had rank at that time [...] She was then quite beautiful, and all we male soldiers did 'a bit of a perv' on [her]. She stood out among the other women in bearing, looks and obvious quality [...] Charmian was obviously not an easy target, which made her seem all the more desirable [...] To my knowledge no one in the men's school course ever got to first base with her. She was always courteous — but reserved [...] both in her relationships with the sex-hungry men in our [...] course, and also in her relationships with other AWAS in her school [...]
>
> Not every AWAS in her school already wore pips. So Charmian was in this way a cut above her fellow AWAS — and so held herself apart. I am sure this was *not* because she was a snob. Her own innate knowledge of her worth, plus her rank, helped her so.[26]

After this administration course, the young lieutenant was transferred to the Directorate of Ordnance Services at LHQ (Land Headquarters), St Kilda Road, Melbourne.[27] Clift later stated that once she was there, the army didn't know what to do with her. And so:

> They gave me to an Ordnance brigadier to see what he could do with me. And all this time I had been writing. You see, you're a writer without knowing it. [The brigadier] had heard that I loved to write, so he gave me a magazine to edit for the Ordnance Corps. And he gave me a great big office with a warrant officer to do my dirty work. I was a little chit! I was twenty, a lieutenant with my own beautiful room in South Yarra. So my last couple of years of the war were great.[28]

Although Clift was actually twenty-one when she went to LHQ, this is otherwise accurate. She worked under Brigadier Howard Kingham, Director of Ordnance Services, editing a magazine called *For Your Information*.

The young lieutenant had fallen on her feet. Technically she was the editor of this journal, but in fact she had to write a lot of the copy herself. She quickly found that she could do the work 'very well', and that she 'loved doing it'.[29]

Indeed, she enjoyed it so much that she felt encouraged to go back to her own writing in her spare time. In her own account of the beginning of her writing career, Charmian Clift states that it was during her army service that she 'began writing short stories'. She had tried the genre previously, of course, but it was now that she started working hard at it. One story which Clift wrote at this time was entitled 'Other Woman'.[30] The prose is lean and controlled, and the piece reveals the compression which the author would later demonstrate in her essays. The subject matter was confronting for the period: as the title suggests, 'Other Woman' dealt with adultery.

The story opens with a woman named Jenny going to the home of her husband's mistress, Sharon. The latter character is instantly recognisable as a Clift alter ego: Sharon has 'a wide, high-cheekboned face' and 'greenish-yellow eyes' which meet her accuser 'defiantly [...] Her voice match[es] her eyes; curiously vibrant and with the same defiant quality'.

Jenny compares 'her own tiny figure — neat and unexciting — with that vital, pagan litheness'. Here we see a very early use of a device which Clift would employ throughout her fiction: that of contrasting heroines — one hard, the other soft. Like all the gentle heroines, Jenny has considerable courage. Deciding to fight to keep her husband, Jenny asks her rival if she loves Michael. 'Love him?' Sharon replies. 'I am bearing his child!' Jenny, who is unable to have children, acknowledges that Sharon has won.

Reading this far, it is possible to see the author playing out a fantasy. The name 'Jenny' makes us think of the author's relinquished child, and in this tale of Sharon who will keep her child and win the man, it is possible to see Clift imagining what her life might have been. Yet Clift was never easy on herself, or on her alter egos. As the story swiftly moves into its half-page denouement, the time is five years later, and Sharon dusts the mirror as part of her 'everlasting housework'. In the clean surface she now observes herself 'looking exactly like a suburban drudge'. Moving on to tidy Michael's desk, she finds a letter, from which slips a photograph. The story ends with the abrupt punchline: 'Through a swirling haze her greenish-yellow eyes looked into the cool sardonic eyes of the other woman'. The message of this irony is clear: the adulterous woman will be paid back in her own coin. Yet it is equally clear that it is always the woman who suffers, while the man escapes scot-free.

Clift's writing was helped at this time by another change of circumstance. In Melbourne, barrack accommodation for Ar-wars was limited, and women over twenty-one were allowed to find their own quarters. Soon Charmian 'achieved one of [her] ambitions', which was to have a little flat of her own.[31] In her own place she could write when she was off duty, and she was free to take part in the liberated social life that was part of the Melbourne wartime scene.

It is hardly surprising that the young lieutenant attracted the attention of various high-ranking officers around HQ. Yet the main advance to Charmian's career at this time came from a rather more lowly figure. One day when she dropped in to the Military History section to see a certain granite-faced major, she happened to meet a short and kindly man who was to take on the role of confidant and 'fairy godmother'.

This was Bruce Kneale, who before the war had been a journalist on the *Argus*. He also wrote short stories, and as the affair with the major flamed and fizzled, the young lieutenant began to bring her writing to Kneale. He suggested that she submit 'Other Woman' to the *Australia National Journal*, a monthly magazine which published stories, features and humorous sketches.[32]

To Charmian's great joy, it was accepted for the May edition. 'And so', she later stated in an account of how she got her first work published, 'joining the army brought about all sorts of wonderful things for me'.[33] Now that she was a published writer, she knew that 'there wasn't going to be anything else, ever, ever, except being a writer'.[34] There was no longer any need for Charmian to dream and wonder about what great thing she would be: she had found the focus for the rest of her life.

It seemed, too, that publication was the entrée to the artistic world which Charmian had wanted to join for so long. When the editor of the *Australia National Journal*, the exotic Mrs Gwen Moreton Spencer, gave an artistic cocktail party at the Menzies to coincide with this issue of the journal, she invited her new author to come.

To others, Charmian Clift might have given an impression of social assurance. At heart, however, she was still the girl who had grown up on the wrong side of town. Scared stiff of the cocktail party, she rang Bruce Kneale, and asked if he were going. He replied that he wasn't too keen. The fledgeling writer confessed that she very much wanted to go, but was too nervous to face it alone. 'All right,' Kneale replied, 'I'll take you'.[35]

At the same time, in May 1945, a former *Argus* colleague of Bruce Kneale's was back in Melbourne on a short leave from Asia. Since early 1942 George Johnston had been travelling the various theatres of war as Australia's first accredited war correspondent. His despatches had given him a fame that is hard to comprehend now that television reporting has overtaken the printed word. Among the many Australians who would hastily open the paper to see what George Johnston could tell them about the places where the boys were fighting was Charmian Clift; indeed, he was her 'favourite war correspondent'.[36]

Naturally, when Kneale mentioned that he was planning to see this old mate, Charmian said how much she would love to meet him. And so Bruce Kneale arranged to have dinner with George Johnston at the Hotel Australia after the arty cocktail party, telling him that there was a girl he really had to meet.[37]

This incident was to provide the seed for the episode at the end of *My Brother Jack* when David Meredith goes alone to Mario's restaurant and runs into Cressida Morley who is dining with his old journalist mate Gavin Turley. In the novel, the war correspondent invites the beautiful young lieutenant to have dinner alone with him at the Hotel Australia the next night — which is also the last night of his leave. The couple meet, and the novel closes, leaving the reader dangling at the beginning of what is clearly going to be a great love affair.

In life, this first meeting was something of a fiasco. Pasting together two versions of a tale which Charmian and George loved telling, it emerges that Lieutenant Clift and Bruce Kneale went to the Hotel Australia ...

> *Charmian:* I had my pips polished and my hat on straight and everything. And we waited and waited and waited [...]
>
> *George:* In the meantime, I [had] met a couple of [...] Army nurses, nice girls I had known in the Middle East. We got on the grog a bit — it was that sort of time. I took these two nurses to the Hotel Australia for dinner [...]
>
> *Charmian:* He came in, an army nurse on each arm, all drunk. He looked at our table [...]
>
> *George:* And there was Charmian and my mate. I realised the gaffe I had made and went over to apologise [...]
>
> *Charmian:* He said, 'Excuse me, I'm as drunk as a son of a bitch.'[38]

It was exactly the sort of opening line calculated to appeal to a girl such as Charmian, who liked her Lancelots to have a larrikin style. Though George wasn't handsome in the classical sense, he was nearly six feet tall and was one of the 'lean and slouchy and brown' sort of Australian men whom this young woman preferred.[39] He also had an exuberant manner, and a fund of colourful traveller's tales. However, while Kneale's two friends found each other very attractive, this was just a brief wartime meeting, and within a few days, Johnston went off to China on his next assignment. Although he had been attracted to the young lieutenant, he had pretty girls all over the world, as well as a wife and baby daughter in Melbourne.

Nor did Charmian Clift eat her heart out for the war correspondent. He was exciting, certainly, with his restless talk of far-off places that she longed to visit, and his reputation as a writer — of four non-fiction war books as well as his newspaper articles — gave him an added glamour. But he was gone, and wartime was lived in the present tense.

Events on the war front now seemed to take on a feverish speed as Germany's surrender brought new hope for those fighting in the Pacific. On 3 September, bells rang across Australia when Japan surrendered. Charmian was swept up in the frenzy as the sober citizens of Melbourne danced in the streets and decorated the trams with streamers. It was three days since her twenty-second birthday. Amidst the excitement of the latter part of this year, the young woman became engaged to a man who was very different from George Johnston. Her own account of this, given many years later, was dismissive:

> I've never been betrothed myself but for once, and that was in wartime, and not formal in any way at all and no parents involved, and the restaurant was sleazy and he fumbled the ring. In any case the betrothal proved to have been an error, although I did like flashing that half-hoop of family diamonds around the barracks for a while, and was quite reluctant, really, to have to give it back.[40]

While nothing came of this engagement, it provides an illuminating insight into what the young Charmian Clift wanted — or thought she wanted.

The Kenny family was one of Melbourne's wealthy and socially prominent Catholic families. It was known for its involvement in culture and the arts, and the two sons and two daughters were educated in music and art. One of the sons, Leo, had had a mild tubercular condition as a child which, though it was cured, caused him to be treated as a bit of a weakling; perhaps it was this that left in him a softness of temperament. The father became a count in the Catholic church, and Leo was pressured by his family to enter the priesthood. The war gave the young man a good reason to leave the seminary. He joined the air force, where he quickly rose to the rank of flight lieutenant.[41] When the war ended, Leo accepted a position as a plantation manager in Malaya. While waiting for his demobilisation, he became engaged to Charmian Clift. The couple agreed that he would go ahead with his plans, and Charmian would join him as soon as she could. They knew that this might take a few months: demobilisation was slow for unmarried servicewomen, and once Charmian was out of the army, she would have to wait until transport to Singapore became available.[42]

Around March 1946, Leo happened to read a newspaper review of an exhibition of paintings by an artist named Edward Heffernan. As boys, Leo and Ed had lived next door to each other, but over the years they had lost touch. Now Leo Kenny contacted Ed out of the blue, and commissioned him to paint a portrait of his fiancée. Soon afterwards, Leo brought to the gallery a strikingly attractive young woman called Charmian Clift.

One of the things that first struck Ed was the class difference between the couple. Indeed, the painter felt that part of Leo's attraction for Charmian was his 'socially very acceptable background'. No doubt this is true. From an early age, Charmian's mother had instilled in her the idea of marriage as a way of moving up the social scale. Yet it was not so much the wealth and position of Leo's family that was important to Charmian as the fact that the Kennys were part of Melbourne's cultural elite. (Ed Heffernan would also remember that 'Charmian wanted desperately to be involved with an art scene'.) More importantly, Leo was himself involved in the arts. In the portrait painter's description of Leo of this time, it is possible to see the fulfilment of the dreams of the young girl who had longed for tirra lirra.

> Leo would have been round about thirty [...] very tall, slightly aquiline features [...] a very good-looking young man, very slender [...] He had a very good mind, he was a very sensitive person, a very good musician [...] He was very interested in art [...] drew and painted reasonably well.[43]

These artistic interests of Leo's included literature. Indeed, he tinkered about with a bit of writing, just as he painted pictures and played music. As the couple showed each other their work, Charmian no doubt felt how wonderful it would be to share a vocation as well as love. This aspect of their relationship was captured in the inscription Leo wrote in a copy of *The Oxford Book of English Verse,* which he gave his fiancée after the couple spent a romantic weekend at Portsea:

March 22nd
Cliftie's Book.
All we writers have large libraries
Portsea again ...
L.K.[44]

This March weekend was in fact a farewell. Immediately afterwards, Leo left Melbourne for Malaya. He was able to console himself with the thought that when she came to join him in a couple of months or so, she would bring the portrait that he had commissioned from his old friend.

When the time came for the first sitting for this commission, Lieutenant Clift arrived in uniform at the portrait painter's home. Four decades later, Ed Heffernan vividly remembered how she instantly infuriated his wife by publicly stripping off her army shirt and changing into an off-the-shoulder blouse. As a subject she was restless, 'almost aggressive in her posing'. Heffernan felt that Charmian enjoyed aggravating his wife — 'She loved stirring situations.' To avoid more domestic trouble, Heffernan decided that it would be easier if the work were done at his city studio. Over the next couple of months there were half a dozen more sittings; or occasionally the painter and his model would go out for a drink instead.[45]

While the portrait took shape, events were also shaping the life of the painting's subject. Like many women and men in the armed forces, Charmian would find that the contacts made in the army would help her establish herself in civilian life. At the St Kilda Road Headquarters, one of the brass hats who was always in and out of the building was Brigadier Errol Knox, the army's Director General of Public Relations. In civilian life, Knox was Managing Director of the *Argus,* one of Melbourne's major morning newspapers. A tough and autocratic boss, he also fancied himself as a talent-spotter. Charmian later described how he 'discovered' the Ordnance magazine and the young lieutenant who was editing it: 'He said to himself, "This is the girl. We're going to have her." So when the war was over he asked me to join the *Argus* — which I did'.[46]

This account is accurate, but it shortens the time span. In fact, it was not until 10 May 1946 that Charmian Clift was demobilised.[47] She immediately joined the staff of the *Argus* — or it is even possible that she started there a little before being 'de-mobbed'.[48] Her Ordnance superior, Brigadier Kingham, also moved over to the *Argus*, where he took up the position of Associate General Manager. Charmian may initially have continued some duties as his secretarial assistant, as well as working in a journalistic capacity on the Women's Supplement.

In late May, Leo Kenny sent Ed Heffernan a cheque as first payment for the portrait commission, and a letter in which he asked his old friend a favour: 'I think Charmian is a bit lonely in Melbourne. Will you shout her a beer for me some time?'[49] Meanwhile, he wrote to his fiancée urging her to hurry up and come to Malaya. Now that she was demobilised, there was no excuse for delay.

But suddenly Charmian began to wonder about her commitment. Certainly, marriage to Leo Kenny promised the fulfilment of her adolescent dream of escaping from her social background. It was a chance to live overseas, and the position of plantation manager's wife would also have appealed: it is easy to imagine Charmian play-acting the role of Mrs Leo Kenny, in a large hat and cool white frock, sitting on the verandah of the clubhouse with a long tinkling drink.

Yet attractive though this lifestyle appeared, the passion to write was stronger than the desire to travel to exotic places. Although Leo saw himself as a writer — and indeed a travel piece on Singapore by 'Leo M. Kenny Ex-RAAF' would appear in the *Argus Week-end Magazine* in July of that year[50] — Charmian believed her fiancé was only an amateur or hobby writer. Worse, she had realised that he assumed her attitude was the same; she knew that he expected her to stop writing once she gave herself up to marriage and, no doubt, full-time motherhood. Charmian's feelings about this are clearly revealed in one of the *Greener Grows the Grass* fragments. In this text, a young journalist named Christine Morley, working in a Melbourne newspaper office, expresses her resentment against her fiancé Leonard, who keeps 'demanding that [she] drop everything and take a plane' to join him in Malaya: 'He says what does my writing matter anyway, seeing I'm not going to write any more once I'm married'.[51]

This issue of vocation versus love has posed a dilemma for many women writers; it is, of course, the theme of Miles Franklin's autobiographical first novel, *My Brilliant Career*. It was while she was mulling over this problem that Charmian Clift discovered what seemed to be the perfect solution: the way to combine writing and love was obviously to fall in love with another professional writer! In this particular fragment of *Greener Grows the Grass*, it is not surprising that in the newspaper office where Christine Morley works there is a journalist named Martin Smith, who writes books as well as articles. The two characters bump into each other one day in the lift ...

On one of her first days in the *Argus* building, Charmian happened to be in the lift when George Johnston got in. Neither of them had seen each other since the brief encounter at the Hotel Australia, twelve months earlier. Charmian later stated that George was so surprised at seeing her that 'he blinked vividly and said an extraordinary thing: "Welcome home". And then bolted out when the lift stopped'.[52]

George Johnston would include an account of this lift meeting in the first draft of *Clean Straw for Nothing*. It gives a sense of Charmian Clift's presence at this time:

> The unexpectedness of this encounter [...] so took David Meredith aback that all he could say was 'Welcome home'. The other occupants of the lift were looking at her, not at him, for she had that invincible calm quality of a woman sure of her beauty, and he was only able to take in those incredible green shoalwater eyes looking at him in steady undismay, and to see the hint of a smile just beginning to touch her wide mobile mouth when, suddenly conscious of the total inanity of his remark, he nodded in quick embarrassment and made a guilty escape down the marble stairs that led to the classified advertisements section.
>
> (Later he was never able to work out why he had uttered that quite meaningless phrase, although for long it remained one of the important, if trivial, links of private affection between them.)[53]

The Cressida Morley who appears in this draft passage conveys the same spirit as the Cressida of *My Brother Jack*. By placing this character at the newspaper office — as her model had been in life — the author had to account for her being there. In the early stage of writing the novel, Johnston intended that Cressida Morley, like Charmian Clift, would be a writer. In this version, David Meredith races off to see his old colleague Gavin Turley the morning after the lift meeting, in order to ask how he can find Cressida. When Turley tells him that Cressida is joining the staff of the newspaper, Meredith asks:

> 'Is it a writing thing?'
> 'Of course.'
> 'I didn't even know she wrote.'
> 'My dear chap, she has quite a formidable talent, believe you me. She has written some short stories which are quite first class, and some poems which are ... well, they're not all that bad either. And she has done a brilliant job of editing this L. of C. bumph.[54]

This draft version of the novel has a great deal more biographical authenticity than the published version. In the latter, the lift meeting and this part of the conversation with Turley were dropped.[55] This change would make an extraordinary difference to the characterisation of Cressida Morley, who simply becomes an AWAS lieutenant 'about to be discharged' — and with no particular employment prospects or ambitions. Without her writing, Cressida would lose her reason for existence. And without writing as a shared passion, the fictional relationship would prove to be a pale shadow of the real one.

It was around June of that year that Charmian was due at Ed Heffernan's studio for what was to be the final portrait sitting. On this occasion, Charmian arrived with a friend to whom she was keen to show the picture. This was George Johnston; the painter had known him slightly at art school. From the moment Ed Heffernan saw Charmian with George, it was 'instantly obvious' to him 'that George was going to be the one'.[56]

To the portrait painter, Charmian's change of partners seemed unfathomable. In his opinion, George was 'rather ratty looking' compared with the classically handsome Leo Kenny. But a romance writer would instantly have seen what was going on. Many years later, when Charmian described how she had seen her wartime experience 'in terms of a novel', she added that this was 'furthered by' her meeting with George Johnston. In these novelistic terms, Leo Kenny was Edgar Linton, or St John Rivers, or Ashley Wilkes; he was the sweet but weak male character who is introduced into the plot only to be swept aside when the real hero — in the form of Heathcliff, or Mr Rochester, or Rhett Butler — steps onto the stage.

Charmian knew the genre, and recognised her hero when he arrived. Yet George Johnston was at heart an unlikely candidate for this role.

8

A Benevolent Steamroller

Somebody [...] once called him 'a benevolent steamroller' [...]
The writer George Johnston, that is.[1]

With this arrival of George Johnston on the scene, it is necessary to freeze the frame in the narrative of Charmian Clift's life, and bring George up to the time of this second meeting, in the middle of 1946. What sort of person was he, this man who was going to be 'the one' in her life? And what sort of environment had he come from?

In an essay about her husband written in 1969, Charmian Clift would describe him as 'a benevolent steamroller'. She quickly added:

> There is obviously a great deal to him apart from the steamroller, or flattening out bit, although I do believe that to be a true observation. Or true in so far as he is inclined to be a conversational bully — being better informed about more things than most, liking to dominate, and having a devastating turn of wit [...] He is also a steamroller in his purposes.[2]

In this same piece, Clift would contrast the different ways in which she and George tended to remember past experience: 'I suspect it is the difference between optimism and pessimism', she noted. The essayist went on to attribute George's general tendency to pessimism or (in Clift's phrase) being a 'Nay Sayer', and her own tendency towards 'Yea Saying' partly to the fact that she 'had a much happier beginning and launching into life'. If *The End of the Morning* is compared with the early part of Johnston's autobiographical novel *My Brother Jack*, the pictures of childhood which emerge are diametrically opposed. In contrast to the outdoor freedom of Lebanon Bay, David Meredith's world is a drab, cramped, suburban one. Cressida Morley's parents may be problematic figures, but they have an enormous presence in the child's world; the young Davy's parents, on the other hand, are conspicuous by their absence. Although Charmian's happy childhood was part of her personal myth (or her Yea Saying), as she attached such significance to her husband's comparatively *unhappy* beginning, it is important to see what this consisted of, and how it affected the man so deeply.

Certainly, George himself believed that his upbringing was miserable. At some time around the middle of 1962 — by which time he thought that his life could well be drawing to an end — he began to make some notes exploring the character of his alter ego David Meredith, who had appeared in the novels *Closer to the Sun* and *The Far Road*, and with whom the author was increasingly identifying. Previous examination of this autobiographical character had been concerned with Meredith's present life of exile in Greece, or with his wartime experience. Now, seeking to understand the 'paradox' of David Meredith's love for his wife, Johnston went back to his own beginnings, and wrote a two-page typewritten note, entitled 'Childhood — "The Dollikos"'. Although in this text the alter ego is not named and the narrative is presented in the third person, this is a reflection on the childhood of the David Meredith character whom the author would soon proceed to develop in the novel *My Brother Jack*. Indeed, the scene appears almost unchanged in the first chapter of that novel.[3] However, in the first draft note — written as a shorthand form of self-analysis — the author also gives his view of the effect that his childhood had had on him. The text begins:

> His mind, perhaps, had been in some way twisted strangely by a childhood which he had not come to understand — or even been prepared to try to understand — until he was a man of middle age. Only then did he come to see the geographical flatness of the suburbs, the emptiness of the sky, the hollow places where companionship should have been, and the imperfections that had surrounded him. And in maturity he was inclined to cling, with a kind of perverse but passive greed, to everything that was antithetical to these earlier formations.[4]

Of course, this isn't necessarily true fact, but it is true interpretation: it is how George Johnston saw his own past. So what was this strange 'twisting' which he believed had happened in his childhood, but which he had repressed until middle age? And how did this internal shaping connect with the external world in which he had grown up?

George Johnston was born in the Melbourne suburb of Malvern in 1912, but within a couple of years the family moved to nearby Elsternwick. The author would later say that he grew up around Elsternwick, Elwood, Caulfield, Brighton and St Kilda.[5] Part of the area skirting Port Phillip Bay, this was originally coastal dune land; as flat as the water in the wide enclosed harbour, it stretches in one endless and unbroken plane to the horizon. In George's childhood, the view of one-storey brick or weatherboard bungalows seemed to 'spread forever, flat and diffuse, monotonous yet inimical, pieced together in a dull geometry of dull houses' with 'nothing to break the drab flatness of this unadventurous repetition'.[6] Johnston's sense of the restrictiveness of this environment is further revealed in a reference in the 'Dollikos' note to the 'fenced and hedged flatness of the suburbs': everything seemed boxed in. While the family home was 'small, dark-corridored' and overcrowded, the young George's 'world' was 'even more closely confined', for he and his brother Jack were pushed out to the small enclosed area of the back verandah known as 'the sleepout'.[7]

The inhabitants of this dreary neighbourhood also seemed to be cut from the one template. Certainly, some were Catholics and the rest were Protestants, but even that difference did not affect their values and aspirations, or the clothes they wore or the food they ate or the way they presented their houses to the street. If the matter of class is vital to an understanding of the Clift family's position in their society, it must also underpin any understanding of George Johnston's family and their social role. He himself would describe the suburbs where he grew up as 'terrifying' in their acceptance of 'their mediocrity'; the overriding problem, as the author saw it, was that these suburbs were 'a step or two higher' than the crowded inner city working class districts, and yet a couple of steps lower than the true middle class areas: 'They betrayed nothing of anger or revolt or resentment; they lacked the grim adventure of true poverty; they had no suffering, because they had mortgaged this right to secure a sad acceptance of a suburban respectability'.[8]

George's family fitted perfectly into this lower middle class environment, for it too had a betwixt and between status. George's father, John George

Johnston, had begun his working life as a labourer, but by the time of George's birth was a maintenance worker for the Melbourne tramways, and later would become a maintenance engineer foreman. George's mother, born Minnie Riverina Wright, had come down in the world by her marriage, for she was the daughter of the editor of the Bendigo *Advertiser,* and had been brought up to play the piano and dabble in watercolours and even oils. She would retain an air of middle class respectability that would be reinforced when her mother Emma came to live with the family, soon after the move to Elsternwick. Although in *My Brother Jack* the author invests this grandmother figure with a restless and even 'reckless' spirit,[9] in fact she was a rather unaffectionate woman from the middle echelons of country town society. Overall, Minnie and Emma would have an eye for small proprieties that would make for a stultifying social atmosphere.

If there is a feeling of déjà vu to this description, that is appropriate. Allowing for the difference of a hemisphere and generation, George Johnston's family background was uncannily similar to that of Sydney Clift.

Within the family, George's father was always known as Pop. Of course, this can be an affectionate term, but in the case of John Johnston it seems appropriate to his temper, which was likely to explode at any moment. Gentle Minnie was no match for him, and would take the line of least resistance. But perhaps he was not like that when they were married, in 1899 ... After their first child, a boy, died at the age of eighteen months, they waited five years before they had another baby. This was a girl, whom they named Jean. Then Jack was born, in 1909: a strong and lusty child, this son wasn't going to go the way of the first. It would not be surprising if Minnie lavished a double quota of love on this surviving boy. In July 1912, another son was born. They named him George Henry.

When George was two years old, there took place a series of events, the cumulative effect of which was to make the young child suddenly feel as if he had been abandoned. Firstly, Minnie's attention and a considerable amount of her affection were withdrawn when she gave birth to another baby. This same year, George's father left home. No sooner had baby Marjorie arrived and Pop gone than George's mother started to disappear from the house for virtually all the time that the young child was awake. On her fleeting reappearances she wore stiff aprons and strange white headdresses that made her seem like a different person. There was a nasty smell to her, too, which the boy would later identify as either iodine or carbolic or ether. It is significant that in George Johnston's fictionalisation of this early period, he actually has the mother figure (also named Minnie) 'leaving her four small children' in order to go off and become an army nurse in France for 'rather more than three years'. He notes that even after her return, she was 'still something of a stranger to us [...] mostly because of her years of absence from us, but also because she was even then not really an integrated part of the household but seemed only to visit us each afternoon or evening in her starched nurse's uniform'.[10] Minnie's disappearance brought yet another change, as George's grandmother Emma arrived to look after the children. In the novel, the author notes that 'the effect of the absences of both [...] parents' made Davy 'something of a namby-pamby' who 'clung to' the grandmother.[11] The same was true in life. And when the whingeing two-year-old attached himself to her skirts, Emma used to dose him with castor oil and send him out into the back yard to play in the small area bound by tall paling fences.[12]

As the years of the war went on, George found words on which to hook some of the changes that had happened to his family life. He learned that his mother was a nurse — actually a Voluntary Aid Detachment auxiliary at the military hospital at South Caulfield. He heard words such as 'Gallipoli' and 'the Somme' as his father moved from one theatre of war to another. But when he was two, it felt as if love was abruptly withheld, for no apparent reason. It is no accident that in another description of Minnie's war work, the author referred to her 'abandoning and neglecting her children'.[13] The separation anxiety which the child clearly suffered from this experience would stay with him all his life. So would an underlying lack of trust in other people. Throughout his life, George would be acutely sensitive to the slightest threat of betrayal or rejection or abandonment.

Even apart from the disruptions caused by the war, the Johnston family home was a loveless environment, lacking in expression of verbal or physical affection, and it would leave George with a difficulty in showing love to the person whom he would love most. In the note entitled 'Childhood — "The Dollikos"', the writer went on to relate an anecdote which seems to have been his only early memory of love. In this, the young boy, playing armies on the linoleum with the seeds of a vine which his mother calls 'the dollikos', causes his grandmother to slip and hurt herself and break a bag of eggs. The boy flees 'in a terrible fear' of 'retribution' to the 'sanctuary' of the wash-house roof, where he sits for over an hour as the old woman rages below. Here, his 'abject fear of the tiny termagant' is weighed against his 'certain knowledge' that he will fall to the ground.

However, when finally the child 'surrenders' and comes down, his grandmother does not punish him at all, but holds him very tightly and kisses him. Johnston notes that 'It was the dollikos which explained to him — although not until many years later — that love existed even in that loneliness.'[14]

What is remarkable about this anecdote is the fact that the author regarded it as an epiphany. If that was George Johnston's only memory of love, it is little wonder that his childhood should create a 'twisting'. At the same time, we see in this story the sort of topsy-turvy behaviour of adults which children find so confusing: after doing something wrong — something which actually hurts the old woman, and causes a visible breaking — the child receives affection and approval. By the same token, however, when he doesn't do anything wrong, the adults seem to go away and leave him and not love him. (Or — an even worse thought — had he in fact done something terrible, which broke up the home? Children often feel this, and take on a burden of blame.)

While this slight tale reveals so much of George's inner feelings, it is also significant that the young alter ego is playing armies. From the time George was two until he was about twelve or thirteen, the Johnston family home was filled with talk and images and physical evidence of war and death and sickness and mutilation.[15] As well as working at the hospital during the daylight hours and often through the weekend shift, Minnie frequently brought home pet invalids to recuperate at *Avalon* for a period of weeks or months or even longer. (A one-legged veteran named Bert Thornton stayed so long that he eventually married George's elder sister Jean.) As a result, 'every corner of that little suburban house' was 'impregnated for years with the very essence of some gigantic and sombre experience'. Among the 'inanimate props' were the crutches and artificial limbs, the walking sticks and 'at least one invalid wheel chair, which perennially cluttered the narrow hallway'[16]. Every flat surface was decorated with war memorabilia displayed on top of the lumpy string doilies that the amputees made.

It was a strange atmosphere that surrounded the boy: overwhelmingly masculine, yet maimed and rendered impotent — symbolically if not actually. In the novel the narrator notes that he and his brother spent 'a good part' of their boyhood 'in the fixed belief that grown-up men who were complete were pretty rare beings'. The house guests were 'amps' or 'double amps', and one had lost his arms as well as his legs and was reduced to a torso and head in a wheelchair. Others were blind. Yet another wore the scars of mustard gas in terrible facial burns, and used to frighten the child with his 'staring silences'.[17] All of these men had been at the Front, and their reminiscences produced nightmares in the mind of the little boy who used to sit so quietly on the verandah as they talked that they would forget he was there. Over the years, this constant exposure to the themes of war and sickness and death would haunt the child's imagination, resulting in a deep-seated fear of illness and dying which would remain throughout George's life.

Yet this wasn't the worst of it. The war was even more sharply realised for the young child in the photographs of the muddy 'wilderness' of the Front, which appeared in the *Illustrated War News*, showing 'corpses sprawled in muck or drowned in flooded shell craters or hanging like cast-off rags on the tangled wire'. Alongside these dreadful representations were the images of German atrocities which the young boy encountered in the cartoons of Louis Raemaeker, a Dutch artist whose graphic images were initially occasioned when he saw streams of Belgian refugees fleeing into his neutral homeland, and whose work was used to stir up popular hatred against 'the Hun'. George Johnston notes that as he 'knew nothing then about propaganda', Raemaeker's images 'assumed a horrible reality, the substance of nightmare translated into printed truth'.[18] In the novel, the young Davy finds the three-volume set of these cartoons hidden — together with the copies of the *Illustrated War News* and other memorabilia — in 'the big deep drawer at the bottom of the cedar wardrobe' in his parents' bedroom. In the narrator's descriptions of his furtive visits to this collection, and the 'morbid thrall' exerted by the Raemaeker texts, there is a sense of the illicit thrill of pornography.[19]

Among the frightening pictures, the author remembered images 'of the bestial Huns disembowelling starving Belgian children'. It is no coincidence that many of the stories told in these pictures are of children being separated from their parents, or of children apparently abandoned and left at the mercy of a huge ogre. But is this enemy really a stranger, or has he somehow swallowed up and become the missing father? In a household without many other books — and especially with no illustrated children's books — it would be surprising if the young boy had not pored over these images of other children, and identified with them. This is particularly likely in the case of a child such as George, whose visual sense was acute.

Meanwhile, as the boy was witnessing these obscenities from the Home Front, his father was actually experiencing the horror that was World War I. After making it through Gallipoli, John Johnston was shelled and gassed in the trenches of France, losing some of his hearing and developing lung problems which would make him prone to bronchitis. More significant were the psychological scars that he brought home with him. It seems that, like many veterans of World War I, Pop suffered post-traumatic stress syndrome (or shell shock, as it was then called) from what he had experienced and witnessed at the battle front. And like many other veterans, he felt that it was shameful or unmasculine to admit to the pain caused by what he had taken part in. Unfortunately, in the case of Pop and many other husbands and fathers, the ongoing trauma had a habit of venting itself within the home.

Although George had felt abandoned when his father left in 1914, the return of this irascible and unpredictable man made the sense of rejection and uncertainty worse, for it is clear that George feared his father through the rest of his childhood, and when the fear finally subsided, it would be replaced by loathing. In *My Brother Jack,* the author dramatises this combination of terror and repulsion in the scene where the Meredith family go to the wharves to greet the returning troops. It is significant that after five years of absence, the father is a complete stranger to the boy:

> I was seven then, but small for my age, and the day was charged, for me, with a huge and numbing terror. This fear was involved with the interminable blaring of brass bands, and a ceaseless roar of shouting and cheering, and the unending trampling past of gigantic legs [...] The climax of it all came when a strong voice, hoarse with excitement, began to shout, 'Minnie! *Minnie!*' and without warning I was seized suddenly and engulfed in one of the gigantic, coarse-clad figures and embraced in a stifling smell of damp serge and tobacco and beer and held high in the air before a sweating apparition that was a large, ruddy face grinning at me below a back-tilted slouch hat and thin fair hair receding above a broad freckled brow, and then there was a roar of laughter, and I was put down, sobbing with fear, and the thick boots marched on and on, as if they were trampling all over me.[20]

Rarely has a passage of adult literature captured so perfectly, from a child's point of view, the sense of smallness and vulnerability and powerlessness that children frequently feel. However, while of course many men can seem giants or ogres to children, Pop Johnston was truly a formidable figure: measuring six foot three inches (190 cm) and weighing in at fifteen stone (over 95 kilos), he stood out even in a line of soldiers, and his bigness seemed to be emphasised by the size of his face, which was left exposed by his early baldness. His nose was large too, and his jug-ears stuck out. It is also true that at the time his father returned, George was a comparatively small boy, for he would not start to shoot up until he was in his teens. But more important than his physical slightness was the sensitivity which is revealed in this passage. George seemed to *feel* things more than his siblings; as if he were a changeling or a cuckoo, he was always the odd one out among the children in his family. Certainly, he was much more thin-skinned than his brother Jack, who was not only three years older and physically much stronger, but who took everything in his stride, and rarely paused for reflection.

This difference in feeling — in the way life was experienced — between the two brothers is relevant to the next bit of the story. This concerns the image given in the novel of the father as 'morose, intolerant, bitter and violently bad-tempered' — so much so that the narrator's 'memories of the period all have the tint of nightmare'. It isn't just that Davy fears violence against himself; in this portrayal, the mother's fear of the father is such that the boy is gripped by 'a very real terror that Mother would be brought to such a point of resentment of her husband's tyranny that she really would run away and leave us all'. To forestall this further abandonment — which would leave him completely 'unprotected', the young boy tries to 'work out ways of murdering [his] father'.[21]

Soon the father institutes the 'system of monthly punishments'. This aspect of the early experience of the young Davy Meredith leaves an indelible impression on readers of *My Brother Jack*. The narrator relates how, as well as 'summary punishments' such as a cuff around the ears or a 'slash with a stick or a strap' for 'offences immediately detected', at some stage his father began to punish the two boys 'for the offences which had *escaped* his attention'.

> So on the last day of every month Jack and I would be summoned in turn to the bathroom and the door would be locked and each of us would be questioned on the sins which we had committed and which he had not found out about. This interrogation would be the merest formality; whether we admitted to crimes or desperately swore our innocence it was just the same; we were punished for the offences which, he said, he knew we *must* have

committed and had to lie about. We then had to take our shirts and singlets off and bend over the enamelled bath-tub while he thrashed us with his razor strop. In the blind rages of these days he seemed not to care about the strength he possessed nor the injury he inflicted; more often than not it was the metal end of the strop that was used against our backs.

This went on for several years, and God knows what damage it did to me psychologically. I remember that from about the twentieth of every month I would behave with the innocence of a saint and the sycophancy of a French courtier in a desperate attempt to prove my rectitude. It made no difference. I was beaten anyway.[22]

But is this fact or fiction? In his biography of the author, Garry Kinnane accepts without reservation the declarations by George's siblings Jack and Marjorie that 'no such beatings took place'. Indeed, the biographer sees the denial of the beatings and of Johnston's whole portrait of the violent father figure as being so important that he deals with this on the first page of his book.[23] This view has now been accepted as 'fact', so that the 1990 edition of the novel includes the following information in the 'Notes' explaining 'differences between the novel and the biographical details of Johnston's life':

Johnston's brother Jack and his sister Marjorie are adamant that their father never used physical violence, nor any kind of systematic punishment. The general tyranny of Mr Meredith is fictional, and is undoubtedly created in order to provide an element of conflict and a harsh environment in which to gain sympathy for young Davy.[24]

Garry Kinnane further notes that the author's 'creation of Jack Meredith senior involved distortions of childhood memories, some deliberate and some probably unintentional, representations of strong feelings, and a considerable degree of pure invention'.[25] Of course it does: that is what fiction is about. But the point is that memory involves distortion at the best of times, and of course it is always particularly distorted when the subject being remembered is childhood. Here the passage about the return of the troops provides a salutary warning: in the act of remembering childhood, perspectives change. Some things get bigger, while other things diminish.

To try to measure the *truth* of it all is like measuring shadows: the information changes enormously over time.

Thus the memory of George's siblings may be true fact for them, but it may not be the same as George's memory.[26] Some people forget painful events almost as soon as they happen; as these people get older, they view their childhood through increasingly rose-coloured spectacles. Other people continue to feel and to see the dark side of their childhood. Perhaps we should wonder whether George's siblings were not trying to protect the reputation of their family, and the memory of both their parents. After all, it is not just the father who is demeaned by the revelation of beatings and bullying.

Whatever *really* happened, it is a fact that in life as well as in fiction, George Johnston would speak of the brutality of his father and of the beatings which he said he had regularly suffered. Not only did George believe in this version of events, but so did Charmian; the story of the systematic punishment distressed her so deeply that when her husband would begin to tell it, she would run from the room in tears.[27]

Kinnane records that George's first wife, Elsie, would also remember how George 'frequently and without affection referred to his father as "the old bastard"'. And while denying the physical violence of Pop Johnston beyond 'the occasional disciplinary whack', Johnston's biographer graphically describes the verbal cruelty of George's father, his 'sarcasm' and outbursts of 'bigotry', the way he 'flew into a rage at any questioning of the value of the war', and his 'virulent hatred' of Catholics and people on the left of politics.[28] Indeed, so fearsome was Pop, so uncertain his temper, that when his elder son married a Catholic girl of Irish descent, he was so afraid of telling his father what he had done that he continued to live at home, apart from his wife, for the first year of married life, which included the period of his wife's pregnancy and childbirth.[29] This was not timid George, but the brave larrikin Jack, the family rebel! It rather undermines the seventy year old Jack's assertion that George's portrayal of Pop was completely unfounded.

Surely George Johnston's depiction of his father both in fiction and in factual reminiscence must connect with the author's reflection on how the mind of either himself or his alter ego had been 'in some way twisted strangely' by childhood experience; as the published passage rhetorically declared: God only knows what psychological damage was caused by the terror he felt in regard to his father. The other significant thing about the way this punishment is described is the fact that the father's behaviour is unfathomable to the boy. While he lives in constant expectation that vengeance will strike, he does not know why it happens. Like the 'dollikos' incident, it is another example of the irrationality of the universe, and the lack of connection between cause and effect. While it probably seemed obvious to Minnie Johnston and to adult friends — and even, perhaps to the two older children — that Pop was still suffering from the war, the reason for John Johnston's violent temper was not known by George until very late in his life — indeed, until after the publication of *My Brother Jack*, and his siblings' remonstrances with him about the portrayal of the father figure. In an interview given in 1968, the author would present a more sympathetic view:

> He was a sad figure in a way. It wasn't till many years after he died that I learned that he had been quite severely gassed on the Western Front, and he lived in a sort of world of private nightmare [...] I think he probably suffered a lot. The result was he took it out on people.

In the same breath, however, George introduced the other significant part of his memory of his father. This was the man's contempt for his younger son because of George's supposed lack of masculinity.

> My father's phrase of unutterable contempt was 'You've always got your nose in a book. Why don't you go out and take up some sport?' He had this obsession about manliness. He regarded me, as indeed did my brother Jack, as a bit of a 'sonk'.[30]

This reflection is particularly interesting because it links the father's attitude with that of the elder brother. In life as in fiction, the young George was very much dominated by the two older males in his home; although Pop and Jack had their own ongoing battles, they were at one in their feeling that George was somehow failing to make the grade in the business of being a man. The charge of being 'a sonk' echoes through the early part of *My Brother Jack*. The expression combined the sense of being sooky or cowardly with being sissy or feminine.[31] A connection with reading and matters of the arts and the intellect was also part of the pejorative contained within this four letter word. Thus when Davy in the novel is about fifteen, he cops it on both counts, and from both his family persecutors:

'You and your blasted books!' [Dad] would snarl. 'All you're doing, my lad, is muddling your mind and ruining your eyesight. Why the devil don't you get out and do something?'

'Just what I keep telling him,' Jack would say. 'He ought to go out and pick up a sheila.'

'At his age. What damn good would that do him?'

'Well it'd be better than sitting around a bedroom all night with those sonky mates of his.'

This was one of the root sources of Jack's hostility. My 'sonky mates' were three boys who had been in my year at technical school [...] Jack had no time for any of them [...] Since I already had crazy ideas about everything which Jack regarded as normal and necessary, and because I was always reading books, my brother's dread was that this companionship would turn me into a homosexual.[32]

The author quickly insists that he himself 'was not aware that homosexuality existed'; but there can be little doubt what is implied when Jack accuses one of these friends of wearing his hair 'like a sissy', and goes on to declare that Davy and his 'sonky bloody cobbers' will 'end up a bunch of tonks'. In a later scene, when the narrator (now aged sixteen) leaves home to stay at Sam Burlington's studio and Jack comes to see if he is safe, the elder brother asks if this 'codger' is 'another' of Davy's 'bloomin' tonk friends'. And when the lad protests that Sam is 'very nice', Jack replies: 'I didn't ask whether he was very nice. I asked if he was a poofter'.[33]

These conversations — these expressions — have the ring of authenticity. In life as in fiction the younger brother was made to feel inadequate in the business of heterosexual conquests. In regard to talking to girls, let alone having sex with them, he was a slow starter, whereas Jack was precocious. Later George would try to model his behaviour on Jack's idea of manhood, as demonstrated by sexual success.

Although George was painfully shy with the opposite sex — even his sisters could easily make him blush — by adolescence he was already starting to reveal the exuberance that people would later comment on, and he certainly was not without companions. Indeed, as in the novel, there were three other boys with whom he shared his interests at this time. Kinnane records how the four boys 'would spend hours in George's room, talking, sketching, reading, building model ships, in fact generally engaging in a boyhood life-of-the-mind, with George at its centre'. One of these friends describes George as being someone with 'too much energy', who 'was always larking about'.[34] In his final years at Brighton Technical School, George was a member of the school library committee and was secretary of the dramatic club. In this context it is perhaps curious that in the second sentence of the note on 'Childhood — "The Dollikos"' — where the author is writing only for himself — he refers to how in middle age he came to see in his childhood 'the hollow places where companionship should have been'. Clearly, looking back, he found something lacking in the depth or level of friendship which he had experienced. Or perhaps, like Charmian, he defines childhood as meaning the pre-pubescent years. Certainly, there are no accounts of him having friends at primary school.

Despite his bookishness and his timidity or gentleness, George Johnston played soccer for his school and later Australian Rules football for the Brighton Presbyterian Church team. While the height which he suddenly acquired in adolescence made him a fast runner, his great energy also helped. Jack Johnston played in the same church team, but relied on his strength and bulk. As Garry Kinnane records, 'the whole family got involved in the football team', with Pop acting as a decidedly partial goal umpire and Minnie running fundraisers.[35] In later years George Johnston would use an analogy of players and spectators as a kind of philosophy.[36] George was in no doubt that he himself was a player in the game of life, and so were the people whom he respected; he also played to win. Yet in regard to the real sport that he played in young manhood, it is possible that he basically went along with the family passion in order to avoid his father's constant complaint that he should stop reading and go and play sport. In his autobiographical novel George Johnston edits out any sporting ability in David Meredith. While this is an economical way of strengthening the differences between the characters of the two brothers, perhaps it also reflects the author's private feeling. After he stopped playing, he did not retain any interest in football, or in any other sport.

The basic path of George Johnston's young manhood was similar to that of David Meredith, except for the fact that the author omits his scholastic success from the fictional account. Thus David Meredith does not complete his final school year and fails his Intermediate Certificate, as do his three 'sonky mates': the boys are linked by 'a deep guilt at having failed at school'.[37] In real life, as Kinnane points out, the author 'completed his final year at Brighton Technical School, and in fact obtained the highest qualification that the school issued then, his Junior Technical Certificate'. While Kinnane sees the 'naggingly depressive tone' of Johnston's portrayal of David's failure in this period as reflecting the author's 'state of mind at the time *My Brother Jack* was written in 1963',[38] this change strengthened the story of the character's rise to literary success by sheer talent. In a similar way, of course, Charmian Clift would also pretend to have left school without her Intermediate Certificate.

It was October 1926 when George Johnston, aged fourteen, left school in order to begin an 'artistic apprenticeship' as a lithographer to the established printing firm of Troëdel & Cooper. The lad had always shown a flair for drawing — like his mother before him — and the family saw lithography as a solid trade that would be suitable for this sensitive second son. Minnie and Emma were particular pleased, because this occupation represented a move up from the blue collar world, and it was a return to the world of printing, with which Emma's husband and Minnie's father had been involved.

Although the 'art' for which George was being trained was the art of drawing advertising posters and labels, he was required to attend classes for a few hours each week at the National Gallery School. Still painfully shy, George did not find it easy to associate with the wild young men — and even more intimidating young women — of the art world, and he preferred to retreat to the solitude of the domed reading room of the State Library. As one of the literary boys at his school, George had had pieces published in the school magazine, and now he continued to write. Like David Meredith, he had a passion for sailing ships; he would read about the old clippers and windjammers, and then write about them. No doubt this interest partly developed from living close to the harbour. It was also connected with aesthetics: these ships were a beautiful combination of solid hull and ethereal, wind-filled sails. Yet surely these ships also represented the wide world from which they had come. The young George Johnston — like the young Charmian Clift, some years later — would dream of catching a boat across the seas to escape from the dreary place in which he was growing up.

It is appropriate that it was this particular passion which would put the young man on the path to his own escape. In 1929, when George was only sixteen, he sent an article about shipwrecks on the southern coastline to the Melbourne *Argus*. It was accepted for publication, and the fee of five guineas was equivalent to what George would earn in three weeks as a second year apprentice. As the budding author began to publish more articles, he developed more social skills and more self-confidence. Though still very awkward with girls, he even began to hang about on the edge of the Gallery School group that clustered around a vibrant young painter named Sam Atyeo.

Of course, 1929 is the year which is usually given as the start of the Great Depression. In fact, unemployment had been rising for some time, but certainly it was now that the collapse of the American and British economies caused a dramatic escalation of Australia's internal economic problems. It is illuminating to use this year as a marker in the life of George Johnston — the year when he had his first writing commercially published, and when he began the move into the world of art and what could loosely be called Melbourne's bohemia. While many other Australians would suffer the effects of the Depression — unemployment, eviction, the search for work, the humiliation of life on the dole or the ill-paid tedium of relief work — for George Johnston this coming decade would be a time of growing success and security, and a time of movement up the class scale.

As the 'great river' of the Depression swirled along its course,[39] George continued to work out his apprenticeship. He also continued to play football on weekends, even becoming secretary of the club. He still lived at home, of course; in those days, it was expected that young people would live with their family until they got married and started a new family. But increasingly he was finding the atmosphere stultifying. After Jack left home in 1931 to join his wife and baby daughter, the situation at *Avalon* became even more unbearable. George longed to find some different sort of life for himself.

The door opened in 1933. George had continued to get occasional freelance articles published, particularly in the *Argus*, and not long after he turned twenty-one he was offered a cadetship with that newspaper. He abandoned his apprenticeship, and started his career. Like most novices, he began on the shipping round.

George Johnston had an amazing aptitude for journalism. Perhaps he had inherited some particular combination of talents from his maternal grandfather, the country newspaper editor, for his success was not just due to his ability to write: many good writers make dreadful journalists. George's extraordinary level of nervous energy was also part of it — he was able to churn out good stories at a tremendous speed, and could get by on very little sleep. But perhaps the main part of his talent was the personal charm and gregariousness that seemed to blossom when George started the job. On the shipping round, George no longer found his stories in old library files, but by talking to people as they arrived from overseas. George had a natural curiosity about every subject under the sun, and his job gave him licence to ask intimate questions of perfect strangers. In his new role, the shy boy became outgoing.

The cadet reporter's work was so prodigious that he quickly caught the eye of the higher echelons, including the redoubtable Errol Knox, who by 1937 would become Managing Director of the *Argus*. Knox made it so clear that George was his favourite, and was being groomed for high things, that George's colleagues nicknamed him 'Golden Boy'. Later this description would be employed without irony, but in the beginning there was a certain combination of derision and jealousy in the use of the term. In this period, journalism was still a gentleman's job, at least on a quality newspaper like the *Argus*. George's colleagues, such as Bruce Kneale and Geoffrey Hutton, had been to private schools and had gone to university. George Johnston's awareness of the class difference between himself and his new associates is signalled clearly in *My Brother Jack*,[40] in which the author combines various colleagues in the composite character of Gavin Turley, who comes from a wealthy, cultured and old established family. Just as David Meredith admires and wishes to emulate Turley, so George Johnston — in order to survive in this world — would need to pick up something of the style of his gentlemen colleagues.

A quick learner, George soon blended into his new environment. Yet while he could joke with the other reporters and interview famous people, he was not at all adept with young women in social situations. One of his old school friends would comment that, at the age of twenty-one, George had still not taken out a girl; and George would be the last of the four friends to be married.[41] Unfortunately, when he did marry, in 1938, he was still at such an early stage of his development that he would choose someone who simply was not suited to the life that he was beginning to make for himself.

His bride, Elsie Taylor, was a friend of his younger sister Marjorie. A pleasant and unambitious young woman from the same sort of background as George, she wanted a nice home and children and an uneventful life in the suburbs. Like many wives of her era, she would be left behind as her husband's career took him into a world where she did not fit. And as in many marriages of that particular time, the war would greatly accelerate the widening of the gap between husband and wife.

In the first couple of years after the outbreak of hostilities, however, George remained at the *Argus*, where he completed his rise up the promotion scale to the rank of A grade journalist. In early 1941 he wrote his first book — a non-fiction story about the battle cruiser HMAS *Sydney* and its crew, which he rattled out of the typewriter in seven weeks. This helped raise morale among the troops and found a ready market with the public. It was quickly followed by two more war books.[42] In October 1941 the Johnstons had a daughter whom they named Gae, for George *and* Elsie.

Meanwhile, George was dithering about whether to enlist for active service — as some of his colleagues, including Bruce Kneale, would do — or whether to wait for a job as a war correspondent, which he had been half-promised. Garry Kinnane describes some of the forces that pulled the journalist in contrary directions before he finally decided to bide his time and make the career move. He suggests that 'in later years George was to experience intense guilt over his decision', and would see it as a matter of 'cowardice' and 'moral "defection"'.[43] In this analysis of George's later feelings, Kinnane is probably right.

Unsurprisingly, it was Errol Knox who in January 1942 appointed George as the *Argus* war correspondent. When he received his licence in February, it was the first such licence issued by the Australian Army in World War II. George always found it a source of pride that his licence was stamped 'Number 1'. As well as appearing in the *Argus*, George's despatches would be syndicated to the *Adelaide Advertiser* and the *Sydney Morning Herald*. As the war went on, freelance articles by George Johnston would also appear in the London *Daily Telegraph* and the American *Time* and *Life* magazines.

Five days after receiving his licence, George was given an honorary ranking of captain, and a uniform to go with it. He was also given a posting to Port Moresby. It wasn't very far away — but it was overseas! As the war correspondent flew off to Townsville for his briefing, it seemed that he had finally escaped from the claustrophobia of the grey childhood suburbs. He had left the settled life behind.

From February 1942 until the surrender of Japan in September 1945, George Johnston travelled the globe. During this three and a half year period, he spent altogether only six or seven months at home with his wife and daughter. Once again, taking on a new role seemed to cause George's personality to open up: now he suddenly found himself a success with women. As early as June 1942, relations between the Johnstons were 'under some strain', according to Garry Kinnane; it was clear to friends that the couple were 'drifting apart' and George told a mate that he had 'grown bored with his marriage'. When George returned for Christmas that year, Elsie knew that her husband was having an affair with a woman in the *Argus* office. After spending most of 1943 in America, he returned again for Christmas, and told his wife that he wanted a divorce so that he could return to a woman in New York whom he loved. At George's suggestion, the couple separated: Elsie and Gae moved to a flat in St Kilda and George went to a hotel. Within a few days, however, he moved into the flat — moving out again soon afterwards, not to return to America, but to take up an assignment in Asia.[44]

This time he was away for fourteen months, travelling initially to India, Ceylon, Burma and China where, in September 1944, he made an extraordinary journey by jeep along the road from Kweilin to Liuchow, at the time when thousands upon thousands of Chinese civilians were retreating from the Japanese advance through a landscape ravaged by drought and famine. The experienced journalist was deeply shocked to see beside the road a hundred thousand human bodies 'rotting in the hot sun'.[45] While few people would fail to be sickened by such a sight, the mutilated and bloating corpses fuelled the particular nightmare which George's memory had carried since his childhood exposure to the pictures in his father's war magazines and the stories that his mother's patients would relate. Yet this was even worse than anything documented by Raemaeker, for these people had not died in battle, but because of the economic dealings of their own government representatives. As Johnston's alter ego would protest: 'Those hundred thousand were all dead [...] because a clique of Kuomintang bastards [...] were manipulating the currency market. They made the best part of eight million American dollars out of their little racket'.[46]

It was as if what the journalist saw on this road was literally an eye-opener. At the same time, the moral sense of this late developer was suddenly awakened. From now on, he would start to wonder what the war was really for. He would also begin to question the role of the war correspondent, and to see it as a rather shoddy job which, like the dealings of the war racketeers, traded upon human suffering.

After this, it was a relief to leave China for a posting to the Middle East, followed by Greece, Yugoslavia and Italy. George Johnston left Rome in January 1945, returned to Burma and India, and finally arrived back in Australia in late April. It was during this leave that he met Charmian at the Hotel Australia in May 1945.

Immediately afterwards, he flew back to China, via India. A couple of months later he took a month or so off to make a journey by pony through the high country of Tibet, where he met the Living Buddha and 'lived with mountain nomads, with lamas, with lowland farmers, with small merchants'.[47] This experience gave the journalist a sense of shared humanity, as well as turning his mind to matters of philosophy and the spirit in a way that this energetic agnostic had not really thought about before.

As George Johnston and his deliriously ill travelling companion, photographer James Burke, arrived late back at the base camp to fly out of Tibet, they found that everything had been dismantled, and the last DC3 was revving for take-off. By luck, the engine stalled. George managed to catch the pilot's attention by firing his revolver. The two boarded the plane, and escaped.[48] Although this was not the most dramatic brush with death which he experienced,[49] George Johnston believed that if he had not caught that DC3, he would never have got out alive from the remote valley. Perhaps this incident concentrated his mind in a very personal way upon the matter of mortality.

By August 1945, the war correspondent was back in western China. It was now that he witnessed something that would affect him so profoundly that he would start to become a different person, although it would be a decade and a half before the full effect would reveal itself. At its simplest, this revelation could be summed up as an awareness of the human price of war; this was a matter partly of horror, and partly of futility. Half of the story had already happened: this was the vision of the exodus to Liuchow, and the corpses beside the road. But now the journalist witnessed the tragedy repeat itself, as a mass of refugees fled back towards where they had begun. As the war ended and the journalist caught the plane out of the town of Chungking, this was his last visual image both of the war and of China:

> An ant-horde of uncountable people disgorging from a central mat of human blackness that looked like a forest of some stunted growth, an immense and hardly believable spreading and scattering and trickling of Chinese moving on dubious destinies across a parched brown map. A million exiles setting out after nearly nine years of war to walk back to homes in distant provinces across a devastated land.[50]

By the end of his life, Johnston would come to the view that there was 'no meaning to anything experienced except that it [had] been experienced'.[51] But in his mid-thirties he still sought to understand the *point* of the thing that had set in motion this vast movement of people. In a brilliant phrase, he would later refer to how 'the chambers' of his 'visual memory carried a war surplus of souvenired images'.[52] This particular image of people struggling and dying down the long road would be the crucial one; while it would fuse with the other journey he had witnessed, on the road between Kweilin and Liuchow, it would also carry the earlier images which Johnston's visual memory had retained from his childhood. The anti-war feeling which he would bring home from World War II had some of its origin in the images that he saw of World War I, via the grisly realism of Raemaeker's illustrations of an earlier exodus of refugees.

For the author, this journey of the Chinese refugees would become a potent symbol. At the same time, this road, this experience, was the starting point of George Johnston's own journey. It was a turning point between what had happened before and everything that happened afterwards. Indeed, 'Nothing has seemed quite real since we flew out of Chungking', the narrator of *Clean Straw for Nothing* declares.[53] Overall, George's experience in western China would leave him with a negative or pessimistic view of humanity and of the 'point' of human life.

It did not help that immediately after seeing the 'ant-horde' of refugees, he travelled via the official peace talks in Manila to Japan, where he witnessed the surrender ceremony on board the US warship *Missouri*. Leaving the entourage of political and military leaders, the journalist went on alone to the town of Hiroshima. Here, as he walked in the ruins of a mission garden where 'all the trees and flower gardens and the shrubs [had] wilted and died as if they had been seared by enormous heat',[54] he again saw what humankind was capable of doing. In moral terms, the war seemed futile if the representatives of justice and democracy could do what they had done at Hiroshima. While the war left George Johnston profoundly disillusioned with the political system, what he had seen in Japan would also give him a very real fear of the developing Cold War; he believed that nuclear devastation could happen again — any time, any place. Twenty years later Johnston would say that he 'emerged from war as a very strong pacifist'. In particular he noted that 'the critical period' had been seeing Hiroshima; this left such a 'profound impression' that 'from that point' he 'became very anti-war'.[55]

Although 'sickened by the waste and misery and suffering of war [...] by the ambitious idiocies of great men and the corruption of ideals', as the journalist prepared to return home he was aware that, in personal terms, peace was 'unwanted'. In the first draft of *Clean Straw for Nothing* the author noted of David Meredith that 'there yet remained a part of him that had not wanted the war to end'.

> As a correspondent he had had a fairly privileged time of it, adventurous and yet with a reasonable choice of either hazard or the lack of it, and he had found little attraction in the thought of returning to the dullness of Melbourne and, above all, the necessity for some uneasy realignment with his wife.[56]

Like David Meredith — and like many other men and women who had served in the armed forces — when George Johnston came home in October 1945 he felt profoundly restless. Everything seemed to be an anticlimax. The last thing he wanted to do was settle back into married life even though, unlike his alter ego, he had a four year old daughter whom he barely knew. Although he stayed at the St Kilda flat, this was only meant to be a temporary arrangement. In fact, when the *Argus* management had recalled Johnston from Tokyo, they had offered him a 'reprieve': he was 'to prepare himself for a two year assignment in South America'. And so, as Meredith tells his wife Helen, this period became 'only a marking time'. There was no point 'even *trying* to settle down'.[57] However, civilian travel was very hard to arrange in this immediate post-war period, and George Johnston had to wait for a berth on a ship to South America. He was writing the odd feature article for his newspaper, but he couldn't really settle to that, any more than he could settle into his home city.

Part of the problem with Melbourne was that it reminded George of his childhood and youth; he was afraid that, after all he had done to 'hack his way out', he could end up back in the thicket. At the same time, the city's complacency seemed even worse because — unlike the other cities he had recently visited — it hadn't 'even suffered'.[58] In a draft of his novel, the author has his alter ego rail against 'this soggy suburban pie crust' that seemed to be 'over everything. The bloody parochialism of the place! [...] The insularity! The deadly bloody wowserism!'.[59] Overall, it was 'a sour, cynical, nasty city', where 'a powerful tide of human dilemma runs beneath the skin of everything'.[60] Yet he 'enjoyed being a part of this dilemma': 'It identified him with the unorthodox and the unstable, with a world slightly out of balance which at all costs had to be prevented from tilting back into the static dullness of the conventional picture'.[61]

Deliberately hanging on to his own instability, George waited through the spring of 1945. Summer came — 'nervy and exhausting and as hard to get along with as a hot northerly'. By March of the new year, the Melbourne autumn was arriving, 'cold and squally',[62] and George was still waiting for a passage to South America. Life in the flat with his wife and child was increasingly claustrophobic, but at least he still had his way out.

Then the escape route was abruptly closed. The *Argus* management decided that, rather than sending their top journalist overseas, they could use him better at home. An editor was needed for the *Australasian Post*. This was the new weekly magazine which was to supersede the moribund country magazine, the *Australasian*. George was promoted in March 1946 to this position, and the first issue of the new publication was released in April.

In the author's mind, this period of six or seven months between October 1945 and March/April 1946 would become such a vacuum that in his fictional versions he would have to manipulate time in order to handle it. In the first two attempts at writing *Clean Straw for Nothing*, Johnston would jump his alter ego from Hiroshima (in what would have been the southern hemisphere spring of 1945) to his return home in the autumn of 1946, with nothing in between, and have him meet Cressida Morley within a few weeks.[63] In the final version, he would bring Meredith back to Melbourne at the time of his own return in October 1945, but it is after only a few weeks of restless wandering and intermittent fighting with Helen and malaise with the newspaper that the journalist contacts Cressida Morley. Both these fictional versions express the real meaning of this period: which is that nothing happened for George Johnston, between the end of the war and his reunion with Charmian Clift. Until that encounter, everything seemed on hold. And then life suddenly started again. It was symbolically and emotionally spring time, though in real life it was autumn.[64]

9

SETTING OUT TOGETHER

'I am glad we are setting out together. Wherever the journey should
take us — I am glad we travel together.'[1]

After their second meeting — in the lift of the *Argus* building —
Charmian Clift and George Johnston fell immediately and
flamboyantly in love. To colleagues observing it happen, it was a matter of
'instantaneous combustion'.[2]

As far as Charmian was concerned, George simply seemed the answer to
all the dreams that she had been dreaming since she first waited for her
'tirra lirra man' to wander along the bank of the reedy North Kiama creek.
Yet if Charmian's philosophy of love reflected her early reading of the
Arthurian stories (mediated by Tennyson), it was far more powerfully
shaped by the Metaphysical poets. Years later, when writing the tale of the
passion between the characters Kathy and Fotis in *Honour's Mimic*, Clift
turned to John Donne for a phrase that would encapsulate the ruthless
intensity of their love. The novel's title is taken from the third stanza of 'The
Sunne Rising':

> She's all States, and all Princes, I,
> Nothing else is.
> Princes do but play us; compar'd to this,
> All honour's mimic; all wealth alchemy.[3]

In Clift's view, love overruled all other considerations if it were the kind of
love that Donne also expressed as being that of 'two souls [...] which are
one': 'if they be two, they be two so/ As stiff twin compasses are two'.[4] At this

time, when she fell in love with George Johnston, Charmian believed that she and he were twin souls.

This is clear from the way in which she depicts her fictional characters Christine Morley and Martin Smith in the section of *Greener Grows the Grass* set in the newspaper office. Although this particular fragment of text covers barely nine pages, the novelist repeatedly stresses the many similarities between Martin and Christine: both are tall, both have a lithe, loose manner of walking, both are endearingly messy, both are planning to go overseas in the near future. Most significantly, both lovers are serious writers (as well as being journalists), and both are caught in unworthy and damaging relationships. In the mirroring of the names of Smith's wife (Leonie) and Morley's fiancé (Leonard — based, of course, on the real Leo), the novelist sets up these partners as a common enemy: both Christine and Martin are trapped by someone who would prevent them from fulfilling their artistic destiny. If love is more important than honour, art overrides absolutely everything.

Naturally, part of George's attraction was the fact that he had published a number of books, as well as being a famous journalist. But Charmian was not some sort of author groupie, hoping to catch some of the writer's glory, or even his talent. George's writing was important to her because it held out the promise that this man would not try to prevent her from doing what she secretly lived for.

Yet another thing in George's favour was his comparative maturity. Although an eleven year age gap is not particularly remarkable, it was significant at the beginning of this relationship. Since her first adolescent flirtations, Charmian had shown a decided preference for older men. This surely connects back to her father, who was such a powerful figure that Charmian needed an exceptional man to live up to the standards which he had set. In the same way, Charmian's sister Margaret commented that as a young woman she couldn't find a boyfriend to measure up to Syd.[5] Although, of course, Charmian would have denied that she shared her sister's hero worship of 'the terrible tyrant', she was equally under his spell.

In regard to Charmian's fascination with this particular older man, the curious similarities between George Johnston and Sydney Clift are surely relevant. As we have seen, there was an affinity between their home environments, despite the fact that these two men grew up a generation and a hemisphere apart. Although George's prestigious white collar job contrasted with Syd's enjoyment of messing about with machines, they were both autodidacts, with a thirst for information about everything under the sun, and George shared Syd's Shandy-like enthusiasm. Both men tended to make a display of their masculinity, in case they seemed not masculine enough. And both were (in Charmian's phrase) 'conversational bullies'.[6] This was not necessarily intended as a criticism. In fact, Syd had trained Charmian so strenuously in the art of his particular kind of conversation that she loved thrashing out ideas with this sort of man.

Most importantly, both Syd and George were larger-than-life characters who held centre stage in any gathering. The difference was that while Syd restricted his audience to the men gathered at the 'Corner Parliament', George's stage was the world. His easy smile communicated a sense of infectious exuberance and vitality, and he had an extraordinary magnetism, which seemed to work equally upon men and women. George's flamboyant style at this time is captured in a description given by Greeba Jamison, who was an *Argus* colleague and good friend of George's:

> He would burst into the big reporters' room, described in perfect detail in *My Brother Jack,* and the whole place was turned on end, particularly for the girls. He would snatch up the best-looking one he saw, grab her on his knee or swing her up towards the ceiling and catch her in his arms; everyone, men and women, would cluster around and George would tell us, with tremendous gusto, a spate of exaggerated adjectives generously sprinkled with bloody (one of his favourite words), great gusts of laughter, of his exploits in the war, Very Important People he had met, women he had made love to. Usually we would repair to the Duke of Kent Hotel across the road in LaTrobe Street and the story would continue over many rounds of beer.[7]

And a great many of these rounds of beer would be paid for by George, whose generosity was yet another reaction against the meanness of his upbringing. Another *Argus* colleague, Geoffrey Hutton, supports Greeba's view: '[George] was the complete extrovert, a man with an inexhaustible talent for making friends, dissolving personal and social barriers [...] He could charm the birds out of the trees.'[8]

This latter phrase would often be repeated in regard to George; as the years went on, Charmian would find this talent difficult to live with. Yet at this time, she was more enraptured than anyone. To this twenty-two year old girl from the backblocks, George Johnston was a man of the world, a traveller whose conversation was crammed with the names of famous places and famous people. She vividly describes him in 'his leaping time — trench coat, beret, dressing gown from de Pinna, pigskin luggage, passport fabulously stamped with nearly every country of the world':

> He could give you, in words, the look and the smell and the taste and the sound of an experience (usually an exotic experience, because he collected exotic experiences the way some people collect luggage labels: like travelling in Tibet and living with the Chinese Communists and visiting the last of the great ivory-painters in Isphahan).[9]

While a relationship with this man offered Charmian the chance to further her vocation as a writer, George also offered the fulfilment of her other dream — of escape. Unlike Leo, who was offering a base in only one foreign country, George promised he would take the young woman to see all the places that he himself had seen, and more. And so to Charmian, the relationship represented freedom. She and George would travel the world, and write, and never settle down and live in the suburbs like ordinary people.

This anti-suburban philosophy was, in turn, a great part of the appeal which Charmian held for George. While her beauty and her youthfulness were important to him, even more important was his idea of her as a wild, free, child of nature — exactly the sort of person who would be depicted in the Cressida Morley passages of *My Brother Jack*. In life as in fiction, the sense of freedom which the young Charmian seemed to embody was the main source of appeal to the disillusioned war correspondent. After witnessing the horrors of the last few years, and after returning to the tedium of post-war Melbourne, Charmian seemed to offer a fresh start. She was 'natural' in a way that he did not see himself as being, and possessed an honesty which he felt he did not have. Perhaps some of this would rub off, and he would lose this lingering guilt that he had always behaved in a rather cowardly and shoddy way — in his childhood, in his marriage, and particularly during his time as a war correspondent.

In seeming to hold out a promise of escape from the past and from suburbia, Charmian represented the antithesis to George's childhood world. Linking himself to her was a kind of guarantee that he would not fall back into the way of life that he hated, because 'with her nothing could ever be entirely conventional'.[10] It will be remembered that, in the 'Dollikos' passage already cited, the author notes how 'in maturity he was inclined to cling [...] to everything that was antithetical' to the 'earlier formations' of flat suburbs, empty sky, hollow companionship, and surrounding 'imperfections'. After this, themes of possession and perfection were introduced. Thus the unnamed protagonist 'searched the world for mountains and rivers', pitched his ambition high, and 'possessed his wife as a symbol of [...] unattainable perfection'. This 'wife' is not the author's (or alter ego's) first wife, but the Cressida Morley character. His love for her was 'the greatest of all the rivers he had discovered', and he would 'permit no flaw in its current'. The author went on to declare that 'the paradox' of the protagonist's love was 'perhaps in his childhood'; this led directly to a description of his family home and then of his only memory of affection and love, the 'Dollikos' incident itself.[11]

As we shall see, this definition of love, which contained meanings of possession and perfection, would have a profound effect on the relationship. While Charmian had been brought up on stories from the Arthurian cycle, it was actually *George* whose notions of love itself and the role of knight and lady derived from the tradition of *fine amour*.[12]

Thus Charmian represented 'the prize' which the hero traditionally wins at the end of his quest. Indeed, George Johnston would use this term again and again in his published and unpublished accounts of the relationship between David Meredith and Cressida Morley. The author always links his alter ego's urge to win this prize with his journey outward from his restrictive upbringing and his shoddy adult experience. While the 'Dollikos' note was written before *My Brother Jack,* the author would develop this self-analysis in some notes which he would write in 1963, when he was preparing to start *Clean Straw for Nothing*:

> [David Meredith] derives from enclosed and puritanical conceptions [...] He is evasive, superficial, not natural in the sense of Cressida's naturalness. Not only has his marriage with Helen been a fiasco and a failure (to some degree self-inflicted), but all his sexual experiences have in some way been casual, inexperienced, worthless, distorted, cheap, contrived, makeshift. Always falling short of what he feels himself to deserve. His love for Cressida, however, is something of almost cosmic difference. She represents the unattainable prize, something more than he can ever hope to have achieved.[13]

There is no doubt about the biographical authenticity of the attitude expressed in this passage. Nor is there any doubt about the extraordinary prize that Charmian represented. Greeba Jamison also gives a vivid picture of the effect Charmian had on her male colleagues at the newspaper:

> Charmian came into the *Argus* office and, believe me, she turned that *Argus* office on its heels [...] She was very attractive, a very beautiful young woman [...] very sexy. I mean, every man who looked at Charmian just, you know, wanted to go to bed with her. You didn't put it like that in 1946, but that's how it was.[14]

All in all, if George were able to win Charmian's love, it would represent both the triumph and the revenge of the boy from Elsternwick — for he, just as much as she, was hellbent on 'showing the bastards'. An added element of satisfaction was their defiance of the many friends and colleagues who shook their heads pessimistically at the developing relationship. These nay-sayers are transformed in *Clean Straw for Nothing* into Gavin Turley's 'warning' that: 'You two would destroy each other. You wouldn't last six months together'.[15] George Johnston was determined to prove them wrong. So was Charmian Clift.

The love affair between George and Charmian set the *Argus* office buzzing with gossip. Apart from anything else, George was still living with his wife Elsie and young daughter, and members of the newspaper staff took sides on the subject. All in all, Greeba Jamison remembers the affair as being 'the *scandale*' of the time, with everyone in the office 'waiting on tenterhooks to see what happened next'.

While Johnston had not made any secret of his previous liaisons,[16] this relationship was different, not only because of the obvious level of intensity but because it was being conducted inside the *Argus* building. ('You wouldn't dare go into George's office without knocking three times', Bruce Kneale declared.[17])

After the relationship had been going on for some weeks, George and Charmian spent a weekend together down the coast. On Johnston's return to the St Kilda flat, his wife told him to get out.[18] This was a gambit in Elsie's strategy to keep her husband, for she just as strongly as Charmian believed that her relationship with George was meant to be. Whenever she had previously taken decisive action, the tactic had worked.[19] But this time,

George's sense of post-war disillusionment meant that he wanted a complete break with his past. And so he did what she suggested — he left.

The two lovers moved together into the raffish Post Office Hotel (known as the Tin Shed Hotel), situated opposite Melbourne's GPO. The blatancy of this cohabitation increased the scandal surrounding the lovers. Although the war had changed many people's attitudes to the issue of sex outside marriage, it was still not 'done' for a couple to live openly in a de facto relationship. And, of course, it was the woman who would be forced to wear the shame. Even for Charmian, this was a bold act.

It wasn't only the love affair that caused gossip. Whereas the main reporting and editorial staff were all on the third floor of the *Argus* building, the *Australasian Post* had two small rooms on the fourth; as the *Post* had no real staff of its own, Johnston would commission articles from the general reporting staff. The *Post* rooms became a kind of club for George and his mates. In this, too, George Johnston acted with little discretion: one night when the crew were carousing, Brigadier Kingham burst in to complain, 'You could hear you lot in bloody Darwin!'[20]

Yet even the high drama of the love affair did not stop Charmian Clift from doing her journalistic work. On 22 June she had her first bylined article published — a portrait of Cecil Beaton for the *Argus Week-end Magazine*. Although both subject and audience required something written in the *Home Beautiful* style, the crafting of this piece reveals the hand of the writer who would become Charmian Clift the essayist. A week later, the young journalist produced an interview with artist Edward Heffernan on the topic of the portrait painter's views on female beauty — and especially the 'real Australian girl'. This was the lead piece for the *Argus Woman's Magazine*.[21]

And in her own time, Clift was still writing short stories. Greeba Jamison (who was also currently writing fiction) remembers that she and Charmian used to have 'long and frightfully serious talks about [their] writing'. Jamison stresses that her colleague was 'dedicated to her writing' at this time and that 'Charmian would have been a writer whether she'd met George or whether she hadn't'.[22] It was Bruce Kneale's job to buy stories for the *Australasian Post*, and he accepted Clift's story 'The Awakening' (discussed in chapter 3). Slight though it is, it was better than most of the fiction published in the *Post* at this time, and it was the only piece to deal with ordinary Australian life. The story appeared on 11 July 1946.

As far as working for the *Argus* was concerned, it can be regarded as Charmian Clift's swan song. Within the next week or so she was called without warning into the office of Errol Knox — the Managing Director and former Brigadier who, of course, was the man who had personally invited her to join the *Argus* staff. Now he told her that she was to leave immediately.

The news barely had time to penetrate the building before it was eclipsed by an even greater sensation. While there are many versions of this event, they all agree in substance with Bruce Kneale's account of the story, which is based on what was told to him shortly afterwards by George Johnston himself:

> As soon as George heard of Charmian's sacking he burst into one of Knox's conferences and said: 'Knocka! The *Argus* says Charmian has got to be sacked!'
>
> And Knox said, 'Yes, George, she's got to go!' [...]
>
> And George said: 'Knocka, if you sack Charmian you can have my resignation here and now!'
>
> And George said to me: 'I was dumbfounded, because Knox said, "Right George, I'll accept it." '
>
> George said: 'You'll accept it?'
>
> Knox said: 'I will accept your resignation, George.'
>
> And so this great thing happened that no one ever thought could happen — that Knox would sack George or that he'd accept his resignation — because George was the Golden Boy — he was the apple of Knox's eye — Knox thought he was marvellous![23]

What caused Charmian Clift's dismissal? The *Argus* management never gave an official reason, and Clift herself never publicly discussed the matter. However, while the sacking was prompted by a mixture of moralistic disapproval for the adulterous affair and a general feeling that Charmian Clift was a disruptive element in the office,[24] the *Argus* management may also have been hoping to get rid of George Johnston.

Although Johnston told Kneale that he was dumbfounded when Knox accepted his resignation, there is something about Knox's calm acceptance — despite his reputation as a man of explosive temper — that suggests that Knox had considered the likelihood of Johnston resigning. In fact, well before the blow-up over Clift's dismissal, there had been a number of arguments between George Johnston and Errol Knox.

The conflict concerned the content and style of the *Australasian Post*. As far as management was concerned, the periodical was intended to express a mood of post-war optimism, but the editorials tended to reflect Johnston's unease about the direction in which Australia was heading, plus his fear that the warmongers were looking forward to the next conflict. The *Argus* management was also disturbed by certain political views that Johnston had brought home from his travels in Asia, particularly his attitude to the war of national liberation that was escalating in China. While he was hardly, in the phrase of the time, a Red, he had talked with Mao and a number of the other Communist leaders, and he believed that the only hope for China was the defeat of the Western puppet government of the Kuomintang. A typical article pointed out that change in China 'will come when the Chinese want it — and in the way the Chinese want it. It will no longer be the prerogative of the West to direct to the East its course of conduct'.[25] Yet this pragmatic and self-determinist view was problematic in the developing climate of anti-Communism. Two decades later, during the Vietnam years, Charmian Clift told a group of Americans that immediately after the war George Johnston had 'predicted every damn thing that has happened since [in Asia]':

> He talked at clubs and in schools and practically stood on stumps yelling, and he wrote a series of articles that didn't get printed because one of his masters went to such elegant Chinese dinners at the Embassy and the articles might offend.[26]

Within a couple of months of George Johnston's editorship of the *Australasian Post*, his political conflict with Knox and the *Argus* management was known to everyone on the staff. Hume Dow, who was a member of Johnston's team, believed that

> It was more coincidental than causal that [George and Charmian] left about the same time. George was getting so fed up with being interfered with in his editorial control that he was going to leave anyway. George warned us he was going to get out. He suggested we get jobs elsewhere and he [said he] wouldn't resign till we got jobs elsewhere.[27]

With George's dissatisfaction being such public knowledge, it is most likely that word had reached Knox. Further, George's suggestion that his colleagues seek alternative jobs meant that the *Argus* faced the prospect of losing some of its best journalists. It would not be surprising if Knox decided to act. Although the office love affair clearly upset the *Argus* management, it also provided a way of disengaging a journalist who was proving to be a political embarrassment, but without giving him any grounds on which to protest. On July 25 the *Australasian Post* appeared without George Johnston's byline on the editorial.

It is illuminating to compare the actual sequence of events with the account given in *Clean Straw for Nothing*. In the novel, the journalist David Meredith returns from war in October 1945 to take up his old position at the Melbourne *Morning Post*. Shortly afterwards, the managing editor, Mr Brewster, tells Meredith that he is going to spike three articles he has written about China because of the anti-Kuomintang line which the journalist has taken. Meredith is simultaneously informed that his proposed trip to South America is indefinitely postponed. As compensation, he is offered the editorship of a new forward-looking weekly magazine.

Canny Meredith sees this whole situation as 'the trap'. Now that he is unable to leave the country, there will be 'no escape' from his marriage, and he will be chained to 'sleazy little securities. Conformity. Safety. The sad suburban rectitudes'.[28] It is now that David Meredith reaches for the telephone and rings Lieutenant Morley at her barracks. This is the first contact between Meredith and Morley since the dinner engagement which provides the romantic cliffhanger at the end of *My Brother Jack*. The two spend their first night together — at the Tin Shed Hotel — and the next morning David tells Cressida that he loves her and asks her to come away with him — somewhere.

> 'What about your wife?' she said quietly.
> 'That's finished,' I said. 'I've left her.'
> 'Then what about your job?'
> 'I'm quitting that too.'
> 'Oh,' she said. 'You are being serious about this, then?'
> 'I've never been more serious in my life.'
> 'But why? What's the reason?'
> 'I don't think I know. Not yet. Not really. I just don't want to be trapped in this bloody place. I don't want to fall into these awful dull ruts. I don't want to end up living in some dreary bloody suburb growing *Antirrhinums*.'[29]

This reference alludes to the description of Cressida in the restaurant scene, where Meredith reflects that the pagan savage 'wouldn't know an *Antirrhinum* from a *Phlox drumondii* or a mock orange if one fell on her!' For this couple, *Antirrhinums* (snapdragons) would become, in life as well as in fiction, a code word for suburbia — which in turn was a synonym for hell.

Cressida is discharged from the army soon after this, and 'something of a scandal explode[s] in Melbourne' when David leaves his wife to live with her. He also quits his job at the *Morning Post*. He wants to send a note saying 'Get stuffed, Brewster!', but Cressida sensibly counsels him to write a formal letter of resignation — which he does.[30]

Although the novel's description of the political background to the whole situation is accurate, the fictional version reveals most by what it conceals. For George Johnston, the dismissal was so devastating that two decades later it could not be allowed even into the fictional record. For Charmian Clift, too, the event remained a shameful memory: like her husband, she never mentioned the episode in interviews. Apart from the birth of Charmian's first child, it is the only thing which these two were keen to keep out of the public record.

It is easy to see why this incident would upset Charmian. Unlike George, she had suffered the ignominy of being sacked — and from a job which seemed to offer everything the young woman wanted. But George should have taken the whole thing in his stride, especially given the fact that he was left with his pride intact, for at least he had taken the initiative. Indeed, as the story was told and retold, he appeared decidedly gallant. '*This is the last time the woman pays!*' he is said to have declared before storming into Knox's office.[31] Furthermore, with his experience and prestige as a journalist, he could have approached any newspaper office in the country and been given a senior position on the spot.

Surely the reason why this episode troubled George so profoundly was because it was a rejection, and the lovelessness of his childhood made him very sensitive to anything that could be perceived as rejection or abandonment. In a sense, Errol Knox was the father figure who had fostered the unlikely cadet journalist. But now Knocka was knocking Golden Boy back. In addition, the dismissal appeared to epitomise the whole damn problem with the post-war world. It proved that the culture of Australian society was mean-spirited and wowserish, seeking to censure passion and happiness. And yet, in this anticlimactic and dreary society where everything seemed to be on hold, the dismissal was at least an event to force the direction of George's life.

If the openly conducted relationship of George and Charmian had been, as Greeba Jamison declared, the *scandale* of the *Argus* office, the dismissal turned the couple's affair into an absolute sensation. If we are to map the myth of Charmian and George's relationship, its starting point is the dismissal from the *Argus*. The couple suddenly formed that archetypal image — lovers whom society punishes or seeks to separate.

To understand why this couple became an Australian legend, two things must be remembered. Firstly, this was the newspaper world. It was the stock exchange of juicy titbits, wild rumours, unsubstantiated allegations, superficial analyses. Secondly, while George Johnston had many mates, there were also a number of journalists who had been unhappy when Golden Boy was given the assignment or the promotion which they felt to be their due. There were people who didn't like Charmian, too: men whom she had rejected; women who felt their sexual territory threatened; snobs. One of the *Argus Woman's Magazine* journalists remarked to Bruce Kneale that 'Charmian was sadly lacking in background'. She was still the girl from the wrong side of the tracks.

And so many people in the Melbourne newspaper world were quietly laughing when Golden Boy and his consort got their marching orders. The telling and retelling of the George-and-Charm story was fuelled by malice as much as by a genuine appreciation of a good piece of gossip in a dull city in the first dreary winter after the war.

It is important to understand this, because as the myth of the Johnstons developed over time, there was always in it an aspect of gloating at their downfall. This links, of course, with the traditional Australian pastime of lopping the tall poppies. But there is something older in it as well. As the journalists who have fed the myth in recent years have persisted in calling the Johnston story 'a Greek tragedy', it must be said that the story is not Greek because Charmian and George happened to reside for some years on the island of Hydra, but because the Comeuppance of Golden Boys and Girls is a popular theme of Greek mythology. That, after all, is what hubris is all about.

In the aftermath of such catastrophes, it is common for the fallen heroes to go into exile. On their dismissal from the *Argus*, George and Charmian had nowhere to go. They stayed on at the Tin Shed Hotel until, after a few weeks, the friendly publican lent them his cottage in the small town of Sorrento, down on the Mornington Peninsula. For Charmian, this was a reversion to habit: in the wake of disaster she always fled to the sea. But this time it was the wrong season, and the southern ocean was grey and bleak. The land was flat.

The relationship with George was also suddenly rather flat and bleak. In their time of living together at the pub, they had been happy itinerants, eating as well as drinking in the bar. But now that they were in a house, George expected her to clean and cook as Elsie had. (Indeed, he would later tell Elsie that he didn't know if he'd be able to stay with Charmian, she was such a sloppy housekeeper.[32])

Another pressure, for Charmian, was being constantly at such close quarters with someone. She had never lived with any of her lovers before. It was difficult to be with someone who expected her to open up her most private recesses. It seems that it was at Sorrento, too, that Charmian first experienced George's jealousy. Certainly, in his own account of this escape to the Sorrento cottage in *Clean Straw for Nothing*, Johnston has his alter ego David Meredith pinpoint this as the time when 'he had become obsessively jealous of Cressida'. He remembers how Archie Calverton — one of the other residents of the Tin Shed Hotel — had come down to the cottage, and David had made 'a quite unfounded accusation of [Cressida] having flirted' with Archie.[33]

The character of Archie Calverton is composed of a number of male friends with whom Charmian had a platonic relationship, but whom George suspected. In the novel Archie plays the role of confidant to Cressida and advisor to David. He stands in for various men who played these roles in life. One such friend may well have visited the couple at Sorrento, and George may have expressed jealousy. Any such incident is in itself irrelevant. This scene is important because it shows that George Johnston himself dated his jealousy as starting from this very early stage in the relationship.

The second point of the Calverton incident in the Sorrento scene of *Clean Straw for Nothing* is that David Meredith acknowledges that the emotion was 'unfounded'. This is also Meredith — and Meredith's model — speaking with hindsight. In the novel, Cressida bites David's finger to the bone when he wags it at her in accusation. This is indicative of how George saw Charmian's resistance to his jealousy. From the very beginning, it was a matter of bone and blood. However, this realisation only came later. In 1946, George simply felt jealous and Charmian simply resisted. Neither knew that this would be a major ongoing conflict in their relationship. Even when, many years afterwards, Johnston came to understand something of the matter, he simplified it in *Clean Straw for Nothing* by introducing a rival to the scene. The issue, however, was not about something as obvious as sex. It was to do with George's all or nothing attitude to love.

While George's philosophy of love already derived from the *fine amour* tradition, the way in which the couple left their jobs at the *Argus* reinforced this, and simultaneously changed the balance of the couple's relationship. By making the gallant sacrifice of his career, George believed that he had done the chivalric thing that deserved the ultimate reward. It was really from this time that George saw himself as having won the 'unattainable prize'; from now on, he would see himself as entitled to claim Charmian as his possession. And yet there was always the sneaking fear that he would lose the prize, because at heart he didn't really think he deserved it. Some other, better man would come along. Although he wouldn't work out the connection with his early background until many years later, it is clear that this possessiveness was directly linked with the fear of abandonment which had developed during the author's early childhood.

Charmian could, of course, have no understanding of any of this, because in her eyes George was the epitome of a successful and outgoing man of the world. He wouldn't have private pains and buried traumas. But from her point of view also, the dismissal had changed the balance of the relationship. She now believed that she owed George a great obligation of loyalty, for he had showed great loyalty by resigning his own job in defence of her honour. This pattern of suspicion and possessiveness — on the one side — and loyalty in the face of all odds — on the other side — would play itself out over the next twenty-three years.

We see Johnston's half of these feelings epitomised in the notes which he made, prior to beginning *Clean Straw for Nothing*, about the relationship of David Meredith and Cressida Morley. As the author moves from the idea of Cressida as 'the unattainable prize' to that of Cressida as a possession, he again makes the link with his alter ego's quest to escape his upbringing:

> And she is his. The most precious thing he has ever owned. To lose her would be to lose everything. Still struggling onward from the dreary little house in Elsternwick, he has gained much, but nothing so precious as this. He cannot afford to lose it [...]
> For Cressida is Golden Boy's real laurel wreath.[34]

Of course, David Meredith's attitudes of possession and ownership in regard to his wife were largely the attitudes sanctioned by society in this post-war period. A great many Australian husbands at this time felt that their wives 'belonged' to them. While there was already developing a sort of underground resistance to such attitudes, it would be a couple of decades before the resistance would really be felt. There are always some people, however, who are in the vanguard of rebellion. For Charmian Clift, any acceptance of being a possession was impossible. Her own ideal — of limitless freedom — was as strong as George's will to possess her. The sides of the battle were freedom versus control.

Were there moments at Sorrento when either Charmian or George wondered what on earth they had committed themselves to? Whatever they privately felt, there could be no backing out after their grand gesture. It would seem like giving in to the whole pessimistic post-war ambience. Moreover, despite the uneasiness of this period, it was at the Sorrento cottage that the couple established the routine of writing together that was to be the cement for their relationship over the next two decades. At this particular time, Clift worked on her short stories. Meanwhile Johnston began a novel called *Moon at Perigee*; set in India, this potboiler features an embittered painter who is redeemed by his love for a girl with Charmian's green eyes.[35]

The image of Charmian and George writing together is a potent one: two people bashing away at two typewriters on the one table. Stacks of typescript — his spilling over into hers; hers ending up in the middle of his — the air wreathed with cigarette smoke ... This is one of the few public conceptions of the relationship of Charmian and George that is absolutely accurate. But into this picture must be put the talking which was a vital part of the writing process. If this image is the key to the relationship, it is also the key to the curious collaboration that took these two authors through more than twenty-one books, a bundle of radio programs, a twelve-part television serial and various other theatre and film projects.

As he worked, George would pass pages of typescript across to Charmian for immediate editing as well as encouragement. At midday, the couple would stop and have a few beers, and George would expound his ideas for plots and characters to Charmian. Alternative lines of development would weave back and forth as the two passed the skein of story to each other. By the end of a session, it would be hard to tell whose idea was whose. At this time of their life, it did not matter.

This was a writing process in which talking was a first or second draft, at least for George Johnston. Charmian was the 'sounding board' on which he tested out all his ideas; years later he would describe her as his 'verbal collaborator' and 'best critic'.[36] In this context, it is interesting to hear Ruth Park's rather terse comment on the writing methods of her husband D'Arcy Niland:

> He was one of those writers able to use selected people as sounding boards. It is not a happy situation for the sounding board, especially when that person is trying to work, and when that person is herself darkly secretive, never speaking of any work until it is completed.[37]

Like Park, Clift was one of these private writers. To understand just how very public a writer Johnston was, it must be remembered that he had learned to write in a crowded newsroom where journalists often shared work as they raced to a deadline on a particular story. In his own words, he 'was very facile and churned out books at the drop of a semi-colon'.[38] Indeed, as his colleague Geoffrey Hutton noted: 'When [George] was hot after an idea he would type like a road drill [...] He was always impatient to hammer out his story to a dramatic finish'.[39]

Charmian Clift's time in journalism had been far too brief for her to develop such rapid and communal writing habits. She was, as George described her, 'a slow, painstaking, very private writer'.[40] She did not show the typescript of work in progress to him, or anyone, although she did sometimes talk to George about the general lines of her stories and characters.

Although this difference between the public method of George Johnston and the private process of Charmian Clift would create problems, these would not appear for a while. And anyway, even when they did, it was still the writing, and especially the talking-about-writing, that would provide the enduring bond of this relationship. To sit together and have a drink at midday and run through the hypothetical alternatives of plots and characters would always be a vital part of the domestic and professional routine of these two.

For Charmian, there was something else about George as a writer which would make up for just about anything. He recognised her as a fellow writer, and indeed for many years he even publicly acknowledged that by literary standards she was a better writer than he was.[41] In George Johnston, Charmian Clift had got what she wanted: a man who allowed her — indeed, encouraged her — to write. Given this, any attempts to intrude upon other private things seemed a minor problem, at least at this stage.

* * *

After a few weeks at Sorrento, the couple returned to the Post Office Hotel. Melbourne was depressing: while it was now October, the weather was still wintery and everyone was still talking about the same old scandal. An added strain for Charmian was the disapproval of George's family. When he took her to meet his parents, and his brother Jack and sister-in-law Pat, she felt as if they regarded her as an adulterer and home-breaker. Although Charmian was perhaps overly sensitive about this, it is certainly the case that Pat was a committed Catholic who could not approve of George leaving his wife and child for another woman. Jack, meanwhile, reacted badly to what he saw as the posh side of Charmian — which of course was the cosmopolitan manner that this small town girl adopted when she felt ill at ease. To someone like Jack, Charmian would seem to be 'bunging on side'. Her manner of speaking would contribute to this impression, especially because her accent intensified when she felt unsure of herself.

The perception that George's family did not like her or accept her would continue to nag at Charmian for years, and George himself would see the situation as a matter of two sides of a family conflict. In *My Brother Jack*, the excruciating scene in which the narrator takes his fiancée, Helen, to a gathering at his parental home reflects his family's reaction not to his first wife, but to Charmian. The 'antagonisms that would never be forgiven' are presented as particularly concerning the narrator, his fiancée and his brother Jack.[42]

For Charmian in 1946, faced with rejection on all sides, the solution was obviously to cut and run. One drab Sunday morning she and George drove one of her army friends to the railway station to catch the Sydney train; suddenly unable to bear it any longer, she suggested to George that they too should get out and go to Sydney.[43] As well as being fed up with Melbourne, Charmian had reason to head north at this time: her father, though still working at the quarry, had been ill recently,[44] and it was more than two years since she had seen her family and her birthplace. And so the couple decided to travel up the coast road and stop at Kiama before reaching Sydney. Charmian had met George's family; it was now time for him to meet hers.

The prospect of bringing George to her home town caused Charmian mixed emotions. On the one hand, she looked forward to showing him her favourite places — and to showing her man off to her family and to those people who had sneered last time she'd come home. On the other hand, however, there was an element of risk involved. Would George still think everything about her was beautiful when he saw the squalid little place where she had grown up? Even more importantly — what if he discovered some of the shameful things about her past?

As it turned out, everything went so well that the couple ended up spending some months in the cottage with Charmian's parents and her grandmother Emma. Although Charmian and George were openly 'living in sin', this did not bother Syd, who enjoyed yarning with George. Meanwhile Amy and George got on famously.[45] However, Charmian's mother was worried that George might return to his wife and child in Melbourne.[46] And so she went out of her way to encourage this successful prospective son-in-law, and to try to ensure that, despite Charmian's troubled past, she would make a good marriage. But while the family had good reason to like George, it is significant that he even won over those North Kiama neighbours who found Charmian herself standoffish and hard to talk to.[47] This is proof beyond all question of George's legendary ability to 'charm the birds out of the trees'.

This honeymoon summer in Kiama was the perfect antidote to Sorrento: blue and gold Illawarra days spent surfing or fishing or lazing about the beach; nights of romance, picnicking by moonlight or lolling in the warm dark sea. This freedom was particularly welcome after the scrutiny that the relationship had occasioned in Melbourne. As to Charmian's happiness, the best indication is provided by the holiday snapshots. In photo after photo, she seems to be bursting with joy and pride, as if she can't quite believe her luck. Even more remarkable is the fact that, for once in her life, she isn't posing for the camera. Her eyes are on her lover.

George's feeling about the harmony of this time emerges in the Lebanon Bay passage of *Clean Straw for Nothing*:

> We have been given our own small vision of Paradise, and this share of Paradise has been contained and complete in itself. There has been no other world around us, no intrusion from past or future, everything has been held in a long pause within the sea and the sand and the winds and the high sky.[48]

At Kiama, George saw the quintessential form of the quality in Charmian which had initially drawn him to her. This was the part of Charmian which he saw as the wild pagan, or the free child of nature with sand between her toes. His sense that Charmian was somehow more 'natural' than himself was affirmed when he saw her against the backdrop of her dramatic childhood beach, which contrasted so strongly with his early memories of flat Melbourne bayside suburbs. This naturalness, as he saw it, was tied up with an ability to live more intensely; and it implied a knowledge of the meaning of life or the reason for living, which he felt was denied to his cramped spirit. But an even more important part of the Kiama experience, as far as George would see it, was that it was here that he witnessed for the first time another extraordinary element of Charmian's 'pagan side'. This was the mystic or dreaming aspect of Charmian; the part of her which was connected with her innermost privacy and longing. For many years, this would rank with the 'naturalness' and 'freedom' and 'honesty' as the reason to love her.

In the Lebanon Bay passage of *Clean Straw*, Johnston has the narrator remember how Cressida at this time 'would stare away, quite withdrawn, as if listening to some music that was only for her ears'. At night sometimes, he would 'follow her dumbly to the edge of the crisping sands' and watch as she communed with whatever it was she was listening for:

> Sometimes she would stand there as if spellbound, staring out across the ocean's slow deep heartbeat to the black platform that supported the prodigality of southern stars, and on her rapt face there was an utter absence of dismay. She seemed to exist, then and there, in her own assured entitlement to freedom [...]
>
> I still remember that infinitely disturbing impression she gave of only awaiting some cue or some encouragement — perhaps even only some other unquestioning human alliance — to release all the forces she was holding in check and reach a pure, rapturous intensity of living that seemed as alien to me then as some far-off foreign land.[49]

This description — retrospective and semi-fictionalised though it is — captures something that would become one of the many paradoxes in the relationship between George and Charmian. Although in the Kiama honeymoon Charmian's private feyness renewed George's sense of the specialness of the woman he loved, this passage is bristling with danger signs as the narrator — alien, foreign, from a far-off land — is left 'dumbly' outside this mystery which perhaps could be released into 'rapturous intensity' by 'some other unquestioning human alliance'. Even this private mysticism is a sexual challenge, charged with the possibility that some other man will provide greater fulfilment. Yet it is also linked with the other challenge of the 'entitlement to freedom'.

For the moment, however, none of these dangers was apparent. And so the couple lingered, exploring the landscape and their new relationship, through Christmas and into the new year of 1947. It was, perhaps, even as late as February before they continued up the coast to the city.

In these post-war years, the shortage of rental accommodation in Sydney was so acute that landlords were able to extort 'key money' amounting to hundreds of pounds in addition to the first week's rent.[50] Unable to find a flat, Charmian and George took a room at a seedy Kings Cross hotel. They had only been there a short time when the news came: on 7 March 1947 Syd Clift died of cancer. Charmian had known he was ill — but not that ill. Down at North Kiama the neighbours were also shocked, and Syd's workmates were very hurt because Amy had kept her husband's death so private that nobody knew about it until they saw the burial taking place in the Bombo cemetery.[51]

While the weeks Charmian had recently spent with her father had been happy, she would never forgive him the tyrannies of her childhood. There was little time, however, to think about the past, for it was around now that Charmian realised that she was pregnant. To some extent the circumstances were the same as those of her pregnancy five years earlier: once again she was unmarried and living in a cheap room in Kings Cross. This time, however, she need not fear the pity which the single girl suffers; this time she was unashamed and overjoyed.

In Clean Straw for Nothing, when Cressida Morley tells David Meredith of her pregnancy, he is beset by a 'flurry of panic'. 'I'm not divorced', he exclaims. 'We can't get married'. But Cressida replies: 'Who said anything about getting married? [...] We love each other, don't we?'[52] Charmian, like Cressida, wasn't bothered about the legalities of the situation, but George was mortified at the thought of having an illegitimate child.[53] He had previously been unable to get his wife to agree to a divorce, for Elsie was sure that sooner or later George would leave Charmian and return to the marital fold. This wasn't a completely irrational hope. However, once Charmian was pregnant, George was able to use this to put pressure on his wife. The divorce process was quick in the immediate post-war climate, and on 28 April a decree nisi was granted. However, the law required that three months elapse before subsequent marriage.[54]

The pregnancy brought to an end the directionless state which the couple had been in since their dismissal from the Argus. They decided that George would move into a furnished room above a Kings Cross restaurant and get a job in Sydney, while Charmian would go back to the healthy environment of Kiama; George would travel down to join her at weekends.[55]

Given his reputation, George soon obtained a position as a features writer on the afternoon newspaper, the *Sun*.[56] Although he would now be earning a reasonable salary, the couple had no savings and would have to find a lump sum of 'key money' in order to secure a proper place to live. Under this imperative, writing became a matter of urgent economic necessity. At George's suggestion, they decided to collaborate on a novel.[57]

Of all the traveller's tales that George had told Charmian, the one that she found most fascinating was the story of the five weeks he had spent trekking through the high valleys of the Ta Hsueh Shan mountain range in remote Tibet. He had also written about this experience, in his Asian travel book *Journey Through Tomorrow*.[58] Both authors could see this exotic background as being good potential for work of fiction. While George Johnston's account of the Tibetan journey was to provide the raw material for the novel *High Valley*, the place and the people would be transformed by Charmian Clift, who drew upon material which she knew like the back of her hand.

The story concerns a young man named Salom, who is very much an outsider figure. Chinese by birth, he was left behind as a child in Tibet by the Communist army, yet when he returns to China, his own people spurn him. An old pedlar tells the youth that he need not be ashamed of his origins, for the Communist army is 'an army of heroes':

> I think it is wrong to regard this army as evil. For it was an army
> made unconquerable by the very fact that it could not live with
> the thought of defeat [...] When a man dies he should seek but a
> single word to be brushed on the tablet above his grave.
> Undefeated. That is the word, boy. *Undefeated*.[59]

On the advice of the pedlar, Salom returns to Tibet to seek out the remote and beautiful Valley of the Dreaming Phoenix. In this high valley, Salom falls in love with a pure maiden named Veshti, who is the headman's daughter. The novel spins into a dozen subplots before the two lovers are cast out by the community. Deciding to live in exile, they ride off towards the mountain pass — only to be trapped in a mighty blizzard. In the face of certain doom, Veshti tells Salom: 'I am glad we are setting out together. Wherever the journey should take us — I am glad we travel together'.

Sweetly virtuous to the last, she wishes 'to become [his] wife'. The story ends 'with her naked body burning under his ...' The last word, however, is left for the Living Buddha who, returning in the spring to conduct the funerary rites over the naked and frozen bodies of the lovers, echoes the pedlar's words with the declaration that: 'They were the *undefeated!*'[60]

Although no drafts of this work remain, there is a considerable amount of both external and internal evidence about its writing. The bulk of the work was done between about March and August 1947, but the polishing was not completed until the end of the year.

Describing the collaborative process, the authors explained that they wrote 'a careful synopsis', and then divided up the chapters so that each section was initially written by one author working alone. They then 'exchanged ideas and rewrote each other's work if necessary', so that the text was 'continually revised as [they] went along'.[61] While both authors individually rewrote and polished their own bits, Clift also acted as editor and arbiter on Johnston's work.

For most of the writing process, Charmian was at the Bombo cottage, working alone on the front verandah table. With his full-time job at the *Sun*, George was not able to get much done during the week. Margaret Backhouse gives a vivid picture of how the couple worked at Kiama on weekends:

> George and Charmian would be sitting at the old deal table [...] each with a typewriter, going for their lives. George would be typing away, typing away, typing away, almost singing as he's going, typing away, give it a little thought, puffing cigarettes, typing away, typing away.
>
> Charmian would do a little bit, think, tear it up, chuck it in the wastepaper basket, get up and walk around, stalk around, and so on, but when she put it down, it was right. And eventually she'd pass over what she'd written to George.
>
> He'd read it, he'd pass over what he'd written — he'd have *this* much for her to read, but she'd have a little bit like that for him to read, you see. And then they'd put their heads together and say, 'Now what are we going to keep and what are we going to cut?' [...]
>
> And there might be a stony silence for a while or something, or one of them might say something rude, *but* they'd come together. And it would be, 'All right, we'll do it this way!'[62]

Johnston's journalistic background had trained him to churn out prose as if for an urgent deadline. Indeed, he had produced the 35 000 word Tibet section of *Journey Through Tomorrow* in only nineteen hours. However, as he readily admitted, this facility caused him to 'grab at the immediate idea or the immediate image', thus producing 'a kind of superficial slickness'.[63] In the writing of *High Valley*, Margaret commented, 'Charmian used to pull him up, you see, because he was inclined to sort of skim along over the top, when he could have gone a bit deeper'.[64]

Again and again, George Johnston paid tribute to Charmian Clift's input. A year after the novel was finished, he stated: 'If there is any quality in this book it is the work of my wife. She is responsible for characterisation and emotional content. I was the journalist who provided the substance, she was the artist who provided the burnish'.[65] And in a biographical note for the book's American publishers he described the collaboration as 'a fair 50–50, I contributing most of the descriptive material as a journalist, she supplying the emotional structure and theme'.[66]

As Margaret remembered this division of labour, Charmian was 'encouraging' George to talk about his time in Tibet, 'and she was taking his descriptions of people and places and all the rest of it, but the people in particular, and *moulding* them into a character'. In 'moulding' her Tibetans, Charmian Clift was able to use local clay. Although the Valley of the Dreaming Phoenix combines Johnston's accounts of S-le-t'o with the miniature geographical model that lay just beyond the verandah of *Hilldrop*, Clift also drew upon people she had known all her life. While Muhlam, the headman of the valley, could be a pen-picture of Charmian's father, there is at times an uncanny similarity between the rest of the clan and certain North Kiama neighbours.

In the heroines, however, Clift literally expressed her self. If the 'elusive' Veshti represents one side of Charmian Clift, the novelist drew upon her more obvious qualities in Veshti's foil, Bitola — 'a vivid, sensuous creature whose beauty [is] the beauty of bombast and colour and being alive'. Like her creator, she is tall and broad-shouldered, and her laugh is 'a husky sound deep in her throat'; her gaze is 'insolent'. With this contrast between 'hard' and 'soft' heroines, Clift developed the device which had already been evident in her 'Other Woman' short story; she would use this same opposition throughout her career as a novelist. In later couplings of female characters such as Meg and Julia, Milly and Kathy, and even Cordelia and Cressida, we can see the mirroring of 'soft' Veshti and 'hard'

Bitola — though after *High Valley* the primary focus is always on the 'hard' heroine.

If Veshti and Bitola are opposites, the heroine and hero are twin souls, and the alienation which sets Veshti and Salom apart from other people of the 'tribe' reflects the experience of the novel's creators. Although Charmian Clift and George Johnston came from very different family backgrounds, both had felt themselves to be outsiders to their families and their environments. With the theme of rejection and exile, the story also reflects the novelists' recent experience. In the scene in which Salom and Veshti, spurned by the tribesfolk, set out desperately to cross the mountains, we can see George and Charmian — drummed out of Melbourne — heading off to an unknown future. And in the Living Buddha's last words we can read a kind of defiant battle cry of the novelists: they had been kicked out of their brilliant careers, and the world had disapproved of their grand passion, yet 'they were the *undefeated*!'

On another level, too, the novel expressed some of the frustration of the writers' immediate past and their concern about the values of the post-war world in which they lived. Although the story is a heady combination of the genres of fairytale, quest, cowboy yarn and exotic romance, this is also a political novel, written well in advance of its time. Prevented by the *Argus* management from publishing his views about China, Johnston tried in *High Valley* to explain something of the situation to Western readers. The book's message is a quiet plea for tolerance. While Salom's moral development is dependent on his learning to respect the beliefs which he personally cannot endorse, the crucial lesson is given by the Living Buddha, who indicts the West for being contemptuous of things it doesn't understand. At the same time, the representation of Salom, the man from the Han country, is one of the first dignified, three-dimensional and positive portrayals of a Chinese person to appear in Australian literature. Such pleas for the understanding and tolerance of Australia's Asian neighbours were to become an urgent theme of Clift and Johnston's work in the 1960s.

By the middle of 1947, George Johnston had managed to rent a poky bedsitter at Manly. After this, Charmian would come up and stay sometimes, and meet some of the new friends George was making in Sydney. However, she continued to spend most of her time down at her mother's house, which she regarded as her permanent address.[67]

One person who made George's acquaintance through journalistic circles at around this time was Allan Ashbolt, who was one of the directors of the experimental Mercury Theatre, along with an actor friend named Peter Finch. Attached to the theatre was a small acting school, and every so often Ashbolt would try 'to brighten up the students' by bringing in 'someone from outside [...] to talk about their life — this was a brain-expanding exercise'. So he rang George and invited him to address a class, and when George turned up he was accompanied by Charmian, whom Allan hadn't met before. The Mercury provided an easy atmosphere for George to speak in, but for Allan Ashbolt — who sat in the audience, next to Charmian — the most memorable aspect of this occasion was the sight of her anxiously watching George on the stage:

> He was a really relaxed, easygoing sort of talker — he spoke extremely well — I mean, he had these students fascinated. He was talking about his big journey — the one towards the end of the war — over in China and Tibet and so on. And he just stood there and talked and talked and talked — as he could! You know, it was an extraordinary gift [...]
>
> What really interested me was that while George was up there in front of the students, talking, Charmian was sitting next to me and she was nervous all the time about him — you know — '*What's he going to say?*' and '*Is he going to do it properly?*'
>
> She was whispering, '*Is he all right? Is he? Is he? Do you think they're following him?*'
>
> And I'd say, 'Yes, they're fascinated!'
>
> '*Are you sure?*'
>
> And she was sitting there and her hands were going up to her face, and I could see the very very deep — not just *concern* for him — but the *feeling* she had for him. It wasn't that she particularly wanted him to be a success with the students, it was just that she didn't want him to fall to pieces or to start rambling or anything like that.[68]

Whether or not Peter Finch was present on this occasion is unclear, but it was at about this time that the actor became a friend of both George and Charmian.[69] However, he certainly did not play the intimate role in the couple's life which the so-called 'Finch character' — Archie Calverton — plays in *Clean Straw for Nothing*.

At the end of July the final papers for the divorce came through, and a week later, on 7 August, Charmian Clift and George Johnston were married at the Manly registry office. In interviews given in later years, the couple would backdate this event to May.[70] This was not an attempt to sanitise the record, for May was still well and truly after the baby's conception. However, May was the month when these two romantics would always celebrate their anniversary. It had been in May 1945 that they had met at the Hotel Australia, and it was May 1946 when they had met again in the lift of the *Argus* building. May was when the marriage of true minds had taken place.

The wedding ceremony was distinctly low key. The bride, 'radiantly and unashamedly with child', [71] wore a light blue sack dress with a pillbox hat. She didn't seem to care what she looked like, but Mary Andrews — one of George's new Sydney friends — thought the whole outfit looked so awful that she insisted on lending Charmian her turquoise brooch.[72] Later that day there was a small party at the home of Arthur Polkinghorne, one of George Johnston's colleagues from the *Sun*.

Despite Charmian's unceremonious attitude to the wedding, marriage itself was terribly important to her. It was a commitment for life. It did not matter that the ceremony was performed at the registry office, with none of the words of the traditional service: as far as Charmian was concerned, she had taken George for richer or for poorer; for better or for worse; in sickness or in health; till death did them part. She would keep these vows, at whatever cost.

A couple of weeks after the marriage, the first full draft of *High Valley* was finished; the authors wanted to have some feedback before the next stage of revision. On 26 August they visited one of Charmian's army friends, Jean Skea, in hospital where she had that day given birth to a daughter, and they presented her with a typescript of the novel for her to read and comment upon. Although they subsequently ignored Jean's literary recommendations, they were keen to have her advice about parenting: after Jean and her daughter were out of hospital the couple would sometimes visit, and George 'bathed, changed, petted and patted [the infant] with all the devotion of a man who had missed his first baby'. George and Charmian's delight in the imminent prospect of their own offspring was 'infectious'.[73]

Having decided that their child was a boy, the couple chose the name Martin, after an earlier preference for Julian; despite Charmian and George's agnosticism, the name was suggested by the fact that the baby was due around St Martin's Day.[74]

It was actually on 12 November, the day after the feast of St Martin, that Charmian gave birth to Martin Clift Johnston at King George V Hospital, Camperdown.[75] As part of her antenatal preparation she 'had painted every toenail a different colour so that [she] would have something nice to look at'. Two decades later, the columnist wrote an account of this event:

> When I had my first baby I had it grandly in the biggest and most modern hospital in Sydney and they were all so damned efficient that they would have aseptically amputated all the joy from such an experience if I hadn't been as stubborn as I am. I still remember with a shudder how they slammed the lift doors in my husband's distraught face while they conducted me coldly and efficiently to the upper regions of pain [...] It was a torture chamber.[76]

Of course, this was not Charmian Clift's first baby, and her first time in a natal hospital had hardly been grand. But Charmian Clift the columnist was not the mother of Jennifer: this was the first child of the public Charmian. And besides, this was Charmian's first real chance to experience motherhood. A delightful example of her cluckiness at this time is a letter which she wrote in the persona of nineteen week old Martin to Jean Skea's infant daughter. This is how the typewritten text appears:

> Dear Miss Skea,
> My Mummie says (ccc I can't call you Lindy becorse we havnt bin intorduced. I think that's a bit oldfashioned becorse as i say to her we live in a modern age mum. But she says back in your box mudguts youve got a lot to learn yet. I dont think that s fair becorse as YOU CAN see i can tipe all right all ready ...
> WIL1 you please thank yOur M8—xxx mummie and daddie for the nice presents. plutos ear tastes even nicer than the side of the bath and you know how GoOd t7-htg that is.
> well cheerio mIss Skea and heres hopping to mAke your accantiance soon. mummie says that isn't right but i dont think she knows anyway ... [77]

This epistle was signed 'Martin Johnston' in a huge scrawl that was clearly done by holding the pencil inside the baby's tiny fist.

Within a few days of Martin's birth, George Johnston's byline began to appear on the 'Sydney Diary' column in each afternoon's *Sun*.[78] Although this was essentially a chat column, it was prestigious and lucrative:

according to Mungo MacCallum, George Johnston now had the reputation of being the most highly paid journalist in Sydney, along with MacCallum himself.[79] Such a column was wonderfully suited to someone of George's gregariousness: it gave him a chance to get out and about and meet everyone who was anyone. It also made people very keen to meet George.

As George developed his new network of social and business contacts, Charmian was left out. By the time she met people, they were already George's friends. While Charmian seemed to most people to be socially at ease, she was in fact terribly insecure about her ability to make friends, and keep friends. From this time, she would start to assume that people were drawn to George, and that they simply accepted her because she was part of the deal. The wretched accommodation situation didn't help, for even after the birth of Martin, Charmian had to go back with the baby to Kiama.[80]

Things began to look up in the new year of 1948, when the couple finally managed to find a two-bedroom flat in a block grandiosely named *Stratton Hall* at 26 Simpson Street, Bondi. The building was liver-coloured brick and the view looked over the rooftops of suburbia towards Dover Heights.[81] Charmian couldn't see the ocean. But the beach was in walking distance and for the moment even the prospect of the claustrophobia of flat life didn't bother her: at last the family had a place of their own.

10

Terribly Difficult Years for a Young Woman

At this point I should have taken wings and started to fly but at this
point also, of course, I was involved in having children [...] I think those
are terribly difficult years for any young woman and for a young woman
who wants to write or paint or anything else, even more so.[1]

Charmian would later write that it was in 1948 that for the first time she
saw 'home' as being somewhere other than the house where she had
grown up.[2] In fact, the family home was in the process of disintegration.
Mardie Emma, now aged eighty-six, needed full-time care and went into a
nursing home in Sydney; she would die in June of this year in the suburb of
Collaroy. About this same time Amy would also move to Sydney. Her main
base was with Margaret in the inner western suburbs, but she often spent
the night at Bondi, where she shared the second bedroom with her
grandson Martin.[3]

For Charmian, the notion of 'home' was a potent one, representing
marriage, family, commitment, love and security. For all her restlessness, she
needed to have a safe and constant refuge, a place where she could retreat.
While not a natural housewife, she was very much a home-maker.

One thing Charmian and George had in common was the joy they got
from sharing their home with other people. From this time they would
begin to develop their reputations as social catalysts, and would frequently
keep Open House at the Simpson Street flat on Saturday nights —
occasions described by one guest as 'generous and flamboyant parties',[4]

at which Charmian would cook up cauldrons of spaghetti while George would ply everyone with grog. Guests were drawn from Sydney's artistic and media circles: Peter and Tamara Finch, William Dobell, Kenneth Slessor, Colin Simpson, Mary and Gordon Andrews, Paul Brickhill, Diana and Mungo MacCallum, Barbara Jefferis and John Hinde, Arthur and Monica Polkinghorne, Wilfrid Thomas and Bettina Dixon.

Although now, as later, the couple did a great deal of socialising, they saw this as part of the creative process. Getting together with other people was for them 'a very great stimulus'[5]; conversation was 'a first draft for writing'.[6] And George Johnston liked to get instant feedback on his work-in-progress by reading it out loud at these gatherings.[7]

It was at one of these Saturday night parties, around April or May 1948, that a journalist colleague named Bill Thomas brought along his twenty-one year old daughter, Antonia Hazelwood.[8] Charmian was reminded of one of her favourite Yeats poems by Toni's thick golden hair, while Toni — who was aspiring to be a writer at this time[9] — was very much taken with this slightly older woman who was starting to make a name for herself. As well as both having a young child, the two women shared a love of poetry, which Charmian would read from books propped up on the taps while she did the washing up, and which she would recite at length to her new friend.

Not long after this, the caretaker's flat at Stratton Hall became vacant, and Charmian arranged for Toni and her husband, Laurie Hazelwood, to get the lease. From the beginning, Toni did not like George. ('I'm biased', she would say nearly fifty years later. 'She was my friend, not him. Not George'.[10]) George reciprocated the dislike. This situation suited Charmian very well: at last she had a friend of her own, someone who could be counted on to like *her* more than they liked her husband, someone who would give *her* loyalty no matter what. In her accounts of her friendship with Charmian, Toni always referred to the line from Yeats to which her friend would frequently allude in a promise that: 'I love you for yourself alone/ And not your yellow hair'.[11]

It was, of course, *Charmian* who wanted to be loved for herself alone, and not for her beauty. When the alliance with Toni began, this was the first intimate female friend that Charmian had had since Thellie Brown. While now it was Charmian who played the role of older and wiser girl, in other ways the alliance was like the early innocent days when Skipper and Buddy would sing along to the *Boomerang Songster* and set each other's hair. Charmian and Toni painted their toenails and went out to afternoon tea in silly hats, and they giggled together and gossiped together and complained about their husbands. On one occasion they even got 'tiddly' together on home brew. This was a novelty for Charmian, who usually only drank in moderation.[12]

At about the same time as the new friendship with Toni, something happened which seemed to Charmian to be quite the most extraordinary and wonderful thing in the world. When she and George had completed *High Valley* towards the end of the previous year,[13] they decided not to submit the text to a publisher but to enter it in the *Sydney Morning Herald* competition for an unpublished novel. The £2000 prize made this the richest literary award in Australia at this time; it had been won in the inaugural year of 1947 by Ruth Park's *The Harp in the South*. Now, in the first week of May 1948, Charmian and George were invited to the office of the *Sydney Morning Herald,* where they were informed that their work had won first prize. This seemed to fulfil the prophecy of the book itself. The two lovers were not just the undefeated, but the triumphant winners! While the money represented a great windfall[14] for Charmian and George, the fact of winning was the main thing.

It was on Saturday 8 May 1948 that the news was officially announced in an article below a bold two-column headline on the front page of the *Sydney Morning Herald* :

'HERALD' NOVEL

PRIZES

Husband And Wife

Win £2000

Some pages later, in the literary section, there was a long and favourable review of the book as well as the judges' reports on the prizewinners and runners-up, and photographs appeared of 'Charmian (Mrs George Johnston) and Mr George Johnston'. That afternoon, the *Sun* carried an article on page 2 headed 'JOURNALIST, WIFE WIN NOVEL PRIZE'.[15]

It was unfortunate, however, that these two writers made their first appearance as novelists together, and in such a blaze of publicity, for it was from this time that the public image of Charmian Clift and George Johnston as a couple united in love and work began to take on a mythic element. As we shall see, this myth would put a strain on the Johnston relationship from a very early time, and by the later years would lock Charmian into a more general disjunction between her public and private lives.

If the romantic myth would be hard to sustain, the public image of the literary partnership contained from the beginning an additional problem for Clift, who was depicted as very much the junior colleague; it was to prove virtually impossible for her to change this perception. Publicity photographs taken at this time showed Johnston as dapper man of the world and Clift as ardent ingénue. This conception of Older Man and Young Girl would become part of the public image.

Two decades after the award, Clift wryly reminisced: 'I was twenty-four and suddenly found myself a literary celebrity except that most people didn't think I'd had much to do with it'. Her husband agreed that 'For a long time there was this sort of legend that I really only put her name to it'.[16]

While Johnston himself paid public tribute at this time to Clift's role in the novel, the origin of this legend is encapsulated in the *Sun* headline, with its reference to 'JOURNALIST, WIFE'. Both the *Herald* and *Sun* articles described the winners as 'Mr George H. Johnston, a Sydney journalist, and his wife Charmian'. In neither of these features, nor in the judges' reports in the *Herald* book pages, was the surname Clift mentioned. On the other hand, both papers played up Johnston's experience as a war correspondent. But if 'Charmian (Mrs George Johnston)' was accorded a minor role, the qualities praised in the novel were those qualities which she had contributed.

The judges' report noted that the work 'derives no advantage from its remote setting', adding that 'the reader feels [...] the working of a higher imagination'. The novel's style was declared to be even better than that of *The Harp in the South*: 'The writing has a real distinction, a sureness and delicacy of touch unequalled so far in the two competitions for novels'. The *Sydney Morning Herald* reviewer declared: 'Don't think, if you have read *Journey Through Tomorrow* [...] that you have covered the material of *High Valley*. To do so would be to see the canvas, but miss the artistry later laid across it'.[17]

Winning this competition represented a major breakthrough in the careers of both Charmian Clift and George Johnston. Although more than half the monetary value of the prize would disappear in tax,[18] the real value of the award was that it brought the novelists to the attention of the critics and reading public of their own country, and even gave them an opening overseas. The novel would be published in Sydney by Angus & Robertson in mid 1949, and in early 1950 the prestigious British company Faber and Faber would bring out their edition — to glowing reviews.[19] Also by the beginning of 1950 the American publishers Bobbs-Merrill would decide to bring out a US edition, with a $10 000 promotional campaign.[20]

Later in life Charmian Clift would often say that perhaps one gets the prize at the beginning, and then has to work for it or pay for it afterwards.[21] As far as *High Valley* was concerned, she would pay for this prize for the rest of her life.

For Charmian, this should have been a doorway, a beginning, a ticket to adventure. She felt that she was entitled to some reward — beyond the money, and even beyond the five minutes of reflected glory which winning had brought her. But there was no new start.

About a month after the *Herald* announcement, Charmian realised that she was pregnant again. Martin was only seven months old, and now she was committed to yet another small human being for whom she would be responsible for many years to come. Rather than taking to the heavens, Icarus was well and truly stuck on the ground. A decade and a half later, speaking of this time in Sydney when her writing was just starting to be successful, the author would say:

> At this point I should have taken wings and started to fly but at
> this point also, of course, I was involved in having children, and
> for many many years I had this dual thing, the frustrations that
> are inevitable with any creative person being tied and bound and
> at the same time struggling, beating one's head against a wall to
> do what one wants to do. I think those are terribly difficult years
> for any young woman and for a young woman who wants to
> write or paint or anything else, even more so.[22]

But this was a retrospective view of the situation. At the time, the young woman's body took over. Through this pregnancy Charmian became 'deliciously, sleepily animal', and was given to listening to 'terribly romantic music, études and sonatas' from the couple's large collection of 78s, and weeping buckets at ballet music, as she liked to do.[23]

A vivid picture of Charmian around this time was given by Ruth Park, who remembered her arriving at one of the annual 'wisteria parties' given by 2UE executive Stan Coleman, to celebrate the 'sumptuous purple' blossoms that draped his apartment balcony each spring time. On this occasion a number of 'toad types' were present:

> At the time of Stan's party, Charmian was pregnant with Shane.
> She sailed in like a ship, the toads tossing about in her wake. Was

she beautiful? Yes. Not extraordinarily, or astoundingly or any of the other words sometimes used of her, but beautiful in a frank, summery way that endeared her to everyone. Her walk, carriage, quick, glancing expressions, radiant health and vitality were what drew the eye. Charmian reminded me of the Winged Victory of Samothrace, and I thought this long before she learned that her spiritual home was Greece. It's queer the things one remembers — she was the first person I ever saw with pencilled eyes, though I expect she used a lead pencil, as eyeliner was unknown in Sydney's virgin fastnesses. I was much taken with the novelty.[24]

During this same period, Ruth found George to be 'always a pleasant, witty and relaxed person, with an attractive voice and a faintly comical nose'. Her description reveals that there was already a romantic myth surrounding the couple:

Oddly, though George must have only been in his mid-thirties then, we younger ones all regarded him as being much older, maybe forty-five, with one foot in the grave. He was the sophisticated Older Man who had somehow snared the love of a young girl. No one doubted that love then.

It was a few months after this party, on 3 February 1949, that Charmian gave birth to a daughter. After considering the name Miranda,[25] the couple decided upon Shane. It was an unusual choice at the time — and particularly odd given that Clift had previously used it as the surname of the adulterous husband in her 1945 short story 'Other Woman', in which the first wife bore the name Jenny, borrowed from the writer's first daughter. This is an example of the way in which both Clift and Johnston would recycle names, moving back and forth between literature and life. A dozen years later, Clift would give the name Miranda to her alter ego in some of the first drafts of *The End of the Morning*. A few years after this, Johnston would use it for the daughter of David and Cressida in *Clean Straw for Nothing*.

For George Johnston, Shane would take the place of his first daughter Gae, whom he barely knew. But what did this daughter represent to Charmian? Perhaps this birth went some way to ease the pain that she had felt at relinquishing her first daughter; alternatively, it may sometimes have made the memory even sharper.

Whatever the case, Charmian had her hands full, with Martin at fourteen months as well as the new baby. She was very affectionate with the children and took pleasure in lavishing books and playthings upon them, making them special toys, and dressing them beautifully. George also loved the children dearly, and both parents were determined that Martin and Shane would have the educational advantages that they themselves had missed. But George could enjoy the children without perpetual responsibility.

A snapshot of the difference in the respective situations of the two authors is provided by the biographical questionnaires which they filled in for the American publishers of *High Valley*. Under 'Occupation other than writing' Johnston noted: 'Journalist with the *Sun*, Sydney, Australia. Former war correspondent and foreign correspondent. Correspondent for *Time*, Inc., New York 1942–43–44'. In this same category, Clift declared: 'Washing, sewing, scrubbing, polishing, ironing, cooking'. Under her 'Hobbies and special interests', Charmian Clift wrote: 'Books, music, paintings — and speculation upon the probable futures of my children'.[26] Despite her devotion to Martin and Shane, Charmian Clift found it terribly frustrating to try to juggle the equally demanding roles of mother and author. As well as this, she had to be both a normal wife and a writer's wife — part sounding board, part editor, part Muse.

The growth of the family also meant that money was getting tight. Towards the end of 1948, George Johnston had been promoted to Features Editor of the *Sun*,[27] but he sent money to his first wife (on a somewhat irregular basis) as well as supporting his new family, and the couple now, as always, spent all their available cash on books and records, food and grog — and other people. While both saw themselves as part of the Depression generation, their early experience did not turn them into penny-pinchers. Rather, with money as with life itself, they kept nothing in reserve. And if they indulged themselves, they also shared their good fortune: despite his growing commitments, Johnston would still shout drinks for all and sundry in the Long Bar of the Australia Hotel, even if he had to put the round on the slate.

Thus despite Johnston's salary, the (tax-depleted) *Herald* prize money, and advances on *High Valley*, writing was still an economic necessity. More importantly, it was a vocation, an addiction — for Charmian Clift probably more so than for George Johnston. In the 'Sydney 1949' section of *Clean Straw for Nothing* there is reference to the comparative critical and financial success of the novel which David Meredith (alone) had recently written:

Meredith's modest success as a creative writer made him, therefore, an envied novelty with an obligation to continue the struggle (which had nothing to do with his success as a journalist), and Cressida tried hard to urge him into committing to the gamble. The creative urge really did gnaw at him, and for a week or two he wavered, torn by the conflict in his ambitions. In the end he stuck to the safety of his position with the *Globe*, on the grounds that he was not justified in jeopardising to such a hazardous and precarious prospect the future of the children, a daughter, Miranda, having by this time been added to his responsibilities.[28]

It was in mid 1949 that the Angus & Robertson edition of *High Valley* appeared. George Johnston already had his name on nine books, including two potboiler novels,[29] but this was a first for Charmian Clift. In the flush of euphoria that any new writer feels on seeing her name on the cover of a book, did she, like Cressida Morley, suggest at this time that the couple should spurn security and try to live off their writing? Quite probably. For the moment, however, writing was a part-time job for both these authors. It was now that they started a habit of working at night after the children were asleep, battering away together at their typewriters on the dining room table until the early hours. But what were they producing?

A side project at this time was a collaboration with the composer Albert Arlen on a musical version of *The Sentimental Bloke*; George Johnston was supposed to write the libretto, and Charmian Clift was also involved to some extent.[30] For both writers, however, novels took precedence over scriptwriting. When *High Valley* won the prize, the *Sydney Morning Herald* noted that Johnston's wife had 'a novel in progress, *The Piping Cry*, a psychological murder set in a city'. Clift may have begun this alone but soon it would become a collaborative effort;[31] it would preoccupy the couple for the next three years.

Although Clift at this stage was still amenable to collaboration, one area of her work which she always kept for herself alone was the autobiographical material set in her home landscape. As she was also a writer who liked to have a number of irons in the fire at any time, it is quite likely that — during this time when the author was herself experiencing a new sort of family life — she returned to the various scraps of autobiographical text which went under the title of *Greener Grows the Grass*, and produced some of the domestic scenes concerning

Christine Morley, her siblings Judith and John, and her parents Alma and Tom, in the cottage and landscape that were directly lifted from North Kiama. And with her mother Amy frequently visiting, and no doubt talking about Margaret's daughters Christine and Judith, it would be little wonder if the names spilled into Clift's texts at this time. It was certainly the case that the author used the Kiama landscape, as well as Christine's diminutive 'Tina', in the short story 'Even the Thrush Has Wings', which was typed up and submitted for publication (apparently unsuccessfully) at this time.[32]

During this Bondi period, Clift also found a new outlet for her talent in radio scriptwriting. This was a peak period for the Australian Broadcasting Commission's Drama and Features department, under the directorship of Neil Hutchison, who had been brought out from the BBC to vitalise this area. On Sundays at 6.30 p.m. on Radio National and on Tuesdays at 8.00 p.m. on the Interstate Network there went to air challenging and entertaining programs which presented social or historical research within a dramatised framework. Regular features were the *Famous Women* series, highlighting the achievements of women through the ages, and the *Radio Diary* series, which opened windows into an extraordinary variety of fictional lives.

The novelist and scriptwriter Barbara Jefferis remembered how Neil Hutchison invited new people to write for the department. The array of talent included Jefferis herself, Colin Simpson, Mungo MacCallum and his wife Diana MacCallum, John Thompson and Patricia Thompson — and Charmian Clift and George Johnston. Hutchison was 'great to work for': while he had 'this terrific ability to fire you up and make you suggest things', he himself also had 'a marvellous ability to suggest work'. Once the subject for a program was decided, he let the writer run with it.[33]

Although, again according to Jefferis, Neil Hutchison was 'very fond of Charmian', and he saw a 'lyric quality' in her work, the role of Charmian Clift — and/or George Johnston — in Hutchison's team should not be overstated.[34] The couple's output was steady but not sensational. The first program by either of them to appear in the *ABC Weekly* radio guide was a piece by George Johnston for the Sunday night *Quality Street* program in late May 1949. From then until the end of 1950 Clift wrote four programs, Johnston five, with another two features written in collaboration.[35] At the ABC payment rate of £25 for an hour length play,[36] the total earnings from this work were a drop in the bucket of the Johnston family expenses, but at least this was a way for Clift to earn some money of her own.

The writer adapted quickly to the new medium, finding this sort of writing easier than the extended prose of a novel to fit into the spaces of her life as a mother and housewife. The collaborative nature of the radio medium also meant that she was able to work with her husband on some of the scripts, without the anxiety which collaborative novel-writing caused her. While the shortness of the period between commissioning and deadline prevented Clift from polishing every sentence to perfection, George Johnston's journalistic method of rapid research and writing was admirably suited to radio work.

Yet the research was just the beginning. The gift which both these writers brought to historical reconstruction was their ability to imagine themselves into the minds of people in distant times and places. The *ABC Weekly*'s promotional blurb for Clift's program on 'The Lady Bright' (described as a concubine to the Han court 'a century or two before the Christian era') noted that the author had 'captured in her script something of the fragile Oriental and almost porcelain quality of one of China's most beloved true stories'.[37]

For Charmian Clift, perhaps the most significant aspect of the radio scriptwriting was that it enabled her to gain some promotion for her own name. For any writer, this matter of making a name is a vital part of establishing an interior identity as an author, which in turn is part of the process of gaining the confidence to develop writing skills. The captions to three publicity photographs in the *ABC Weekly* program guide show an interesting development. In the first — August 1949 — the scriptwriter is named 'Charmian Johnston'. Four months later, in December, she is 'Charmian Clift, wife of Sydney journalist George Johnston'. After another four months, not only is her photo on the front cover of the radio guide, but it is labelled 'Charmian Clift, Australian Author'! Although the accompanying article went on to describe her as 'the wife of ...', this was the first significant recognition given to Charmian *Clift*.

And yet the images themselves tell a rather different story. The first — a head-and-shoulders portrait taken during a photo shoot on Bondi beach — shows Charmian, with her glowing health, looking like an advertisement for a food or beverage.[38]

The second photo is, in context, even more extraordinary. This was to promote her 'Diary of a Modern Woman' which, as we shall see, was concerned with the issue of a woman's right to be free to choose a career in preference to wifedom and motherhood. Yet here is Charmian, sitting with

Shane on one knee and with Martin pushing up at her other knee, as she reads a picture book to her children.[39] Rather than illustrating a program about women's rights, it looks like a promotion for the BBC children's series of this era, *Listen With Mother*.

The third image — the full cover — was to promote 'The Lady Bright'. This time, as Charmian looks ardently into the far distance, she gives an impression of the inspired soul rather than the healthy body. She is indeed the Lady Bright, the 'courageous and beautiful girl' who 'inspired poems, plays, operas and novels' and whose 'grave in the Gobi desert is the one place where green grass always grows'.[40]

Although we see a different Charmian Clift in each of these three images, all give the impression that professionally she is a beauty — perhaps one of the actresses who play the characters in the programs — rather than an author. What a contrast it is to see the photograph of Barbara Jefferis which the *ABC Weekly* ran at this same period.[41] Again, this is very 'feminine' compared to the portraits of male authors in suits looking serious. Barbara wears a floral frock and sits gracefully on the carpet in front of a huge vase of flowers. She is attractive and smiling broadly — but in her hands is a script, and the pose of this picture implies that the camera has captured an author reading her work-in-progress.

Of course, Charmian Clift colluded in her public image. Her experience posing for Margaret's portfolio, and later posing as a professional model, meant that when a camera was pointed at her she took on whatever role seemed appropriate to the place and occasion. And yet just as it sometimes seemed that she wrote in her husband's shadow, she also suffered as a writer from being in the shadow of her own public image. Her confidence in her work and talent could not have been boosted by the fact that the ABC program guide highlighted her work so frequently because of her photogenic face.

At the same time, the radio work wasn't real writing — not according to Clift's definition. It didn't satisfy the need within her to write extended passages of prose, and to go back over them and craft them into the shape she wanted. It didn't allow her to explore the depths of character, or to write the descriptions of place which were so essential to her particular style.

In other ways, too, Charmian was unfulfilled. By at least the end of 1949 — the second year at the Simpson Street flat — she was getting that familiar trapped feeling. The flat itself did not help. An endless vista of red bricks and tiled rooftops was not Charmian's favourite view, and it was hard to be cooped up inside the flat with two little children. She often took Martin and Shane to play on the beach, but it was all a far cry from the glamour and adventure that George had promised her. Like her alter ego character Sharon in the short story 'Other Woman', she felt she was becoming a 'suburban drudge'.

Far more stultifying than the architecture or the routines of married life was the social and political climate of Australia in this era. Speaking of this particular time, Charmian Clift later declared, 'I wanted desperately to leave. I didn't like Australia a bit'. At that time the country had, she felt, 'that very nasty feeling of post-war'. It was 'more prosperous than it had ever been' but seemed 'money-grubbing and greedy', 'cynical with the disillusionment of peace' and 'all the values [she] thought were important didn't seem to be there any more'. Besides, it was 'a cultural desert' where 'creative nourishment' was 'scanty'. And the licensing laws were 'barbarous'.[42]

In this post-war period, Australia was increasingly becoming uncomfortable for anyone of left-wing sympathies, as the Cold War witch-hunt began to spread. As in America, the arts were seen as potential breeding grounds for Communists or fellow travellers and, under a growing political climate of suspicion, Australia was becoming an unhappy place for artists, writers, musicians, actors, and creative people generally. In *Clean Straw for Nothing* this is reflected in a curious incident in which a British spy named Crossley tries to recruit David Meredith to become an anti-Communist secret agent in China; after the journalist refuses, he asks what will become of the fat dossier on him which Crossley has prepared. The spy replies, 'I shall probably hand it over to your Commonwealth Security people'. This episode would seem to be completely fictional, given Johnston's known antipathy for the anti-Communist side in the Chinese civil war. Certainly, ASIO currently maintain that they have no file on George Johnston.[43] (Of course, there is no way of checking this.) The likelihood is that the attempted recruitment was something which happened to a colleague of Johnston's and which the author worked into his novel in order to create a parallel between the political climate of suspicion and the narrator's own developing suspicion — for Meredith perceives Crossley to be one of his wife's 'regulars'.[44]

In this part of the novel Johnston also evokes the 'feeling of suffocation, of smothering under some soggy heavy blanket of timid conformity and dullness' current at this time. This perception was increased by the sense of antipodean isolation — 'that torturing affliction of feeling too far away from where anything important is happening, lost on the hidden undercurve of the world'.[45] Meanwhile, the very real worry about the atom bomb made some people feel that if they didn't hurry up and get to Europe, they might never see it: after all, the leader of the recently formed Liberal Party, Robert Menzies, called for the use of nuclear weapons to break the Berlin blockade in 1948.[46]

And so, while Charmian Clift and George Johnston were desperate to get out, they were not alone in their feelings.[47] More and more of the couple's friends kept heading off. Peter Finch and his wife Tamara had gone in October 1948.[48] Ruth Park had given them a farewell luncheon party at the Hotel Australia, at which Charmian, 'joyous and a little tipsy', had started 'excitedly anticipating' the time when she and George would also escape to London.[49] But by the end of 1949, Ruth and D'Arcy had set off for London too,[50] and Charmian and George were still stuck in Sydney.

On 10 December 1949 something happened which made the prospect of remaining in Australia even more insufferable for both Charmian and George. This was the election to the House of Representatives of a government composed of a coalition between the Country Party and the Liberal Party, under Robert Menzies. Its sweeping majority of seventy-four seats to Labor's forty-seven (and one Independent) had been won on an anti-progressive platform which included the dissolution of the Communist Party. The real agenda was the destruction of the trade union movement.

For anyone of left or even small 'l' liberal tendencies, this election spelled danger. For Charmian, the new prime minister represented the style of government which she would later characterise as 'Authoritarianism. Australian brand, I mean. Paternalistic brand, I mean'. She would personify this as 'Father' or (ironically) 'Dear Papa'.[51] In her use of this term we again see the political legacy which Syd Clift had bequeathed to his rebellious daughter — not so much by his rhetoric of freedom as his practice of domestic tyranny.

From the time of this election, the Johnstons' urge to leave Australia became imperative. Paradoxically, the Cold War which was the background to the new climate of anti-Communism would provide their escape hatch. In early 1950 Charmian and George learned that in another year or so they too would be able to get out,[52] for at this time Johnston's employer, Associated Newspapers, offered him a well-paid promotion to head their European office in London for a period of three years or so. They wanted an experienced journalist over there, because of the deteriorating situation in Berlin. The job would start early in 1951.

The year-long experience of living under Menzies would be an important part of Charmian Clift's political development. It would also be tied up with the resolve which would lead her to spend the major part of her adult life away from her homeland. On Hydra a decade and a half later, Charmian would repeatedly question a young Australian friend, Bet Hall, as to whether things were 'really all right now, back there'.

> She told us how she'd left Australia under a cloud — that there were questions asked about her in Parliament because she did an ABC radio broadcast called 'Change Another Pound', about the high cost of inflation in Australia, and it was the time of Menzies, and questions were asked in the House about this.[53]

This story may have been embroidered by Charmian over time, but in fact she did write a program named 'Change Another Pound', which went to air in late June 1950. While it seems unlikely that the matter was actually raised in Parliament,[54] it is clear that the writer felt herself to have been chastised for her politics. Perhaps she was called to account by the ABC hierarchy, who in turn may have suffered the ire of the new conservative government. Certainly, this was the last program which Charmian Clift wrote for the ABC at this time. The incident seems to connect with the story of the *Argus* dismissal and exile from Melbourne: Charmian in trouble, and leaving under a cloud. And indeed she would also speak to Bet Hall of leaving Australia because she was uncomfortable 'because of George's divorce and subsequent marriage to her, and she'd felt that she was sort of thought of as a homebreaker and so on'. It was the whole atmosphere of the country — social as well as political — that seemed to cramp and confine her.

With these sorts of ongoing social and political concerns as well as the daily domestic crises which any mother faces, the demands of the present usually kept the past at bay for Charmian. Sometimes, however, it was impossible not to remember. And on at least one occasion the secrecy became too hard to bear.

Christmas was always a difficult time, because of the cruel irony that when the rest of society celebrated the birth of a child, Charmian remembered the birthday of the baby she had lost. Perhaps to compensate, she always made a fuss of Christmas for Martin and Shane. In these Bondi years she and Toni would 'go into a spin' making 'whole wardrobes of dolls clothes, rag toys and other bits of glamour' in their preparations for Christmas parties.[55]

It must have been Christmas 1949 that Toni came into the flat on one occasion to find Charmian weeping. In one telling of this story, the tears were prompted by a radio script which Charmian was writing on the subject of the baby in the manger. 'It's lovely', Toni had said on reading the piece. 'But what's the matter?' And Charmian told her about the baby whom her mother had forced her to give up. She spoke of how she sometimes searched the faces of little girls in the street, wondering if they were her daughter.[56] In another version of this story, Charmian wrote an ABC radio program about an adopted child; it was this that made Toni decide that she herself couldn't be a writer, because she couldn't use personal experience in such a way.[57]

The variations highlight some of the difficulties with oral history. In fact, in March 1950 an ABC radio play did go to air with the title 'Problem of an Adopted Child'. It was a dramatisation of the pain and confusion of an adopted girl as she grows from childhood to young womanhood.[58] This program was not, however, written by Charmian Clift, but by another friend of Toni's — Barbara Jefferis. The question is: how did Jefferis come up with the idea for this feature? Forty years and scores of radio programs later, she says:

> I would *love* to know! What I am certain of is that *I* didn't suggest it. It wasn't an interest of mine — I didn't know anyone who was adopted — but somebody suggested it and I thought it would be interesting to do. The idea certainly didn't come to me from Charm. It must have come from Neil [Hutchison] as a suggestion, I think — you know: 'Why don't you do ... ?'

What Barbara Jefferis did was go to Crown Street Women's Hospital and interview the matron, Miss Edna Shaw, who spoke freely about the unmarried women who came to the maternity wards and who subsequently gave their babies up for adoption. 'Do you try to match up the babies with the adopting parents?' Jefferis asked.

Matron shrugged: 'Oh, we *try*, but there's so little you can find out!'[59]

Given that Edna Shaw most probably knew of Charmian Clift's connection with the ABC, she may have found this question a little close to the bone. In fact, the matron had matched a particular baby with her own brother and sister-in-law: Charmian Clift's daughter Jennifer was Matron Shaw's niece and goddaughter, Suzanne Shaw.[60]

Of course, Charmian Clift did not know this. And — at the time of the interview with the matron of Crown Street Women's Hospital — Barbara Jefferis did not know about her colleague's illegitimate daughter. However, not long after the program went to air, Toni Hazelwood told Barbara Jefferis the secret which Charmian had confided in her. Toni added that Charmian had said that she just wished the child could know that her mother was Somebody.[61]

If the content of Barbara Jefferis's program touched a sore point in Charmian Clift's past, Clift and Johnston collaboratively wrote a program which seems to have come out of a developing concern in their present. For the *Radio Diary* series, other members of Hutchison's team produced a wide range of topics such as 'Diary of a Spieler', 'Diary of a Beautician', 'Diary of a Jesuit', 'Diary of a Negro', 'Diary of an Alcoholic', and even 'Diary of a Shanghaied Sailor', but Clift and Johnston came up with a 'Diary of an Unhappy Marriage'.

For the content of this program, which went to air in February 1950, we are reliant upon the synopsis in the *ABC Weekly*:

> It tells the story of two very ordinary people in an ordinary marriage which should have been compatible and happy, but for some reason or another is not.
>
> The narrator becomes the pivot when he questions each in turn to find the cause of the trouble. At length he is able to trace the initial error back to the beginning of the marriage, when — through pride, perhaps, lack of understanding, intolerance — each has allowed a triviality to develop into a major problem.
>
> The Diary, covering seven years, provides no solution to the problem, but rather becomes current in event and complexion, with the listeners playing the major roles in an attempt at individual solution.[62]

It seems somewhat ominous that a couple who had been married for only two and a half years should even be thinking about unhappy marriages. Further, the fact that this program was concerned with trying to trace the problem back to its 'trivial' beginning could seem unimportant, if it were not for other evidence that something was already beginning to go wrong in the writers' own marriage. Charmian's friend Toni presents a picture of Charmian at this time as exuberant and fun-loving and George as moody and quick to criticise his wife.[63] Barbara Jefferis, on the other hand, saw George as 'the sufferer in the relationship'. Yet she too felt that already things had soured badly.[64]

This sense that the problems of the Johnston relationship were incipient from a very early stage is further evident in the notes which George Johnston wrote in late 1963 in preparation for his novel *Clean Straw for Nothing*.[65] While there is need for care in using this document, it does illuminate the biographical relationship upon which the second book of Johnston's trilogy was based. The status of the material as notes means that it is very close to the author's interpretation of the characters' models. Of course, this does not mean it is an accurate account of Charmian Clift's feelings or behaviour, but we can fairly take it that Johnston's representations of the feelings of David Meredith are based on self-analysis.

By the time the author had completed this novel, he believed that the genre of the literary novel was undergoing a shift in its very nature. In an important interview about this text, he noted that 'the serious novel must more and more become a question of self-examination'. It was 'a form of confession'. It was 'only in the form of autobiography, of one kind or another' that the novel could 'survive'.[66] An escape clause is provided by the phrase 'of one kind or another'. But this is significant testimony about the kind of fiction — or non-fiction — that George Johnston was attempting by the last years of his life. The degree to which this material, both in the notes and the novel, aims at confession and self-examination deserves respect. Not many men, particularly of George Johnston's generation, would have been willing to lay bare their souls or their psyches in this way — or at least not in a permanent record; the writer left these notes among his papers as part of the record of the writing of his trilogy. Certainly, it would be wrong to use George's 'confession' as some kind of indictment against him; at the same time, if he has written so openly about either his own faults or the faults of a man with a very similar background and character, it would be ridiculous not to take his interpretation into account.

The notes open with David Meredith's attempt to 'search for a beginning point' of the failure of the Meredith/Morley marriage. Johnston asks: 'What had happened to them during all those years?... to Cressida, who had changed into a completely different person?... to himself, David Meredith, who also had changed (been twisted?) into a different sort of person?'

Both in these notes and in the novel which eventually grew out of them, the first problem to emerge is that of possessiveness. It is in the 'Sydney

1949' section of the novel — immediately after the birth of the couple's second child — that Johnston has his alter ego narrator move into his second major description of suspicion and jealousy. By now it is a lot more developed than in the Sorrento phase, but again the author uses the character of Calverton as a convenient focus, along with the sinister rival, Crossley. By this stage the honesty, which was originally one of the reasons why David loved Cressida, is becoming a thorn in his side:

> The problem, of course, was that Meredith was obsessively jealous and Cressida obsessively honest. He loved her so totally that he had to possess all of her, even when the totality of that possession hurt excruciatingly. There were times when he would have been happy to be lied to, placated, soothed, so long as he was endorsed in his ownership, and reassured, for he was haunted always by an abiding fear that he could not hold her, that she would slip away from him into some other man's possession [...] To arm himself against this threat he had to try to know, even if the knowledge was a form of masochism, everything about her. He would question her about her life before he had come to her, screwing the sick tension of his stomach into a grinding knot. Cressida, on her part, with a love that was far less demanding, was perfectly willing to concede him his ownership, for her loyalty to him was as unqualified as her fidelity, but her honesty forbade her to grant to him a retrospective possession, and perhaps this was what rankled with him.[67]

Again this passage sets Cressida's 'loyalty' and 'fidelity' against David's 'possession' and 'ownership'. The preliminary notes for this novel reveal even more nakedly the author's analysis of his feelings. This section is concerned with the early part of the relationship:

> Cressida, long admired, pursued, sought after, will without any particular coquetry continue to court admiration as she has always done, openly and naturally. And David Meredith will interpret this, <u>once she is his</u>, jealously. His reaction is as natural as her belief.[68]

The author goes on to say that Meredith's 'jealousy, however indefensible in cold-blooded logical terms, is just as natural and deeply embedded in his formative past as Cressida's original honesty'.

He is jealous, but tries not to show it. He is even at times mistrustful, although less of Cressida than of life itself, for, to him, how could any man not covet this jewel in his possession? And if Cressida continues to be beautiful, alluring, continues to court and bask in the admiration of men ... The perils are infinite.

In this reference to the 'formative past', the author alludes to the combined sense of the lovelessness and the flatness or emptiness of his early experience. Again and again, George's early sense of abandonment keeps coming into play: it wasn't really his wife he was suspicious of, but love, or perhaps life itself.

At the time of meeting her husband, Johnston notes, Cressida had known 'nothing of the moody, opportunistic evasionist of *My Brother Jack*'. Her lover had seemed 'the very epitome of gaiety, glamour, of the heady excitements of the time'. But now he was different, in a way that she could not yet understand. This was in fact a phenomenon of the time: many women found that the men they had married in wartime proved rather different after peace was declared. But with George, it wasn't just World War II that had shaped him, but the earlier war, which had haunted his childhood.

One of the most cogent and sympathetic witnesses to the torturous effects of George's upbringing is Allan Ashbolt, who happened to grow up at about the same time as George, in the neighbouring suburb of Caulfield. Ashbolt speaks of the effect of war on his peer group: 'A whole generation whose lives had been built around memories — through fathers, mothers, aunts, uncles — of the First World War' and who grew up, once the Depression came, 'expecting to be involved in a war'. And so 'George was carrying this weight around with him — he could never really get his mind away from his memories of growing up'. In his observations of the early relationship between George and Charmian, Ashbolt states:

I could see that *she* was the emotionally developed one in that partnership, and that George — partly because of his background [around] Caulfield — did not have great gifts for intimacy. This was a problem which developed over the years. It is a strange thing to have to describe. It didn't mean that he lacked affection, love, deep devotion, but he very often had no way of expressing this. Basically he was very devoted to Charmian, but at the same time very watchful, very suspicious — never quite sure that really, she belonged to him in any profound way — always fearful that she might break out.[69]

* * *

'Well, you know,' Ashbolt concluded ruefully, 'there it was!' — implying that in that description lay the kernel of the whole problem with the relationship.

It is fascinating that in this description Charmian — still only in her mid twenties — emerges as the 'emotionally developed one'. Indeed, throughout Ashbolt's reminiscences of the couple in this period,[70] there is a sense of Charmian mothering the emotionally starved and needy child, giving him the assurance which he so desperately needed so that he would not feel abandoned. But Ashbolt could not have known how desperately Charmian herself craved love and affection, and how George's lack of the 'gifts for intimacy' would make her feel unwanted.

This is where the insecurity of both partners created a strange sort of abrasion. On the one hand, while George feared that some other man would take Charmian away from him, he needed to feel that she was desirable to other men, or she would lose some of her value. George's vicious circle connects with an equally problematic and circular pattern in Charmian's behaviour. After her marriage, Charmian continued to cause — or allow — men to react sexually to her. This was still her response to the insecurities of her childhood and adolescence, her way of trying to make people love or like her — or at least notice her. The more George's personality and prestige won *him* friends, the more she felt that she had to play the only card she had: her sexuality. Now, however, a new element was added. Feeling trapped by suburbia, by marriage and motherhood, and feeling hedged in by George's suspicion, the natural outlet was frivolity. But this incited even more suspicion, which in turn made Charmian feel more hedged in. This is how Johnston, in the notes for the novel, described the restrictions:

> Resentment begins — this is according to her own stated belief [...] when she finds herself 'trapped' in marriage. The first child triggers it off — a realisation quite suddenly and alarmingly that her true roots are in a kind of pagan liberty [...], that she has never really wanted marriage and the responsibility inseparable from the state of marriage. She has not wanted to be possessed, hedged in, denied the right of any wild creature to run freely and hide in solitude. In context with her secret beliefs, 'trapped' is perhaps not an overdramatic word.[71]

No, it wasn't. In his repeated reference to Cressida's complaint of 'trappedness', George Johnston is picking up one of Charmian's refrains.

(It had also been his own charge against his first marriage.) The author's use of the word 'possessed' is just as revealing. The problem of freedom versus ownership — incipient in the relationship since the first days at Sorrento — had become a running sore a few years later. Yet for all his pages of analysis, Johnston never seems to realise the paradox that the so-called 'natural' and 'pagan' side of Cressida, which was the prime source of her attraction for David, was the very thing which David immediately wished to contain.

In this constant summoning up of 'young Cress with sand between her toes', 'the barefooted pagan on the mile-long beach', Johnston is following the authorised version of the childhood of Charmian Clift which she herself promulgated.

> The pivot of this, the real freedom, as it were, is almost an atavistic race-memory of the Saturnalia, the Golden Age, the days of the young, irresponsible, unattached, free-living, free-loving Cressida of the golden beaches.

Yet, as we have seen in Part I, Charmian's childhood — free though it certainly was — was underpinned with various elements of unhappiness. It was these elements which George Johnston inadvertently reactivated.

In noting the difficulty which she felt to exist in the Johnston marriage, Barbara Jefferis remembered observing 'a complete change' in Charmian's attitude to George in the brief span of these Sydney years:

> At the beginning, Charmian used to quite literally sit at George's feet — she'd just curl up beside him and gaze at him while he talked, when they were first married [...] She thought that absolutely every word that George spoke was a pearl of wisdom.
>
> And there had to be a change, and it was hard on George when it came, I guess. Because it wasn't very long before she was challenging everything he said.[72]

This description is uncannily similar to accounts, given both by Margaret Backhouse and by Charmian herself, of how the young Charmian challenged and questioned everything that Syd Clift said. It has already been noted that one of the elements of Charmian's initial attraction to George was the fact that he was cut from the same cloth as her father. From an early stage in the relationship George began to fill the niche in Charmian's life that her father had once filled.

While Charmian herself may never have seen the parallel between her relationship with her father and that with her husband, certainly George Johnston was aware of it, although without seeing its full significance. In discussing how Meredith's jealousy is just as 'natural' as his wife's courting of admiration, the author traces the latter to Cressida's background. This crucial biographical passage makes it clear that Charmian had told George some of the unhappy aspects of her family life and childhood:

> Her need to be courted and admired, her everlasting wistfulness for a wanton freedom, swim up out of the mile-long beach of childhood, out of the running freedom of her own solitudes, the miseries of playing a second fiddle to somebody else, the pressures to escape from binding family tyrannies into a bigger and unrestricted world of gaiety and glamour and excitement. Married, she still knows very little of the David Meredith of *My Brother Jack,* and so when she finds herself back in a restricted world with binding family tyrannies, it is perhaps natural that she will begin secretly to resent the figure of the warder.[73]

If in the references to 'tyrannies' and 'the warder' George Johnston here hints at a connection between his own role and that of his father-in-law, the reference to 'the miseries of playing a second fiddle to someone else' brings to mind Charmian's relationship with her sister Margaret. In fact, George inadvertently combined aspects of the two people who had thwarted the child Charmian and made her miserable. He simultaneously took on the mantle of Syd the terrible tyrant, and of Meg the golden favourite. In this marriage which was also a literary partnership, Charmian was back in the role of junior. Once again, she was in the shadows while someone else stole the limelight. And once again she felt ruled by an overbearing male authority figure.

After raising this important double spectre, George Johnston returns in mid-paragraph to the matter of Cressida's reaction to her feeling of 'trappedness':

> The immediate, and perhaps the continuing reaction is to bring loyalty to bear and force the resentment underground. The husband is blamed and yet made not to blame [...] To conceal

and camouflage the beginnings of resentment [...] the emphasis is placed on the loyal, sharing, generous, uncomplaining, and dedicated wife. <u>But from this point nothing is forgotten nor ever will be.</u>

The interesting thing about these notes is that they provide a window, not just into a relationship — whether real or fictional — of the post-war period, but into the mind of a man who was reacting to certain sociopolitical undercurrents which were starting to ripple the pond of male assurance a decade and a half later. Johnston, writing in 1963, was able to catch a glimmer of what the issue at stake really was.

As this passage continues, the underlying gender politics of all this are suddenly revealed, as the author notes that Cressida's 'feeling of "trappedness" ' is — at a later stage — 'translated (twisted?) into what seem to be more markedly suffragist attitudes — freedom of will, of creative effort, equality of the sexes, rights of personal privacy'. Here 'suffragist' is of course the key word: in 1963 the terms 'feminist' and 'women's liberation' were not yet current, so it was necessary to use an old word for a new mood.

As he goes on to describe how Cressida erected 'the first secret walls' against her husband in this early period of the marriage, it becomes clear that the freedom is internal as well as external:

From now on 'personal freedom' [...], 'invasion of privacy', 'assertion of masculinity', jealousy etc., will all be seen (and sedulously stored away and preserved) as genuine affronts, bruises, woundings, as genuine causes for resentment, as valid reasons for incompatibility. Because they are opposed, or to her <u>seem to be opposed</u>, to her inner conception of <u>an entitled freedom</u>. Which she has been obliged to sacrifice.

Charmian Clift and George Johnston were important transformational figures. Again and again we find them in the advance guard of changing movements of cultural history. In a way, they are emblematic figures who allow us to see a sort of personification of social change. To a great extent the underlying problem in the Clift/Johnston (or Morley/Meredith) marriage was a conflict of roles and rights that is at the front line of the so-called battle of the sexes. It was as if this couple, in the 1940s and 1950s, were playing out a test case for a confrontation which would not come to the fore in most Australian marriages until the 1970s.

Charmian Clift, with her passionate belief in her *right* to freedom, and George Johnston, with his equally strong sense of entitled ownership, were extreme examples of two opposing forces. As Johnston points out, neither could help these feelings, which were shaped by their contrasting backgrounds as well as by their gender. The half generation age difference was a further reason why these two sometimes saw things differently. The difficulty — perhaps the real tragedy — was that because of the time in which Charmian and George lived, the opposed issues of freedom versus control were seen as individual idiosyncrasies or faults, and not as symptoms of a broader and more ordinary conflict. Again, George Johnston in 1963 was starting to understand:

> It may be argued that [Cressida] is fundamentally, by instinct, and even by upbringing, a natural pioneer of changing values. (Is Simone de Beauvoir a valid and genuine prophet of the same change in values? Is Doris Lessing?) The point is that David Meredith, at heart and by instinct, emphatically *is not*.

The work of writers such as de Beauvoir and Lessing would provide a political framework which would enable some women to move beyond the personal aspects of gender conflict, to see oppression as the result of a complex patriarchal system. For Charmian Clift in 1950, however, this framework was not available. Consequently the anger, the resentment, were all focused on the spouse. But because Charmian was a woman of her own time, there was also a sense of guilt and puzzlement at the very fact of this resentment. After all, she had the husband she had wanted; she had two beautiful children; she had good looks and good health; she had enough money for books and records and other little luxuries as well as essentials. So why wasn't she happy? This confusion — which Charmian Clift was never really able to resolve — comes through in a radio program which she wrote in late 1949. This makes it clear that Clift was thinking about the issue of women's freedom within marriage in a way that went beyond any particular concern with herself, her husband, and their marriage.

'Diary of a Modern Woman' is a fascinating artefact from this era.[74] Even the title rings with the post-war feeling that there would be a New Woman, liberated from the pre-war expectations of a life devoted solely to housework and motherhood. She would take her place in peacetime alongside men, just as she had been their equal in wartime. But the title is ironic: the writer shows just how little has changed since the old un-Modern days.

This play is concerned with the problems of a woman, named Emily Baker, who tries to combine a career as business executive with the duties of housewife and mother.

The listener eavesdrops on an argument between Emily and her husband Michael, who wants his wife to toss in her job, bring the two boys home from boarding school, and 'establish a family atmosphere'. Emily objects: 'I have too much of a sense of duty to my children, to my womanhood and — if it comes to that — my marriage, to dream of giving up my job'. Michael protests that if Emily left work, she could take it easy, read books, go out ...

> *Michael:* You'd have fun, and I'd have a home and a wife.
>
> *Emily:*   So that's it! What you'd have, you mean, is an unpaid
> housekeeper! [...] I thought you really believed that
> marriage was a partnership — that a woman had as
> much right to her individuality as a man. You make me
> sick. All men make me sick! Beastly, egotistical, selfish.

This is tough stuff for 1949, and the message is reinforced as the program's female narrator points out that Mike 'doesn't really understand Emily at all'. As both the female narrator and the scriptwriter present the situation at this stage, the problem in the marriage is clearly with Mike: 'He wants to have his cake, and eat it. He wants Emily to be brilliant and beautiful, but he also wants her to be a little more comfortable with it'. Unfortunately for Michael, however, Emily has always been independent.

At this point, a male narrator interrupts. 'Why on earth', he asks, 'did Emily marry and have children?' After all, 'she's always been smart enough and attractive enough to get along by herself'. 'That, my friend,' replies the female narrator, 'is the trouble'.

Yet it is the scriptwriter herself who is in trouble. As the character of Emily and the female narrator turn upon each other, the subtext of the play is that an independent woman will be split in two; the struggle for independence leads to self-destruction. Overall, the confusion of the play's argument is indicative of the writer's inability to find a clear answer to the question she has set herself: why *should* a woman with Emily's ability and independence marry and have children at all? Of course, the same question could be asked of the scriptwriter.

While the emotional and time-consuming demands of marriage and motherhood conflicted with Charmian Clift's passion for her work, another problem was the extraordinary expectations which both she and George placed upon their relationship. It was as if they had to live up to an idealised myth of marriage. This ideal union was, of course, the sense of the couple united in love and literature which had been promoted by the publicity surrounding the *Sydney Morning Herald* award. According to Garry Kinnane, 'they both shocked Neil Hutchison by openly declaring that they "made love every night", often the consummation of an evening's writing together'.[75] This was the kind of statement which furthered the mystique which surrounded these two. If the Melbourne myth was of Love Persecuted, the Sydney legend was Love Triumphant. Given Charmian's pride, it would have been hard to admit that in fact she had a marriage which was suffering the normal difficulties. George would later declare that:

> Cressida's tragedy — more, the whole Meredith tragedy — is that she concealed and withheld for too long what to her was the truth [...] The real trouble is that the husband is misled, and for years will continue to be misled, into a state of proud and sometimes careless complacency, firmly believing his relationship with Cressida to be, not only satisfactory, but rare to an almost unique degree among his contemporaries.[76]

As well as keeping up the pretence of a perfect marriage, there seemed to be another burden placed upon Charmian. This was the requirement that she be happy. There is a poignant passage in *Honour's Mimic* where Kathy, reflecting on the 'sweet time' after childbirth, remembers: 'She had wanted the babies and wanted them quickly, so glad and relieved in her own happiness in them, the happiness like a proof to offer Irwin. See, Irwin, I *am* happy. Truly I am.'[77]

For Charmian, too, having the children was a way of convincing herself that she was happy in her marriage. And so, like Cressida, she brought loyalty to bear and forced the resentment underground. At the same time, the sense of partnership remained so strong that she would still (in Barbara Jefferis's words) 'make the running for George' — would create the moment for him to read his latest work-in-progress or tell his latest amusing anecdote. And if anyone other than Charmian herself should ever criticise or question George, she would be the first to fly to his defence.

Although Charmian's smile was sometimes forced in the later Sydney years, she could always cheer herself up again with the expectation that perfect happiness would be found after another new start. Through the dragging months of 1950, as Menzies established himself on the Australian political stage and anti-Communist hysteria began to take over, Charmian sustained herself with the knowledge that she would soon be off to a new life in a new land, where her marriage and her writing and mothering and absolutely everything would suddenly be wonderful. This time, it wasn't just a matter of escaping from something, but the belief that she would be arriving *at* something. This was the escape overseas of which she had dreamed as a young girl as she sat on Bombo beach, gazing at a ship that floated like a matchstick on the far blue horizon.

11

AN OUTSIDER LOOKING IN

I liked England, I was very happy in London, excepting that again there
was the feeling of being bound and constrained, […] and I felt that I
was an outsider looking in, never part of it, never part of the London
I wanted to be part of, because I wasn't free.[1]

In *Honour's Mimic*, the heroine Kathy reflects upon her escape at the
age of seventeen from the country to Sydney, and then her further
escape:

> Sydney had not been big enough, after all, but there had been so
> much time ahead of her at twenty to find It, the Big Thing,
> whatever it was she was going to recognise the moment she came
> across it. It had to be somewhere else, somewhere farther on, and
> at twenty she had set out again, across thirteen thousand miles of
> seas and oceans […] because London would be big enough to
> contain the wonder or the sign that it was her inalienable right to
> claim as her own.[2]

This attitude which Clift attributes to Kathy was something that she
herself felt. At the age of twenty-seven she 'still had that childhood ambition
to go further and see more' and she knew that 'whatever the Big Thing was,
it wasn't here in Australia for [her]'.[3] The allusion to 'the wonder or the sign'
which the alter ego sees as 'her inalienable right to claim as her own' should
not be taken lightly. This Big Thing or wonder was the personal Grail which
Charmian Clift was seeking: while of course she didn't know what form it
would take, she believed that everything would make sense once she

discovered it. Whatever it was, it was connected with the mystic sense of oneness with the universe which she used to experience as a child; it was about an internal sort of freedom, involving the deepest privacy. But it was also, as this passage shows, connected with Charmian's childhood sense of specialness. This sign that was waiting somewhere in the universe had *her* name written on it.

It was with these huge expectations — as well as the belief that the fresh start would renew her marriage — that Charmian Clift set off with her husband and two children on the *Orcades* in mid February 1951. As the ship sailed out from Sydney, she waved goodbye to the Harbour Bridge thinking (she later remembered), 'I'll never see that again!'[4]

Rhetorical though this was, it underlines Charmian's sense that she was going for good. In fact, she should have expected to see her homeland again in three years or so. George Johnston's appointment was only for this period and certainly *he* thought they would be returning after this time. In his biography of Johnston, Garry Kinnane stresses the importance of this 'projected return', and declares that 'Johnston and Clift were not expatriates' in the 'full sense' — meaning, in Kinnane's terms, that they did not reject their own culture and did not set off intending to live in exile.[5] It is true that George Johnston was not planning permanent exile, and by his own account (given in a 1965 radio interview) he 'probably wouldn't have done it under [his] own steam' (that is, without a job to go to). Yet he did feel there was a sort of mutual rejection going on. 'The country seemed to be rejecting us', he explained, then added that it was maybe a question of 'Australia rejecting us or us rejecting Australia'. The main problem that George highlighted was that 'There didn't seem to be an appreciation of the arts'.[6] For Charmian Clift, however, unhappiness with her homeland covered every aspect of life, from the political to the personal. When she set off on the *Orcades*, she was leaving Australia and suburbia and Menzies and the misery of her own past — perhaps not for ever, but with no thought of returning in the near future.

By coincidence Greeba Jamison, Clift and Johnston's colleague from the *Argus* days, was heading for Europe on the same ship: 'It was a first time overseas for Charmian and [she] was off to see the world — you know — it was the world was her oyster and she was very excited about getting to Europe, getting to Europe, getting to Europe'. Jamison also gives a vivid sense of Charmian, who had changed in the four years since Greeba had seen her:

It was quite obvious to me that Charmian had matured considerably, and she was very much the caring mother. She and George were still — to use that old-fashioned word — were still lovers — they behaved in a very lover-like way together [...] I remember them at night going up to the bow of the ship to watch the stars and the moonlight on the water, and they were very romantic still.

And Charmian was not — you know — perhaps *flaunting* her sex as she had done [...] in the *Argus* days. She was still extremely attractive and [...] oh, she turned men's eyes every time she walked along the deck, but she was certainly not making any effort to have any affairs on the ship, or anything like that. She was very much George's wife, and Shane and Martin were toddlers.[7]

This portrayal of Charmian as devoted wife and mother is a nice one, as is Jamison's picture of Charmian's shipboard style:

She dressed very smartly — a little touch of the bizarre, perhaps, but mostly I seem to remember her looking awfully neat and chic and almost sort of Parisian in her spic and span sort of dressing, but a little bit unusual — she didn't dress quite to the current fashion, she dressed as — you know — Charmian Clift. And the children too — I find it hard to put into words — but they looked sort of *different* from other children and you'd see her walking along the deck with one in each hand as it were — quite a spectacle, really.

'She dressed as Charmian Clift ... Quite a spectacle, really'... This acute description captures the way in which Charmian Clift would consciously wear herself in a role.

Photos of the ship's fancy dress party sent back to Amy Clift show Martin and Shane decked out as an artist (in a smock, and carrying a palette) and his naked model.[8] They won first prize. Nothing wrong with that, except for the sense that these costumes were designed to display the interests of the parents who were featuring an artist and his model in their current novel-in-progress. It was as if, even at the most trivial level, these two writers could not resist the temptation to perforate the membrane between life and fiction — and to go all out for the prize.

* * *

On the drizzly day of 15 March 1951, the *Orcades* arrived at Tilbury. George Johnston's new status as head of the London office of Associated Newspaper Services was immediately apparent when the family was met at the docks by a black hire car with uniformed chauffeur.[9] The office flat was not available yet, so the family was put into a hotel for some weeks before moving in early April to a flat at Cliveden Place, SW1 — just off Sloane Square in fashionable Belgravia. Later the family moved into a pleasant flat that occupied one floor of a converted Georgian mansion on the Bayswater Road, overlooking Palace Gate and Kensington Gardens.[10]

Late winter was 'still gripping [England] harsh and the aftermath of war was still glumly apparent'.[11] Bomb sites gaped, and the facades of wrecked terraces grinned like broken teeth. Yet this first experience of London more than lived up to expectation. In 'The Man in the Corner', an unfinished short story written in London, Clift gently satirises her initial enthusiasm in the bounding naivety of a character named Liza:

> 'How long have you been here?' the girl asked, surveying them without great interest.
>
> 'Three weeks,' Liza said gaily. 'It's heaven. *So* grey and drizzly, and the buses so incredibly red and the stalls of daffodils so incredibly yellow. The incredible people! We feel like extras in an Ealing film. Sitting in pubs for hours with our eyes on stalks.'[12]

To a young Australian filled with Dickens and TS Eliot, even the fog smelled 'right, just right, just what a London fog ought to smell like'.[13]

If England was the source of Charmian Clift's literary heritage, London was also the centre of her contemporary publishing world. After *High Valley's* success in 1948, Charmian Clift and George Johnston had been invited onto the list of the American literary agency Ann Watkins Inc., and in September 1949 they had established a relationship with Watkins' British associates, Pearn, Pollinger and Higham Ltd. This latter relationship, which was to continue happily through the rest of their careers, was in particular with the agent David Higham.

On 2 April 1951 Higham met his two newly arrived Australian clients for the first time, finding them (he told his American associates) 'very pleasant indeed'. The two writers outlined for him a quite extraordinary writing schedule which he sent on to the Ann Watkins agency:

(1) Clift/Johnston — a longish novel of modern Australian life (about 140 000 words) to be ready by the end of the year. Title THE PIPING CRY.

(2) Johnston himself, by the autumn, an 80 000 word novel entitled PAGODA […]

(3) Charmian Clift herself, by the autumn, a 60 000 word novel at present entitled A WALK TO THE PARADISE GARDEN [sic].[14]

It is important to note that from her first meeting with her literary agent, Charmian Clift made it clear that she was proposing to work alone, as well as in collaboration with her husband. As far as George Johnston's workload was concerned, this was in addition to 'thorough' revisions to his potboiler *Murder by Horoscope* (recently returned by the US firm of Dodd, Mead). He had also promised Angus & Robertson that he would finish the script for Albert Arlen's musical of *The Sentimental Bloke,* to which he had been committed since 1948. The composer — now also in London — was becoming impatient.

Although this program sounded crowded, the two authors led Higham to believe that 'all these works are well forward and require finishing and revising in the main'. In fact, of the promised novels, *The Piping Cry* was certainly well under way. But what was the status of Clift's solo novel? The phrase 'at present entitled' is suggestive. According to her army friend Nona Wood, as early as 1943 Charmian was saying that she had written a story under this title.[15] This author had a habit of recycling titles and character names like a frugal housewife, and this would not be the only time when a short story title would later be borrowed for a novel. Given the claim that *Walk to the Paradise Gardens* was 'well forward' it seems likely that she had decided to put this title onto some of the old material from *Greener Grows the Grass*. Perhaps now that she was far removed from her family and from the unhappiness of her past, the author felt able to go back to this autobiographical novel and finally complete it. The fact that she did not mention *Greener Grows the Grass* to her agent suggests that by the time she met David Higham, she had already finished with the work under that title. Certainly, there is no word of this novel in later agency files.

A couple of days after this initial meeting with her literary agent, Charmian had her first glimpse of the Continent, when she and George went to Paris for the weekend with Mary and Gordon Andrews, two of their friends from the Sydney scene.[16] Gordon Andrews was one of the designers of the new South Bank complex. He was just one of the many Australians 'being excited' in London that year, along with others such as Paul Brickhill, Peter Finch, Loudon Sainthill, Pat and Cedric Flower, Albert Arlen and Sidney Nolan. Charmian would later remember that she 'used to think that the most desirable state of being that could be imagined was to be a young and talented Australian in London':

> Weren't we healthier, more vital, more buoyant? And didn't we have so much enthusiasm, so much talent that it was frustrating to the point of actual discomfort to keep ourselves within decent British bounds? We kept bursting out all over the place. I thought we were like a lot of healthy Antipodean sponges, sopping up everything that touched us, good and bad and smelly and all [...] We were enchanted, amused, excited, indignant, frustrated, discouraged, and sometimes contemptuous.
>
> Australia [...] seemed very far away.[17]

There was clearly no cultural cringe among this enthusiastic bunch of Antipodeans, who frequently assembled at each other's flats, talking immoderately, drinking copiously, encouraging each other with dreams of success. They also gathered at gallery openings and first nights, mixing with even greater celebrities — one photo shows a very dapper George Johnston apparently berating 'Larry' Olivier (friend and later rival of Peter Finch), and on another occasion George met Salvador and Gala Dali.

Networking came in handy at all levels. It was through the connection with Mary and Gordon Andrews that Martin and Shane — now aged three and two — began to attend the Montessori kindergarten which the Andrews children also attended. Martin would always retain happy memories of this place, where he drew pictures of ancient battles and learned to grow watercress on the windowsill.[18] Shane was a gregarious little girl, and quickly began to enjoy the opportunity to play with her many new friends. The children's schooling freed Clift for a few hours each day, and she would later describe how she and Mary 'used to roster ourselves for duty chores with our assorted children, like picking them up from school and walking them in parks [...] and riding them around on those buses so vehemently red in all the grey, or traipsing them through museums'.[19]

By the end of April, George Johnston had fully settled in to his new position. On 2 May he began a daily 'London Diary' column for the Sydney *Sun*, in which he recorded a mixture of major international events and odd jottings. The next day, the Festival of Britain opened, hitting England (Johnston noted) 'like a jab in the arm with a hypodermic needle'. That June was the sunniest for many years, and the locals celebrated the Festival with 'a welter of outdoor fancies': 'Londoners have been dressing up as Pickwickians, Elizabethans, street-criers, mid-Victorians, Morris dancers, knights-errant, Edwardians, Shakespearian and Chaucerian characters until one's mind is beginning to boggle'.[20]

Despite the Festival atmosphere, England in 1951 was still operating under a system of ration cards and queues for everything — 'even for Welfare State cod-liver oil and orange juice for the children', Clift complained.[21] Johnston's salary, however, was comparatively high and there was enough money for concerts and theatres, and for books and records and Victoriana bric-a-brac, and when summer came the couple bought a car and 'explored the English countryside'.[22]

In her column reminiscences of this London period, Charmian Clift dwells upon the pleasures and the pageantry, but at the time she was well aware of a rather grimmer picture. Associated Newspaper Services had not sent a leading war correspondent to London in 1951 to cover the Morris dancing. In mid May, George Johnston noted that in his local pub the night before, 'people in nine different groups were talking about the possibilities of World War III'. By the end of July he was recording his 'inescapable impression that America's policy-planners have decided in their own minds that World War III is inevitable'. And in November he reported that 'there is good reason to believe that Russia expects World War III to begin about the end of 1952'. At this time Johnston stated that 'war and peace [was] the main topic of conjecture in London, with the betting at evens either way'.[23] It can't have felt very safe to have taken the children to the northern hemisphere. And as the Johnstons' flat was right opposite the Soviet Embassy,[24] it was rather difficult to turn a blind eye to the situation.

If the political scene was worrying, there were domestic pressures as well. At first the relationship between Charmian and George seemed to improve, as both enjoyed exploring the unfamiliar environment. Charmian made a new role for herself as a London sophisticate; George also had a new cosmopolitan style, befitting his station in life. Posed publicity photographs of the two authors in their flat show each sitting in turn in the same armchair in front of a wall covered with books, pot plants and pictures.[25] Charmian, wearing an elegant dress and shoes, has her hair sleekly pulled back. She reads a glossy art magazine. George, looking like an English gentleman, wears a dressing gown over his suit. He reads a newspaper. There is something slightly bizarre about seeing these images juxtaposed: unlike the Sydney images of the literary partners squashed close together typing, they are now separate, and reading rather than writing.

In public, the couple were busy establishing their image. A picture of Charmian Clift's style and the effect she had on people is given by the journalist Nan Hutton, who described Charmian sweeping into the International Journalists' Club, one night in 1951:

> I had never seen her before, but when the Canadian correspondent [asked] 'Quick! Who is she?' I said instantly, 'That's Charmian, George Johnston's wife.'
>
> George looked as thin and elusive as ever, but Charmian looked like the Queen of Sheba. I forget what she wore — something long and simple with a gold band around her full throat. It was her face, strong boned and mobile, the set of her firm shoulders and her voice, talking to George low and throaty but penetrating.
>
> I have never forgotten this first sight of Charmian looking beautiful, and the instant recognition because she fitted her description so exactly.[26]

Perhaps the most telling aspect of Hutton's description is the shorthand identity assigned to Charmian: 'George Johnston's wife'. Understandably, George relished the boost to his esteem which Charmian's London style created. In *Clean Straw for Nothing*, the narrator remembers of Cressida:

> At least I had *this*. This possession beyond price, this unflawed perfection, this prize among women [...] When one was afflicted, as one frequently was in London, by feelings of inferiority, one had only to take her out to the theatre or a party to have one's ego inflated to the *n*th degree by the extraordinary admiration she would evoke by her striking beauty and the sheer charm of her personality.[27]

At the same time, the narrator reflects, his wife was 'a good and intelligent talker, a charming hostess, a warm and sensible mother' and 'a keystone of reassurance'. A perfect wife, in fact. But despite the author's insistence on Cressida's dutifulness, he seems almost inadvertently to raise again the problem of the difference in male and female attitudes.

In a passage of *Clean Straw for Nothing* dealing with the first year in London, Johnston raises the topic of Cressida's views on marriage via the device of a playscript which the unmarried actor Archie Calverton brings along to discuss with his married friends, the Merediths. This play seems to owe something to the theme of Clift's 'Diary of a Modern Woman' radio play, for Calverton notes that the 'theme is that modern man stubbornly refuses to acknowledge his changing state, which is being brought about by woman's refusal, or disinclination anyway, to be submissive any more'. In response, Cressida declares that:

> A woman can be submissive to a man for any number of reasons. Because she wants to. She's that sort of person. Because it suits her, makes her life easier [...]
>
> A woman might also be submissive because of loyalty, or a love big enough to forgive shortcomings, or simply because of a wish not to hurt. Or, if she has children, because of her family. Or even finding herself caught in a trap, with no way out, and making the best of it. Or simply just not having any alternative.[28]

Although this sounds fairly compliant, Cressida Morley goes on to resist the notion that 'it's a woman's *job* to be submissive'. She also laughs when the husband in the script complains that he and his wife 'don't seem to be able to coincide any more':

> Surely he's not suggesting that marriage has to be a permanent amalgam!
>
> Two-in-one, eternally fused! A gold ring on a finger doesn't create a chemical change. It doesn't turn people into something else. They're still people, two distinct people. Everyone finally is a private human being, and everyone finally has to live with himself. Or herself.

While at the time of this conversation David Meredith simply boasts that he has 'the ideal marriage and the perfect wife', the narrator — looking back at this conversation from the viewpoint of 1968 — declares that 'in that trivial discussion [...] there was the first hint of Cressida's secret and deeply buried feelings, the first fugitive glimpse [...] of futures not yet shaped for us'.[29]

It is irrelevant whether such a discussion took place in the real life of Charmian and George in 1951. What is important is that Johnston dates his sense of his wife's 'secret feelings' and her insistence that even in marriage one is a 'private human being' as first occurring — or first being evident to him — in this initial year in London.

It does seem that it was in London that Charmian brought her loyalty to bear, even more strongly than before, and began to conceal her unhappiness in a show of compliance. She also began to retreat into her very deep interior recesses. The insistence on privacy in Cressida's speech is absolutely Charmian, as is the emphasis on the apartness of marriage partners. The sense of staying in marriage because of family responsibilities could also be applied to Charmian at this time. And as for the trap — that too would be a theme of Charmian's London years. But again, all this is a retrospective view. It puts a pattern to something which, at the time, would have been experienced as a series of things that lay somewhere on the scale between happiness and unhappiness.

In this first year in London, Clift sat for a portrait to the Australian expatriate painter Colin Colahan, who lived in Whistler's old house in Tite Street. Of this sitting, the author later remembered:

> He often played Mozart's *Requiem Mass* while he painted me because he couldn't quite believe that I would always cry at exactly the same point, but I always did. I was filled to bursting with excitement, and I felt very young and very muddled and very choked with being excited and young and muddled, not to mention Mozart and Whistler's house and Nell Gwyn and London London London.[30]

This is the kind of Clift story which seems to invite speculation, especially given the fact that a couple of years later Johnston used this incident of crying during the *Requiem Mass* in a short story of that name, which ends in the murder–suicide of a married couple.[31] Before drawing any conclusions, it must be remembered that Charmian also 'wept buckets' at ballet music. It is best to take the author at her word here: as well as youthful excitement, and being overwhelmed with all the new experience, a key word for these London years could be 'muddle'.

If the marriage was already under some strain, there was more urgent pressure in regard to the literary partnership. Although at the 2 April meeting with their agent the couple had promised *The Piping Cry* by the end of the year, within a few weeks David Higham wrote to say that the

Johnstons' American publisher, Bobbs-Merrill, wanted to know 'whether there [was] any possibility of the manuscript being in their hands by November 1st. If so, they would plan spring publication'. In his reply, George Johnston wouldn't guarantee to meet this schedule, but he did encourage the American publishers to hope for the book by then.[32]

In July the pressure intensified: Bobbs-Merrill asked David Higham 'to say that if they don't get the book until [January] it would have to be published in the autumn of 1952 which would be the most competitive time of the year'. Although David Higham urged: 'Don't hurry this important second novel, but make sure it is as good as it can be',[33] George Johnston wrote back on 1 August, promising that *The Piping Cry* would be with Bobbs-Merrill by the 1 November deadline:

> Charmian and I are both very excited about [the novel]. We think it is going very well indeed. With 150 pages behind us and the story rolling along in great style, we are both more than satisfied, and we feel now that we shall be able to give you a *real* novel.[34]

Towards the end of August, Johnston wrote to George Ferguson, of Angus & Robertson, explaining that work on the script of *The Sentimental Bloke* had been put aside because he and Clift were 'working flat out on completing the novel *The Piping Cry*' (which would also, of course, go to the Australian publishers). Johnston described this urgency as 'a very good thing':

> The deadline has forced us really to attack the problem, and the book itself is going along marvellously. We are both very excited indeed about it and I feel sure that you will like it too [...]
> We both feel confident that this time we shall be delivering to you a *real* Australian novel which might cause quite a stir out there.[35]

The typescript of *The Piping Cry* finally arrived in America in late October.[36] On 5 November David Higham had a meeting with George Johnston, who delivered a second copy of the novel for the agency to assess in regard to its suitability for serial publication, and then pass on to Faber. Higham noted that Johnston had another copy for Angus & Robertson 'and will let us know what they decide'. At this meeting, Johnston promised that his novel *Pagoda* would be 'ready next year'. When Higham inquired after

Clift's solo novel *Walk to the Paradise Gardens* (which should have been completed by now according to the schedule outlined in April), Johnston stated that it should be finished by Easter.[37]

These last few months of work on *The Piping Cry* had been a terrible scramble, yet Johnston was already committing himself and Clift to another race towards deadlines. Money wasn't the prime reason, as book sales were a second income. For George Johnston, however, accustomed as he was to the speed of the journalistic world, there was a feverish necessity to publish quickly and often. It would seem that he simply could not understand that Charmian Clift's writing pace was much slower, and that deadlines — which spurred him on — caused in her a form of paralysis of the creative faculties.[38] He also probably couldn't understand why she was so slow: after all, she only had to look after the flat and the children, while he had a newspaper office to run and urgent news stories to file, and he could still churn out a few thousand words a day on the side.

The oddity, really, is not George's attitude but that of Charmian: it does seem strange that she allowed her husband to make extraordinary commitments about deadlines on her behalf. Indeed, she allowed him completely to manage the business side of their work. Although in the beginning the agents' letters were addressed to Mr and Mrs Johnston, they were sent to George's place of employment. It was George alone who replied, and soon both Higham and the American agents were writing to him alone, even when the business concerned a collaborative project. The agency files contain no letter from Charmian Clift until January 1957.

All in all, Charmian Clift and George Johnston had invested a great deal in *The Piping Cry*, which had been their major writing project since the middle of 1948. Despite the authors' confidence, and despite the fact that the book had been scheduled into the American publisher's spring list for 1952, Bobbs-Merrill rejected this novel. As the records of the Pearn, Pollinger and Higham agency for 1952 and 1953 are missing, it is not clear whether the typescript was actually sent to Faber and Faber and Angus & Robertson, or whether the American rejection caused the writers to withdraw the book.[39]

Although all copies of the typescript have subsequently disappeared, quite a lot can be gleaned from the reports of the two Bobbs-Merrill assessors.[40] These make it clear that this novel contained prototypes of the characters of Cressida Morley and David Meredith. There are affinities between its plot and the plots of two of Johnston's later Meredith novels,

Closer to the Sun and *Clean Straw for Nothing*, and it foreshadowed the experimental structure which Johnston would use in two books of his trilogy. As *The Piping Cry* was a collaborative work, these connections carry implications in regard to the literary relationship.

But firstly, why was it rejected? One assessor, Harry Sterk, decided it was a 'maybe book' ... 'not a certain yes or a certain no'. Yet he paid tribute to Clift's contribution:

> It will be years before we have a manuscript better written [...]
> The 'burnish' Charmian Clift knows how to apply is ever present
> and passage after passage is evocative and revealing [...] We
> won't see Bohemian and middle class life in Australia so well
> depicted for a long time [...]
>
> The main characters are meticulously and effectively
> developed.

The second assessor more forthrightly declared that despite 'stretches of good writing' the book would 'lose money'. The 'sales handicap' which worried the publisher lay in the structure of the novel, which began with the ending and then unfolded the story of the hero's past life through a patterning of revelations. This is akin to the structure which Johnston would use in *Clean Straw for Nothing*, and the projected structure of the author's unfinished last novel, *A Cartload of Clay*. It is easy to see why Bobbs-Merrill thought that such a structure would be 'inevitably puzzling' to their middle-brow American readership.[41]

As to the characters and plot of *The Piping Cry*, we are reliant upon the publisher's assessor, Harry Sterk. The main character is an artist, Adam Reeves (named, of course, for the art materials). Though he is the only child of a middle class family, his early environment — like that of George Johnston and of the fictional David Meredith — is narrow and thwarting. He defies his father and goes to art school, where he meets up with Kettering, who plays the rival-and-friend role which Calverton plays in Johnston's trilogy. On his return from the war, Reeves finds that Kettering has given up art in order to make money in advertising. Reeves also abandons his art and begins to work in the advertising agency.

And yet, ambitious still to be a major painter, Reeves subsequently leaves advertising and acquires Lily — his model, mistress and Muse. This character is very much a prototype of the enigmatic Cressida of *Clean Straw for Nothing*. Now Adam Reeves' second ambition — as strong as his desire to become a great painter — is to 'come to a possession of Lily beyond the physical'. In his obsessional desire utterly to possess Lily, he comes to believe that she is betraying him with Kettering. Much of this suspicion 'may be entirely subjective and with no foundation in fact but it is real enough to Adam'. His 'own doubts and self-distrusts make him know that Lily will eventually leave him'. And so, 'knowing' this, he acts in a way that makes it happen: it is in fact his jealousy and coldness which drive Lily away.

At the artist's solo exhibition, the paintings sell quickly but the reviews of the show, while praising the artist's technical skill, accuse him of being 'uncertain, immature, without a message'. It seems that Reeves's failure as a painter might stem from the same cause as his failure with Lily. On one occasion she tells him that he has no pity, that he has emotions but that they are all 'retrospective'.

The romantic plot of this novel has connections with that of Johnston's later major novels *Closer to the Sun* and *Clean Straw for Nothing*. In all three, the tragedy is based on a similar pattern of suspicion and betrayal. In all three of these novels, too, the hero (or anti-hero) fails because he cannot open himself to love.

If *The Piping Cry* is a bit like a prequel to the later fiction of George Johnston, it is also very close to the pattern of behaviour which was slowly building up in the lives of its two creators. This novel was written, however, a decade or so before the behaviour pattern was to reach crisis point.

It is not completely surprising for writers to seem to predict events in their own lives. If literary characters are 'real', in the sense of fully realised, then there is a limited number of ways for them to behave. And if these characters are derived from aspects of the writer, then it is possible for the writer to mimic the character, for in real life as in fiction it is hard to act 'out of character'. An element of self-fulfilling prophecy can also operate, or fiction may be a means of developing the writer's attitude to life. Yet while *The Piping Cry* seems to ring a warning bell about the possible outcome of obsessive suspicion, this clearly went unheard.

Perhaps the creators were too busy assessing a different sort of damage. After the instant success of *High Valley*, the rejection of the new novel was particularly hard to take. Indeed, as Clift later said in a rare public reference to this incident, 'We thought that all we had to do was do it again. It didn't prove so easy'.[42] While *The Piping Cry* is significant biographically because of its themes, it is also important because the knockback brought about a change in the direction of the careers of Charmian Clift and George Johnston.

In regard to George Johnston's writing, the rejection confirmed his tendency to write popular rather than literary fiction. After this he would turn his back on the material he knew, and aim to produce action-packed stories set in exotic locations and featuring traditionally masculine and adventurous heroes. It would be a decade before he would return to the sort of material and method that the couple had trialled in *The Piping Cry*.

Although the rejection did not turn Charmian Clift away from Australian material, the experience of writing this book combined with the book's failure increased her sense of frustration with the process of literary collaboration with her husband. This would become even more extreme as Johnston aimed more and more for the popular market. The trouble was that Clift could not just bail out of collaboration, because of the contractual rights which the couple's various publishers exerted. In the flush of excitement over the acceptance of *High Valley*, the authors had signed contracts with all three of the book's publishers — Bobbs-Merrill in the United States, Faber and Faber in the United Kingdom, and Angus & Robertson in Australia[43] — promising to deliver two more collaborative books. This three-book contract was like a debt which Charmian Clift could not pay off; no matter what she did, she seemed to get no further ahead. Despite three and a half years work on *The Piping Cry*, she still faced the prospect of collaborating on two more novels with Johnston. Meanwhile, she couldn't get on with her own novel.

Her solution, as we shall see, was to do the tedious slog of research and to workshop the stories and characters with her partner, but to leave most of the actual production of prose to Johnston. Although the option arrangement would force Clift to lend her name to two more joint works, *The Piping Cry* was the last completed novel on which she worked in full partnership with Johnston.

The rejection of *The Piping Cry* was like a black cloud over Christmas 1951 and the New Year of 1952. It seemed to match the sleety skies of Charmian's first English winter. No longer did the fog seem romantic. And it was so cold and wet all the time that she couldn't take the children outdoors, so the three of them were constantly cooped up together in the flat.

Greeba Jamison was only in England for nine months, and while she saw a bit of the Johnstons and visited their home, she was not a particular confidante. Yet from even this amount of contact she discerned that there was 'some disillusionment' for Clift:

I don't think Charmian was altogether happy in that London period — she hated the climate to start with [...] My impression is she also had periods of great loneliness in London because she was shut up in the flat with two little children. George was working top speed [...] He would have been working all the hours of the day and night and on call. You see, because of the time lag, a London correspondent for an Australian newspaper gets telephoned at 2 o'clock in the morning because it's deadline in Melbourne or something. He was a very busy journalist, and I'm under the impression Charmian had many lonely weeks and months during that time in London.[44]

Jamison was also aware that George's absence wasn't always due to work. There was 'a girl here or there', she remembered. In London, George reverted to the behaviour he had practised in the *Argus* office, when married to his first wife: flirting with the pretty junior female employees, and sometimes doing more than flirt. In *Closer to the Sun* — the first autobiographical novel about David Meredith, written a few years earlier than the trilogy — the hero admits to himself there had been 'other women, occasional women' while he and his wife were living in London.[45] This earlier text is considerably more critical of Meredith than the later version.

Did Charmian know? Possibly not yet. Not quite. But she knew she was home alone, and George was out with other people. At the same time, George was still suspicious of Charmian, in particular making a fuss about her friendship with the family's charismatic doctor.[46]

If the weather was often bleak and the domestic situation was lonely and miserable, there was also a sense of being in an alien society, and of still being on the periphery. Clift later described the situation this way:

I liked England, I was very happy in London, excepting that again there was the feeling of being bound and constrained, held by little children in an apartment or taking them to school or bringing them home or walking them in parks, and I felt that I was an outsider looking in, never part of it, never part of the London I wanted to be part of, because I wasn't free.[47]

We will come later to the matter of freedom, but first there is this outsider theme again. In the fragment of story called 'The Man in the Corner',[48] Liza, a young Australian woman, and her husband, John, do not fit in at all with the British people at a smart party. As well as feeling alien, they are made to feel the combined condescension and envy which their colonial status evokes. The story suddenly takes a strange and nightmarish turn as a man with a 'tiny, foetus-like head' and 'not quite human hair' manifests himself in the corner, and insists that he has met the Australians before. He is a collector of stuffed birds (or perhaps something more sinister). Somehow Liza and John are hijacked into a panel van and taken at lunatic speed for a ride through London. The fragment ends before the destination of the journey becomes clear, but the feeling of claustrophobia and 'the almost tangible air of corruption and decay' is very real, as is the sense of the great difference between the couple and their bizarre British hosts. But if here the Australians are described as 'normal people' and the English are aliens, the experience underlines how alien the author felt herself to be in this place.

Although Charmian's feelings of alienation and claustrophobia in London were greatly to increase, by this first winter of 1951–52 she was already disillusioned enough to know that the Big Thing that she was seeking wasn't in England. She was already in the process of fixing her mind upon another place which might contain her personal Grail. Where else but in the cradle of Western art and democracy? George had been briefly to Greece as a war correspondent in 1944 and since the beginning of the relationship had been promising Charmian a trip there. But Charmian was thinking of more than a holiday. In this first winter in England she spoke to Greeba Jamison of going to live in the Greek islands. Johnston spoke of this too, but Jamison 'always had the impression Charmian was deadly serious — she wanted to go to that Greek island. To George it was a bit of a dream [...] But she was dead set to go'.[49] It is hard to resist the temptation to evoke here a memory of the night of the 'squeegee board', when Clift sat in the army hut interrogating her destiny. Was she, in this bleak winter, occasionally thinking of 'an island south of Budapest' that was waiting for her?

On Boxing Day 1951, George Johnston noted in his 'London Diary' column that although there had been 'at least six occasions over the last twelve months when the cold war could have been converted into a hot war overnight', the prospects for peace were now better. All in all, he concluded, 'we have skated over an awful lot of thin ice in 1951'.[50]

In the relationship of Charmian Clift and George Johnston, too, there had been a bit of skating on thin ice in 1951. The ice would get even more patchy over the next three years in London.

* * *

On Wednesday 6 February 1952, King George VI died. With the accession of England's young Queen, the press immediately produced the pretty notion that there had begun a new Elizabethan Age which would achieve 'glory such as the first Elizabeth inspired'.[51] This would prove much more successful than the previous year's Festival of Britain as a morale boost to a nation still recovering from the war. The drama and pageantry of these events pleased Charmian, who confessed herself 'Cavalier enough' to be delighted by 'all the bravery of uniforms and drums and flags', despite her Roundhead politics.[52]

Soon there was for her a much greater source of excitement, for in late April George kept the promise which he had made at the very beginning of the relationship: he took her travelling. The couple left Martin and Shane at an exclusive children's country holiday establishment, run by the wife of Jomo 'Burning Spear' Kenyatta, and while the children went exploring with their hero, young Peter Kenyatta, their parents set off to Europe for a month or so.[53]

As she travelled, Charmian Clift recorded the journey in little scraps of handwritten notes — sometimes in small notebooks, but just as commonly on the backs of envelopes, drink coasters, restaurant bills and the like. After returning home, she would type up these notes into a kind of travel diary.[54]

From the very start of the journey, Charmian began to record her impressions. It was springtime, and on the roadsides wild flowers blossomed among the tidy rows of small white crosses which were a reminder of the recent ravages of war. Charmian and George drove through northern France and Luxembourg into Germany, where they travelled up the Mosel Valley to Koblenz, then down along the Rhine and into Austria. Here the couple stayed in the little town of Feldkirch in the Vorarlberg, where their window looked out on a mountain called Wildekaiser — Wild Emperor. Clift would glean material for a short story, and would store up memories of the Tyrol which, years later, would creep into her writing again and again.

> The Arlberg Pass was open but only just, and all the peaks were pure and dazzling above the dark smudges of spruce and larch and fir, above the huddling wooden villages and the needle-spired churches, and the air was so crisp that words tinkled in it: there were carved wooden shrines on tall posts in the snow, with little offerings of maize cobs and buttercups and drifts of blue forget-me-nots, quite improbable.[55]

Driving down through the Alps, the two travellers reached Italy, where Clift felt — as she had felt in the early days in London — that the whole experience was too incredible to be happening. 'The first time you sail up the Grand Canal through Venice', she later wrote, 'it's not that you couldn't have imagined it. You actually can't believe it'.[56] From Venice they headed south through Bologna, Florence, Siena, and Orvieto to Rome, where George Johnston had spent three months during the war. After a few days sightseeing among the ruins, the couple headed along the coast towards France.

By now, Charmian Clift had seen plenty of famous sights but the high point of the whole journey — the 'sight' remembered by both her and George for the rest of their lives as the quintessence of the whole trip, to be told to their children,[57] to be transformed into fiction — was an incident which occurred during the night in the small fishing town of Lerici. Here the couple's window looked out over the town square and beyond to the Gulf of Spezia, where Shelley had drowned a hundred and thirty years before.

On this night in Lerici, the bells in the marketplace clock tower set up a crazy, uncoordinated clamour as a full orange moon rose in the sky. Below the travellers' window, in the town square, restaurant tables were pushed together for a reunion party. As the couple slept fitfully, the noise mounted, and then into the voices was woven a high, haunting music. Rising, opening their shutters and looking down into the moonlit square, the couple saw that the source of the sound was three thin men in round-crowned hats and long shabby coats, who jigged as they played upon two violins and a pipe. The music died away as the diners began clapping, and suddenly the two watchers realised that the musicians were 'three *old* men'. In her typed travel notes, Clift continues:

> Later, when we had returned to our beds, they played again, and now it was a gay tune that persisted in my sleep, endlessly repetitive yet constantly refreshing. The bells were somehow mixed up in it, pealing with laughter at the ironical pipe, ever higher, ever clearer, leading them on with such joyful absurdities that they crashed out demented, discordant chimes and were suddenly quiet. We awoke together. The music was fading, lightly, lightly, the strings thrummed and the pipe danced on six notes that were the distillation of youth and spring and crushed flowers, and when we crept to the window we saw that the table

below was quite empty, and across the square the three old musicians were walking away (still we did not see their faces). The very tall old man was still in the middle, and as they played they bent their knees and shuffled from one side to the other in time, but their legs looked very thin and very infirm, old men's legs, and I stood at the window and wept as they slowly shuffled into the dark shadows past the clock tower and were gone from us. Still we stood, listening, until we could no longer be sure whether we still heard the vibration of a thin high note ... a reed ... Pan in the moonlight ... all youth ... all beauty ... and I was still weeping when I returned to my bed.[58]

This incident would have an extraordinary meaning for Charmian Clift — and indeed for George Johnston as well. Both writers would store it up, and would later use it in fiction. For the moment, however, the travellers drove on around the coast into France, to Marseilles, and then headed on through 'the enchanted silvery towns of the Loire valley', where the landscape was 'done in washed watercolour as Italy is done in oils, the Loire as delicate as Italy is strong in colour'.[59] Finally, there was Brittany, and then the car-ferry back to England.

It is hard to convey the importance for Charmian Clift of this first European pilgrimage to what she saw as 'the source'.[60] She would draw upon her hoard of memories of this trip in piece after piece of writing for the next seventeen years.

But if this journey provided material, it was also the means whereby Charmian Clift — slowly, and at this stage unconsciously — began to develop the form that was to be her forte. This is evident in the travel notes, which Clift typed onto sturdy punch-holed paper that fitted in a black loose-leaf folder. Although some of these notes (including the first Lerici page) have been lost, in the six and a half extant pages — written up from the handwritten scraps but still a fairly unrevised piece of writing — we see for the first time Charmian Clift confidently writing as Charmian Clift. That is, we have here the writer who would within three years produce her first travel book, *Mermaid Singing*, and who, more than a decade later, would discover in the essay the genre which might have been invented for her.

The values which would make Clift's travel writing and her essays so special were not simply the much-praised lyrical qualities of her prose, but something idiosyncratic to Charmian Clift's way of looking at things. While part of this was Clift's eye for tiny and apparently inconsequential details, it was also the essayist's gift of relating observations back to the personal. There was also an ability to convey the freshness of each experience, and a sensuousness that went beyond the purely visual. Of northern France, for example, she wrote:

> The dilapidation of the French farm buildings. Everything dust-coloured and peeling — or that lovely faded Reckitt's blue — the workmen's overalls blue too — whole blue-clad families out in the fields together — they might have been Chinese coolies [...]
>
> The roads were long and straight and tall poplars met at a point miles away. You just put the car's nose at that point and put your foot down on the accelerator and chased that point on and on and on. If you stopped by the way to go into the bushes at the side of the road the leather of the upholstery was hot when you got into the car again. We had the wind scoops open the whole time. There seemed an enormous amount of sky, with big lazy whoofs of cloud.[61]

A further quality of Clift's was her insatiable curiosity as to the how and why of things. 'Round haystacks with a slice cut out of them, like a cake,' she noted of the Loire valley. 'What implement do they use to cut it so cleanly?' And there was revealed the kind of fascination with, and respect for, the business of manual labour which is also found in the paintings of Millet:

> How satisfying it is to watch an expert at his work, and how beautiful are the trades of the sea. At Lerici the folding of the nets was a complicated matter, and it took two men to handle each net [...]
>
> The brown boy in jersey and striped trousers stood in the boat and his mate on the jetty, and they unwound the net from its coil on the jetty and refolded it into the boat [...] There didn't seem to be any order about it, but I suppose there was [...] Any work done expertly looks easy.[62]

Although Clift typed up her notes of this journey and put them in a folder, at this stage she saw this sort of writing not as a literary product in itself, but as a means to an end. That end, of course, was fiction.

It was perhaps a year or so later that Charmian Clift was to write two short stories prompted by this 1952 journey. However, it is convenient to discuss this work here, not least because its failure to fulfil the promise of the travel notes serves to underline the fact that fiction did not come as easily to Charmian Clift as descriptive, first person narrative. In one of these stories, 'Wild Emperor',[63] a weak little English woman, Doris, comes to join her mill engineer husband, Harry Piggott, at a guesthouse beneath Wildekaiser mountain. A parallel is drawn between the woman, who is imprisoned in her marriage, and Josef, the landlord's tormented son, who was recently a prisoner of war.

Part of the problem with this story is that it lacks a clear and sympathetic character focus. Clift's main fictional piece from this European trip, 'Three Old Men of Lerici',[64] also doesn't quite come off as a story because the writer's sympathy swings back and forth between the female protagonist and her lover in a way that blurs the story's meaning. However, in biographical terms 'Three Old Men of Lerici' is a key text.

Clift's lack of sympathy for the heroine is clear.[65] Ursula is selfish, snobbish and short-tempered. Narcissistically preoccupied with her own ageing body, 'She never wore a watch; the thin threadlike pointers frightened her somehow, spinning so fast. Like wearing one's death on one's wrist'. Ursula realises that it has been a mistake to come on a hectic European tour with her young and adoring lover Freiburg;[66] apart from the exhaustion of travel, Ursula is continually offended by Freiburg's 'tendencies towards vulgarity'. Despite this, she has 'high hopes' when the couple arrive at Lerici. These expectations are quickly shattered when Ursula discovers that the twelve outdoor restaurant tables at their hotel have been reserved for a reunion. Opting for a tray alone in the room, she sarcastically sends Freiburg off to eat at the Shelley Restaurant.

Now there begins Clift's fictional reworking of the incident involving the three musicians, as perceived through the eyes and ears of Ursula. The bells start to ring, and Ursula finds their clamour to be a torment. Yet she does manage to sleep, for when she first hears the pipe it is 'very thin and far away, and so high it [is] almost beyond the threshold of sound':

> There was nothing else, neither laughter nor bells, but after a time a faint thrumming rose and fell behind the reed, like the beating of innumerable tiny wings over a summer pond. Ah, don't! Ursula cried silently. Don't hurt me like that. But the little wings were beating in her head, and the pipe pierced her like sunlight.[67]

She stumbles to the window to 'put out' the mysterious winged thing, but sees that 'all the diners [are] turned towards a lively triangle at the head of the table':

> There, ludicrous in their age and poverty, three very old men in round-crowned hats and shabby coats bent bobbing shoulders over pipe and strings, jigging out a measure to their own music. Their thin old legs bent, fragile and brittle-looking as twigs beneath their flapping rags, shuffling out a spritely parody of youth, and as they shuffled they tilted their heads, each in a listening attitude, as if they were translating some secret thing they heard in the night.

While this 'secret thing' is to become of great importance to Ursula, the pipe summons up the pipes of Pan himself, which are seen as holding the key to ultimate meaning.[68] But the meaning is lost. Ursula is just in the act of receiving illumination when the text breaks off:

> Ursula felt — she ought to feel — outraged. It was as if an outrageous thing was happening to her. As if ... *why*, she thought, groping feverishly on the outskirts of memory, *I know* ...
>
> But just as her mind stumbled in surprised recognition the strings twangled into silence and the last high gurgling note of the pipe floated out to sea and was gone.

As the noisy party resumes, Ursula knows 'It [is] over'. Shivering, colder than she has ever been, she realises that 'She would always be cold now'. Her earlier fears about her own ageing attractions, about her lover's fidelity, return. She visualises Freiburg, happy on the sand with some young Italian beauty, not even hearing the extraordinary music.

> *But then*, she thought, with an old familiar envy stirring tiredly, Freiburg hears it all the time.
>
> He heard it all the time. But that was *it* of course! That was this thing about Freiburg. That was what she had resented in him all this time — and envied — calling it vulgarity. She was always distracted by the discordant notes, but Freiburg was simple and humble enough to hear them as part of the pattern. And it seemed suddenly to her that if one could only hear it the pipe played always — if one knew how to listen, as Freiburg did.[69]

As Ursula wakes again, the music is fading, and Freiburg sits on the window ledge, puffy-faced and reeking of cheap wine. Holding his drunken chestnut head, Ursula looks out, and sees the retreating figures of the three old men, as depicted in the travel notes. And now the author's own tears at this scene are bestowed upon the young man: 'Freiburg's maudlin tears had soaked through [Ursula's] nightgown. She could feel them spreading hot and wet across her bosom, as if her heart had burst'.

The last sentence is a triumph, linking the two lovers into the one body and suggesting a Madonna and Child pose,[70] but it is unfortunate that the adjective 'maudlin' undermines the validity of Freiburg's weeping, and also alienates the reader from Ursula, who seems as snobbish as she was before her experience. All in all, the reader is left wondering exactly what the writer was trying to say in this story. Is it that the Freiburgs of this world hear the music all the time? And are the Ursulas damned never to understand? Further, is the music simply beautiful, or was Ursula right to panic, to feel the music as a form of pain?

As Garry Kinnane has shown, George Johnston drew extensively from Clift's travel notebook for the section of *Clean Straw for Nothing* entitled 'Notes from an Expatriate's Journal'.[71] While this use of Clift's material is part of the biographical record, the differences in emphasis and intended effect between the Lerici texts of Clift and of Johnston[72] are just as revealing.

In the Lerici passage of *Clean Straw for Nothing*, the clock on the marketplace tower is working, and the whole incident — fey though it seems — is presented as a real event placed in real time. In Clift's story, on the other hand, both Ursula and the reader have no sense of what time it really is, for 'the clock on the tower [has] stopped at nine minutes past seven'.[73] By stopping the clock, Clift sets her story in a time void which allows magical things to happen.

In regard to the weeping, there is another shift in meaning. In the travel notes, after referring to 'Pan in the moonlight ... all youth ... all beauty'... Clift simply concludes that she was still weeping when she went to bed. Johnston, however, through the voice of David Meredith, moves into a snatch of philosophising and then to an extended description of the weeping:

> Pan in the moonlight, and youth, and beauty ... So much of
> Europe is a beautiful dream, too. But are good dreams any easier
> to understand than nightmares? I think perhaps Cressida

understands. She is awake beside me for a long time, quite still, staring up into the cool play of shadow and moonlight in the high dim room. Her cheeks are wet and she says nothing. It is a long time since I have seen that secret rapt expression on her face, not since Lebanon Bay, when she would stand at night on the ocean's edge and look out across the dark heartbeat of the Pacific.

I would like to talk to her, but I feel awkward, and to talk would be a kind of intrusion, and I do not, in any case, know what to say.[74]

For David Meredith, the incident ultimately serves to reveal once again his apartness from his wife. It reminds him of their difference.

Overall, it is clear that Charmian and George, looking down from their window, also perceived the sight in the moonlit square very differently. It would seem that for George Johnston, what happened at Lerici was simply an exquisitely beautiful experience of sight and sound. For Charmian Clift, this same experience was a mystic event which seemed to happen outside the normal laws of the universe. Furthermore, it connected with something which had been worrying her since she was a young girl, and which would continue to nag at her for the rest of her life. This was the sense that there was some meaning just beyond her grasp. At the same time, the three old men of Lerici were, for Clift, a reminder that we are all stick figures, transients, here one minute and gone the next. Time was so short: and life might never reveal its ultimate meaning.

12

LOSING IDENTITY

I did very little work of my own because I didn't have time, also in a sort
of sense, in some peculiar sense, I felt at that time that I was losing my
identity completely, I wasn't quite sure who I was. Nothing was
happening in the way I wanted it to happen.[1]

When Charmian returned to England after this European trip, she felt
uneasy at the comparison: the effects of war had been so terribly
evident in France and 'anguished Germany', and Britain seemed to be
suffering less,[2] despite the ongoing queues and shortages. Or perhaps it was
a certain complacency and placidity in the English themselves which was
troubling her. There was a bit of guilt, too, for the Johnston family's
circumstances were particularly comfortable. The Bayswater Road flat was
rather posh, and household help was provided a couple of mornings a week
by a redoubtable Cockney charlady named Mrs Dapp.[3]

In this summer of 1952, the flat above that of the Johnstons was leased by
a young woman named Jo and her husband. The building's small lift
opened directly into both flats, and very soon the two women were seeing a
great deal of each other. This friendship, like the earlier Sydney friendship
with Toni, developed out of the propinquity of flat life, and through a
common experience as mothers of young children — for soon after her
arrival, Jo gave birth to a daughter, and eighteen months later to a son. Like
the friendship with Toni, this relationship with Jo was to continue, despite
geographic separation, until Charmian Clift's death. As these were the only
deep and long-term relationships which Charmian ever formed with other
women, it is interesting that in both cases it was very much a domestic

friendship. Indeed, both these relationships could be described as sisterly — in the family sense, rather than the feminist one. This was the sort of loving and accepting and mutually helping relationship that nice sisters in traditional families have. Again it is possible to see Charmian compensating for the failings of the Clift family.

In Charmian's friendship with Jo, we see a very generous side of her: in January 1954, when Jo was in hospital having her second baby, it was Charmian who looked after the toddler Andrina, and Jo related that when her husband died suddenly six months later, 'George and Charmian almost "adopted" me and the kids'. From her observations of Charmian over the period from mid 1952 to the end of 1954, Jo remembered:

> Charm was a wonderful mother. She seemed to have endless patience and there was always an endless stream of small school friends in and out of the place. Martin was already showing signs of his extraordinary abilities and these although encouraged were never exploited [...] His great love was his lead soldiers with which he staged real battles — laying them out in battle order taken from the history books he had found and using cushions as hills and scarves as rivers etc. It was fascinating to see and Charm always encouraged him in a matter of fact but serious way — letting him leave the 'mess' even if it was in the middle of the dining room floor! Both he and Shane painted and drew wonderful imaginative pictures and were taken to concerts at this early age.[4]

These 'extraordinary abilities' of Martin, who turned five in November 1952, were intellectual. 'He was fascinated by archaeology', Jo added, 'and used to visit the British Museum to discuss all kinds of things with the Curator at regular intervals'. By the age of six 'he used to write the most beautiful poems and stories'; 'he had already read a great deal and seemed to understand what he had read'. Though obviously the child had inherited his intellect from both his parents, it was Charmian who gave Martin the kind of encouragement which caused him to develop his imagination, even indulging his passion for King Arthur to the extent of sewing for him a suit of mail made of tiny individual chain-links.[5] George, meanwhile, envisaged an academic career for this brainy child, whom he nicknamed 'the Professor' — to Charmian's considerable annoyance.[6]

Shane was also obviously very clever and imaginative and would enact all sorts of imaginary dramas with her large collection of dolls, for which

Charmian would make clothes out of scraps of material. However, neither George nor Charmian seemed to recognise or encourage Shane's intellectual gifts to the same degree that they fostered those of their son. It was as if Shane's role was to be the sort of free-spirited child of nature whom Charmian portrayed in the stories of her child alter ego. Of course, Charmian saw this sort of role as an ideal, but it would nevertheless have the effect of making Shane feel that Martin received special treatment — not just from their parents, but also from the other adults whom this odd little boy would engage in earnest conversation about subjects that Shane found boring. The little girl could not be expected to see that her brother's bookishness and preference for adult company reflected the fact that he was painfully shy with his peers, whereas Shane made friends easily and could play with other children from sunup to sundown, taking a leadership role in the games just as her mother had done in the childhood gangs of North Kiama.

The trouble was, in London both children had to spend most of their time inside. On many afternoons, Charmian and Jo and the children would cross the busy road to the park, 'armed with Marmite sandwiches and tricycles and dolls' prams',[7] but this sort of experience did not give the children the outdoor freedom that was part of Charmian's definition of childhood. She would complain that it was 'impossible for them ever to move out of the front door without an adult to accompany them' and that Martin at seven could give her 'an interesting and lucid account of the life cycle of a tree but couldn't climb one'.[8]

Overall, Jo's picture of the 'inside' world of the flat, where she would see Charmian's indulgence of her children, is supported by Cedric Flower, who with his wife Pat sometimes used to babysit. He described Charmian as 'a devoted mama'.[9] But indulgent and devoted though she was, the needs of the children were keeping Charmian away from her writing.

In these London years, the author was having a very frustrating time: starting things and being unable to finish them, starting them in a new guise and again finding them fail. Very little of Clift's solo writing from this London period was ever finished, and none of it was published in her lifetime. As a result there is a gap of eight years between the publication of *High Valley* and Charmian Clift's next real book, *Mermaid Singing*. This is a significant hiatus in the career of a new writer, particularly one as committed as Clift. Was the reason simply the demands of being a mother and housewife?

In retrospect, it seems that the primary thing that was blocking Clift's work was the need to produce two more collaborative novels with her husband in order to satisfy the terms of the contracts which the authors had signed with their three separate publishing companies in three countries. Since the failure of *The Piping Cry*, these contractual obligations had become an albatross around Clift's neck. She couldn't properly concentrate on her own work while she still 'owed' other work. Of course, the real problem was that she hated collaborating with her husband, whose writing process and prose style were wildly different from hers. This difficulty was not helped by the fact that George Johnston loved his wife to work with him, even on projects that weren't officially joint novels. It was hard to refuse to assist him, because he was the breadwinner and she wasn't involved in a major task of her own. Thus the whole thing became a vicious circle: the less Clift wrote, the less she was able to write.

It was under these conditions that in mid 1952 the couple began a new novel, entitled *The Big Chariot*. A tale of heroism and adventure set in seventeenth century China, this was a return to the exotic territory which had proved so successful with *High Valley*.

If Clift worked with Johnston on the actual writing of a text, his production speed meant that she was left behind. There were also arguments about literary matters which spilled over into the personal relationship. She therefore decided to adopt the more lowly position of research assistant. After dropping Shane and Martin at school, she would race in to the British Museum and frantically make notes on historical background material until it was time to hurry back and pick up the children again. During these London years she also did the research for another China novel of Johnston's *(Pagoda)* and for another collaborative historical novel, entitled *Barbarian*. Neither of these got much beyond the research stage. It is little wonder that, years later, when describing how weary she had grown with collaboration, she declared, 'I felt like a literary hod-carrier'.[10]

As both the plot and prose of *The Big Chariot* are very much Johnston's work, it is not necessary to deal with them here. It should be noted, however, that beneath all the historical swashbuckling, this novel — like *High Valley* — was an attempt to educate readers about the people and politics of contemporary China. The authors' foreword claims: 'It is, in its picture of the struggle of a traditional idealism against a vigorous, brutal and machine-forged tyranny, not without its parallel today'.[11] In George

Johnston's view, of course, the contemporary tyranny was the Kuomintang. Given the trouble that his views on China had previously caused, it was brave of Johnston to keep sticking his neck out in regard to this issue.

Another endearing quality is his confidence: for a self-avowed pessimist, George Johnston was capable of the most extraordinary wishful thinking in regard to his own work. Less than a year after his misplaced hopes for *The Piping Cry*, he was writing to Albert Arlen that the new novel might well be 'the big one' that would crack the bestseller list and attract the attention of 'the Hollywood Moguls'. *The Big Chariot*, he wrote, 'represents all our aspirations, and could change our lives completely'. Johnston used this as an excuse to call off the collaboration with Arlen over *The Sentimental Bloke*, telling him to find another librettist.[12]

The Big Chariot was completed at the end of 1952 and by February 1953 had been accepted in America, Britain and Australia. It was published in the United States by Bobbs-Merrill in March. The Angus & Robertson Australian edition followed in August 1953, and Faber and Faber brought out the British edition in September. At first it seemed as if this novel might go well, but once again all the hype came to nothing. Although the book was favourably reviewed, sales in all three countries were disappointing.[13]

The best outcome of the book for Charmian Clift was that it brought about a meeting with her greatest living poetic idol, TS Eliot, who as a director of Faber and Faber invited the two authors to the 'most memorable' afternoon tea that Charmian ever had:

> I even remember what I wore, and that I carried a fresh pair of white gloves in my handbag in case a fleck of soot or grime should stain the ones already on my hands, and that as we approached the door in Woburn Square I prickled all over with electric tingles, like small shocks: my hair might even have stood on end if it had not been so carefully coiffed and secured by a stylish hat. One does not meet idols every day, particularly not for tea.
>
> The room was very large and filled entirely with piles of books. Books on shelves, wiggly piles of books on tables, wobblier piles in stacks on the floor, and out from behind them crawled (quite literally on all fours) J. Alfred Prufrock in person.
>
> He was looking, he said, for his Nobel Prize Citation, which he seemed to have mislaid.[14]

For the girl from the wrong end of town who had sat on the woodblock chanting poetry and dreaming of the world beyond her tiny valley, this meeting was one of the high points of the London experiences.

It was at the beginning of April 1953 that the couple received their first copies of *The Big Chariot*. That very same week George Johnston switched his allegiance to the next project, declaring in a letter to Aubrey Cousins at Angus & Robertson: 'We've already launched out on a new novel, *Barbarian*, which we think will be the best yet'.[15] Although Johnston saw this as a collaborative project, all the meticulous research notes are by Clift and the twenty opening pages are clearly by Charmian Clift writing alone — and in her most lush mode.[16] *Barbarian* is overtly set in the Tigris-Euphrates valley at the beginning of civilisation, but Clift drew once again upon her beloved local landscape: the reedy riverbank has the same rich smell as her depictions of the North Kiama creek, and the gentle boy-hero Kish brings to mind Charmian's brother Barré.

On a more direct level also, Charmian Clift returned to Kiama in her writing during these London years. It has already been noted that the novel *Walk to the Paradise Gardens*, which the author on a number of occasions promised to her agent, probably represented a development from the old autobiographical Kiama material about the Morley family. Although it is clear that Clift took the typescripts of the various versions of *Greener Grows the Grass* to London, the textual evidence suggests that she abandoned this directly autobiographical material for the moment, and chose instead a small incident from her Kiama memory bank as the starting point for a new story.[17] This was the memory of the mad woman Selina, whom the Kiama kids used to spy on as she roamed around the edge of the quarry. In the woman's past there was supposedly some Gothic tragedy, which the novelist now began to spin into a tale which would fit very nicely with the romantic title which she had borrowed from Delius.

But why was Charmian Clift going back again and again in her writing at this time to her own landscape, her own family, her own beginnings? After all, now that she lived a cosmopolitan life in London, she had realised her dream of escape from that small town background. Surely part of the answer is connected with Clift's unhappiness. In London she felt so cramped and cold, so lonely and lost, that she sought happiness and security through summoning up the myth of her free and sunny childhood world. But it was also as if she could not move forward — either personally or as a writer — until she had got this early experience down on paper, and given it closure.

* * *

During these London years, the relationship between George and Charmian was being severely tested. In the first David Meredith novel, *Closer to the Sun*, the hero muses upon how he and his wife Kate had come 'perilously close' to the end in London — though he didn't see it until they left. Nor had he seen 'how deeply he had wounded her'.[18] Later, Kate herself refers to 'the nightmare years in London', when 'gradually she had lost [her husband] as earlier the children had lost him'.

> Gradually, then less and less gradually, she had seen him as a figure growing dimmer and stranger, as tired eyes meeting hers or evading them across a breakfast table which he never saw; seen him as chemist's prescriptions, as benzedrine to stay awake and phenobarb to go to sleep; seen him as lies told in a thick voice on a telephone late at night; as car doors slammed by drunken friends, as tensions and stresses exploding in unreasoning angers or damp-squibbing into dreary silences, as bewildering terrors, as restless eyes staring from a cold bed at a darkened window; seen him also in the shape of herself, growing more shadowy, growing desperately lonely, growing colder, seated waiting on the edge of a bed — a woman left to her own devices, with nothing to devise.[19]

This is a pretty accurate description. In these London years, George was under considerable pressure, and it was Charmian who had to provide the emotional support during his crises, as well as working on his books and her books, and running the household. Mrs Dapp may have done the dusting, but it was Charmian alone who did the evening shift with the children.

In order to put in the hours required by daytime journalism and late-night writing, George Johnston — like David Meredith — relied on amphetamines as well as alcohol and nicotine to keep kick-starting the Muse, and then had to use barbiturates in order to sleep.[20] In the 1950s, the use of such drugs was not regarded as either bohemian or particularly hazardous. However, the combination of work pressure, lifestyle, prescription drugs and alcohol did take its toll on Johnston's health: after all, in 1952 he turned forty. As the author describes this time in the life of David Meredith, by the end of the second year in London the strain of the two jobs was 'beginning seriously to tell on him' and the hero 'pushed himself very close to a breakdown' during the writing of his China novel.[21]

Meanwhile, the thought of Greece continued to burn like a torch through the darkness of London life. According to Garry Kinnane, at some time in 1952 Sidney Nolan had taken the couple to meet an elderly woman named Clarisse Zander, mother-in-law of the painter Carl Plate.

> Mrs Zander had been on an archaeological tour to Greece, which included a visit to Hydra, which she found not only beautiful but cheap, and she pointed out that it would make an ideal retreat for a writer to go to and 'write something worthwhile'. The Johnstons had taken note of this.[22]

In the following year, however, there was no time to explore this possibility. With the Coronation due in the summer of 1953, Johnston's annual springtime leave was reduced to two weeks. The couple spent this April fortnight with their friends Ursula and Colin Colahan on a tour of the vineyards of the Bordeaux region. However, even this was work of a kind, for Johnston had wangled the trip at the French government's expense in return for promising to write a magazine feature which Colahan would illustrate. Although, as with the 1952 trip, Charmian Clift would store up happy memories which she would later draw upon in her essays, two weeks simply wasn't a long enough break, and the presence of the Colahans meant that George and Charmian weren't alone together.[23]

As soon as they returned from the French vineyards, Johnston wrote to ask his editor at Faber and Faber for a copy of WA Wigram's *Hellenic Travel*, which 'we desperately need because Charmian and I are planning a trip to Greece within the next twelve months for the purpose of getting additional material for another novel'.[24] In addition to Wigram's guide, the couple started reading Homer and Herodotus and dipping into commentaries on the Greek myths and popular books about archaeology. Their enthusiasm spread to Martin, who began to transfer his loyalties from King Arthur to Perseus.

The dream of Greece helped the Johnstons get through this year in which George's workload became particularly burdensome, and Charmian in turn had to provide increasing support. While the lead-up to the Coronation required thousands of words to keep Australian readers fully informed about their new Queen, it was not just the volume of this work which exhausted George Johnston. As a republican, the act of writing reams of Royal rubbish seemed to highlight the pointlessness of journalism, particularly when his articles about the Cold War were being subbed down to pap or spiked.[25]

On the great day in June, Charmian and the children had a long and weary wait in the covered stand outside the Abbey until they saw the golden coach roll past. But George had a far worse time inside. That morning, Shane had used her daddy's braces to hang a rebel doll out the nursery window; this was not discovered until after George had left. So he was forced to spend the day holding up his enormous hired tail-suit trousers as he sat next to Rebecca West (with whom he had quarrelled in print), and watched peers of the realm guzzle breasts of grouse while he pined for the sandwiches which he had left in his car outside the Foreign Office. Meanwhile, he was quite out of synch with the lavatory roster. This went on for nine hours.[26]

It would be enough to turn anyone off journalism — and George was already moving in that direction. Earlier this year, in his correspondence with Angus & Robertson about *The Big Chariot*, he had revealed his dissatisfaction with his current employment, asking for an increased royalty rate and large print run because '*The Big Chariot* [...] may be the means [of] getting out of journalism at last and devoting myself full-time to authorship'.[27]

The Big Chariot didn't provide this escape, but the circumstances which would precipitate Johnston's departure from journalism were beginning, although he didn't see this at the time. In September 1953, as a chatty preamble to a letter asking Aubrey Cousins at Angus & Robertson to send his first wife £25 to cover outstanding alimony, Johnston wrote: 'No doubt you know all about the Battle of the Titans and the GREAT MERGER out there between us and the S.M.H., and over here we are naturally rocking to the repercussions'.[28] Johnston could joke about 'the rumblings and shudderings of our little newsprint empire' but this was no small, or laughing, matter. Associated Newspapers Limited, Johnston's employer, had done a share deal with the Fairfax family company which resulted in the editorial management of the *Sun* newspaper passing over to the *Sydney Morning Herald*. Within two weeks of Johnston's writing this letter, the London office was put under the control of Anthony Whitlock, and George Johnston was demoted to the position of second in charge.

Ageing tends to be particularly difficult for those who have won recognition and success in their youth. In the world of Australian journalism, George Johnston had been a prodigy. At forty, however, he was looking distinctly like a has-been. This demotion was almost more humiliating than the circumstances under which George had left the *Argus*:

at least then he had been able to storm off in a mood of righteous indignation, but this time there was no great principle involved. And this time he had to stay. Or did he?

Since the success of *High Valley*, Charmian Clift had been urging her husband to get out of journalism so that they could both try to live by full-time writing. The reason Johnston always gave for not doing this was that he had to be the breadwinner. The problem was that while he stayed in journalism, and while he stayed in London, the family needed not just bread but butter, jam, cream and caviar to go on it. And a chilled bottle of hock on the side. The only solution would be a double break: to leave journalism, and to leave city life behind. This would be like the 1946 escape from Melbourne, but on a far grander scale. Under these circumstances, the idea of Greece began to burn even more brightly.

In the unproduced television play *Bed of Thorns*, written in the early 1960s, George Johnston gives an insight into his state of body and mind at this time through the depiction of Charles Collins, a businessman in his early forties who is thoroughly exhausted as the result of a takeover bid. As Collins comes out of the tube station on a wet and cheerless winter evening, he hallucinates that he sees a rocky Greek landscape. When he returns to his comfortable Bayswater Road flat and tells his wife Janet of the vision, she tells him that he's 'been in a state of jitters for months'. She sends him off to see a doctor, who declares that Charles is 'in a highly neurotic and very run-down condition' exacerbated by 'this filthy winter'.[29]

In fact, in this winter of 1953–54 George Johnston suffered a drawn-out bout of bilateral pneumonia.[30] Already his chest and lungs were proving to be his weak spot. All in all, as the doctor told the fictional Charles, the sooner he took the long-delayed holiday to Greece, the better.

And so when George's annual leave came in April 1954, the couple went to what Charmian would describe as 'the land of our dreams'. This love affair with Greece, she noted, was 'founded on a sort of romantic bookishness, fed through the years on Sophocles, Homer and Thucydides, Strabo and Herodotus'.[31] Already completely under the power of the Homeric legend, the couple were planning a comprehensive tour of the sites of ancient myth rather than a restful seaside holiday. And like the vineyards trip, this would be a working holiday, gathering material for fiction and non-fiction which would pay for the expenses. As usual, the children were boarded in the holiday home; it wasn't the best solution, for Martin always complained about the food, and Charmian always missed the children,[32] but without any relatives in England, there was no alternative. The itinerary was too hectic for young children to enjoy; and besides, the couple desperately needed some time alone together.

Charmian and George set off by train on 26 April.[33] Although the Orient Express totally failed to live up to romantic expectation, everything suddenly brightened as the couple saw the dawn breaking on the snowy top of Mt Olympus.[34] They were in Greece!

Before Charmian and George had left England, Martin — now aged six and a half and 'serious about his heroes' — had given them a letter to pass on to Perseus 'if you have time, of course'.[35] If Martin could write to Perseus as other children write to Santa, his father's attitude was nearly as credulous. Describing in a feature article how he and his wife went 'holidaying with Homer', George Johnston promised that 'You can find the myth and magic' of Ancient Greece, but 'There is an act of faith to be performed first: you must *believe* in Homer [...] You must believe that he is dealing, in essence, with historical truth'. Some years later, George Johnston would start fashioning his own myth out of a combination of life and legend, and featuring David Meredith as Odysseus the journeyer.

For the moment, however, George and Charmian were happily following in the footsteps of their bardic guide. Making as their headquarters the beautiful little town of Nauplion on the Gulf of Argos, they spent about a week visiting the legendary sites in the Argive Plain, catching local buses on 'the road that the Seven Against Thebes marched along, that proud and unruly Alcibiades drove along on the way to the Nemean Games', or meandering around the 'fairyland' beauty of the old Venetian harbour at Nauplion. From here it was a short boat trip to the island of Hydra, which Mrs Zander had recommended to them. With its Italianate architecture it was very beautiful, but although the couple spent a romantic night there, it was Nauplion that most attracted them as a possible future residence.[36]

Over the next four weeks the pilgrims moved on — 'filling in the gaps' — to Sparta and Pylos, to Epidauros and Aegina, to Rhodes and Patmos and Delos, to Crete and finally to Delphi, where it was 'almost impossible to doubt' that Homer had come to wash himself in the 'clear waters of Castalia' before walking 'on ahead of you, slowly, climbing up toward the sacred place'.[37]

Although George Johnston laid on the local colour with a trowel in order to sell this experience to a travel magazine editor, there is no doubt that this journey to Greece was for him something special. For his travelling companion it was an absolute conversion. Apart from all the resonance of myth and classical literature, Charmian could feel the sun and the wind and the sea for the first time in three years, and the people were friendly and spontaneous after the stuffy English. Suddenly she felt in touch with a part of herself which had seemed left behind in Kiama. She would describe this first brief glimpse of Greece as being 'as overwhelming as only love at first sight can be'.[38]

Surely it had to be possible to find some sort of way for the family to come and live in this place where Shane and Martin could run wild and free, as she had done in Kiama. And think of the educational opportunities, too! Cedric Flower remembered the couple raving about the benefits of taking the children to the source of culture,[39] and their friend Jo declared:

> It was because of [Martin's] intellect that the family decided to go to live in Greece. His intellect could be channelled into learning a new language and strange customs etc instead of getting bored in a school where his fellow pupils were still learning to read.[40]

From the time of their return to England in late May 1954, the decision was pretty well made. There were just a few small questions to answer. Where exactly would they go? And when would they set off? And how would they raise the money? As we shall see, Charmian and George had a particular way of making important decisions. First they would mull over a dozen alternative prospects, apparently weighing pros and cons and swinging between wildly different solutions. They'd do it. No, they wouldn't. Yes, they would. But they'd do it this way. Or that way ... And then they would suddenly discover some 'reason' — often apparently trivial — which caused them to take the plunge and do what they had secretly been wanting to do all along.

Just before they had left for Greece, Johnston had sent a note to their agent David Higham mentioning that '*Barbarian* (by both of us) is [...] well under way' and adding that there were 'a lot of things' that he would like to discuss. Did these 'things' include the possibility of a change to full-time authorship? Certainly, at the couple's next meeting with their agent, in mid June, there was an important discussion about the direction of both writers' careers. David Higham's memo of this occasion reveals that Clift and Johnston announced that their collaboration was to end:

> Except for one book in the fairly distant future — *Barbarian* on
> the short side — they intend to write separately from now on.
>   *A Walk to the Paradise Gardens* (70–80 000 words) by Clift
> ready end of Nov.[41]

The agent added that a proposed novel by Johnston, *The Cyprian Woman*,
would also be ready by the end of November. This novel with a Greek
background had been on the author's mind for at least six months; indeed,
one of the reasons for the recent trip had been to gather material for it.
David Higham's memo also recorded that Clift would be sending in some
short stories. These were the two stories from the 1952 trip — 'Wild
Emperor' and 'Three Old Men of Lerici' — which Johnston would submit
in September 1954 along with two stories of his own.[42] Nothing came of
this, and apart from one later short story — 'The Small Animus', written as
a spin-off from *Mermaid Singing* — Charmian Clift seems to have
abandoned the short story form around this time.[43]

In regard to the decision to write separately, the proposed novel *Barbarian*
would pay off the contractual obligation. Despite the sense of relief which
Clift must have felt now that her desire to write solo was acknowledged, she
had no hope of meeting the November deadline for the *Paradise Gardens*
novel. Apart from anything else, the three months of summer school
holidays were for Clift 'the time of tension and nightmare and tight controls'
— a time when she had to put aside her own work in order 'to concentrate
on the least desperate measures for keeping the children amused and
healthy'.[44] For George Johnston, on the other hand, summer was the most
perfect time to work. In this silly season of the British press, it was possible
for him to squeeze novel-writing into office time, especially as his personal
secretary, Mary Buck, was always happy to retype his final copy.

Under these conditions Johnston was able to complete *The Cyprian
Woman* by early October 1954. In this text, the author borrowed the name
Christine from Clift's autobiographical novel *Greener Grows the Grass*, and
developed her journalist/writer character into a kind of caricature of Clift
herself. George Johnston's Christine is a thirty year old writer: tall,
beautiful, intelligent, independent, successful ... but also predatory and
promiscuous. Having destroyed the masculinity of her husband, she turns
her sights upon the novel's hero, Stephen Colvin, who in turn loves a young
Greek maiden, Erica Konstandis, who is as constant as her name. In the
unsympathetic portrayal of Christine, George Johnston for the first time

produced a sexually aggressive female character who could be identified as a version of Charmian. That he borrowed the name of one of her alter egos seems to have added insult to injury. Certainly, Clift abandoned this name for her alter ego after her husband had used it. However, she would retain the surname 'Morley', and would use it again when she returned to her autobiographical narrative around 1962.

If in his fiction George Johnston was already portraying a marriage in which the wife is wanton and the husband is cuckolded, in real life it was George who was unfaithful at this time. In order to escape from the restrictions of the flat, it had become the custom for Charmian to take Martin and Shane to stay for a few weeks each summer at a bed-and-breakfast farmhouse in the Cornish hamlet of Zennor, where they could engage in the rustic rituals of bell-ringing and square-dancing, pasty-making and storytelling, as well as paddling and playing on the beach. In this choice of Cornwall, with its 'mad, wild, romantic coast', it is again possible to see the Kiama influence, and during these 'wet grey summers' Charmian tried to give her children something of the freedom and the closeness to the earth and ocean which she herself had experienced as a child.[45]

While these innocent pleasures were in progress, George in London was having an affair with a very pretty young typist from the office, who boasted of the relationship to other colleagues, citing as proof the gaudiness of her boss's underwear.[46] George Johnston was perhaps seeking to reassure himself that, despite turning forty, and despite his demotion, he could still cut some sort of glamorous figure. In the early David Meredith novel, *Closer to the Sun*, Johnston has his alter ego wonder if his involvements with other women in this period had been 'moments of magic [...] or only interludes of escape from tension and fear'.[47]

This affair in the summer of 1954 was so public that, even if Charmian had been unaware of her husband's earlier flings with girls in the office, she knew of this one. The incident was deeply humiliating. It was a reminder that she too was growing older: if George was over forty, she had turned thirty, while her rival was still under twenty. The situation was reminiscent of the set-up which Clift had proposed in her 1945 short story 'Other Woman', in which the young woman who commits adultery is transformed by a few years of marriage and motherhood into 'a suburban drudge', and discovers that her husband is in an adulterous relationship with another young woman.

During this same period, George was still accusing her of infidelity in thought if not in deed. In one of the London 1954 sections of *Clean Straw for Nothing*, Johnston includes a protracted account of David Meredith's jealousy of Cressida's friendship with Calverton. Once again, this composite character is used as a hook on which to hang the suspicions. This time, the jealousy reaches a new level of intensity.[48]

In another section of the novel dealing with this same period, the author points to the London experience as one of the milestones in the relationship of Cressida Morley and David Meredith: 'Clearly it had been in London that the seeds of pain were sown, that the breach in their personal relationship, never at that time expressed nor even hinted at, began insidiously to encroach upon their love'.[49] As explanation, Johnston notes that 'their lives together had begun to take separate courses'. David had been 'very much occupied' with his work in Fleet Street and with the writing which he (alone) did at night, and so 'was, for the most part, happy'. The narrator adds that: 'It was a different matter for Cressida, whose activities were both constricted and restricted'.

Paradoxically perhaps, despite her loneliness Cressida in London 'had a strengthening concern to hold herself within her privacies'. There was also in her a deep longing, but 'what she yearned for she presently did not know'. Although privately very unhappy, Cressida had to 'still strive to keep up the appearance of happiness so that David could continue to believe in its reality'.[50] Yet as Cressida defensively retreated into her inner spaces, this awakened her husband's jealousy. In his discussion of this 'London 1954' experience, Johnston opposes Meredith's possessive sexual jealousy of his wife to 'Cressida's own possessiveness of that silent uncommunicated world in which her own myth was harboured, creating dreams which became, at times, more powerful than realities'.[51]

Cressida's 'myth' (other passages make clear) is her belief in her entitlement to freedom, which Johnston, through the consciousness of Meredith, repeatedly describes as being unrealistic, something 'which has never existed for anybody'. From his earlier belief that freedom was the best part of Cressida, Johnston's alter ego had by now come to see it as a flaw.

Of course, Charmian herself believed that she had actually experienced limitless freedom in her childhood: for her, it was not unrealistic to long for it. In her own retrospective account of these London years Clift noted, as we have seen, her sense of being 'an outsider looking in, never part of it, never part of the London I wanted to be part of, because I wasn't free'. While she refers to the constraints of child-minding, clearly this sense of lack of freedom went far beyond the time limitations which motherhood imposed upon her. In some way the lack of freedom caused an all-encompassing sense of alienation, of being outside the place and the action. She went on:

> I did very little work of my own because I didn't have time, also in a sort of sense, in some peculiar sense, I felt at that time that I was losing my identity completely, I wasn't quite sure who I was. Nothing was happening in the way I wanted it to happen.[52]

Clift's comment here about 'losing [her] identity completely' should be taken fairly literally. On the surface she appeared to have a strong sense of self at this time — and indeed, she appeared to her friend Jo to be happy — but all the indications are that in the last couple of London years she was not just profoundly miserable, but lost.

If her statement above is reversed, part of the reason for this is revealed: *because* she was doing very little work of her own, she felt that she was losing her identity. Charmian Clift was one of those authors for whom writing is as vital to life as breathing: if she wasn't expressing herself through her work on a regular basis, she stopped being herself, and everything else seemed to get out of kilter. And when she was unable to write, there grew over time an unfocused feeling of loss, as if some vital part of her identity were missing. This in turn would lead to a loss of self-esteem and self-confidence.

It was also the case that Charmian *had* lost quite a lot of her identity in the move to England. As Johnston pointed out in his notes on the relationship between Cressida and David at this time: 'He is still a "somebody", she feels herself more and more becoming a "nobody", or, at best, no more than an appendage to her husband'.[53] Back in Australia, Charmian Clift had started to establish her name as a writer; in London it cut no ice to have won a novel prize awarded by a daily newspaper in the Antipodes. In Australia, too, she had had the radio work to back up her fiction, and she had happily dealt with Neil Hutchison about program ideas and business matters. In London she left even the administration of her career to Johnston. It was as if the loss of identity was a vicious circle: because she was apprehensive about her literary status, she effaced herself, which had the effect of lowering her power to control her status.

As well as all this, it is surely no coincidence that at the same time as Charmian Clift felt herself to be losing her identity, there was the development of the first of George Johnston's fictional versions of her: initially Lily in the collaborative novel *The Piping Cry*, and then the predatory Christine Lambert in *The Cyprian Woman*. Although there is no evidence of Charmian complaining about the Lambert portrayal, it is not hard to see why she might have been hurt. It is not uncommon for family and friends of authors to feel a mixture of pain and violation when they find pieces of their character or aspects their experience turning up in a novel. This is particularly the case, of course, with authors who work in the genre of realism, and especially with those who are themselves recognisable as characters in their texts. When people take exception to what they perceive as transgressive fictional portraits, it is not necessarily the 'bad' or 'obvious' things that they mind. The author may inadvertently make public some apparently trivial thing which the character's model felt to be intimate or private or domestic. At the same time, the author may firmly believe that she or he has 'made up' the character, or has developed it as a composite, and may even be unaware of what has been borrowed or used.

While all of that can be difficult, it goes with the territory of being in a relationship — whether as friend or spouse — with that sort of writer. No matter what Charmian's occupation, she would have ended up in her husband's fiction because he was the sort of writer who drew directly from the people around him. The vital thing, however, is the effect that this had upon Charmian Clift's professional life. She too was an author who drew from life. She too used herself as her first model. But the very look of her 'self' — the external and internal shape — was changing in the skilful hands of another artist. It was as if her fictional identity — her imagined self — was being sucked into another text. And when the process was finished, the character was so changed that Charmian could no longer herself inhabit or use that fictional space. Ultimately, the real character would even seem to change.

It is no coincidence that it is in the 1954 passage of *Clean Straw for Nothing* that the Cressida character really starts to separate from her model. Initially she just seems empty, as she increasingly exists as an appendage to her husband; and then the author fills the vacuum by drawing a parallel between Cressida Morley and Emma Bovary.

Looking back on these later London years in *Mermaid Singing*, Clift refers to the bars of the cage that had surrounded her and her family. She concludes: 'Now the bars had become so close and numerous that you couldn't see out any longer or remember how the sky looked or whether there was anybody left in the world who walked free'.[54] It was obviously time to cut loose and start a new life somewhere else entirely.

Since his September 1953 demotion, Johnston had periodically battled with the editorial policy of his new masters. On one occasion, for instance, the main boss in Sydney, Rupert Henderson, found 'unacceptable' an article in which Johnston put both sides of the issue on the Wolfenden Royal Commission on homosexuality. In reply, Johnston sent them a piece on London sewers, telling his London superior, Anthony Whitlock, 'If they don't like what I write for them, I'll give them shit!'[55] During this period George had been angrily handing in his resignation every so often, and then changing his mind. It seems that by about mid 1954 he had 'heard a rumour' that Rupert Henderson was 'fed up with his uncooperative attitude and was planning to call him home'.[56] Anyway, he had been in London longer than the original posting of three years, so he could expect to be recalled some time soon. In a sort of reprise of the *Argus* situation of mid 1946, it was time for George to jump before he was pushed.

According to the Johnston legend, it was quite out of the blue that George conceived the idea of taking his family to Greece, where he would write full-time. This is how the story goes, in the version given by the author's biographer, Garry Kinnane: One day in September 1954, George happened to be walking down Regent Street when quite fortuitously he ran into Wilfred Thomas, an old colleague from the ABC who was now part of the expat circle in London. Thomas told George of a radio program that he was in the process of making at the nearby BBC studios; hearing that the program concerned Greece, George asked if he could listen. So Thomas took him into the recording studio. Thomas's program was an examination of the ailing sponge-diving industry on the Greek island of Kalymnos; it was intended to promote a plan for Greek divers to migrate to Darwin, where pearl-divers were needed. The idea was that they would soon earn enough money to bring their families out. According to Thomas, as soon as George Johnston heard the program he immediately declared: 'Do you know, I've been looking for a book to write that would get me out of Fleet Street, and this is the one!'[57] And so the couple 'immediately began to make plans'; within two months they were in Greece.

Thomas's account to Kinnane has only Johnston present at the moment of revelation and decision, but in *Mermaid Singing* both the narrator and her husband George hear the program in the BBC studios. In Charmian Clift's atmospheric telling of this tale, it is clear the couple had been already thinking about going to Greece, but her story suggests that it was essentially a matter of coincidence and luck that they met their old friend and heard the Kalymnos tapes.[58] Garry Kinnane's version reinforces this notion of the luck of the Johnstons. Indeed, at this point he refers to how 'the gods had smiled on them' twice already — with the *High Valley* prize and the London job. He describes this encounter with Thomas as 'their third stroke of luck'.[59] Thus the lives of Charmian Clift and George Johnston seem like a fictional story, in which coincidences happen, and a *deus ex machina* appears at just the right time to push them in the right direction.

The real story is less economical — which was why it was deliberately edited and reshaped by Clift. It makes the couple appear much more responsible for their actions, and reveals how long and seriously they had considered their plans before finally deciding to migrate to Greece. The difference between the legend and the real story highlights the fact that, even if a text is labelled 'non-fiction' and has in it characters called 'Charmian' and 'George', this does not mean that it is not a literary object, shaped by a writer's hand.

While the Clift version referred to above is from the text of *Mermaid Singing* with which Australian readers are familiar, the considerably different version appeared in the American edition of *Mermaid Singing*. This account, published some time before the British/Australian edition, was the original completed text; as we shall see, the British editors wanted the volume of words reduced, and so the author chopped off the first five chapters — amounting to forty-four pages in total — and rearranged all the business of the reasons for the move into a couple of pages deftly inserted as a flashback in chapter 2. Although, of course, the American text was also a crafted portrayal of events, it fits with the other clues that the Johnstons had long been considering Greece — going all the way back to their conversations with Greeba Jamison in the winter of 1951.

In this American text, the order of events leading to the decision to go to Kalymnos is that by a certain time (in fact, probably around September) the couple had resolved to leave London and live in Greece. At this stage they had 'nothing more definite in the way of plans than that [they] were "going to Greece"' — possibly to the town of Nauplion, or maybe to Hydra or Santorini or Mykonos.

The trouble was that besides a place to live we did need an initial writing project that would occupy us for the first six months or so and provide some sort of insurance against our second year, when we might well have come to the end of our financial resources.

It was at this point that a radio producer friend, knowing their interest in Greece, invited them both to the BBC studios to hear a program about Kalymnos and its impoverished sponge-divers. After hearing the tapes, the couple sensibly went away to do research, but could not 'find out much more about the island'.

Nevertheless we were fired by the story.
'At least,' we said to each other, 'we can go down there and see for ourselves. We aren't committed to stay if we don't like it.'⁶⁰

And so, the narrator repeats, the island of Kalymnos had 'fired [their] imaginations and bolstered [their] flagging courage [...] in London at the time of indecision'. In fact, even after this, the couple did not intend actually to live on Kalymnos, for Thomas told them right from the start that that particular island was 'only a bare rock' and 'no place for gently nurtured children'. He advised them that the neighbouring island of Kos was 'quite possible from the point of view of amenities', and so that was where they decided to live.⁶¹ They would be able to commute to Kalymnos and gather material.

The decision about Kalymnos set the couple to 'adding up [their] resources'. Yet, there was another moment when faith failed. The American version of *Mermaid Singing* opens with George, having done the sums 'all through the miserable, squabblish afternoon', declaring: 'Well, that's that! [...] It was a nice dream, I suppose'. The money required was short by at least one thousand pounds. The text rings with authenticity as George, overwhelmed by their lack of funds, immediately goes out into the 'soggy October night'⁶² to buy two bottles of Margaux. While her husband is out, Charmian bathes the children and puts them to bed, then admits her defeat by ordering the coal for the forthcoming London winter. After George returns, the couple get out their holiday slides and are overwhelmed by longing. It is only now that the narrator asks her husband how long they could live on their funds in hand, if they 'cut right down'. A year, maybe, he tells her. She replies that even a year in Greece would be worth it: 'They couldn't take it away from us once we'd had it'. In this passage 'They', of course, represent all the powers of suburbia and respectability, the nameless system which Charmian always feared would get her in the end. George is still worrying whether 'one has a right to gamble the children' when the narrator decides to cancel the coal, the very next morning.[63]

This account fits with other biographical details. Kinnane gives October as the probable date for Johnston's final and serious resignation from his job.[64] Once this had been done, and the couple had really burnt their bridges, they became 'intoxicated' by their 'folly': 'We might be mad, improvident, reckless, irresponsible, shiftless, rootless, but we were going to Greece. By God we were!'[65]

Now there was a scramble to get as much cash together as possible, by selling possessions such as the car and some of their records and old clothes. Kinnane notes that Johnston managed to get Rupert Henderson to agree, 'since he was wanting to bring [Johnston] home anyway', to give him the return fare in cash rather than a ticket from England to Australia.[66] Perhaps Henderson, like Errol Knox at the *Argus* at an earlier time, was only too pleased to get rid of this talented but difficult employee. All in all the Johnstons were able to muster together about £1000, plus their return fares to the United Kingdom. Clift described this as enough money 'to last for about a year if [they] managed very carefully and stayed healthy'. Although they thought that 'it might just be possible to live by [their] writing when [their] capital ran out',[67] the official version of the plan as told to David Higham was that they would be away 'for about a year' — and then, presumably, they would return to England, if they hadn't earned the money to stay on. Higham noted: 'They mean to write a novel about the sponge-divers in Greece who lost their living because of synthetic sponges, went to Australia to pearl-dive, but couldn't because of the tide. It is a joint book and should be ready in April'.[68]

Despite the decision to write separately which the Johnstons had discussed with their agent in June, the proposed novel was to be a collaboration. It is clear that they had decided to abandon the ancient historical novel *Barbarian*, and to remit their outstanding contractual obligations by way of this new project. From this plot synopsis outlined to Higham, it is also evident that the authors projected that the pearl-diving scheme was to fail. This prognosis came true sooner than they had imagined.

A few days before the Johnstons were to leave, friends assembled at the Bayswater Road flat for a farewell party. The guests included old friends from Australia such as Peter Finch, Pat and Cedric Flower, Paul Brickhill,

Colin and Ursula Colahan, and Johnston's colleagues and employees, including Anthony Whitlock, Nigel Palethorpe, Hazel Tulley, Victor Valentine, the devoted secretary Mary Buck and the attractive young typist Patricia Simione. The party was well in progress when Wilfred Thomas arrived with his wife Bettina Dixon and announced that he had just had a phone call from Canberra to say that the scheme for Greek divers to migrate to Australia had been cancelled. The whole rationale for the novel, which in turn was to give some sort of plot or purpose to Johnston and Clift's own migration, went up in smoke.

There was a moment's terrible silence. For George Johnston, this must have seemed justification for all his cautiousness and pessimism. For Charmian Clift, however, there could be no second thoughts. She had to act quickly to stop her husband from changing his mind at this crucial moment. While the exact wording differs slightly from testament to testament, the essence of her reply was: 'But we can't back out now — I've already cancelled the order for the winter coal'.[69]

This casual response to a major problem rightly became part of the Clift legend. For Charmian, who had already ordered the coal and cancelled it during the early change of plans, there could be no going back.

On 25 November 1954, having reduced their belongings to two typewriters, a small bundle of work-in-progress, a box of lead soldiers, an emergency supply of dolls, and a few clothes, there set off by aeroplane Charmian, George, Martin, Shane and Dear Guy.

Dear Guy?

Earlier that month, in a brainwave of a scheme to dispose of all the old clothes and rags, Charmian had helped Martin and Shane make a very large and very special Guy Fawkes. Indeed it was so special that when Guy Fawkes Night came, Martin refused to allow his friend to go on the bonfire. And when it was time to set off, he refused to leave the effigy behind. His indulgent mother gave in, of course. And so Dear Guy set off with the family to start a new life on a remote Greek island.[70]

England had let Charmian down. She had gone there in a mood of fervent expectation, believing (like her character Kathy in *Honour's Mimic*) that there she would 'find It, the Big Thing, whatever it was she was going to recognise the moment she came across it'. But England had turned out to be too cramped, or perhaps too prosaic, to contain the 'wonder or sign that it was her inalienable right to claim as her own'.[71]

Now, in the manner of a religious convert changing sects, she knew that she'd got it right. Indeed, the signs were already starting. When she and George had gone, in early November, to the Greek consulate to organise their paperwork, they had anticipated 'weeks of running backwards and forwards with forms and documents and photographs and signatures and arguments and explanations'. To their amazement they found the consulate was 'working on the old pre-Menotti, pre-Kafka system, for all the world as though people were still human beings and individualism had not vanished from the land'.

Even more auspicious was the greeting of the vice-consul, who received the couple with the words: 'My name is Moses. You understand? Moses. I think that I lead you now to the promised land'.[72]

This was exactly what Charmian wanted to hear.

PART III

THE PROMISED LAND

13

ANOTHER WORLD

We were making a venture, less to another country than to
another world, to a 'new life'.[1]

Icarus flew over Kalymnos. Ovid describes how, after the boy and his
father had passed over Delos and Paros, there lay below them Kalymnos,
'rich in honey'. It was at this time on his journey that Icarus found his
confidence in his wings, and 'began to enjoy the thrill of swooping boldly
through the air'.[2]

Charmian, flying into Greece rather more prosaically in a BEA Vickers-
Viscount on 25 November 1954, was perhaps nearly as exhilarated as she
viewed the 'wild snow-capped mountains' of the 'promised land'.[3]

At first, in Athens, staying at the Hotel Majestic, all seemed to be 'going
wonderfully well' (George wrote to Jo, back at the Bayswater flats).[4]
November can be bleak in Greece, but this first week the sun shone so
brightly that the children went swimming day after day. Fortune, too,
seemed to shine upon the writing venture, for on 28 November George
Johnston received from his agent the news that offers had been made for his
novel *The Cyprian Woman* by both Faber and Faber and Collins, with the
latter offering the better terms and showing much greater enthusiasm. This
news was particularly welcome because for some time Johnston had been
wanting to change from Faber to Collins, whom he regarded as having the
best fiction list in England. He immediately cabled Higham to 'ACCEPT
COLLINS',[5] and that night he and Charmian went out on the town. George
told Jo: 'It's nice to have £250 coming in the first week of being on one's
own! Very encouraging.' And the celebration 'couldn't have been nicer':

> Charmian and I went to a Cretan taverna [...] (wonderful wild dancing and music and beaut people) where we both got high as kites, with memorable hangovers next morning. Charm finished up the evening dancing traditional Cretan group dances with some Cretan soldiers back from Korea.[6]

He also reported that 'The kids are crazy about Greece [...] and generally having the time of their lives. Mart, to our astonishment (and relief), has fallen madly in love with Greek food [...] Shane dances around in ecstasy'. Even more good news was that the couple had managed to secure in advance a flat on the island of Kos, to which the family travelled on 2 December. It was there that things fell apart. The accommodation above the landlady's quarters provided no cooking facilities and no privacy. The December sunshine changed suddenly to the biting wind and sleet of a Greek winter.[7] By now the children were tired and fractious, and Martin's passion for Greek food was tempered by the absence of peanut butter.[8] Meanwhile, Charmian was realising the enormity of the step that she and George had undertaken.

And then it seemed that fortune stepped in again in the shape of a man named Manolis, who spoke enough English to assure his 'brother and sister' that he would find them 'one good house' on Kalymnos. They went on the next boat, despite the dangerous weather.

> We came to the island of Kalymnos in the small grey caique *Angellico*, belting in around Point Cali with a sirocco screaming in from the south-west [...] It seemed to be a fine brave way of making an arrival [...]
>
> Our lean friend and self-appointed guide, Manolis [...] said with the air of a patriarch who had brought his tribe to the promised land: 'My brother and my sister, we come now to Kalymnos.'
>
> And so, indeed, we did.[9]

For Charmian, it wasn't just Greece that was the end of the journey but this particular place in Greece. In her heart and in her head and in her soul, Charmian Clift knew that Kalymnos was the Promised Land, for it was her own personal landscape writ large. Here the fat of the Kiama pastures had been picked off by storms over millennia, so that the bones of the land were bare. Here the cliffs had been blasted not by mere quarrymen and gelignite, but by earthquake — perhaps by the very earthquake which had brought down Knossos and Mycenae. Here even the sea possessed a frenzy that made treacherous Bombo seem tame.

The affinities which Clift felt between the two places were so strong as to be almost uncanny. Clearly, then, the Big Thing was here somewhere. And though Charmian was not so presumptuous as to think that she herself would necessarily find it, at least and at last she was looking in the right place. Part of this miracle which she was seeking was to do with her relationship with George. Now that they had finally shaken the dust of suburbia from their heels and pledged their lives to their vocation, surely the marriage would prove to be everything she had once believed it could be. And if she performed the rites correctly, she might find the ultimate meaning for which she was searching. Perhaps she had a sense that this time it was Do or Die. To Charmian Clift, thirty-one seemed old. Time was starting to run out. The thing she was looking for was not the sort of wisdom which Tiresias gained after a long life. It was, rather, the sort of thing for which you had to 'go down to the sea and wait and listen'.

> How to say [...] that we were looking for a mermaid? How to explain that we were civilisation sick, asphalt and television sick, that we had lost our beginnings and felt a sort of hollow that we had not been able to fill with material success. We had come to Kalymnos to seek a source, or a wonder, or a sign, to be reassured in our humanity.[10]

And again the signs were right. Within half an hour of their arrival, Manolis found them a house right on the Kalymnos waterfront. Although there was no bathroom, and the lavatory was 'as noisome as [Charmian] had expected', the couple immediately decided to rent it. 'We had come to a point where we had to stop and sort ourselves out', she later noted.[11]

In *Mermaid Singing*, Charmian Clift would describe in loving detail the yellow house on the harbour and the family's settling in; the establishment of friendships with the neighbours; the first skirmishes with the plumbing; the selection process whereby a woman named Sevasti claimed the role of 'household prop'; and the ups and downs of the children's adjustments to Greek life. However, the writer had been on the island for some months before she began to shape this account into something to be read by strangers. At this early stage, she simply assumed her normal work habit of making lots of little notes, keeping a detailed but spasmodic journal, and getting to grips with her surroundings through letters to friends. While Charmian regarded conversation as a first draft for writing, conversation via correspondence was also a part of the writing process. About a week after arriving on Kalymnos, Charmian wrote to her 'Dearest Jo' a letter which is very much a first draft not just for *Mermaid Singing*, but for subsequent letters to other friends:

We have rented a house on the quay, overlooking a harbour filled with orange and yellow and blue caiques; the house costs us about £6.10.0 a month, which is regarded by our friends as extortion on the part of the landlady. They are all scouting around for a cheaper one [...] In the meantime I am most happy, and would pay much more for the view. Kalymnos is much more beautiful than we had anticipated. Great stark pepper and salt mountains and the town huddled beneath them around the harbour — the houses blue and yellow ochre and brown and pink — simple cubes like a child's drawing — and casuarina trees along the waterfront. Our house is over a big cellar filled with sponges — Shane spends a lot of time there flirting with the young men who sit around all day with big shears, clipping the sponges smooth. We have three bedrooms and a living room and a kitchen and a lavatory — furnished with the barest essentials — beds, a table and four chairs, a few pegs to hang things on, a saucepan to cook in, and four knives, forks and spoons. The cooking is done on an open charcoal grate and a primus; I am forced to improvise a great deal. But in all my problems I am helped by the local women (wonderful creatures in black dresses and headscarves) who come bringing me little gifts of preserves and fruit, or extra saucepans and dishcloths and even odd chairs and tables. My household help is a beautiful worn Donatello-ish creature called Sevasti, who cleans up our bare rooms and carries water (no running water here) in those marvellous earthen pitchers, and does our washing. She is a widow (husband killed in the war), and like most of the women has a family of six — the few shillings I pay her each week mean the difference between staying alive and dying of starvation. Most of the population is hungry most of the time — no one eats more than one meal a day, and I am often ashamed. But that doesn't mean it is a sad island. In fact it is very gay, and George and I drink a lot of retzina and everyone sings in the tavernas. The sun shines hot as hot (not today — today there is a wild purple sky, and clouds rolling down over the mountains, and all the caiques are tossing on a rain-lashed sea — very elemental and wonderful) — but most of the time it is hot — like a perfect English summer, but cleaner, and one is reluctant to do anything but sit around under the casuarina trees drinking endless cups of coffee. In the morning I go to the market — where everything is fresh and cheap and beautiful (Portobello Road seems very dull in comparison) and you can buy fresh fish at 6d for two kilos, and little glossy green peppers and wonderful vegetables of all kinds, and dried vine leaves for dolmadhes, and strings of garlic, and tangerines as big as your two fists, and baskets of fresh lemons, and crisp little cabbages for salad. Nothing costs more than a few pennies [...] My milk is brought by a small boy with a battered can — he comes by donkey each morning over the mountain, and I am regarded with some awe because I buy a kilo every day. None of the local kids have milk or eggs ever — excepting perhaps on feast days. But they are a beautiful lot of kids, every day dozens of them invade the house to play with Martin and Shane and dress and undress Shane's dollies. They run messages for me and teach us all Greek. They have lovely names — Calliope, Themolina, Anna, Drossos, Petros, Georgio, Michaelis — and our two, after a couple of bouts of homesickness, are settling down to enjoy the sunshine and freedom and play [...]

We have done a lot of visiting — very formal eating of preserves and drinking of little ouzos, and other wonderful rambunctious meals of fish and soup and retzina that probably used up the whole week's rations. Can't tell you how kind the people are, and unbelievably gentle. Next time I'll tell you about their pretty little houses, with built in beds and striped rugs and wonderful primitive embroideries. Too much to tell, and I must write thousands of letters to let people know our address.[12]

The wild weather of this particular day was a prelude to what was to come. Through the rest of December and all of January, Charmian revelled in 'tempestuous seas, storms that split the heavens open, wild singing, drunken revels'. She would remember these two months as a time when 'everything [was] elemental, furious, beyond the edge of normality and control'.[13]

It was, of course, something beyond normality and control that Charmian was craving. And while she loved the variability of the weather for its own sake, the rhythms of the seasons were particularly significant on Kalymnos, where the whole social and economic fabric of the island was linked to the patterns of the weather.

Of the 14000 people who lived on this small barren plot of land — a mere ten miles long and five miles wide — 1500 were sponge-divers. The rest were the wives and children of sponge-divers, the widows and orphans of sponge-divers, the crippled boys and men who once used to be sponge-divers, and the merchants who lived off the sponge-divers by selling the hard-won product or by servicing and provisioning the boats. The sponge-diving season would begin just after Easter each year, with the boats setting off during April and May for their seven-month summer exile at sea. As the winter drew in, the boats would return again. Through December and January, the divers would be flush with money; they would also have time on their hands. This was their annual rest and recreation break, which they would spend drinking and gambling in the tavernas. Two authors seeking to research sponge-divers could not have come to a better place at a better time. In her account of that winter, Clift also noted: 'I know that we worked very hard, but in my memory we are eating and drinking and singing and dancing wildly in lamplighted blue rooms among crowding dark faces'.

And so — eating and drinking and singing and dancing — they started work immediately on the novel. The process of collaboration for this project was a variation of the way in which the partnership had worked on *The Big Chariot*, with Clift as 'literary hod-carrier' and Johnston writing up the material. But whereas with the earlier book Clift had gathered her information from secondary sources, now she collected it from life around her. In essence, she was her husband's eyes and ears. Despite the language barrier, she was able to draw from the divers the necessary background material, and with her anthropologist-like perception she observed the nuances of the taverna groups which revealed the extraordinary bonds and hierarchies that operate in Greek men's society. She also made available to George her notes on the island landscape. While Clift was note-taking, Johnston immediately started getting the words down on paper. From the start they rolled off the typewriter with miraculous ease. Only three weeks or so after renting the house, Johnston wrote to his agent in terms that were hopeful, to say the least:

> We have settled very happily into Kalymnos and the book has begun and is well under way. We are both tremendously excited about it. It is far far better than we had even dared to hope, and we both feel this time that we are on to a winner. The big problem is to make our writing justify the theme, which really is one of epic dimensions.
>
> [...] We hope it will work out as a real best-seller, but then I suppose one hopes that with every book! This one, however, excites us far far more than anything we have ever written before, and we have great hopes for it.[14]

He also expressed his 'hope that it will be done by about the end of April', noting that till then the family would stay on Kalymnos; afterwards they would 'probably move closer to Athens, probably to the island of Hydra', which had rather more in the way of amenities.

This novel in which so much hope was invested was called by its authors *The Kalymnian,* expressing their emphasis on its hero, a Kalymnian sponge boat captain called Manolis;[15] it was later to be published in the UK as *The Sponge Divers* and in the US as *The Sea and the Stone.*

While George Johnston hammered out the words of this 'epic' story, Charmian played the role of writer's wife as well as writer's sounding board. As her letter to Jo reveals, it was she who did the marketing, and who learned to cook under island circumstances. She also looked after Martin and Shane, who had considerably more trouble fitting in than Charmian's first letter would suggest. Frustrated by their inability to communicate with the other children, they were also bewildered by the poverty of their playfellows, and for the first couple of months 'Martin's shoulders drooped and he was given to spasms of uncontrollable panic', while Shane 'became surly and sulky and defiant'.[16] As well as helping the children through this difficult adjustment period, Charmian spent three hours each morning 'supervising their lessons and forcing them to learn Greek'.[17] In the manner typical of the children of migrants, Martin and Shane would soon pick up the language fluently from their peers and would eventually deride the way their parents spoke. However, it was Charmian who was the first to deal with the language. Despite some problems in regard to transliteration from the Greek to Roman alphabet, the many Greek phrases which Clift includes in *Mermaid Singing* show that she got a certain grasp of the language very quickly — even if this remained more or less the range and level of Clift's Greek. George Johnston's command of Greek was even more rudimentary.

With the beginning of February, everything seemed suddenly to change. Now sun began to slice through the grey clouds and the winds tossed kites instead of sleet. By now, too, the first round of adaptations to the new way of life had been made. Once again, Charmian wrote to her Dearest Jo:

> We've settled in here completely. It now seems the most natural thing in the world to fetch water in the big red lyeeni instead of turning on a tap [...] and to run the kitchen fairly efficiently with a bit of charcoal and two pots and a grater. Why I needed all those pots and pans and dishes and strainers and mixers and manglers I can't imagine. And washing machines! And refrigerator! And a gas stove! Sevasti is better than any washing machine ever made — she is a superb laundry service, with darning thrown in, and patches for Martin's jeans, and the duckiest bright blue circle on the backside of George's best daks, where he sat on a nail. We live the rich full life — eat like princes and drink like Kalymnians and George at least works like buggery. Marvellous book coming, Jo. Big, wonderful, crammed-full and spilling over book — the sort of book that I always knew he would write one day if he had a chance. He can't help writing it superbly — he's saturated in the atmosphere and the people and the drinking and the talk and the singing and the stories and every day when he sits down to work it just pours out onto the typewriter. I walk on tiptoes and shoo the kids away and keep him well fed and pray the magic holds until the book is finished. I work too when I can — in fits and starts. No flow yet — what with marketing and cooking and schooling the kids every morning and so on — but tomorrow the brats start proper school with all their little friends, and maybe I'll be able to get down to it then. George's book is so good that anything I do is of minor importance anyway.[18]

One of the common misconceptions about the Johnston relationship is that Charmian was perennially jealous of George's output and success. This letter, where she speaks from the heart to her closest friend, is crucial evidence to the contrary. Another noteworthy feature of this passage is the way Charmian Clift genuinely seems to put only a small value on her own work. There are surely two separate but linked factors operating here: firstly, the vulnerability and tentativeness that the author always felt about her work; secondly, the way in which women in general and women artists in particular tend to devalue their labour. Even in this private account to another woman, Clift does not whinge or complain about the endless domestic routine interrupting her writing.

Along with this growing warmth of February, it was now that Charmian felt that the family was 'beginning to be accepted'.[19] Writing to Jo, she added:

> It's rather nice [...] that no one stares at us any more. As curiosities we have lost our interest value and are accepted everywhere on the same basis as all the other Kalymnians, excepting perhaps that a little extra kindness is always added.

There is a bit of wishful thinking here. The Johnstons were not Kalymnians, and had the luxury of deciding how long they would stay on the island — while most of the locals were flat-out trying to get permits that would enable them to escape to the promised land of Australia.[20] However, Charmian was already in full Greek mode: photographs show that the sleek London cosmopolitan had been transformed into a totally different woman, with bare legs, full skirt, and big shopping basket. She wears no make-up, allowing the freckles on her nose to shine through her suntan, and her hair has been cut into a simple style that makes her look young and fresh. She also looks splendidly healthy, and not since the photos from the Kiama 'honeymoon' of late 1946 has she looked so natural and so happy.

This fits with *Mermaid Singing*, where she notes that 'we felt well — actually, physically, consciously well'. Though she and George stayed up late carousing, 'there was no need to take benzedrine to stay awake or barbiturates to go to sleep'. They 'came to terms with time again', away from the pace and pressure of the city treadmill. Best of all, they established a regular work rhythm, working from Monday to Saturday.[21]

It was among all the excitements of this February that Charmian started to become aware of the ancient pagan world that lay beneath the surface of contemporary Greek life. Her first taste of this was the strange festival of *apokreas* — a season of excessive feasting and dancing, when surrealistic revellers 'wandered about the town in little bands — men padded lewdly with pillows and dressed as women, women hobbling in seamen's boots and scarecrow jackets':

> Often while we were eating our supper they would file quietly up the dark stairs and assemble around us in a silent circle. Their faces would be covered by hessian or sheeting with eye slits cut in it, or by baskets hung with fishnets and tassels. Around their waists they all wore girdles of dead, headless fish or the skeletons of fish, or a bunch of dried, queer-shaped gourds, or even saucepan lids [...] They would caper and leap around the table quite silently. And then they would hit the saucepan lids with sticks and rattle the gourds in every corner of the room, and then they would bow and go out as quietly as they had come.[22]

On Kalymnos, the three weeks of *apokreas* provided the last chance to celebrate marriage or baptism, for after this there was Lent, and after Lent, Easter; and after Easter the husbands and fathers and fiancés went away for seven months — and might never come back. So in this short carnival season Charmian and George attended wedding upon wedding — indeed, there were eight on one Sunday alone — and dozens of christenings. They accompanied the islanders for a day of dancing in the courtyard of the church at the inland village of Chorio, and on the last Sunday they took part in 'a wild day of feasting and dancing on the threshing floor of Brosta'. (Both of these events made their way into the novel in progress). As if all this revelry were not enough, Charmian's February letter to Jo records that:

> We give some pretty good parties ourselves too — we ask maybe eight people or twelve and by ten o'clock there are fifty, and the man with the tsabuna as well, and someone goes out and buys another gallon of retzina and I go out to the kitchen and put on another pot of spaghetti, and someone remembers the words of another old Kalymnian song or the steps of another old dance, and on we go — men, women and kids — singing and dancing and eating and drinking as if the world was young again.

After stuffy London parties, it would not be surprising if all this went to Charmian's head a bit. Years later, in his '*Clean Straw for Nothing* General Notes', George Johnston would describe what he felt to be the initial effect of Greece on Charmian Clift's alter ego Cressida Morley:

Charmian in Sydney, 1941.
Top and below: working as a photographic model.
Bottom right: working for Bjelke Petersen Physical Culture Studio.

Lieutenant Clift (c. 1945).

Charmian and George on their 'honeymoon' at Kiama, summer of 1946–7.

Charmian and George at Bondi, 1948–50.
Top right: image used in *ABC Weekly*, 13/8/49.
Bottom right: image used on cover flap, *High Valley*.

Charmian with Martin and Shane — image used in *ABC Weekly*, 24/12/49, to promote Clift's radio program, 'Diary of a Modern Woman'.

Charmian and George at work in London (early 1950s).

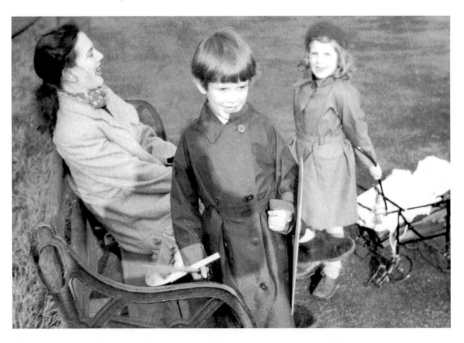

Charmian with Shane and Martin in a London park (early 1950s).

Charmian with Shane and Martin on a cold summer holiday, Cornwall
(1953 or 1954).

Charmian on her European holiday, spring 1952.

Above and left: life in the London flat (early 1950s).

Below and bottom left: the 'Holiday with Homer', spring 1954.

Here is a world of heady excitements, of life and laughter, of gaiety, of glamour, almost in a way that earlier world of 'sand between the toes'. There are no restrictions, there seem to be no fences, even the family tyrannies are no longer binding in the way they were, challenge and a delicious kind of peril can almost change them into being fun. This is a heady brew for a woman long sobered by moral, physical and spiritual confinement. (The secret things are still all there, stored away, undisturbed.) Given a taste of freedom she will want to drain the cup. It is her long-denied right.[23]

While this description of Charmian's liberation is spot-on, the writer neglects to mention that he, too, at this same time, was caught in the 'heady excitements' of Greece. At these Kalymnos parties and taverna nights, George as well as Charmian took an enthusiastic part in the dancing, and he even 'rendered (but richly!) "Waltzing Matilda" or "The Road to Mandalay" '.[24]

But now February was over, and *apokreas* too. As the island swung into the strange quietness of Lent, the two writers established a work rhythm such as they had never previously achieved. 'At some time in the long vacuum of Lent we finished the novel', Clift notes in *Mermaid Singing*.[25] She would later reflect that 'It was a strange book because it was written from day to day': 'You looked out of the window and saw a storm raging, anchors dragging, men struggling, and that would go into the book next day. It was blow by blow'.[26] And in the travel book she explains that 'the story' of the novel 'was all around us. We were living in it. We sipped morning coffees with our characters, and at night we sat with them in the tavernas, sharing copper beakers of retzina and platters of barbunia'.[27]

Indeed, people encountered in the novel crop up again in Clift's travel book — though often names switch from one character to another, and two or three real Kalymnians are frequently merged together to make one fictional sponge-diver. The whole process was somewhat akin to the way in which certain dramatist/directors produce a play by workshopping the plot in conjunction with the cast. Charmian Clift and George Johnston loved being on the stage doing the research with their actors for this drama; and the process seemed to speed up the production of the book, as well as giving the story extra zest and authenticity.

Looking back with the privilege of hindsight, it is possible to see the Kalymnos novel as an early step along a road which would take both writers — both people — to a dangerous conclusion. From this point on, the writers would start, imperceptibly at first, crossing back and forth through the thin boundary that divides fiction from reality. As they did so, this sense of 'living in' the story would grow stronger and stronger. And as the people around them started to become characters, so would the writers themselves. This was different from the way in which these two writers had previously used aspects of themselves or each other as fictional models or alter egos: now both the time and the emotional distance between real events and fiction would begin to shorten, so life was able to appear on the page almost as it does in a newspaper. (Not for nothing had both these authors started as journalists.) And if the story happening around the writers wasn't eventful enough, then it was in their hands to gear up the plot a little. Thus the writers, by the act of writing so immediately and 'realistically' about the real life that was happening around them, could change the real plot to fit the fictional story.

All this, however, was for the future. At the moment, this sort of docudrama method seemed like a miracle. After all, it took Johnston only three months to write the 450 typed pages (approximately 130 000 words) of the Kalymnos novel. On 29 March he posted the typescript off to his faithful former secretary, Mary Buck in London, for retyping. By the first week of May, one copy of the clean text would go to David Higham at the London agency and another to Bobbs-Merrill, the American publishers, who were keen to include the book if possible in their autumn list.[28]

In regard to British publishers, Johnston was hoping that a way could be found to publish the book with Collins; however, 'this being a joint novel, options will be held by Faber in England', Johnston wrote to Higham. The loophole was that the Faber option was 'on terms to be agreed': if another publisher offered better terms, then the writers were not bound to proceed with Faber. However, Collins was unlikely to make an offer for the novel because, under the agreement which Clift and Johnston had made with the Australian company Angus & Robertson at the time of *High Valley*, A&R had the option to the couple's collaborative work in the territory of Australasia, and Collins would not want the book if they couldn't profit from Australian as well as British sales.[29] Johnston therefore wrote a chatty letter to George Ferguson at A&R, apologising for not being in touch since moving to Greece, and drawing upon old mateship to ask a favour:

If you were willing to waive your option in the interests of a couple of Australians who now have to earn their bread and butter (margarine!) we could offer it to the English publisher most likely to succeed with it.[30]

Although the collaboration had been undertaken in order to fulfil the last obligations of the three-book contract, it is clear that the couple at this stage really saw this novel as a joint book.[31] However, their attitude would later change. In 1960, in a letter to his daughter Gae, George Johnston claimed that *The Sponge Divers* 'was really his book, "the two names having been left there as an obligation of contract" '.[32] If Johnston became keen to take full credit for the work, Clift became just as eager to disavow it. In her 1965 interview for the National Library, she declared:

Actually, of course, [*The Sponge Divers*] was a phoney collaboration because I was beyond the stage where I could collaborate any longer. I wanted to work in my own way. This was probably very egotistical but most writers have this.[33]

And in two newspaper interviews, also in the 1960s, both writers played down Clift's part in the writing of *The Sponge Divers*. While Charmian continued to note that her job had been to 'learn the language and bring in information' to her husband,[34] the journalist Alan Trengrove was told that the collaboration had only lasted through three novels (ie *High Valley*, *The Piping Cry* and *The Big Chariot*). 'By then', Trengrove wrote, 'they realised they were "killing each other". Their styles were too much at variance'.[35]

By this time, Clift and Johnston had come to believe that it was during the writing of the Kalymnos novel that they had realised the enormous difference in both their writing styles and their literary aspirations. In fact, because they had kept to their separate spheres, there hadn't been trouble in the production of *The Sponge Divers*. As we shall see, it was another text that brought the revelation that they were poles apart.

Certainly, in March 1955, both writers were pleased as punch with the new book. However, this time when Johnston described the project to David Higham, he somewhat tempered his enthusiasm:

We both feel that this is far and away the best novel yet, and the one that will have the most popular appeal, but sad experience prompts us to a cautious view: we are building no castles in the air. Nevertheless, we feel that it has come off, and are very happy with it.[36]

Meanwhile, Johnston also raised with his agent for the first time the problem of taxation. This — as much as any personal problems — was to become instrumental in the failure of Clift and Johnston's brave attempt to live as writers in Greece.

With the novel off their hands, the writers slipped into a strange state of limbo.

> Emptied at last of the energy and effort we had summoned and expended day by day and week by week for so many months, we were left with those gaping hollows of purposelessness which seem to be the natural seepage tanks for all the sly frets and fears which can only be kept dammed up by work.[37]

It is easy to pass over this acknowledgement by Charmian Clift of the effect that not-writing had upon her. For a writer — such as Clift — for whom 'work' is a matter of expressing an essential part of being, then the act of not working starts to undermine the essence of identity. It is little wonder that anxiety fills the vacuum. The author had already had some experience of this during the London years, and a decade later would suffer the full force of it. For the moment, however, it was a fairly short-term experience.

This time, too, there was a very real cause of anxiety. After all, the fate of the novel — its acceptance or rejection — would decide the fate of the whole venture. Charmian noted: 'It was for somebody else now to decide whether we could go on living in Greece'.[38]

It would seem that for George, this decision was less vitally important than for his wife: certainly, he was very keen to stay, but he could see an end to the Greek sojourn. In his March letter to George Ferguson, he declared: 'Our present plans are two years here and back to Australia'.[39] Charmian Clift, on the other hand, seems never to have put any time limit on living in Greece; and if they did have to leave, she didn't seem to be thinking of Australia as her next destination. For the moment, 'affected by a pervasive melancholy', she was storing up every bright fragment of Greek life in case she might lose the lot.[40] But now the 'vacuum of Lent' was suddenly filled to the brim with the excitement of Easter.

In Greece, of course, Easter was spring, and the resurrection celebrated by the Orthodox Church mimicked the rebirth of the landscape and everything that lived in it. Charmian had experienced other northern hemisphere springs as a city flat-dweller, or as a tourist; this was the first time that she went through a winter and then saw around her bare trees burst into blossom, saw in the marketplace the daily arrival of new lambs and vegetables and fruit. And, after the dramatic rites of Good Friday and Easter Saturday, the customary Greek sense of starting a new year was heightened on Kalymnos where, after the Easter festivities, the sponge boats began to set off for their long working season.

This rush of spring fever seems to have given Charmian Clift her own miracle of rebirth: out of the blue, the jottings and observations and journal notes and letters that she had been writing since her arrival in Greece all started to come together in her first, her quickest, and arguably her best solo book — *Mermaid Singing*. Through April and May, Charmian Clift worked easily. Back in London, attempt after attempt at writing had come to nothing. This time, the shape of the book was provided by the subject matter itself. Although there was very careful selection and editing and rearranging in this seemingly artless presentation of life on a Greek island, the backbone of the plot was the immutable pattern of the seasons and the corresponding rituals and festivities. Thus the writer didn't have to worry about what to say next, and could concentrate on how to say it.

After the years of collaboration, and after the London failures, it was a glorious feeling for Clift to have a book of her own happening at last. The sense of good fortune was intensified in mid May, when the American publishers Bobbs-Merrill accepted *The Kalymnian*, describing it (Johnston told Higham) 'as "a magnificent piece of work", a "superb novel", "*quite* a book", and so on' — apart from the title (which they promptly changed to *The Sea and the Stone*) and some 'dirty words' (which they chopped out). This acceptance brought the promise of an advance of $US500 on signature of contracts, with an additional $US500 when the book was published in autumn. (As it turned out, the money was to be held up for some months.)[41] As well as the rave reaction, there was even talk from the Americans about the possibility of the book (and its setting) interesting the film studios. This was music to George's ears.

While George was to continue to worry about whether the family could stay on in Greece, the novel's acceptance by the American publishers was enough assurance for Charmian that 'a second golden untouched year stretched ahead of the first':

> 'It's all right!' we assured each other again and again, both of us suddenly sick with relief. 'It came off. It's all right!' [...]
>
> We had done what we'd come to Kalymnos to do — we had earned ourselves a slice of time. Now we could transfer ourselves to one of the islands we used to dream about — Mykonos maybe, or Santorini, or Hydra, or Spetsai. We could send for our books and pictures and establish a proper working base.[42]

...Yes, but not quite yet. By now, Shane and Martin had settled happily into school and were speaking fluent Greek; being that little bit younger, Shane had even picked up the language without a trace of an accent. At school speech day they had both performed a recitation, to the pride of their parents.[43] Martin had already found for himself a new bunch of heroes in the *pallikaria* and the *klephtika* — freedom fighters and bandits from the time of the Turkish occupation. And both children had taken to the outdoor freedom of island life, where they could swim and run around in absolute safety, without any adult supervision. While the children wanted to stay on Kalymnos, their parents were not ready yet to start looking for another island. And besides, where would they find another Sevasti? So they decided to stay for summer, and enjoy themselves.

For Charmian, part of the enjoyment was this sort of holiday job she had given herself, of writing about life on Kalymnos. She was still reticent about mentioning her work to agents or publishers.[44] However, in mid May, when Johnston wrote to tell Higham about the American acceptance of the novel, he added in a postscript: 'Charmian is proceeding famously on a sort of light-hearted solo travelogue book, *Mermaid Singing*, which I think is going to turn out to be really something. This, of course, will not be ready until late this year'.[45]

Meanwhile, George's post-novel restlessness continued. He tinkered about, making the requested cuts to *The Sea and the Stone*; over the next couple of months he also wrote a film treatment of the story, which he sent to Peter Finch (to pass on to the British company Rank) and also to the American agency, for submission to Hollywood film scouts.[46] In addition he started writing a sequence of short stories which he envisaged as *Tales of the Aegean*. The first three of these were finished and posted to Mary Buck for retyping by early May; soon the author would send off a fourth.[47]

At the same time, George was very worried again about the future. By June, the reassurance of the American acceptance seems to have been completely undermined by the fact that there was no news about the reaction of the British publishers. Towards the end of the month he wrote to David Higham expressing his concern 'at hearing nothing':

> You will appreciate, I am sure, our anxiety that some decision should be reached soon. We have now been over seven months in Greece, with virtually no income coming in and a fairly steady drain on our not very substantial resources. We shall soon be approaching the stage where it will be necessary to make plans either to stay on here or return to Australia: obviously to make plans, we must have some picture of future expectations [...]
>
> I am sorry to sound a little edgy and impatient, but all the details of our present and potential economic circumstances, and the whole structure of our gamble in throwing in the job in London and coming to Greece to freelance make it imperative that (a) we should turn out as much material as possible as quickly as possible, and (b) that there is the least possible delay in marketing this material, if it is marketable.[48]

When a cable arrived from Higham in early July to say that both Collins and Faber wanted the novel, Johnston accepted the Collins offer with alacrity, but immediately started to fret about the agency's failure to report on the short stories.[49] While he sat around biting his fingernails, he started 'helping' Charmian with her book. Although there had been squalls and skirmishes between the two authors during their various collaborations, the real rift over writing happened in this summer of 1955. By the time Pat and Cedric Flower arrived for a visit, around mid July, Charmian Clift was thoroughly fed up with the situation.

The Flowers themselves were in a rather unsettled state at the time. En route from England back to Australia, they had a berth on a migrant ship from Piraeus to Sydney, but had to wait until the rest of the passages had been booked. At first it seemed a splendid idea to have a bit of a holiday, catch up with George and Charmian; but after a while it began to feel as if they had been there a hundred years. For a start, Pat and Cedric were not impressed with Kalymnos; living with other people is particularly difficult (Cedric Flower noted) if the hosts 'are working, correcting manuscripts and so on'; and life with the Johnstons had an element of drama to it at the best of times. 'Though they were marvellous, of course,' Cedric quickly added.

By now, *Mermaid Singing* was a completed text, though still undergoing revision. Charmian gave the typescript to Cedric to read, asking him if he would do some little pen and ink sketches to accompany the narrative. Meanwhile, she was still going through the work in her habitually painstaking way, making corrections, adding bits, cutting bits, moving passages and whole sections around. As usual, she and George were working with both typewriters at the same table — which also served as the dining table — and from time to time George would lean over and pick up her typescript and start reading little bits out loud, making suggestions as to how the text could be made more colourful, more descriptive, generally more catchy.

Charmian bore this in silence. And then one day she confided her misery to the guests. Cedric Flower remembers:

> 'I can't stand it', [she said]. 'George keeps going over and correcting it all.'
>
> And Pat — who was a writer herself — said, 'Well, you've got to stop that, you know. You can't have George doing that — it's *your* work — you've got to tell him.'
>
> She was terrified to tell him. Knowing how touchy George was. But she summoned up courage one day over a drunken lunch. George was absolutely *stunned* — absolutely stunned. *Hurt* — you know? He was terribly put out. In fact he didn't talk to Pat and I for about a week — which is embarrassing if you're living in somebody's house, on their charity and all of this. It was an *awful* situation.[50]

Cedric Flower's punchline to the anecdote is important: 'I don't think he touched anything she wrote after that'. After another pause, Flower added, 'But it rankled, like anything'.

George Johnston's feelings in this matter must be understood. Apart from the grievance which anyone feels when 'help' is rebuffed, Johnston had never before had to confront the enormous differences between himself and his wife which were raised by this matter of the *Mermaid Singing* manuscript. Firstly, there was the issue of working methods. Since his days as a cadet journalist, Johnston had been accustomed to giving his copy for comment to others, fresh off the typewriter, and to seeing and commenting on the work of the other journalists at the desks around him. This habit had remained, and although he had developed a thin skin about criticism, he was still prone to read out a first draft at the drop of a hat. Indeed, he showed Charmian first draft work every day — and she was accustomed to going over it like a sub-editor, toning down his excessive adjectives, discussing the material and helping him refresh his mind as to the particular look and sound and feel of the things which they had experienced together. So why was it different when *he* went through *her* work, putting adjectives in and trying to discuss the descriptions?

The difference, of course, was that she hated the process. To the same extent that George Johnston was an intensely public writer, Charmian Clift was a private one. At the same time, this issue opened the whole can of worms labelled Literary Taste and Style. This matter of adjectives — the number of them, the placing of them — and descriptive passages in general summed up the completely variant styles of these two writers.

As well as differing in style, Clift and Johnston were aiming their work at completely different audiences. As Cedric Flower noted in regard to *The Kalymnian* (which he read in typescript at this time), George Johnston was writing for Hollywood — producing a story that aimed at attracting film interest. So it was all big and splashy, with descriptive passages that were intended to sound like a great film set. The writer's voice was a shout, intended to be heard by a million ears. The primary intention was to make money. In *Mermaid Singing*, on the other hand, Charmian Clift was writing in the first place for herself (in the notes and journal passages) and (by way of letters) to a few close friends. When this material began to be shaped into a book, she kept the same intimate voice, with the effect that each reader feels personally addressed and drawn into the small circle of the writer's world. As to her aim, it was simply to produce the best book that she could write. It has to be pointed out that at this stage Clift had the luxury of producing art, while Johnston had the responsibility of feeding the family with his work.

In some ways, *Mermaid Singing* represents the finest work that Charmian Clift would ever publish. Yet although it received a good critical response in Britain and America, it did not hit a popular chord. This was largely because *Mermaid Singing* was a book ahead of its time, in regard both to its structure and to the attitudes which it expressed. As for the former, it is significant that the book's American publishers would refer to 'the experimental feature of the manuscript'; even at contract stage they foresaw sales difficulties.⁵¹ The problem — for publishers and readers — was the way in which the author moves backwards and forwards through time, following a roughly chronological pattern from winter to summer, but letting the subject matter send her off at tangents.

One memorable example of the trapeze-like swings of the text occurs in the description of the family's first Christmas in Greece. This winter story is barely started before being interrupted by the arrival of the writer's son, Martin, at the height of the following summer, when the account is being written:

> Our own Kalymnian Christmas had of necessity been a makeshift business —
>   'But *Mum!*'
> Martin, wearing only a very small pair of patched blue shorts and carrying a string of fish threaded through their gills, had just arrived with Apostoli and Georgouli to make more bait [...]
>   'What is it, Marty?'
>   'Why are you writing down that stuff about its being makeshift?'⁵²

Again and again through *Mermaid Singing*, this sort of immediacy is used to position the writer as the wide-eyed wonderer, relating whatever unfolds as she sits typing at her window, overlooking the waterfront. This technique comes across as a kind of literary photorealism. Clift's practice here was also very different from normal autobiographical writing, in which the author knows the shape of events up to the time when she begins putting the text onto paper. Although Clift used novelistic licence in the portrayal of character (including her own), and although of course she used all her writerly skills in the selection of subject matter, as far as the plot — or shape — of *Mermaid Singing* is concerned, there is no artifice to the apparent artlessness: as she wrote, the writer truly did not know what would happen from day to day, or at the end of the 'story'.

This method of using happenstance gave the text a great sense of urgency and freshness. *Mermaid Singing* is also remarkable for the personalised authorial voice. Here for the first time readers are invited to enter the private world of this writer, who speaks intimately to each one of them, as she might perhaps write to a real friend such as Jo. At the same time, it is in *Mermaid Singing* that Charmian Clift for the first time lets loose her remarkable gifts of prose lyricism. And yet while it is so personally and lyrically written, *Mermaid Singing* also reveals the curious questioning mind of its author, as she connects her observations and her reading to make original suggestions about the continuing pagan influence in Greek Christian culture and about the relationship between men and women in Greek society.

In order to assess the originality of *Mermaid Singing*, it is necessary to consider it in the context of its genre and its time, particularly as sales would prove to be poor in the very period when the British market was craving books about Greece. While the war had given many British people their first taste of travel, post-war rationing tested the patience of the nation. As a result, middle class Britons began to travel to the Mediterranean in search of sun and food. Those who could not afford this luxury took surrogate holidays by means of books. The popularity in the 1950s of books about Greece ran the whole gamut, from scholarly works such as Robert Graves's *Greek Myths* (published in 1955) to fiction such as Mary Renault's novel *The Last of the Wine* (1956), which was set in Ancient Greece. Meanwhile, Elizabeth David's *Book of Mediterranean Food* was revolutionising English dinner parties. Naturally, there was also an excellent market for travel books.

Although English travellers had been publishing accounts of their journeys to Greece since Byron's day, the first of the modern Greek travel books to be published in Britain was Lawrence Durrell's *Prospero's Cell*. A nostalgic evocation of the poet's life in pre-war Corfu, this came out with Faber and Faber in 1945. In 1950, Penguin published a British edition of *The Colossus of Maroussi*, by Durrell's friend Henry Miller.[53] In 1953, Faber published Lawrence Durrell's *Reflections on a Marine Venus*. The following year, another British traveller, Robert Liddell, published his *Aegean Greece*. Essentially a guide book, this was read for pleasure as well as information.

It was 1956 that saw the publication of the Greek travel book that instantly capitalised on this developing market. In *My Family and Other Animals* Lawrence Durrell's younger brother Gerald gave *his* version of the family's five-year sojourn on the island of Corfu in the balmy days before the war. Here the author cleverly combined a sun-drenched landscape with three other things that British readers love: childhood, animals and whimsy. The book was a runaway bestseller, with three hardback editions coming out in the year of publication, followed by four more over the next two years. In 1959 it was published in paperback by Penguin, and was reprinted at least once a year for the next couple of decades.

The year after this book's publication, the elder Durrell released his third and most successful Greek travel book, *Bitter Lemons*. A pro-British account of Cyprus during the time when the Cypriots rebelled against colonial rule, this was exactly what a great many English people wanted to read in 1957.[54]

If we compare the publishing history of the Durrell books in Britain with that of *Mermaid Singing* and its successor, *Peel Me a Lotus*, it is impossible not to feel deep sympathy for Charmian Clift. Part of the trouble was bad timing. *Mermaid Singing*, written in 1955, was to suffer a series of mishaps which meant that it would not appear in Britain until the beginning of 1958, by which time both the Durrell brothers' books had found their place in the market. Although Clift's book received excellent reviews, it sold fewer than 1500 copies in the first three months.[55] The publishers as well as the author were very disappointed.

In America *Mermaid Singing* at least avoided the time lapse and came out in 1956. But there, too, it received strong reviews and limp sales, with fewer than 1200 copies being distributed during the first year.[56] The main problem was the 'experimentalism' of the text which the publishers had noted when accepting the book.

Another reason for the poor sales performance of *Mermaid Singing* — and indeed of all Charmian Clift's books, fiction as well as non-fiction — was the fact that the author lived permanently in Greece, unlike other people who wrote about the place. While Clift could not meet with her publishers and agents to discuss business matters, she was also invisible to the public. This problem was compounded by Clift's nationality. The British market is not inclined towards books by 'colonials', and Americans prefer an American perspective on things. Meanwhile, in the author's homeland, very few copies of the book were ever distributed; *Mermaid Singing* would not be published in Australia until 1970.[57]

Overall, it was unfortunate for Charmian Clift that George Johnston had broken with Angus & Robertson and the British Faber and Faber in order to give the collaborative novel *The Sponge Divers* to Collins. If *Mermaid Singing* had gone to Faber in Britain and Angus & Robertson in Australia, Clift may well have picked up better sales. But she had burnt her bridges with Faber, and the more downmarket Collins rejected the text.[58]

Yet while all these factors were weighed against the book, the main reason for the commercial failure of *Mermaid Singing* was the fact that the author's social and political attitudes were far ahead of the times. Forty years after its writing, *Mermaid Singing* speaks now with a very contemporary voice. It is illuminating to compare the portrayal of Clift's Kalymnians with that of the Greeks in other 1950s travel books. Lawrence Durrell's depiction of the 'Cyps' as 'uncomprehending children' reveals an attitude of class as well as race; this is further bound up with a position of colonialism. Thus when the writer gets a job teaching English at the Nicosia gymnasium, which has a British curriculum, he refers to the staff of 'devoted and loyal men who had spent years teaching the lesser breeds their alphabet'.[59] Meanwhile, Robert Liddell in *Aegean Greece* advises readers that when taking the boat to Hydra, 'it is much better to travel first class', because the other passengers 'are more travelled than the lower classes, and are much less likely to be sea-sick'.[60]

There is no contradiction between this kind of racial snobbery and the celebration of Greeks as Noble Savages. It is this latter outlook that we find in Henry Miller's book, where the local people feature either as simple repositories of the age-old virtues or, in the person of George Katsimbalis, as a 'colossus', a character who is symbolically larger than life. In fact, Miller's archetypal Greek was a cosmopolitan intellectual, and fluent English speaker.

In the account of the younger Durrell, too, it is only educated and English-speaking Greeks who become true friends; the rest of the locals are Noble Savages, or buffoons. Charming though his story is, we never forget that young Gerald, in the eyes of the Corfiots, is 'the little English lord'; and never does this lord refer to the islanders by any term other than that of 'peasant'. (Even their dogs are 'peasant dogs'.)

There is a world of difference between these attitudes of Clift's contemporaries and the sensibility expressed in *Mermaid Singing*. In the essay-like section concerning the crippled sponge-divers, the reader is introduced to eighteen year old Panorimides Katapoulis. Then there follows the agonising account of watching from the house as this boy makes his first walk after leaving hospital, held between two other youths.

> They turned him around under our balcony, awkwardly and gently, and the three of them walked back the way they had come. It took them fifteen minutes to get as far as the war memorial, but they walked right in the centre of the street and they looked neither right nor left nor gave a single greeting to the

strollers who watched their progress interestedly. I stood at the window and wept until long after they had disappeared from sight, the two straight boys in the black diver's caps and the twisted boy propped between them, the boy who didn't wear a diver's cap any longer. That was one of the few times I thought I would have to go away from Kalymnos.[61]

This is no emblematic Greek sponge-diver, but someone real and dignified, revealed by the compassionate eye of the beholder.

But it is the ear as well as the eye that reveals the writer actively going out to meet the local people halfway. Italicised phrases of Greek leap out from nearly every page of *Mermaid Singing* as the writer revels in using the correct words for foods and boats and greetings and festivals and places. Curiously, though both Durrells boast about how well they speak Greek, there is not a Greek word in either *My Family and Other Animals* or *Bitter Lemons*, and the Greek characters speak either a standard English (in Lawrence's book) or (in that of Gerald) a combination of archaic English and the most execrable and fawning Gringlish.[62]

In contrast, when Charmian Clift does Greek–English dialogue, the 'mistakes' are not exaggerated, and the vital role of the translator is honoured rather than ridiculed. We get the feeling that it is the *xeni* — foreigners — who are inadequate for not speaking Greek, rather than the bilingual Greeks who are stupid for speaking imperfect English. At the same time, we get a sense of moving back and forth between the two languages. And when the writer puts down a lengthy dialogue between her friends Yanni (the village carpenter) and Sevasti (the 'household prop') on the complex subject of differing male and female attitudes to married life, the writer candidly tells us:

> I am reporting this conversation as if I had clearly understood every word. In fact I suppose that even at that time my Greek was still at the stage of a few nouns and phrases [...] and conversations were conducted with bits of Greek, bits of English, grimaces, gesticulations and goodwill. But it is true that with people you love there is a wealth of understanding, of communication and response, that transcends the difficulties of language.[63]

'*With people you love*' ... that is the essence of it. Charmian Clift could love a Greek maid, for she saw her as an equal.[64]

This dialogue between Sevasti and Yanni leads us to yet another unique quality in *Mermaid Singing*. If the author's attitude is revealed in matters of ethnicity and class, it also shows itself in regard to gender. In Clift's portrayal, Greek women are the forthright and formidable managers of their households, the de facto heads of their families. They are tough, vibrant and bawdy as well as being pious and pure. They are very different from the occasional Greek women whom one meets in the books of Miller and the Durrells.

Clift's account not only shows the strength of these women, but it is directly concerned with the relationship between the sexes, which it presents as an age-old and irreconcilable conflict. As Sevasti argues with Yanni, we see how far the writer herself has come since she wrote the radio play about the marriage problems of the Bakers:

> 'Blah Blah! Blah! Big mouth Yanni! What do you know about marriage? What does any man know about marriage? Your lot only have the fun of putting the babies into us. You don't have to bring them out, or feed them, or weep over them [...] How do *you* know what a woman wants? Marriage is slavery, that's what marriage is. It's a broken back and a broken heart and work from morning until night [...] There's no end to the pain of it, there's no rest in it.'[65]

Yet despite this pain heaped upon them, the Kalymnian women, in Clift's account, have two sources of strength. Firstly, there is their communal life — at the well, at the baker's oven, sharing stories, giving support. This links with an older strength, which Charmian Clift may have been the first popular writer to document.

Some reference must be made here to Robert Graves's two-volume compilation *The Greek Myths*. The introduction to this work argues that the old triple goddess (virgin, mother and crone) continued as a powerful presence in the Greek religion even after the invading Hellenes of the early second millennium BC instituted their own male gods in order to reinforce the patriarchal society which they were putting in place of the old matriarchy. Graves asserts that, after considerable upheaval, 'the familiar Olympian system was then agreed upon as a compromise between Hellenic and pre-Hellenic views', with the old triple goddess reappearing in new guises.[66]

On a number of occasions in *Mermaid Singing*, Clift reveals the influence which Graves's argument had had upon her.[67] But Clift goes beyond

Graves's aim — which is to prove that the old myths contain and reveal a history which was once new and living. Charmian Clift turns this proposition inside out, declaring that it is the *myths* which are still new and living, in the history that is happening right outside her window. And so she takes Graves's theory and applies it to contemporary Kalymnian society, showing how the pre-Olympian beliefs continue to run through the culture. On this island, Clift declares:

> One can see the worn threads of the old pattern [...] in its essentials older than recorded history, going back to a misty time when masculine subjugation to an all-powerful Earth Mother led to masculine revolt and the goddess was overthrown [...]
>
> These dark atavistic currents still seem to swirl through the everyday life of Kalymnos [...]
>
> It is impossible not to be aware of the deep and profound difference between male and female here [...]
>
> I think that here women are never quite regarded as human beings. They are of a different species — the female species, the mysterious Other Ones whose femaleness is derided and despised, but who must be kept under lock and key in case they work a magic. It is all very dark and ancient and filled with the cold white beams of the moon, the fear of blood and three spits for the evil eye. In the churches the dark, hard God of Byzantium thunders His creed of male supremacy. In the tavernas and coffee-houses and shipyards and the crowded diving boats [...] it is substantiated. But in the Kalymnian houses the triple goddess lurks still upon the hearth and bedshelf, smiling lewdly among the *ikons*.[68]

Although writers such as James Frazer and Robert Graves provided the grounding for Clift's analysis, there is surely here also an influence of Simone de Beauvoir. The English translation of *The Second Sex* had been published in 1953, while Clift was living in London. As this instant bestseller was widely reviewed and discussed, it is inconceivable that she did not read it. With its proposition of Woman as the Other, forced into a secondary and inferior position because she is always seen in relation to Man, it was calculated to appeal to Clift, for this thesis fitted her own experience like a glove. Here on Kalymnos, however, she was able to see women who — while still the Other — used their apartness in order to assert supremacy. Was it possible that in this supposedly primitive society, Woman was the first sex?

Here it is necessary to avoid anachronism. In the last decade or two, a certain section of the women's movement has sought origins in the matriarchies of Ancient Greece, particularly in the Mother Goddess cult. While Charmian Clift drew historical connections between the power of women under the old matriarchy and the power of twentieth century Kalymnian women, she was not some sort of forerunner of the New Age Mother Goddess worshippers. Although feeling the links between herself and the other wives and mothers of the island, she acknowledged the distance between herself and the possessors of the old powers and traditions.

One night, for example, as she sits in the taverna — the sole woman except for the proprietor's wife, Golden Anna — the men's conversation turns to women's business. Does the foreign woman know, asks Fortes, 'how to put the devil in a bottle?' When she confesses her ignorance, old Costas Manglis tells her that 'All Kalymnian women know'. The other men hastily cross themselves and look uncomfortable. Meanwhile, Golden Anna 'quivers with silent laughter' but will not explain anything to the foreigner, who 'is inclined to be cross and governessy and demand explanations'.

> George is grinning. 'Go on,' he says. 'You're jealous. You can't have it *both* ways. You traded in devil bottling for trousers and a cigarette holder.'
>
> There are enough grains of truth in this gibe to irritate me. But some old ineradicable knowledge lingers, like a worm burrowing secret tunnels in the validity of my sophisticated scorn and amusement.
>
> If I stay long enough in Kalymnos it is not improbable that this old second memory might quicken.[69]

But she didn't, and it didn't. The worm would keep burrowing, but Charmian Clift was a product of her time and place, and while the Greek experience was to shape her way of viewing her marriage and her womanhood, her feminism would ultimately have more in common with that of Simone de Beauvoir than of Golden Anna.

If *Mermaid Singing* expresses the strength of Greek women, both in modern society and in the ancient past, another aspect of the book's uniqueness in the contemporary travel genre lay in the fact that it expressed a female domestic viewpoint. Charmian Clift approaches her female 'characters' not just from the standpoint of a woman writer and traveller, but that of a woman who shops, cooks, cleans, looks after children, and generally lives the life of a wife and housewife and mother. Although there were other women travel writers in this period — notably Rebecca West, Rose Macaulay (whose novels Clift adored) and Freya Stark — the invariable 'gimmick' is that a *woman* should go on a difficult journey by arduous transport in a remote and dangerous place. Splendid as they are, the books of these other writers celebrate the extraordinariness of individual and atypical English women who set off to have men's adventures, rather than the strength of a large group of 'ordinary' non-English women who stay home.

Here, Clift was breaking new ground in the travel genre. Again this worked against sales. In the 1950s, people taking a holiday by means of a travel book did not wish to read about women doing the chores. It was a different situation thirty years later, when another Australian woman migrated to Greece and wrote a book about her domestic life. When Gillian Bouras's *A Foreign Wife* was published in her homeland in 1986 it received a warm reception, being reprinted the same year, then again in 1987, 1988 and twice in 1990. The problem with *Mermaid Singing* was that it was written three decades before the market was ready for an Australian woman's account of living in a Greek village.

Meanwhile, in this summer of 1955 Clift continued to work on the manuscript, in between swimming and enjoying the island with her family and her Australian house guests. The Flowers, however, were not nearly as impressed as their hosts were with the Kalymnian lifestyle, and they volunteered some advice:

> Pat had a long talk to Charm and said, 'Charmian, you can't live in this primitive awful place any longer, you know. Suppose the kids get sick ...' There were no doctors, no dentists, no nothing. And they'd finished the novel. They had no further cause to be there. So we said, 'We'll look after the kids. You go and find somewhere civilised.' So off they went.[70]

It was now the beginning of August. A couple of weeks before, there had been what George described as 'a minor earthquake'; the Johnstons, like their Greek neighbours, had gone down to the beach to spend the night in safety. No sooner did the couple leave Kalymnos on their house-hunting expedition than a major earthquake devastated the mainland town of Volos, sending shock waves down the Dodecanese to Kalymnos where the Flowers suddenly felt uncomfortable about the responsibility of looking after Shane and Martin. There were bedbugs too (which Sevasti blamed on the foreign visitors), and then two telegrams arrived for George, who of course couldn't be contacted.

Luckily, after about five days the couple returned, raving about how 'they'd found this *marvellous* uninhabited island called Hydra [...] And they'd rented a house and it was to be up stakes and off!' This, of course, was the island which Mrs Zander had recommended in 1952, and which the Johnstons had visited during their Homeric holiday in 1954.

There was more cause for enthusiasm when the telegrams were opened. One was from Johnston's former London newspaper office, asking him if he would go to Volos for them and report on the aftermath of the disaster. It was nice to feel wanted. And even nicer to be able to refuse: for the second telegram carried the news that one of the recently written short stories, 'The Astypalaian Knife', had been sold by the American literary agency to *Cosmopolitan* magazine for the extraordinary sum of $US850. There is no record of Johnston's reply to the newspaper office, but it is a fair assumption that it was written in the same high-handed tone as his next letter to his London literary agency, in which he pointed out their error of judgement in regard to his short stories. In *Clean Straw for Nothing*, Meredith notes in a checklist of events that he 'refused, on principle, the Volos earthquake assignment'.[71]

Looking back, it is possible to see the conjunction of these three things — the 'discovery' of Hydra, the rejected assignment and the windfall of money — as determining the length of the sojourn in Greece, and with it the future of the whole family. When he rejected the Volos job, Johnston effectively burnt the last of his journalistic bridges, so that when he was to try to break back into the London newspaper scene in 1960, he himself was to be rejected. But that was for the future, and even George Johnston didn't worry that far ahead. For the moment, the story money assured Johnston that it was really possible to stay in Greece, and make a living. It was time to celebrate — and get moving to Hydra.

14

THE COMMITMENT

This is the island to which we are committed.[1]

Hydra (pronounced Eethra) is proof of the real estate agent's maxim that the three most valuable aspects of any place are location, location and location. With its precipitous mountain slopes, its arid soil, its sparseness of vegetation, and the bareness of the rock face that rises like a fortress behind the town, the island would appear to offer little attraction. Though its name promises water, this is false advertising: volcanic thrusts have buried most of the springs and there are only a few sweet wells. Perhaps this is the reason why the island was ignored by the ancient Greeks; when it was finally settled — as recently as the thirteenth century AD — it was by immigrant Balkan shepherds. So impossible was it to subsist off this barren rock that these shepherds became seafarers and traders, adventurers and pirates. As well as having a safe harbour, the small island was nicely positioned — convenient to mainland Greece, and on the route to the Black Sea, to Africa and Egypt, or even to Italy, Spain, France and points further west and north.

During the Napoleonic Wars, the Hydriot corsairs made a fortune by running the blockades and selling Russian wheat to the highest bidder. They brought a treasure-trove of furniture and art as well as gold back to the island, and then built mansions to house their spoils, creating a town which is amongst the most beautiful and individual in Greece. But all this wealth won from war went back to war. In 1820 the island was fabulously rich and supported a population of 30 000; within a decade it was bankrupt, for Hydra sacrificed everything to the War of Independence against the Turks.

Greece was freed, but Hydra sank into stately decline; by the 1950s its population had dropped to 3000.

For Charmian Clift, this sad and splendid tale was part of the beauty of the place, as was the sense of a landscape frozen in time. There is a hint of the glass dome image — the sense of relics preserved — as she describes the harbour town:

> In appearance, the town today must be almost exactly what it was in the days of its merchant princes, for practically no houses have been built in the last 120 years. It rises in tiers around the small, brilliant, horseshoe-shaped harbour — old stone mansions harmoniously apricot-coloured against the gold and bronze cliffs, or washed pure white and shuttered in palest grey: houses austere but exquisitely proportioned, whose great walls and heavy arched doors enclose tiled courtyards and terraced gardens [...] Above the town the mountains shoot up sheer.[2]

Yet although this passage — from the first chapter of *Peel Me a Lotus* — gives a sense of unspoiled timelessness, the writer was to witness a different reality before the first year was over. Things were changing on Hydra, and once again the island's location was to be its fortune. With the rise of the mid-twentieth century city of Athens, and particularly with the opening up of tourism in the early 1950s after the conclusion of the Greek Civil War, Hydra was just entering its second boom period. Only thirty-five sea miles from Piraeus, with a pretty little steamer going to and fro every day, the rock was perfectly positioned ...

By the time Charmian Clift and George Johnston moved to Hydra, it was already too late. By the time they realised this, it was doubly late — for by then they had bought a house right in the middle of the tourist trail.

At first, when the couple arrived in late August 1955, they simply rented a place near the harbour. Pat and Cedric Flower were still with them — still waiting for transport back to Australia — but within a few weeks the news came that their ship was ready. At the farewell at the Hydra waterfront, Charmian suddenly burst into tears. 'I'm pregnant,' she blurted.[3] The tears were just Charmian being Charmian. After all, on the trip to the French vineyards she had wept when saying goodbye to the mayor of Bordeaux.[4] Naturally a farewell to friends would bring buckets, no matter what her own circumstances.

But pregnant she was. By Charmian's reckoning it had happened on the night of the July earthquake back on Kalymnos, when the family had slept on the beach.[5] This gave the conception a mythic specialness (with Poseidon, of course, presiding as god of the sea and earthquakes). Despite these good auguries, Charmian had mixed feelings about having another child. Here she was, finishing the first book she had ever written by herself; her other two children — now aged six and eight — were going to school; at last she faced the prospect of whole mornings of her own in which to write. At the same time, the family was still living from hand to mouth. It would be little wonder if Charmian didn't sometimes feel bitter and frustrated, if she didn't anguish over the situation or occasionally 'babble incoherently that age-old prayer of women: Let me off, please, Lord! Let me off this time and I'll never do it again!'[6]

Years later, in her interview for the National Library, Charmian Clift mentioned her discovery at this time that she was 'going to have another baby', and added: 'This plunged me back into a long long tunnel which I thought I'd just got clear of'.[7] This was Clift on a bad day, expressing years of resentment about books that could have been written, choices that could have been made, freedom that could have been enjoyed. At the time of this pregnancy, although Charmian did rail against the implications another child would have for her professional life, the coming birth was also a source of happiness in her personal life. For Charmian and George, this conception was physical proof of the renewal — in their relationship, in their lives — that had begun since moving to Greece. It sealed their commitment, to each other and to the family unit, and this in turn led to the kind of grand scheme and romantic gesture that Charmian loved.

Only six months earlier, George had told George Ferguson that the plan was for two years in Greece, after which they would go back to Australia. George may even have been counting 1955 as the first year of this Greek sojourn. This would have meant a return as soon as 1957. Suddenly, however, this future was abandoned. The unexpected prospect of the new baby, coming at the same time as the move to the beautiful island of Hydra and the successful completion of two books, made the couple so euphoric that they decided to buy a house in order that the family could live in a home of their own. The only sticking point to this grand scheme was the fact that there was no money, apart from the windfall that had come from the sale of the story 'The Astypalaian Knife', and that would be needed for Charmian's confinement. There was no doctor on Hydra and George was determined that his wife should go to a hospital in Athens for the birth. Charmian, on the other hand, did not want to leave Greece, and she was particularly loath to return to her homeland. At this point, therefore, she used her own health and safety as her bargaining card: her solution was to spend the windfall money on a house, and then forget about gynaecologists and hospitals and have the baby at home, with only the help of the local midwife.[8] This was no mean decision in a society where there were no painkillers beyond ouzo and aspirin, and where complications would result, at the very least, in the arrival of a bunch of black-clad *gorgones* spitting furiously to ward off the Evil Eye.

And so, from the first weeks on Hydra, as Shane and Martin settled into new friendships and a new school, Charmian and George started house-hunting after the morning's stint at the typewriter. As to work, Charmian Clift was still polishing *Mermaid Singing*. It was posted off to the American publishers Bobbs-Merrill by the end of the year, together with the graceful little pen-and-ink sketches that Cedric Flower had done for it.[9]

Before the Kalymnos book was quite finished, Clift decided to do an Hydra book, even jotting down a page of notes describing the food and weather and island rituals of September. Despite the usefulness of such material, Charmian Clift was never a systematic journal-keeper. October of 1955 sped past without an entry, and it was not until December that the author did another page of descriptions — this time of November/December combined.[10] By February 1956 she was making her observations straight into the first typescript draft of the book which she originally called *A Handful of Quietness* (borrowed from Ecclesiastes) but later renamed *Peel Me a Lotus*. It was a decade since her reading of Tennyson's poem had given her the phrase which she would use for the book title; but here in Greece she would often think of the *lotophagi* — or lotus eaters — the race of people in the *Odyssey* who feed upon a fruit called the lotus, a taste of which makes travellers to their shores lose all desire to return to their native land. This myth summed up her attitude to her own foreign sojourn: as far as she was concerned, there was no desire to return to Australia.

Meanwhile, in November, amid 'Storms. Broken shutters banging. Rain in torrents'[11] there arrived a couple of friends whom George and Charmian had known in London and had urged to come to the island. Sidney Nolan was by now beginning to make a name for himself in the galleries of London and New York, but was not yet making serious money. His wife

Cynthia was the sister of John Reed, the wealthy Melbourne art patron; after working as a nurse, she had become a writer, with two novels published by this time.

Sid Nolan and George Johnston, sharing a similar lower middle class Melbourne background and having no artistic territory in common, got along famously — swapping anecdotes of childhood, and reminiscing about the dreary Melbourne bayside suburbs where they had both grown up. Cynthia Nolan and Charmian, on the other hand, had very different class backgrounds and similar aspirations; they were not natural soulmates.[12] However, it was not the two women who threatened to come into conflict, but Cynthia and George.[13] Fortunately, there soon arrived a couple of strangers. These were Patrick Greer — a little Irish ex-teacher and writer whose frequent rejection by publishing companies provided the other authors with solace in their darker moments — and Greer's cheerful Australian wife Nancy Dignan, who provided distraction when arguments started to become personal.

By December, as the mountains of the Peloponnese in the distance became covered with snow, the six resident *xeni* were a tight little group. Through this stormy Hydra winter, they would meet at least once a day at the back of the Katsikas brothers' waterfront grocery story, where some tables crowded together amongst the barrels and boxes provided them with a cosy clubhouse. At night they often got together at a taverna. There were visits, too, between the Johnstons' rented house on the waterfront and the mansion, high on the hill, which the Greek painter Ghika (Nikos Hadjikiriakos) had lent to the Nolans.[14] All in all — given the terrible proximity — even cynical Cynthia admitted that 'We really get on rather well'.[15]

Wherever they were this winter, these Australians would drink retsina and sometimes they would sing. 'But mostly we talk', Clift noted, 'individually, severally, and at last all together, hurling and snatching at creeds, doctrines, ideas, theories'.[16] Not surprisingly, a lot of this talk was of Greek legend. In particular, Charmian passed on to Sid the two-volume *Greek Myths*, by Robert Graves, that she had devoured while living on Kalymnos. Nolan also borrowed the Johnstons' copy of Homer. Another current favourite was *The Living Brain* by W Grey Walter,[17] a neurological-cum-philosophical treatise regarding human biology and human perception. This also was passed on to the artist. A decade later, Clift observed:

What was curious, and in a special way intoxicating, was to have this vast field of mythology, and even vaster field of experiment within the human mind, given back to us, transformed, made applicable quite personally to each of us. [Sid Nolan] helped us to believe in our different talents by showing them to us in a quite new and unexpected way. He acted as a catalyst for our own tentative ideas and theories.[18]

Although, as we shall see, this catalyst factor was to be very important in regard to Johnston's work, Clift would seem to underestimate the input that Nolan in turn got from his friends. Sid Nolan, like Charmian and George, had had little formal education; like them, he was always hungry for knowledge. For all three of these autodidacts, classical literature and history were something which they had discovered for themselves; this meant that they were able to see these old ideas afresh and synthesise them into their own work in new and personal forms. Cut off from the outside world, unable to read the newspapers or understand the radio broadcasts, the foreigners began to chat and argue about the characters and events of the legends as if they were not just real, but contemporary.

In particular, the *Iliad* immediately absorbed Nolan, and he got the idea of doing a series of paintings about Troy. The site of the legendary battle was, of course, across the Aegean, but Nolan's Troy also incorporated his own native landscape. Johnston wrote later that:

[Nolan] was able somehow to associate the great Trojan epic tragedy with drought paintings he had done, with an Australian background of parched earth, dust, prickly vegetation, death, heat, bones [...] In images separated by the width of the world and 3000 years of time, he sensed a parallel, indeed a mutual poetry concerned with human struggle.

He wanted to paint Troy, he said, in its pitiless heroics, in the true brutality of its images.[19]

As the winter storms battered the town, Nolan worked feverishly at experimental oil and ink sketches on paper. Whenever Charmian and George clambered up the hill to the old villa, there would be sketches carpeting the floor. Johnston later remembered seeing:

Hundreds and hundreds of studies concerned with nude figures interlocked and grappling, centaur-like horsemen, dessicated skulls and bones in formalised masks and helmets, the harsh edges of the dry rock and brittle, snaggled vegetation against burning bright skies.

Despite the proliferation of sketches, Troy had Nolan on the run. On one wild night he 'flung his sketches down and cried, "You can't paint it! You need metal and a forge. It's got to clang!"'

The breakthrough would begin to come in April, when Johnston lent Nolan a recently published article by another Australian writer, Alan Moorehead, who was living on the neighbouring island of Spetsai. This piece, from Moorehead's as yet unpublished book *Gallipoli*, drew parallels between the Australian campaign of 1915 and the Trojan battles. 'It was like unlocking a door', Johnston noted. It would take Nolan another few years to get the ideas onto canvas, but this was the genesis of his *Gallipoli* series.

If Nolan now saw a way to fuse these two potent myths and present the old story in a new and Australian light, a door had also been nudged open for George Johnston. Although the link was not as immediate and obvious, it was during these months of discursive talking with Sid Nolan about Homer and the Australian identity and growing up in flat Melbourne suburbs that George Johnston began to see mythological connections with his own story. For him, the *Odyssey* was the key text, for the connection *he* made was to see himself as Odysseus the wanderer. Johnston's retelling of the myth — like that of Nolan — would be unidealised and Australian, and just as Nolan incorporated suburban images of St Kilda bathers into his Troy/Gallipoli, Johnston would set the opening of his epic in the soulless suburbia of lower middle class Melbourne. While the writing of it was still a few years off, it was during this winter that the seed was sown for Johnston's trilogy. But all this was for the future; at the moment it was Nolan's work that was the focus for the myth-lines.

If Johnston's conversations with Nolan were focused on Homer, it would be wrong to think of Charmian as being on the fringe. She had her own myth to discuss with the painter, for it was during this winter that there began the game of dividing people into 'Daedalus types' and 'Icarus types' (as discussed in chapter 2).

Of the six original players of the game, George and Cynthia were followers of the careful engineer and maze-builder, while it was Charmian who most exemplified the spirit of Icarus. As for Sidney Nolan, he also liked to identify with the high-flyers and the risk-takers, and it was he who turned the Icarus story into a kind of battle cry, urging the others to 'Fly then! Bloody well soar, why don't you?' when rejection slips or fear of failure overtook them.[20] And it was Sid who during this winter immediately incorporated this particular myth into his work, producing a series of sketches that would catch Charmian's eye during visits to his studio:

> Icarus occurs again and again. The same haunting naked figure soars above fanged rocks and wide, dark seas, sometimes just rising from the ground, sometimes a speck floating high against a burning ball of sun, frail as a dragonfly. And always on the ground, earthbound and staring upwards with sorrowful yearning eyes, is the lonely figure of the Minotaur — a man's body with a bull's head with the wide tapering horns curled upward and the formalised white flower of Crete blooming fresh between his sad human eyes.[21]

'There are shields too', she added as an afterthought: for Charmian, even Troy paled beside the Icarus story.

Through this wild winter, house-hunting had continued. At last, in the new year of 1956, Charmian and George found what they were looking for. It was not one of the villas of the old Hydriot merchant princes, but a solid middle-sized house built by a sea captain in 1788. (George was to find the coincidence of the date with Australian history to be auspicious.) Now began a nerve-wracking six weeks of dealing with Greek banks and Greek bureaucracy. It is little wonder that Charmian, by now heavily pregnant, sometimes felt overcome by anguish or just sheer panic. But finally in February the couple paid the drachma equivalent of 120 gold pounds and took possession of the house by the well.

According to the myth which would soon begin to flourish, this house was the last bargain on Hydra. Its cheapness would be reiterated in newspaper reports and travellers' tales, building up a picture of this lucky Australian couple living dirt cheap in their remote paradise in a house that they had purchased from the fee for a single short story; indeed, the Astypalaian knife which had inspired Johnston's story was mounted on the wall in pride of place. As with many of the Clift/Johnston myths, Charmian and George themselves started this one; they didn't seem to realise that this sort of tale feeds an established perception that writers are paid vast amounts for doing very little. It is not the sort of image that endears authors to the Australian public.

In fact, at the exchange rate prevailing at the time, the house cost $US1300 — more than half as much again as the $US850 windfall from *Cosmopolitan* magazine. In later tellings of the house-buying tale, the fee for this story was actually increased to $1300,[22] as the point of the tale was to highlight the protagonists' good fortune, as well as their impetuousness and bravery. They were actually braver — or even more foolhardy — than their memory of events suggested, for the rest of the money came from the contingency fund which had been set aside to pay the fares back to London if everything should go badly wrong.[23] At the time of handing over the money, Clift noted:

> There it went! Our last little bit of capital, our going-back-to-civilisation money, our reserve against children's illnesses, tonsils or appendix operations, dental disasters — or that never-mentioned contingency that might arise if all does not go well at the birth of this new baby of mine and I have to be carted off dramatically to Athens in a caique.[24]

Little wonder that, standing at the back of Katsikas's store half an hour later, she found her mouth 'gone dry with surprise and terror' as she realised that 'in spending all our capital we had indeed burnt the last boat. Had one really intended to commit oneself so irrevocably?' But for Charmian, the question was only rhetorical. The next moment she is happily announcing again that 'This is the island to which we are committed'.

Commitment. Along with loyalty and privacy, it was one of Charmian's key 'things'. Making a commitment gave her the sense of reassurance which she so desperately needed; it was something to balance against her impulsiveness. It connected with her feelings about marriage, family and security. This particular commitment of the house was a testimony in stone and mortar to the relationship which Charmian saw as binding herself, George and the children. In addition, it was a way of holding George in Greece, for Charmian was well aware that while he had a romantic love for the place, he was not really emotionally suited to a life of exile and economic insecurity.

Apart from the financial side of the house purchase, there were other risks. While anti-British feeling was intensifying on the island of Cyprus, this was to be just one of the political hot spots of 1956, along with the crises of Suez and Hungary. All in all, buying the house had been a very 'Icarus' thing to do. When Sid Nolan offered a sketch as a house-warming present, there was no doubt of Charmian's reply: 'Yes, please. An Icarus if you can spare one. I'd like Icarus aspiring on that wall'.[25]

While the Johnston myth was to make the house a symbol of the couple's defiance of caution and convention, it really was a romantic building. Set in the neighbourhood behind the waterfront, it looked onto a small cobblestoned square at the centre of which was a brackish well where the local women and children would gather to collect water for washing. The house itself was the traditional Greek square white block, with blue shuttered windows at ground and first floor level. The second storey was invisible from the street, for it was set back behind the wide roof terrace. Though not the 'marble mansion' which would be described in the Australian press,[26] it was a beautiful place, and most importantly a place where many people felt at home.

Entering not by the heavy front door but through a door in the side wall, visitors stepped into a small courtyard with grapevines and fruit trees; later Charmian would plant a bougainvillea that splashed scarlet down the outside wall. From the courtyard a door led into the house, and down a couple of steps. Blinking at the sudden change from sunlight, guests now found themselves in a large, cool cavern, cut right into the island rock. Here, divided into three sections by archways, were the kitchen and living area, each section up or down a couple of steps from its neighbour.

Whitewashed walls, dark ceiling beams, cool flagstones ... This was the area that Charmian would transform into the kind of Mediterranean kitchen found in lifestyle magazines — except that this was twenty years or more before the peasant vogue began. Here, strings of garlic and huge earthenware pitchers were set off by glowing Arachova rugs, comfortably sagging chairs, and Greek *objets trouvés* ranging from a two thousand year old amphora to a crazily ornate birdcage. On the walls were old lithographs of the Heroes of the War of Independence, a set of antique pistols, and paintings by visiting artists — including the little Icarus sketch. At a time when Australian domestic architecture enforced an apartheid system between the kitchen and the living area, this was a woman's workplace which allowed the cook to be at the centre of the party.

Moving on upstairs, on the first floor were the bedrooms. And then above that, the whole of the second storey was the studio, leading out to the terrace where the view stretched across the gulf to the mountains of

Troezen on the Peloponnese. At the time of purchase, this top floor had two rooms, but soon the new owners had the intermediary wall knocked down to make one big work area.[27]

Beautiful though it was, the house, like all old houses, would need continual care and maintenance. In the beginning, it also required considerable renovation: it had been vacant for sixteen years and had a leaking roof and no glass in the windows. Every room needed painting. There was also the costly and complicated matter of having a bathroom and flushing toilet installed in a country where plumbers and plumbing supplies were a rarity; and even when it was done, the system was always fragile, apart from the fact that it took half an hour or so to pump enough water for the day's needs.

All of this took money. Over the next nine years, the house would be like a difficult child, constantly demanding attention. And, of course, the more attention given to it, the more its family loved it. For the moment, in February 1956, the race was on to get enough of the renovations done so that Charmian could move in before the family got bigger: the baby was expected on 12 March.[28]

As she waited, Charmian received in early February the wonderful news that Bobbs-Merrill had accepted Mermaid Singing, and would publish it in their fall list (ie around September). Now, with her first solo book accepted, Clift began to handle her own business correspondence with her American publisher and agent. However, she still usually left Johnston to deal with David Higham, though occasionally adding a separate note in the envelope. While it was convenient for Clift to leave this part of the work to her husband — especially in regard to all the tedious tax matters — it did diminish Clift's ownership of her work by putting Johnston into the role of interpreter. In regard to this US acceptance of Mermaid Singing, for example, he told Higham: 'This of course is not a novel — rather a personalised family travel story of life on Greek islands with a couple of small kids. It is, I think, very nice'.[29]

In accepting the book, Harrison Platt, the Bobbs-Merrill editor, advised the writer that he would want 'a few cuts and some slight revisions'.[30] Clift decided to hold back from sending a copy of the typescript to her British agent for submission to the British publishing market until she had made the alterations for the American edition. This would prove to be misguided.

In March, as the renovations progressed at snail's pace, gales periodically cut the island boat service and the Hydra midwife sojourned in Athens. Luckily, the baby obeyed all Charmian's instructions to 'Hold off! Hold off!'[31] A sudden new worry was the political situation, as the British governor on Cyprus arrested the highly popular Archbishop Makarios and had him deported to the Seychelles. While on Cyprus itself EOKA (the National Organisation of Cypriot Fighters) waged guerilla warfare against colonial rule, in Athens there were noisy demonstrations and Union Jacks were burnt. On Hydra, schoolchildren were taught songs about *Enosis* (union — with Greece, of course — was the ultimate aim of the Greek Cypriots) and youths scrawled EOKA on walls.

In such a situation, it was hard for the Johnstons to explain that as they were Australian, not British nationals, it wasn't really their fault. Fortunately, they had their children as insurance policy. By now, Shane spoke Greek as fluently as any of her peers, and she was clearly identifying as a little Greek girl. She had made friends with dozens of children at her new school, and spent her spare time in the world of safe but unsupervised play of the island *paithia*, or children. Already it was becoming clear that Shane and her elder brother were chalk and cheese. Martin was much more reticent about making friends with other children, and — perhaps because he had been that little bit older than Shane when he migrated to Greece — he would always keep one foot in the English-speaking world and the other foot in the new world of Greece. As time went on, this would have the effect of reinforcing his distance from his peers, as he explored the English language either in conversation with adults, or through books. This in turn would increase the gap between Martin and his sister who, as they grew up, would have less and less in common.

As early as this second year in Greece, a kind of snapshot of the difference between these two siblings was evident in their varied reactions to the Cyprus troubles. Eight year old Martin — still loyal to his remembered English schoolfriends — was distressed when his headmaster, as well as the other children, began to denounce all English as butchers and barbarians. Yet he would be chosen by his teachers to carry a wreath and recite a poem in the procession for 25 March, the day that celebrates Greek Independence. Shane meanwhile had cast off any identification with her past along with her ballet shoes and London party frocks. She ran exuberantly through the back streets with her *parea* (or gang) of other seven year olds, 'shouting Cyprus catch-cries and death to the English with every appearance of intense enjoyment'.[32]

But even the presence of the children wasn't enough to allay the suspicion of authorities towards the foreign residents. The Johnstons, together with the Nolans and the Greers, were summoned to the police station three or four times in March. This was the beginning of the nerve-wracking dependence on the goodwill of the police that any foreign resident in Greece has to bear. From this point on, everything concerning the Johnstons — from their personal behaviour, to their choice of friends, to their occupation, to their income from abroad — could be taken into account in order to determine whether or not their residence permits would be extended or revoked. Possession of the house made the situation even more fraught for Charmian and George. In *Closer to the Sun* and in *Clean Straw for Nothing*, Johnston expresses the anxiety and degradation caused both by the regular visits to have permits renewed, and by the unpredictable summonses to the police station at the whim of the local police. In the latter novel, a passage set in 1956 depicts the kind of 'threatening harangue' which the whole family suffered whenever the emotions of the Cyprus issue set the police chief into one of his 'wild rampages of xenophobia'. Such episodes made George feel that, despite all their attempts to settle in Greece, they were still aliens, and would never belong.[33]

What with these personal and political pressures, it would be little wonder if Charmian became thoroughly fed up as the weeks progressed and still the baby delayed. The 'March' chapter of *Peel Me a Lotus* concludes with a passage which reveals something of the contradictions she was going through:

> My face is cold turned up to the cold stars. Inexorable and orderly they move across heaven, star beyond star, nebula beyond nebula, universe beyond universe, wheeling through a loneliness that is inconceivable. Almost I can feel this planet wheeling too, spinning through its own sphere of loneliness with the deliberation of a process that is endlessly repeated, a tiny speck of astral dust whirling on into the incomprehensibility of eternity. How queer to cling to the speck of dust, whirling on and on, perhaps at this moment even upside down. There's no comfort in the stars. Only darkness beyond darkness, mystery beyond mystery, loneliness beyond loneliness.
>
> Wrapped in its own darkness and mystery and loneliness the child in my body turns, as though to remind me of mysteries closer to hand. And I go spinning on through space, enveloped by mystery, ignorant as a sheep as to why I am being used in this

way. On the dark little terrace under the dark mountains I have a childish desire to shake my fists and shout into the impossible emptiness between those wheeling stars, 'This is all very well, but who am I?'[34]

While this description opens with a mystic sense of being at one with the universe that is reminiscent of the little girl starbaking on Bombo beach, the final cry suggests the frustration of the writer and mother whose very existence seems sometimes to be swallowed by the demands of others.

And yet Cynthia Nolan noted that, as Charmian's 'hour' approached, she was 'admirable truly'. By now, 'some or most of the bitterness and frustration and anguish', which had been brought on by the prospect of motherhood, had gone.[35] This sense of calm and resolution was no doubt helped by the fact that when April came, everything suddenly fell into place. The house was now livable, and the family moved triumphantly into the first home they had ever owned. The weather cleared. The midwife returned. There was now also the support of a young Greek woman named Zoe, who was engaged to help with the washing and domestic chores. And when Charmian finally took to her bed, Martin sat watching over her through the whole afternoon, and read to her five chapters of *The Iliad* without pausing for breath.[36]

This anecdote highlights the way in which the Homeric legend had become a kind of family bible, with at least some of the family members internalising the myths that make up the Homeric canon. The consequences of this were for the future. At the moment, it was clear that the new child must have a Homeric name. Martin plumped for Agamemnon, if the baby were a boy; luckily George and Charmian considered the likely outcome if the family were to move back to Australia and 'Aggie' had to face a school playground. And so 'Jason' was chosen, as a heroic name that would be acceptable in both Greek and Australian cultures. In the meantime, the child was nicknamed 'Booli' or 'Boo'.

At last, on 3 April, 'Jason arrived at 6 a.m. within three quarters of an hour and with the aid of Zoe and the midwife', Cynthia Nolan wrote to Pat.

> The latter crooned over Charm and rubbed her stomach with alcohol during the event, and gave her two tumblers full of ouzo after [...] Jason is very like Charm, same build and same big mouth and bone formation of the face — but the longest fingers I've ever seen — what does this portend? and I'm not sure he

isn't going to catch George's nose [...] Knowing what an adoring mama Charm is I think she is now all pride in this third wonder. The poor girl has certainly had a bad time of resentment and rage behind her. George is absolutely thrilled.

Shane was also particularly excited about having a baby to dress up and carry about and play with. As time went on she would form a very close bond with her little brother, and would be his ally in the family, despite the gap of seven years between them.[37]

Naturally Charmian was also thrilled now that the waiting was over. The passage about the birth in Peel Me a Lotus is a miracle of lightness, with the writer's joy shining through the description of the infant. Here the intensity of emotion is highlighted by the unsentimentality of the physical details and the telegraph-like concision of the prose: 'His eyes are beautifully blue and swively. He looks more like a tadpole than anything else. The house is filled with an immoderate happiness'.[38]

As Easter brought the annual Greek ritual of cleansing and rebirth, Charmian — with her regained sense of her own body ('how light it feels, how oddly uninhabited') — felt as if it were she who had just been born.[39] And now, as the weather warmed up, she was back in her element. At the swimming hole one day, George watched from the rock shelf as Charmian dived 'from the highest rock above the cave-lip, willing [her] spread arms to hold [her] arched in air'.

> It was a day to attempt the unreasonable, so close it seemed, so almost within one's power to defy the laws of gravity. Launched in an arc above the waiting sea it seemed possible that one might hang there for a moment before the downward plunge [...] or even soar on, on and on like a bird soaring across the brilliant gulf.
>
> 'What's the damage, Icarus?' George asked mildly, helping me out. But the damage proved slight for the joy of the aspiration — a grazed shin scraped on the ledge that plummets down below the cave, and a foot full of sea-urchin spines.[40]

But soon the private joys of the swimming hole had to be shared. With May, the Nolans left and the summer visitors began to arrive. In Peel Me a Lotus, as Clift records the influx over the months of June, July, August and September of this year, there is a sense of amazement expressed as the writer notes the way 'this beautiful little port' is being 'discovered'.[41] Years later, Clift would take an almost proprietorial attitude to the island's popularity. Back in Australia in 1969 she would tell a journalist from *Walkabout:* 'We were the first foreigners who bought a house [on Hydra]. In a way we started a colony. Now there are hundreds of writers and painters there'.[42]

In fact, the Johnstons were not the first foreigners to buy an Hydra house,[43] and when they arrived in 1955 the island had already been 'colonised' by a small and changing band of foreign residents, including those who stayed at a government-sponsored art school in one of the waterfront mansions. In addition, there was already an annual summer influx of foreign tourists, and the island was also a yachting resort for Athenian millionaires and their friends such as Winston Churchill and Princess Soraya. It was also becoming a popular film location, for in the summer of 1955 the Greek film director Michael Cacoyannis had made *The Girl in Black* on the island.

It was therefore somewhat naive of Charmian Clift to be surprised as the midday boat from Athens increasingly unloaded travellers from Europe and America. Though most were island-hoppers, staying only a few days before moving to the next Aegean port of call, the 'colony' of Johnstons and Greers was now increased to a dozen or so regulars. These included a pretentious American remittance man, a stinking Russian sculptor, a clutch of serious Swedes of both sexes, and a French artist named Jean-Claude Maurice. Although from the moment of his arrival Clift picked him as being 'dangerous', she also found his predatory antics funny. Again and again through *Peel Me a Lotus* she pokes fun at 'Jacques' (as she calls this character), and when at last a gang of Greek men punch out the teeth from his beautiful smile, it is no surprise to the reader to learn that the teeth are caps and the smile is false.

Clift's description of the difficulty of coping with the influx is heartfelt. This was the first time that she found 'her' tavernas full of shouting strangers, 'her' shopkeepers short-tempered and understocked, 'her' waterfront full of gawping sightseers, and — most significantly — 'her' private swimming hole at the cave full of foreign bodies, both human and inhuman. As the debris of decaying melon rinds, rotten tomatoes, cigarette butts, torn paper of all-too-obvious origin, and dubious rubber objects drifted down to the shark net to join the festoons of intestines and offal that had floated back from the slaughter yard, it was clear that paradise was lost. Meanwhile, week after week, the weather became hotter and hotter, and Hydra's water supplies — including the vital storage cistern underneath the Johnston house — dried up.

The Johnston money was drying up too. Buying the Hydra house in a lump sum had taken virtually all the couple's savings; any money left over had gone on the very expensive plumbing and the other vital repairs. At the same time, it had been very difficult for either author to write while dealing with the combined disruptions of house-hunting, waiting for the baby's birth, and living amidst renovations. And now there was the lack of sleep and general exhaustion of life with a new baby.

Despite the interruptions, Clift continued with the Hydra book while she gently nagged her American publisher for the edited version of the Kalymnos text. It didn't arrive until mid May.[44] It was only at this stage that Bobbs-Merrill drew up the publishing contract. This offered the same terms as those previously granted for *The Sea and the Stone*, except that the advance was reduced from $US1000 to $US500 (half on signature; half on publication). The publisher advised Clift's American agent, Ivan von Auw:

> *The Sea and the Stone*, up against the judgement of the market place, didn't do very well. It disappointed those of us who admire the Johnstons' work, and we felt it deserved better. But the record remained.
>
> Charmian Clift's new book is an experiment for all of us [...] Some of our editors who read it [...] like the writing very much. We strongly recommended that the House undertake the book. Against us we had the experimental feature of this manuscript and the sales record of the last one.[45]

Charmian Clift was always amenable to editing, but preferred to rewrite passages rather than simply to accept an editor's cuts. Although it seems that only a few changes were suggested for *Mermaid Singing*, it took four weeks before the revised text was ready to send back to America. At the same time, Clift sent a copy of this altered text to David Higham. Johnston, writing separately to the agent, told him that they wanted it sent to Collins 'without delay'; a personal letter of praise for *The Sponge Divers* had recently arrived from William Collins himself, so the couple had decided that Collins was their favourite publisher. Johnston also wrote directly to William Collins ('more or less on Charmian's behalf, since she is tangled up with the baby at the moment') to flag the fact that a typescript by Clift would soon come from the London agency to the publisher.[46]

This personal appeal was in vain: *Mermaid Singing* was rejected by Collins, and David Higham began submitting the typescript to other publishers. As the agency correspondence for the latter half of 1956 is missing, it is impossible to be sure of the timing of this rejection, or the reasons for it; nor do we know how many other publishers were approached. Although the painfulness of this must at least have been somewhat ameliorated by the fact that the book was coming out in America, the time lost through all this would prove damaging to sales.

Meanwhile, Johnston's work was going through a slow patch. Since the short stories of mid 1955, all he had produced was a detective novel, *Twelve Girls in the Garden*. The first in a series featuring a pixie-like professor of archaeology named Professor Challis, the fact that these books were written solely to keep the family pot boiling was underlined by the pseudonym — Shane Martin — under which they were published. Though *Twelve Girls* was posted to Higham in March 1956, it wasn't until June that the work was submitted to Collins.[47]

Even more frustrating was the fact that the English edition of *The Sponge Divers* was still not published. Ready for release in June, the book was held up until August because William Collins had liked it so much that he did not want it published 'until a reprint was ready, and a big publicity campaign organised in Australia'.[48]

What with all these delays, there does not seem to have been any money at all coming in over the first half of 1956.[49] By now the tax situation, which had begun to bother Johnston on Kalymnos, was revealing itself to be an enormous problem, and was to cause yet another delay in payments due. In April Johnston wrote to Higham asking if there were any way 'of evading this iniquitous English tax system which virtually cuts our income in half' while not allowing the writers to offset any writing or living expenses against it — and while these particular taxpayers received from the British government nothing in the way of services: 'On paper we are now earning a passable living wage, but when the tax is taken off it spreads very thinly. There was something once about "no taxation without representation", wasn't there?'[50]

Higham wrote back that his accountant, Monica Preston, advised that there was now a reciprocal tax agreement between Britain and Greece; the couple could claim exemption from British tax if they were paying Greek tax.[51] Johnston was delighted, especially as Greek tax was 'very low', and allowed deductions for children and working expenses. In mid June he advised Monica Preston that payments of royalties should be held up until 'this Greek tax matter' was worked out; at that time he believed he had 'the matter in hand, and the necessary papers are being examined and inquiries made in Athens'.[52] As it turned out, the labyrinthine nature of Greek bureaucracy would mean that Clift and Johnston were never to be able to fill in the exemption forms. They would continue to pay up to half of their British earnings to the British government for the rest of their stay in Greece. They would also pay roughly a third of their US earnings to the American government.

While no money came in between January and June 1956, the July royalty statements were frightening. Although there was enough to live on for the next six months, the writers suddenly came 'face to face with the plain bleak realisation that perhaps [they were] going to go on being poor!'[53] Since making the romantic decision to live in Greece and be full-time writers, this was the first time that George Johnston and Charmian Clift realistically assessed their financial situation and prospects. The eighteen months up till now had had a feeling of holiday, of temporariness, of looking around and, Micawber-like, waiting for things to turn up. It was only now that the writers could start to see some sort of pattern to their royalty payments, and that pattern wasn't very reassuring. No matter how hard they worked — and no matter how well they worked — the financial odds were stacked against them. They always blamed the tax bill, but their isolation added to their financial problems, for they were unable to promote their books. Nothing could be done about this, in the absence of money for annual trips to London and New York. Thus poverty bred poverty and the spiral of financial trouble could only get worse.

It is here that the timing of the house purchase becomes significant. With hindsight, it was clearly premature to have bought a house after barely fourteen months of life as freelance writers in a foreign country. Were Charmian and George themselves thinking this in mid 1956? Probably. In the July chapter of *Peel Me a Lotus* Clift makes a bleak assessment:

> We can maintain the situation, hold the fort, provide a home and food, but what effort even so much has cost already and will cost yet — only to maintain — and perhaps — the dismaying thought has to be faced — perhaps there is to be nothing more! Dear God, what a world of difference there is, after all, in living simply because you choose to and living simply because you must.
>
> Caught. Marooned. Incredulously we try to accept the fact that we really are marooned, castaways on a little rock.[54]

Now the brave statement from February that 'this is the island to which we are committed' was repeated in the harsh glare of summer light:

> Did I say I was glad to be committed? What ignorant chittering. Sometimes, looking out at noon at the brazen, clanging mountains, I am secretly appalled. It is a terrible landscape. Mummified by heat, all the juices dried out of it, naked, hairless country.

For Clift of course, place and persona were always intertwined, so from the description of this sunburnt country she shifts immediately to a scrutiny of the physical effects on George and herself:

> We are suntanned, but how scraggily thin we are, how nervous, and what an astonishing number of new lines there are, tension lines, worry lines, that are scored deeply and for all time [...]
> And where has our patience gone, our good humour? We are nervous, inclined to irritability, to sudden explosions of violence; we are captious, querulous, and tired.

It isn't sounding very different from the descriptions of their old city tension, when they lived in London. And indeed, if there George Johnston had been on a treadmill of journalism that kept him away from his novel-writing, now he was on just as much of a treadmill as he churned out potboilers as well as trying to find time to write a *real* novel — *the* real novel that he knew was in him somewhere.

Charmian was guiltily aware of the pressures George was under — 'doomed to write not what he wants to write but what he knows will sell. For him, creative freedom is still a will-o'-the-wisp'. This in turn put the pressure back on Charmian to take on the major burden of housework and childcare so that George could write as well and as much as possible. It is clear that at this stage she still saw her husband as the professional full-time writer, and herself as a housewife who wrote when she managed to find a little bit of time in between her other chores. During this summer, 'her' time was usually in the afternoon siesta period, when Shane and Martin would be off somewhere, the little town would fall into a 'hot, white silence', and even the baby would sleep. It was difficult for both partners to work, 'stripped to shorts and streaming rivulets of sweat'.[55] But in the cooler morning period, when ideas came faster from a fresh mind, Charmian was busy with her first job.

Indeed, a paradox is that in her own written accounts of family life, she does not write at all. 'While I work', she says (meaning 'do the housework'), 'I can hear the dull thudding of George's typewriter up in the studio — that familiar intermittent chatter that has been the background to all my married life'.[56] And in the description of the daily regime, she notes that from dawn, when the baby wakes, 'duties are strictly divided'. While she tends the infant, makes sure the older two are dressed and fed and ready for the day, and sets off to do the shopping, George is already writing. This is a division of territory as well as of time. While 'the studio is [George's] action-post for all the morning', she refers to the kitchen as '*my* morning action-post',[57] even using italics (a rare thing for Clift) to stress the difference. Although Charmian adored the house, its purchase had brought a great deal more work for her: tidying and cleaning for a family of five in a three-storey house is no mean feat. Little wonder if she asked 'What creativeness in this?'[58] — and if she secretly longed to be the one upstairs, thundering away at the typewriter.

Little wonder, too, if somehow there seemed to be less time to spend with the new baby than there had been back at the Bondi flat when Martin and Shane were infants and Charmian had had more energy, more modern appliances, the support of a mother and close female neighbour, and less of a feverish urge to write a book. Certainly there were neighbours here who were willing to help, but that tended to make Charmian's situation worse.

Besotted though she was with Greek customs, and despite her admiration for the matriarchal strength of Greek women, Charmian Clift had no time for Greek practices in regard to infant welfare. No sooner would she put Jason — or Booli, as he was still usually called — outside in the courtyard to lie 'browning in his basket like a joint in the oven',[59] than the gate would open and in would flock a host of women from the square. Picking the baby up and clucking over him (and maybe spitting three times, to ward off the Evil Eye), they would chide his errant mother for not feeding him the instant he cried, for not wrapping him in heavy swaddling bands, and for her dangerous practice of letting the air and sun touch him.[60]

What with this cultural criticism, combined with lack of sleep, it is small wonder that the July to September chapters of *Peel Me a Lotus* form a record of mood swings, from joy in the baby and general happiness with life to anxiety and sometimes even sheer panic. A great deal of this stress was frustration about the lack of uninterrupted time for working. Feeling this restriction as a lack of freedom, in these months it sometimes seemed to the author that her future appeared as 'a vista of lines full of diapers going on and on for ever'.[61]

Over the next few months, the issue would gradually resolve itself. Already, Zoe was employed to help with the heavy work of cleaning and washing. This was an intermittent job: the young Greek woman would frequently pop in for a couple of hours, but she didn't come every day. Indeed, in July Charmian would note that 'an answer to the problem' of handling her two jobs would be 'to ask [Zoe] to come every day to look after the house and the baby, but we can't really afford full-time help'.[62]

Zoe was probably only in her late twenties, but she was already a widow, and her husband had died before she had borne any children. This was an unusual and difficult position for a Greek woman to be in, because a childless woman was virtually a woman without identity or purpose. Given the way in which all the local women regarded Jason as being 'their business',[63] it is hardly surprising that Zoe in particular regarded him as 'her' baby. While she lavished upon this infant all her need for nurturing, Zoe also gained high status by being in charge of this first foreign baby ever to be born on the island. Soon she was popping into the house even when there wasn't a particular paid task to be done. She would offer to mind the baby. As time went on, Zoe would take upon herself more and more of a mothering role. Meanwhile, Charmian would regard herself as a thoroughly modern sort of working mother who employs a nurse or nanny.

Certainly the other two children were thriving. The *paithia* of Hydra had total freedom to play and explore, and to Shane and Martin it seemed that the streets and courtyards and mountainside and little coves of the island were a kind of vast adventure playground. Yet unobtrusively, in the background, there were always adults around, keeping watch on the children. If child-minding was a communal responsibility, so was the feeding of children. Shane and Martin would be given bits of food through the course of the day as they passed through different courtyards.

It is easy to see how this kind of safety and freedom in the enclosed area of an island seemed to Charmian to be an ideal way of spending childhood: it was like her idealised version of her own childhood Eden in the little valley of North Kiama.

Meanwhile, as this Hydra summer wore on, the financial worries meant that Clift had to keep slogging away at her book about the island. August is usually the hottest month in Greece, and August on Hydra is particularly relentless. The positioning of the little town, with its back to the breeze of the Meltemi, makes it far hotter than the neighbouring islands of Spetsai and Poros. And the bare burning rock which encloses the port reverberates and traps the heat.

The combination of 'heat, waterlessness and decadents' had a terrible effect on George.[64] These 'decadents', of course, were the foreign 'artists', more and more of whom arrived as the weeks went on. Few ever produced any art, but they dropped names and talked about what they *would* do — and meanwhile bludged money from George, who was as generous as ever despite the fact that he was churning out another Shane Martin novel so that his family could survive. As the holiday season reached its peak, a summer sexual pattern of one-night stands and covert liaisons was evident, and there were taverna brawls — explosions of temper and jealousy — as the foreign colony went 'a little mad'.

The whole atmosphere of licence had a predictable effect on George Johnston. In *Peel Me a Lotus*, Clift describes her husband brooding through 'the sweaty windblown watches of the night', threatening to sell the house and move back to London: 'From being a gregarious, warm-hearted, talkative, generous and romantic fellow he has become suspicious, moody, unfriendly, irritable, and despairing. His work too is causing him concern'.[65]

Although she attributed this distress and distraction to the heat of summer plus the 'decadents', there was a particular decadent upon whom George Johnston focused his anger. This was Jean-Claude Maurice, the French artist whom Charmian describes under the name 'Jacques'.

It is easy to see in Maurice just about everything that Johnston hated and despised. As an existentialist who claimed to be in Sartre's circle, he was from the group of people whom George Johnston summed up under the word 'pissants'. While Johnston saw the academic discipline of modern philosophy as a matter of time-wasting pretentiousness,[66] he perceived the libertarian ideals of existentialism as a threat to the fabric of order and the family, and as a proclamation of a selfish freedom without responsibility. George Johnston would have detested Jean-Claude Maurice if he were old and ugly; the fact that the Frenchman was young and beautiful made everything far worse. And so, on top of all the other worries of this summer, George began to suspect that there was some sort of liaison developing between Charmian and Jean-Claude.

It is clear that, at this time, there were no grounds for such a suspicion. In the July chapter of *Peel Me a Lotus* there is a damning description of the

Jean-Claude character, concluding with the declaration in regard to the 'decadents' that 'I refuse to acknowledge them as my spiritual brothers'.[67] By August, Clift was observing that 'the atmosphere seems bad, sick somehow, and it permeates the whole town'.

Worse was to come. By September, summer tourists usually start to leave Greece, but September 1956 on Hydra only brought a larger and more extraordinary crowd: no less a person than Sophia Loren arrived, complete with personal entourage and a whole American film crew, for Hydra had been selected as the location for the film *Boy on a Dolphin*. Over the next few weeks the island entered 'a state of occupation', and Charmian looked on as 'her' waterfront now became a film set, with the resident *xeni* as well as the indigenous inhabitants providing 'local colour'.[68] Buildings were renovated, or demolished, or even built; water was piped into the island by tankers; lavish parties were held; and as well as foreign bums and drifters, there now arrived the idle rich, come to watch the circus.

At last, in October, the rains came, filling the Johnstons' underground cistern and sending the film crew scuttling back to the States. As the waterfront settled back to normal, it was time to get down to a winter season of hard work. While George kept up his demanding schedule, he also continued the drinking and worrying of summer.

Clift, meanwhile, had reached the difficult stage of her second travel book. It was at least encouraging that the American edition of *Mermaid Singing* was now out — looking very attractive with its Cedric Flower illustrations — and *The Sponge Divers* was at last on sale in Britain and Australia. Although Clift had written the monthly sections of *Peel Me a Lotus* as the events and seasonal changes were happening, it was now that she began reorganising and polishing her material. Having begun the book with the moment of house-buying in February, she chose to conclude her account in October, looking forward towards the coming winter. In order to provide a nice round shape to the book and to tie off the loose ends of the 'characters', she brings 'Henry' and 'Ursula' back to the island in the October section and has *them* start house-hunting. In fact, Cynthia Nolan was never to return to Hydra; Sid did return this year, but only for a few days, and in December. Charmian barely saw him, for she was sick in bed with flu.[69]

As the year drew to a close, there came the wonderful news that *Mermaid Singing* had been accepted by the British publishing company Michael

Joseph. The editor, Roland Gant, declared the book 'delightful', though he stipulated that there would have to be a certain amount of cutting in order to reduce the book's length (and cost). By this time, too, the book was being 'widely and appreciatively' reviewed in America, the Bobbs-Merrill editor told the author.[70]

This should have been a very happy Christmas for Charmian — the first one in her own home, the first one with her new baby, the first one with a book of her own on the market — but there was a new worry. No sooner was she over the flu than George came down with something much worse. Writing to the British literary agents in the New Year, Clift noted that 'George has been terribly sick with a bout of pneumonia over Christmas — oh, the isles of Greece!'[71]

In retrospect, it is possible to see this pneumonia (which George had also suffered in England) as a forerunner of the successive complaints that would affect him over the next few winters. The link would finally be made between these disorders and tuberculosis, which caused the weakness of George's lungs that made him prone to bronchitis and pneumonia. His very heavy smoking exacerbated these chest problems, and increasingly made it hard for him to breathe with his damaged lungs.

With the benefit of hindsight we can also see, by the end of this first year on Hydra, all the factors that would eventually lead to the failure of the whole Greece venture: the poverty/tax nexus; isolation from business contacts; the decadence and disruptiveness of the summer tourist season; the claustrophobic clubbishness of the resident foreign colony; the exhaustion caused by dealing with primitive conditions ranging from long-term water shortages to the daily pumping of water; the difficulty of maintaining a family home in a society with different cultural values; George's health problems; George's jealousy; Charmian's frustration at the lack of working time; and the establishment of a lifestyle in which drinking a few glasses of retsina and sitting down and talking to friends would be part of the ritual of going shopping or collecting the mail.

Charmian Clift and George Johnston did not, of course, have the benefit of hindsight. At this stage, the setbacks had not established a pattern. For them — even for the pessimistic and cautious George — there was always the hope that the next boat would contain the letter with news of the big break into fame and fortune. In the meantime, nothing much could be done. In July 1956, Charmian was declaring:

Thank God we *are* marooned, that there is no question of going back. If there was a chance of escape I suspect that George might take it. He was never made to fight a holding action. Out and attack for George, and lavish the spoils. It's hard for him to be caught like this. I watch him sometimes hating the mountains. He looks baffled, and uneasy, and afraid.[72]

By August, as we have seen, George was actually threatening 'to sell the house and move back to London'.[73] This was not really an option: it would have been a terrible upheaval to move the children and all the belongings for the third time in eighteen months; and besides, George simply had too much pride to run back to Fleet Street — or Australia, for that matter — with his tail between his legs. The threat to sell the house was, rather, a kind of trump card that George would play when he feared that he might lose Charmian. It was very effective.[74] This threat would intermittently be repeated throughout the rest of the time on Hydra.

Whatever George Johnston's haverings and second thoughts, Charmian Clift was still committed to Greece. At a moment of doubt, in *Peel Me a Lotus*, the author reminds herself 'how grey it all was' in London, and then shifts to a statement of commitment that expresses her Icarus-like aspirations:

Ask nothing of it and the soul retires, the flame of life flickers, burns lower, expires for want of air. Here, in the midst of all our difficulties, life burns high. Though it seems sometimes that we make no progress towards the ideal, yet the ideal *exists*, and our energies are directed towards it.

Despite the plural pronoun, this sort of aspiration could well imply a lone enterprise; yet Clift immediately links the whole notion of commitment to her children — and does it joyfully, without any rancour or sense of the family tying her down: 'The very presence of these three eager living little creatures reminds us that we are committed to life: this house — so bare yet — is an affirmative statement'.[75]

Later, in one of the terrace at night-time scenes which she does so beautifully, she describes the children sleeping:

With thin, naked brown arms flung wide and sun-bleached heads gleaming silver in the starlight. Looking at them sweetly sleeping one has a little unreasonable stirring of faith again.

Through them we are committed wholly to life: the enterprise is sound. One can work a little longer, try a little harder.[76]

And finally, if faith failed and even family wasn't a good enough reason, the commitment — to live by writing, and to live in Greece — had by now built up its own momentum, and could not be gainsaid. By now 'the decision' was 'irreversible':

> In our own small ways we are all embarked on our journeys; why, even while we are dithering indecisively about the state of the tide and the inadequacy of our victualling we are already shooting out on the current, out and away into the wide blue frightening loneliness of freedom.[77]

It was this freedom which Charmian would begin to explore during her third year in Greece.

15

A LIFE FOR OURSELVES

I think that after that second year we began to really build
a life for ourselves.[1]

If 1956 was the year of commitment to living in Greece, Charmian would
come to see 1957 as the time when the family really established
themselves in the new land and the new life, and when she herself at last
found the liberation that she was seeking.

> I think that after that second year we began to really build a life
> for ourselves and it was a wonderful sort of life, in a way. For the
> first time in my life, apart from the time when I was a very young
> girl, I found time to do my own writing, I found time for a social
> life, I found time to look after my family properly. The days are
> very long there and life is very easy, very wonderful.[2]

It is clear that in this paradigm, happiness is dependent upon the
management of time so that Charmian's own needs, and the needs of those
who depended upon her, could all be met. If this is reminiscent of the
attitude of Emily Baker — the 'modern woman' of the post-war era whose
life Clift imagined in her 1949 radio program — this juggling of priorities
would also be familiar to any professional woman of today. Like most
professional women, Clift's ability to do her two jobs was dependent upon
finding support with child care.

In the winter of 1956–57, Zoe began to be employed on a full-time basis;
her main task was to look after Jason while his parents worked. The young
widow's role started to expand very quickly as she took the prestigious baby

with her when she went out shopping, or visiting the homes of other women. As a result, in this early time when the infant was learning language by hearing it spoken and trying to mimic the sounds, Greek was his mother tongue. Meanwhile, his real mother was 'just someone whom [he] wouldn't have known very well'. George was also just an adult figure, seen occasionally. 'George and Charmian, or one or the other, or both, were there, or down at Katsikas's, or [wherever]'. Jason points out that 'because it was a three-storey house, the writing room wasn't just the next floor but the next floor again, and generally Zoe didn't do much about up there — I presume under instructions'.³ Of course, by the time the downstairs part of the house was in use, Jason was asleep.

As Charmian reminisced about her 'wonderful sort of life' in Greece, she made it clear that 'time for a social life' was a priority, as well as writing time. In this regard Zoe also provided the vital backup. Already there was no need to worry about the two older children, for if they came home from school and found their parents out, they could wander down to the port and find them at Katsikas's. Meanwhile, Zoe was happy to have Jason for a little longer, and soon she was taking him home with her to sleep for the night.

Along with work time and free time, it is significant that Charmian identified the third component of the 'wonderful sort of life' as having the time to look after her family properly. She may have delegated, but there were a great many jobs that she did herself, such as the daily marketing and the preparation of meals for family and up to a dozen guests.

> Even to keep a semblance of order in such a big house is an all-day job. Upstairs and downstairs, to sweep, to pick up children's litter, to tidy, to ferret out dust ... marketing, making meals, cleaning up after them ... the baby needs attention, the pot is boiling over, the kerosene stove has blown up in your face again, Shane can't find her clean socks, your hands are covered with charcoal and no water in the tap ...⁴

Like most mothers, Charmian was the person responsible for administering and organising the business of family.

Under the new work system, Clift really got a rhythm up during the early months of 1957. In late March, as she continued to polish the Hydra book, she received page proofs of the British edition of *Mermaid Singing*, including the cuts that the editor, Roland Gant, proposed. He noted that he 'took rather a long time over it because [he] enjoyed the book so much that [he] found it difficult to know what to take out'.[5] This was little consolation, for the author did not like his suggestions. Her answer to Higham, to pass on to Gant, shows that Clift was very aware of the sort of book that she had produced:

> By eliminating the reasons for our flight to Greece, they have turned the book into just another travel story, which I never intended to write. People like Robert Liddell can do that sort of thing much better than I could ever hope to do. If you have read the American reviews you will have noticed that the reviewers' interest in the book was on the score of the personal problem of escape [...]
>
> Would you please tell Roland Gant thank you for liking the book, and that I know it is a grisly job hacking someone else's work.[6]

The writer was also bothered by the form of the cutting, which 'left a few choppy, disconnected paragraphs in the beginning'. She 'honestly could never agree to letting them stand as they are'. Instead, she promised to undertake a major rewrite. As we have seen, Clift would drop the first five chapters, dealing with London and the move to Kos, and start the book with the arrival on Kalymnos. It would be a great improvement.

Her first priority, however, was to finish the Hydra book. Around the middle of April 1957 she posted a copy of the typescript to David Higham in Britain, and another to her American agent, Ivan von Auw.[7] The author's celebration at completing her second book coincided with Easter, always the high point of the Greek Orthodox ritual calendar. This year, as Charmian joined the noisy crowd greeting the arrival of the new light from Jerusalem outside the church at midnight on Saturday, she felt herself to be at a new beginning with her work.

As soon as the festivities were over, she set herself to making the required changes to *Mermaid Singing*, posting the parcel of corrected proofs to Higham's agency in early May, together with publicity photographs of herself and Kalymnos which the publishers had requested. In the same mail she separately sent a letter to the book's editor, Roland Gant, notifying him that the parcel had been posted. Despite her care, disaster would happen. But for the moment, the author was delighted to be rid of all her outstanding revisions. She had that most magnificent of things: a clear desk. Now she could start a new project.

Years later, she would tell a journalist that after she wrote the two travel books, she 'thought it was time for THE novel'.[8] And for this first novel by Charmian Clift alone, what could she write about, but Kiama? She had actually known for some time what she would turn to when *Lotus* was done, sending word to Angus & Robertson at the end of the previous year that after her current book she 'plan[ned] one with an Australian setting'.[9] It was now time to go back through the folders of old drafts that she carried around with her, and to pull out the various bits and pieces of *Walk to the Paradise Gardens.*

Towards the end of April, there was good news from the Higham agency that a film option on *The Sponge Divers* had been taken by a British firm, Zonic Productions.[10] Both authors saw this film interest as proving that 'at last the decision to move from London was being financially justified'.[11] And yet, for the moment, the Johnstons' bank account was down to a few pounds. One afternoon at this time Charmian was so overcome by money worries that she spent several hours weeping as she played a record of Brahms' 4th Symphony over and over.[12] The next day, George received an airletter from the American publishers William Morrow giving him 'the wonderful news that *Twelve Girls in the Garden* [had] been taken by the Dollar Book Club for their October selection with a guarantee of $10 000 (split 50/50 between author and publisher)'.[13] As David Higham declared when he wrote to congratulate the author, 'This is real money, isn't it?'[14] However, it wasn't as good as it seemed. In the short term, the deal meant that the expected publication advance of $500 on the novel — already due — was put off, and there was considerable paperwork to be done before the $5000 came through; this sum in turn lost ten per cent in agency commissions, then another thirty per cent in tax.[15] But in late April 1957, when news of the money arrived, it seemed splendid.

Encouraged by the prospect of riches, George Johnston had another bash at persuading the Greek bureaucracy to tax him in that country, as this would ensure his exemption in Britain. Again, he completely failed — complaining that he felt he would be obliged to devote his whole life to the task, 'since the Greek authorities can't find the proper precedent and, in any case, their modus operandi derives directly from Sisyphus'. In desperation, he asked that Higham chase up money owed — such as the royalties on *The Sponge Divers*, none of which had yet been paid to the writers — and put it into their account without deducting tax. This letter — which puts the bank balance at £3 10s — forcefully expresses the paradoxical situation in which the couple found themselves at this time:

> Charmian and I are at the moment at a point of success with our writing higher than we have ever before achieved — but we have no money we can immediately draw on [...]
>
> Ah well, it's a queer business, writing and, after all, there are ups as well as downs ... We're broke, but we do *feel* very rich for a change — and things do seem to be going wonderfully for us now.[16]

Under the sway of these great expectations, Clift made a disastrous mistake in regard to *Peel Me a Lotus*. Over the previous year or so, the Johnstons had been getting fed up with their American publishers, Bobbs-Merrill, because book sales came nowhere near reaching the authors' hopes. When Clift sent off the *Peel Me a Lotus* typescript, Johnston told Higham that:

> Charmian's *Mermaid Singing* which had wonderful reviews all over the States, turned out to be a complete flop, and a little money from royalties which we had expected this month turned out to be non-existent. We are breaking all connections with Bobbs-Merrill from this point and have written to America accordingly. To be published by them is to indulge oneself in a sort of literary suicide-pact![17]

However, the American agent was obliged to offer Clift's book to Bobbs-Merrill, for they had an option on it. His letter to the author alludes to the difficulty of selling her books in the States:

> *Peel Me a Lotus* is a fine book, but I'm not sure how saleable a book it is in American terms. It doesn't seem to me exactly the kind of book to take a strong stand on with Bobbs-Merrill, for fear we might be out of the frying pan into the fire. In any event [I] will try to get a larger advance on this than they paid on *Mermaid Singing*. Unhappily, the sales report on the latter is very discouraging, only 1180 copies have so far been sold [...] Bobbs-Merrill certainly made a very handsome book out of *Mermaid Singing*, and I think believed in it and tried to sell it, but this is not an easy kind of book for the American market.[18]

Harrison Platt, the editor at Bobbs-Merrill, was delighted to hear that Clift's new book would be coming, noting that although they had been 'disappointed by the initial sales record' of *Mermaid Singing*, there seemed to be 'some continuing interest'.

> It is also noticeable that the best reception the book has had is in college bookstores. Charmian seems to be building a place among the young intellectuals and the artists — not enough of them yet, but a growing group.[19]

Given the publisher's ongoing commitment, it would have been wise to stay with them, not least because this would further encourage them to sell *Mermaid Singing*. However, Clift advised her American agent to push Bobbs-Merrill for a 'substantial advance' and an advertising guarantee; if they refused, this would allow her to get out of the option clause on her contract, and publish elsewhere.

Meanwhile, work began to slacken off as spring turned to summer, and the new season's crop of visitors began to arrive. By now, as well as the Johnstons and the Greers, the long-term resident foreigners on Hydra included an English poet, David Goschen, and his wife Angela, and a Swedish writer named Axel Jensen and his wife Marianne. Charles and Ruth Sriber, whom George and Charmian had known in Sydney journalism circles, had arrived to live in Athens (and later Icaria); the couples would sometimes stay with each other. This summer the English novelist Elizabeth Jane Howard stayed on the island for several weeks.

Another new visitor this season was Grace Edwards, a large and quietly spoken American with a doctorate in divinity and a passion for folk culture. After a life sheltered by middle class affluence and academe, Greece — and Hydra in particular — was an eye-opener; she fell in love with the country, and with the easygoing lifestyle available to a resident foreigner. Quickly becoming a member of the Hydra inner circle, she was dubbed Big Grace, to differentiate her from another woman (now called Little Grace) who was already living on the island. From the start, Grace got on wonderfully with George; with Charmian, she was always considerably less comfortable.[20] An anecdote of Grace's about her first meeting with Charmian is very revealing.

In this story, Grace was sitting with the foreigners at a table outside Katsikas's, as everyone waited for the midday boat to arrive from Athens. Grace had only been on the island a day or two, and although she already knew George Johnston — indeed, he was sitting at the table — she had not yet met his wife, who had been in Athens for a couple of days, doing the banking and shopping. As soon as the steamer docked, Charmian Clift strode around the waterfront to Katsikas's, walked straight up to the group and, without waiting for an introduction to the new foreigner, she launched in. Grace remembered: 'She [...] arrived right in the middle of a conversation we were having [...] and immediately took charge with an awesome confidence and female aggression, directing her attention solely at the men present.'[21]

To the quiet American woman, this signalled rudeness and sexual competitiveness. In fact, Charmian was reasserting her claim over her territory. Already she saw the Hydra waterfront as her patch, and after having been away for a couple of days she had to make sure that she hadn't lost any ground. Charmian's sense of ownership was inextricably tied up with her sense of belonging, and of being for the first time in her life an insider. This attitude would be expressed in the autobiographical account Clift would give for the National Library tape archive in 1965. Immediately after her comments about building a life in Greece, Charmian declared:

> Of course, we were about the first foreigners who lived on that island, and later, winter after winter and summer after summer, others came drifting in, buying houses, and there began to be established a foreign colony [...] On that island for the first time I didn't feel like an outsider looking in, because I had built something for myself that was mine.[22]

'Something for myself that was mine.' The personal pronouns say it all.

And as the years in Greece went on, Charmian's need to 'own' the Hydra scene would become more and more evident. In her eyes, it was she who gave the thumbs up — or down — to new arrivals. If we can see this as a form of compensation for a lonely childhood as an outsider, this vetting didn't go down well with all the visiting *xeni*, particularly those who were not admitted to the Katsikas group.[23] Soon, some would derisorily be calling Charmian 'the Queen Bee of the *agora*'[24] — rather as her mother had been nicknamed 'Lady Muck' in North Kiama. But if there is a parallel with Charmian's mother, surely we can also see something of Syd coming into play. Charmian may have left the little valley and journeyed to the other side of the globe, but — like her father before her — she was happiest being a big frog in a little puddle. Or a small town girl in another small town.

Certainly, she revelled in the social life of Hydra, far more than she had ever enjoyed the London scene. There was something about both Charmian and George that seemed to slot into Greek cultural notions of celebration, in a way that most *xeni* couldn't manage. They expressed *kefi* — an untranslatable word that embraces the spirit seen in the dancing or the singing or the plate-smashing. Moreover, their economic lifestyle of feast or famine was normal in a society where many families put their groceries 'on the slate' while the men ventured away to sea for months in the hope of finding sponges. Thus it was perfectly acceptable for George to run up large bills at Katsikas's, and pay them when the book harvest came in.

Overall, Charmian was entitled to feel that she and George were building a life that was uniquely theirs. And as she rejoiced in this life over the summer of 1957, George was also enjoying himself. Certainly, to Grace Edwards, looking back on this summer, it seemed that the Johnstons were happy in their relationship. Indeed, it was a peaceful high season, memorable largely for the fishing dinghy that George purchased when the first bit of Book Club money arrived. This satisfied the ambition that George had cherished since his teenage years, when he had written pieces about ships for the Melbourne *Argus*. With the advent of the *Slithey Tove*, as Charmian christened the vessel, the Johnston family and their guests were able to explore little coves away from the busy tourist trap of the swimming hole near the town.

For Charmian, the only real trouble this summer concerned the *Mermaid Singing* revisions. On 1 July, nearly two months after posting them, the author wrote to Higham noting that she was 'starting to worry slightly' because she had received no acknowledgement of the parcel of proofs.[25] It turned out that it had not arrived, and although editor Roland Gant had received her accompanying letter, he hadn't chased the matter up. Not surprisingly, Charmian Clift was 'terribly distressed': 'What are we to do now if it doesn't turn up? Have they duplicates? I don't suppose it matters much about the photographs, but the thought of doing all that dreary revision again makes me feel quite ill'.[26]

Of course the publishers blamed the Greek postal service. Whatever was to blame for the disappearance of the proofs,[27] if the writer had been able to meet with or telephone her agent and publishers, the problem would have been identified and solved within days rather than months. As it was, the rewriting all had to be done again, and it was not until January of the next year that the English edition of the book came out.[28] This delay in regard to the publication of *Mermaid Singing* also caused *Peel Me a Lotus* to be held up in Britain, for Higham felt that he should not offer it to Michael Joseph until they had brought out the earlier book.

Meanwhile, through the summer of 1957 Clift was sticking to her decision to find a new American publisher for *Peel Me a Lotus*. In an effort to help, Elizabeth Jane Howard wrote to her own US publishers, Random House, introducing Clift. Under the author's instructions, the American agent pushed Bobbs-Merrill to increase their advance.[29]

As the high season drew to an end, money was becoming tight again. How could it not? George was as generous as always, shouting round after round of drinks for the large groups that assembled at Katsikas's, and frequently giving cash hand-outs to indigent foreigners. His position as husband, father, house-owner and published author made him appear so well established that some of the foreign artists tended to treat him as a sort of *paterfamilias*, whose duty it was to provide when they were in need. At the same time, of course, they didn't particularly respect him for his easy generosity; indeed, some despised him for being saddled with kids and domestic worries, while others looked down from their ivory towers at an author who was crass enough to write for commercial publication.[30]

So why did George Johnston keep giving 'loans' and shouting the whole mob? To some extent this simply expressed his adherence to Australian notions of hospitality and mateship. Neither he nor Charmian could look the other way when someone was short of money for food or a drink. Yet it was also by profligacy that George celebrated his own escape from the penny-pinching and mean-spiritedness of his upbringing. At the same time George, just as strongly as Charmian, needed his prime position in the Hydra foreign colony to be acknowledged. By constantly giving help that ranged from drinks to cash to advice about accommodation and other practical matters, Johnston confirmed his position as leader in this small community.

Although later summers would deplete the bank balance even more, by the end of September 1957 cash was so low that George Johnston wrote to the Higham agency in the hope that a bit of money from the *Sponge Divers* film option might be expected soon. His letter crossed in the mail with one bearing the bad news that the film was off — at least for the moment. The agent offered to 'have a word with Collins' to rustle up some money in the short term.[31]

It was this same week that Charmian Clift received from Ivan von Auw in America the news that Bobbs-Merrill had turned down *Peel Me a Lotus* under the difficult contractual requirements which she had set. Noting that their attitude towards the manuscript had been 'rather reluctant' in the first place, the publishers explained that they would have taken it in the hope that a novel might be forthcoming.[32] As Clift's agent had tactfully tried to warn, the book's fate was now very uncertain.

It was too late for regrets. As autumn brought the beginning of the couple's heavy working season, Charmian Clift started to labour in earnest on the novel, *Walk to the Paradise Gardens*. After so many false starts, the task was rather daunting. Yet even despite the recent setbacks in the publication of her two travel books, she had confidence now as a solo author. With the new life and new freedom that she felt she had won by the end of this third year in Greece, this surely was the chance to fulfil her vocation as a novelist.

The winter of 1957–58 was harmonious, but as always the rain and chills had an ill effect on George's health. The old stone house was damp and draughty, and impossible to heat effectively from top to bottom; the studio overlooking the terrace was particularly prone to the weather. George still passed off his seasonal ailments as colds and flu, with maybe a touch of bronchitis. There was no doctor on the island, and there was little point catching the boat through the wild weather to Athens in order to be told to go home to bed. It seemed more sensible to buy antibiotics — which were available in Greece without prescription — and dose himself. If at the same time he felt miserable, that was either a side effect of the drugs, or the natural result of the illness.

And yet while this was the line George took in public, the literary evidence suggests that he was privately starting to worry about his recurring ill-health. Certainly, the book that he produced this winter reveals a deep sense of anxiety, coupled with a feeling that it is impossible to reverse some impending fate. This novel, originally titled *The Horde* (but published under the title *The Darkness Outside*), was begun towards the end of 1957; it would be sent off to the British and American agents in May 1958.[33] Despite a string of rejections and editorial problems with the series of archaeological detective stories, this was another work with an archaeological setting. Yet unlike the Shane Martin books, this was a serious attempt at producing a literary novel.

Set in a dig in Iraq, where six archaeologists — four male, two female — are searching for evidence of a lost Sumerian civilisation, the text reverberates with a sense of doom, disease, disaster, disintegration, and shortness of available time. As the archaeologists work frantically to complete the year's digging before the annual flooding of the Tigris, an old Englishman wearing a frayed suit is inexplicably found lying nearly dead in the marshes. Hearing the sick man's delirious tale of some coming invasion, the archaeologists become prey to the forces of superstition and darkness. When the Arab workers get wind of this fear, they take the transport and escape — leaving the six marooned in the desert.

While the image of being marooned is reminiscent of the *Peel Me a Lotus* description of feeling like castaways, Johnston's choice of title for this novel — *The Horde* — was even more obviously derived from his deep uneasiness at Hydra's annual invasion of summer barbarians. Throughout the book, the themes are those which would, over the next decade, preoccupy the author in both his private life and in his fiction. From the opening chapter, there is a sense of alienation, of being 'strangers in the desert', coupled with a sense of the impermanence and pettiness of human existence. Expressions like 'fatal inevitability' and 'jinx' become more and more prevalent in the novel, and it is clear that the author can find little source of hope. As the river steadily rises, and the recent golden discoveries of the dig are increasingly threatened with deluge, the sense of being trapped is linked with the sense of time running out. Eliot Purcell, the middle-aged director of the dig, has to decide to 'put away [his] own prize [...] for somebody else to discover'.[34] Meanwhile, as the archaeologists lapse into transgressions that range from sexual licence to betrayal to suicide, Purcell increasingly flagellates himself for his own 'uneasiness, shame, guilt, anger' and, somewhat later, for 'all [his] moments of ineptitude, irresolution, obstinacy, cruelty, procrastination, callousness'.[35]

If this foreshadows the self-castigation that would mark David Meredith's introspection in Johnston's trilogy, the novel's ending has a strange echo of the conclusion of *High Valley*, as Purcell and his young lover Grace die alone together in the desert, and their bodies are not found for some months. Yet despite the inevitability of the doom, a sense of hope and courage has been provided by Purcell's commitment to 'get[ting] on with the job'. No matter if 'epidemic has brought Europe to its knees', or if 'the hordes of Asia are marching upon us', Purcell declares: 'We will continue with our work, and be grateful for the privilege'.[36] And that in the end is his victory: as well as preserving and cataloguing the treasures of the dig, Purcell has left his testimony of events in his first-person narrative account.

Sensational though this plot may sound, the beliefs and values expressed in it would underpin the rest of George Johnston's life. 'We are trapped, aren't we?' declares one of the *Horde's* characters. 'Absolutely trapped [...] And time runs out.'[37] It could be the author's motto for the next few years on Hydra. To understand George Johnston's future actions, it is necessary to grasp something of the curious combination of overwhelming fatalism and hard-working practicality that had overtaken him. While this text shows the writer taking himself and his work with a new level of seriousness, it also represents his first use of a first-person narrator in a major work. This literary mode would soon become extremely important for the author as an instrument for personal examination. This self-examination would in turn change not only the way he viewed his life, but the way he lived it. As Johnston turned the microscope onto himself, he would also turn it onto his wife.

If George was already feeling threatened by an annual horde of invaders, he was in no state to face the coming season. With hindsight, it is possible to see that George's unstable health, together with his private worry about his condition, was having an effect on his temperament and general attitude. In turn, these concerns were already starting to cause a distancing — both sexual and emotional — between George and Charmian. Yet because the health problem wasn't acknowledged, let alone properly diagnosed, it was impossible for either partner at this stage to see where the trouble was beginning. There was just an unmentionable gap that they politely skirted around.

In the light of this developing situation, it is hardly surprising that the tourist season of 1958 was the first truly bad summer for George Johnston and Charmian Clift. Grace Edwards certainly noticed a change in the couple's relationship. Since her happy holiday of the previous year she had settled permanently in Athens. Returning to Hydra in the summer of 1958, she found that the first foreign bar had opened on the island. And by now, she commented, Jean-Claude had come.

Jean-Claude Maurice was, of course, the person whom in 1956 George Johnston had suspected of having — or wanting to have — an affair with Charmian. The French artist hadn't been on the island in 1957. This summer he returned, and George's suspicions were validated. Or was this rather a matter of self-fulfilling prophecy, with Charmian Clift — after carrying the blame for a liaison that didn't exist — finally succumbing? (Shades of Lily's behaviour in *The Piping Cry*.)

To understand the attraction that Maurice held for Charmian, it is useful to flick back to her portrayal of him in the travel book. From the moment of his arrival, Jacques (as he is called) stands for youth. Into the group of foreign residents who are worried by the passing years arrives this newcomer who makes 'everyone conscious of time':

> He came off the morning boat, a rather short young man with a beautiful brown throat and a sun-bright head. His feet were bare, and he wore only a pair of patched jeans, a rag of a scarlet shirt, and one gold ear-ring.
>
> Rather slowly and sleepily he shuffled along the quay, carrying a big artists' portfolio, a mule saddle-bag in bright stripes and a tabby cat in a netted basket. Had he chosen to arrive in the faun-skin of Dionysus, wearing an ivy-crown, and carrying a fennel wand, the effect could hardly have been more electrifying.
>
> 'Do you think that young man is *real*?' asked Ursula.[38]

As well as youth, the Frenchman represents hedonism and sheer animal beauty. He is exotic, artistic, narcissistic, and splendidly untrammelled by partner, children, or even baggage. If he is the cat who walks by himself, he is also a creature from another world. But most of all, he is pure pagan.

Although Jacques is only a minor character in Clift's travel book, every mention of him is a variation on these themes of youth, beauty, wildness and Dionysian freedom. The writer adopts the stance of a respectably married older woman who finds the young Frenchman's promiscuous sexual displays funny — for she herself is outside the circle of his prey. After brief encounters with visiting foreign girls he begins to 'stalk' the naive young American woman Katherine. The writer finds this amusing too, observing one day the hysterical Katherine scrambling up the hillside away from her seducer, who is apparently too idle even to follow her.

As the summer wears on and tempers start to fray, the author becomes fed up with the Frenchman's cadging of money from her husband. Now the very mannerisms that once stood for freedom are quite sickening:

> How offensive, how artificial and silly his provocative, shuffling walk, his skin-tight pants, his jasmine flower, and that damned ear-ring. How intentional it all is — the slow eyelids, the enigmatic smile, the shirt arranged to display the better the golden mat of hair on breast and belly, the irresistible glance that

flicks on and off like a traffic light, the interesting touch of *angst*. Not Dionysus after all, the fleet, the free, the beautiful, the ever-young — but only a little curly dog in season, whose imperative it is to sniff after any and every lady dog.[39]

Given the attitude revealed in this passage, how was it that — two summers later — Charmian had an affair with the model for this character?

It would be making too much of the situation to look for deep reasons. The whole point was that this was a summer romance — a diversion — time out from the responsibilities of being a wife and mother. Charmian's fling with Jean-Claude was a parallel to George's own liaison with the pretty young typist in the London summer of 1954. Of course, society did not apply the same standards to matters of male and female sexuality and fidelity; and George followed the mores of his time. For most husbands, the situation would have been miserable and humiliating; for George Johnston, with his personal history of feeling abandoned and certain worries that he was beginning to have about his virility, it was particularly painful.

Yet if Jean-Claude's initial attraction was his youth and beauty, Charmian found in him something beyond his toy-boy appeal, for he seemed to encapsulate the type of freedom that Charmian was seeking. In George Johnston's novel *Closer to the Sun*, the character Achille expresses Jean-Claude's philosophy: 'I believe in life, in existence, that is all. In being what I am. It is enough'.[40] Existentialism gave a veneer of intellectual respectability to Jean-Claude's lazy hedonism. At a slightly later time, the catchphrase for the young man's attitude would have been 'Do your own thing'. In 1958, this idea seemed new and liberating; and indeed, Jean-Claude was a harbinger of the so-called sexual revolution. Although this is usually associated with the 1960s, the change in values had of course been slowly gathering strength since the war had challenged established attitudes to sexuality, morality and gender roles. By the late 1950s, little pockets of rebellion were starting to break out.

While Jean-Claude was a prophet of liberation, he also came from a world that seemed to Charmian the epitome of sophistication. As the Frenchman name-dropped the doings and sayings of Jean-Paul Sartre and the rest of the *Temps Modernes* group, Charmian soaked up a romantic atmosphere of Saint-Germain-des-Prés and the artistic Left Bank of Paris. And of course, the ideas of at least one of Jean-Claude's associates were particularly interesting to Clift.

As well as endorsing Simone de Beauvoir's views on women as the second sex, Charmian Clift could find parallels between herself and George, and Simone de Beauvoir and her lifelong partner Jean-Paul Sartre, for both were couples who shared work and life. It was widely known that de Beauvoir and Sartre had an 'open' relationship, in which both partners publicly had affairs with other people. This was the philosophy of freedom that Jean-Claude Maurice spoke about. To George Johnston, it represented a threat to values such as 'morality, family, law'.[41] To Charmian Clift, it seemed to show a way to have the best of both worlds. Why couldn't you feel complete commitment to a long-term partner and at the same time have a totally separate relationship with somebody else?

One vital difference, of course, between the situation of these two women was that Charmian Clift had children and a house to look after, while Simone de Beauvoir operated alone, from a hotel room. But apart from these domestic responsibilities, the concept of an open relationship was anathema to Clift's husband. It is no coincidence that, in one of his private analyses of Cressida Morley's desire for freedom, George Johnston wonders to himself whether Simone de Beauvoir is not a 'prophet of the same change in values' as Cressida Morley. Of course, George Johnston, like his alter ego David Meredith, was 'emphatically not' in agreement with these values.[42] It was a matter of generation, as well as gender. George Johnston took as his intellectual role model the American writer F Scott Fitzgerald, whose attitudes epitomised the relationship between the sexes in the period between the wars.

The very landscape of Hydra seemed designed for intrigue. Down its network of narrow lanes and cul-de-sacs, there was ample scope for chance meetings or assignations. Yet it was also a town for spies and whispers. A rumour could jump like wildfire from the *agora* to the back streets in a matter of minutes.

And so, in the summer of 1958 the foreign colony of Hydra thrilled with the gossip of clandestine meetings between Charmian and Jean-Claude, of jealous rows between George and Charmian. To understand the level of excitement caused by this affair, the dreary propinquity of island life must be grasped. For everyone — including the protagonists — the drama was a relief from the boredom and claustrophobia that always set in during summer. (A couple of years previously, Cynthia Nolan had aptly commented: 'Hydra in summer, full of myths I could never raise more than a yawn over'.[43]) While the *xeni* always thrived on gossip about the incestuous relationships within their little group, there was of course a special thrill to this particular story: as the queen took her golden young consort and the king stormed and railed, there were some courtiers who were delighted.

This was a summer of violent explosions and dramatic reconciliations. An Hydra resident later recalled the time when 'Charmian had a flip' with a Frenchman:

> George was so upset about him that he actually packed up and set forth in a motor boat, fortunately driven by one of his friends. He drove him round and round the port till George had cooled off: we stood around and cheered when he came back.[44]

The most striking thing about this description is the public nature of the dramas. Increasingly, it was as if the amphitheatrical harbour setting was a stage on which the script was played out for the bored crowd of *xeni* who doubled as extras and audience.

This is an appropriate place to take the testimony of Patrick Greer, who in 1980 wrote a piece about his memories of the Johnstons on Hydra for the *London Magazine*. While the tone throughout seems embittered and jealous, there is some truth to Greer's depiction of the inflammable nature of the Johnston/Clift relationship, and its effect on the other foreigners.

> In the early days I'd had 'a thing about Charmian', as [George] rightly guessed and publicly announced. My admiration was obvious and open and I'd never tried to do much about it out of a quite genuine desire not to interfere, maybe disrupt something that seemed to be going, if a bit bizarrely, rather well [...] It took about a year of their company before [my wife Nancy and I] realised that interference was exactly what they wanted. They needed the conjugal drama, preferably a public, quayside enactment of it. Whether they were conscious of the desire, or drama occurred in spite of themselves, it was difficult to know.[45]

Greer moves on to *Clean Straw for Nothing*, and especially to the book's preoccupation with 'the history of men coming under the spell of Cressida, a tale of her suspected or real infidelities', and then he again asserts that he was 'one of the first in a series of people who were encouraged to have a thing about Charmian'.

This reference to encouragement seems to sit oddly with the jealousy that George Johnston also exhibited in regard to his wife. And yet Greer's suggestion rings true. Charmian was still George's prize — and there was little point having a wife who was beautiful and sexually alluring if other men did not appreciate the fact. Further, it was symptomatic of George's insecurity that he had to keep testing his wife. Still believing that he did not deserve someone like Charmian, he had to check up on her all the time. And like his narrator Eliot Purcell in *The Darkness Outside,* he feared that he might have to put away his golden prize for other men to find. Patrick Greer goes on to note that some visitors responded to this 'encouragement':

> Inevitably certain of the players in this casual comedy wished to take their 'part' to its logical conclusion (the Johnstons had a great capacity for pursuing anything to its illogical conclusion), and so, once more, the whole foreign community, the natives as well, in so far as they could be enlisted, were involved in a struggle to keep the Johnston Family united, the Holy Grail Johnston Flag Flying, George might be about to do away with himself again.

This depiction of the foreign colony involving themselves in the 'struggle to keep the Johnston Family united' fits exactly with George Johnston's fictional portrayals of friends weighing in with advice and support for his alter ego David Meredith, who must continually be calmed down, talked around, convinced of his wife's love for him, and persuaded to give the marriage another chance. While Meredith's wife leads a lonely life, with no one to act as supporter, David Meredith always has any number of people in his corner, ready to cheer him on, offer advice about tactics, and mop up the blood between rounds.

And what of Patrick Greer's suggestion that 'George might be about to do away with himself again'? Although there is no evidence of Johnston ever staging an attempt, he was flirting with the idea of suicide in the fiction he was writing at this time.[46] We can probably also take as fairly autobiographical the scene in *Clean Straw for Nothing* in which David Meredith — provoked to despair by his wife's infidelity — stands at the edge of the cliff overlooking the sea-cave and thinks of suicide as 'the one certain escape from the trap, from failure, from responsibility, from the unending precariousness of economic hazard, from ill health, from the whole unbearable rigour and peril of going on'.[47]

The intention of such threats was to increase the pressure on Charmian to stay, and not abandon him. Part rhetoric, part romance, George's talk of suicide was something from the script that was increasingly being played out in real life as well as on paper. In the cliff-top scene in *Clean Straw,* Meredith tells himself 'with a kind of relish' that if he were to take such action, there would be 'a tincture [...] of romantic drama'. Yet it only takes the narrator 'a matter of moments' on the cliff before deciding against suicide as 'too cold and sinister and lonely'; and besides, it is 'intolerable to contemplate' that he should not be able to see his wife again. Here again we see the bondedness of these two: life together might sometimes be fraught with immense difficulty, but the concept of being separated by death was insupportable.

Through this summer, as the public dramas went on, Charmian Clift was privately suffering the worst rejections of her writing career. In March the British publishers Michael Joseph — who had recently brought out *Mermaid Singing* — had turned down *Peel Me a Lotus.*[48] Now the folly of leaving Bobbs-Merrill became terribly apparent, as every six weeks or so there came a letter from the American agent Ivan von Auw carrying news of another publisher refusing *Peel Me a Lotus.* Meanwhile, in July the book was further rejected in Britain by the publisher James Michie.[49]

This was all very hard to bear. On a personal level, *Peel Me a Lotus* meant a great deal to the author, for it was the story of the birth of her new child and her love for the first home that she felt to be truly her own. In terms of her development as a writer, Clift saw the text as being her best work so far. After the critical acclaim of her first travel book, she had been confident that she had done an even better job the second time. And in commercial terms, too, the author felt that she had jumped through the right hoops. This second book was less structurally complicated than the first, so must surely be more suited to the popular market. Like Gerald Durrell's bestseller, it had lots of funny scenes about the foreign colony. That was what readers wanted, didn't they? Especially Americans. She had put lots of funny Americans into it.

In her attempt to understand the market, Charmian Clift could not have got it more wrong. And her eagerness to correct the 'faults' of her first book led her astray. Although *Peel Me a Lotus* exhibits the extraordinary tone and phrasing that marks Charmian Clift's literary voice, this second travel book is not as fine as its predecessor.

The first problem is the book's structure. Dutifully heeding the publishers' comments about the 'experimentalism' of *Mermaid Singing,* the author made the new text follow the calendar and move simply through the events, with no time jumps and few digressions. Apart from the fact that digressions are this author's forte, the problem with this structure is that while some months are terribly busy, others are slack. To give them all equal weight in the text, the writer was forced to condense some wonderful material; thus, with all the excitement of moving house and having a baby in April, Easter becomes a single paragraph, shunted over into May. Another difficulty was that the experience documented in the Hydra book — unlike that of the Kalymnos book — did not have a natural shape. To declare in the opening sentence 'Today we bought the house by the well' was a catchy starting point, but the 'journey' of the family living in this house would not actually have an end until 1964, when the Johnstons returned to Australia. Thus the text had to be written before the story found its own shape.

While both the urgency of production and the imposed time frame affected the book's structure, a certain genre problem within the text reduced its sales potential, for *Peel Me a Lotus* is an example of anti-pastoral in a form of literature that typically follows pastoral conventions. Despite some extraordinarily lyrical depictions of Hydra, the lasting impression of the island is of a searingly hot place full of superficial and vindictive people. Even worse, the author reveals her own anxieties and unhappiness. Although it is possible in a travel book to detail hardship and ugliness and even — as in *Bitter Lemons* — to show paradise being lost, there must be some Arcadian element which makes the reader feel that he or she is taking a vicarious holiday. Yet on top of the depiction of the relentless landscape, there was something else that was just too un-Arcadian. While Clift had verged on this in *Mermaid Singing* with her concentration on the female side of life, she went too far for the market in her second book. In *Peel Me a Lotus* the amount of domestic material is increased as the writer/narrator details the relentless grind of chores in between the bouts of lotus-eating:

> From a real adversary courage flows into you. But there is no lifting of the heart when all you are asked to fight are bed-bugs and garbage cans and stinking drains [...]
>
> What creativeness in this? Here is no progression, no building towards some ideal summit, but only a perpetuation of the present. The clean becomes soiled, one makes the soiled clean, the clean becomes soiled again [...]

> A housewife is a housewife wherever she is — in the biggest
> city of the world or on a small Greek island. There is no escape.
> She must move always to the dreary recurring decimal of her
> rites.[50]

While this sort of litany of daily life might be expected to miss the mark
with men, it is interesting — given Charmian Clift's later popularity among
women for just this sort of domestic detail — that it apparently went down
even worse with female readers of the 1950s. When the British publisher
James Michie rejected the text, he noted regretfully that he personally had
liked it, but he hadn't been able to get his female manuscript assessors to
'back up his views'.[51]

Meanwhile, in *his* rejection letter Roland Gant from Michael Joseph had
pinpointed another problem when he noted that 'Charmian Clift seems to
have lost that original freshness of approach and interest in the Greeks
rather than the visitors'.[52] Notwithstanding Gerald Durrell's success, it seems
that the British market had had enough of books about foreigners living in
Greece, and now wanted to know about the indigenes!

The worst problem of all, however, concerned the depiction of a
particular section of the foreign community. Clift's naivety combined with
her sharp eye and her powers of verbal mimicry led her to portray the
American visitors with all their pretensions and prejudices and verbal ticks.
The worst is a character named Mrs Knip, who goes around asking
everybody: 'But what are you doing it for?' In this needle-sharp depiction of
the insensitive busybody who single-handedly sets out to judge and civilise
both islanders and foreign colony, Clift managed unwittingly to attack the
whole value structure of Middle America.

It is little wonder that, again and again, American publishers praised the
book's prose style but declared that it would be very difficult to sell. Over
the next eighteen months, the manuscript would be rejected in turn by
Dodd Mead, Farrar Straus, Harper's, Little Brown, Morrow, Putnam,
Random House, Rinehart, Simon and Schuster, and Doubleday.[53] *Peel Me a
Lotus* was never to find a place in the US market. It is a tribute to the
author's complete lack of commercialism that she would never quite
understand what it was that she had done wrong.

It was hard for Charmian Clift to keep working on her novel *Walk to the
Paradise Gardens* through the summer of 1958, while there still seemed no
prospect that her previous book would ever be published. However, when

the summer visitors left — including Jean-Claude Maurice — she started to see an end to this novel on which she had laboured in fits and starts since at least the London years.

The text takes on a new resonance if it is borne in mind that the final version was written during this unhappy year, for this story is an exploration of two failed marriages. Using the device of two heroines which she had begun in *High Valley*, Clift contrasts Julia, the wife of successful architect Charles Cant, with Meg, married to Roy Tressida, who is the proprietor (and, by his name, symbolic 'king') of a ramshackle little camping park named Paradise Gardens on a beach just outside the township of Lebanon Bay. Julia, who grew up in the house where Meg now lives, appears at first to be confident and gregarious. She is dark-haired, well-groomed, wealthy, childless, and seems free of constraint or care. Meg, with ash-blonde hair and an air of shining purity, has a young daughter whom she adores and protects.

While themes of infidelity and guilt are easily discernible, a deeper thread is concerned with another kind of fidelity as the two women in the novel put up with miserable marriages in order to protect and support their vulnerable and inadequate husbands. At the start of the novel, Julia is engaged in a desperate attempt to rescue her marriage. 'Let us love each other!' she nearly cries out loud to her husband on the first day. 'Before it's too late!'[54] Charles, like the author's own husband, has a nagging fear of failure, and believes that time is running out for him. He is holing up in Lebanon Bay while he awaits the announcement of an architectural competition that he has entered. Despite her support for her husband, Julia wants also to win her own free identity.

In the early stages of the holiday, she discovers a new and happy self: for years, her 'natural talent for joy' has been 'vitiated by Charles's mockery', and she has given up her own pleasure to that of Charles, enjoying herself only 'vicariously or retrospectively or qualifiedly'.[55] She wonders now: 'Why should she spend all her life watching things? Why should she not participate also?' No sooner has she made this claim for herself than she gets drunk and ruins everything.

> But why, why should it always be like this for her? Why, whenever she tried to break through out of the public image of Charles Cant's wife — to be herself, Julia, distinct, separate, acting independently — did humiliation or disaster befall her? [...] She

watched herself in some oblique interior way [...] And 'Oh! Oh!'
she cried to Charles Cant's wife in misery, 'That is all very well,
but where am I?' [56]

While Julia's spouse is cold and pompous, callous and hyper-critical,
Meg's husband Roy plays strange and complicated power games to keep her
under control. On one occasion, he tells his wife:

My father used to thrash me once a month regularly. I think I
might have mentioned it to you before. In the bathroom. With a
razor strop. Because he knew I must have been up to some trick
or other he hadn't found out about.[57]

Clearly, here the author was incorporating one of George's anecdotes of
childhood. It is implied that it is this background which produces the
insecurity that in turn causes the fictional Roy to harass his wife about her
fidelity until at last she does commit adultery.

As the plot unfolds, and the lives of the two unhappy couples mingle
over a summer holiday season, various tensions rise to the surface. The
catalyst is provided by Con, a guileless young Greek waiter for whom Julia
conceives a passion that is less to do with sexuality than with emulation: she
would like to share his innocent and unquestioning acceptance of the
world, and his ability to experience sheer joy. However, Con himself loves
not Julia but Meg, who in turn falls in love with Charles, who makes love to
her but is incapable of loving anybody but himself.

At times the novel reads like a tragic rendering of *A Midsummer Night's
Dream*, as the lovers chase each other through the nights of barbecue and
dance. Yet the novel's symbolic landscape pays tribute to Dante.
Throughout the book, images of Paradise and Hell are juxtaposed, and as
the plot warms up, bushfires ring the township and the wind whips a
sandspray 'as hot as the breath of inferno'.

A further influence is classical Greek drama. Here, as in a Greek tragedy,
the characters seem to have no alternative but to act as they do, and their
actions form a kind of ritual that leads to a predestined disaster. Their fate is
connected with the story of Selina — remembered from Clift's own
childhood, and resurrected from the drafts of the novel written in London
— who used to stand on the cliff edge of the quarry, waiting for the return
of her lover who (according to rumour) had been helped over the edge by
the woman's jealous husband. In this text the situation is reversed when

Meg stands and watches as her admirer Con pushes her husband Roy over the cliff.

Beyond the dramatic plot line, the novel is primarily concerned with Julia's quest for herself, as she seeks her own meaning. Thus in the presence of Con, she finds herself wondering:

> Why was he so happy? What did he know that she didn't? And why, *why?* did she have this queer, unaccountable feeling of being on the verge of recognition of it? Yes — almost as though she had only now realised the value of something she had thrown away, but could not yet remember what the thing itself was.[58]

To some extent, Con is a reworking of the character of Freiburg from the author's short story 'Three Old Men of Lerici', in which Ursula realises that her naive lover hears the music of the pan pipes all the time. The lament of both Julia and of Ursula reflects the author's own feeling that there was some vital thing that she simply was not recognising.

Despite the misery of this summer holiday, Julia does move tentatively towards a state of acceptance: 'What other people's preferences are, what their opinions of us are, don't really matter. Only what we are'. Taking courage from this new understanding, she feels that 'she had come to the end of a probation and the beginning of real life'.[59]

At best, however, Julia must be satisfied with this personal and private victory. When her husband fails to win first prize in his professional contest, his smooth facade breaks; as Charles makes no progress towards humility or wisdom, the result is simply a realignment of forces, with Julia now the stronger in the relationship. It is ultimately the alternate heroine who comes out best, for Julia reflects that at least Meg has been 'lifted from the ordinary and the dull into the romantic climate of high tragedy'.

> Things had happened to her. Unforgettable things. She would never have to rest dry and lonely outside the stream of life. Even if she could not keep her head above water, even if she was bruised on the rocks, or caught at last in the whirlpools, she was part of it, for ever and ever.[60]

In this image, which reflects Clift's description of flirting with death in the tides of the sea-cave, the author makes yet another affirmation of her Icarus belief that it is better to live dangerously than not to experience life at all.

As the autumn of 1958 set in, Clift worked in her laborious way, moving backwards and forwards through the text of this novel, polishing, editing, rewriting, revising. It was so painstaking, so slow.

Although Jean-Claude Maurice had left, the relationship between Charmian and George was still difficult. George was naturally bitter, and kept going back over the affair. It did not help that in his work he was unable to move ahead or turn his mind to a new project. In July he had received the welcome news that *The Horde* had been accepted in Britain by Collins, but the editor required considerable changes — including a new title. At the same time Helen King, Johnston's editor at the American publishing company William Morrow, wanted the book 'subject to revision'.[61] By early September Johnston had done 'a complete rewrite' incorporating all the Collins editor's suggestions.[62] However, in November the author received the miserable news that Helen King at Morrow now didn't want the book. In writing to Higham about this, Johnston also advised him that 'Charmian is very close to the finish of her novel, *Walk to the Paradise Gardens*, which I think Michael Joseph might very much like to see'.[63]

At last, in December, the tide of bad luck seemed to be turning, as David Higham wrote to tell Charmian that Hutchinsons had made an offer for *Peel Me a Lotus*. In her reply, she declared that 'The offer seems like a special Christmas present, since I'd given poor old *Lotus* up long ago'. The author then went on to mention for the first time her work in progress:

> I think you will be pleased to know that I have just finished a novel — that same old one I have been promising you for years, and still the same old title — *Walk to the Paradise Gardens*. George and I like it, and since there is nothing frightening about it from a publisher's point of view, and since it has an Australian setting, which I believe is awfully fashionable these days, I think we ought to be able to place it all right. Now *Lotus* is placed there doesn't seem to be so much of a hurry, and I might take another month for the final polishing bits.[64]

To her final flourish of 'very best wishes from us both for Christmas', Charmian adds a comment that clearly comes straight from the heart: 'This has been a year of great difficulties and much hard work, and it is so nice that it ends so happily'.

16

ALMOST FOUNDERING

I do not like to think much on those years because we
almost foundered [...] As he fined down alarmingly
in weight [...] he also fined down in character, persona,
or whatever you call it. And of course this in a way was
alarming too — for a wife, that is, who found she was married
to someone else entirely.[1]

As 1959 opens, it is timely to take stock of the professional position of
these two writers. At the age of forty-six and with sixteen books
published, George Johnston could be regarded as a writer at the mid-point
of his career. At thirty-five, Charmian Clift still had only one book published
under her own name, but there were also three collaborative publications as
well as another book under contract and a solo novel that was nearly
completed. At this stage the couple should have been able to rely on backlist
royalties for a certain level of survival, with advances from new titles topping
up their bank account. In fact, what was happening was that they were living
off their advances — or on credit, in the expectation of advances. The
problem was that book after book went out of print after its first edition.
Sometimes George Johnston's work scored good reviews, and there was the
occasional sale of an edition to a book club, but his novels never sold well in
the bookshops. And Charmian Clift's solo sales had barely started.

While the poor result from so much hard labour was demoralising, even
the occasional financial upswings brought certain adverse effects. When
something of George's made good money, it was always unexpected; and

invariably it was for a text that the author himself did not value. This feeling of life being subject to irrational fate was exacerbated by the daily ritual of going down to the port at midday and waiting for the boat to bring the mail. Would there be 'money or the promise of it? More bills? Acceptance or rejection? Success or failure? Hope or despair?'² Whatever the outcome, the situation called for a drink at Katsikas's.

The unpredictability affected everything. In George and Charmian's correspondence, great happiness and terrible worry alternate from letter to letter, from week to week. Many accounts of this period tend to the gloomy side, coloured as they are by George Johnston's own testimony in *Clean Straw for Nothing*. Yet it must never be forgotten that the Greek sections of this text were written some eight or nine years after the events portrayed; by the time of writing, Johnston's physical condition was so bad that it caused him to forget the happiness that had also been part of the Hydra experience.

Certainly, the year began with desperate financial worry. On 3 January, Johnston wrote to Higham that 'once again we have come to the end of our financial tether'. The couple had received none of the English royalty money which had accrued in the past year, and were 'now rather desperately in need of some'. At the same time the author wrote to Higham's accountant, Monica Preston, asking her to pay off the arrears of the previous year's tax but to 'leave the taxation on this year's earnings [...] to be cleared up in due course', and simply pay money owing into the couple's London bank account. The agency was unwilling to do this, and immediately paid the tax department £269 0s 5d. Johnston was devastated, writing back a fortnight later that the situation remained 'intensely worrying':

> You will see that out of £257–18–10 I receive £61–3–9; while out of an earning of £102–19–7 Charmian receives £64–14–7. This meagre return comes from five books in circulation or accepted, two foreign translations, one sale of foreign serial rights, an earlier novel, and certain magazine extracts. For this, and all the work it represents, the return in total is £125–18–4, which I'm sure you'll agree is hardly worthwhile.³

Johnston went on to ask that remaining advances due (amounting to £475) be paid into the bank without deducting tax, warning that 'if this is not done, our situation here will become quite impossible and we shall have to sell up and get out'. At the same time, he promised to 're-start the weary round' of trying to persuade the Greek authorities to tax him in that country. In conclusion, he reminded his agent that 'as Charmian has pointed out, a writer's life on a Greek island is not all peeling lotuses'.

Indeed, a few weeks later Charmian would tell David Higham that it was 'bitterly cold' and they had 'stoves roaring extravagantly all over the house'.[4] Although wood was very expensive on Hydra, the investment seemed worthwhile: so far, George had got through the winter unscathed. However, he had been losing weight for some time and his lean frame was becoming painfully thin.

Yet against these various difficulties must be balanced the joy that both Charmian and George got from their work at this time. At the end of January, Charmian returned to Higham the signed contracts for the UK edition of *Peel Me a Lotus*, commenting that she had heard from the editor at Hutchinsons and he seemed 'friendly and ready to be co-operative'. After the double revision of *Mermaid Singing*, she was hoping for an easy editorial run on this second book. At the same time, she commented that George 'has just started a new novel, so is at his happiest'.[5]

The new novel — called by its author *The Islanders* — would be published under the title *Closer to the Sun*.[6] While this would represent a new stage in the development of George Johnston's writing, it would also be extremely important in biographical terms. In the creation of this text, significant changes would be wrought in the relationship between fact and fiction, life and the portrayal of life, the private sphere and the public sphere. This in turn would change the way in which Charmian Clift and George Johnston lived their lives. For the location, characters and plot of this work the author drew directly from his own recent experience. Set on a Greek island, this novel tells the story of an expatriate Australian writer whose wife has an affair with a French artist and pseudo-intellectual.

It was in this book that Johnston began to develop the character who would prove to be his most successful alter ego. This, of course, was David Meredith. Unlike the Johnston heroes of the past, with their varied ethnic backgrounds — Tibetan, Greek, Chinese, American — and their exotic occupations — sponge-diver, warlord, archaeologist, film-maker — this time the author set out to portray a character who was like himself. While Meredith shared many of the same concerns as his model, including a need to examine the alienation of the expatriate existence, Johnston was still seeing this alter ego from the outside. In this text, David Meredith is portrayed in the third person, and the author still occupies the role of omniscient narrator. It would take a few more years and another novel before Johnston would see and speak directly through the eyes and mouth of his alter ego.

It was also in this book that Johnston first expressed his sense of personal identification with Odysseus the journeyer. The seer-like Erica Barrington tells Meredith that he is 'still sailing in search of something that lies over the sea-rim'; he will perhaps find what he is seeking, but he will also want to sail back home.[7] Thus the author began to use the Homeric story as a way of exploring his personal preoccupation with exile and repatriation. In the novel's last scene, when a sponge boat captain sets sail late in the season with a makeshift crew, Meredith observes that 'You had to make your own journey with whatever crew, whatever provisions you could get. The importance was in the journey, in the sailing out and the sailing on, in the grip of your own hand on the tiller'. This idea is so important to the hero — and the author — that it leads to the novel's philosophical resolution:

> All right, the talent of David Meredith might not be as great as he might wish it to be, nor his marriage as romantic, nor his island as idyllic ... but he had brought off his own stand for the right to hold the tiller in his own hand, and by God! this was something [...] Since they were committed to the journey, then they would sail this way ... and perhaps [...] he would find what he was seeking and recognise it when he found it.[8]

This metaphor of life as journey would become the main philosophical notion that George Johnston would pursue for the rest of his own life. As he continued to write, the myth of the Odyssey would become more and more important. Increasingly, however, Meredith-Odysseus would appear as a lone traveller.

As to David Meredith's unfaithful wife, the author looked not just to his own wife, but to her writing. He borrowed from *Peel Me a Lotus* the name Katherine (which Clift gives to the young American woman whom the Frenchman stalks), and bestowed it in the form of Kate upon Meredith's spouse. For those who have read both texts, the description of the arrival on the island of Achille Mouliet — as the Frenchman is called in Johnston's novel — evokes a familiar feeling, for again he appears from the boat crowd wearing the small gold earring and carrying a bulging portfolio of drawings and a tabby cat in a string bag. (In this version the cat is 'one-eyed'.) The pagan aspect of the young Frenchman is even more overtly signalled: 'His brown face was the face of a faun, or of an old Greek god, a face with the pagan look of an ancient angel. In fact he was on the verge of looking almost too pagan to be really believed in'.[9]

As the plot of *Closer to the Sun* unfolds, intimacy develops between Achille Mouliet and Kate Meredith. This leads to a seduction scene in which Johnston brings in the full import of Dionysian imagery, as Kate Meredith follows the Frenchman up a hot and rocky hillside (in a reverse of Katherine's hysterical flight from Jacques in *Lotus*) to a romantic ruined windmill.

> He had almost reached the crest of the ridge, so that from her lower viewpoint his body again was thrown against the sky, a complete form that was tawny-brown and capped by gold silhouetted godlike against the empty shining hugeness of the sky, and smiling that haunting, far-away smile at her, and calling to her, 'Come. We are almost there. Come. You are so slow.'
>
> He looked exactly like the bronze image of the god Dionysus she had seen once in the Louvre, the god young and naked and beautiful [...] Was this how the ancient women had felt, following him upwards and upwards into the lonely mountains, these women in *ecstasis*, the mad women, the Maenads, Thyiads, lost to all but the sense of orgiastic licence, of frenzy and abandon and the naturalness of physical love ...?[10]

Like a Maenad following Dionysus, Kate Meredith is drugged with ecstasy. She does not choose to take Achille as a lover in preference to her husband: she has to. While this might seem a gesture of forgiveness, what Kate Meredith loses in this portrayal is her free will. This is very different from the attitude that Clift expresses towards her own heroines when they commit adultery. Meg, Julia, Kathy — in their various ways they acknowledge what they have done, and expiate their sin or shame.

A decade later, Charmian Clift would make an extraordinarily acute assessment of *Closer to the Sun*:

> I don't think it was a good novel, but it was a very important one to me because it was halfway honest — that is, honest for half its length, when obviously uncertainty engulfed him and he retreated into story-line and the old trick of dazzling observation.[11]

That Clift was able to make such a generous comment is a tribute to her own honesty. Johnston himself would say of this first portrayal of David Meredith: 'I lost my nerve, and the character turned out not to be me at all'. On another occasion he would tell his old friend and colleague Elizabeth Riddell that with this first David Meredith novel, as with the second one, *The Far Road*, he had 'compromised'. 'Halfway through each book I had got cold feet. I broke their backs in the middle. I didn't have the confidence to do it right'.[12] At the time of writing the book, however, the good half was good enough to encourage the author in the belief that this time he was really writing something that mattered.

In biographical terms, the essential thing about *Closer to the Sun* is its point on the trajectory of George Johnston's fictionalisation of the real experience of himself and his wife. Although aspects of Charmian Clift had been appearing in the female characters in Johnston's fiction since the green-eyed heroine of his 1946 potboiler, *Moon at Perigee*, this new text went deeper and further into private matters. Also, the characters were far more immediately identifiable when placed in their 'real' setting.

Of course Clift was a writer too, and she also drew on the people and world around her. However, while aspects of George's character or experience would appear in the two husbands portrayed in Clift's novel *Walk to the Paradise Gardens*, Roy Tressida and Charles Cant were clearly composite characters, made up of so many bits and pieces that the 'George-bits' were not easily recognisable. Further, the plot and setting of the book were so far removed from the writer's adult life that it is unlikely that readers would make any biographical connections.

In her travel books, Clift took real experiences from the family's life and put them straight onto the page, and in these first-person narratives she even called her characters 'George', 'Martin', 'Shane', 'Booli', and so on. The difference is a matter of genres and conventions. In something which purports to be a non-fiction memoir written in the first person, the reader accepts that while the portrayals are based on real people, there will be embroidering and bias. But in a novel which is supposedly 'made up', everything seems bigger and bolder and somehow more authentic. For someone who finds herself in such a piece of 'fiction', the experience can be devastating, for it seems sure that the reader will accept the work as being 'true'. It is like hidden camera documentary, as opposed to the documentary interview done with the consent of the subject. The fact that the particular privacy intruded upon in *Closer to the Sun* was a sexual one — and that the incidents reflected badly on Charmian — made the whole thing even more humiliating.

Given George Johnston's habit of handing his typed pages to his wife for instant editorial feedback, the production of this novel severely tested Charmian Clift's forbearance. To read each day about herself — and not quite herself — doing things which she had done — and not quite done — was unnerving as well as mortifying.

Meanwhile, through these first months of 1959, Clift herself kept at her slow and steady polishing of *Walk to the Paradise Gardens*, while also dealing with the slight revisions required by the editor of *Peel Me a Lotus*. Around Easter, she sent the typescript of her new novel to her agents in both Britain and America.

At the end of May, her American agent Ivan von Auw wrote back excitedly that 'The jinx seems to have broken first crack out of the box'. Harpers were 'very enthusiastic' about *Paradise Gardens* and offered an advance of $1500.[13] In writing immediately to David Higham to tell him the news, the author declared: 'I am, of course, quite immoderately happy'.[14]

Within a month or so, there was even more good news. Hutchinsons in the UK — the publishers of *Peel Me a Lotus* — also accepted the novel, although offering terms that weren't as good as those previously given. In her response to her British agent Clift queried whether this implied a 'want of confidence in the book'. She herself at this time was uncharacteristically sure of the value of her work:

> I have all sorts of writing plans, and shall probably go on producing a novel a year for many many years to come. I think *Lotus* was better than *Mermaid*, and *Paradise Gardens* better than *Lotus*, and I know the next one, *Honour's Mimic*, is going to be better than *Paradise Gardens*. I have, you see, enough confidence in myself at least.[15]

Stressing that she found the new terms offered to be 'rather humiliating', she even wondered whether she should seek yet another publisher, and mentioned how 'difficult' it was 'from this distance, without any personal contact, to have a proper sort of relationship with one's publisher'. In the letter's conclusion, however, Clift is buoyant again as she announces: 'Am starting work on the next one in a few days. Do you like the title? It's from Donne'.

George was also delighted at her success. In his own business letter to Higham in this same mail, he concluded: 'Charmian's beginning to do very nicely under her own steam, isn't she? I'm overjoyed'.[16]

Through this summer of 1959, George Johnston worked like a man possessed. One reason was that for the first time, he was really exploring both his talent and himself. In late July he outlined 'the writing situation' to Higham, noting that 'for several months' he had been 'flat out' on his novel, which he described as 'by far the most ambitious thing I've yet attempted, and which I have great hopes for'. The author added that he was currently doing the final revision, which he hoped to have completed within the next month. He explained that he had been putting off the next Shane Martin, but as soon as the real novel was done he would begin 'immediately' on the potboiler; he had 'already worked it out'. It was to be titled *The Far Face of the Moon*.[17]

The author was most encouraged by splendid reviews of *The Darkness Outside* which now began to appear in the British press. While Muriel Spark called the book 'a highly distinguished nightmare novel' and J B Priestley described it as 'perhaps the best novel yet in its field', the critic from the *Daily Express* declared: 'George Johnston can write like Joseph Conrad. How fresh and vital it is!'[18]

However, if success was the carrot causing George Johnston to write in earnest, fear was the stick. He wrote this first David Meredith novel in the belief that this might be his last chance to secure his reputation as a novelist. At the same time, he regarded the book as something that the family could live on for a while if he should die — as he feared he would — in the near future. Although this summer the financial situation was 'all right for the time being',[19] Johnston was desperately trying to build up a bit of insurance. The reason for this fear was evident every time he looked in the mirror.

After scraping through the winter, in March George had suffered a bout of what he self-diagnosed as 'Asiatic flu'.[20] The combination of illness and the nervous energy that he was pouring into his work seemed to be sweating more and more weight off him, and by this summer of 1959 he was — by his own description, and that of others — looking like 'a Belsen victim'.[21] He was privately convinced he had cancer,[22] but was not admitting in public that there was anything wrong with his health. This was partly because he was operating under that form of superstition that holds that disease will go away if it is ignored. At the same time, he didn't want to stop work until his novel was finished: he felt he couldn't interrupt the flow for trips to Athens to see doctors and have tests, let alone to go into hospital for an operation. While anyone would have been frightened and worried under these circumstances, George had his own particular phobias about illness and death and hospitals, which went all the way back to his childhood experience of living in a home that seemed to function as a hospital outpatients department.

Throughout this time, Charmian was deeply worried about George's health, and repeatedly begged him to go to Athens to see a doctor.[23] But George refused even to admit to his wife that anything was wrong with him, and was very prickly if she raised the subject. This unmentionable anxiety deepened the distance that had developed between the couple over the previous year. As always during summer, George was prone to be tense and nervy and subject to sudden fits of temper. All this, of course, was exacerbated by the increased drinking and carousing, the late nights and hangovers, that went with the high season.

It is clear from Johnston's own accounts to friends that by this time he had withdrawn from virtually any sexual relationship with his wife. He attributed this to his illness, which made him less able as well as less inclined. His biographer notes that he told Grace Edwards that he was 'A one time a year man'.[24] It also seems that by now the author had developed a superstitious idea that sexual performance diminished writing potency; or perhaps this was an attempt to look on the bright side of the matter. In imagining how this physical problem affected George, we again have to remember his childhood. Certainly, most men in their mid-forties would feel their masculine identity to be threatened by the prospect of impotence. But this was particularly demoralising for someone who had grown up with the dominant males of his family making him feel that he had failed to make the grade in the masculinity stakes. And now all the effort that George had made to become a man seemed to be to no avail. Of course, this whole equation between sexual potency and masculinity and, further, between sexual performance and a successful marriage, was a furphy. But in terms of the social attitudes and mores that had shaped George Johnston, the man had to be able to perform.

Yet another effect of the illness he was suffering would have been drenching night sweats[25] — which George no doubt attributed to flu or fever. It would seem that at this time, he often took to sleeping apart from his wife. No doubt this was to prevent her sleep being interrupted, or to avoid giving her this 'flu'.[26] However, the natural result of all this was to undermine companionship, especially as he refused to discuss any of this with Charmian.

As if all this weren't complicated enough, the self-examination that George Johnston was undertaking created its own form of distancing, as the author increasingly became absorbed in his private considerations. In *Closer to the Sun*, he considers this situation from the point of view of David Meredith's wife, giving her Meredith's brother Mark as sounding board:

> David, having asserted his right to a personal destiny, was no longer predictable. How could they, his brother and his wife, hope to understand him when he was grappling and groping to try and understand himself? He had been her husband for eleven years. She had lived with him and loved him and shared or endured all his changing forms of thought and belief and conviction. Yet now, more than ever, he was subject to a range of subtleties far beyond even her grasp.[27]

This long passage of introspection concludes with Kate's reflection that 'He had become lately much removed from her, lost to his own perturbing self examination'. A hundred or so pages further on, Kate and Mark again consider the difficulty of understanding David in his recent state of withdrawal. This time Kate directly expresses her feelings about the situation:

> 'I don't expect you can go through eleven years of marriage without getting a few scars, a few bruises ... on both sides, I mean. There are gaps left, little hollows, concealed wounds [...] certain little curtains of secrecy behind which we hide ourselves from each other [...] moments when we should talk to each other, and we don't ... we skirt around it very carefully and come back to smile at each other, and the gap is left there behind us and we never have to look at it again. Lately it's been happening often. He's so preoccupied ... worried, I think. He doesn't talk about it. We just move around the gaps. We're always very polite about it. We're so careful to consider each other's feelings that the feeling itself gets rubbed away to nothing.'[28]

It is curious that when the author took on Kate Meredith's point of view, he was able quite clearly to see what was happening, but when he was being either David Meredith or himself, he went on being blind to the effects of his self-examination.

Naturally, when his relationship with Charmian diminished, George began thinking, as David Meredith does in this novel, of the temptations open to 'women left to their own devices'.²⁹ Johnston's suspicion increased, and he began to accuse his wife of infidelity, and even to repeat these allegations to the rest of the *xeni*. According to Johnston's biographer, 'if he had drunk too much, [he] would at times let his bitterness and jealousy to come to the surface, and gabble publicly about his wife's "wampum belt" of male scalps'.³⁰

The result was predictable. This summer a liaison began between Charmian and a visiting American named Chadwick, who would later provide part of the model for Cressida's lover Galloway in *Clean Straw for Nothing*. Like Jean-Claude Maurice, Chadwick was by way of being an artist: essentially having a long holiday on the island, but producing an occasional sketch in order to give a sense of purpose to the venture. Charmian's predilection for artists reflects her early wish to be an artist herself: just as her fictional character Julia wanted to *be* the object of her desires, Charmian was able vicariously to be a painter through Maurice and Chadwick.

In Chadwick, too, as in Maurice, Charmian Clift chose someone as different as possible from her husband. Indeed, she would never turn her eye to anyone who could really be competition for George. Similarly, she never saw any relationship as impinging upon what she had with George: her commitment to the unit of family and the habit of married life was total. But she did believe in separate spheres. Naturally, George didn't see the situation in the same way at all.

October always brought some relief from summer frenzy. This year, as the water cisterns began to fill, as the tourists began to leave, George Johnston finished the novel on which he had worked so hard. By now he was having difficulty breathing, and his weight had dropped to 8 stone 10 pounds, from a top weight of 11 stone 12. He admitted that he didn't have 'the bodily resistance left to fight back even a common cold'. At last, he gave in to Charmian's pleas and allowed himself to be 'leg-roped' off to Athens.³¹ It was early in October when he saw Dr George Anastosopoulos in his surgery and was X-rayed at a clinic. After a nervous week back on Hydra, he returned for the verdict on his health.

At this point, the natural focus of the story shifts away from Charmian Clift to George Johnston, for it was he who experienced the drama of travelling to Athens in order to be given — it seemed most likely — a death sentence.

There is almost too much information about what George was thinking and feeling on this day, for he would write about it in three separate fictional accounts.

But what of Charmian, stuck back on Hydra? Wasn't she also awaiting a verdict? Didn't her fate and future hang in the balance? Despite her fight to retain her own privacy and separateness, the sense of loyalty that Charmian Clift felt towards her husband was such that any wound to him was a wound to her. This union of the couple was so strong that it was irrelevant whether Charmian was loving — or even liking — George very much in this period. He was simply part of her, and part of the combination of marriage, home, family, that her security was vested in.

On a sheerly practical level, too, the possibility of George's death — or even a severe illness requiring operations and lengthy convalescence — was for Charmian deeply worrying. How would the family survive? Her own earnings were not enough to keep them all, and indeed the family could not manage if George were even to have a six-month respite from work. More immediately, if hospitalisation were required, how would they pay the bills? And was the Greek hospital system good enough? Overall, the problem threatened to cause the very thing which Charmian feared most — the necessity to sell this house that was her home and leave this world of her own where she felt she belonged for the very first time.

On top of all this, if George weren't around, the entire responsibility for the family would rest upon her. As well as the usual difficulties that any parents face, a particular problem for these parents was that of communication.

Jason — now three and a half — was still under Zoe's care; for him, the notion of 'family' at this stage was 'simply Zoe', for the age gap between the young child and his siblings seemed 'gigantic'. As well as taking part in Zoe's network of communal visiting, Jason was already making his own independent visits. He remembers 'a lot of time running around in a somewhat feline way':

> I loved all the mothers and their kitchens. I would go from one
> house to another, being given many meals a day, and I would
> hang around the kitchens, with the women. And I remember that
> while I was alone, I never felt lonely, but all my memories are
> either of me doing these things alone, or with adults — with
> Greek adults [...]

I think what probably happened was that in the early years I just stuck with Zoe, and followed her around. But the island being small and self-enclosed — a safe space — almost my earliest memories are of running around alone, being sure to come back by the time Zoe was to take me home.[32]

Obviously, Jason felt loved and cared for by his dozens of mothers, but the increasing problem for his birth mother was that she did not share her youngest child's mother tongue. Charmian's own Greek had not progressed beyond its first-year-immigrant level. It was fine for shopping and for exchanging pleasantries with the locals, but that was about its limit. The fact that she and Jason thought and spoke in a different language made communication very difficult.

The older children also communicated with each other in Greek. This made it very hard for their parents to adjudicate their frequent battles. With Martin turning twelve and Shane aged ten, the two elder siblings had a stormy relationship, and it wouldn't be long before the generational battles of adolescence would start.

This was all part of the complex business of raising a family away from one's homeland and home language. If anything should happen to George, it would be Charmian's responsibility alone.

After the week of apprehension about the X-rays, George Johnston returned to Athens and arrived at his morning appointment, only to be told to go away and come back again that evening for the results. The patient naturally assumed that his doctor was postponing the moment of truth. He spent the day walking the streets of the old quarter of Athens, sure that the diagnosis would be terminal cancer.

However, when George went back to the surgery that evening, he was told that he merely suffered from tuberculosis. Although the disease was in both lungs, the doctor maintained that it had been caught early enough and was completely curable. The patient could go home to Hydra the next day, but he would have to return to Athens very soon to begin a course of treatment.

A week later, on 26 October, Johnston wrote to Monica Preston, the accountant at the Higham agency, telling her that he had TB, 'but fortunately reasonably early and quite curable'. He was leaving that day for Athens 'to begin the cure tomorrow'. He added: 'I'll be up there for three weeks and then I'll be able to come back here to the island to continue the inoculations. All will be well, but it does involve us in an immediate crisis'.

The point of the letter was to ask the accountant to 'put the tax deductions aside until later in the New Year', and pay into the London bank account all the money available to date. (Once again, the negotiations with the Greek tax officials had ground to a halt.) The situation was desperate: 'At the present moment we have nothing', Johnston declared, and he begged Monica to bank the money owing 'with the utmost speed, because this is a crisis which cannot be avoided, and at the moment we are very broke indeed!' Johnston also noted that he had 'written privately to Billy Collins asking him for a loan of £200 or preferably £250', and ended by sending 'love from us all'.[33]

On 27 October, George began the cure. He was required to visit Dr Anastosopoulos's surgery once a day for an injection of streptomycin; apart from that, he had to have rest and quiet and regular meals, and was meant to stop drinking and smoking. He stayed with Grace Edwards in her apartment in the Athens suburb of Metz, overlooking the leafy green of the cemetery.

For Grace, this was a very pleasant time. Unlike most of the resident foreigners, she led a celibate life, and she enjoyed having a man in the house for a change. With a regular income from her American inheritance, Grace was financially well off compared with the Johnstons, and she liked to buy imported delicacies to tempt George's appetite; it suited her fine that George was on a regimen that limited his drinking. Even though he didn't stop smoking, he did manage to cut down a bit.

If George was to continue such a regime back home on the island, he would need to control his emotions better than he had over the last few years. He told Grace that when he returned, he 'was never going to play the role of jealous husband again'. He wasn't 'going to let her bug him'.[34]

Although the doctor had ordered rest, he was agreeable to the idea of his patient working for a couple of hours a day. While staying at Metz, the author wrote the first version of a short story titled 'The Verdict'. He also completed the Shane Martin potboiler *The Far Face of the Moon*, a tale of jealousy and betrayal featuring a green-eyed nymphomaniac and an impotent hero who has killed his wife because he was unable to tolerate her serial infidelity. The author would post this to his agents in Britain and America in early December.[35]

During George's convalescence, Charmian came to Athens to visit her husband at Grace's place. Chadwick accompanied her to the city, but he did not come to the flat in Metz. Whether or not Charmian actually spoke about her liaison to George, the Athens foreign colony loved gossip, and news of the American's presence would soon have come to George's ears. Certainly, his jealousy was freshly aroused at this time. In fact, if George was worrying about Chadwick, Charmian was probably jealous of George's friendship with Grace,[36] and even Grace would concede that Charmian's habit of flaunting her infidelity revealed her need for reassurance. In this particular situation, Charmian may even have feared losing George. After all, he had been rejecting her for a year or more, and now he was cosily domiciled at another woman's place. At the very least, this would threaten Charmian's territoriality. Grace would later make no secret of the fact that she had wanted George to remain living with her, although she would always stress that she saw this as a platonic arrangement.[37] Did Charmian feel that this sort of idea was being considered?

In Grace's view, there was nothing sexual in her relationship with George, and so there was nothing for Charmian to concern herself about. For Charmian, however, sex was not what she shared with George: her relationship with her husband was based on talking — especially the talking about writing that went on after the morning's work session. If Charmian felt that Grace was taking over her own position, this wasn't far from the truth. George and Grace would sit on the balcony together at midday and have a drink and some *metzethes* while George discussed with his hostess what he had written that morning. The discussion would continue at the end of the day. During this time at Metz, George talked a lot to Grace about his distant past, as well as about his present unhappiness with life on Hydra and with his marriage. The two friends also shared a passion for archaeology and ancient history, although George's interest was at a more popular level.[38] In the way the relationship was developing, Grace was taking over Charmian's role as George's sounding board and intellectual companion. While George sometimes said that Charmian had educated him about literature and art and culture, it may have seemed that this very intelligent woman with her high level of academic achievement might be able to do the job better than Charmian could.

At the same time, Grace's position as someone who came from an upper-class family and who had inherited 'old money' would have caused Charmian's childhood sense of inferiority to come into play. Apart from this, Charmian knew that Grace didn't much like her, or approve of her.[39] Grace was very much George's friend, and Charmian still saw her associates as being divided into the vast majority of people who were in George's camp, and the few whom she could trust to take her side. One of the reasons why she turned to people like Maurice and Chadwick was that they could at least be relied upon to support *her*, and not George. During her years in Greece, Charmian had no woman friend to provide the Toni/Jo role. Her most intimate associates on Hydra were drawn from the foreign colony's small circle of homosexual men.

Altogether, while Charmian's fling with Chadwick appeared to be thoughtless or even callous, from Charmian's point of view it seemed that George also was having a relationship with an outside person. At the same time, her liaison did not mean that she was not desperately concerned about George, or that she was not committed to his care. When he was ready to come home, she again went to Athens, where the doctor showed her how to use a hypodermic syringe so that she would be able to treat her husband. She practised on a potato until she felt she was skilful enough; she was to become so good that many Hydriots would come to her for their injections.[40]

As to the timing of George's return to the island, there is no exact date available, but it clearly occurred only a few days before 8 December, when he wrote to David Higham a cheery letter beginning: 'Back from Athens and well on the way to a full recovery, I hope, and I am now able to continue what remains of my treatment at home'.[41] It was six weeks since he had set off to Athens for what was intended to be a three-week cure.

It is time to consider the fictional tellings of this part of the story. Obviously, it is not a question of testing the 'truth' of these narratives: fiction is always true, according to its own laws. However, the fictional portrayal of the role of the Charmian character in George Johnston's published tale of this illness would contribute a vital part of the myth that surrounded the real Charmian. By the time the tale had been told again and again, it would be incorporated into the biographical record.

The first fictional version was a short story titled 'The Verdict', which George Johnston wrote at Grace Edwards' place in November 1959.[42] Like *Closer to the Sun*, this was a third-person account concerning the author's alter ego, David Meredith. The story opens as Meredith leaves the surgery of Dr Georgaikis, having been told to return that evening to hear the results of his X-rays and receive his verdict. Despite his certainty that the diagnosis will be terminal cancer, Meredith has 'no feeling of alarm at all'.

Indeed, the sensation was one of elation and relief, of having come to the final resolution of a long and difficult problem. He felt exhilarated, touched with an almost jubilant excitement. He felt himself at last to be a man cleansed of misgivings.

In this state of calm, Meredith sits reflecting at a cafe in Constitution Square. He is happy to consider that he is not obliged to write any more novels.

He no longer found it necessary to prove anything — either to himself or to anyone else.

This of course was the basic reason for the extraordinary, weightless feeling of release. Release, yes, rather than relief.

As his thoughts turn to his wife, he gratefully observes that Kate is 'both capable and attractive, and she would be all right'. Now, over two pages, there is a moving account of Meredith's love for his wife, whose fidelity is not in question. Although he reflects that 'the prospect of losing her had occasionally [...] racked him with nightmares of anguish, jealousy and remorse', he acknowledges that 'as far as he knew' there had never been 'the slightest warrant' for these worries.

Meredith moves on from here to consider the 'mutual' effects of his illness. 'Over the last two years', he admits, 'there had been forces at work [...] forming subtle changes in their relationship' — even though 'nothing of it had been discussed'. Among the ill effects he counts the fact that 'future plans were never considered in any very long-term perspective'. Another unfortunate result was 'his own restless, driving obsession for work'. This in turn had led to his 'nervous and physical exhaustion', and even his excessive drinking. 'More important still', Meredith observes, the illness 'ambiguously excused him from those sexual responsibilities which a husband normally owes to his wife'. Indeed, they had even 'agreed that "sex and creative writing seldom mix"'. The truth of it was, of course, that he, in his weakening physical condition had cringed away from any physical contact with her out of sheer fear of inadequacy and humiliation, loving her desperately yet afraid to touch her'.

At this point in his reflections, Meredith sets off walking through the old Plaka section of Athens. After some hours he stops at another cafe. Suddenly he feels fear. At the same moment there arrives a casual acquaintance, an air hostess named Nitza. She is unwilling to stay and have a drink with him: she can't be late for work because there was a plane crash the previous day, killing all the passengers. As she hurries off, a terrible feeling of aloneness hits him.

The story ends, leaving both David Meredith and the reader waiting for the verdict. By now, the hero's sense of calm and release has completely evaporated. Not only does he fear death, but he desperately wishes to cling to life, in the figure of the youthful and ebullient Nitza.

The extant version of this text is clearly a revised and completed story. Four years later, however, the author returned to this story of 'The Verdict'.[43] This was after he had completed the autobiographical novel *My Brother Jack,* and while he was tinkering about with ideas for the sequel, *Clean Straw for Nothing.* By now, the wife of David Meredith had undergone a name change — from 'Kate' to 'Cressida' — so over this early typescript the author substituted in handwriting the name 'Cressida' for that of 'Kate'. Apart from that, the editorial changes to this first body of text were minimal. However, five additional pages of typescript were added directly after the original ending. These would significantly change the import of the story.

In this second telling, after the air hostess Nitza leaves, the author has Meredith retrace his steps back to the surgery, where Dr Georgaikis tells the patient that he suffers from a 'tubercular condition' but that it will be cured in 'a matter of weeks'. Despite this good news, Meredith walks bleakly out into the Athens night: 'He knew that nothing had been resolved and he had to begin all over again. He felt so miserable he could have cried. He put his head down in his hands and wished that he was dead'.

In this account, as in the earlier version, Meredith's relationship with his wife is happy. Therefore the reader can only assume that the source of the hero's misery is the whole wearying business of life, and in particular the grind of trying to survive as a writer.

No such conclusion can be drawn from the third version of the narrative. Here both the source of Meredith's concluding death-wish and of the illness itself are made crystal clear: it is all the fault of his wife Cressida. This third version, which is placed as an early section of the novel *Clean Straw for Nothing,* was written in Sydney around 1968. This was the only version of the story to be published in the author's lifetime.

The incident again begins as David Meredith steps out of the doctor's surgery, with ten hours to fill before he receives the verdict on his condition. The first hint of a changed attitude comes when Meredith thinks of his wife, at home on the island. In both short story narratives, this is a comforting idea, but in *Clean Straw for Nothing* it leads to Meredith wondering 'if *he* would be there, with her in the kitchen'. Nameless though 'he' is at this stage — for this is the first section of the book to be set in Greece in 1959 — the reader is told: 'It was quite a definite feeling [Meredith] had about Cressida, more than just a vague suspicion'.[44]

Moving on to the cafe at Syntagma (Constitution Square), Meredith sits down and reflects. Significantly, this new piece of text appears:

> It all went back, of course, to the affair with Jacques — had there been an affair? he had never really known, although Jacques had been emphatic enough — and all the anxiety and the drinking that winter, and then the pneumonia, and the dreadful precariousness of their position in Greece, and his fear of having to be forced back again into society.

After the two separate references to Cressida's infidelity — in the past with Jacques and in the present with the as yet unnamed lover — the author has to cut the long passage about Meredith's love for his wife, and about the strains and distancing (including Meredith's impotence) that the illness has placed upon the couple's relationship. The *Clean Straw for Nothing* narrative moves straight into the walk around Plaka, and the meeting with Nitza. The last part of the second version of the short story is lifted directly into the novel text, complete with Dr Georgaikis's cheerful diagnosis, Meredith's return into the night, and his wish 'that he was dead'.

In literary terms, the second and third versions of this narrative benefit from the irony that a reprieved man realises that what he wants is death. In biographical terms, however, it is important that only the first version be considered in regard to the state of mind of George Johnston in late 1959, when the events of the story were happening.

The major part of the rewriting concerns, of course, the change to the role of Meredith's wife. Even though George Johnston knew of Charmian's infidelity at the time he wrote the first version of the story, he did not choose to include it in the fictional record. By the time of the novel, the Charmian character is shown as unfaithful at the very time that her husband is under his death sentence in Athens. More significantly, she is presented as being the *cause* of his illness, through her past infidelity with Jacques (despite the fact that Meredith isn't sure that an affair had happened). Later in the novel, David Meredith again traces his illness back to his suspicions of Cressida and the French existentialist in the Merediths' 'second year' on the island. The biographical connection is with Johnston's unfounded suspicions of Charmian and Jean-Claude in 1956.[45]

It is this passage that suggests that from Johnston's first encounter with Jean-Claude Maurice, his jealousy was aroused. In *Clean Straw for Nothing*, Meredith reflects that, although he had suspected an affair, he had held his tongue and 'worked all the harder and tried to smother suspicion and joined the interminable round of drinkings and dancings and parties'. The narrator also remembers how, when Jacques left in the autumn, he assured Meredith that he and Cressida had never been lovers (again following the facts of the matter in regard to 1956). Indeed, even Meredith in the novel's present time seems inclined to believe that Jacques had been speaking the truth — and yet the narrator still has it both ways.

> Soon after [Jacques] left the island the combination of worry and overwork and the hysterical saturnalia of the foreign colony, and the whole messy muddle of my neuroses, took its toll. I became ill at a Christmas party, developed double pneumonia, and didn't leave the house for six months. This led to the tuberculosis a few years later.[46]

Of course, in the New Year of 1957 George Johnston did indeed come down with a bad bout of pneumonia. However, to present this as *leading* to tuberculosis is part of the fiction. In fact, even the illness of the winter of 1956–57 was not necessarily linked to the particular worries of that time: George Johnston's medical history of pneumonia and respiratory trouble went back to the London years at least. More importantly, tuberculosis is an infection of the tubercle bacillus, which causes tiny tubers to grow in the lungs; it is not a development of other lung problems. At the time of diagnosis, George used to make a joke of mimicking Dr Anastosopoulos's heavily accented 'H's as he quoted the doctor saying: 'You have a little bug called "Hoffman"!'[47] It was thought that George had most likely picked up his 'bug' during his army service, particularly the time he spent in Asia.[48] While the author was obviously aware of these facts, it suited his fictional pattern to link David Meredith's illness with his wife's infidelity — or possible infidelity — with Jacques in 1956.

But in regard to the fictionalising, this was not all. If Cressida in the novel is blamed for causing her husband's illness, she is in addition blamed for stopping his cure. In other sections of this novel concerning Meredith's life in Greece in 1959, Johnston would pick up the notion of Cressida's continuing infidelity while her husband was undergoing treatment. When Dr Georgaikis prescribes the rest cure, Meredith stays with Big Grace (who carries her real name into the fictional account). The patient makes a good recovery until Grace throws a party, to which Cressida and her lover — the American painter Galloway — both come. After his wife leaves Athens, David Meredith's 'detachment and composure' drain away. He begins smoking heavily, and starts drinking again; he eats and sleeps less; and as his drugs don't mix well with alcohol, he stops taking some of his tablets. It is not long before he cuts short his treatment by a month because he is unable to bear the thought of Cressida with Galloway. He admits to Grace that the doctor is not pleased about the matter, but declares that 'Cress can give the needles'. In the face of his friend's remonstrances, David agrees that returning early, before the treatment is finished, 'could be dangerous'. But he '[has] to go'.[49] Thus once again the import of the fictional account is to blame Cressida for her husband's ill-health.

The danger of this, in a novel which in many ways is so nakedly autobiographical — and which includes real and easily identifiable people, such as Big Grace — is that the reader makes the jump of completely identifying Charmian with Cressida, and thus blames Charmian Clift for the failure of this initial attempt to cure George Johnston's tuberculosis. This fictional telling has by now been written into the biographical record, with Garry Kinnane informing readers:

> Johnston's period of rest with Edwards was to have been for at least three months, but he missed the children, and was plagued by thoughts of Clift and Chadwick. After six weeks he could stand it no longer, and decided to return to Hydra.[50]

As we have seen, the original time frame for treatment was three weeks, and it was always intended that after a short period under the doctor's daily observation, Johnston would continue the injections and the treatment at home. In fact, he stayed in Athens for more like six weeks than three; there is no evidence that he was ever meant to stay for three months. That this whole scenario of guilt and responsibility was created at a late stage and for fictional purposes is highlighted by the fact that in 1964, when Johnston wrote a long autobiographical account, he declared that after he became ill in 1959, Charmian had 'cured him'.[51]

* * *

Certainly, it was terribly distressing for George Johnston in Athens to know that his wife was having an affair back on the island. It is little wonder that, when he returned home in early December 1959, there were terrible scenes of accusation. Many years later, Carolyn Gassoumis, one of the Hydra foreign colony, would tell an Australian journalist that 'George's reaction to the affair was not a bit as he described it in the book'.

> I was around when the love affair occurred that George describes in his novel, when he went off to Athens to see about his TB and Charmian had that devastating affair with an American [...]
>
> He was furious. Threatened to leave her, once and for all. George was always doing that.[52]

However, it wasn't long before Chadwick left the island, and things settled down. Charmian had the responsibility of administering George's daily shot of streptomycin, but it was up to George to monitor his own drinking and smoking, to take his tablets, and to make sure that he got enough food and rest. Over this Christmas and New Year period, the regimen went very well. Garry Kinnane notes:

> In the early months of 1960 Charles Sriber came across [George] in the office of Chandris Shipping Lines, arranging to have his books sold on board their ships, which did regular runs to Australia. According to Sriber he was back to his old chirpy self, and said his health was 'clean' and he was 'feeling marvellous'.[53]

Meanwhile, the news of George's illness had spread to Australia, and he received letters of concern from old friends, family, and his first wife Elsie. In February 1960, George wrote to his daughter Gae, now a university student; the mood of this letter is cheerful in regard to health, and ebullient as far as writing plans are concerned:

> My dearest Gae,
>
> This is just a brief little note out of the distance and silence to let you, and of course Elsie, know that I'm still surviving and making slow but fairly sound progress. I'm still having daily needles of streptomycin and I guess I'll be taking all sorts of drugs for many months to come, but at least I can be treated at home now, and I have got a little of my weight back — not all

that much, alas, but at least a start towards that complete recovery which I know now is only a matter of time.[54]

Johnston went on to say how 'very, very touched' he had been by Elsie's letter, and to urge his daughter to write and tell him her future plans. As to his own future, Johnston was decidedly optimistic:

I have an idea your Old Man might turn out to be a real novelist yet! I have a feeling of being on the verge of writing something really worthwhile, but this sickness does make you pretty groggy (not the sickness so much, I think, as the effect of the drugs which are stuffed into you every day), and of course there has been in this last five or six months a shattering loss of time and money. However if we can hold out a little longer I think we'll see brighter times ahead.

Johnston concluded by noting that there was a 'possibility' that he would be going back to London 'for a time in early summer': 'And I am even vaguely thinking of a return to Australia for a time — the isolated life here is beginning to wear in some ways — but it is still too early to be definite, as much depends on health and money'. Although the first-person pronoun is used here, this doesn't mean that George Johnston was thinking of these plans in regard to himself alone; this letter was directed at Elsie as well as Gae, and George always minimised references to Charmian when writing to his first wife.

This letter to Gae also hints at a dilemma that would affect the patient's recovery. The fear of death seemed to have concentrated his creativity. And while he had been assured that his disease was curable, he continued to worry that time might be short. Both these things made George Johnston want to put more hours and effort into his writing. Yet he also believed that his prescribed drugs were seriously undermining his ability to work. Therefore he soon began to cut back on his medicine, or to take it spasmodically. The irregular dosage of the antibiotics would prove particularly harmful in the long term. While the drugs did not succeed in defeating the infection, the patient's body was getting enough of a dose to build up an immunity. Of course, George did not have the medical knowledge to know what he was doing to himself.

Anyway, his whole focus was on his writing. The author was now beginning something of immense importance to him, something that had been at the back of his mind since the war ended and which was taking shape under the title *The Far Road*. This was the story of the journey he had made as a war correspondent through China, when he had seen the hundred thousand corpses of refugees rotting beside the road; in many ways this was the story of the beginning of the author's personal journey. But would he be able to do it justice? As with *Closer to the Sun*, he was again drawing upon autobiographical experience, and again he explored this experience through the alter ego character of David Meredith.

Charmian would later claim 'a personal pride in the book' because she had 'nagged him' into writing it.[55] Part of this nagging, of course, involved making herself available as sounding board and emotional backup as George got this horrific tale down on paper. The months of anxiety had interfered terribly with Charmian Clift's own writing. *Peel Me a Lotus* had been released in Britain by December 1959, and had attracted very good reviews. The novel *Walk to the Paradise Gardens* had an easy passage through the editorial process. It would be published in both Britain and America in 1960, again to excellent reviews. Although this must have been encouraging, there was no real progress on *Honour's Mimic*.

It was now five and a half years since Charmian and George had left England for Greece. It was more than three years since that consolidating period of 1957, when Charmian had really felt that the family were establishing their own sort of life in the new land. Although she would have been too proud to admit it, things were starting to come unstuck. As well as the ongoing economic worries, there was something happening within the relationship between Charmian and George. It would be easy to point to things such as Charmian's summer liaisons or George's illness as being 'problems' that were straining the marriage. Certainly, those things didn't make life easy. But it would seem that what was going on was more complex, and more interesting.

By the summer of 1960, Charmian Clift was finding herself involved in a strange form of adultery. Over the last couple of years her husband had changed so much that she found herself married to a different person. If George had ever been the 'tirra lirra kind of man' that the young Charmian had dreamed about, then he certainly wasn't that man any longer. Looking back from the perspective of 1969 on this change, she attributed its cause to the illness that had begun to afflict her husband a decade earlier:

Some words of Gerard Manley Hopkins come to me here. 'Sickness broke him.' But I'm not sure whether sickness broke him, or, in a cruel sort of way, made him. He raged against it for years, despaired, became bitter and hating and not easy to live with [...] I do not like to think much on those years because we almost foundered, but I do like to think on those years because in those years he began to write in a different way. To me, a truer way. Perhaps he thought he had nothing to lose any more. Perhaps he thought if people didn't like what he was and what he thought and what he felt they could bloody well lump him. The necessity to charm, to please, to entertain, to be approved [...] dropped out of his make-up like so much unwanted baggage, and as he fined down alarmingly in weight [...] he also fined down in character, persona, or whatever you call it. And of course this in a way was alarming too — for a wife, that is, who found she was married to someone else entirely.[56]

The illness, and the drugs taken to combat the illness, were responsible for an enormous change in George's manner, in his aspirations, and in his whole way of writing. Contrasting this new husband with the brash war correspondent whom she had met 'in his leaping time', Clift noted that in those days he would tell you all about an exotic experience, 'but he couldn't or wouldn't tell you how it felt'. She added:

Perhaps he was afraid of how things felt. Certainly he shied away from any written expression of his own emotional reactions to things and settled instead for what he thought his reactions should have been if he had been in the skin of an elderly professor of archaeology or however he was disguising himself for that particular novel.

But from the time George became aware of his illness, he would set aside the outlandish disguises. From now, the only mask would be that of the alter ego, David Meredith. Of course, this too was a disguise. But it would become increasingly difficult to distinguish it from the writer behind it. At the same time, George Johnston would become so involved with exploring 'how things felt' that he seemed to be making up for lost time. Meanwhile, he would retreat more and more into his work. George himself would express the situation this way:

> For three years a writer may have a deep commitment to a
> private world of his own. It is pretty hard to jell the fundamental
> things of marriage, like companionship, sharing drudgery, and
> bringing up kids. If two people are involved in the same sort of
> problem over any length of time, it could mean that they are
> living in intellectual cells, in which there is not much room for
> the realities of life.[57]

While the 'realities of life' came second to the fictional process, it was
George who spent more time in the 'intellectual cell'. As well as carrying
most of the domestic responsibility, the main pressure on Charmian now
was George's mortality. From 1959, Charmian would live with the
unspoken fear that perhaps her husband only had a few years left; from this
time, she would start to put her own work on the backburner so that
George could get his done. Yet the issue of the division of labour in this
partnership wasn't just to do with time. It was as if there were a certain
finite well of creativity available in the household, and if one partner used it
up, there was nothing left for the other to draw upon.

If Clift found herself married to a different person, the fundamental
cause was not the depth of Johnston's commitment to his 'private world',
but what he was doing — and becoming — in this fictional world. Since the
onset of his illness, the writer's main work had started to become an
extraordinary exercise in lay psychoanalysis, through the exploration and
development of the fictional character of David Meredith. This exercise
allowed George Johnston to feel release, in the way that many patients feel
better after telling their problems to a trained therapist. At the same time,
the very act of writing down his troubles provided an escape. He could for a
few hours forget his fear of dying by entering an alternative world, one in
which he had control of the character's destiny.

As the author explored his own life through the story of his alter ego, a
two-way process began. Through the relentless analysis and rewriting of his
alter ego David Meredith, George Johnston was making himself afresh. And
as this alter ego had a wife — based on Johnston's own wife — changes
were also being wrought on the role that Charmian Clift was expected to
play. At the same time, a shift would happen in the balance between fact and
fiction, and between private and public spaces. With the writing of *Closer to
the Sun* in 1959, George Johnston began to use autobiographical parts of
himself and his experience in David Meredith; very soon, however, instead

of the character following the model, the reverse would start to happen, and Johnston would start to transform himself into his character. Simultaneously, of course, he began to transform Charmian into Meredith's wife; it is not surprising that she, too, would sometimes seem to act like her fictional counterpart.

Meanwhile, work went on hold again as the high season got into full swing. In this summer of 1960, visitors to Hydra included a poor young Canadian poet and folk guitarist named Leonard Cohen, who gave his first formal concert at Katsikas's grocery store. Concerned about his poverty, the Johnstons had him to stay for some time in the spare room; later, when he managed to find a cheap house to rent, Charmian and George gave him a large work table, a bed, and pots and pans for his new home.[58]

At the same time, the Johnstons' own poverty was shocking a wealthy upper-class English couple called Didy and Peter Cameron, who introduced themselves to the Johnstons on the recommendation of Elizabeth Jane Howard. Didy Cameron was also 'shocked' by 'George's frail condition'.[59] She felt that George should get a second opinion on his illness from specialists in England, and she urged that the children should have more educational opportunities than those available on Hydra. The fact that George had already been thinking in terms of a visit to London made him receptive to such suggestions.

By the end of this summer of 1960, the two couples had agreed on a house swap: George and Charmian would have Peter and Didy's country farmhouse, and in return the Camerons could use the Hydra house as a holiday place, when they weren't living in their London residence. In the past Charmian would have resisted any move from Hydra, but the situation had become so desperate that even she was willing to give it a try. Clearly something had to be done, if the relationship was to be salvaged.

17

PLAYING THE ROLE
ASSIGNED

In this weird dream-world everyone slips into a Role ...
Queerest, and most terrifying of all, one finds oneself unprotestingly
playing the role assigned.[1]

By the end of October 1960, the Johnstons had moved to a Tudor house
on Charity Farm, near the small village of Stanton on the border of
Gloucestershire and Worcestershire. Charmian would later describe this
whole venture as 'insane'.[2]

Certainly for the children it was a very different way of life, especially for
Jason, now aged four and a half. His mother would later remember that 'He
spoke only Greek, and he had never been off the island of Hydra in his whole
four years [...] Of course, he panicked, grew thin and nervous, unconfident,
clinging, whiny'.[3] No doubt at first there was some culture shock. Yet Jason
himself remembers adapting quickly and painlessly to the new way of life:

> I'm afraid I do not remember pining for Zoe. It was just: 'Well,
> that's over, and now we've got a new thing.' And so I became
> closer to Mum, because she was just the only figure there ...
>
> Ironically perhaps the biggest difference for me was that the
> life in England was such a smaller world. There was no longer a
> whole island to run around in, there was just this one little
> farmhouse, where I was in the house with Charmian all day, and
> Martin and Shane were off at school, and George was sometimes
> there but often not — I have no idea what he was doing.

The technological difference been Hydra and England particularly struck Jason when his mother took him to the market town of Stanton, where there was a place with milk vending machines.

> It was just incredibly exciting because I could get chocolate milk at any machine and I was allowed to do the coin and work it myself, and that was just miraculous! And the other thing that was miraculous was the twin-tub washing machine. And the third thing — which never struck me as miraculous, I suppose because there are no moving parts or anything that a boy can fiddle with or take apart — was the television. And basically I think I learned English from Bill and Ben the Flowerpot Men.[4]

Meanwhile, Martin was not finding school in England to be the stimulating experience that well-meaning English people had insisted was necessary for him. In fact, after the summer holidays of 1960 Martin had happily started at the Hydra high school, which was run by a liberal and well-educated female principal who fostered drama and the arts.[5] As far as Martin's English education was concerned, there were enough books and writers coming into the house to satisfy his interests. Alas, one thing the Greek education system didn't offer was the 11-plus examination, which all British children had to sit in order to be slotted into the 'right' secondary school. Lacking the marks which would have gained him a place at an academically oriented grammar school, Martin was required to attend Winchcombe Secondary Modern — an experience which he would always describe as 'sheer unadulterated hell'.[6]

For Shane, now eleven, it was perhaps even harder to adapt to school in England, because Greek was so much her preferred language that she wasn't accustomed to reading and writing and spelling in English. Separated from her large network of island friends, she was lonely and isolated.

Charmian also was very unhappy. Although the Cotswolds countryside was picturesque, her taste by now was for the bare bones and radiant light of Greece. She missed the sea, and the winter cold seemed everlasting and unendurable. Given George's history of pneumonia, and his proneness to colds and respiratory illness, the dripping climate was dangerous as well as unpleasant.

Nor did the visit do anything to counteract the isolation Charmian Clift had been living in for six years. The nearby village may have been 'so old, so mellow, so authentically Jacobean as to be breathtaking',[7] but it offered less in the way of culture or company than did Hydra, for at least on the island there were other artists and intellectuals to talk to. While George was able to get up to London on the train, Charmian had to stay home and look after the children.

For the first time in six years, Charmian Clift was a full-time housewife and mother. In an essay describing how she felt during this period in England, the author uses the word 'marooned'. There were a few outings to the homes of various friends of the Camerons, but the two Australians had little in common with men wearing tweeds and driving Bentleys or ladies who rose at the end of dinner 'with that twitch of the trailing skirt that summoned all females at the table to retire and leave the gentlemen to their port'.[8]

If everything from the education system to the class system made life at Charity Farm unhappy, the misery was compounded by the same problem as always. Clift later commented that the exchange of houses failed because 'the essential ingredient (that is to say money) was missing, we having counted on a batch of royalties which proved to be non-existent'.[9] These non-existent royalties included those which Charmian Clift had expected from *Peel Me a Lotus* and *Walk to the Paradise Gardens*. As it turned out, sales were poor for both books. Also, Johnston had expected to receive an advance on *The Far Face of the Moon*, but his British publishers rejected the novel at this time.[10] Meanwhile, the British edition of *Closer to the Sun* was released this year, but proved to be (in the author's words) 'such a flop'.[11] The American edition was not due out until mid 1961.

And so George went cap in hand to Fleet Street, to ask his old colleagues for work. He later told Colin Simpson:

> I thought I could easily get back into the newspaper world. After all, I'd run a news service in London, I had a lot of mates in Fleet Street — or I thought I had. It was, 'Wonderful to see you again, George!' and then, 'Haven't been too well, I hear. What are you now — forty-nine? Let me have a word with the Editor. Phone you Monday.' You know, 'Don't call us, we'll call you.' It was a young man's world.[12]

While this rejection hurt George's pride, Charmian also felt it terribly. Through the final months of 1960 she turned all her energies to encouraging and supporting her husband in the writing of his China novel, *The Far Road*. The subject matter was so grim that this wasn't an easy task, but it would prove to be the vital exploration and catharsis that George Johnston would need to do at this stage of his writing career. 'I loved that novel', Charmian would later declare. 'I stood up and cheered for it'.[13] In gratitude for her support, the book's dedication reads: 'For Charmian, In Earnest'.

Johnston finished *The Far Road* not long before Christmas, and sent it directly to Collins. This brought an advance of £300, which the author managed to extract from the publishers immediately, even though contracts hadn't yet been signed.[14] Johnston had already begun a new Shane Martin detective story, under the title *A Wake for Mourning*.

Although Charmian Clift was acting as sounding board for her husband's writing, as far as her own work went, nothing was happening. This was like the last time in England, when her writing was blocked. Again, the difficulty seems to have been tied up with the writer's sense of the loss of her own identity. She would touch on this in an essay, remarking that 'a very curious thing happens' if you live in a house that belongs to other people:

> We found, by living in their house, that we began living their lives [...] It all ended badly, as these things are bound to do [...] Because of course you can't turn into somebody else by living in somebody else's house and using somebody else's personal things and following somebody else's life pattern. It is all make-believe.[15]

It may seem strange for Charmian Clift to complain about living a life of 'make-believe'. Wasn't this what she had been doing since she was a child? And didn't she also in her 'real' life exchange roles from stage to stage, from costume to costume? Certainly. But Didy Cameron's role wasn't fictional; and besides, it didn't suit Charmian. She was not landed gentry: she was a quarry worker's daughter from the wrong side of town, and her only really happy times at Charity Farm were spent with the farm hands. When the lambing season began, she would sometimes go out into the achingly cold dawns and help with the birthing; walking home she would feel 'exultant and good and fulfilled'.[16] Or as she roamed around the house in 'the prowling hours', she would hear 'the low buzz and burr of voices' of Jack and Harry, returning from the fields:

> And sometimes they would come in and let me look after the damp new lamb in front of the fire, and I would give them mugs

of tea and cider, and we would sit and talk, as I knew we would, of lambing seasons past, and country lore, and tales of love and revenge and supernatural happenings.[17]

By the New Year of 1961, prospects looked very bleak. Over the next four months, Charmian and George would go around in circles, making plans and breaking plans about where to live, what to do, how to survive. The £300 advance on *The Far Road* disappeared as soon as it arrived. Although there was no rent to pay on the farmhouse, the Johnstons had assumed responsibility for the Camerons' household expenses, including the wages of various 'retainers', and the cost of living was exorbitant after Greece.[18] School uniforms and books had to be bought for the two older children; all the family needed new footwear and warm clothing. And then there was Christmas — and George and Charmian would always spend lavishly on presents for the children.

By early February, when he submitted the typescript of *A Wake for Mourning* to Collins, Johnston also 'sent out an SOS' for another £300 'on general account'. On Higham's recommendation, this money was given as a loan.[19] It appears that one of the reasons George wanted this extra cash so urgently was to pay Charmian's fare back to Greece.[20] When David Higham wrote to the author this February, he noted that the Collins editor had 'mentioned that Charmian was going back to Hydra to sell the house'.[21]

This plan — to sell the Hydra house and settle permanently in England — seems crazy. After all, the children were hating school, Charmian was miserable and unable to write, George couldn't get journalistic work and was suffering from the climate. Perhaps the couple were so demoralised that they didn't know what they were doing. The fact that they did not contemplate a return to Australia shows that they still hadn't forgotten how stultifying and censorious their homeland had been.

Although Collins were willing to lend money on account of the new Shane Martin novel, they would only take the book if Johnston agreed to undertake major revisions.[22] Meanwhile, he had also sent this novel directly to Helen King at Morrow. By the third week of March, she had written back to the author, declining it.

At some stage between mid February and the end of March, the Johnstons made a new decision about their future. As usual, an apparently trivial event would push them to do what they — or at least Charmian — had secretly been wanting to do. On this occasion, the trigger was set off when the family went to the cinema in Stanton and saw their friend Melina Mercouri starring in the film *Never on Sunday*. The sight of Greek sun and light made them decide to go back forthwith.[23]

However, this time the couple needed a bit of extra moral support if they were to act on their impetuous idea. Who better to help them chase the sun than Sid Nolan, the man who was always urging his friends to 'bloody well fly'? In an essay about the artist, entitled 'The Rare Art of Inspiring Others', Clift mentions that when they saw Nolan in London during this time the 'encounter was necessarily brief', but 'it was long enough to give us the courage to make a decision that had seemed, until then, too dangerous and difficult to contemplate'.[24] This can only have been the decision to return to Hydra. At some time during this period in England, Nolan also gave some practical help, by sending his old friends an art book with a number of £5 notes interleaved between the pages.[25]

On April Fools' Day, George wrote an answer to Higham's six week old query as to what they were doing: 'Such a time of doubts, decisions, changes of plans, indecisions, etc., that it's only now we have something definite to tell you. We are definitely going back to Greece about April 15th'.[26] Now there was a scramble to borrow the money for the air fares. Perhaps some of the £300 borrowed from Collins in February was used; Johnston also got a loan from an old journalist colleague, Vic Valentine.[27] Although in *Clean Straw for Nothing* this money for fares plus a gift of 'a thousand quid' to set them up again in Greece is given outright by the so-called Peter Finch character, Archie Calverton, this is pure fiction, included in order to develop the role that Calverton plays in the novel as Meredith's confidant and rescuer.[28] In fact it is unlikely that Charmian and George even saw Peter Finch during these months in England.

And so, with borrowed money, they 'ransomed [their] way back to Greece' (as Clift put it). But before they went, of course, they threw a party, to which Charmian invited the Bentley set as well as her farm-hand friends and the Camerons' retainers and locals from the pub: 'And the lady of the Manor danced with the gardener and our daily char with the Squire, and at one point everybody sang, all together, marvellous Cotswolds songs until I was bursting with tears and didn't want to leave ever'.[29] Of course not. No matter how miserable a time she'd had, Charmian was still hopeless at saying goodbye. She had cause to cry again a few days later, when the little steamer approached Hydra and Charmian caught sight of her island, her homeplace:

> As the ship came in towards the wharf I could see a crowd of people. I thought 'Who's on board, I wonder?' and 'Probably some politician', because people were holding up placards. When we got nearer I could read the placards, and I started to blubber. They said 'Welcome home to the Johnstons' and 'You've never been away!'[30]

Now, instead of a farewell party there was one of welcome, and tables were brought out to the front of Katsikas's and there was dancing and singing through the night. One black spot in the happiness was the fact that the couple still had 2000 drachmas on the slate at the grocery shop, and they had returned from England without the money to pay it. But the Hydriots were as delighted as the *xeni* community to have the Johnstons home again. At the party that night, one of the Katsikas brothers took George aside and — despite the outstanding loan — slipped a wad of notes into his hand, saying 'You take this and pay us when you can ... A man like you can't not have money. You take it, you order whatever you want from us ... We know everything will be soon all right. You must take it, because you are our friend'.

Although the immediate financial pressure was eased, there was nothing in the bank, and no prospect of anything coming in. In the two years or so since the beginning of 1959, Charmian Clift had published *Peel Me a Lotus* and *Walk to the Paradise Gardens*. George Johnston had published *The Darkness Outside* and *Closer to the Sun* under his own name, and *The Myth is Murder* under the Shane Martin pseudonym. He had also completed *The Far Road*, *The Far Face of the Moon* and *A Wake for Mourning*. Despite this productivity, the couple were, if anything, worse off financially. It was indeed, as Johnston told Higham, 'a pair of rather worried people' who had returned to Hydra around 16 April 1961.[31]

For the three children, life in England had been so miserable that it was sheer joy to be home where the sun shone. Even twenty years later, Martin's memory of the relief of being back on Hydra would ring out as he delared that 'We settled back very very very happily indeed'.[32] Martin rejoined his high school class 'just in time [...] to do the final exams for first year', while Shane, now twelve, was in her final term at her old primary school. She instantly slotted back into her wide network of friendships and relationships. Jason remembers that:

Shane really was intricately linked into the social structure of the island — with girlfriends and boyfriends and gangs and things going on. It was a social sort of life. An entirely Greek life. That was one of the differences between Martin and Shane. Shane had no interest in the adults and their artistic pretensions and all that. Only in the Greeks.[33]

Meanwhile, Jason himself had returned speaking only English, 'and no Greek whatever'.[34] Of course, as he rejoined his old playmates and began again to speak Greek, he 'lost most of [his] English'. And yet this time, he remembers, he 'never lost it completely'. One of the main changes brought about by the Charity Farm sojourn was that by the time he returned, Jason's view of the family unit had expanded to include 'Zoe plus Mum and Dad, Shane and Martin — and Tripod'. (Tripod was the family's three-legged cat.) Within this grouping, it was Shane whom Jason saw as his ally. After this return to Hydra, Jason would sleep at night in the family home, and would only occasionally stay at Zoe's.[35]

Yet another change for Jason was that he would start primary school when the holidays were over. Shane was also about to undergo a rite of passage: she would start high school at the same time. Despite the fact that she had lost most of her last year at primary school because of the trip to England, she would top the high school entrance exam at the beginning of the new school year — and be rewarded by her proud parents with a record player.[36]

But that was still for the future. As the children settled back into island life, their parents spent the first couple of weeks wondering if they had done the right thing in returning with no prospect of any income. In the confusion of changing plans, the authors had neglected to tell their American agent that they were leaving England. It was to Charity Farm, therefore, that Ivan von Auw sent a cable on 26 April bearing the amazing news that the Literary Guild had chosen *Closer to the Sun* as its October Book Club selection, with a guaranteed payment of $US25 000, to be split equally between author and publisher.[37]

This news did not reach Hydra until 30 April. The next day was May Day — always a time for celebration in Greece. George spent some of the day writing at length to Higham:

> This is absolutely wonderful news, isn't it? I can't tell you how thrilled I am, especially because — as I think you know — we

went through rather a desperate time in England [...] Now, suddenly, there's room to move and time to work.[38]

After some business details regarding ongoing projects, Johnston concluded that it was 'Strange to think that had the news come a fortnight earlier we should probably have stayed on in England. Now, at least, we shall be able to visit regularly'. This comment is strange in itself, for it suggests that the only thing wrong with the visit to England had been lack of money.

With this good news, Charmian could also enjoy her homecoming. After all the lost writing time in England she was keen to re-establish a rhythm of work. In a quick meeting with Higham before leaving, Johnston had promised the agent that 'Charmian will finish [the] novel when back'.[39] It was two years since she had started *Honour's Mimic*, and it was beginning to try her patience. For Charmian Clift to write, she needed to feel free of pressures. Because she had to work so hard at crafting her apparently spontaneous lyrical outflow, she needed more uninterrupted time than George Johnston, who could sit down at the typewriter and — no matter what was going on in the background — let the text spill onto the page.

For the moment, however, in the early summer of 1961, George Johnston had no particular project as a burning priority. He had recently completed a television play,[40] and was tinkering about with revisions to the Shane Martin detective novel *A Wake for Mourning*. Meanwhile, although Ivan von Auw had explained to Johnston that his share of the Literary Guild money was not actually due until January 1962, the author was understandably keen to receive at least some of it. In May 1961, von Auw collected $US2000 from Morrow and paid it into the Johnstons' bank account (after taking out his ten per cent commission plus the money owing for tax). Telling his client that the publishers were 'aware' of his 'precarious financial situation', the agent added: 'Let us hope that it is now relieved for all time'.[41]

This was a slim hope. Most of this money went to paying off debts (which amounted to as much as £1500[42]), including some of the money borrowed for the family's fares back to Greece. In July, Johnston got another $US1800 advanced.[43] This summer of 1961 was a particularly expensive one, as Charmian and George celebrated their return to their home in Greece by embarking on major building renovations. As always, the moment they had money, they spent it.

The cost of living on Hydra was also continually being inflated by the increasing wealth of the visitors. In May, the island suddenly became front page news in America when Jackie Kennedy arrived for a visit. This set the seal on Hydra as one of Greece's most popular holiday destinations. Given the island's new prominence, sales of *Peel Me a Lotus* should have boomed. The problem was that the book had never been published in America; it had never been distributed into Greece; and it had gone out of print in England. In early June, Charmian Clift wrote to David Higham asking him to 'do something about having *Peel Me a Lotus* reissued or resold somewhere else':

> Fantastic things are happening to this island, which by next year may well become one of the most fashionable resorts in the world, and *Lotus* is the *only* book about it. I am asked a dozen times a week by tourists where they can buy a copy [...] It seems crazy that it should be out of print just now, when [...] the tourist expectation is fabulous for the summer.[44]

David Higham replied that while no one could bring *Peel Me a Lotus* out before 1962, he would do his 'very best to see what can be done about getting it onto the market again in some form'. However, he was 'anticipating some difficulties'. Although the initial print run of 3000 had run out, there was hardly enough interest to warrant a reprint.[45] Only a month later, Michael Joseph decided to remainder outstanding stock of *Mermaid Singing*, as sales had by now 'virtually ceased'.[46]

But to return to Clift's description of the tourist season — what did she mean by terms such as 'fabulous' and 'fantastic'? Certainly tourism was booming, but it was really just a development of the phenomenon that had been happening since the Johnston family had arrived on the island. The thing that seems to have changed is Charmian Clift's attitude. While in *Peel Me a Lotus* she laments the arrival of every new crowd of visitors and speaks disparagingly of the wealthy yachting set, now she seems to have become star-struck, goggle-eyed, bedazzled — like the adolescent girl back in Kiama, who was fascinated by the silvertail set at the Oddfellows Hall dances.

Charmian Clift was not alone in her enjoyment of the proximity of the rich and famous. George Johnston could also sometimes get carried away with the island's star tourists:

> Everybody comes to Hydra, and there always seems to be plenty of time to talk to them and get to know them. Peter Ustinov, Henry Fonda, Garbo, Jackie Kennedy, Onassis, Callas, Queen Soraya, Olivier, Churchill, Chagall, Liz Taylor, Tennessee

Williams, Steinbeck, God knows who else! They all come here. Writers, musicians, sculptors, painters, scholars, archaeologists, scientists, engineers, con men, crooks.[47]

This is George Johnston in his role as public myth-maker: these comments were made in an article promoting the author's work, and no doubt he sought to bask in a bit of reflected fame. It is certainly true that the Johnstons' associates were interesting and artistic, and included some famous names and some wealthy Athenians. However, they were not in the elite class mentioned here. When the international yachting set arrived, they ate and partied on their boats, and did not sit around outside Katsikas's.

At the same time as he stressed the Hydra high life, George Johnston also emphasised the privations and pleasures of the simple life, which was the other half of the public image he liked to promulgate. After the series of names and occupations, he immediately went on: 'Still, one has to rely a lot on one's own resources. No telephones, no TV, no roads going anywhere, no cars, no cinema to speak of, no cabarets. The simple life. It has its pleasures, and it has its problems.'

As well as the excitement of the high season, this was a time when the Johnstons were able to exercise their particular skills of communication — of giving out, and taking in. Charmian later remembered:

> Our house, although in a sense it was isolated, was always brimful of people. For ten years we were never without guests. We never knew how many we would have for lunch or dinner; sometimes it was just the family, but more often fourteen people. And in a way this was for us a very great stimulus; we were cut off from the world but we had, in fact, on a very remote Greek island a much more vivid social life and much more intellectual nourishment than we ever got out of Sydney or London or any big city; also a more constant flow of young people through our lives than most writers.[48]

George Johnston also would stress the 'stimulus' he got 'from other people', adding: 'You are always grabbing people for phrases, witticisms, characters, ideas.'[49]

And yet, for all the input which these two writers got from their visitors, it is also clear that perennially acting as host consumed a great deal of time. Charmian Clift in the essay 'An Old Address Book' would make a more realistic assessment of the situation. She began by commenting on her habit of exchanging addresses with passing strangers — some of whom would 'look in' when 'passing through', as she had 'begged them to do':

> More often they sent their friends, or friends of their friends, with letters of introduction, and their names too are written into my old red [address] book [...] How many luncheons and dinners they must represent, how many picnics to that jewelled bay called Bisti, [...] how many visits to tavernas that mere tourists never found, how many times we must have related the history of our long island sojourn, explained again about the children's education, conducted tours of our house, walked people through tourist shops to protect them from being cheated, found hotel rooms, farewelled steamers at afternoon or dawn [...] Surely we must have needed those strange people in some way or we would never have gone to such trouble ... needed them momentarily, I mean, perhaps to convince ourselves that our lives were as meaningful as we hoped they were, or, perhaps, selfishly, to preserve a reputation for hospitality of which we were proud.[50]

The essayist touches a vital nerve here. After living in Greece for seven years or so, even Charmian would sometimes secretly wonder if the poverty and privation were really worthwhile. It was reassuring to have people arrive to gasp at the beauty of the house, to express envy at the freedom of the couple's lifestyle.

Insofar as the Johnstons were known back in their homeland, it was not so much for their writing as it was for the curious fact that they lived on a Greek island. By the early 1960s, Australian tourists were beginning to join the throngs who arrived on Hydra. Because of the political situation in Egypt, Qantas planes now landed at Athens instead of Cairo, and a number of tourists took advantage of the stop to get off and do a bit of sightseeing. In an early synopsis for the second book of his trilogy, Johnston would express the effect that this had had on him:

> One day [Meredith] walks down to the little waterfront to wait for mail. Off the ship come a long line of tourists. They all have Qantas bags over their shoulders. Kangaroos. The faces he remembers. The accents [...] Australia is forced back on him

whether he likes it or not. More and more Australians pass through the island.[51]

Hearing that an Australian couple lived on Hydra, these tourists would often ask to be taken to what was known as 'the Australian house', and would knock on the door and expect a personalised tourist information service. On one notable occasion, the visitors were a large delegation of the Australian Dried Fruits Board and their wives. These were the sorts of Australians with whom George and Charmian would have had nothing in common, back home; yet here, the shared nationality made a bond that would at least last through a night on the town, a session at Katsikas's. Returning to Australia, these visitors would pass on stories of this strange couple who had 'gone native'. (Geoffrey Hutton commented that George Johnston 'had become a peepshow for Australian tourists'.[52]) For Charmian, these visits would start the rhythms of the Australian language moving in her head. For George, the tourists would provoke memories of the blokes who used to come to his childhood home. In the synopsis quoted above, Johnston noted of David Meredith: 'Gradually he crawls out of his hiding place to ask the questions'.

As well as jetsetting celebrities and dinky-di Aussies, Hydra of course was still a favoured resort for artists. Again, the Johnstons lived up to their reputation for hospitality. In the essay about her address book, Clift remembered that as well as the passing acquaintances there were 'other names':

> French, Italian, Swedish, Norwegian. Poets and painters and potters and novelists. I remember these better because I connote them with long early-morning sessions over the kitchen table, cups of coffee, making up spare beds, the lonely, the lost, the desperate, the raging dreamers, the sick and the desolate, the stifled, the suffocating. Did we give them anything, I wonder, except momentary comfort?[53]

It is typical that Charmian would wonder whether she and George had *given* anything to these people, rather than asking what they had gained. Certainly Leonard Cohen, who had returned to the island to buy a house in the summer of 1961, would remember what the Johnstons had given:

> They were extremely helpful to all young people coming to the island. Many stopped at their table at Katsikas bar, to drink with them and get advice — on everything from where to buy their kerosine to what chemical to use to stop the toilet smelling.
> They were the focal point for foreigners on the island.

They had a larger-than-life, a mythical quality. They drank more than other people, they wrote more, they got sick more, they got well more, they cursed more and they blessed more, and they helped a great deal more. They were an inspiration. They had guts. They were real, tough, honest. They were the kind of people you meet less and less.[54]

Although Charmian and George loved helping people, and loved sharing their home and their island, what a strain it put on these hosts. It was often Charmian who took on the full-time role as summer tour guide, while George still got his mornings at the typewriter.

In this summer of 1961, the constant flow of guests were a particular strain. In August, Charmian would tell Jo:

Our house has been gutted [...] all summer and everything covered in rubble [...] We've built a fireplace, and a wall of cupboards, and a verandah, and altered the bathroom door and heaven knows what, and in another week we will have a beautiful clean white shell we can begin filling with the very few lovely things we want to keep. I've given all make-shift and make-do things away. All this building has been fairly strenuous, and through it a constant stream of visitors, and the island more crowded than I have ever known it, and now a film company (Mercouri and Dassin) with attendants, hangers-on, hopefuls and hostesses, and the normal Hydra summer dramas as well. So about six weeks ago my metabolism screamed in protest and I am now being stuffed with very expensive drugs, and curled up in my empty white house like a snail in a shell, waiting for it all to blow over.[55]

This August, Charmian turned thirty-eight: her body was starting to rebel against late nights and long drinking sessions. It is interesting to see how the tensions and fights that would consume George were to Charmian just 'normal Hydra summer dramas': a kind of seasonal hazard, not to be taken too seriously.

And yet the couple scraped through this particular summer with their relationship in fairly good order. In this August letter to Jo, Charmian commented with her customary generosity on George's Literary Guild windfall, as well as his more recent additional successes:

Yes, it's true that George has come into dollars, twenty five thousand of them (but we have to halve with the publishers) [...] This, as you can imagine, has made a Difference to Our Lives. He's also had his TV play bought [...] and a cable yesterday says *The Sponge Divers* has been taken on a six month option for a film [...] I am thinking in cliches like It Never Rains But It Pours, or To Him That Hath Shall Be Given, etc. [...] It couldn't have happened to anyone nicer or more deserving (I'm not thinking about the money either) and I am still cheering.

George himself was so happy that around October he wrote to his first daughter, Gae, inviting her to come and spend some time with the family when she finished university. In a letter sent shortly afterwards to Elsie, he noted that he still weighed under nine stone. Although suffering 'a lack of energy' he claimed he 'did "feel pretty fit", was enjoying "the joys of peace", and believed he had "some pretty good books coming up" '.[56]

Despite the cheery tone of this letter to Elsie, George was not at all well, and his condition deteriorated during October and November. Apart from his obvious thinness, his breathing was laboured and he suffered from coughing fits and emphysema, which were exacerbated by his heavy smoking. It was sometimes hard for him to get up and down the steep lanes and steps of the hilly town. By early December, however, he was able to assure David Higham that he was 'now back to pretty good health after a month or two of retrogression'. He had been working fairly hard these last few months, and had just sent Collins the revisions to the Shane Martin novel *A Wake for Mourning*. He was also 'well into a complete re-write' of *The Far Face of the Moon*, which was 'coming along excellently'.[57]

Charmian had also been hard at work on her novel since the end of the long school summer holidays. Jo and her husband Peter Meyer visited in September, but in her August letter Charmian had warned that she and George would 'both be very hard at work'. She added: 'This is important. Getting back to work I mean, on the principle of chasing a streak of luck while it's running, also for our own discipline'.[58]

By the end of the year money had run out again, and in early December Ivan von Auw cabled his client another $US1800, representing the advance on the American edition of *The Far Road* as well as an extra $500 from the Book Club money.[59] So far, $US4500 of the Literary Guild money had gone.

In the new year of 1962, Charmian Clift broke her resolution never to work with George again, and embarked on a new joint project. She told Jo:

> We are at the moment doing another collaboration (extraordinary, this) — a perfectly factual anatomy of Hydra to be called *The Serpent in the Rock*. By this time all the damage is done. Whatever we write won't alter the influx of tourists, and we figure that if we don't write the book someone else will, and nobody can know the place as well as we do.[60]

In describing the work to the American agent Ivan von Auw, Johnston would also stress the book's market potential, and would describe it as a 'new kind of treatment for this sort of a book'. He added: 'We know of no other "anatomy" like this that has been attempted anywhere'.[61]

No copy of the text is extant, but Martin Johnston described the book as being partly a personal testimony of the kind his mother had done in her earlier travel books, and partly a historical and geographical exploration of the island and its customs. Martin himself had done a considerable amount of the research — reading and translating historical sources and local folktales. It was to one of these that the book's title referred: it was said that deep in the harsh rock of Hydra there dwelled a serpent which, if roused, would exert a terrible vengeance.[62] Perhaps this was a legend not meant for *xeni*. Anyway, it was not to prove a good omen. For Clift, the usual difficulties of collaboration with her husband were increased by the fact that the book was written under terrible time pressure, for the authors aimed to submit the text in time for publication in the spring of 1963. She was forced to try to match her output with that of Johnston, while simultaneously editing the text and collating the research material.

In early February 1962, George told David Higham that his health had 'kicked back' on him again.[63] Once again he succumbed not during the excesses and tensions of summer, but during the quiet season, when the winter damp got into his lungs. Another trigger for the relapse was worry. Again, however, the cause of the anxiety was not Charmian's behaviour, but the author's work. The specific problem was the new David Meredith novel, *The Far Road*.

George Johnston had had good reason to believe in this book. Soon after its British publication in January of this year, it picked up a 'most splendid review' in the *Times Literary Supplement*.[64] Yet by the third week of February the author was upset enough to write to Billy Collins 'to say how disappointed' he was about promotion and sales. He reminded the publisher that this book was 'very important' to him personally, adding that 'if this one just peters out it will be the third one in a row for me'.[65] In fact, this novel would prove to be a complete failure, in commercial terms.[66]

As he fretted about the fate of the novel that meant so much to him, Johnston was still 'plodding on' with revisions to *The Far Face of the Moon*.[67] Clearly the author's enthusiasm for this potboiler — on which he had been working since 1959 — had long since waned, but he was still trying to turn it into a saleable product. Overall, the strain of this worry and illness exacerbated other problems and led to flare-ups of tension. While any kind of argument or confrontation was kept to a minimum in front of the children, it is clear from allusions that both George and Charmian would later make about this period that there were times when the relationship seemed almost to be beyond hope of rescue.[68]

It is clear, too, that Charmian felt that the root cause of the difficulty was George's sickness, and George's understandable resentment of his sickness. In her description of his 'rage' against his physical condition, she explained:

> He was, of course, affronted and outraged by the corruption working in his lungs. And there were times when he was affronted and outraged by anybody who didn't have corruption working in his lungs. (Or so it seemed then: it was the impression he gave.) Why did it have to pick on him? Him of all people who had never been sick in his life.[69]

As Charmian was closest to him, she naturally was the one who affronted him most by her health and sheer physical vigour. And with Charmian's easily provoked sense of guilt, it wouldn't take much for her to start to feel some element of responsibility. At the same time, her loyalty to her husband was, if anything, increased by his debility. No matter how unbearable the situation became, she could not leave him under these circumstances.

There were other domestic tensions too, as Martin and Shane reached adolescence. Jason remembers how his two siblings 'just couldn't stand each other'. By now, the differences in their attitudes, tastes, interests and beliefs were so extreme that there was a 'complete mutual incomprehension'. For the most part, Shane and Martin were able to keep out of each other's way, for 'the openness of the island' meant that 'you could actually have a lot of privacy'. But if they were 'forced to be in each other's company', there would be instant fireworks:

Shane and I would start singing a snatch of some particularly horrible little pop song, and Martin would come in with a *klepht-*y sort of adult thing and [say to us]: 'Oh how commercial — you're fucked!'

And then it'd be: 'What would *you* know? You're just a little snob!'

And it would all start.

It was very polarised, and I have to admit that I completely took one side — namely Shane's — for whatever reason — perhaps the fact that she was that one year closer to me — maybe because Martin was so self-consciously a little adult, while we were still happy to be children a bit — or for whatever reason.[70]

Of course, this sort of friction — especially over musical preference — is a standard part of family life in a house with teenagers. For Charmian and George, however, these disputes were particularly wearing at this time, when they were doing their best to maintain civility in their own relationship. And, of course, all the arguments between the three children were in Greek. Although the parents would know the gist of what was going on, they would not be able to intervene and adjudicate fairly.

As well as these ongoing domestic worries, Charmian had another source of anguish at this time. Her own mother had for some time been suffering from senile dementia and had been living with Barré and his family at Woonona, near Wollongong. By now, Amy had completely lost her memory. Over the years of exile, Charmian's correspondence with her mother had dwindled, and by the last couple of years there seemed little point writing as Amy didn't even know those around her.[71] The dropping off of correspondence did not imply a diminishing of the bond.

Soon there were money worries as well. Previously, Johnston had been told that the Literary Guild money was due at the end of January 1962.[72] In March, Ivan von Auw informed his client that the publishers would be happy to advance another $US2500 (of the $US8000 owed), but 'under the terms of the contract the money wouldn't be payable until next fall's royalty statement'.[73] The author was 'rather disturbed' by this, stressing that 'we have made commitments on the assumption that the money was payable after January 31st'. He pleaded that at least $US4000 be remitted as soon as possible to their bank account.[74] Von Auw managed to send this sum, but he and David Higham exchanged correspondence wondering what their client did with his money. They decided that in future it would be better if they tried to help him make his money last by withholding some of it from him.[75] The author did not explain why he needed so much money, but it is obvious that it was to pay local builders and tradespeople for the extensive house renovations.

By the end of May the text of *The Serpent in the Rock* was ready to send off to the agents in Britain and America. Johnston told David Higham that he thought the book to be 'rather something'. In this letter, Johnston also commented: 'Health picking up again, and on the whole feeling pretty well again.'[76]

With the travel book done, Charmian Clift could return to *Honour's Mimic*. She had so often started this work and been forced to interrupt it that this time she hoped for a clear run. By the end of June, Johnston reported that she was 'back in full stride now' on the book.[77] Surely this time she would finish it?

The writing of *Honour's Mimic* was taking the author to a new level. As the novel opens, Australian-born Kathy, aged thirty-one, has left her publisher husband and two young sons in England in order to come to a Greek island where she plans to spend some months in the home of her English sister-in-law Milly, who has married a wealthy English-educated sponge trader. While the author uses her favourite device of counterpointed heroines in hard Kathy and soft Milly, this time all the author's sympathies lie with the hard character. In this regard, Kathy is pure diamond. With her cropped red hair (barely hiding a scar on her skull), her thin white face, the gash of lipstick on her wide mouth, her skinny legs tucked into stretch pants, the heroine's body has been stripped down to the bone; her soul also, we feel, has been laid bare, the nerves exposed. It is as if Julia from *Walk to the Paradise Gardens* has decided that she can no longer tolerate her comfortable middle class life with her safe, dull husband and has simply — cracked. Indeed, when it is revealed that Kathy is convalescing after a car crash, the reader feels that there is some mystery to this accident; or was it perhaps not an accident?

This brush with death provides a link between Kathy and Fotis, a failed diver whom no captain wants to recruit for the coming season. On his last voyage, Fotis felt fear, and it stalks him now like a curse. Both he and the foreign woman are in a reckless frame of mind, as if their experience has broken some sort of barrier; both have moved outside the limits of normal society. 'We are alike', Kathy thinks, recognising Fotis as another 'desperate one'.[78]

As the two meet in a ruined Byzantine palace above the town, Kathy, 'having nothing else to give him', tells the diver: 'That car accident. I was trying to kill myself'.[79] When Kathy and Fotis fall in love, all other considerations become irrelevant. Drawing on the John Donne poem that provides both title and epigraph, the author depicts a passion so overwhelming that even honour is devalued into 'mimic'. Thus Kathy is heedless of her reputation, and doesn't spare a thought for her husband and sons; Fotis could not care less about his pregnant wife and eight hungry children.

After a time of furtive assignations, Kathy moves to a rented peacock-blue room above a taverna, where she and Fotis become Donne's lovers, in their own all-encompassing sphere. Yet there can be no happy and domestic ending for these two. In order to restore her lover's pride, Kathy throws shame to the winds and goes to beg from her brother-in-law a position for Fotis as a diver on one of the family boats. When the boats leave in the fourth week of Lent, Kathy faces the loss of the lover she has sacrificed. As she returns from the wharf, she is spat upon by one of the local women; she barely feels the first stone that hits her.

While *Honour's Mimic* presents the apotheosis of the author's view that love overrides any other consideration, this is not a romance novel. Indeed, the novel's main originality lies in the way the author breaks one of the essential rules of that genre by having her heroine love a man who is far below her on the class scale, and who comes from a different ethnic and cultural background.

Lady Chatterley's Lover is the literary comparison that springs to mind (especially given the influence of *Sons and Lovers* on *The End of the Morning*). Yet in *Lady Chatterley*, DH Lawrence is at pains to emphasise that the gamekeeper Mellors 'might almost be a gentleman'; he looks 'like a free soldier rather than a servant'; he seems to the heroine 'so unlike a gamekeeper, so unlike a working man anyhow'. Although at times he speaks in the local vernacular, this is a deliberate choice; the rest of the time, he speaks with 'no trace of dialect'.[80] Mellors can even read and write so well that at the end of the novel he is helping a trainee schoolteacher with her lessons.

Compared with this, Charmian Clift's Fotis is authentically working class: although he too has been a soldier, the author does not make him out to be anything other than a poor and illiterate Greek sponge-diver. Unlike the clean and white-skinned Mellors, Fotis is swarthy, and doesn't wash too often. His use of English is spare, broken, like his rocky landscape. 'I'm being your husband, Ketty. Me!' he tells the heroine.

If the volume of the passion in this novel is tuned as loud as it was in *High Valley* and *Paradise Gardens*, the writer this time avoids the screech of melodrama. The ultimate meaning of the story is that there can be no escape for the lovers: they will be forced to endure their separate fates. The author wisely avoids any temptation to tidy up Kathy's ending: will she return to her husband (would he have her?) or will she perhaps again try to kill herself? That isn't what the book's conclusion is about. It is, rather, that when Fotis goes off alone to confront his terror, to meet his fear — to risk his life — Kathy will be with him. She promises that:

> 'He will conquer even the smell of fear because of me. Because I will be with him waking and sleeping, I will crawl with him along the bottom of the sea, I will be the air that he breathes, I will be his lungs and his eyes and the pump of his heart. I promise you this.'[81]

By arranging Fotis's place in the sponge fleet Kathy is giving him 'the chance of retrieving the right to live with himself'. Thus, ironically, in the end honour is given pre-eminence over love. If Donne provides the title, it is another Metaphysical poet, Richard Lovelace, whose message seems to echo through Kathy's renunciation of Fotis. 'I could not love thee, Dear, so much,/ Loved I not Honour more'.[82]

Some readers have speculated as to whether this novel is autobiographical, in the sense of drawing from an account of some liaison of the author's with an actual sponge-diver.[83] Such an idea misses the meaning of the passion that is coded into this novel. The love here is not primarily about sex, but about a bonding of twin souls. Ultimately, Kathy's promise on behalf of Fotis — which her lover does not even hear her make — was Charmian's vow in the face of her husband's illness. It is surely no coincidence that all the imagery in this declaration is of lungs, air, and breathing, at a time when the man whom the author herself loved was struggling for breath.

Every time Charmian Clift established a good work rhythm, summer intervened.

Peter Finch was in Greece this year, for the filming of *In the Cool of the Day*, and managed to get to Hydra for a few days with his old friends. (This short visit would be spun out into those passages of *Clean Straw for Nothing* in which Calverton stays on the island and acts as confidant to David Meredith.) Meanwhile, Hydra began to fill with Warner Bros film people, and by the first week of July the whole island was 'submerged under a Hollywoodian madness'. The film crew were even using the house next door to the Johnstons as a location, and the little square reverberated with the noise.[84] This wasn't unusual. Every year now, Hydra assumed the nature of a permanent film set between the months of June and September. In the twelve months from mid 1962, no less than three American films shot on the island were due to be released.[85]

In *Peel Me a Lotus*, Clift had written an account of her first experience of the takeover of the island by film-makers who transformed the public area of the waterfront into 'the queerest fantasy world'. In this 'make-believe waterfront', mobile cameras and actors trundled up and down, and many of the locals (both Greeks and *xeni*) were co-opted into playing themselves as 'extras', pretending to greet each other as they pretended to buy vegetables from the market stalls, and often repeating their actions over and over between 'takes'. At the same time, 'sometimes the waterfront [was] still a real waterfront', where the locals could market, greet their friends, or go about their normal business. The difficulty was telling which bit of the *agora* was which, and which friends were really being themselves, as opposed to acting at being themselves. The author concluded that 'In this weird dream-world everyone slips into a Role [...] Queerest, and most terrifying of all, one finds oneself unprotestingly playing the role assigned'.[86]

If the number of Hydra films was growing, the standard was dropping. This debasement was symptomatic of the wholesale degeneration of the island, and especially of the foreign colony. Of this period after the return from England, Martin would later remember:

> Life on Hydra was [...] better in a material sense, less good in an emotional sense. The foreign community was getting bigger and bigger and beginning to tear itself apart with internecine squabbles and bitchery and all sorts of sexual and alcoholic tangles, and generally beginning to be a pretty unhealthy sort of place in which to live. My parents more and more felt this.[87]

In particular, the couple would start to be concerned about the effect on the children. Yet Martin's view here is probably shaped by hindsight. At the time, the children cheerfully exploited their membership of both worlds.

There was good pocket money to be made, not just from acting as extras in films,[88] but from running errands for the film company and translating for the tourists. Even Jason would set up 'a little side-line [...] as interpreter for the tourists'. He adds: 'It was a little secret between Shane and me'.

Certainly, Jason remembers this period of his childhood as being 'a time of extraordinary freedom'; really the only difficulty was what to do during the afternoon siesta time when the island would be 'almost deserted' and he would wander about by himself. By early evening he would assert his 'little feline habits', turning up at the kitchens of various Greek houses for his dinner — or dinners. And eventually he would gravitate down to the waterfront to meet up with his parents, who would feed him again.[89]

Towards the end of this summer, the publishers began to bring in their verdict on *The Serpent in the Rock*. In August, Raleigh Trevelyan at Michael Joseph was 'extremely sorry to have to decline the book' but he did not feel it to be 'one for [their] list'.[90] This was a double blow, for Michael Joseph had published *Mermaid Singing*, and Trevelyan had been the editor at Hutchinsons who had handled *Peel Me a Lotus*. In America, where the authors had felt sure of great success, the reaction was just as negative. The editor at Harpers wrote:

> [The authors'] love for their way of life on the island comes through well — and so does a picture (but their picture) of the island — and I found much of the book fine reading. *But*, in spite of the tourists now flocking to it, Hydra is really not worthy of a whole book. It has very little past, and I suspect its present, small scale at best, is fleeting.[91]

While this reaction highlighted the book's subject matter, David Higham's reader complained about the length; the agent recommended that the authors cut 20 000 words from the total of 90 000 before the text be offered to another publisher.[92] Over the next couple of months, *The Serpent in the Rock* would also be refused in America by Little, Brown and by Doubleday.[93] It was never to be published.[94]

The book's rejection was a severe blow, more so for Charmian Clift than for George Johnston. It was a couple of years since she had had anything published, a couple of years since she had had any income of her own. She had interrupted her real work in the hope of buying time by producing a money-spinner — and all she'd done was lose time. In critical terms, the response was even more upsetting, for travel writing was Clift's specialty.

Moreover, this round of rejections happened at a bad time for Charmian: at the end of September 1962 her mother died in hospital at the age of seventy-five. The death certificate gave the cause as '(a) Dementia (b) Arteriosclerosis (c) Myocardial degeneration, senility'.[95]

For Charmian, the impact of this death was very powerful. Syd Clift may tend to steal the limelight in Clift's accounts of family life, but it is Amy who emerges as the dominant figure. Although the love which Charmian felt for her mother was strong, other emotions were tangled up in it. After all, it was Amy who had favoured her first-born daughter over Charmian; Amy who had been the driving force behind sending Margaret to art school; Amy who had thought Charmian could make her own way, and become a schoolteacher. All in all, Amy Clift may have given Charmian her love for poetry and her urge for travel and adventure, but it was also Amy who had made Charmian feel second-rate. And to some degree it was Amy's extraordinary reticence about matters of the body that had caused Charmian to develop her complicated attitude to sexuality, which at one moment would seem to be defiant of conventional morality and at the next would seem to agree with small town notions of shame and guilt. Perhaps most painful of all, it was Amy who had pressured Charmian to give up her own first-born child.

While Amy's death stirred up old memories, old pains, it also meant that these memories could be publicly explored, in fiction. For this autobiographical writer, there was now a dramatic opening up of subject matter. In the past, as we have seen, Charmian Clift had tried again and again to write Amy's story and the stories of her own young self, but always she had run into a brick wall. Charmian could not write in depth about her family while Amy was alive, because she couldn't bear the thought of hurting her mother with a portrayal of the pain which she herself had felt as a child. Now Charmian's way was open. Or — more likely — the way had been open for some months. When the news of Amy's deteriorating condition began to arrive from Margaret and Barré, Charmian returned in her mind to that double country of her past — Kiama and her childhood. Once Amy lost the ability to read and remember, Charmian was free to write.

Although officially she was hard at work on *Honour's Mimic*, it is clear that around the middle of 1962 Charmian Clift made a new start on the telling of the Kiama story. In this new Kiama narrative, the prose and dialogue is a quantum leap ahead of the rather wooden style of the various texts of *Greener Grows the Grass.* And whereas in the earlier versions the alter ego had been an adolescent, this time the author took her character all the way back to childhood. In this new account of the Morley family, the father's name remains 'Tom' but it is now that the mother's name changes from 'Alma' to the wonderfully appropriate 'Grace'. The children's names become Shakespearian (like that of their creator). Now 'Judith' becomes 'Cordelia', after Lear's faithful daughter,[96] and dull 'John' changes to 'Ben', short for 'Benedick'. The best is saved, of course, for the heroine. The young pagan is no longer Christine, the Child of Christ, but Miranda, daughter of Prospero the magician. The maritime connotations of the name perfectly suit the beachcombing girl from Kiama.

Of this Miranda material, only fourteen pages (largely unconnected) remain. A five-page opening passage of this work bears the title *The End of the Morning* — borrowed from the much earlier short story. Mixed in with these drafts, there are also three pages (page 20, page 27 and an unnumbered page) written in the first person. Of course, Clift had used first-person narrative in her two travel books. By using it now for her alter ego, she was narrowing the gap between her fictional and non-fictional personae. She was identifying with and claiming the alter ego as a close part of her self.

This new relationship with the character needed to be formalised by a new name. Although the narrator of these three pages is not addressed by name, it was surely at this time, with the change of narration from third to first person, that Miranda Morley was transformed into *Cressida* Morley.[97] It is unlikely that 'Cressida' came as a bolt from the blue, for elements of the name in the forms of 'Chris' and 'Tressida' had been appearing in the author's fiction for a long time. It was now, however, that Clift chose to use this name with its wonderful literary ancestry: Homeric, Chaucerian and Shakespearian. At the same time, the diminutive 'Cress' sounded fresh and green; like Miranda, it also had watery connotations.

But what of the other association of the name 'Cressida' — the identification of the Shakespearian Cressida as a fickle jade? Would Charmian choose this name for herself?[98] Any concerns we might have about Charmian Clift's attitude to the name are dispelled by Rodney Hall, who stayed with the Johnstons on Hydra in early 1964 and discussed at some length with them the writing of *My Brother Jack*, including the appearance of Cressida Morley at the end of that novel. He declares: 'The use of the name would have been hers'.

She *loved* the name. Charmian was one of those life-loving people who take things in with an appetite and I remember she said, 'I've always wished I was called "Cressida". I've always loved the name "Cressida" '[...] And I remember her saying, 'And of course it has the advantage that she was so *wicked!*'[99]

Overall, these three creative decisions — to go all the way back to the alter ego's childhood, to use a first-person narrative, and to call the hero/narrator 'Cressida' — represented a crucial breakthrough in this long-delayed work-in-progress. It appears that it was now that Charmian Clift wrote the greater part of the earlier of the two extant versions of *The End of the Morning*, in which Cressida tells her tale from her own point of view.[100] This dating of both the novel's beginning and Clift's origination of the name 'Cressida Morley' is confirmed by the author herself. In August 1968, Charmian Clift would apply for a Commonwealth Literary Fund fellowship in order to write 'a novel of a semi-autobiographical nature, set [...] on the south coast of New South Wales and titled *The End of the Morning*'. The author would go on to declare:

It was begun six years ago, before my husband started *My Brother Jack*, and set aside so that he would be free to complete his own project. [It] is about a girl called Cressida Morley, who has appeared already in *My Brother Jack* but I invented her first.[101]

While there was no reason for Clift to tell the anonymous Commonwealth Literary Fund assessors that she had 'invented' Cressida if she had not, the use of the specific date of six years rather than 'a few years' suggests that she was very sure of the timing: and of course six years before 1968 takes us back to 1962. This matter of the dating of Clift's unfinished novel is more important than it may seem, for it raises certain considerations in regard to the writing of *My Brother Jack*.

What was George doing during this summer of 1962, as he waited to hear the publishers' response to *The Serpent in the Rock*? In June he had sent off the newly revised version of *The Far Face of the Moon*. For the first time in his writing career, he had no project to which he could immediately turn his hand. In fact, he had been engaged on no major piece of fiction since he had finished *The Far Road* in England in late 1960. This represented a significant fallow period in the working life of this usually prolific author.

After this 'rest period', and after the trial runs at serious work in the two David Meredith novels, *Closer to the Sun* and *The Far Road*, George Johnston at last felt himself ready to do something really important. Ever since returning from war in October 1945 he had been wanting to write a novel about an alienated artist in the post-war world.[102] Despite the failure of his first attempt at this in the collaborative novel *The Piping Cry*, the author had continued to mull over the idea. Meanwhile, the clock was ticking. Although his health through the summer of 1962 wasn't too bad, Johnston lived all the time now with the knowledge that his illness was chronic and recurrent. If he didn't do the novel soon, it could well be too late.

Dissatisfied with the way in which he had lost his nerve halfway through his two previous David Meredith novels, George Johnston now began to make some notes exploring the character of this alter ego, with whom the author was increasingly identifying. The author also returned to the idea of trying to trace the breakdown of a marriage back to its first causes. This time, after considering the failure of David Meredith's great love affair, Johnston would ask himself the vital question: was there something about David Meredith that made him not very good at love?[103] A consideration of this question took the author back to his own beginnings. It was around this time that he wrote the note entitled 'Childhood — "The Dollikos" ',[104] discussed in chapter 8.

Although it was only now that George Johnston began putting onto paper his analysis of the effect of his unloving childhood environment, it is clear that he had been nutting away at some of the connections for years. In *Peel Me a Lotus*, for example, Clift describes George 'talk[ing] in a wild spate of words' in the exuberant time following the birth of Jason and the move into the new house. While this talk was of all sorts of things — 'of masters and slaves, cities and people, journeys, meetings, partings', and so on — Clift concluded that:

> [He] talks of all the arrivals and all the setting-outs, as if his life was a knotted ball that he is madly unravelling backwards ... all the way back to the flat suburban streets and the flat suburban houses behind the safe silver wire fences and the child waiting in the bathroom for his father to enter with the razor-strop to administer the ritual monthly beating. 'For the sins,' his father said, 'I have not found out.'[105]

Here George is not Odysseus but a kind of Theseus, following a ball of twine that leads him through the labyrinth of claustrophobic Melbourne suburbia — to the monster that is his father! It is symptomatic of the changes that had been happening to George since the onset of his illness that he was now ready to start exploring this labyrinth — even confronting this monster — by way of the written word as well as the spoken word. This was exactly what the author was doing in the 'Dollikos' text, and perhaps in other notes about his childhood, which have not been preserved.

But while producing this sort of fragment of autobiographical analysis was helping George Johnston clarify his thoughts, it wasn't taking him any further into a novel. There was no trigger for the plot — no opening. And so, fearing that he might die before he was able to make his autobiographical testimony in the form of a successful novel about David Meredith, Johnston considered a rough and ready solution. What if he just gathered together a number of unfinished semi-autobiographical fragments into a kind of loose anthology, called it *The Meredith Papers*, and published the text as it was? The author went so far as to write an introductory piece in which he presented himself in the first person as an anonymous book editor assembling the remaining papers of a dead friend. This friend was a writer who had 'given himself the fictitious name of David Meredith' and who in these text fragments 'studies himself in the way a professional writer would study a character he has imagined'! This statement turns inside out the whole business of the alter ego, and makes it clear that 'David Meredith' is just a facade or mask: behind the name is a real person — by profession a writer — who has been examining his real self. Thus the fiction is really non-fiction.

The 'editor' goes on to tell the reader that these papers begin with the short story 'The Verdict'. This was to be followed by 'the draft of a novel or novelette' which the dead author had been 'proposing to write'. As well as this there would be 'drafts of dialogue, entries in a journal, fragments of a play, observations, quotations, random thoughts jotted down as they must have occurred to him, even the text of an imagined suicide note'.

> Yet all these things are pertinent to the core and theme that runs right through every page of *The Meredith Papers*. The dissection of a man in search of himself with himself as pathologist — post-mortem, as it were, if one looks at it another way, on a dead love.[106]

As George Johnston continued to bash his head against the brick wall of his major work, a couple of things started to show him an opening.

Given the way in which George and Charmian discussed story ideas together on a daily basis, it can hardly be coincidental that George Johnston began putting his mind to his childhood at the very time when Charmian Clift went back to her own autobiographical novel about her origins. But this wasn't all. As earlier discussions of material from *The End of the Morning* show, Clift's projected novel is concerned with two sisters: while Cressida Morley is the heroine of the tale, her qualities and personal characteristics are highlighted by the contrast between Cressida and her elder sister Cordelia. Earlier, in some of the drafts of *Greener Grows the Grass*, Clift had explored a similar parallel between the two sisters Christine and Judith. This, of course, was a variation on Clift's favourite novelistic device of contrasting hard and soft heroines.

Thus in Clift's autobiographical work-in-progress George Johnston could see a model or framework for the fictional exploration of two contrasting siblings as they developed through childhood and adolescence. Certainly, in *Closer to the Sun* Johnston had written about two Meredith brothers.[107] But the failure of the first Meredith novel stemmed in part from the fact that the author had made David's brother into another David: both men are writers, and the only real difference is that Mark is commercially successful while David is struggling. Besides, this novel was only concerned with the brothers as middle aged adults. Clift, on the other hand, was again asking in *The End of the Morning* the question that she had been posing for more than a decade: how can two same-sex siblings, with the same upbringing, turn out to be opposites?

By coincidence, as George Johnston around this time was thinking about his childhood and family, he received a letter from Joy Russo, the daughter of his brother Jack. This niece had read a feature article in the Australian press glamorising the Johnstons as expatriates living the good life on their idyllic Greek island, and she was prompted to write a letter to her uncle reminding him that his stay-at-home brother was also a valuable person.[108] As we have seen, through childhood and adolescence George Johnston had a rather ambivalent relationship with Jack. While the younger boy had looked up to his brother as a bit of a hero and even protector, George had also felt — or been made to feel — inferior to the older boy in the areas of masculinity that both Jack and their father thought to be important. Meanwhile George's own areas of aptitude and interest — especially reading and writing — were derided and devalued. Since reaching adulthood, the two Johnston men had moved in very different directions. Their ambitions, their attitudes, their life experience, their choice of wives, their lifestyles — everything was chalk and cheese. This difference formed a kind of textbook example of the nature/nurture question that Clift was asking in regard to the childhood development of two sisters. Why had the two Johnston boys turned out so very differently? In his first page of jottings for this novel, the author would note: 'You see what I am trying to get at is what made Jack different from me. Different all through our lives, I mean, not just older or braver or not as clever'.[109]

And so George Johnston, as he considered the effect of his childhood in the 'Dollikos' text, came to realise that, if he wanted to write about the post-war David Meredith and the failure of Meredith's great love affair, he should begin at the real beginning and write a novel which took the hero up to the time that the author had previously seen as his starting point. Suddenly he realised he had a conclusion to his story: the meeting between David Meredith and the woman who would turn out to be his 'prize possession'. Now, via Joy Russo's reproach and Charmian Clift's example of a novel dealing with the childhood of contrasting siblings, Johnston found the focus that he needed: he could tell the story of his alter ego David Meredith by contrasting him with his brother Jack. However, he would reverse Clift's balance of sympathies: in his text the soft character, Davy, would steal the limelight — and the story — from the hard character, Jack.

In another way, too, it seems that Charmian Clift's new start on her autobiographical story in *The End of the Morning* had an influence. At this time, as we have seen, Clift made the decision to rewrite her narrative in the first person — to present the world of the novel from the inside, to deal only with that material which the narrator/hero had personally observed and experienced, and to dispense with any pretence of authorial objectivity. If this mode opened the way for Charmian Clift, it also seemed to George Johnston to be the key. Although in the novels *The Darkness Outside* and *The Far Face of the Moon* he had allowed his heroes to narrate the story, he had always used the third person for his David Meredith material — even recently, in the 'Dollikos' note. Now he also made the decision to look at his childhood and family from inside the perspective of his alter ego.

As this summer of 1962 turned to autumn, George Johnston began to let the memories flow. For this storyteller, it was only natural that a great deal of the reminiscence was done out loud, in conversation with his usual sounding board. This was the thing that he and Charmian loved most: talking and talking, thrashing out ideas for story, for characters, for themes, for locations, for ways of telling a tale. And on one of these occasions at this time, the pair 'talked for thirteen hours straight [...] and came up with an idea that turned into a novel called *My Brother Jack*'.[110] It was now that Charmian Clift put aside her work on *The End of the Morning* in order to give all her time and energies to talking George through his past.

18

SOME INSCRUTABLE BOND

Some inscrutable bond held them together. But it was
a strange vibration of the nerves, rather than of the blood.
A nervous attachment rather than a sexual love. A curious tension of
will, rather than a sexual passion. Each was curiously under the
domination of the other. They were a pair — they had to be together.
Yet quite soon they shrank from each other.[1]

Whenever members of the public or the media talk to an author about a particular book, the most common question is 'Where did you get the idea from?' Many authors develop a story to enable them to explain the creative process. Often, when such a story has been told a number of times, it will seem to the author to be the full truth, because memory will set aside the extraneous details. In this way George Johnston was to develop a public legend about the time when the inspirational light bulb flashed, and the novel *My Brother Jack* was begun. The following version was given in an interview with Joan Flanagan in January 1969:

> Alone in the house and very sick — I thought I was going to die — I examined this whole thing of life and achievement. I thought of the books I'd written and I suddenly felt that not one of them amounted to anything.
>
> I thought to myself: 'Why don't you write something worthwhile?' So I got up out of bed, still sick, and I went downstairs, shaking with fever, and I wrote the first page of *My Brother Jack* exactly as it was printed.[2]

Eighteen months later, Johnston would tell the story somewhat differently in an ABC broadcast for secondary students who were studying the novel:

> I had been absent from Australia for many years, I was living on a Greek island, I was seriously ill with tuberculosis, and I was homesick for my native land. As a way of trying to overcome the long dragging hours of confinement in a sickbed, I set myself the task of trying to remember a street in Melbourne I used to walk along in the early 1920s, when I was a ten year old schoolboy. Although I had virtually no distractions, it did not come easy. However, I persisted, and gradually — I thought at the time miraculously — the street reassembled itself in my mind, bit by bit, shop by shop, house by house, the most minute detail, people and things I had not thought about for forty years. Not only the street but the house I had lived in, its occupants, the contents of its drawers and cupboards. After about three weeks I wrote it all down, and this still stands, without a word altered, as Chapter One of *My Brother Jack*.[3]

Certainly, these accounts are emotionally true, for they link the author's physical sickness and his homesickness with his exploration of his past. However, it is clear that when the author wrote the first page — or first chapter — of his novel, this was the culmination of an intensive period of preparation, much of which was done by way of discussion with Charmian Clift.

In another interview, the author revealed something of the way this discussion worked, as he expanded upon the 'monumental feat of recall' which he had had to undertake in order 'to bring back Melbourne, Australia, in the grip of the Depression':

> It was tough — but if I gave myself to memory it worked in a most uncanny way. I'd try to remember a street, and soon I'd be able to bring back all the shops.
>
> And though Charmian was eleven years younger than I, she could remember the Depression as a little girl. I'd ask her, 'What sort of clothes did your sister wear? What sort of slang did you use?'
>
> Gradually this whole nostalgic world began to re-emerge. But was it a fantasy world or a valid memory? I had no way, on Hydra, of knowing.[4]

For this project of 'recall', the author could have had no better assistant, for Charmian Clift possessed an extraordinary visual memory. While she was able to call up a whole landscape like a toy town inside her head, she had also developed a method for summoning visual memory by walking herself step by step through a landscape. This is displayed in the opening section of The End of the Morning, where Cressida traces her regular walk to the quarry to deliver her father's lunch. In regard to Johnston's account of recreating in his mind the street he used to walk along as a ten year old, this was surely the result of the sessions of reminiscence, in which Charmian elicited memory by asking questions.

This anecdote of Johnston's also reveals how he drew upon Clift's memory bank in the creation of the novel's atmosphere. Through the many drafts of her own autobiographical novel, Charmian Clift had been developing her store of material about Australian life in the period between the wars. Again her visual memory came into play, enabling her to conjure up the minute period details that give a writer's work a feeling of authenticity.[5]

After weeks or even months of this process of remembering, there came the day when the author got out of bed, and sat at his typewriter, and produced the opening of the novel, pretty much as it would be published. At the same time, he wrote a page of handwritten notes, neatly headed 'MY BROTHER JACK'. These record details of the interior of the family home, and places seen on the walk up the main street.[6]

This must have been around the beginning of October 1962. On 11 November George Johnston would write David Higham a long business letter concluding with the first hint about the project given to either of the author's agents: 'I am 100-odd pages out on another Johnston novel, of which I will tell you more later, and in pretty good health generally'.[7] When the author was engaged on a book, he had a standard writing 'target' of three finished pages of typescript per day.[8] The production of a hundred pages suggests that he had been writing for about five weeks. Although this letter to Higham indicates that the author was not undergoing a particular health crisis at this time, he was of course chronically ill. By mid January 1963, looking back a few months, George would tell his ex-wife Elsie that he had been 'more or less semi-invalid and housebound since the end of October'.[9] Certainly, as winter set in, Johnston did succumb to his customary seasonal bout of severe respiratory illness, and he continued to write the novel while in very bad health and suffering from the side effects of prescribed drugs.

Through this stage of work as well as in the initial 'recall' stages, Charmian's input was constant. By now George had moved his bed as well as his work into the downstairs living room, as it was cheaper to keep just one fire going. This room was on two levels, with a step next to the table where the author worked. In his January 1969 interview with Joan Flanagan, George Johnston gave an account of how he and Charmian worked together in this room:

> That entire winter I was sick — I couldn't leave the house — and we kept a fire going in the [room]. We had a man coming down every day with a load of wood on a donkey. We kept that fire going twenty-four hours a day for seven months.
>
> Charmian sat on a stone step on a cushion and we talked and talked and remembered and remembered and I wrote *My Brother Jack*.[10]

In another account of their way of 'collaboration through talk and criticism', the couple remembered 'once talking without pause — except for some drink', for more than a day during the writing of this novel.[11]

Through the whole of this winter of 1962–63, Charmian Clift drew the book out of George Johnston. As well as sitting on the step in her role as sounding board, she also sometimes assumed her customary place on the other side of the work table and helped write and collate the research notes, just as she had done with the other collaborative novels and more recently with *The Serpent in the Rock*.

In the journal that George Johnston used for his trilogy, the section devoted to *My Brother Jack* includes some pages in Clift's bold handwriting; these show something of the way in which she worked with her husband. On one page, Charmian Clift has written a list of Australian expressions, such as 'Stone the crows', 'That'd be a turn-up for the books', 'getting spliced', 'Strike a bloody light!' and 'skite'. There are also two pages of character notes, which include these observations:

> Jack was a character born for ardent adventure.
> (The stage was never big enough.)
> He was hamstrung by circumstance, and by his own innate nobility.
> He could have acted out some passionate Conradian drama, in South America, say, or some unnamed island, of which he would

have been king. Looking down the years, one likes to think this. Circumstances were against him. Circumstances are against all of us. One way or another [...]

Jack's 'just and passionate spirit'.[12]

This may simply be Clift acting as amanuensis. But it reveals that even the character of Jack himself was a subject to be thrashed out by both authors talking together.

Of course, so was the character of Cressida Morley. As we have seen in chapter 7, the depiction of the young woman during her AWAS training at the golf course also reveals the input of Charmian Clift. Yet it appears that Clift was also involved in the characterisation of Helen Meredith. Later describing this character to Rodney Hall as 'a concoction of ours', Charmian went on to explain that she and George had 'got together' to make sure David Meredith's first wife Helen was not like George Johnston's first wife Elsie. The reason was to spare Elsie any pain or embarrassment.[13]

Although in this case the author was keen to distance the fictional character from the model, there was no attempt to disguise the author's parents or siblings. Most notably, George's brother carries his real name into not just the book, but its very title. By putting his brother into the novel under his own name — and in such a significant role — George Johnston considerably narrowed the distance between fiction and fact, between public and private. In a sense, he was doing what Charmian had done in the travel books — putting in family members under their real names, fictionalising other names, and selectively presenting material through a first-person viewpoint.

The final part of Charmian's input into the novel was more directly editorial, for she commented on the text, page by page, draft by draft, as it rolled off the typewriter. A year later, the couple would explain this process to Rodney Hall, after he had read a copy of the typescript. The description they gave is strikingly similar to the way in which Charmian's sister Margaret had described the couple's 1947 collaboration on *High Valley*:

Charmian had given up all her work for *My Brother Jack* and she sat on the other side of the desk. And he'd bash out the pages and pass them over, one by one, and as he wrote them she read them. And then when they took coffee breaks and things, she would immediately feed back. And she [said] that the main thing she used to say to him was: 'Is that really true?' [...] Her input was basically biographical stuff. Her input was to say, 'Come on, George, you've written lots of fiction that may not last. But this is important — let's get it right.' And she said that all the way through she was saying, 'Is that *true*?' And he felt challenged, and a lot of the stuff he re-wrote.[14]

To mention all this is not to take away the authorship of *My Brother Jack* from George Johnston, for he himself acknowledged Charmian's input. As well as describing his wife as his 'verbal collaborator', Johnston would say that 'in a very real sense' *My Brother Jack* was 'Charmian's book'.[15] Telling another journalist how his wife 'encouraged' him to write *My Brother Jack*, the author added: 'It was virtually a collaboration'.[16]

Yet if Charmian Clift's way of working on this book was akin to the way she had worked on earlier collaborative texts, there was a difference to her sense of involvement. This time there was a great urgency, and the knowledge that a greal deal was at stake. She believed, just as George believed, that this might well be his final chance to produce a book that was really worthwhile. This project was George's life, not just because it told his story, but because it represented his chance of life after death. Any sacrifice seemed worthwhile, in order to let him have this chance.

At the time, it didn't seem to matter if she put aside her own autobiographical novel, because she would have plenty of time to work on it. At this stage it also didn't seem to matter if her own alter ego character of Cressida Morley appeared in George's book; anyway, this would only be a small role, and towards the end. In all this, Charmian was making the kind of selfless sacrifice that her heroine Kathy makes for her lover Fotis in *Honour's Mimic*. She would be with him, 'waking and sleeping', and she would 'crawl with him across the bottom of the sea', and she would give him 'the chance of retrieving the right to live with himself'.

Indeed, at this time the author was also trying to do her final revision of this last part of this novel. In his 11 November letter to Higham, Johnston reported: '*Honour's Mimic*: Charmian says "Close to the finish and going well"'. Around this same time he also mentioned her progress to Ivan von Auw, who wrote back: 'Happy to hear Charmian is nearly finished with her novel'.[17] Yet this was the sort of breezy way in which Clift would say that work was progressing when it wasn't. In fact, she would not complete this book until the same time that George completed his novel.

George Johnston, on the other hand, was forging ahead. In December he wrote to Robert Knittel, the editor at Collins, who was still reluctant to accept *The Far Face of the Moon*, despite all the revision that had been done. The author blithely noted that he was considering withdrawing this earlier work, because he was so confident about his new book:

> I am well into another novel which I know is far far better than anything I have tackled before [...] All I can say to you [is] that the present novel — for the moment entitled *My Brother Jack* — is immeasurably the best thing I have ever done, and it is certainly the novel on which I would be prepared to stake my writing future.
>
> It may be three months or so before it will be ready for you to see [...] As it shapes now this is going to be a *big* novel: it is, moreover, an Australian novel set against a big canvas: it might be controversial but I am sure it will be read.[18]

Although this author had so often engaged in wishful thinking about the great prospects of his work, this time he knew that he was writing a very different type of book. So did his partner. By the Christmas of 1962, Charmian as well as George believed that that mythical beast — the Great Australian Novel — was coming to life in their living room.

It is necessary to understand the level of Charmian Clift's personal investment in the creation of this novel if we are to understand the tension that would later develop over this work, over the characterisation of Cressida Morley, and over the whole matter of the ownership of shared personal experience and the right to use it for fictional purposes. This in turn would cause problems in the relationship between Charmian and George. Finally, the success of this novel would prove to have a serious effect on Clift's own future as a novelist.

As well as making notes for her husband in his work-in-progress journal, Charmian Clift kept a rather spasmodic notebook herself. Into this went drafts of prose, passages copied from books, brief notes on the structure of projected pieces of writing, shopping lists and personal reminders, and passages of writing that hovered on the border between diary jottings and notes towards fiction.

One night during this period Charmian Clift spent a couple of hours writing a rather strange set of notes. While the handwriting suggests that these pages were written over a few glasses of wine, this raw first draft text provides valuable insight into her frame of mind. In this same journal the author had already drafted out the last scene of *Honour's Mimic*. Now she would write a testimony which has occasional fleeting connections with that novel, but which concerns a relationship between a man and a woman who are definitely not the book's two lovers. It would seem that the unnamed protagonists here are, if not quite Charmian and George, then perhaps Clift's version of Cressida and David.

> They had a curiously exhausting effect on each other: neither knew why. They were fond of each other. Some inscrutable bond held them together. But it was a strange vibration of the nerves, rather than of the blood. A nervous attachment rather than a sexual love. A curious tension of will, rather than a sexual passion. Each was curiously under the domination of the other. They were a pair — they had to be together. Yet quite soon they shrank from each other. This attachment of the will and nerves was destructive. As soon as one felt strong, the other felt ill. As soon as the ill one recovered strength, down went the one who had been well. And soon, tacitly, the marriage became more like friendship. Platonic. It was a marriage, but without sex. Sex was shattering and exhausting. They shrank from it, and became like brother and sister. And the lack of physical relation was a secret source of uneasiness and chagrin to them both. They would neither of them accept it [...]
>
> Glancing at her quickly, with searching and anxiety, and a touch of fear, as if his conscience were always uneasy. He quivered with a sort of cold, dangerous mistrust, which he covered with anxious love [...]
>
> There was an aloneness, and a grim little satisfaction in a fight, and the peculiar courage of an inherited despair.
>
> His life was a rattling nullity and her life rattled in null correspondence [...]
>
> His cold, uncanny grey eyes, with their uneasy grey dawn of contempt
>
> She had longed to die, positively.
>
> her hot, confused, pained self
>
> His look was neutral, sombre, hurt.

He felt her aloneness as a sort of shame to himself. He wanted at least the pretence of intimacy. The thought of it filled her with aches, and the pretence of it exhausted her beyond belief [...]

A sort of dense maleness, positive, strong.

This time of dark, palpable joy.

devastating fits of depression which seemed to lay waste to her whole being

He looked — cancelled, annihilated

She had passed into another, denser element of him, an essential privacy

Whitehot with love for him

A mind as rough as a cat's tongue

The clean smell of the sea

It was a fate unique and their own; the capacity to bear it appeared to them the privilege of the chosen.

And like a man bound treacherously while he sleeps, he woke up fettered by the long chain of disregarded years [...]

It was as if they themselves, the selves who recognised each other, were being shouted down

The dim drowning sense of some shapeless disaster.

She had wanted her life shaped then — immediately — a decision — a force[19]

Although the text breaks off here, it is clear that it originally continued.[20] Whether or not this is essentially a diary passage or a fictional draft, it is directly applicable to Charmian Clift's personal situation. Clearly, the relationship between these two is 'exhausting'. And yet this passage is also the most amazing testimony to the strength and complexity of an alliance between two people. Brother and sister, the 'he' and 'she' of this text were bonded on an emotional seesaw: when one was up, the other was down. By referring to it as their 'fate', the writer indicates that she sees it as being out of the hands of the two antagonists to control or improve the situation. Indeed, this serves to highlight the specialness of this couple: this fate was 'unique', the 'privilege of the chosen'. This lack of control over their destiny is repeated twice more: they themselves — their real selves — the selves they used to know and be — are being 'shouted down' by some nameless others. And in the poignant, unfinished ending, the female character longs for something to come from outside and push the plot and characters in a new direction.

If this relationship is a seesaw, so of course is the emotional state of the writer of these notes. Charmian Clift was someone for whom 'dark, palpable joy' and 'devastating fits of depression' could exist side by side.

In January 1963 George Johnston wrote his own account of the marital relationship in a letter to his ex-wife. A few months earlier, Elsie had belatedly answered George's suggestion (made in October 1961) that Gae might visit the family on Hydra; Elsie had opposed the idea, fearing that George was trying to win Gae's affection away from her. Now George wrote back to say that the situation was such that he 'couldn't and wouldn't ask Gae to come here':

> The blunt fact is that I am undergoing a rather serious crisis, and it is rather a toss-up at the moment whether or not I shall be selling the house here and perhaps returning to Australia. Everything now is rather in the lap of the gods and dependent on a book which I am working on now rather desperately (a long and perhaps important book about Australia) but which will probably take me another couple of months to finish.[21]

After summarising his recent financial and health crises, the author went on to admit that 'Queerly, the effect of all this has been to make me write better, I am sure, than I've ever written in my life, and if I can pull off what I'm doing I think it might make everything worthwhile'.

> Anyway, all this, as I say, is in the lap of the gods. The fact is that Charmian and I have been grappling with a domestic and emotional crisis for some little time and although for the sake of the kids we are desperately trying to see it through for a bit longer it is all rather difficult and in a sense (to me, at least) there doesn't seem to be much hope of it being resolved. (Maybe it's just me who can't make these things work out!)

Given that these comments were directed to Elsie, the description of the level of 'domestic and emotional crisis' was perhaps overstated. George tended to appeal for sympathy when writing to his ex-wife. Notwithstanding this, the proposal to sell up and return to Australia was serious. Although in this letter it is presented as a sort of fail-safe mechanism to be activated if the book did *not* work out, it is clear that, from the time he was midway through writing *My Brother Jack*, George Johnston had realised that he must go back.

If homesickness provided part of the reason for writing the book, working on this text intensified to a painful degree the author's sense of longing for his homeland. The knowledge that he was possibly terminally ill increased this: if he were to die, he wanted to do it on his own soil. Furthermore, through the act of writing about Australia and talking to visiting Australians, George Johnston had begun to remember and value aspects of the Australian way of life and attitudes — and to contrast these with the attitudes he disliked, which were expressed by members of Hydra's foreign colony. Describing this emotional turnaround some years later, he told Elizabeth Riddell that he 'began to feel that if salvation was anywhere — though increasingly doubting that salvation existed — it could be found back in the gumtree and kookaburra womb'.[22]

Discussions with Australian tourists also whetted Johnston's interest in the current state of his homeland: it seemed that the country was no longer as parochial and stultifying as the place he'd loathed and left in the early 1950s. In particular, he considered Australia 'the greatest country in the world for young people' and he wanted 'the kids to be in it'.[23] George was particularly keen that the children should have the educational opportunities that he himself had lacked. There was the feeling that 'we were going down the plug-hole [...] and willy-nilly dragging [our] kids along to a future that was quite unpredictable'.[24] Language was a particular issue: Martin would remember that while his parents felt that English language universities 'seemed better' than Athens university, another 'strong inducement' was that Jason should have more opportunities to learn English.[25] Finally, George Johnston's confidence in his current work was also a deciding factor: in the past, he had not wished to go back because he feared that his old colleagues and friends would see him as a failure; now he felt he could return, if not with glory, at least without ignominy.

All these reasons for returning to Australia were growing stronger and stronger in George's mind at the opening of 1963. But the January letter to Elsie gives the impression that George alone was planning to sell the house and return — leaving, it would seem, Charmian and the children in Greece without a roof over their heads. Was this the plan? Had George and Charmian at this time decided on a separation? Certainly it is the case that George tended to think of the house as being *his* property, to sell if he wished, and he probably did sometimes think of escaping alone. But it was always part of his plan to make an escape for the children as well. And anyway, it wasn't only George who was thinking about Australia.

In her National Library interview, Charmian Clift rounded off her account of the years in Greece by foreshadowing her return:

> This sort of life is, as they say, fabulous, it is idyllic, it has so many things to recommend it, and of course for the children it was wonderful beyond belief [...] But eventually one runs out of creative nourishment, I think. We were not taking in so much any more. We'd taken it in. I think we'd given out too much too, we weren't very capable of giving anything out any more. Also, it never came off in the grand manner as one had so fondly dreamed. We were living precariously still, from year to year. With children growing up, all this sort of thing becomes very difficult. Also [there was] their education to be considered. And then finally, costs of living rose and rose because the foreign colony got more and more and more fashionable, more and more people, film stars, all sorts of people, began coming there, and our cheap little island that was ours was ours no longer.
>
> Then we both — and I think this is quite quite strange — began to get homesick [...] We began thinking about Australia, I think first for the children and then because George was writing a book called *My Brother Jack* which made us think about Australia and talk about Australia, and try to remember Australian slang and so on, and through my own children I kept going back to my own childhood and my own beach and the sort of happiness I had then.
>
> Finally — in some trepidation, admittedly — not quite sure, we thought it was time for us to come back again. By this time I'd written four books alone, two travel books and two novels. I didn't feel that staying in Greece I had anything more to write about and I desperately needed to discover or rediscover something. I think George felt the same way, too.[26]

George, of course, had been hankering after Australia for some years,[27] but this account does make it clear that the idea of returning was also independently beginning to occur to Charmian — even if hindsight and a wish to please her audience made her exaggerate her own desire to return. However, while both Charmian and George were starting to think in terms of a return, the subject would not be a matter of open public discussion until much later in the year.[28]

It was around late March 1963 that George Johnston finished writing *My Brother Jack*. He had worked on it for eight hours a day, seven days a week, for six months or so.[29] Not long after this, Charmian and George were visited by a young Australian, Mungo MacCallum (son of their old friends Diana and Mungo MacCallum senior). Hospitable as always, the Johnstons insisted that Mungo stay for a few days before going back to Athens to meet, and marry, his fiancée Susan. By Easter the young couple had established themselves on Hydra, for they had decided to spend summer on the island. They would remain until about September.

Mungo remembers that when he first arrived, the manuscript of *My Brother Jack* had recently been sent to Collins. Although there had been no word yet from the publishers, the couple were already jubilant at the book's prospects.[30]

George Johnston was drained to the bone after completing his arduous task, but he allowed himself no rest.[31] Since starting *My Brother Jack*, he had known that the story he wanted to tell was so large that it would have to be done as a trilogy.[32] Still fearing that time was short, he immediately got cracking on the second book. Mungo remembers that during this summer of 1963 George worked 'all the time', in a regular routine from 8 a.m. to noon every day: 'He was already quite well advanced into the next book [...] He always intended to do a follow-up. He used to quote the epigraph a lot — "Drunk for a penny, dead drunk for tuppence, clean straw for nothing"'.

George Johnston's seriousness about his work — as opposed to the frivolous attitude of the rest of the Hydra foreign colony — made a deep impression on the young Australian who was himself tinkering about with a novel. Always happy to encourage a young writer, George talked to Mungo about his own work. It was at this time that the author revised the short story 'The Verdict', changing the name of Meredith's wife from 'Kate' to 'Cressida' and taking the story through to the doctor's statement of reprieve.[33] Over the next ten months or so, the work on the new novel would take the form of the character notes discussed in chapter 9. The author also produced his first draft of the opening; this consisted of at least thirty pages.[34]

Meanwhile, what was happening to *Honour's Mimic*? As agency records for 1963 are missing, we can only guess at its completion date, but it is clear that this novel, begun in such hope in mid 1959, was also completed and sent off by Easter 1963. Charmian Clift would later describe how difficult it had been to write this book:

> I write very slowly, I always have done, and the last novel I wrote
> [...] took a terribly, terribly long time. This was something to do
> with the fact of running out of creative nourishment because I
> ran into an absolute writing block, and it took me about three
> years, in little jumps, to finish that book.[35]

In fact, the production time for *Honour's Mimic* was closer to four years.
After all this difficulty, Clift should have been ecstatic at its completion.
However, the celebrating was reserved for George's novel. It is symptomatic
of the situation that Mungo MacCallum remembers the 'great delight' when
the readers' reports on *My Brother Jack* arrived and the novel was accepted,
and he remembers any number of conversations about the rosy future of
George's book. Yet he cannot remember hearing even the title of Charmian's
novel being mentioned.

At some time over these months, *Honour's Mimic* was accepted for
publication in the United Kingdom by Hutchinsons, who had previously
published *Walk to the Paradise Gardens* and *Peel Me a Lotus*. The typescript
was also submitted to American publishers, but it was never published
there.[36] As with *Peel Me a Lotus*, the Greece portrayed in this novel was not
the paradise that American readers wanted to read about.

Now that *Honour's Mimic* was done, Clift's next project should have
been *The End of the Morning*, which she had set aside the previous year in
order to help her husband with his novel. But the author was finding it
impossible to get back into her work. Mungo MacCallum recalled that, in
contrast to George Johnston's regular work hours and productivity, 'At
the time, Charmian Clift wasn't writing'. He went on to relate the one
exception: 'I remember once Charmian arrived down at the waterfront
and announced she'd finally started writing again. She said: "I've written
two hundred words — but they're really *lovely* words!" That was the last
we heard'.[37] This anecdote reveals that Charmian Clift wasn't just having a
holiday: something was stopping her from writing, and the fact of not
writing was bothering her. But no sooner did she start than she stopped
again.

If during the writing of *Honour's Mimic* Charmian Clift had experienced
times when the well of her creativity had seemed to dry up, the situation
was to become far worse. The summer of 1963 was the beginning of an
ongoing and ultimately devastating period of block in regard to fiction-
writing that this author would suffer for the rest of her life. The significant

thing is not the summer slackness, but the fact that when the autumn of 1963 came, there was no return to work. Apart from post-novel limbo and domestic uncertainty, something else was affecting the author's ability to get words onto paper.

With hindsight, it is possible to perceive that Charmian Clift's rapidly developing block was connected with George Johnston's writing. Part of the problem was all the fuss going on about *My Brother Jack*. Commenting further on Clift's idleness over this summer, Mungo MacCallum noted:

> I think she felt it was George's hour of glory with *My Brother Jack*. She felt he'd beaten her, outdone her. She was blocked a bit: how could she follow an act like that? I think she felt they'd done lots of things together, and now George had done something that she wasn't part of.

Immediately after making this assessment, Mungo stressed that Charmian was 'very generous in her praise of *My Brother Jack*'. He recalled an incident in which 'One day people were talking about writing and someone said something about "We're all still waiting for the Great Australian Novel". And Charmian said, "No, we're not — George has written it!" '

However, while the force of the limelight on George had the effect of casting his wife into the shadows, the real issue was not what George had done in the first book of the trilogy, but what he proposed to do in the second. The material upon which George Johnston had been working since finishing *My Brother Jack* was in itself enough to make Charmian Clift baulk at her own work. The extant notes for *Clean Straw for Nothing* written at this time[38] begin with a page in which the author searches for the 'beginning point' to the breakdown of the relationship between his alter ego David Meredith and his wife. This was the same old question which Johnston had been worrying at for a long time, but now a significant level of blame was laid on the female character. From the assertion that 'It was near enough to the truth to say that she had destroyed him sexually and destroyed him physically', the tone is set for the portrayal of Cressida that would appear six years later in the published novel, in which Cressida's infidelity causes Meredith's fatal illness. The repeated use of the verb 'to destroy' is strong stuff. Yet perhaps the most problematic aspect of this short passage is the phrase 'near enough to the truth'. It was this kind of appeal to veracity that would blur the boundaries between the fictional and real personae of Cressida and her model. Taking the narrator's truth to be the truth of the author, many readers take the completed work as memoir, despite the author's standard disclaimer at the front of the text.

From here, Johnston went on to observe that in regard to Meredith's wife, 'it had been simple to settle for the lay diagnosis of schizophrenia, because there had always been this split personality thing in her right from the beginning'. But now, as the notes move into five densely typed pages of 'Particular Notes on Cressida', the author deduces that in fact there were not two but 'three Cressidas' housed within the one woman.

Certainly, these notes were not for publication. However, there is no way that Clift could not have known the material upon which her husband was working: these pages were not produced in a secret sanctuary, but either at the living room table or in the joint studio. If the boundary between the real Charmian Clift and her fictional counterpart had been breached in the portrayal of Kate Meredith in Johnston's novel *Closer to the Sun*, from the time of these notes the situation became even more complicated.

The issue was not simply the fact that the character of Cressida represented such a direct lifting of certain parts of the model. Nor was it just that this was an unflattering portrait. After all, Clift had coped with Johnston's portrayal of the predatory female author Christine Lambert in *The Cyprian Woman*. The problem that was arising now was that Charmian Clift regarded Cressida Morley as being her own alter ego character. And if Johnston was developing Cressida — how could Clift? It was as if there were two sculptors chipping a figure out of the one block of stone, but one sculptor worked much faster than the other, so that his side of the shape was developing while the other side was still inchoate. At the same time, the slow sculptor happened to be the model for the figure, and so felt particularly frustrated at the way in which the other part of the work was shaping up. Little wonder if the slow sculptor couldn't work. And little wonder if the model felt distressed by this distorted image that she could see coming to life before her eyes.

As the summer of 1963 turned to autumn, the Johnstons' plans were becoming increasingly uncertain, while they continued to discuss whether or not to return to their homeland. It was like the situation towards the end of the Charity Farm sojourn: once again Charmian and George were making two or three different decisions every few weeks. Certainly, there were a lot of complicating factors to be weighed up if two adults and three children and a mountain of possessions were to move from one hemisphere to another.

And besides, at least one of the children didn't want to go. Shane had few memories of her birthplace and was dead set against the idea of leaving the island that was her home and the home of all her friends. In particular, she was in love with a young Hydriot man and — with all the passion of a fourteen year old having her first love affair — she felt that she could not bear to be parted from him. Apart from that, moving to Australia meant leaving her language and her culture. The terrible memories of going to school in England didn't help.

To Jason, the whole idea was at first quite unimaginable, but soon he started to feel 'a great curiosity' as his parents made 'a bit of a conscious effort' to engage his interest. Around this time, they began giving him Dr Seuss books and encouraging him to write on the English typewriter as well as the Greek one, and then George started giving his younger son maps and '*facts* about the new country'.

> I remember a distinct impression that everything about Australia seemed so weird. They had money that wasn't decimal. They had weights and measures that I was going to have to start to learn — about inches and fathoms and rods and poles and perches. They had this weird thing called constitutional monarchy, which I didn't understand. You know, I was given this sort of encyclopaedic approach: 'This is your new land, that you're going to go to. And [so you have to] learn all about it!'
>
> And everything I learned about it just sounded fascinating and weird and kind of wrong.[39]

If Shane was opposed to the move and Jason was confused, Martin was fairly happy to return to the country which he could still remember. He had actually retained a sense of being Australian, which was evident, for example, in the way he linked his feeling for the Greek *klephts*, or brigands, and their ballads with Australian bushrangers and Australian bush ballads, which he knew intimately from the Stewart/Keesing edition of *Australian Bush Ballads*.[40] Of course, Martin's view of Australia was as weird in its way as that of his seven year old brother. Although intellectually he knew that it was an urban, coastal and technologically advanced society, Martin envisaged Australia as a wide brown land full of bullockies and brumbies and country town shoot-outs of the kind familiar from the old Westerns that frequently showed at Hydra's open-air picture cinema.

Anyway, to the children it often seemed not worth thinking about Australia, because the plan would change again. For the parents, yet another major stumbling block to the emigration was the perennial problem of lack of money. In the latter half of 1963 there was not enough to cover airfares to Australia, let alone the cost of setting up a household there. The only possible way to get the money was to sell the Hydra house — but then where would the family live while they waited to go to Australia? And what if Australia was awful? Perhaps the solution would be to send George on alone to assess the situation and establish a base. There is no record of Charmian's switches of plan over this period, but George's correspondence provides an outline of some of the variations which were considered, even if these letters are coloured by his mood swings.

In September 1963 Johnston wrote, after some years of silence, to George Ferguson at Angus & Robertson, to ask the publisher to help 'push' *My Brother Jack* — which Collins were intending to distribute into Australia in January 1964. He added: 'I don't yet know how plans will work out, but Charm and I are trying to get back to Australia on a visit early next year'.[41] Presumably at this time the idea was that they would have a look at the place together, and if they liked what they saw, one or both would return to Greece to collect the family and handle the house sale.

The next month, George's first wife wrote to tell him that their daughter Gae was to be married in December. In early November George wrote back to say that he would be coming to Australia for the mid January release of his novel, but he would not be able to get there in time for the wedding. In this letter, as in the one written at the beginning of this year, he implied that he alone would be returning to Australia, leaving Charmian and the children on Hydra. He concluded:

> You gather from this I am not particularly happy. I don't at all want you to think I am making suggestions, but perhaps it would interest you to know that I now often find myself thinking how nice it would be just to go back to you.[42]

Elsie must have felt triumphant at this comeuppance for Charmian. After twenty years, she had not remarried, and she lived in the same flat where George had stayed during his wartime leave; indeed, her life was still that of the war bride, waiting for her husband to come home. If Johnston was Odysseus, Elsie was Penelope. Around this time she started to send George socks, with letters worrying about whether he was keeping warm through the winter. Predictably, this infuriated Charmian, who was heard to declare: 'Elsie is waiting for George to come back! That woman thinks that this is just a temporary aberration in life, and it'll all go back to normal'.[43]

However, the impression George gave Elsie was not necessarily the truth. It was at the same time as this November letter to his ex-wife that the author wrote to an old journalist colleague, John Ulm, who was now the Chief Press and Information Officer for Qantas, employed at the company's Sydney office. The gist of Johnston's initial letter was to ask Ulm if he could arrange a free ticket to Australia for the launch of *My Brother Jack*, in return for which the author would give Qantas a 'quid pro quo' by way of mentioning the company during press and television interviews. When Ulm replied that the company would need something more concrete by way of a contra deal, Johnston immediately wrote back offering to 'bind [himself] to a firm contract concerning publicity in a book'. While this makes it clear just how desperate George Johnston was for an airfare, he was not after a single escape route. He rounded off his request by saying that it seemed to him only a slim chance that Qantas would be interested in his offer, 'So can I be barefaced and suggest that if anything can be done, can a return-trip be kept in mind, since I will probably have to get back here?'[44]

Obviously at this stage the idea was that George would go to Australia in order to help the sales push for *Jack*, and then return to Greece to help Charmian sell the house and bring the family back. A couple of weeks later, a new variation on the plan was developed when Collins suddenly decided to change the Australian publication date for the novel from January to early March 1964, in order to tie in the book's promotion with the Adelaide Festival, to be held at that time. As part of the promotional plans, the publishers arranged for Johnston to be invited to speak at the Festival. At this stage, Qantas agreed to pay the airfare, but only one way.[45] On 12 December, George — who was clearly writing with a view to Elsie's reading the letter — told his daughter Gae:

> You may be interested to know that we shall *all* be returning to Australia next year [...] I'll go out around the end of February and will stay on out there, and the three kids will follow out with their mother about June. Homesickness has become too much for us, and we have decided that this side of the world no longer offers what Australia might. And I think the kids are now very eager to

finish their schooling in their own country and try the Australian way of life as a change from all these years of living in Europe.[46]

This made everything sound a little more definite and less complicated than it really was. Certainly, Shane was still totally resistant to the move. And although Martin was keen to go, he would remember that the idea was that his father would go back for the Adelaide Festival 'but he would also act as a sort of scouting force for the rest of the family and report on what he saw in Australia, and if it seemed good, all the rest of us would come back'.[47] If it didn't seem good — then George would return, and the family would stay on Hydra.

George, however, had already made up his mind, and the main parts of the plan as outlined in the letter to Gae were followed. George would return by plane in February, and Charmian would stay to settle up matters in Greece and bring the family out later in the year. In effect, this meant a quick escape for George, while Charmian faced a tedious process which would take the better part of a year. It was she who would have full responsibility for the children during this time, as well as responsibility for the house, the packing, the whole enormous upheaval. The big decision may have been made, but Charmian also faced a hundred small decisions about the matter every day. And besides — Charmian was still torn between going and staying.

Although she may have felt that the creative nourishment of Greece had dried up, she was still in love with the place. And the Hydra house was the home she had made, so carefully, so beautifully. Now she had the heartbreaking task of un-making it.[48]

In the New Year of 1964 Charmian and George acquired two new young Australian protégés. It was in early January that Rodney Hall happened to rent a cottage on Hydra with his wife Bet and five month old daughter. Of a different generation to the Johnstons, the Halls had never heard of the writers Charmian Clift and George Johnston, and certainly did not know that the couple lived on the island. They soon found out:

> We encountered them one morning in the bar at the back of Katsikas's. Charmian and our baby fell in love on the spot. We were invited to the Johnstons' house for a party [...]
>
> The guests at the party were all expatriates from one country or another — mainly the United States — and were all determined, in their isolation, to be seen to be having a good

time. As the evening gathered momentum, people got dressed up and played charades and then sat round the semicircular fireplace exchanging cosmopolitan opinions. This was pretty heady stuff, until George put on a record — Haydn's trumpet concerto — on their crazy little portable player. The music came out sounding so reedy it made me laugh. I said that, anyway, the work was brinkmanship between cheerfulness and vulgarity. All hell broke loose. George took such offence at this and at 'the type of Australian' (his description) that it showed me to be. To our astonishment he ordered us out of the house. Charmian, ever loyal when George took a stand, rushed to support him. The expulsion was, characteristically, thoroughly public. So out we went into the night, disgraced, the pram bouncing along Hydra's cobbled streets, with our beautiful baby still asleep despite the hubbub, to our cold cottage. It was mid-winter at the time.

Next morning, after we had discussed the drama and decided the misunderstanding was crazy because we had liked them both enormously, we agreed that we must do something about it. So I set to work typing up a fair copy of the seven poems I had written since our arrival on Hydra, and attached a cover sheet dedicating them to George and Charmian.

Ceremonially, we walked round to their place to present the poems. They were out. The best we could do was leave the folder there and return home. Then, about an hour later, we heard penetrating and musical cries hallooing in the street outside. Curious cries that floated nearer and then farther away and nearer again. More curious still, the syllables resolved themselves quite clearly into our own names. We opened the outer gate of the courtyard and called back. A moment later, Charmian, who had only the vaguest idea of where we were living, appeared round a corner bearing a basket filled with fruit, cheeses and flowers. She had been wandering the labyrinth with her gifts (images of ancient Greece were always tangible when you were with Charmian).[49]

Charmian insisted that they come straight back over to her place. There was another dinner, and 'That began it all', Rodney declared. 'We sort of fell in love with them — we just loved and loved them'.[50] Although Rodney and Bet Hall only knew Charmian and George on Hydra for a couple of months, their testimony is particularly interesting because they both speak of the strength of the Johnston relationship, and the very great areas on which the two agreed. As the time drew near for George's departure, Charmian invited Bet and Rodney Hall and their baby to move into the large studio, saying: 'Come and live for as long as you like — you'll be good company'. Rodney remembers that 'Life in Charmian's house was filled with these dreadful arguments, jubilant reconciliations, and erratic mealtimes'.[51] Despite the volatility of the situation, Bet Hall was impressed by the warmth and courtesy that existed between their hosts.[52]

This was, of course, a particularly trying time. Discussions about returning to Australia were still going on, and George and Charmian frequently asked their young guests 'for news of how things had changed in the years of their absence and whether or not the wounds of the Cold War fanaticism had healed'. To Rodney it was clear that the couple still 'felt very wounded and injured about Australia, and very alienated'.

Meanwhile, George was being pressed to set his departure date. In mid January *My Brother Jack* was published in the United Kingdom. The critical reception was so favourable that Collins decided to increase the copies being shipped to Australia to 8000.[53] Ken Wilder, the manager of the Australian branch of the company, sent the author a cable reading 'PUBLISHING IN AUSTRALIA 5 MARCH STOP IN PROCESS ARRANGING YOUR STAR BILLING WITH ALAN MOOREHEAD PATRICK WHITE NOLAN ADELAIDE FESTIVAL [...] VERY DESIRABLE YOU ARRIVE SYDNEY LATE [...] FEBRUARY'.[54]

Johnston had already written to Billy Collins announcing that the whole family was moving permanently to Australia, and towards the end of January he also wrote to David Higham, telling the agent the travel plans for the first time. These were essentially the same as those which he had outlined to Gae in early December, but now there were specific dates: 'We are leaving Greece and returning to Australia to live. I shall be flying out about the 24th of February and Charmian will follow with the children around June or July, probably by sea'.[55] Charmian was still privately havering about this decision, but there can be no doubt as to her public compliance in the plan. This letter, although written by George Johnston alone, was very much a joint business letter. A couple of weeks later, George wrote to his first wife announcing: 'We're selling up here and returning to Australia permanently'.[56]

The couple had already started testing the real estate market by advertising the house in classy magazines in the United Kingdom; they had absolutely no idea what sort of price it would fetch. And they had also begun the process of applying to the Australian Embassy for immigration to Australia for Charmian and the children: the only way they could afford to get back was to become migrants under the scheme of assistance which provided passages for ten pounds.

Although George was desperately keen to leave Greece, he was anxious about the journey. The years of respiratory problems combined with heavy smoking caused him to suffer emphysema so badly that by now he could sometimes barely walk uphill; he was well aware that such a long trip in a pressurised aircraft could be dangerous for someone with his breathing difficulties. Bet Hall remembered that 'he was quite alarmed by the notion' of flying; 'he knew it was a big risk'.[57]

It was therefore a highly charged scene when Charmian farewelled her husband at Athens airport on 22 February. Was this perhaps the last time she would ever see him? No, George was a survivor; surely he would get through this, as he'd got through his other crises. Perhaps it even seemed as if he was making an easy escape, while Charmian was left to bear all the problems of the move. Altogether, it was a difficult day to get through — and no sooner had George gone than a strange coincidence occurred...

Rodney Hall, who had accompanied the couple to Athens, had arranged to meet Charmian after George had flown out, so that they could catch the boat back to Hydra together. Rodney arrived early for this meeting, which was at 'quite a smart coffee shop'. Soon after Charmian joined him, he became aware that a man across the room was staring at him with 'an intense, extraordinary look'. He remembered: 'It was amazing! A total stranger! I thought: "God! What's that?" It was unmistakeable — it couldn't have been aimed at anyone else but me'. After a little while, the stranger came and presented himself at the table where Rodney and Charmian were sitting.

> And Charmian went absolutely white. She was just sitting there and she went white, and she was speechless.
> And then she took his hand and I realised that she knew him! It was a great relief to *me*, to find there was a rational reason for all this. And Charmian said to me, 'Can you excuse me for a moment?' So I got up and went out in the street for five minutes because she obviously had something she needed to say [to this person].

I came back, and he'd gone. She was sitting there and I sat down with her and we just took up chatting — I thought she looked a bit shaken.

Later, as Rodney accompanied Charmian home to Hydra on the boat, he was aware that 'She was obviously very upset'. The next day, the man whom Rodney had found so strange at the Athens cafe turned up at the house. It was Jean-Claude Maurice. Although Charmian had invited him to visit, this was not a resurrection of the old affair. He stayed a day or so with her, then left and found accommodation elsewhere on the island.[58]

George Johnston, meanwhile, was having a 'triumphal return' to Australia (he told David Higham), with 'highly favourable publicity' on television, radio, and in the print media.[59] This publicity machine had been set in motion by Johnston himself, and continued to be driven by the author. As it would also affect the public reaction to Charmian Clift's homecoming, it must be mentioned here.

Joan Flanagan — then a young secretary in the publicity department of the Sydney office of Collins — remembered the unique nature of the *My Brother Jack* campaign. She explained that Collins was 'a very hospitable publishing company'. In addition to this, she noted:

We were just at the end of the colonial thing. When a writer arrived in the country you could get a lot of press.

And George was so smart. Before he left the island he'd sent out complete articles that he had written — professional articles, ready to go into print — so stories could be placed ahead. They were what you would call 'colour pieces' on life in Hydra. We collected them into a press kit, which Collins didn't have at the time. We placed it everywhere [...] And he sent photographs of himself and Charmian and the family — photographs on the island and of the island. It was contrived, but ...

And George sent all the contacts. That was the other thing he sent. Every single person who might be able to help, from the old days. We had the English reviews [...] And of course the book was sent to the right people.

The *My Brother Jack* publicity was amazing, really. George was always laconic and gentle, but quite a man for knowing what he wanted, and he'd get it.[60]

This campaign would mark a new stage in the development of the Johnston myth. In particular, the photographs would create an extraordinary picture of the couple's life on Hydra. Joan also recalled:

> They came in with such a gust of — well, publicity, but also of expectation. Everybody was waiting for these people who had lived this storied life. We thought these were people who had led an idyllic life on an island, and produced all this work and — you know, you can tell the story any way you like.

If part of the legend was provided by pictures of the Greek isles with Charmian as a sort of gypsy queen, another part of the legend was the image of George as the suffering artist, whose commitment to the dream had imperilled his life. This was dramatised on his first day back in the country when, after a heavy schedule of interviews followed by a big party at the Collins office, George lost his voice shortly before he was due to appear on a late night television variety show. Luckily his old mate Sid Nolan — in Australia for the Adelaide Festival — was present at the welcome party, and came to the rescue. Viewers that night were regaled with the image of the host interviewing a ventriloquist act, with Johnston sitting wheezing and Nolan speaking for him.

Nolan, of course, was a skilled showman, and he had told George some of the tricks whereby an expatriate could win the affection of the Australian public. However, George also brought to this publicity campaign his own knowledge of the way the media works. For some, he overdid it. Twenty years later, one journalist would refer to this promotion as 'too much George Johnston all at once'; another writer would refer to the 'carefully engineered hero's welcome'.[61] This kind of reaction would eventually cause certain journalists to attempt to lop off the heads of the Johnston tall poppies. But for the moment, the media were happy to run with the story of the exile who returned to praise everything he saw.

After the tumultuous reception in Sydney, George moved on to Melbourne, where he visited Elsie and his family as well as doing a new round of interviews that played up the angle of the Return of the Home Town Boy. He then moved on to Adelaide, and the Festival.

As George travelled he sent ecstatic messages back to Charmian and the children in what Martin would describe as 'absolutely dithyrambic letters, paeans in praise of such aspects of Australian life as motels'.[62] One such epistle, which Johnston also sent for publication to the *Age Literary*

Supplement, gives an indication of the sorts of things he thought would impress the family. Overall, his main emphasis was on the 'Continental' influence on Australia, as well as 'a real metamorphosis in attitude' on the part of Australians towards 'Continentals'. In particular, he singled out the Greek influence 'like signs printed in Greek along the streets and in the shops, and real bouzouki music drifting up from cellar cafes […] and all those popular Athens pulp magazines […] on sale in the newsagents [and] soccer teams called […] Hellas and Olympiakos'. While admitting that 'some solid hypocrisies linger yet from the old days of hard-core wowserism', he was at pains to stress that 'after the tired, cynical, disillusioned Old World' Australia was 'a nation walking onwards, briskly, […] and with head well up'. After further praise of Australia's affluence, architecture and lack of class divisions, the writer concluded: 'Of one thing I'm absolutely certain. The children will adore it here. And it's the right place for them. I can't wait for their arrival'.[63]

Such an appeal was carefully geared to cover every angle, from Shane and Jason's fondness for Greek pop music to Martin's support for his favourite soccer team and to Charmian's political concerns about her homeland. However, as far as Charmian was concerned, the praise fell on deaf ears. According to Rodney Hall, she didn't want to hear how wonderful everything was back in Australia.

> She didn't expect [George] to stay when he came back here. That was the simple fact […]
>
> While we were there, and George was sending these ecstatic messages back saying what a wonderful time he was having, she was very delighted for him but she was very resistant to the notion — quite verbally resistant — saying 'As long as he doesn't want us to move back home!' What her reasons for that were I don't know, but she just loved the life in Greece.[64]

To Bet Hall, it seemed that Charmian's feelings about returning to Australia were 'mixed': 'I think at times she was absolutely joyous about it, and couldn't find out enough about Australia'. On the other hand, there was the old Cold War anxiety, and — extraordinary though it may seem — Charmian still tormented herself with the fear that people blamed her for running off with George. In particular, she still worried about the way George's family regarded her. On top of this, Charmian was anxious about going back and beginning all over again, at the bottom of the ladder. Yet overall, Bet felt that Charmian was reassured by George's messages.

On any day, Charmian's feelings swayed back and forth between staying and leaving. One of the main factors pushing Charmian towards going was tremendous worry about Shane. Her boyfriend was soon due to leave the island in order to do his National Service, and Shane was talking of becoming engaged to him. Bet recalls:

> Charmian got the wind up because she decided that she couldn't see Shane turn into one of those black-clothed wives confined to the house and ruled in that terrible chauvinist society [...]
>
> Shane was a big factor, I think, in Charmian's own return here. One of the really big things Charmian wanted to do was give Shane the experience of what Australian society was like [...] A big part of Charmian's reason for returning was that as a mother she wanted to disentangle Shane from what she saw as a fatal decision.[65]

Shane naturally didn't see the situation this way, and threatened that if the family left, she wouldn't accompany them. It must be remembered that at this time, Shane was just turning fifteen. This was the age at which Charmian had defied her own mother by dropping out of school instead of going on to become a schoolteacher. For Charmian, who had lost the chance of furthering her education and who had suffered so much pain through the circumstance of her first pregnancy, it was devastating to watch her daughter wanting to throw away her chances in an even more irremediable fashion.

If the matter of leaving Greece or staying was terribly difficult for Charmian, it also seemed to the Halls that all the fuss over the publication of *My Brother Jack* meant that 'some new complexity was happening in that always complex relationship' between Charmian and George. In his introduction to *The World of Charmian Clift*, Rodney Hall stresses Clift's input into that novel, then adds:

> But now the novel was about to be launched, her manner was touched with loss. It had become George's book entirely. She was a combative personality — as he was, too — and I think she sensed already that *My Brother Jack* had put him beyond her reach, beyond competition. Up till then she could claim (as George often claimed for her) that she was actually the better writer. But now it was as if she felt he had been lifted to another level by the breadth and integrity of this novel.
>
> Charmian's losses began, from that point, to accumulate.[66]

Rodney remembered how his attention was drawn to Charmian's sense of loss by her good friends Chuck and Gordon, who had known the Johnstons for many years.

> I remember Gordon saying to us when Charmian wasn't there, about her situation, 'Well, it's very tough for her. As a *writer*, she's been in rivalry with George all these years, and she's always held her end up and she's always had some comeback. She's had her own books, and his have never really done anything that hers haven't done. But now, he's suddenly in a different league altogether. And she's bereft, as it were, professionally as well as personally.'
>
> And that's stayed with me. Obviously I wouldn't have remembered it if I didn't at the time think there was a lot of truth in this — that *My Brother Jack* in fact delivered a blow to Charmian and Charmian's own sort of status in that partnership.[67]

Expanding on this memory, Rodney Hall pointed out that it wasn't just the fact that a book of George Johnston's was doing far better than anything that Charmian Clift had written, but that it was this particular book — on which she had worked behind the scenes.

> She [had been] working for him — with him — on something which, in the printed sense, she got no credit for. George used to in person be very fulsome about her part in *My Brother Jack*, saying he couldn't have done it as he did it without her. But of course that doesn't show up in the book. I mean, there's no acknowledgement at the beginning of the book [...]
>
> Yes, she had been a partner in that book in a way that they'd never done before. They'd been partners in writing before, but this was a subordinate role. So already in the course of this book — partly because of his illness — she adopted a subordinate role. She was supporting him in order for him to get something important done before he died.
>
> And I think also another very important factor for her was that there was a big gap between her and his family, and that she'd had to imaginatively live in the life of that family and give that family credence and give that family status — which she'd

willingly done — but I think that actually cost her as a person a great deal [...] I got the impression she'd not liked or been comfortable with the family. She had felt that they'd seriously disapproved of her, and had also thought that she was snobbish into the bargain [...] And one of the things that had cost her was that she'd had to undergo the kind of humility of helping make a family member a hero of a book that would last — as she once said to me — a hundred years.

And I think that cost much more than one could see on the surface. That was a surrender of something important to her — because George had always felt under pressures from his [first] wife and from his family — pressures that she was very sensitive to.

This analysis of Rodney Hall's perceptively touches on so many of the things that would preoccupy Charmian Clift over the rest of her life. The problem was not just that George's novel had taken off while her own work floundered, but that she was not receiving due credit for her part in that collaboration. Even more important is this issue of being in a subordinate role; this brought back the old pain of playing second fiddle in her own family.

The assessments of Clift's reaction to *My Brother Jack*, given by both Rodney Hall and Mungo MacCallum, bring to mind the description of the couple in Clift's notebook: the seesaw nature of the relationship which meant that 'as soon as one felt strong, the other felt ill'. Despite his frail body, there can be no doubt about the strength of George Johnston during this post-*Jack* period. If George was up, the concomitant effect was for Charmian to be down. Although she seemed her confident and outgoing self, the down side was expressed in her most private area — her work. From this time, her assurance in her own novel would seem to dwindle.

Although Charmian was still privately dithering about the move, she began the process of applying to her own country for immigrant status. This brought its own misery when Charmian and the children went to Athens for the medical examination which was required by the Australian government. Forced to wait naked in a room with other female applicants, Charmian was 'absolutely appalled' at the indignity inflicted upon shy village women. Martin also found the procedure 'very humiliating'.[68] Overall, the immigration process did little to reassure Charmian about life in Australia.

Not long after this, the Halls left Hydra to continue their travels. It was really only now that Charmian had to face George's absence. For anyone accustomed to the normal separations of marriage — the daily nine or ten hours in which the spouses work in different places; the weekend times when each partner pursues separate interests or sees different groups of friends or family; the business trips and even holidays spent apart — it would be very difficult to comprehend the effect of the separation of Charmian and George. Day after day, they worked in the same place, and when work was finished, they socialised together. They had no separate circles of friends or family. They had no individual interests, hobbies, sports or pastimes. And since coming to Greece, the only time they had been apart was the six weeks of George's medical treatment in 1959.

Argue though they might, they were as bonded as a pair of Siamese twins. And now that bond was cut. George in Australia was missing Charmian and the children, but there was a great deal of hubbub around him and his book; and besides, he was in a new place, and was doing unaccustomed things, meeting new people. For Charmian, still in the family home with the children, trying to follow familiar routines, the separation was far more noticeable.

Suddenly there was no one to talk to — or no one immediately at hand. At any time this would have been difficult, but it was particularly hard under current circumstances, in which Charmian was expected to organise the family's move and deal with all the uncertainties which this move involved. Perhaps the most stressful part was suddenly to be forced into the role of single mother of three children — particularly given the relationship between Shane and Martin, and Charmian's own arguments with Shane over the whole matter of the move to Australia. Zoe was another complicating factor: the departure of 'her' family would cause enormous changes to her life, to her finances, and to her status, and she was understandably reluctant to lose Jason. At times Charmian had to exercise all her tact to try to ease Zoe's resentment.[69]

As Charmian struggled alone with this complex situation, she was constantly receiving letters from George detailing his successes and travels, and telling her about the interesting people he was meeting. After taking part in the Adelaide Festival, he made trips to the Kimberleys and Cape York and Darwin. He also went back to Melbourne, again visiting his family and his first wife, with whom he now began corresponding in an increasingly intimate fashion — even writing to her on the occasion of their wedding

anniversary, congratulating himself on remembering the date.[70] From late
April to June he stayed in luxurious circumstances on the grazing property of
Matt and Sheila Carroll at Coolah, on the western plains of New South Wales.
Here his health underwent a remarkable improvement, for he had 'absolutely
nothing to do except ride a bit and shoot a bit and write a lot and go to bed
early and get up early', he wrote to Elsie.[71] Although Charmian would not
have known the details of George's correspondence with his first wife, she
would have assumed that in his Melbourne visits her husband saw the
woman who — as far as Charmian was concerned — was still trying to get
George back. But beyond any specific jealousy, George's accounts of the new
friends he was making would have raised Charmian's customary anxiety
about the way in which George's charm won people over to his 'side'; by the
time she arrived, everyone worth knowing would already be George's friend,
and there would be nobody left for her.

All this must be taken into account in order to understand an attachment
that Charmian now formed. It would seem that, on the day in Athens when
Charmian had coincidentally met Jean-Claude in the smart cafe, the
Frenchman had introduced her to a companion, an Englishman named
Anthony Kingsmill. There can only have been time for them to have
exchanged a few words, but Kingsmill would later remember that he arranged
to meet Charmian again at a cafe a few days later. When this second meeting
occurred isn't clear. Perhaps it was when Charmian went up to Athens for the
medical examination. According to Kingsmill, Charmian invited him to come
to Hydra, and after a week or so he did. She met him at the port, and took him
back to stay in the house.[72] There must, in fact, have been a bit of a time lag, for
by the time the Englishman arrived, the Halls had continued on their travels.
Anthony Kingmill would remain with Charmian until she left the island.

The picture of Anthony Kingsmill given in the biography of Leonard
Cohen — with whom he was to become very friendly — shows the source
of his attraction to Charmian, for he is described as a 'painter, drinker and
gifted conversationalist':

> The adopted son of the English writer Hugh Kingsmill, Anthony
> was plagued by the unknown origin of his biological father [...]
> Kingsmill ended up on Hydra after going to art school in
> London and spending some time in Paris. Dapper and short,
> with soulful grey eyes, he would frequently quote long passages
> from Tennyson, Wordsworth and Shakespeare [...] To the colony

of romantically damaged men on the island, he announced that all sex was metaphysical.[73]

What with the art school background, the problematic father, the habit of poetry-quoting and the particular predilection for the Metaphysical poets, Anthony Kingsmill was like a made-to-order Clift hero. There was also an appealing larrikin element, manifest in Kingsmill's wild drinking bouts, and Cohen described how his friend would endearingly 'break out into a little softshoe shuffle whenever he was elated or drunk'. After living so long with someone who could barely walk, it was a relief for Charmian to have a companion who could match her own energy. Furthermore, he was an adult to whom she could talk, at a time when she found herself being reduced to the level of squabbling with the children or walking on eggshells around Zoe. And in fact the domestic situation did become easier, as Martin — who was furious about Kingsmill's arrival in the house — went to spend some time with friends in Beirut. Shane, on the other hand, hoped that perhaps her mother might now stay in Greece with Anthony, and then Shane herself wouldn't have to leave.[74]

Perhaps Charmian was thinking a little along the same lines as Shane: if she fell in love with someone, then that would be a reason to stay in Greece. Certainly, Anthony was begging her to stay on Hydra with him. Unfortunately, she couldn't manage to reciprocate his feelings. He was a fun companion and an attractive escort, but as a man who 'survived largely on charm and commissions of never-to-be-completed work',[75] he could not equal George. Anyway, George was her husband. There could be no one else in the long term.[76]

To add to Charmian's difficulties over this summer of 1964, she was finding it hard to support the family and settle up the final bills.[77] Although *Honour's Mimic* had been published in Britain and Australia in late March, this did not bring money for the author. The novel received very favourable reviews in both countries, and by August sales would reach 2000, but Clift's mid-year royalties amounted to only £56.[78] With the house still on the market, it was clear by now that it was not going to be easy to sell. To make matters worse, Charmian managed at this time to set the kitchen on fire. There was no serious damage, but a lot of soot and smoke had to be cleaned and the whole area had to be whitewashed.[79]

Packing was a heartrending task. So many of the treasures so lovingly collected over a decade had to be given away, as well as boxes and boxes of books. Some things, however, just could not be discarded; among the cargo was the elaborate birdcage, the ship-maker's model of a fat-bellied caique, the 2000 year old amphora and also, of course, the paintings by artist friends, including the Nolan sketch of Icarus and the Minotaur, given as a housewarming gift so very long ago.

Even more heartbreaking than the packing were the farewells, to places as well as to people. And throughout this whole time there was such ongoing rigmarole associated with the migration process that it was hard to feel that Australia actually wanted the family.

> By the time a migrant — and I am including myself and my Australian-born children in the term — actually boards the ship that is to carry him to his brave new world the audacious bite of decision has long since been blunted, if not altogether gummed up, on the toffee apple of bureaucracy. The freshness of adventure has worn off and uncertainty, alas, is practically all that remains.
>
> There were times when it was necessary to support each other in sadly faltering convictions.[80]

At last, at the end of July, the family was ready to leave, 'but still tied emotionally to what we had abandoned'. After the last goodbyes on Hydra they caught the ferry to Athens, then boarded the *Ellenis*, together with a thousand other souls, 'including families of English migrants, Greek proxy brides, be-shawled and bemused grandmothers shrouded in shapeless black and already wailing ritually, and young Greek labourers with the sturdiness and aggressiveness of Cretan bulls'.[81]

For both Charmian and George, Cavafy's poem 'Ithaca' had a very special significance, and both were fond of quoting key lines from it.

> Always keep Ithaca fixed in your mind.
> To arrive there is your ultimate goal.
> But do not hurry the voyage at all.

It was George, of course, not Charmian, who liked to identify with Odysseus the wanderer, who spent so many years returning from the Trojan War. Yet it was Charmian who made the slow and arduous journey by sea back to Australia. And it was Charmian who returned, like Odysseus, to find herself a stranger in her own land.

PART IV

RETURN TO ITHACA

19

An Odd Sort of Migrant

All migrants, I think, are optimistic, or, anyway, hoping like blazes
that they've really done the right thing. And we were odd sorts of
migrants, in that we were migrating to home, which from [thirteen] years
and half a world away could be distorted by the curve of the earth,
memory, and couriers' reports, into Utopia or Hicksville.[1]

In the story of Rip Van Winkle, a man falls asleep during a solitary ramble
in a remote mountain area. Waking after twenty years, he returns to his
home town to find that the world has completely changed. In illustrated
adaptations, contrast is drawn between a handsome young hero setting off
and a long-bearded ancient returning, but the main interest of the original
story is not in the physical changes that the townsfolk see in Rip Van
Winkle, but in the changes — particularly technological changes — that the
hero observes in the town.

Charmian Clift, returning to Sydney after so many years — most of
which had been spent in a remote and technologically primitive place —
was a kind of latter-day Rip Van Winkle. In the various public tellings of
the story of her return, however, the emphasis seems to be not on what
Rip Van Winkle saw of the town, but on what the townsfolk saw of Rip
Van Winkle.

It is hard not to be surprised at the cruelty of the descriptions which have
been given of Charmian Clift on her return. Here, for example, is Johnston's
biographer describing the 'shock among the friends and family at what they
saw':

Friends such as Toni Burgess and Cedric Flower could hardly believe the change in her. It was not simply that she was older, but that she seemed to be a different woman. The beautiful, confident, stylish Clift who had gone abroad with such hubris thirteen years earlier had vanished and been supplanted by a flaccid, overweight, terrified matron with scraggy hair and no stockings. The huge, white smiling teeth were now brown and rotting. Moreover, as was soon to become apparent to all, she had returned with a drinking problem. Cedric Flower recalls her fingering her hair over her face in a defensive, nervous measure, and looking as though she wanted to become invisible.[2]

Kinnane goes on to describe the welcome home party that George had arranged for the night of Charmian's arrival. Here, in the house that George had leased, were gathered 'all the old friends' from the Saturday party nights at Bondi: 'Arthur and Monica Polkinghorne, many other journalists, the Flowers, the Nolans, the Drysdales, the MacCallums, Alan Moorehead, Toni Burgess':

When Johnston and Clift entered the room, MacCallum recalls, it was obvious that the whole occasion was a disaster — she was so afraid and nervous that she could not, or would not, smile at all, and she 'just stood there quivering', looking as if she'd been bound up in some dreadful corset.

Suzanne Chick presents an even harsher portrait, drawn from the testimony of Toni Burgess. Again, the scene is the night of the welcome home party:

When Charmian first opened the door to her friend Toni, her appearance was a terrible shock. She had changed. Her once confident demeanour had gone. Frightened green eyes looked defensively out of a ravaged, sun-damaged, drink-damaged face. Her once strong white teeth were discoloured and decayed. Her hair was dry and thin. Across the bridge of her once straight nose was a scar, a break-line.

The beautiful young woman of style and flair, who had left Sydney in triumph, had returned middle-aged and apprehensive.[3]

It could be said that the next stage of the Clift myth really takes off with this first picture of Charmian arriving back in Australia. It is therefore worth asking what people really saw, and why they remember that they saw this monstrosity.

As to the appearance of Charmian Clift at this time, photographs taken just before she left Hydra show a healthy and attractive woman, full of energy and life. Her body still looks good in a swimsuit. Her face is glowing, and her hair — cut in a simple style — is shining and certainly not 'thin' (if that means thinning). In one photo the teeth are widely displayed; perhaps they are somewhat discoloured by nicotine, but they are not the rotting stumps suggested by the descriptions above. As to the nose, it seems as straight as ever, and even later close-up photographs show no scar line.

When Charmian arrived in Sydney, she was exhausted. And yes, she was terrified. She was terrified of people looking her up and down and making exactly the kinds of judgements that they made. This crowd of old friends and colleagues had watched each other enter middle age gradually, at the same time as their own selves had been ageing, but in their eyes Charmian had sailed off a young woman — and sailed back as a middle-aged one.

It was not just old friends, however, who had to adjust the reality to their expectations. Even perfect strangers found that Charmian had 'changed', for she was the inadvertent victim of the publicity campaign that George had unleashed earlier in the year, in preparation for his own triumphant homecoming. To the young Collins publicist, Joan Flanagan, the photographs of Charmian in Johnston's publicity material were extremely vivid; she remembered that 'Charmian sort of burst upon us with this wonderful legend that George had sent ahead'. Naturally, Joan was disappointed when the model did not live up to her image:

> Because she came in with the wash — the publicity wash associated with George — we expected this raving beauty — her photographs had come ahead — and anyway she wasn't — a different woman arrived.
>
> When she walked in, she looked *different* to me. She looked different from what I'd expected. It just wasn't the same. I was disappointed that she wasn't as charismatic and confident and beautiful as she had been.[4]

Joan stressed that 'I'm not being critical of her — to me, writers don't have to look like anything in particular'. It was Charmian's *manner* that was different from Joan's expectations, more than her appearance.

The first time I saw her, I remember her arriving at the door of the office looking hesitant and uncertain, where I'd expected her to look vibrant and confident. I went: 'Is that *Charmian*? Is that *her*?' I didn't recognise her from the photographs.

The whole focus on Clift's appearance again shows the way in which the myth undermined the real woman. Just as the photos in the *ABC Radio Guide* in the 1940s had distracted people from the talents of the scriptwriter, now the natural effects of age were used to convict Charmian of some kind of failure.

In fact, a change would occur in Charmian Clift's appearance after her return to Australia. On Hydra, she was very fit, for she was constantly walking up and down the hilly town, but in Sydney she lived the typical sedentary life of a writer. Within a year Charmian would put on about a stone in weight. Despite the statements of her detractors, however, she was never fat, and certainly not 'flaccid'. She simply put on the covering of flesh which was the inherited pattern of her body type: she had once observed her mother's face broadening with age, just as her own was beginning to do.

But the initial criticisms are to do with more than face and figure. The 'no stockings' line alerts us to one aspect of the problem. In Sydney in 1964 middle-aged and middle-class women — even women of an artistic social circle — had a certain code of appearance that involved stockings, step-ins, high-heeled shoes, fashionable outfits, and hair-dos which were the product of the hairdressing salon. Charmian's style on her arrival broke every article of this code. In her Greek mode she was accustomed to being bare-legged, and bare-faced, to wearing no corsets (Kinnane's comment is particularly ironic), to washing her own hair, letting it dry in the sun, and snipping at the ends every so often with a pair of nail scissors. This mode was so unfamiliar on an adult woman that observers could not recognise it as a form of female beauty. The situation was like a reversion to the time of Charmian's adolescence, when her appearance was not of the kind that was fashionable.

Of course, Charmian Clift was particularly perceptive to the various codes of dress and style. From the moment she saw the other women who came to greet her, she knew that in their eyes she looked wrong. And so she wanted to hide herself.

It is now time to shift perspective and see what she saw.

It was a wild, wet night.

It was her forty-first birthday.[5]

It was a time of arrival in her homeland — a homeland from which she had fled for political as well as personal reasons, a homeland about which she still felt very ambivalent.

It was also a time of reunion with her husband. Although she knew he had missed her, Charmian was also waiting for the private scene which would erupt when all the people left: the scene of questioning and recrimination, when she would have to answer for her affair with Kingsmill.

What did she see at this party in her new 'home' — in this rented house where she hadn't even unpacked? If those gathered saw a woman who had changed considerably from the one they had known years before, this woman herself saw a crowd of people who had made a sudden jump to middle age. She also saw complete strangers, new friends whom George had made over the last few months. Even when she realised that people 'were all still recognisably themselves', she perceived a gulf of difference between these old friends and herself. They were 'that much more prosperous, or at least established ... "Assured of certain certainties," [she] thought with a sneaking envy. They were all so very much at home in this land'.[6] And once again, Charmian Clift was outside the window, looking in. She must have wondered why on earth she had left her island home and friends and a man who loved her, in order to come to this place where she did not fit in.

Over the next few weeks, Charmian Clift would shape herself into a new role. This time it was a transformation from Island Peasant to Sydney Sophisticate. Within a few days Charmian would go to the hairdresser, and she would start to buy a whole wardrobe of new clothes. Instead of sun-faded cotton skirts and shirts, there were tailored linen dresses and suits, stockings, heels, the appropriate constricting undergarments. One part of her was bemused as she considered 'to what discomforts women have submitted through the ages in the name of fashion'.[7] And yet the part of Charmian that had once been an elegant city-dweller was also revived. She declared that she was 'prepared to enjoy spike heels after bare feet, hair lacquer after salt-dried tangle, formal dresses after old pants and parched shirts, civilised drinks after the rough and resinated island wines, the company of people actively engaged in their own society after the company of people who had repudiated theirs'.[8]

This new Charmian Clift can be seen in its apotheosis in the publicity photo that would appear on the front cover of her essay collection, *Images in Aspic*, published only a year after her arrival. Here the hair looks as if it has been cut in a salon; the make-up has been applied in magazine-model style. But it is the hat that sums up the change.

In photos from Greece, Charmian wears a wide-brimmed straw hat that is just a fisherman's or peasant's hat, sometimes with a scarf tied around it. The hat in the *Images in Aspic* photo presents itself as a discreetly expensive milliner's version of a straw peasant-style hat. Here, however, the brim has been trimmed back so far that its function of providing shade is lost; the crown has been extended so high that it would easily crush and break; the ribbon is neatly attached; and the whole thing is designed to be worn at a ridiculous sideways angle which makes the wearer appear to be quirky and individual. The required angle also limits the wearer's vision to one eye. Just as the hat, by metamorphosing from straw worker's hat to lady's fashion item, has lost its whole *raison d'être*, so did its wearer lose some of her reason for being when she changed into a Sydney lady.

This whole matter of style — of how Charmian looked — will run like a thread through the next few years of her story. As time went on, the Charmian Clift style would become part (though rather an uncomfortable part) of the new alter ego. To Joan Flanagan, it seemed that even after Charmian had bought new outfits, she still didn't look right: 'I always remember her as being oddly dressed. I just have a memory of her being in something like a suit that was oddly out of tune'. Joan adds that this nonconformity 'quite suited her' and indeed 'She was really — she was her own self'.[9] But was she? For the moment, in these first few hectic weeks, it was more a matter of a little girl dressing up.

Of course, this exterior remodelling was accompanied by significant interior readjustment. But in the initial flurry of arrival, there wasn't time for Charmian to pause and take stock of herself. It was like the first few weeks when she had arrived on Kalymnos. The difference was that now she was ten years older, and did not believe that she had arrived in the Promised Land.

At least it was easy to adjust to the comforts of modern life. The house that George had rented was furnished and recently renovated, and after the primitive arrangements in Greece, it was the 'sheerest luxury to run hot water taps, to see a bath filling', to have a permanent supply of electricity and gas, and even 'flushes that flush'.[10] The problem was that this house was situated in the affluent suburb of Mosman on the northern side of the harbour, so the rent was exorbitant; from the beginning the couple began to look for alternative rental accommodation, while keeping in mind the hope of buying a place when eventually the Hydra house sold. This added to Charmian's feeling of impermanence as she unpacked the treasures from the trunks and tried to turn the Federation style Sydney house into some sort of facsimile of the Hydra home.

One of the reasons George had chosen Mosman was the good state schools in the area. Although the third and final term of the school year had started, all three children were immediately enrolled, so that normal family life could get under way as soon as possible. There were various adjustments for them all to make, both socially and academically.

Jason — now eight and a half — had found the long and exciting boat journey to be a useful transition between Hydra and Sydney. While the family slept together in a cramped cabin like the rest of the £10 migrants, they ate at the captain's table; as a result of this difference in status, Jason had begun to readjust his notion of his national identity, thinking: 'Oh, I'm not Greek — I'm one of these English people'. By the time of his arrival, the 'funniness' of his spoken English was still 'commented upon', because 'it wasn't the funny English of someone who can't speak English', but 'it was made all the more funny because it was basically all right but there were these odd little things'. And so, still speaking 'funnily', he went into third class at the local primary school, where he experienced something of the reaction that any non-Anglo child would have received in this monocultural and middle class institution at this time:

> Just the *fact* that I came from Greece and had a different background — I was assaulted about it. So that encouraged the kind of idea of: 'Don't even talk about it!'
>
> [For example] there was talk of religion in the playground. And at first I'd happily say, 'Oh, I'm Greek Orthodox'. I soon learned not to say that, and to say, 'I'm Church of England'.[11]

Yet as well as this suspicion of nonconformity, there was also a kind of latent resentment of the new student's wide and unusual experience. His teacher's initial attitude was: 'I hope you don't think you're smart!' While Jason's parents would also suffer this sort of attitude from some quarters, it is interesting to see even a child regarded as a tall poppy that needed to be lopped.

Meanwhile it had been decided that Martin would attend North Sydney Boys' High School and Shane would go to North Sydney Girls', both selective schools with a high academic reputation. Martin went into fourth year (the second-last year of the five-year Leaving Certificate system) and Shane into third year.[12] It was hard to start a new school in third term, and at first it seemed to Martin like Winchcombe Secondary Modern all over again. The value of a Greek high school background was completely disregarded, and he found himself placed in the lowest academic stream.

Shane 'just wasn't happy' (Jason remembered).[13] She was desperately missing Hydra, as well as her boyfriend and all the friends she had grown up with. More specifically, she was annoyed to be going to an all-girls school, and she hated the uniform. Like her mother, Shane had really had enough of schooling by the time she was fourteen, and she found the experience claustrophobic and boring.

Yet, as always, Shane quickly made friends — not necessarily from within the school confines; over the next few years her wide circle would be very multicultural as she was drawn to other young people who were not from the Anglo-Australian mainstream. And at the boys' high school there were enough other oddballs for Martin also to find a peer group quickly. By the time of his seventeenth birthday, in November, both older children had a large group of friends to invite to the party.[14] By the end of the year, Martin had got himself promoted into the A class.

Overall, Jason remembered that after the family settled into Australian life, 'the whole feel was that we were turned into more like a "normal family"'.

> [My parents] were more like normal parents, who sort of had a job, as opposed to being around Katsikas or physically being three storeys up and you didn't know what they were doing. And the family unit seemed more like a unit, because you're not just running freely around an island.
>
> I mean, with hindsight, you could say that we were all to some extent constricted — but to an eight year old, that meant 'normal'. It certainly wasn't the breezy easy feel it had been.[15]

Maintaining this kind of 'normality' wasn't easy for the household manager, who felt the lack of the automatic backup that had been provided on Hydra, either by Zoe or by neighbours. Within a month of her arrival, Charmian came down with a feverish cold so severe that she rang for a doctor, whom she had chosen at random. This general practitioner — who was to become the family doctor over the next six years — remembered that on this particular afternoon Charmian was in 'some distress' because 'she didn't have any help' and she was due to collect Jason from school. (George was away on a trip somewhere at this time.) As the doctor visited her daily over the next week or so, he was aware how hard it was for her to run the family without any support.[16]

Meanwhile, the bank balance was empty. While the resettlement was costing a great deal, it was also clear that ongoing living expenses for a family of five in Sydney were going to be exorbitant. In fact, the family had for months been living on borrowed money — or borrowed time.

When George had arrived back in Australia in late February, he already owed £500 to Billy Collins personally.[17] This money was soon gone — not least in supporting the family back in Greece — and so the author accepted all sorts of commissioned projects. At the same time, the success of *My Brother Jack* meant that the publishers started pressing the author for the sequel. In late April, while he was staying on the Carrolls' grazing property at Coolah, George offered Collins a deal, through his agent David Higham. If the publishers were to pay 'an immediate advance on the as-yet-unwritten sequel', this would allow the author to 'get cracking' on *Clean Straw for Nothing* 'without any economic anxieties, almost at once'.[18] Although the £500 loan was still outstanding, Billy Collins was happy 'to grubstake' the author for the new novel, offering terms that were rather extraordinary given that he had not seen a word of the typescript. These were £500 on signature, £500 three months after signature, and £500 on delivery — with the delivery date a mere seven months hence, in January 1965.[19] George replied that he found the offer 'very excellent', and promised that *Clean Straw for Nothing* was 'already under way, and there should be no difficulty in my delivering to Collins well before the end of the year'.[20] This deal with Collins over the second book of the trilogy would become an albatross around George Johnston's neck.

Despite the author's show of confidence, there had been little progress on this novel since the notes and the thirty-page first draft which Johnston had produced in Greece between the summer of 1963 and his departure in early 1964.[21] Only two weeks after promising Higham that there would be no difficulties, George had told Elsie that he was 'wrestling with this bloody novel', adding: 'I am rather depressed by the thought that perhaps *My Brother Jack* was the ONE book I had to write, and I can't do another'.[22] Unable to deal with this large creative problem, Johnston continued to take on short-term projects.

By September 1964, the first £500 advance on the unwritten novel had gone. The author reminded Higham that the second £500 was due in early

October.[23] Yet the novel had not progressed. It was now vitally important for Charmian to earn the money to pay the weekly household bills while George battled to meet his impossible January deadline. Fortunately, an offer of some freelance writing had come when she was still in Greece. Although this work would prove to change Clift's life, at the time it just seemed a way of making a quick bit of cash until she was settled enough to resume the real work of her autobiographical novel-in-progress.

During George's scouting foray to Melbourne after his homecoming, he had met up with an old journalist friend, 'now an important newspaper editor' who, George later noted, had got in touch with Charmian 'to ask if she would write "some regular pieces"':

> He was not at all sure what these pieces were to be ... sort of essays, he thought ... anything she liked. The point was, he explained, that he was not looking for a woman journalist, but a writer. The daily press needed some writing, real writing, from a woman's point of view.[24]

Most commentators have assumed that this editor was John Douglas Pringle and that the newspaper in question was the *Sydney Morning Herald*, but this is not the case.[25] It was, in fact, the Melbourne *Herald* which initially employed Charmian Clift as a columnist. On 6 November 1964 her first piece was published in that newspaper. At that time the Melbourne *Herald* and the *Sydney Morning Herald* had an agreement whereby they could use each other's material. Thirteen days later, on 19 November, this same essay appeared in the *Sydney Morning Herald*. Over the next three months, Clift's column would regularly come out in the Melbourne paper before appearing in the Sydney one. In mid February 1965 a new pattern was established, with the essay appearing first in the *Sydney Morning Herald*'s Thursday Women's Section, and then a couple of days later in the Melbourne *Herald*. As these pieces were commissioned at the Melbourne end, they were also sub-edited there,[26] and at this stage it was the Melbourne paper that paid the author.[27]

The most important thing was the brief: it was a job description that was perfectly tailored for Charmian Clift. While she had never written short pieces before, the mode of the essay — with its idiosyncratic point of view and its apparent discursiveness — was akin to the mode that Clift had practised in the travel books; and of course 'real writing' was right up her alley. From her very first column piece, Charmian Clift immediately found her voice: assured, intimate and intensely personal. It was so close to the voice of the writer's alter ego narrator Cressida Morley that she would be able, when appropriate, to lift passages from *The End of the Morning* straight into her column.

In this first piece, appropriately titled 'On Coming Home', the writer assessed some of her impressions gained over the first two months. It was an unusual viewpoint, for someone to be both native-born and newcomer; as the writer herself would later express it:

> All migrants, I think, are optimistic, or, anyway, hoping like blazes that they've really done the right thing. And we were odd sorts of migrants, in that we were migrating to home, which from fifteen years and half a world away could be distorted by the curve of the earth, memory, and couriers' reports, into Utopia or Hicksville.[28]

For the rest of her life, Charmian Clift would continue to ask whether Australia was indeed a Promised Land or the end of the earth. She would turn her rare skill of social observation and analysis upon her own country and compatriots, just as she had examined the people and customs of Greece in her two travel books. As she did so, the initial optimism would start to wane.

In these first few weeks, the writer noticed how 'over and over again' a certain statement was reiterated with complacency. 'The old place has changed quite a bit since *you* saw it last'.[29] She would turn this statement into a series of questions. Had Australia changed since the early 1950s? If so, how? Were these changes superficial or profound? For better or worse?

The first change that people pointed out to her was a European influence. 'They said: "It's the migrants that've made the difference. We've got a real Continental way of life now"'.[30] Of course, this was the 'metamorphosis' that George had singled out as the most significant development in Australian society when he had written his enthusiastic epistles back to the family in Greece. Charmian was sceptical then, and remained so, even after her return:

> Yes, there is an obvious European influence [...] But may I suggest that a Continental 'way of life' which so many Australians consider we have achieved (rather, it seems to me, like earning a Boy Scout's merit badge) cannot be printed on a menu card. It is a matter of the spirit.[31]

The second area of change to which people drew Clift's attention concerned urban growth, and in particular the city skyline. To this, Rip Van Winkle replied that 'Surely it would be a matter of marvel and wonder only if skylines had remained exactly as they were fifteen years ago'. In fact, the size of the city appalled her, and through the next years Clift's voice would ring loud and clear against the red brick sprawl of suburbia and the high-rise developments around the harbour, both of which she saw as reflecting poverty of the spirit as well as architectural bad taste.[32]

A third change from the post-war world which Charmian Clift had left was the sheer amount of consumer goods, especially the volume and variety of available foodstuffs. But for someone of Charmian Clift's political proclivities, the development of a highly consumerist society was not necessarily an improvement. After living in a place where every resource was precious, there seemed to be so much waste in Australia. It is not surprising that a frequent concern of Clift's column over the next five years was the disposal of garbage.[33]

Although Charmian Clift knew that the unpardonable sin would be to criticise ('Yes, I know I can go back to where I came from if I don't like it'), she nevertheless perceived fundamental problems in the society, caused by the very affluence and security which she was meant to admire. Over the years of her exile she had 'kept a cliche-image of [her] countrymen and women — frank, fearless, independent, astringent, tough, highly original'. But now faces seemed to have softened, and she found the qualities which she associated with the Australian image to be missing. 'Certainly the qualities one has always associated with Australians do not appear to be reflected to any marked degree in cultural achievements as opposed to material ones'. With this reference to culture she moved on to matters of national identity:

> I suppose that what I have been really looking for is evidence of a spiritual change — a burgeoning and a bursting of the image qualities into a real cultural and social flowering, spiky and wild and refreshing and strange and unquestionably rooted in native soil. Not just Australian singers, but Australian singers singing Australian songs, not just Australian dancers but Australian dancers dancing Australian dances, not just Australian actors, but Australian actors acting Australian plays written by Australian

writers expressing Australian ideas and challenges in Australian idiom. Not a 'Continental way of life' but an Australian way of life developed naturally from its landscape, climate, and its own heritage.[34]

To soften the harshness of her evaluation, Clift pointed at this early stage to a sense of 'hope and expectation', and she used a word which she would use again and again: 'There *is* a feeling of imminence here'.

This was Clift the optimist. In fact, she would keep on waiting and hoping for the arrival of real change, but would grow increasingly restless at the lack of fulfilment of this promise. While hindsight reveals that the feeling of change which she intuited was the spirit that would be manifest in the election of the Whitlam Labor Government in 1972, that shift in political consciousness was still a fair way off.

Over the next few months, Clift would find other flies in the national ointment. One was the Australian practice of social (or antisocial) drinking. How she longed for the easiness of her midday sessions with George at Katsikas's grocery shop: if the couple wanted a drink and a talk now, they had to catch a bus to a pretentious red brick hotel, where Charmian was not allowed to enter the public bar.[35] This segregation of the sexes in pubs was indicative of an attitude which still relegated women to the grade of second-class citizen — a condition of 'sexual apartheid in employment, wages, social standing and moral judgements'. Clift wondered 'a little impatiently how much longer it is going to be before society faces up to the fact that women are fully-fledged members of the human fraternity, and as such entitled to participate in its economic, social and cultural life on terms of absolute equality'.[36] In the segregated society of Greece, Charmian Clift had been accustomed to absolute equality with men: by being a *xeni*, she was outside any local rules, and in the bohemian expatriate circles of the foreign colony, women were expected to be liberated. It was a rude shock to arrive back into Australian society and find herself once again expected to be seen and not heard.

If the position of women had barely advanced, Charmian Clift quickly discerned the same old attitudes in regard to race and ethnicity. Despite people's praise for the new 'Continental way of life', within six months the columnist was wondering 'whether in fact the tolerance [was] as genuine as it first appeared to be'. There seemed 'a weird sort of ambivalence about it, as about so many other Australian attitudes'. She believed that Australians needed to move beyond tolerance or even praise into *welcoming* the newcomers.[37]

But if Australian attitudes to Europeans still smacked of the past, the feeling about Asia combined the old White Australia views with a new paranoia which saw the Asian nations as a series of dominoes falling one by one to communism in a southward momentum propelling straight for Australia. On 10 November 1964, the Prime Minister, Sir Robert Menzies, introduced conscription for twenty year old males — including the provision that they would serve overseas. Under a bizarre intake system, birth dates were to be placed in a lottery barrel, and those whose date was drawn were to be drafted. A few days later, Clift wrote an essay 'On Lucky Dips' deploring as 'extremely sinister' this method of gambling with young lives; this piece was apparently rejected by her Melbourne *Herald* employers.[38]

In April of the following year, the federal government announced that Australian troops would be sent to Vietnam. For Charmian Clift, this revived memories of the immediate post-war situation, in which George had been reviled — and perhaps even sacked from the *Argus* — because of his support for the national liberation movement of China. Soon she was publicly opposing Australia's role in the Vietnam War as well as conscription, and urging that Australians extend friendship and welcome to Asian people. Just as her cultural nationalism was in advance of its time, so was her view of Asia as 'the place where one lives'.[39]

At the same time as she started work on the newspaper column, Clift took on another and even more demanding project. This also had its origin in the intensive networking that George Johnston had done on his homecoming: looking up old friends and colleagues, seeking new outlets for work.

Neil Hutchison, who had been in charge of ABC Radio Drama and Features when Clift and Johnston had written radio scripts back in the Bondi days, was now in charge of Television Drama for the ABC. Sitting next to George Johnston on the plane back to Sydney after the Adelaide Festival, Hutchison had proposed the idea of adapting *My Brother Jack* for television. Johnston was very keen on the idea of a television adaptation, though he would have preferred to see his book translated into a film. Neil Hutchison had in his ABC department a group of young employees who were equally enthusiastic about the proposal. One of these was Storry

Walton, who was Hutchison's choice as producer/director for the series. His preferred scriptwriter was George Johnston himself: not only had he written the novel, but he had had some experience with scripts.

At this early stage Hutchison faced, however, a fair degree of controversial discussion in his own department, because the senior staff thought that Johnston would not be able to do the adaptation. Further, they did not see *My Brother Jack* as television drama material. Storry Walton remembered that 'Their problem was that *My Brother Jack* didn't have an action-based through-line — a very traditional kind of naturalistic dramatic flavour. It had still centres, and dwelt on character'. Meanwhile, Johnston himself began to have 'doubts' about his ability to do the script adaptation. Part of his concern was that he was 'too close' both to the book and to his own story; it would be difficult for him 'to take the additional step of adaptation'. This was made particularly hard because Storry Walton wanted the actor Ed Devereaux in the role of Jack; this would make the television Jack a much older brother than the one in the book. As well as this, Johnston wanted to get on with the sequel rather than plough the same ground again. Walton recalls that the whole matter of the adaptation had reached this rather difficult point when Charmian Clift arrived back in Australia.

> And they together agreed, long before they confided in anybody else, that Charmian really ought to write it.
> I think it was the right decision, because first of all Charmian was at one remove from the Johnstons' story. Secondly, she had an extraordinary facility. She grasped ideas very quickly [...] She also had a marvellous ability with dialogue. She had a feeling for the vernacular of the period. And lastly she was quick — and you had to be quick in the way in which that serial was made.[40]

Indeed, speed was essential. The ABC was eager to screen the show while the book's popularity was still running hot, so the deadline was terribly tight. This job would engage most of Charmian's time from about October 1964 until the show went to air in August 1965. Although it presented her with a new challenge, it meant collaborating again with George. Moreover, it required Charmian to put herself imaginatively right inside the Johnston family. While Storry Walton thought that Clift's 'remove' from the family made it comparatively easy for her, this was not in fact the case.

The first bridge to cross was the matter of the novel's discursiveness, and the requirements of adaptation, particularly in relation to the character of

Jack. In a speech given in about July 1965 to scriptwriting colleagues, Charmian Clift explained the reasons for the quite significant changes that were made. After noting that she wouldn't want to 'meddle with' *My Brother Jack* as a book — 'Anyway, since I've been involved in it from the beginning I have done my meddling long since and far away' — Clift went on to point out that a television serial is limited 'by time, budget and by the medium itself'.

> So what I did eventually was to take the portion of the book I found most significant — the years of the Depression leading up to the War — [...] and to cram into this as much of the earlier part of the book and as much of the later part of the book as I could without overloading it. Oddly enough this is the period in the book itself where [...] Jack himself is absent [...] So I have had to invent a lot of incident that doesn't actually occur in the book [...] What I have tried to do [...] is to stick to the truth of the book, the essence of it, and present it in terms more dramatically suitable to that little viewing screen than long chapters of narrative.[41]

While George was consulted at every stage, both the character and role of Jack in the television serial are quite different from those of Jack in the novel — and it was Clift not Johnston who 'invented' the television Jack. He was her character in both senses of the word, for not only did she write him but he was a kind of male alter ego. While Charmian Clift drew upon some of her own qualities to develop the engaging larrikin who steals the show, her comment that 'Jack, who is the hero, needs to be present' highlights one of the main differences between book and serial. Jack is not the hero of the novel, but a sort of measuring stick for David: hence his absence from so much of the story. In a script, as Clift points out, this couldn't work, and so it was Clift who wrote for Jack the role of a truly Australian working class hero, of the type whom she unashamedly declared herself to adore.

With this change to Jack's role, there must also be a change to that of his younger brother. Although David is still used as the first-person narrator, and although David's eyes remain the lens through which the audience views the story, the necessary shift to third person involved in the film medium means that viewers are much more free to make up their own minds about the contrasting qualities and characters of the two Meredith brothers.[42]

This task of adaptation was a deeply personal and involving matter, which wrung an enormous amount from Charmian Clift. It was a kind of reprise of the original experience of helping her husband with the writing of *My Brother Jack*. Once again, she put aside her own family novel, *The End of the Morning*, in order to work on the Johnston family story. Again she drew upon her own store of Depression material and used it in her husband's story. The authenticity of the television serial relies upon a myriad of details of setting, diction, costume and general feel for the period which were the product not just of Clift's memory of her own family home but the twenty years she had been detailing this domestic life in the various Kiama novel drafts. This was Clift's most precious literary resource, and there was a danger that when at last her own book was done, it could seem that she had used George Johnston's material.

If the scriptwriter put her own family experience into the Meredith story, it was of course sometimes painful for her to enter into the Johnston/Meredith family so wholly. Her job now was nothing less than to present this family — which she saw as disapproving of herself — as an Australian legend. While this was hard for Charmian, it was also not easy for George to let his story — both fictional and real — be adapted. For both of them, it was back to the old mode of collaboration through the verbal thrashing out of ideas. But this time Clift had the last word. Walton remembered:

> They really did work as a team on the development of all the synopses. And there was discussion — adamant discussion — on every episode, until the moment it was delivered. George read everything, they talked about it, commented on it, but in the end she put her stamp on it, where it was necessary. There was a kind of agreement that if they couldn't resolve a point, then we would run with Charmian's view. It didn't happen very often.[43]

As well as facing the possibility of upsetting George, the feelings of the real Jack and his wife Pat had to be considered. 'They were the grey ghostly judges', Storry Walton vividly recalled, 'that sat just outside our circle all the time that it was being made'. In fact they had the power of veto, for the serial of *My Brother Jack* could not go to air without a signed clearance from them that they would not sue for any aspects of the portrayal of their fictionalised characters. Jack and Pat came up to Sydney to see the filming of Episode 1 — but still delayed their permission.

The urgency of the deadlines increased the tension. At an early stage of the project, this was the schedule:

> End of December 1964 — casting and treatment 10 episodes
> January — working on final episodes, dialogue etc
> February — camera scripting, film scripting in detail
> April — filming — Melbourne[44]

In the event, this schedule was revised somewhat, but to write ten half-hour episodes between about October and February was terribly tight, especially for someone who had never written a television script — and, indeed, who had not watched television until a few months earlier.

Walton attributed Clift's success to a natural talent for the medium, noting that 'Had she lived longer, Charmian Clift would have been one of the best screenwriters that Australia has ever produced'. He added that 'Charmian also really had a great producer's eye':

> She was potentially not only a good screenwriter but also a good producer. She collaborated naturally after a while in the discussions about sets and costume and so forth. She played a very important role in that. It wasn't just left to the rest of the professional team.[45]

The scriptwriter was also involved at every stage of rehearsal and shooting. This level of collaboration was unusual in the 1960s Australian television industry, but Charmian Clift managed to cross the barriers. She waited patiently on the studio floor right through camera rehearsal in case any last-minute changes were needed to the script, and she even sat in the control room during shooting. Storry Walton found this novel experience of a writer's presence 'extraordinarily helpful, especially with someone who could make a quiet, cool appraisal of the dramatic process'. He added that 'One of the great tributes to Charmian's integrity and her personality was the fact that there was such a bond of trust built up between her, her director-and-producer, and the actors'.

Indeed, the actors adored both Charmian and George, and the whole of the shoot became an emotionally involving experience, for they were aware that they were acting the lives of real people. Early on, just after the casting had been decided, the Johnstons held a special cast party at their home. As the actors came in, Charmian and George succeeded in identifying everyone by role.[46]

After years of slowly working on the travel books and novels, with no deadline beyond the desire to finish, and no editorial input until the text was complete, it was an enormous change for Charmian Clift to be suddenly involved in two separate projects — the column and the script — which required the writer constantly to meet deadlines, and to lay open her work either to journalistic sub-editing or to the collaborative criticism and changes that are the norm in the television industry. It was, of course, particularly difficult to do this when so many other adjustments were going on. At times it seemed as if there was no space left for the personal part of the writer's life.

During the third weekend of November 1964, however, Charmian managed to grab time to make 'a sentimental pilgrimage'. Since arriving back she had had reunions with her sister Margaret and brother Barré. Now she and George went down to Kiama, where they stayed (like Julia and Charles in *Walk to the Paradise Gardens*) in the rambling old Brighton Hotel. If any return to a home town brings back odd memories, Charmian Clift's homecoming was particularly strange, for she had been rewriting the place and the people during her seventeen year absence. And so similar was contemporary Kiama's appearance to that of the town that she had been fictionalising for two decades that in her essay about this visit (written for the local paper as well as the Melbourne and Sydney *Herald*s) she included her standard description of Lebanon Bay, lifting the passage directly from *Paradise Gardens* and *The End of the Morning* into the newspaper text.[47]

As well as visiting the graves of her father and grandparents in the Bombo cemetery, she met with a number of old acquaintances — including her girlhood friend Thellie Brown — who came to the lounge of the Brighton to have a look at how Charmian had turned out. If most were not impressed,[48] it wasn't Charmian's fault. Just as she had tried as a child to be liked by the locals, she tried terribly hard on this occasion to strike the right note. In an interview for the local paper, she declared that she and George had decided 'to build a "writer's retreat" in or near Kiama, where they could work in peace and quiet'. She also told the *Kiama Independent* journalist that she was 'now writing a new novel, *To the End of the Morning* [sic], based on her childhood in Kiama'.[49] This was a very forthcoming statement for Clift to make — to actually name a work-in-progress in a press interview — and it shows how serious she was at this time about the book, and how sure she was that she would complete it. Indeed, the two projects were obviously coupled in her mind: build the 'retreat' and write the Kiama novel in it, with her landscape all around her. What could be better? For the plan to happen, it would be necessary to sell the Hydra house, but perhaps a place in Kiama might almost make up for leaving Greece?

It was a grand idea — and if it had come off, it might just have provided the haven for her self and her writing that Charmian needed. But there was not enough money, and soon the idea was set aside in the continuing struggle to live by freelance writing while organising a family.

The new year of 1965 kicked off with a bad omen. Since George Johnston's return to Australia, there had been no particular crisis in his health, although he was still very thin and he wheezed frequently with his emphysema. In March, however, as he was travelling in western New South Wales researching the text for the coffee table photographic book *The Australians*, he became so ill that he had to book into Mudgee hospital for a couple of weeks. As he had feared he was suffering a recurrence of his tuberculosis, it was a relief to discover it was bacterial pneumonia.[50] However, both he and Charmian were living and working at such a hectic pace that the reprieve would be short-lived.

In April there was great excitement when *My Brother Jack* won the Miles Franklin Award.[51] Although the novel had already achieved great popular success, the winning of this literary prize seemed to George Johnston affirmation of his dream of writing the Great Australian Novel.

Publicity in relation to this prize spurred on the enthusiasm of everyone involved in the television serial. This same month, Charmian and George went to Melbourne for the filming of the outdoor location scenes of *My Brother Jack* which could not be done in Sydney. At the same time, Clift met with her employers at the Melbourne *Herald*; it is indicative of the esteem in which they held their columnist that they paid for a penthouse suite for her. During this visit, George took his brother Jack and sister-in-law Pat, and also his sister Jean and her husband Bert, out to dinner at Florentino's. Although Charmian always felt uncomfortable with George's family, it was vital that Jack and Pat be kept happy at the moment, so that they would sign the *My Brother Jack* release. There seems little doubt that Jack got considerable pleasure from keeping his brother and sister-in-law dangling on this matter. Consciously or unconsciously, it was a way of paying George back for his years of absence and his neglect of their mother. As usual, George and Charmian struck the wrong note when they tried to woo Jack. Fifteen years later he was still complaining about the expensive dinner at the 'clip joint': 'They gave me spatchcock, no bigger than a sparrow, a spoonful of spinach and half a potato'.[52]

While Jack would sneer about this dinner costing £100, he had no idea of the sacrifice that had gone into paying for such a meal. At around this time the combination of the family's precarious financial situation and George Johnston's commitment to the second book of the trilogy caused Clift to take on a new role as a radio broadcaster. Anne Deveson, a young radio journalist who had a morning news and current affairs program each day on the commercial station 2GB, had already met Charmian on a few social occasions. Deveson was aware of Charmian 'being lionized' and 'feted all around Sydney': 'Everybody wanted a piece of Charmian.' It didn't surprise Deveson, therefore, that 2GB should offer Charmian Clift work; what did surprise her was Charmian's reaction:

> I remember meeting her at a party and she was talking about [the forthcoming 2GB job] and she said she felt sick at the thought, because she hated broadcasting, she hated performing in public — which interested me, because she didn't appear to be like that when you met her socially, because she held the floor.[53]

Anne arranged to have coffee with her colleague on the first day she came into the studio, and soon the two women were regularly having a chat and a coffee after both their programs had gone to air. It was clear that the only reason Clift was doing the work was financial:

> Charmian talked quite a lot about the need for her to go out and earn and this obviously meant her doing things that she hated doing — or said she hated doing — and as they often made her sick I think she really did hate doing them.
>
> I remember actually hearing [Charmian] being sick in the lavatory before going on air [...] I am quite sure that she did find it an enormous strain. Part of that may have been that she didn't want to be doing it anyway. George was writing — George was working on *Clean Straw* [...] It was part of that tension between her and George that she wanted to be writing as well.

In fact Charmian Clift was not very good in this particular medium, for the discursive turn of her mind which came across so well in the essays was not appropriate to live radio. Anne Deveson remembered: 'As a broadcaster, she was all over the place, in that she would be passionate and intense and fascinating, and then she'd lose the plot'. Her conversational style was often unsuited for a form of radio in which she had to break every four minutes for an advertisement. All in all, Clift 'found the whole commercial scene difficult to handle'. 'She didn't understand the milieu' and 'she felt she was sort of prostituting herself'. This wasn't a matter of snobbery: she was concerned about the quantity of advertising of all kinds that besieged consumers, and at around this time wrote a very forceful essay on the topic.[54]

And so, after a short period — perhaps only a few weeks — Charmian Clift resigned from 2GB. However, it would only be a month or two before financial necessity would again compel her to work as a broadcaster.

The pressure of the radio work on top of the television scriptwriting and the weekly column was so great that in May 1965 Charmian suffered a bout of pneumonia. Despite this, she didn't miss a single newspaper deadline. In a letter to David Higham written this month, George described the general frenzy of his and Charmian's lives:

> I've sat down to write to you a dozen times, somebody has popped in, the phone has rung, something has happened, then puttings off and the gaps of impossible commitments, the problems of kids, new schools, looking for new houses, dental appointments, catching up on years of island living [...] masses of other domestic problems which you don't want to hear about, and both working very frantically. This is a very different world from an island in Greece [...]
>
> There is a mass of things to do here, the only problems are to get the time and the necessary readjustment to them. Life has been very unsettled and it is very difficult to get to any real creative work.

Indeed, Johnston had just abandoned a two hundred page draft of *Clean Straw for Nothing*, and had told Billy Collins that he had decided to put work on this novel completely aside for the moment. As usual, one of the main causes of the furious work pace was the need to pay off debts: 'Living here is costing the earth, and will, I'm afraid, until we can get our own place'.[55] The Hydra house still hadn't sold.

On the personal front, also, problems kept arising. In June Charmian was suddenly confronted with the death of her brother Barré who unexpectedly suffered a coronary at the age of forty-two. She had seen him twice since her

Charmian in Kalymnos, 1955 — with George and Sevasti (*above*) and the family (*below*).

Hydra.

Charmian in the Hydra house (c. 1957).

Jason (1956–7) with Charmian (*top left*), Shane (*top right*), Zoe (*bottom left*) and George (*bottom right*).

Charmian on the terrace of the Hydra house (c. 1958).

Jason, Shane and Martin (c. 1959).

Charmian with Shane and Jason (c. 1960).

Charmian with George (c. 1962).

Charmian in Sydney, 1965 (image used for cover, *Images in Aspic*).

Charmian consulting with George about the script for *My Brother Jack* (1965).

Charmian with Martin and George at Mosman (c. 1967).

Charmian at Mosman, 1968.

return but had been too busy for any extensive catching up with him: there would always be time later, when things had settled down. The years of separation did not soften the blow of Barré's death for Charmian. Rather, it brought back the intensity of her relationship with this person who had been her 'first and best friend', and 'almost [...] twin'. All the old stories came flooding back, and memories of that imprinted Kiama landscape, and just as she had lifted passages of *The End of the Morning* into the Kiama essay of November, she now lifted passages about their shared childhood into her very moving obituary essay for her brother. While in this essay Clift makes no differentiation between the 'fiction' of the novel and the 'non-fiction' of her column, the timing is also significant: she could let readers share even in the immediacy of her grief.[56]

The next month — July — this cycle of illness and crisis moved in even closer. Now George's reprieve of earlier in the year proved false. He came down with a severe chill, on top of his normal breathlessness and frailty, and on 10 July was admitted to Royal North Shore Hospital for tests. On 22 July — two days after his fifty-third birthday — he wrote to Jack and Pat:

> [The tests] finally came through on my birthday to disclose — wouldn't it! — that I've got the TB actively back again — this time in the other lung, and quite a bad set of cavities. So it's going to be hospital for me and I'll be in at least three months, and probably longer, which coming at this time is a pure bastard. They're giving me a brief temporary reprieve so that I can go home to make the necessary domestic, economic and professional arrangements so that Charm will be able to cope while I'm out of action — poor Charm! — so I'll probably be let out tomorrow for about three weeks, and then I'll come back in here again. Isn't it all a sheer bastard, when things were just going so well, especially for Charm![57]

George was readmitted in mid August. In fact, he would remain in hospital for not three but eight months, until April 1966. However, in a way this institutionalisation relieved him of any immediate problems and gave him the sort of freedom that he had longed for in his story 'The Verdict'. It was, as he realised, 'poor Charm' who had to sacrifice her writing in order to deal with the economic and domestic crisis.

After only a year's respite, she was back in the situation of being a single mother of three children. This time, however, there were far more demands on her time than there had been on Hydra, for she was also the family breadwinner. Now the income she earned with the weekly column was needed to pay the household bills. It was a fortunate coincidence that around this time Clift was offered a new contractual relationship in regard to her weekly column.

John Douglas Pringle had moved from the position of editor of the *Canberra Times* to the editorship of the *Sydney Morning Herald* in June 1965.[58] He remembered that, fairly soon after his arrival at the new job, Angus McLachlan, the managing director, came up with the idea of taking Charmian Clift on. 'He said: "Let's get her!"' Pringle added that 'When Angus suggested we should "get her", this struck me as the beginning of an entirely new arrangement'.[59] This decision was relayed to the redoubtable Maggie (Margaret) Vaile, Women's Editor of the *Sydney Morning Herald*, who remembers that Pringle came into her office one day and announced that he had 'pre-empted [her] authority a bit' by engaging Charmian Clift. Maggie was delighted. Under this new arrangement, both the pay cheque and the sub-editing were the responsibility of the *Sydney Morning Herald*. After this, Clift's copy went to Maggie on a Saturday, was published in the *Sydney Morning Herald's* weekly Women's Section on the following Thursday and appeared in the Melbourne *Herald* on the subsequent Saturday.[60]

The important aspect of this story is the fact that the decision to employ Clift on a regular basis came from the top: not many freelance columnists are engaged on the specific orders of the managing director. This is particularly significant because by this stage Clift's column had shown itself to be considerably to the left of the editorial policy of the Fairfax-owned *Sydney Morning Herald*, which was committed to supporting the government position on Vietnam. By mid 1965, Clift had criticised a number of key elements of Australian society, including its consumerist mentality — a radical position to take in a section of the newspaper which aimed to sell an enormous range of products to consumers. In July she would publish her first piece making clear her opposition both to conscription and to the war in Vietnam.[61] Although it seems that her opposition to National Service had been censored the previous November, by now her following was so strong that she had won for herself a lot more freedom.

For the Fairfax management, the bottom line was that Charmian Clift attracted readers, and this in turn helped sell newspapers and advertising. In September of this year, the Clift column would be moved to the prime position of page 2 in the Women's Section, opposite the social notes. At the same time the large retailer Grace Bros, which had formerly advertised only intermittently in the *Sydney Morning Herald*, bought the major advertising space on this page 2–3 spread on a regular basis, specifying that its advertisements were to be placed near the Clift column.[62] This support from a major advertising subscriber, coupled with the regular volume of Clift's fan mail and the fact that her views were known when she was engaged, all helped to strengthen Charmian Clift's editorial freedom.

If Clift was in two minds about contracting herself in a long-term way to the strain of the weekly deadline, George's illness tipped the balance. At about this same time, Clift also accepted an offer made by Anne Deveson's husband, Ellis Blain, to be one of the regulars on his ABC radio program, *Let's Find Out*.[63] This was a two-hour daily discussion show about topical social and political issues, and each day Blain would have a different female commentator as his partner. Deveson remembered:

> She would appear about once a fortnight — there was a fairly loose roster system — and she enjoyed that much more [than commercial radio] because she had the support of an extremely experienced broadcaster and somebody who shared her views, and she was back in a familiar milieu — she was back in the ABC — she wasn't having to contend with a commercial environment which she found so difficult.[64]

It would not be long, however, before the familiar anxiety about performing on radio would arise. For the moment, the radio work was another thing which had to be shuffled into Clift's schedule.

Like any working mother, Charmian had to juggle the needs of the family as well as the demands of her job. Although *My Brother Jack* was in the can, Charmian still often had work commitments through the afternoon, and in the evenings she visited George in hospital. The two teenagers could more or less fend for themselves, but Charmian's most pressing problem was who would be in the house to look after Jason when he got home from school, and through the evening. She was not able to take him to the hospital with her, because children were not allowed to visit TB patients. A solution was found when an invitation came from Jack Johnston's daughter Joy and her schoolteacher husband Felix Russo for Jason to come and stay with them and their large family at Longwood, near Euroa in Victoria's 'Kelly Country'. George thought:

It would be a wonderful break for him to be with other kids and an organised family life during what is bound to be a pretty confused and difficult time over here. This would give Charm a bit more mobility and independence to cope with the domestic and economic problems while we get over this little crisis. As we shall.[65]

To Charmian, although this meant splitting the family, it did seem for the best, under the circumstances. It also offered an opportunity for Jason to experience the kind of Australian country childhood which she always idealised. Another advantage was that it took Jason out of the infection zone. There was always the fear that the other members of the family would catch tuberculosis, and Charmian and the two older children had to have regular chest X-rays because of their contact with George.

Whatever else this crisis brought, it exerted the necessary pressure on Jack Johnston to sign the television release form. It also served to strengthen the ties between Charmian and her husband's family. On 17 August she wrote a letter to Jack and Pat thanking them effusively for their 'sympathy and love and kindness' in the crisis. She went on:

On the business of the telly play I think and worry and wonder a great deal about you both. It is, of course, fiction. But it's fiction based on fact. *I* think the Jack and Sheila that the viewers will come to know are the nicest people in the world [...] It's strange and unprecedented on this that we've had people bawling like babies in rehearsal, and even the producer, Storry (whom you met) was in tears as the last episode was put on tape. So whatever I've done I know it isn't unsympathetic. I only think about the publicity and the pressures and all that and hope you don't mind too terribly much. I feel that this is such an important venture, and it means so much to so many people and has proved without a doubt that we *can* make world standard television here that it is worth it whatever. On the other hand it isn't worth it if it embarrasses you two or worries you or anything like that. I do hope so much that it doesn't. I love Jack and Sheila myself, and have written their parts with love. And I know that all Australia is going to love them, and indeed the whole Meredith family.

Sad news for last. George came down yesterday with a terrible attack of pleurisy, and was bunged back into hospital a week before he meant to go. Actually it's probably good, because now he'll *have* to give up worrying and working and fretting and just lie on his back and get well.

Ah well.

See you soon, I hope, and in the meantime [...] I know you can't love the serial as much as I do, but I hope you will feel how I feel about those two marvellous people.

Love, Charmian[66]

It is no wonder that Charmian was so nervous about Jack and Pat at this time, for it was only a few days later — on Saturday August 21 — that the first episode of *My Brother Jack* went to air.

The next weekend, Charmian made the trip south with Jason to Joy and Felix's place where she spent a couple of days settling her son in and saying goodbye. It is indicative of the stability and love within the family unit that Jason simply remembers the 'fun' of the train trip with his mother, and then his instant adaptation to life with his cousins at Longwood, with no feeling of being rejected or abandoned.[67]

Given Charmian's feelings about the importance of keeping the family together, this separation was a terrible wrench. And as she set off back home, a transport strike left her stranded alone at night at a country railway station, with three and a half hours to wait for her train. To add to the bleakness, it was her birthday.[68] Only a year before, as she had struggled off the migrant ship, it had seemed at least that the family was reunited, whatever other difficulties of adjustment lay ahead. Now, with George in hospital and Jason with relatives, the family unit — the thing in which Charmian vested her commitment — had crumbled. The symbolic meaning of this first birthday on Australian soil was expressed in the aloneness, the darkness, the waiting for something which was delayed, and delayed again and again.

20

A LONE WOMAN

A lone woman in a world filled with jeopardy, [she] is deeply concerned
with 'security' (although not at any price) [...] and with her
reabsorption into the Australian scene as it impinges on her own life and
problems. She is brave. She is gay. Only to herself would she confess her
fears, doubts, trepidations and insecurities.[1]

During the filming of *My Brother Jack* there was so much publicity
about the series that a critic would declare that he could 'recall no
Australian dramatisation [...] which came to us after such prolonged
fanfare'.[2] Working against this excellent publicity was the ABC's scheduling
of the show. As Jack Ayling, lead critic for *TV Week*, declared:

> ABC TV has a certain winner in the new Australian series *My
> Brother Jack* — but trust the public service?! [sic] The series is
> slotted at 8.50 Saturday nights, running slapbang into the middle
> of the *Mavis Bramston Show*. How silly can you get?[3]

The revue-style comedy of the *Mavis Bramston Show* — starring Gordon
Chater, Carol Raye, Barry Creyton and the gang — was 'the most popular
Australian program devised since the beginning of television'.[4] The situation
was made even worse by starting *My Brother Jack* at 8.50, when *Mavis* had
already been running for twenty minutes, and by putting *Jack* after the low-
rating *Four Corners*. There was also strong competition from the other two
channels, which were trying to win viewers away from *Mavis Bramston* with
the American cowboy shows *Wagon Train* and *Gunsmoke*. All in all, the

series couldn't prevail against the competition. The real Jack was quite correct when he wrote to the ABC advising that 'Most everybody agrees with us — it's first class entertainment and 7.30 p.m. on Sunday night would really have been a fitting time for it'.[5]

Unfortunately, there were other problems that could not be laid at the door of the programming department. Initially the show got a favourable response from the critics. After viewing three episodes at the ABC studios, Jack Ayling stated in *TV Week* : 'I say unequivocally that *My Brother Jack* is the finest serial ABC-TV has produced [...] The series ranks with any serious production made in Australia'. He added that 'George Johnston's wife, Charmian Clift, has most ably conquered [the] obstacle' of adaptation. 'As the woman who transformed that novel into a TV script her efforts should be long remembered'.[6] However, after Episode 3, critic Frank Doherty in the rival *TV Times* headed his column with the warning: 'Not enough action in Brother Jack'.[7] The next week he complained that '*My Brother Jack* ambled through another episode'.[8]

This was a reaction against the whole style towards which Storry Walton and his film sequence director Gil Brealey had been aiming — a style modelled on 'documentary realism'. Walton explained that it had been a 'very self-conscious decision' to have longer scenes, which allowed the characters to talk in a naturalistic fashion. The problem was that this was unfamiliar to most Australians, and many viewers shared Doherty's desire for a faster pace and an action-packed plot.

Those involved in making the serial were not daunted. Two decades later, Walton would still be pleased by the critical and public response, and by the serial's landmark features. He pointed out that there had previously been no attempt in Australian television to make something over ten episodes, with such a large cast and with up to thirty per cent shot on film. At the same time, 'nothing had been done which got so close to Australia's working class idiom'. Furthermore, the budget 'came in very well at the end'. And though this serial did not immediately begin a spate of Australian realistic drama as its creators hoped, Walton believed that 'the flags that *My Brother Jack* flew in 1965 were unfurled again when the Australian cinema got off the ground in the late sixties and early seventies'.[9] This is no wild claim, for the production unit provided a training ground for a number of young hopefuls of the film world, including Richard Brennan (later a film producer and director), Bob Ellis (screenwriter and critic) and Albie Thoms (independent film-maker). Thoms' estimation of Clift's scripts stressed their sociopolitical importance:

I think [the scripts] contain some of Charmian's best work, reinterpreting as they did the '30s and '40s. In retrospect this seems most important, since there was a strong movement in Australian society at that time to break from the shackles of the Menzies era and embrace new ideas. The book and, perhaps more significantly, the TV series contributed to this process by helping us to understand the immediate past.[10]

It would only be later, of course, that these long-term gains of the serial could be assessed. For Charmian Clift at the time, it was enough that the very first thing she had written for television was going to air — and appearing as if by magic in people's living rooms. The response encouraged her to want to go on writing for this medium.

Indeed, by September 1965 she and Johnston had already put together a proposal for a television drama series which they called *Coastline*. This had a very imaginative format of thirteen episodes, each of fifty minutes, loosely 'threaded together' by a recurring location along Australia's 'fantastically photogenic' and variable coastline. The writers declared: 'Stories will be adult, original, sophisticated, dealing basically with genuine and contemporary human problems, and treatment where necessary should be unconventional'. Amongst the unconventional aspects was the suggestion that 'much, or all of the series will be on film' (ie shot on location) and the writers asked that 'consideration might seriously be given to filming in colour, so that black and white prints could be made for general first release, and a highly profitable second sale made for colour TV at a later date'.[11] If here we see these scriptwriters looking to the future, the broad perspective of Charmian Clift and George Johnston is evident in the way they saw themselves as writing for the overseas as well as local market.

In September 1965, as *My Brother Jack* went to air and as the proposal for *Coastline* was submitted, Charmian Clift was ebullient about her work prospects. In one of her rare letters to David Higham she summed up the year since her arrival:

Dear David,
Sorry about the long silence. This has all been so new and so invigorating in a mad sort of way. I think I like it. At least it is a country where you can still make things happen instead of waiting for them to happen. I have been making my own sneaky little

revolutions, first, by writing essays for the weekly presses to be read by people who don't know an essay from a form-guide, but absolutely love it, and second by barging into television with a ten part serial of *My Brother Jack* that is getting rave notices from astonished critics who didn't seem to know that we could make good television in Australia. All this has been tremendous fun and tremendous hard work and all in the first year back, so at the moment I am taking stock and considering what to do next. Here I am high-priced help and greatly valued and I suppose I could go on writing television or start pushing a film or turn to straight theatre (which I'd like to do, actually). On the other hand I have a half-finished novel which I'd like to get done — excepting that there's so little from novel writing in the way of daily bread, let alone jam or gravy, that I don't know whether I can afford to. I don't know whether you know that George is back in hospital with a recurrence of the old wog and will be there probably for six months on present prognosis. It's rather a blow just at this time, but at least they say they can cure him really this time, and I suppose we must regard it as time to be used to the best advantage possible. He'll be able to work, though not under any pressure — I hope he'll get on with the novel, but I suppose that depends on his emotional climate (he is even more disillusioned about novel-writing than I am, and I know the Elizabethan Trust want him to write a play). Anyway, we'll see. The most important thing is for him to get well again […] Greece seems far far away and I haven't had time to miss it yet. This is nice too, and just as foreign. The children have adjusted rather well (excepting perhaps for my daughter, who thinks Australian men crude beyond belief and swears she's going back to Europe as soon as she can raise the fare). But the eldest is on his way to Sydney University with (on present marks) a Commonwealth Scholarship to see him through, and the youngest is as happy and busy as a small boy should be, and nobody is really pining. MBJ is still getting the most amazing publicity, particularly since my telly serial has started — and at the moment we are all praying the BBC is going to buy it and give it another boost in England. American sales are, as usual, disappointing. Love, David. George I'm sure will write to you himself.

Charmian[12]

It is strange that Charmian did not mention in this letter that her address would soon be changing. With George and Jason away, there was no need for the large and expensive house in Kirkoswald Avenue, which anyway was too much for her to look after. Although the Hydra house was sold at around this time, it would take a while for the money to come through; the prospect of buying a house in Sydney, when family life was so unsettled, seemed very complicated. The best interim solution was to rent a flat. In her first break since the start of the column, Charmian took two weeks off in the middle of September to look for suitable accommodation, and by the end of the month Charmian, Martin and Shane had moved into a brand new red brick building situated on the major thoroughfare of Ben Boyd Road in the suburb of Neutral Bay, a few kilometres from Mosman. In 'Getting With the Forward-Lookers', Clift gave an ironic description of the block of flats:

> Every corner bulges with tiers of white iron balconies, of which some have a Harbour view and some do not because, while this building was still under construction, it apparently seeded some red bricks on the plot next door, which took root and flourished and are at this moment growing up layer by layer into an identical building (whose balconies, of course, will have a Harbour view until another one grows alongside).
>
> Anyway, I don't care about that, because the lowest east bulging balcony does have a Harbour view, and that, temporarily (and for reasons which seem to have been mislaid somewhere in the sheer hysteria of moving from one place to another), is mine, and I intend to grow morning glory on it and take very chic public breakfasts and evening aperitifs at a white iron table when I can afford one or acquire one and I am designing some very forward-looking gowns (or robes) for this purpose.[13]

This account reveals as much about the persona that Clift was assuming for her column as it does about the block of flats. The essential qualities of this particular alter ego are cheerfulness and courage ('This [experience] is, of course, an exhilarating sort of challenge'), combined with elegance and style ('We have some marvellous pictures that would look absolutely gorgeous on the mushroom-coloured walls if one only dared to desecrate them with nails'), and a certain dippiness ('There is also a very expensive carpet-shampooing machine that I was conned into buying by a very brisk saleslady who called one day, and of which I am terribly ashamed, since I don't have the sort of carpets that need shampooing').

As to Charmian Clift's real feelings about this move, she would later even admit in the column that this 'determinedly cheerful piece' about being forward-looking had been written 'in a mood of rampant self-pity'.[14] She was, quite understandably, unhappy about the new place.

The problems weren't just with the building, but with the complete lack of privacy: for all three, the lack of space was very hard to bear. The relationship between Shane and Martin had not improved, and the totally different philosophies and lifestyles of these two continued to grate — particularly in the area of musical taste. Shane had left school by now, and found a job in a film studio, but it was her 'ambition [...] quite literally to be a gogo dancer on *Bandstand*'.[15] She and her girlfriends spent a lot of time practising their dancing to the sort of pop music that featured on that television show. They wore the uniform of mini skirts and high boots, pale lipstick, black eye make-up, and long straight blonde hair that was so fashionable with that peer group. In this aspiration, Shane was once again unconsciously revealing how similar she was to her mother, who at the age of fifteen had practised the latest songs with her girlfriend Thellie and dreamed of being a dancer, or maybe a nightclub singer in a long lamé dress. In contrast to his sister, Martin's taste in music was for the political protest songs of Bob Dylan and other folk singers of this time. In appearance, Martin was by now about as tall as his father, and although his frame was strong, he was very thin. He wore heavy black spectacles, and his hair was longer than school regulations allowed. Naturally, when Shane's friends and Martin's friends were together in the living room of the flat, there was mutual incomprehension, and a battle over the record player.

Of course, these sorts of conflicts between teenage siblings are absolutely normal, but it was difficult for Charmian, who was not only a working mother but a mother who had to conduct her working life from this same living room. Her 'study', where she wrote everything from television scripts to the weekly essay, consisted of one section of the long refectory table — or it would be, when the table eventually arrived. As the flat was unfurnished, Charmian now had to find the time and the money to go out and Start Afresh, purchasing everything from stylish Czechoslovakian glasses and an enormous refrigerator to a lavatory brush and a plastic kitchen tidy.

However, if flat life was difficult, the actual location of the new home was an eye-opener to the newcomer. Within easy walking distance of the

Neutral Bay Junction shops, the area had a 'quirky sort of character' that was 'a blend of the raffish and the smart'. Unlike the inhabitants of Mosman, Charmian's new neighbours represented a considerable ethnic diversity — at least in terms of Australia in the 1960s. This was for Charmian Clift the 'first approximation' of 'a neighbourhood' that she had lived in since her arrival in Australia.[16] Despite Charmian's pleasure in discovering her new neighbourhood, the stress of moving caused her to come down with a bout of pneumonia which left her 'confined to barracks for a couple of weeks' in early November.[17] This at least meant that she was able to write a letter to her old friend in London:

> Dearest Jo — it seems such a long long time since I have been in touch with you, and sad that I never seem to have time to write to my friends when I write every day to all sorts of silly people on social committees who only want me to make speeches to bored ladies in floral hats or stand on public platforms and talk about the Pill. I firmly refuse to waste any of my valuable time on that sort of nonsense, but the letters have to be answered if only to say Not on your life, mate. So many things have happened since I wrote to you last. First, and most awful, is that George is back in hospital again with three great holes in his lung — the lung that was supposed to be the good one — that were only revealed by a new X-ray process and quite by accident. Nobody knows how long they've been there — it could be years — but it does explain a lot of things, and thank God they've been discovered and the curing process is in hand. The short cut is surgery, which doctors here seem very blithe about, but we are fighting that one. On the other hand, if no surgery, he is going to be incarcerated for another six months, which is pretty damned depressing. He is not, as you know, a patient man, and while he can work gently for a couple of hours a day he is not allowed to work under any pressure (which is the only way he *does* work well), so he is feeling very depressed, frustrated, and isolated, although I've taken this flat very close to the hospital so I can see him every day. On the good side all my hard work the first year back is paying off and I can look after the rest of us without him having to worry about earning money. I have a radio programme now as well as the weekly newspaper column, and the TV presentation of *My Brother*

Jack was so wildly successful that I have more TV offers than I could possibly cope with. Also I am working on a play, under the auspices of the Elizabethan Trust, and very excited about that. Unfortunately, all this terrific pressure of work is beginning to catch up and I am recovering now from my second go of pneumonia in six months, which means that I too am a bad TB risk from now on and have to curtail activities to absolute essentials — like earning a living. I live in a sort of Limbo. Temporary flat, temporary life, the family fragmented. I've sent Jason down to stay with his cousins in Victoria for these six months, since he isn't allowed to see George or George him and I have to work so hard I don't have time to make up for that. Actually he's loving it — real country life and country kids and their father the headmaster of the little country school — but I miss him something awful — and am at present house-hunting around with a view to getting us all back together again as soon as George is let out of the bin. Martin and Shane and I muck along in this wildly modern flat with buttons and gadgets everywhere but no furniture except a bed each and a desk for me to work on and a table to eat off and piles of books higgeldy-piggeldy all over the floor. Shane is working in a film studio learning editing and cutting and sound-mixing and all the technical side of film making and is happy for the first time since coming back here — very independent and filled with technical jargon and buying her own clothes and being really very pleasant and growing extraordinarily pretty — not pretty exactly, but very kooky and chic and individual, and I like her more than I've done since she was a tot. Martin is in the middle of the dreadful and all-important matric, out for every scholarship he can get, and nervous to the point of twitches in spite of his incredible record this year. He'll do marvellously, but just at the moment we are all suffering with him. He is quite enormous and wears his hair very Beatly and his shoes very pointed and his pants so tight he practically has to soap his legs to get into them, and is ardent about colour-questions and civil rights and the Peace Corps and everything proper to his age and intellect. He'll be all right [...] What else can I tell you? I don't know whether I like this country or not, but for the moment I'm stuck with it so I try to make the good things work for me, and at least I can do things to make the cultural climate a bit more exciting. I mean, you can still *make* things happen here instead of sitting around and wondering why they don't happen. This, of course, is exhausting, but if you manage to carry a few people along on a wave of enthusiasm some of them keep on going and something comes out of it all. There is some nice ordinary painting going on, not much in writing or in theatre, TV is coming along and the film industry seems to be reviving. I hear sometimes from the old Hydra crowd, but since the house has been sold I don't have any emotional ties there and the news seems to come from another planet. At least I am certain that I like this better than that, which is a good thing to find out I suppose, even at my age. I am mad to go to Asia for a trip, and am trying to arrange this for next year, as soon as I can hand over the home fort to George for a bit. One is so disturbingly conscious of Asia here, and a bit frightened, and a bit excited about possibilities. No more room. Much love, Charmian[18]

Although Charmian was being determinedly cheerful, this letter reveals the pace and pressure of her existence. And at this difficult time there was suddenly an unanticipated worry about money. When Collins drew up their six-month royalty statements for the second part of 1965, they held back Johnston's payment owing on *My Brother Jack* (approximately £450) because he had failed to deliver *Clean Straw for Nothing* as he had promised to do in return for the £1000 which had been paid in advance on this unwritten novel. Writing in mid November to advise his client of this, David Higham noted that 'under the agreements, they are strictly not entitled' to act in this fashion, and asked if the author found it acceptable.[19]

A letter thundered back from Thoracic Ward No. 3, Royal North Shore Hospital. Johnston found 'the set-up disturbing AND improper'. He reminded his agent that Billy Collins himself had authorised the payment to 'grubstake' his novel, then proceeded to explain that he had written about 120 pages before putting the work aside, with the approval of Billy Collins, who had told him 'to wait till it "came"'. (This was essentially the same draft which the author had mentioned abandoning in his letter to Higham, back in May.)

It was not coming well, partly because I was physically and mentally exhausted by the tremendous running about on the homecoming promotion of *My Brother Jack,* partly because the unsettlement was not conducive to thoughtful creative writing, and mostly because (quite unknown to me at the time) I had redeveloped active TB and a new and largish cavity in my previously sound lung. On top of this, with Collins' total approval, Charmian and I were for months involved in getting MBJ on as a national TV serial [...] The fact remains that virtually a whole year has gone on *My Brother Jack.*[20]

Johnston went on to explain that when he had come into hospital he had 'tried to tackle the novel again, but this proved hopeless, in an eight-bed ward with a typewriter balanced on the edge of a bed, and under constant heavy drugs and sedation'. The author added:

I think I have, while in here, worked the novel out in my mind now, and will go at it full spate as soon as I am discharged — I do deeply WANT to — but that is the situation. (Quite a lot of other plans and writing projects, both Charmian's and mine, have had to be postponed or given up altogether as a result of this hospitalisation.)

He concluded by reiterating that the withholding of the *Jack* royalties against the *Clean Straw for Nothing* advance came as a 'complete shock' to him, 'especially as we were banking on these royalties [...] for the payment of our taxation'.

The simple fact is, David, that I have largely got myself into this state of health by trying to get CSFN written and at the same time to devote all other energies to the promotion of Jack. But I cannot write CSFN unless I can give it my best. It MUST be the best thing I have ever done.

This indicates how very seriously George Johnston regarded the writing of the second book of the trilogy. To the list of reasons for not writing it he might also have added fear of failure: it is always hard to satisfy critics and the public with a sequel, and *My Brother Jack* had been taken up with such fervour that it would be a hard act to follow. Although Johnston declared in this letter that he thought he had now worked the novel out in his mind, he was in fact still having desperate trouble with his material — not least because for the first time in his life he was trying to work alone, without Charmian as sounding board. Of course, he couldn't tell his agent any of these problems, because he had to get the *Jack* royalties — urgently.

David Higham immediately took the matter up with Sir William Collins, who agreed that stopping the money had been 'entirely wrong', and ordered that the outstanding royalties be paid forthwith. The matter of the advance on the unwritten work could be delayed until April of the following year, when the next set of accounts would be done. Billy Collins also wrote personally to George Johnston, to reassure him.[21] As things turned out, the publisher would keep extending the deadline.

Although this problem was overcome by Christmas, it had caused Charmian as well as George a month of terrible anxiety. And when the money at last arrived, it went immediately to the Taxation Department, to pay off tax owing on money earned by the *My Brother Jack* television serial. Again the couple were caught in a cycle of robbing Peter to pay Paul. As always, they were broke, despite the fact that they were earning fairly good money. In 1964–65 George Johnston's income had been £2107, and in 1965–66 it was £1564. By now, Charmian Clift was contributing more than her husband to the household economy. In 1965–66 her income was £2250.[22]

Apart from the tax debt, the establishment of the flat had cost a great deal, and ongoing household costs were high, for Charmian was glad-handed with her teenage children, who in turn had acquired their parents' habits of generosity and hospitality. The new refrigerator was constantly being emptied by the many teenagers who buzzed in and out of the flat.

In these circumstances, the payments for the weekly column and the fortnightly radio sessions on the ABC *Let's Find Out* program assumed a great importance. If the sums in themselves were comparatively small, at least the money was regular. Yet the cost to Charmian Clift was high. In regard to the fortnightly radio broadcasts, Anne Deveson remembered that after a certain time of Charmian working with Ellis Blain, 'again much the same things began to happen [...] in that she clearly found it a great strain — she used to get very nervous — he said she was sick once or twice'.[23] Despite this, she would continue working on this program right through her time at Ben Boyd Road.[24]

The pressure of the regular column deadline was also by now starting to take a toll. As well as the stress of meeting these commitments, the author naturally resented the fact that this ephemeral work was keeping her away from work on *The End of the Morning.* As her letter to her agent had made clear, there wasn't enough 'daily bread' in novel-writing. Although it was pleasing to see the republication of thirty-six of the newspaper pieces in the anthology *Images in Aspic,* this was no compensation for the autobiographical novel which the author had had to put aside.

Another strain on Charmian at this time was a particular type of loneliness. Life without George might have been more peaceful, but it was not the life to which Charmian was accustomed. This December, in a list of things which she would like to have been doing, the columnist revealed how deeply she was missing her unique relationship with her husband:

> Most of all, I would like to be sitting around [the] new and splendidly monastic table and benches with George Johnston, talking and talking and talking for hours at a stretch (we talked for thirteen hours straight once and came up with an idea that turned into a novel called *My Brother Jack*) and drinking very cold beer and inventing plots for novels and plays and stories.
>
> [But] I can't sit around the table and talk to George Johnston because George Johnston is in hospital and hospitals aren't conducive to our particular sort of talking and don't have cold beer and wouldn't allow thirteen hours for working out an idea.[25]

On 18 December, George was permitted to leave hospital in order to spend three weeks with his family over the Christmas/New Year period.[26] However, the joy of reunion was tempered by the fact that the doctors had now told George that his condition was so bad that surgery could not be avoided. The large and irregular doses of antibiotics that the invalid had taken in Greece had made his tuberculosis resistant to drugs. For George, this was like the period in 1959 when he had awaited the 'verdict' on his health: he would later admit that 'once again' he had 'expected to die'. And just as the earlier expectation had caused Johnston to undertake a major assessment of his life — both personal and professional — this new encounter with mortality would also prove to be an emotional watershed. While the prospect of such major surgery would have been worrying for anyone, this was once again a time when George's early experience came into play. Hospitals, surgery, mutilation, abandonment, aloneness, fear: all these categories had been collapsed together in the mind of the child who had once been George. It was only natural if memory flooded back in odd combinations.

For Charmian also, of course, this was a nerve-wracking time. As someone who had never had even a minor operation, the thought of George's surgery was horrific. Meanwhile, she had to keep up her regular column work and try to hold the household together, for the sake of the two teenagers. It was a gloomy Christmas anyway, with 'the small boy' away, but Charmian was cheered by Jason's present of an audiotape of himself and his cousins 'singing their carols and thumping out their piano pieces and chanting their Christmas messages'.[27] He had settled very happily into life at Longwood, where he had 'high status' in the family in the role of eldest son and second oldest child[28] — a pleasant change after being for so long regarded as the baby of his own family unit.

In the first week of the New Year of 1966, George went back to hospital, and on 14 January he underwent the massive surgery which he would later dub his 'shark bite'. This involved a resection of the apical segment of the right upper lobe of his lung; a few hours after the main surgery, it was necessary to perform an emergency tracheotomy, to enable the patient to breathe.[29] For two weeks George lay in the post-surgical 'recovery room', hovering between life and death, alternating between waves of pain and moments of drug-induced relief, unable to speak because of the tubes in his throat. In this fortnight when his mind moved in and out of consciousness, George Johnston experienced a series of hallucinatory insights into both the meaning of experience and the structure of his novel.

The full details of George's revelations disappeared once he began to recover. Yet enough memory of this experience would remain for the author to believe that he had gained a significant 'clarification' while in the recovery room of the intensive care unit. Speaking of this some years later to Elizabeth Riddell, Johnston would declare that at this time he had 'got control over the theme of *Clean Straw*'. He added: 'I could handle the story. I understood how to do it'.[30] In a 1969 interview with Joan Flanagan, the author would also describe the post-operative period in hospital as the 'turning point':

> For two years, I'd been trying to do a sequel in the narrative style
> of *My Brother Jack*. If it had been finished, it would have been a
> novel of 850 pages. I had a major surgery and once again I
> expected to die and once again I didn't. And suddenly the whole
> thing became clear.[31]

The author went on to say that during this period he 'seemed to be existing in a series of slots of pain, overlapping like the spokes on the whipping machine which used to be displayed in the window of the old Coles Book Arcade in Melbourne'. At that point, he 'could see very clearly what shape [the novel] was to take'.

Back in the ward after this fortnight in intensive care, Johnston managed to write a couple of pages based on the insight he had gained. So important was this 'clarification' that he treated this passage as a new start to his novel.[32] It would be nearly two years before the author was ready to expand this fragment into the form it takes in the 'Sydney, 1966' passage of *Clean Straw for Nothing*, but through this period the insight would remain in the author's mind.

In the novel, Johnston describes two separate recovery room revelations. The first is to do with the meaning of experience and time. This passage (from the completed novel) was copied almost verbatim from the opening passage that the author had written in 1966:

> Meredith had to try to piece it all together, seeking it where he could in the narrow tight slots of clarity lying between the great fields of pain flinging out of himself and away and back into a past where it no longer hurt [...] There were times when he felt the whole secret almost to be within his grasp.
>
> There was neither night nor day in the windowless Recovery Room [...] so that time existed only as an abstract in the endless flinging recession of the sheets of pain dropping into a past composed entirely of fragmented things that he didn't have to go through any more. He felt elated at this discovery that all experience, even the most painful, turned into something that no longer had to be experienced.[33]

As he lies in this room, unable to speak, Meredith wishes he could communicate this 'revelation' to Cressida, of whom he is aware from time to time, 'standing beside the trolley [...] sterile-capped and masked'. The text moves on to a description of some of the other patients in the recovery room. One is dubbed 'the social woman'.

> Meredith thought of her as the social woman. She was a terrible mess of crushed bones beneath the sheet and she had a face that had once been very beautiful and was still comely. She was only

flickeringly conscious. She looked to be about the same age as Cressida, only more tired, which was understandable. A number of different men visited her, all staring down without ever saying anything, their eyes above the white masks hurt and helpless. Meredith thought of them as the woman's lovers, although they could have been only business associates or relatives. In the circumstances who they really were didn't matter.[34]

Although in this scene Cressida herself is the very model of the solicitous wife, it is the ravaged beauty and supposed promiscuity of the 'social woman' that is important to David Meredith's dream state. It is difficult not to feel that this woman takes Cressida's place — becomes Cressida — in the hallucinations.

After this comes the second revelation. Again the insight is foreshadowed by a description of the pain. The text moves into a description that links with the author's account given later to Joan Flanagan. This hallucination took the form of a childhood memory:

When he had been a small boy in Melbourne there had been two little mechanical mannikins in the window of Cole's Book Arcade, dressed as Jack Tars [...] which worked at a kind of windlass thing which flung over, rhythmically but jerkily, oblong boards printed with statements like COMIC BOOKS, FICTION FOR ALL AGES, GAMES AND PUZZLES, NOVELTIES AND STATIONERY, THE GROTTO AND AQUARIUM, GIFT BAZAAR. Meredith was reminded of this by the way the sheets of pain moved, as if there was a toy windlass inside him, moving it out of him in flinging, slapping jerks. At first, in the shadowy clefts and apertures between the jerks, the remembered ghosts had gathered, but later they had all vanished to make room for the clarity of the revelation. It was the clarity that was the special thing about it.

The author's use of the term 'whipping machine' in his verbal description of this hallucination is a clue to what was happening inside the patient's memory under the effect of drugs and pain. Surely the 'flinging, slapping jerks' were mimicking the rhythm of the razor-strop wielded by his father, and the two little 'mannikins' remembered from the shop window represented himself and his brother; indeed, they were *Jack* tars. As with

My Brother Jack, the author's painful memory of his childhood was the trigger that set off the writing of fiction. This movement of the pain, and the movement of the oblong boards manipulated by the Coles Book Arcade mannikins, would provide the author with a metaphor for the movement he needed for his novel. More than eighteen months later, he would develop an additional metaphor for the book's structure.

In biographical terms, the importance of George Johnston's experience in the recovery room is threefold. Taking it now in reverse order: there is the structural method suggested by the advertising boards which 'rhythmically but jerkily' move on, allowing room for 'ghosts' in the 'apertures' between the printed information. This would lead to the author's decision to chop his chronological story into fragments, told essentially from the point of view of Meredith in the present looking into the past. This method would allow the novelist to avoid one of the problems he had been having with the earlier drafts which was that, if he told the whole story sequentially, it was going to be 'longer than *War and Peace*'.[35] This 'windlass' method would enable him to wind the story quickly through a large timespan. The greatest boon, however, of a fragmented method is that it allows a writer to be even more selective than usual in the shaping of the story. For an author using such a method, the decision about what to leave out becomes as important as what to include; for the reader, however, there can be no way of knowing what happened in these gaps in the story.

George Johnston always seemed to find this structural insight gained in the recovery room to be a bolt from the blue. In fact, this approach was very similar to the structure which he and Clift had employed in *The Piping Cry*. More recently, in *The Meredith Papers* (discussed in chapter 17), the author had planned to put together a series of fragments of material, like jigsaw pieces in a box, and leave it to the reader to fashion the picture.

In yet another account of the story of his 'clarification' — given in September 1969 to the journalist Kay Keavney — the author noted that it was during this hospital time that he had realised that 'above all' the book would be 'a love story'. He added that it was also in this post-operative period that he had come to a crucial decision in the matter of characterisation. 'To some extent', Keavney reported, 'it was his own love story, with Charmian, but his character of Cressida was fictional too. For this reason he would not make her a writer'.[36]

This is where the second significant aspect of the recovery room experience kicks in. Now the double-sided figure of Cressida as noble wife and 'the social woman' with her multiple lovers and shattered face comes into play. (It is no coincidence that Cressida is masked.) In the first draft of the novel (discussed in chapter 7), Cressida Morley had been by vocation a writer of poetry and stories, as well as earning her living as a journalist.³⁷ As the author decided to leave out this part of the character's experience, she would become like the idle ruined beauty, for she would have no occupation, let alone vocation. From this time, as the book dealt predominantly with the relationship between David Meredith and Cressida Morley, it would also deal with the infidelity of this idle beauty, and her betrayal of her husband.

But how could a writer get around the issue of the possible pain which such a portrayal might cause to the model for the fictional character? It is here that we find the third factor of the recovery room experience which impacts on the biographical story. In order to be able to write this fictionalisation of the Cressida character, the author would draw upon his revelation that 'all experience, even the most painful, turned into something that no longer had to be experienced'. This sort of idea had been floating around in George Johnston's philosophy ever since his meeting with the Living Buddha in wartime Tibet. But now, as Johnston faced pain and the possibility of death on a daily basis, it became the closest thing that this agnostic had to a creed. A few years later, Martin Johnston would note that, towards the end of his life, his father's philosophy came down to 'the central acceptance of the fact that there's no meaning to anything experienced except that it has been experienced — and that is perhaps enough'.³⁸

Now the author had two ways of justifying his decision to write whatever he wanted to write without worrying whether it would hurt anyone. Firstly, no one's pain could be equal to his own sufferings: he had been to hell and back, and carried the scars upon his body to prove it. Even more importantly, his revelation declared that all pain *meant* nothing — just as experience meant nothing. The present simply turned into the past, in the way that the little signs on the mannikins' windlass flipped over and over — or, indeed, in the way that the prayer wheels of Tibetan Buddhism turned in the wind. Everything disappeared ultimately into the mists. Onto the belief in the irrelevancy of pain and experience was transposed a feeling that the present, too, was irrelevant. Only the past mattered any more, as both Johnston the novelist and Johnston the person relived his own story. This enabled him to feel the pains of the past with the immediacy of the present, while simultaneously denying that the telling of this past could cause real pain in the present — for neither the present nor pain really existed.

This, then, was the import of the 'clarification' or epiphany which Johnston experienced in the recovery room after his surgery in January 1966. Despite the intensity of this, the author would still not be able to get the novel down on paper. For over eighteen months, until about September 1967, Johnston would experience what he would later describe as 'a gigantic writer's block' in regard to this work.[39] However, the author's whole near-death experience, together with what he perceived as the meaning of the revelations, would start to shape both his attitude to life, and the way in which he would behave towards his wife.

Anxiety about George's health as well as worries occasioned by the political situation led Charmian Clift to write as her New Year piece for 1966 an essay that revealed some of her deep concern about the future. The title — 'On a Lowering Sky in the East' — set the sombre mood:

> It looms ahead portentous as years go, dark in colour as a lowering sky, shot with ominous flickers that might presage real lightning bolts, uneasy with rumours of economic recessions, readjustments, restrictions, sanctions, deepening military commitments, grave predictions, hints from high places that things might have to get worse before they get better.
> And the slaughter continuing.[40]

This sentence stands as a paragraph alone, in terrible emphasis. The writer then goes on to catalogue some of the horrors she sees in daily newspaper photographs:

> Babies not only abandoned but burned with napalm, fleeing women bloodied and torn, screaming faces, young boys bound under viciously kicking boots or smashing rifle butts: the horror is blunted by such constant repetition: we turn to the sport or the gossip concerning television celebrities or the social pages.

While this piece revealed a new strength of political concern in the Clift column, there was soon to be a political change on a national level. On 20 January, Sir Robert Menzies announced his retirement from the position of Prime Minister. For Charmian Clift, this had a deep symbolic significance. Would this at last be the end of the Cold War atmosphere that she had loathed for so long? It was soon clear that there would be no immediate improvement; if anything, things would be worse, for with Harold Holt at the helm, the country would tend more and more to woo the friendship of the United States, offering increasing commitment of troops (including conscripts) to Vietnam as proof of fidelity.

The dark and brooding persona revealed in this essay was part of Clift the columnist. Another part of the columnist's persona was the determinedly cheerful — but still concerned and compassionate — flat-dweller and mother of teenagers. In the early months of 1966 this second character was fleshed out into a fully developed alter ego as Clift began to write the first drafts and treatments of a television series entitled *Kate Perrin's Life*.[41] The proposal was for this to be twenty-six episodes, each of thirty minutes. Although the cover page of Draft Submission No. 1 (dated 30 May 1966) noted 'Proposal for an ABC-TV Series by Charmian Clift (or Charmian Clift and George Johnston)', it was Clift alone who had taken the project to this stage. Or Clift alone, with Storry Walton in the role of sounding board.

While this series would never be produced, the draft scripts form an important part of Clift's television work. They also provide biographical insight into how Clift viewed herself and her world at this time. Described as 'situation comedy/drama set in contemporary urban and suburban Australia', *Kate Perrin's Life* would have been a kind of television dramatisation of the weekly column — complete with current political concerns and family crises. Eschewing the unsavoury aspects of Johnston's character Kate from *Closer to the Sun*, this new Kate is a splendid heroine in the Clift tradition.

> Leading character of the show is KATE PERRIN, an attractive 'interesting' woman around forty. She is a writer of considerable ability, and a widow. She is sophisticated, has travelled abroad, but is something of an oddball — intellectual, original, passionately human, unconventional, deeply concerned for her own individualistic values, rather Bohemian, and more than somewhat disorganised. She is both wise in the humanities and impractical in everyday matters [...]
>
> KATE is the mother of two children. BEN, who is aged nineteen, is doing an arts course at university. POLLY, the daughter, is aged seventeen.

Kate Perrin is in fact closer to the real life model than any of Clift's other alter egos, except for the child Cressida Morley. (Storry Walton affirmed that 'Clift wasn't adapting anyone — it was Charmian coming through strongly and boldly'.) Kate's 'back story' was also borrowed directly from the life experience of her model — with a dash of the art school experience of Charmian's sister Margaret thrown in:

> Kate was born in a small South Coast seaport town, completed a high school course, and went on to study art and fashion design, but married young and did not continue with this as a career. When her two children were still quite young she went overseas with her husband, a newspaperman. During the next twelve years or so she lived variously in London, Paris, Rome, Athens.

In order to make the character a single mother, the scriptwriter dispensed with the newspaper husband 'in an automobile accident on the autostrada', which had occurred a couple of years earlier. Now, 'impelled by a sense of isolation, loneliness and downright homesickness, [Kate has] returned to her native land'.

> Although loyally Australian she is still not quite at home in Australia. She is concerned for her children, but also concerned for her own career and her own individuality as a person [...] She is also a little lonely. The trouble is that she simply has too much on her plate with the flat and the children, her job and her personal life.

If this character description is starting to sound like a cry for help from the author, it continues in a vein that reveals a terrible loneliness:

> With her late husband Kate had lived a very happy and colourful married life, and while there is no morbidity in her memory of this past association, she has not yet met another man who fulfils her particular requirements. Yet she is often alone and lonely: it is likely that she would welcome a genuinely romantic affair, and even a second husband if the right man came along [...]
>
> Kate, a lone woman in a world filled with jeopardy, is deeply concerned with 'security' (although not at any price), with Ben's education, with Polly's fecklessness, and with her reabsorption into the Australian scene as it impinges on her own life and problems. She is brave. She is gay. Only to herself would she confess her fears, doubts, trepidations, and insecurities.

The setting for all this was the living room of the Neutral Bay flat, described as 'chaotic in an interesting way'. The 'general air of disorder' is 'created largely by the activities of the young'. These 'young' were a vital part of the series. In the characters of Kate's two adolescent offspring, Charmian's own two teenagers are unmistakeable, and the friends of 'Ben' and 'Polly' were important as catalysts for action. As from week to week they brought their problems to Kate, the series could engage with new contemporary issues such as 'examination problems at school, university, protest demonstrations, the blight of suburbanism, teenage sex and morals, delinquency, conscription, racial prejudice, surfies, folk singers and beatniks, long hair, the go-go life, and what-have-you'. The multicultural neighbours in the flats dropped in with other problems for Kate to sort out. It was these problems — plus some of Clift's own difficulties as a single mother and home-grown migrant — which went straight into the story treatments.

Twenty-five years later, Storry Walton had no doubts about the potential significance of *Kate Perrin's Life*: 'Here was Charmian setting up what would have led the field in serious political situation comedy/drama. It was such a good idea — such a good idea! It was in advance of its time!' In discussing Clift's scripts for contemporary stories such as 'The Demo' and 'The Call-up', Walton declared that the serial 'was going to be a wonderful opportunity to do in television what *Blue Hills* had successfully done in radio' — ie comment on topical issues as they arose.

However, the actual nature of this social commentary was going to be far to the left of any discussion ever raised on Australia's most popular radio serial. This was the problem, for the ABC. Storry Walton explained that initially Clift was 'encouraged' by the national broadcaster to write treatments of the series but 'she was never paid for them', and 'the ABC in the end in fact reneged' on the whole idea. Clift's political attitudes were the nub of this refusal. Walton referred back to the 'nervosity' which some people had initially felt about George Johnston's left wing views, adding that in regard to the *Kate Perrin* series, 'There was a feeling among some of the script editors in the ABC that Charmian was radical'. Walton notes that 'I thought the ABC should have embraced Charmian [...] and gone out of their way to secure her', but in fact the reverse happened. 'After *My Brother Jack* she didn't get a good reception [at the ABC] ... There was a lot of nervosity about — about her'.[42]

Although it is hard to pinpoint the timing for all this, it is clear that in the first six or eight months of 1966, as Clift produced the main storyline for the *Kate Perrin* series, she did feel encouraged, not least by Walton himself. Further encouragement was given by the actor Googie Withers, who 'expressed enormous personal interest in the proposal' and said 'she would be greatly interested in the role'.[43]

The writing and rewriting of this series would continue spasmodically through 1966 and most of 1967, during which time encouragement would gradually change to rejection. In retrospect, it is clear that if the series had gone ahead, it would have been an absolute ground-breaker in terms of its presentation of an independent single mother living in a multicultural Australia. Three and a half decades later, the issues explored in the *Kate Perrin* scripts are still considerably more challenging than those presented on any current Australian family sitcom.

Over March–April 1966, as Clift worked on this first Draft Submission for *Kate Perrin*, she had her longest break from the column: for five consecutive weeks, readers of the Women's Section of the *Sydney Morning Herald* were informed that the columnist was ill.[44] As her November letter to her friend Jo had revealed, since coming back to Australia, Charmian had suffered from a predisposition to chest infections and flu, to which the hectic pace of her lifestyle made her prone. The amount of time spent at the hospital didn't help. Apart from this, Charmian was (according to her GP) in basically good general health. However, throughout these years she regularly sought medical advice in regard to decidedly unpleasant symptoms of menopause, including menstrual disorders and hot flushes. She also complained of depression, which the doctor attributed largely to the anxiety caused by George's chronic illness.[45]

Sometimes the amount of pressure became insupportable. As a result, Charmian's drinking was becoming a form of escape and self-medication rather than a way of socialising. Sometimes Charmian drank to give herself confidence to go on radio or speak in public. She would also sometimes have a few glasses of wine or whisky in order to numb the terror of the weekly column, or to kickstart the flow of ideas. Yet another reason was to escape from the many pressures and problems that were daily heaped upon her: intoxication provided her with the 'time out' which she couldn't get in any other way. But of course the alcohol was itself a depressant, and hangovers brought on self-recrimination as well as headaches and nausea.

During her break from the column in March–April 1966, Charmian made preparations for George's return. He was discharged from hospital on

21 April.[46] The flat was a dreadful place for convalescence, what with the cramped circumstances and the noise of two teenagers and their waves of visitors dropping in at all hours, especially as Martin was now at university and making new friends to bring home. It was Charmian who had the unpleasant job of cramping the style of her two older 'young'.

And in any case, George was not at all well. While his body had not fully recovered from the trauma of surgery, the ongoing prescribed drugs left him woozy and depressed. Under these conditions he knew there was no hope of returning to work on *Clean Straw for Nothing* for quite some time.[47] This delay understandably made him impatient and sometimes ill-tempered.

For the moment the best course of action seemed to be to join Clift in the scriptwriting ventures, initially by adding his name as possible co-writer of *Kate Perrin's Life*.[48] It is typical of the professional sharing of this couple that Clift would immediately allow Johnston into the scriptwriting team. As usual, collaboration was frustrating. By now Clift was considerably more experienced as a television scriptwriter; and besides, George Johnston's natural talents did not lie in the area of television drama.[49] However, he had innovatory ideas for documentaries, some of which were made.

Both writers showed a good understanding of the importance of the television medium. At this time, many Australian authors regarded this form of entertainment as lowbrow, and would have nothing to do with it. But Charmian Clift and George Johnston were proud to be seen as communicators of ideas. Speaking to members of the Australian Writers' Guild, Clift told scriptwriting colleagues:

> A writer's business is communication, and he would be an idiot if he didn't use every medium at his disposal as a channel of communication. A novel communicates to some thousands of people [but] that little screen is in every living room. The potential audience is in terms of millions. It would be crazy not to exploit it. If you think it's not good enough or the standard is too low, or you can't bear to associate art with commercialism [...] make the standard better [...] Whatever the difficulties or obstacles, I think we just have to dive in. And do it anyway.[50]

In July 1966 George Johnston told *Sun* journalist Alan Trengrove that both he and Clift were 'turning their eyes to television writing'. He explained: 'The field of communication between the creative person and the public is being taken over by television. The only people who can lift standards on television are writers. We both can see that the challenge is there'.[51]

For these two communicators, media interviews such as the Trengrove piece were also part of the job. Although this particular interview was given by George alone at the Neutral Bay flat, the piece was part of a series entitled 'Partners'. A rather ugly photograph of the couple holding a copy of *My Brother Jack* was captioned 'Charmian Clift and George Johnston — that comparatively rare phenomenon: a successful husband and wife writing team'. This was a standard part of the public image of these two, and indeed the 'hook' or 'angle' of many of the newspaper stories was the presentation of Clift and Johnston as a kind of pantomime horse. While this image went all the way back to the publicity surrounding the *High Valley* prize in 1948, it was bolstered by the picture of the happy family that Clift herself created in the newpaper column. Yet it was developing into a myth which Clift was finding increasingly wearing.

By agreeing to be interviewed for trivial feature stories such as this one, Charmian Clift and George Johnston laid themselves open to criticism from the highbrow literary establishment. The derisory comments about the couple which occasionally appear in Patrick White's letters reveal the extent of the divide between the two sides of Australian literary culture. In one of these remarks, White inadvertently hits the nail on the head:

> Every time one opens a paper [the Johnstons are] in it, but I suppose that is so they can continue to have it good. One wonders what one might do in similar circumstances. I don't *feel* I could turn into a Johnston, but I have always been able to sit back and get on with what I wanted to do, without any of the material worries.[52]

Clift and Johnston's belief in communicating was one reason why they appeared so frequently in so many different media outlets. Another reason was their political beliefs. Unlike Patrick White, who at this time was publicly silent about contemporary issues, Clift and Johnston would use any opportunity to try to alert the Australian people to concerns ranging from the Vietnam War to censorship to architectural ugliness. However, the major reason why George would give an interview such as the Trengrove one would be in the hope of boosting sales, and hence the royalties, of *My Brother Jack*. Unlike White, neither he nor Clift could sit back and get on with what they wanted to do.

In this *Sun* interview Johnston noted that Clift was 'trying to write an autobiographical novel', adding: 'It is half-finished, but her other work intrudes'. Of course, *The End of the Morning* had also been described as 'half-finished' in the interview given to the Kiama newspaper over eighteen months earlier. Not only was 'half' a considerable exaggeration, but it is clear that this work had not progressed since Clift had returned to Australia. The whole feeling given in this article is that novel-writing was a luxury that simply could not be afforded.

Meanwhile, George's arrival at the flat caused well-meaning friends to intensify their campaign of nagging Charmian to find a house to buy — preferably somewhere up the leafy North Shore, where life would be peaceful for her sick husband. This infuriated Charmian. Why should she come back to so-called civilisation in order to bury herself in suburbia?[53]

However, the move could be postponed no longer. Through the winter months of 1966 Charmian began house-hunting in earnest. By August she had found a place. Unfortunately — from her point of view — it was situated in suburban Mosman, in a 'decorous tree-lined street that was muted in key almost to somnolence'. She longed for a water view, but this place had no outlook at all. Yet there was something about this tall, slender white house which had a steep-pitched slate roof and wide shingled bay windows, a funny little porch at a side entrance and a general air of shabby neglect. It was, she concluded, 'amiable [...] It wasn't a house to look out of but to live in'.[54]

And so the Johnstons bought 112 Raglan Street, Mosman. In fact, the house's layout was not very convenient: the stairs would prove difficult for George to climb because of his breathing problems. The house would also need a considerable amount of costly renovation. However, in terms of atmosphere it was a splendid choice: in an odd way this place had a rambling similarity to the Hydra house, and it soon brimmed with friends and hospitality as the Hydra house had.

In November 1966 settlement on the property took place, and Charmian bade farewell to the Neutral Bay skyline that she had grown to love.[55] Once again the belongings were packed into trunks and tea-chests, then unpacked again amidst the chaos of carpenters and painters.

In the September holidays, Jason had been up to stay in the flat.[56] When the school year finished in December, he left his cousins in Victoria and came back to Sydney, to rejoin his parents and siblings.

As the family celebrated this Christmas of 1966 together in their own place, it seemed to represent at last the homecoming of the exiles. And yet for Charmian this very togetherness emphasised a certain absence. Since returning to Australia, her thoughts of her relinquished daughter had begun to take on a new sharpness. In this city where that episode of her life had occurred, it was natural that she would sometimes wonder what Jennifer was doing or where Jennifer was living. The anniversary of her daughter's birth at Christmas intensified this anguish of uncertainty. Of all the burdens that Charmian carried, this was by no means the heaviest, but it was one which she had to bear completely alone.

21

FINDING AUSTRALIA

Finding Australia is a queer and emotional business.[1]

Charmian Clift always enjoyed the chance New Year gave of wiping out all the errors of the past and starting afresh. In her New Year essay for 1967 the columnist wrote feelingly of this 'recurring seasonal moral audit' and the 'sort of palpable aura of splendid intention'.[2] But it was in a letter to Joy and Felix Russo, written on New Year's Day, that Charmian expressed her real joy this year, her sense of optimism now that Jason had come home and the family was at last reunited and in their very own place.

> It is so good to start this year with such profound thankfulness for so many things, and not the least of them that the small boy is with us again and we are a family under our own roof for the first time in years [...]
>
> The house is proving to be everything we hoped, though far from finished yet.[3]

For Charmian the greatest attraction of the house was a small room on the ground floor, next to a little side porch. This would be her study; the addition of a divan meant that she could sleep there at times when George was particularly ill, or when she needed to work late or start at dawn. Twelve months earlier, belting away at her typewriter on the long communal table in the flat, she had used Virginia Woolf's famous dictum that a writer needs a room of her own as theme and title of an essay bewailing her difficult existence.[4] Now, in February 1967, she recycled the title and essay opening but was able triumphantly to declare:

And so I have achieved it. After twenty years of belting somebody else's cast-off typewriter in corridors and corners or in my lap for the want of better work-space I not only have a typewriter of my own, but actually a room of my own.[5]

The new typewriter was a portable, with a fancy font which mimicked spidery handwriting; she used it particularly for letters, but sometimes also for her essays. As to the room, it was 'quite small and monastic', 'painted white, with a sloping wood ceiling and a sash window'. One whole wall of her 'cubbyhole' was taken up by splendid bookshelves of Queensland maple. And on the door were the 'decorations and warnings' that had been somewhere about her workplaces for the last ten years: 'a scrawled chalk Icarus, pink and white, that was sent to me once when I was feeling low', an announcement of her first novel, and a sign saying 'Do Not Disturb'.

Through the whole of 1966, neither George nor Charmian had corresponded with their literary agent in London. Kindly David Higham had written four times, begging:

> Do, my dears, let me have some news of you. I have none and am constantly worried about George's health. One line to say that he's so much better and that you're both happy and well — and even working on books — would cheer me enormously.[6]

Of course, they couldn't write to reassure David of any of these things, but their silence is mainly indicative of the fact that neither was working on a novel. To write and say this would increase their sense of failure. At last, in February 1967, David wrote that he 'would be grateful for any news' whether good or bad.[7] George's reply shows just how bleak things had been — but again there is the sense of optimism that now a new start was under way:

> Dear David,
> Guilt and contrition! I don't really know how I can write to you at all! One can merely say, David, that since the operation (that went rather worse than we had expected) it's been a bit of a battle getting well again, and I'm still a good deal below par so far as energy and respiration are concerned. But vertical now, at least. Lots of other problems, too — readjustments to this rather special way of life, economic troubles, and until recently, difficulties of accommodation. However we have now purchased

an old house and had it done up and are very pleased with it. Room for all and room to work. All this adds up to the reason I stayed out of touch — I couldn't bring myself to write when I had nothing to say that wasn't rather dispiriting. I think things will be looking up from now on. I haven't yet got back to the sequel to MBJ and have really been only pottering around on reasonably undemanding things — book reviews, odd articles, TV work — and to keep the pot boiling Charmian has been involved in a weekly newspaper column and a daily radio session, so she too has done no creative writing [...]

I can't really tell the shape of work this year at the present stage, but am very hopeful of getting back soon to *Clean Straw for Nothing*, but anyway I'll keep in touch from now on. I do apologise for what must have seemed like a churlishness, but was really only a pretty deep depression.

Much love from us both, and do forgive,

George[8]

At the bottom of this he scrawled in handwriting: 'Actually, we are both feeling much better now — and will survive. Even in this very curious antipodean rat-race'.

George Johnston's main project at this time was an ABC documentary which took the interesting form of George interviewing the painter Russell Drysdale while Drysdale painted a portrait of the interviewer.[9] Since returning to Australia, George had become very friendly with Tass (as the painter was known to his friends) and his wife Maisie, and the documentary was filmed at the Drysdales' house at Bouddi, in the bush overlooking Brisbane Water. In this casual portrait of two blokes who sit around and drink and smoke while they chat about painting and writing and life, a captivating sense of George's particular conversational charm emerges. And yet this laconic piece is charged with tension, for as the viewer watches George — skeletally frail and often gasping for breath as his long nervous fingers play with cigarette or beer can — there is a feeling that he might die at any minute. It would be hard not to be moved by it.[10]

In May, Charmian took her three weeks annual leave from the column. Previous 'holidays' had been spent at home, reorganising the household, or had been wasted on illness. Now for the first time since returning to Australia she managed to get a holiday away from family reponsibility and away from city stress. She went north, to a landscape of rainforest and rock shelves, where there was 'no mail, and no desk pad scrawled with appointments and reminders, and newspapers came so late as to be scarcely worth opening'.

Charmian returned from her holiday not just personally refreshed, but also with a renewed feeling for her country. Her experience of Australia had previously been limited to Sydney, Melbourne, and her Kiama heartland. This trip north gave Clift her first taste of the variety and vastness of the landscape. She concluded her first essay after her return home with the observation that 'Finding Australia is a queer and emotional business'.[11] It would only be a few months before she would set off again, on a longer journey of discovery.

Despite this new love for the physical side of her country, Charmian Clift was by this time profoundly disillusioned about many aspects of Australian politics, Australian life and Australian people. As the third anniversary of her return from exile approached, the essayist pulled together many of her criticisms in a 'Report from a Migrant, Three Years After'.

> It is interesting now to look back on the things we wrote three years ago. The words 'challenge', 'excitement', 'vigour', 'vitality', 'opportunity', occur often. Also 'a sense of imminence'. I wonder whatever happened to that? Or were we, with bridges burned behind us, doing a desperate bit of wishful thinking?[12]

Often in conversation Clift would rage against the complacency of Australia and Australians.[13] Now she would declare that while she still thought the country 'so prodigal in opportunity', it was 'yet so unheroic, bland and even meek in the character of its people'.

> There is so little anger here. I suppose, as Bernard Shaw said, nobody will trouble themselves about anything that doesn't trouble them.
>
> And, mostly, Australians seem to be untroubled. Most Australians, that is. Far from being anti-authoritarian, as I had always believed, they actually seem to derive a sense of comfort and ease from unquestioning submission.

The writer then moves on to a list of 'the things that have happened in the last three years, the things that have become acceptable just by the acceptance of them'. This list includes conscription; commitment 'to a war that [...] is extremely nasty and strictly none of our business anyway'; higher prices and lower standards of consumer goods; 'worse public transport'; 'further despoliation of natural places'; the 'tragedy' of Jorn Utzon's departure from the Sydney Opera House; 'present curtailment of educational facilities and unpleasant hints of future curtailment of civil liberties'. Under this umbrella of civil liberties, Clift cites the censorship of films and books, and the stifling of Australian initiatives to write and direct and produce local television programs.

While acknowledging that 'there is protest', Clift worries that it 'seems to be spasmodic protest, and not sustained'; 'nor does protest ever become a whole mass movement, as in America'. All in all, she wonders when she too 'will stop asking questions, meekly heed authority, and settle for the adequate, the pretty and the approximate instead of demanding the good, the true, and the beautiful'.[14]

Fortunately, this migrant's unhappiness would soon be at least temporarily eased by a journey of discovery across the continent. This came about through a project in which George Johnston was initially involved.

After the success of the Drysdale documentary, a plan was hatched between George Johnston, Allan Ashbolt (head of Television Features in the ABC) and Storry Walton for a much more ambitious work. Sidney Nolan was due to arrive in Australia in August for a retrospective exhibition at the Art Gallery of New South Wales, to commemorate his fiftieth year. The proposal was developed for a documentary in which George Johnston would talk to the painter while accompanying him on a kind of retrospective journey to some of the places where Nolan had lived and painted. George was the obvious person to do the job of interviewing Nolan and writing the voice-over narration: not only was he an old friend of Sid's, but he could draw parallels between his own lower middle class suburban Melbourne background and that of his friend.

Storry contacted Nolan, who was keen to be the subject of a biographical film. Everything was ready by the time the artist flew in to Sydney on 15 August.[15] Unfortunately, in all the planning, no one had realised that Sid's affection for George — and to some extent Charmian — had considerably waned since the Hydra winter of 1955–56.[16] With this film in 1967 would come the ending of the old relationship — at least from Nolan's side.

'The whole situation was very peculiar', according to Allan Ashbolt, who was executive producer of the documentary. Part of the trouble was that over the years Nolan's social and political stance had become deeply conservative, while the Johnstons' attitudes hadn't changed. Ashbolt, who had known Nolan in New York in the late 1950s, inadvertently hit the nerve of this difference when he met with the painter in order to outline the shooting schedule. At the beginning of the discussion, Ashbolt said to Nolan:

'Before we go on, just let me ask you something ...'

Already George and Charmian had been deeply involved in the anti-war movement, so I said to Sid, 'How would *you* feel about taking a stand on this issue?' And he looked absolutely stunned — really! — and I thought 'Here we go, we're off to a great start!' [...]

So my relationship with Nolan ended at that time, and I wasn't sorry about it, either. I mean, he was just really bound up in himself and determined to stay on the conservative side of politics.[17]

Soon there would be worse problems than political differences, but at the beginning everything seemed to be all right. There was a splendid night when Charmian and George were present with Nolan at the Art Gallery of New South Wales as pictures were uncrated and hung and the painter looked at work which he hadn't seen for years.[18] A couple of weeks later, George accompanied Sid to Glenrowan to reminisce about the Kelly paintings. Back in Sydney for the mayoral reception at the town hall on 7 September, George gave the official speech of welcome. This was recorded and later transcribed by the documentary team:

This'll be a very brief speech. Siddie and I are very very old friends, we're both fugitives from Melbourne and we have followed a strange pattern — excuse my breathing, it's something wrong with me — and we went to the same schools, played in the same footie teams, both the sons of tramdrivers, and it's a very great honour to think that one of us, starting five years behind scratch on me, has achieved from Melbourne a civic reception in the city of Sydney.

(LAUGHTER)

... I am very proud indeed to be associated with him.

(APPLAUSE)[19]

Perhaps it was now — as George drew parallels between himself and Sid — that the painter decided he didn't want George in *his* film. Or perhaps the problem was the way George instantly won the sympathy of the crowd with his broad Australian accent, punctuated by his wheezing breath. Whatever the cause, Allan Ashbolt remembers that early in the shoot there was 'a sudden dislike on Nolan's part for George and Charmian':

> He thought that they were simply exploiting him.
>
> He had too big an opinion of himself, that was the problem. And he thought that they shouldn't have been intruded into this film. He would have preferred a documentary only with Nolan in it. And a few friends saying kind words. That's what he wanted [...] Because this was going to be Sid's fiftieth birthday and this was his present to Australia, and he didn't want these intruders mucking it up![20]

It appears that neither George nor Charmian was ever aware of the change in Nolan's attitude to them.[21] Perhaps their need to believe in Nolan was too great. Over the years Charmian had made the painter into a sort of guru, using his 'Bloody well fly!' philosophy to reinforce her own Icarus tendencies. And George, as we shall see, could still wring a great deal of meaning from a simple comment by the artist.

The next stage of the film itinerary was a visit to the site of Nolan's Central Australian paintings. By now it was becoming clear that George couldn't get the film's subject to open up and talk on camera. At the same time, the pace was proving too much for George's health; he certainly was not fit enough to go on the gruelling location shoot to the Centre. The only solution was for Charmian to be brought into the project. She was, Storry Walton remembered, 'the person best able to talk with Sid — to unlock Sid'.[22] This was not an easy job, for she had once described Nolan as 'not a wonderful story-teller' and 'not a good conversationalist — he only worries ideas around'.[23] Besides, for someone who hated talking on radio, it was absolutely nerve-wracking to interview someone on camera. However, the job had to be done, and as usual Charmian picked up the reins when George was unable to hold them. In mid September, she flew to Alice Springs with Sid and Storry and the crew.[24]

Although the shoot would only take about two weeks, Charmian Clift would be away from home for about six weeks altogether, and her journey, which progressed from the Centre to Far North Queensland, would be for her as important as her European discovery tour had been, back in the summer of 1952. Once again, she kept notes of her pilgrimage — jottings about landscape and climate, facts about people and places, together with occasional reminders to herself about how she was feeling. While the 1952 travel notes had become a resource for future fiction, these 1967 notes were instantly transformed into nine essays which form a discrete whole in the oeuvre of Clift's column writing. Like the best travel writing, these pieces tell as much about the internal journey of the traveller as they do of places seen and things encountered. In this case, the journey was an awakening — a revelation. 'If I cry my beloved country, what country is it and how shall I cry it?'[25] By the end of the trip, Charmian Clift was closer to an answer to this question.

It was metaphorically perfect that the first 'chapter' of this quest was entitled 'The Centre'. The traveller was initially awed by the size of the country. This sense of alienation was heightened by the awareness of the 'black shadow-weave of the disinherited' who moved through the town. As a child, Charmian Clift had known Aboriginal families living in humpies up on the Bombo headland. More recently, she had become friendly with Faith Bandler and Kath Walker and other activists. In Alice Springs, however, for the first time as an adult Clift saw the squalor to which Aboriginal town-dwellers had been reduced. 'I want to say "I'm sorry,"' she wrote in her first travel essay. 'Apologise. Absolve myself'. She concluded that 'Here in the thriving Alice, the guilt hurts intolerably'.[26]

Within a couple of days the film crew had all moved to Ayers Rock. It was the Olgas, however, which provided the ultimate spiritual experience. On one particular day a ranger escorted Charmian Clift, Sidney Nolan and a small contingent of the documentary crew up through one of the gorges. At first the party all fanned out, and as Clift walked alone through the early morning, listening to the silence, she realised she was 'not proofed against immortal longings'. The walk continued to the top of one of the strange red rocks, 'in the middle of what look[ed] like an Elizabethan herb garden'.[27]

Reflection on this garden and on the geological age of the landscape would prompt a strange conversation between Charmian and Sid about notions of paradise and immortality. As the camera rolled, and Charmian led the conversation from Coleridge's paradise to Kafka's idea of paradise, and then on to the artist's Prometheus paintings, she reminded him that he had 'travelled all the way back to the Greek myths'. With her reference to paradise, she finally managed to unlock the painter, and as Sid burbled on for the film, Charmian herself fell completely silent.[28] As her essay about this occasion reaches this moment, the author announces: 'I don't think I want to write about it at all really. I would like to keep it to myself and never tell a

soul'. It is clear that this was one of Charmian's moments of epiphany —
like the moment at Lerici — when she glimpsed something of what she was
always seeking. By the end of the day she would decide that the whole
venture of 'making a film in this paradisiacal herb garden' was
'presumptuous'.[29]

At the beginning of October, when filming in the Olgas was completed,
Nolan and the documentary team headed south to Melbourne.[30] Clift flew east
to meet a couple of friends of Tass Drysdale's, who had recently spent some
time with his colleague Ray Crooke and Ray's wife June at their home outside
Cairns. Believing that Charmian needed an extended break, Tass urged her to
go and stay with these friends. Charmian's hosts expected a city sophisticate;
they were amazed at the vulnerability of the woman who arrived.[31] June would
later remember that 'Charmian and I [...] communed instantly'.[32]

As well as wanting to explore her own country, Charmian was looking
for copy for the column. The Crookes and other people in Cairns started
recommending interesting places she should visit. When her hosts suggested
she go for a jaunt to Thursday Island, where they had once lived, she begged
June to accompany her. June was happy to go, but first of all Charmian set
off alone[33] to a place which initially seemed as hellish as the Olgas had been
heavenly.

This was a frontier settlement, less than a year old and with a population
of approximately 150; this unlikely place had been settled because a
company had set up a refrigeration and packing plant to service fourteen
prawning boats which trawled out in the Gulf of Carpentaria:

> Karumba is a name on the map of Australia, a dot on the mouth
> of the Norman River where it flows into the Gulf of Carpentaria
> and the hawks hang over the mangroves and the sandflies are
> murder. Thousands of jellyfish pulse on the tide, and the opaque,
> oily-looking water harbours huge coarse repellent fish, mud-
> crabs as big as large platters, sharks by the hundred, and still,
> they tell me, a few old and sagacious crocodiles.
>
>   It is sinister country. Evil to me since I react violently to
> landscape and am repelled utterly by this one that seems to be
> saturated with a sort of thick grey heat. The river here is broad,
> sluggish, yellow-grey in colour. The mangroves are green-grey,
> dense and heavy. And the blue-grey sky seems to have a tangible
> skin of heat on it.[34]

The writer may have been 'repelled utterly', but it is with the arrival at Karumba that her prose lifts and soars. Now she found the subject that was her forte: people. And what people! There was something about these prawn fishermen that reminded Clift of Kalymnian sponge-divers, and even the boats reminded her of Greek sponge boats.[35] This, of course, was the ultimate accolade.

And just as Charmian had quickly won the friendship of the sponge-divers during that first winter on Kalymnos, now her enthusiasm and lack of snobbery caused the men and women of Karumba to welcome her into their midst. By the time we have read the two Karumba essays we feel that we, too, have met Linda and her mother Evelyn in the packing shed, Graham from the CSIRO, Laurie and Tuppence from the boat *Ulitarra*, Laurie's wife Marion in the caravan park and their son little Stevie, and even 'the mysterious Mrs Pawlowska over the salt-pan' who stuffed the crocodiles that adorn Kath's bar. This sense of familiarity — on the part of both writer and reader — is heightened by the fact that Charmian Clift links herself with the townsfolk as she joins them in their work: 'We sort into wicker baskets', she tells us, and later, 'We stow the stores in the galley' and 'We all skate and slither and slide through the curling white mists' of the ice house. It is interesting that Charmian Clift, who saw herself always as the outsider, was so easily able to feel an insider amongst people such as these; the reason, of course, was that these were misfits and outsiders escaping from the larger community. In the bar of Karumba's one drinking establishment, she declares:

> This is the way a bar should look, and the faces around the bar look the way faces should look [...] Tonight nobody is wearing a disguise of any sort. Perhaps up here nobody wears disguises at all. And that, heaven knows, is an odd thought.[36]

All in all, for the first time since being back in Australia Clift felt that the imminence she was seeking was being fulfilled:

> There is, in spite of the boredom and monotony and heat and sandflies, an air of high excitement about this place [...]
>
> There is an atmosphere of challenge and adventure and high hope and endeavour that is about the most refreshing and exciting thing I have struck in Australia. In this most unlikely place a town called Karumba is away to a flying start. And Australia is a more exciting place than I ever dreamed.[37]

If Karumba was away to a flying start, so was Charmian's journey. After meeting up with June Crooke, she now headed north to Thursday Island, off the tip of Cape York. Although the writer found it 'not a lovely island' in terms of its geography,[38] again it was the people who really made the place for her: pearlers and islanders, living people and the dead whose exotic names she traced in the graveyard.[39] There was also, of course, the ocean itself: this was the first time since leaving Greece that Charmian had been able to indulge herself in sea worship. And as well as this, there was easy companionship with June, friendship of a kind that was rare for Charmian to experience. In the evening, sitting on the frangipani-strewn verandah of the hotel, the two friends would sit 'laughing until we have laughed ourselves into gravity again and peace and wonder'. To add the final seal of escapism to this holiday, there was even a fling with a naval officer who would continue to pursue Charmian after her return home. It was a nice boost for the morale. Mostly, however, the time on Thursday Island was a time of escape from care.

Twenty years later, June would also remember the holiday as a very special time:

> This little scenario fate had unexpectedly dealt us deliciously sharpened our receptive nerve-ends, heightened our perceptions, and our totally contrasting recent urban past only assisted in illuminating rather than dulling our perspective on each day's experience. Well ... as Charmian said, we were two reluctantly-domestic mums on the loose, and why not!
>
> All the same, we were over the rim of the world, and of course we had to return to its harrassed/harrassing centre.[40]

June 'accepted that', but Charmian found it difficult to contemplate. It even felt anticlimactic to return to Cairns. However, the Crookes' home on a beach north of Cairns provided a buffer zone between the journey and the return to Sydney. Trying to identify just what it was that was so different 'up there', Clift decided it was the people, and what made them special was that they had this quality of 'realness' which she would increasingly emphasise over the next couple of years.

> People seem more like real people in the northland. Perhaps because there are so very few of them, and each one of the few has so much space to move in that everybody is quite distinct,

individual, a figure in a landscape. It is not that the people are really larger than life, or even, I think, unduly eccentric. It is more the feeling that nobody in the north is anonymous. Perhaps there is something in this sense of being wholly and identifiably oneself and nobody else at all that lures so many pressurised southerners north.[41]

'Being wholly and identifiably oneself and nobody else at all' ... The phrase resonates with paradox as we think of Charmian Clift putting on her column persona in order to write this. Soon, she would also have to return to being those other people she had to be: guest speaker and social commentator, mother and wife and city-dweller. In her public persona as essayist she put a brave face on the need to return to Sydney, but in private she broke down. June remembers that:

There were moments before Charmian finally boarded the plane south from Cairns when I felt very anxious for her. She wept and was so loath to return to Sydney! It seemed she would have given almost anything to avoid returning. I didn't fully understand this at the time.[42]

Amongst her unhappy protestations were her fears about what would happen to her relationship with June and Ray when the Crookes moved to Sydney, as they were planning soon to do:

'Oh I know what will happen,' she said more than once. 'You'll come to Sydney and George will charm you both — he charms all the ducks off the pond. He always does.' This was said as if in bitterness, which really made me wonder about George.[43]

Of course, June did not realise that for twenty years Charmian had felt that nearly all the couple's friends were essentially George's friends, and that they supported George and took George's side. While this reflected Charmian's general insecurity, as well as her family background as the unfavoured child, it was by no means an imaginary or paranoid reading of the situation. The 'charm' of George's personality — his ability to make new friends in an instant — seemed if anything to have intensified as his sickness took an increasing toll of his physical capacities. At the same time, his sickness and his obvious physical frailty naturally won him a great deal of support and sympathy, while most people seemed to pay little attention to Charmian's suffering and Charmian's needs. It is little wonder that she feared that she would lose her special relationship with her own new friend.

It was also not surprising that she was loath to go back to all her burdens. And yet the hope of making a personal fresh start took her home again, where it seemed (despite 'familiar irritations [...] like people welching on the washing up, and people not picking up their own litter'⁴⁴) that the stage was set for renewal on a number of different fronts.

While Charmian was away, George Johnston had started work again on *Clean Straw for Nothing*, which he had not touched since writing down the fragment of recovery room revelations of January 1966. For some months the author had been steeling himself to a return to the book, which had to be done for contractual reasons, apart from Johnston's own desperate desire to finish the trilogy before he died.

Two things that happened in August 1967 would provide the break through the 'gigantic writer's block' which the author was suffering in regard to this work. In April 1967 Johnston had decided to apply to the Commonwealth Literary Fund (the precursor to the Literature Board or Fund of the Australia Council) for a fellowship to support him while he wrote the novel. When that year's applications were due in August, he submitted one, posting it on 21 August. In this application, the author noted that his reason for applying was 'largely concerned with health'. At present he was receiving a 100 per cent Repatriation War Pension; his surgery of the previous year had left him with 'a good deal less energy'; he wished 'to be able to concentrate these reduced energies <u>fulltime</u> on the writing of the novel' for a whole year, 'instead of, as now, having to use the energies in writing articles, book reviews, TV scripts etc. as a means of earning income sufficient to support my family'. In regard to the purpose of his application, Johnston stated that he wanted 'to write the second in a planned trilogy of Australian novels'.

> The second novel — provisional working title CLEAN STRAW FOR NOTHING — will cover the period 1945 to 1965 and like the first novel will be deeply concerned with the social background of the times. Its central theme will be a study of Australian expatriation — the forces which drive an Australian away from his own country, the gains and losses arising out of expatriation, and the forces which finally draw him back again to his native land.

Like MY BROTHER JACK it will be to some extent fiction of an autobiographical character, with the same character of David Meredith continuing his quest for self-fulfillment, the two novels thus providing a continuous social background from 1919 to 1965.[45]

This does not even mention the 'love story' between David Meredith and his wife Cressida, which Johnston knew was going to be the focus of the book. Indeed, everything suggests that this will be a social realist novel dealing with expatriation, rather than the personal angle of Meredith's marriage. Johnston was careful to phrase his CLF application so that his project sounded safe, and directly in line with the track record of his past work; he also clearly felt it would be more attractive if he emphasised the universal theme rather than the private one.[46]

For the same reason, this submission implies that the novel's structure was to be a conventional linear narrative — similar to that of *My Brother Jack* — which would follow the hero/narrator through a chronological account of his explorations. As the author described his 'big canvas', he gave no hint that he might be contemplating the sort of fragmented structure, modelled on the idea of a windlass moving 'boards' or 'sheets' of text, that had come to him during his recovery room insight. In fact, George Johnston would soon receive another revelation about how to compose his 'canvas'.

This new insight would develop from a comment made to the author on the night after he posted his application. This was 22 August, the night on which George Johnston and Charmian Clift had spent some hours with Sidney Nolan in the Art Gallery of New South Wales, as the work for the painter's retrospective was uncrated. At one stage, when Sid and George were looking at the impasto technique of some of the paintings, Nolan explained: 'What you do is lay on the colours underneath. But then you have to cut into them'. From his own account, the writer 'understood without understanding what the artist meant'. Nevertheless, he 'stored away the knowledge'.[47] Within a few weeks, George Johnston would remember this idea of cutting into colours and would develop it into a new metaphor which he would find more useful than that of the Coles Book Arcade mannikins winding on the 'sheets' of past events.

In regard to the timing of all this, the act of making the application to the CLF readied the novelist for work, and at least got him typing down the themes again. This was the first breaking of the block. Then there was the encounter with the person whom Johnston regarded as a kind of literary godfather of his trilogy, for in Johnston's mind the conversations with Nolan in the Hydra winter of 1955–56 had led to the initial idea of writing a modern Australian Odyssey. Three weeks later, when Clift went away with the film crew, the author started writing. It was no coincidence that this break through the 'block' occurred when Charmian Clift was away from home for two months; without Cressida's model in the house, Johnston had the imaginative space which he needed to work on the fictional character.

The opening passage of the novel, set at a party of film people on the Queen's Birthday weekend in 'Sydney, 1968', gives us the first 'sheet' of the story. In fact, the date was 1967: when the novel was finished, Johnston would change the dates so that the latest present time of the novel all takes place in 1968. At this party, one of the film-makers commits the social solecism of asking the novelist David Meredith why he isn't writing. Meredith replies, 'I'll tell you why I am not writing', but is distracted and doesn't explain.[48]

The next 318 pages become the writing that *isn't* being done. This was the novelist taking the pressure off himself — breaking the block, sidestepping the fear of failure — by telling himself that there were no expectations upon him. He wasn't writing a novel! He was just fiddling — tinkering ...

In the second passage (also dated 'Sydney, 1968') the narrator Meredith expands upon the kind of 'not-writing' which he plans to do. He tells the reader:

> Once you have traded in experience for the memory of experience there's no difference any more between the lies and the actualities: you might as well have it the way you would have liked it to have been: given enough time you'll come to believe genuinely that this was the way it really did happen. Which is very good for the soul, especially when it's showing signs of shrivelling a bit.[49]

The narrator goes on: 'If I try to set it down in a kind of random journal, it won't really be going back to writing'.

With the declaration that this is a journal, the author begins to play around with genre; from this point, the boundaries between fiction and non-fiction will be increasingly blurred. Three decades later, the successes as well as the controversies of postmodernism have conditioned readers to this kind of game with genre in a text that positions itself in the area of literary fiction. In the 1960s, however, the notion of the unreliable narrator was not current. One of the assumptions which readers of that decade would make about a 'journal' was that it would tell the truth, at least insofar as the fictional journal-writer saw it. So what about the declaration that the narrator is going to 'have it the way [he] would have liked it to have been'? This confusion is compounded when, straight after the promise that this will be a 'journal', the narrator notes that he is 'just trying to work it out, rather, to get it straight before it is too late. Before falsification and delusion take over, like a lulling anaesthetic blandly easing one into the desired oblivion'. This clearly implies that the reader is to believe David Meredith's integrity. Indeed, these jottings are presented as a last effort at truth by a man who hasn't got very long to live. The implication that this is a dying man's testament gives added authenticity to the text. All of this goes to the heart of the way in which this novel would be read — as essentially a truthful story. A further blurring of the boundaries would be created by the connections and correlations between the characters of David Meredith and Cressida Morley and their non-fictional models. Many readers would take this to be not just a journal but a memoir.

While Charmian Clift was away on her travels, George Johnston wrote on at a fast rate, moving from 'Sydney, 1968' to 'Melbourne, October, 1945'. Here he reworked some of the material from the opening of the earlier drafts (discussed in chapter 8). It was also now that he changed the date of David's meeting with Cressida from the autumn of 1946 back to the spring months of 1945. After a passage set in 'West China–Japan 1945', the novel picks up again in Melbourne that same October, in a passage transferred so directly from the first draft that it does not really make sense in the new context.[50]

At this point, under the heading 'Sydney, 1966' the author included the passage that he had written in hospital in early 1966, after the hallucinatory insights he had experienced in the recovery room. In the next section, dated 'Athens, 1959', the text moves into the beginning of Meredith's illness. This 'beginning' or cause is the section dealt with here in chapter 16, where the reason for David Meredith's illness is laid at the door of Cressida's infidelity. However, it would seem that at the initial stage of writing the novel — when he was still unsure whether the fragments would lead anywhere — Johnston simply collated in the short story version of this incident, 'The Verdict', which makes no mention of Cressida's adultery. In these two inserted sections the narrative was written in the third person, unlike the first person of the first five passages of the work.

By this stage the bundle of typescript would have appeared decidedly fragmented to this orderly writer, who was accustomed to producing a text which was tidily divided into chapters of roughly equal length. In particular, the shift between first- and third-person voice was an unusual practice for a novel of this era. What would readers make of it? Indeed, what could the author himself make of it? How could he forestall criticism that this was just a collection of bits and pieces? It is no coincidence that it was immediately after this that the author came up with a new metaphor to describe the shape and movement of his work.

Remembering Nolan's comment about cutting into colour, Johnston's mind switched from the Coles Book Arcade mannikins to another childhood toy: the kaleidoscope. Through the voice of his alter ego he reassured himself that 'It will all come together, I am sure, like the pieces of a mosaic or the scattered chips in a kaleidoscope'. The author now had something even more haphazard than the jerky but rhythmical movement of the sheets of pain or the advertising boards. With 'the shaking of the fragmented chips, the patterns forming at random' he could really break up his material and select what to include, what to leave out.

George Johnston would come to find the kaleidoscope image so useful that, in a 1969 interview about the writing of the novel, his memory would shift this insight back to the time of the recovery room clarification, replacing the metaphor of the Coles Book Arcade figures. In this account of the creative process, the author went on to stress that in the kaleidoscope form, 'Time followed an emotional rather than a chronological sequence'. He added: 'The concept was exciting, but dangerous. Remove chronology, and to some extent you remove tension, suspense. So you must seek your tensions in other areas — in the characters, the themes'.[51] The concept was indeed dangerous, for once chronology is removed, the whole pattern of cause and effect can be reversed.

In this short expository passage, the narrator again repeats his assertion that 'I am not trying to write, just setting things down to get them straight'.[52] Thus again Meredith is claiming the integrity — the non-fiction veracity — of his account. The reference to getting things 'straight' would surely be read as meaning in order, including in chronological order of cause and effect, but, of course, the author had dispensed with chronology. At the same time, the genre-game that this isn't a novel but just the unstructured and random memories of the narrator increases the sensation that this is a memoir. Of course, the text was not random. Through virtually all of the book, it is clear that the author was writing the sections sequentially, and revising as he went, in accordance with his normal method. Despite their chopped appearance, he was not writing pieces as they came into his mind, then slotting them together retrospectively. Again and again, internal evidence shows the 'flow' from one passage to the next. While in every way this compilation is highly ordered and extremely selective, the pretence of 'randomness' would also ultimately affect the reception of the text: readers in the 1960s were not alert to the necessity to read the spaces or gaps between the pieces of a fragmented story.

From this exposition of the kaleidoscope method, the story picks up again in the Melbourne spring of 1945 and takes us through the beginning of the love affair to 'Lebanon Bay, 1946', where David and Cressida spend their paradisiacal honeymoon.

As Johnston was writing the novel through September–October 1967, he was also writing the first draft of the narration for the Nolan documentary, based on transcripts of the sound tapes which the film team was sending him within days of the sequences being shot. Receiving a copy of the conversation that Charmian had had with Sid on the top of the Olgas, the author immediately culled this into his 'journal', but put David Meredith with Cressida and the Nolan-character, Tom Kiernan, at the top of the rocks. For some reason that serves no discernible artistic purpose, he backdated this 'Central Australia' passage to 1965. This leads (via the artist's reflection that there was 'no room for Paradise or poetry' in post-war Sydney) to sections headed 'Sydney, 1946', 'Sydney, 1948', 'London, 1950' and 'Sydney, 1949'. In these passages a hurried account is given of the early — and happy — years of the Merediths' marriage.

Suddenly again it is 'Sydney, 1968' (actually Sydney 1967), and a new passage opens with the word 'Today'. This is truly a journal entry. Meredith interrupts his 'whizzing through the last eighteen years' with some reflections on the friends from university whom 'Julian' (the Martin-character) has brought home, and who infuriate the writer with the Bob Dylan song which they keep playing over and over.[53] There is a very significant biographical clue in the text here. Meredith notes: 'I have kept pretty much to my room because Cressida is due back today and I want to be as fit as possible'.[54]

'Due back from where?' the reader might well ask. In the novel there is no reference at all, in either the preceding or following sections, to Cressida going away anywhere at this time. As the 'Central Australia' section of the novel is dated 1965, she can't have been *there* — not for three years! — and as Meredith takes part in this journey to the Centre, he wouldn't be so looking forward to his wife's return that he would wish to rest in preparation. So where has she been?

Of course, the answer is clear from the biographical record: this was written on the day in early November 1967 when Charmian was due back from staying with the Crookes. It is here that we must draw a very important line in the sand: this is the extent of the novel which George Johnston wrote while Charmian Clift was away. In the published text, it comes to a hundred pages.

On 27 October — as Charmian was about to return from her travels — George Johnston received the news that he had been awarded a Commonwealth Literary Fund fellowship for twelve months, valued at $6000. Payments would be made monthly in advance, and would commence on 1 January. (As tax was deducted at source, this would result in a payment of $374 per month.) In his letter of acceptance, Johnston wrote: 'I really do not have words to convey my feelings'.[55] Apart from the usefulness of the money, the fellowship was an honour, and seemed to the author to be further proof that he was accepted by the literary establishment of his country. This was wonderfully encouraging — and on he worked.

A few days later Charmian arrived home, suntanned and rested and unable to stop talking about the North. As always, she was delighted at her husband's success, and there was rejoicing on all fronts. George was so pleased to see Charmian's happiness that he wrote to June Crooke on 6 November, thanking her for giving his wife 'this rare and I think extremely special interlude in her life'.

> She doesn't know I am writing this letter to you, but I have been so moved by her obvious immensely deep feeling and love for you that I feel it would be churlish of me not to thank you for all your warmth and kindness to her. Charm is a rather special sort of a person, I think, but she has always been a bit of a 'loner', very particularly where other women are concerned, and in all the

21 years I have been with her I have never known her to have such rapport and compatibility and love with another woman as she so clearly has with you. She came back looking ten years younger, walking on air, and still bubbling over with joie de vivre. I do hope, June, that she has been as good for you as you have been for her. And I do thank you for your extraordinary kindness. The whole trip up north seems to have flicked some switch in Charm and given her back so much that is real and valuable and tender and marvellous — she has had a pretty shitty time of it in the last few years — that it is almost as if she has been reborn.[56]

Two days later, when a painting of Thursday Island arrived as a present from Ray, Charmian herself would write:

My very dear June — it was, after all, an incomparable time, vibrant enough to be young in, and perhaps middle-aged married ladies and mothers-of-three don't often please the capricious gods who mete out such experiences. I feel I ought to make a small libation at the least [...]

Home was walking into love and radiance and days and nights of celebration and fatted calf and everybody saying everything all together and at full belt, and I suppose we shall all have to exhaust soon but at this point there is no sign of flagging — I seem to have mislaid ten years and my darkest burden of melancholy. Perhaps this is a temporary situation, but I am wallowing in happiness while it is here.[57]

The letter was interrupted by the arrival of Storry Walton, and again the Thursday Island stories had to be told, and immediately Storry was 'inflamed' and plans were spun 'to make wonderful documentaries' about the place — although (Charmian warned June) the ABC wouldn't have any money for this till next winter and 'knowing the ABC [...] the idea could go down the plug-hole between now and then'.

Here, in this happy babble about work plans of her own, Charmian went on to declare: 'G's novel is well under way and I have read it and like it very much indeed. People are so pleased about the Fellowship, which is nice and warming'. In regard to the extent of the novel which George had written while his wife was away — and which Charmian read immediately on her return — it is significant that the portrayal of both Cressida Morley and of the Merediths' marriage is benign in this part of the text. Also, this includes none of the material that Clift saw as her own fictional stockpile.

Amongst the busyness of her return, Clift had found time to see her editor John Douglas Pringle at the *Sydney Morning Herald*. He was 'very pleased' with her (she boasted to June) and 'fascinated by T.I.', telling her she could write as much as she liked about her trip and offering to reimburse her for her travelling expenses. 'Only', she told her friend, 'I think I will keep a very great deal for myself'. This brought her again to her good intentions for a Fresh Start:

> I will pretend for a little while that I am still on Safari in the tropics, although from the number of telephone calls it is evident that the game is really up and importunate people know I am home again. I have made splendid resolutions about public platforms and charitable luncheons and television interviews, also about losing a stone of weight, and brisk walks, and keeping fit. I wonder how long it will be before sloth and muddle overtake me again. I feel so good that I would like to go on feeling good, and feeling private too and not public property.

After some more family chat — including affectionate references to her 'great lumbering baby' hefting himself onto her lap — she tells her friend: 'Dear June, I can't thank you, because there aren't any words for that. But we will never lose each other now, and I will love you very truly and dearly always'.

For a short time it seemed as if this friendship was going to blossom via a regular correspondence. Only ten days later Charmian wrote again, obviously in response to a reply of June's. She was glad June's girls were to come home soon: 'I have a theory families should be families, no matter what the difficulties, and love and hate and squabble close-in'. She continued in a vein that is pure Charmian in her mode as eternal sprite:

> Let us never never never, darling June, have anything to do with middle age. It doesn't suit either of us a scrap. Keep all your tapers lit and blaze away like a forest of candles — you might burn out sooner but it will be a brave bright showing and you will cast a lot of warmth and radiance.[58]

It is typical of Charmian, too, that she would move from this personal declaration straight into Tass Drysdale's praise of Ray's latest exhibition, and again to the minutiae of family life: 'Poor G is in the middle of tooth extractions, Martin is in the middle of exams, Shane is in the middle of love, and I am in the middle of plans'.

These plans included doing something about the depression which she periodically suffered. In November 1967, Charmian began to consult a psychiatrist. The timing of this is important, as is the fact that the decision to consult someone came from Charmian herself. Her general practitioner was sure that it hadn't been *his* idea that Charmian seek professional help; he suggested that the psychiatrist in question was 'well-known [...] at that time, and so she may just have gone to consult him because she'd heard that he was a good doc'.[59] The psychiatrist in turn reported that Charmian was suffering from 'depression and anxiety'. The family doctor understood that Charmian's consultations with the psychiatrist 'continued for some months'.[60]

While it is not known what cause the psychiatrist ascribed to the patient's state of 'depression and anxiety', it is clear that she made no extraordinary personal revelations to him.[61] However, to the family doctor it appeared that there were two different reasons which could account for Charmian's ongoing emotional state.

On the one hand, the GP did to some extent associate Charmian's depression with the menopausal problems of heavy menstrual bleeding, and hot flushes and sweats which she had been suffering since she first began consulting him in September 1964.[62] Certainly, some of the behavioural symptoms which menopausal women can experience include deep unhappiness, low self-esteem, mood swings, sensations of sudden panic or of lingering anxiety, a proneness to tears, extremes of irritability, a general feeling of being on edge, and a feeling of confusion. However, as the collective authors of *Our Bodies, Ourselves* note, 'the link between depression and menopause' is a 'particularly damaging [...] myth' about the climacteric.[63]

Yet the family doctor looked beyond the stereotype of 'middle-aged women's problems'. Reflecting many years later on his patient's situation, he observed:

> This is probably thinking in retrospect, I suppose, but there were plenty of apparent reasons [for Charmian's depression] — there was the menopausal reason, but I think much more significant was the burden of caring for George. And there were the three children in the background all the time, and if you talk to the

families of people suffering from tuberculosis, there is always the
fear that they will become infected. That's another aspect too.

But just the sheer physical and emotional effort of caring for
someone who is slowly, very slowly, but obviously progressively
dying is an exhausting business — and the depression is just a
reaction to the pressures of that sort of life.

On top of this, the GP felt, were the strains which the relationship itself
imposed, and the strains which Charmian imposed upon herself in regard
to the relationship. In particular, while the 'responsibilities and efforts'
required of Charmian were becoming 'intolerable' — 'that was the upfront
reason for Charmian's depression' — it was clear that Charmian was unable
to set these responsibilities aside, and simply walk out on George and the
marriage.

She had old-fashioned values — and whatever happened to
George, she was going to stick with him [...] Charmian had
taken a vow 'Till death us do part' and she was determined — or
perhaps not even consciously determined — but my
understanding was that she felt it was her responsibility to care
for him for ever.

As well as the pressure exerted by Charmian's attitude to her marriage
vows, her doctor was aware that 'she was the breadwinner, and had been for
quite a long time'. But beyond all these reasons, she 'wasn't able to run away,
she couldn't leave, because of the children'.[64]

The issue of the children was increasingly at the foreground of quite a lot of
Charmian's anxiety and stress. Within a few weeks, the kind of honeymoon
of the family reunion was over, and the familiar conflicts had re-established
themselves. Although the Raglan Street house was large, it didn't offer the
private space that the family had had in their Hydra house and their
extended yard of the island town. It must also be remembered that the
house functioned as a workplace for Charmian and George, and to some
degree for Martin, who as a student had irregular hours. This meant that
there were often three adults at home during the daytime.

The house further served at times as a nursing home or convalescent
hospital. The irony was no doubt very sharp for George: after growing up in
a home full of sick and dying people, he was now the invalid in his own

children's home. The situation wasn't easy for George, but it also wasn't easy for the children — particularly the older two, who were noisy and untidy and argumentative, in the way of young adults. And increasingly Charmian became drawn into arguments with them. In most households, it is the mother whose dreary role it is to nag about chores not done and litter left lying about, and this was even more the case in the Johnston household, because George had for the most part moved beyond this kind of engagement. At the same time, because she couldn't bear anyone hurting George, Charmian would fly to his defence if the kids ever did start rowing with their father — so it would be Charmian again at the forefront. And she would also try to arbitrate the arguments between the older two, to ease the general strain, but would end up in the thick of it.

Jason remembered the sort of conflict that would erupt between his sister and brother, who still 'loathed each other':

> To a large extent it was mitigated because they were just doing different things. [But] even in a big house, if either or both had their friends around, it was particularly bad, because Shane and her friends would despise Martin's hairy hippy friends, and his studenty friends would despise her 'bourgeois' friends — et cetera et cetera.[65]

By now the difference between these two siblings, which had once been a matter of personality and taste, had taken on a political dimension. No longer did Martin simply adopt the stance of the intellectual, aloof from society's problems, lost in a poetry book or a chess game. By the end of his second year at university, he was starting to be concerned about a welter of issues of liberation and social justice, ranging from opposition to censorship to opposition to conscription and the Vietnam War. Although in his campus life Martin was more associated with the arty group around the student newspaper than with the organisations and meetings of the student left, he certainly spoke the rhetoric of the times, which was also the ideology of the music that he played.

Paradoxically, it was Shane who in terms of temperament was far more suited to being the family rebel. But with Martin staking out the territory of the current youth revolution — just as he had much earlier claimed a kind of birthright to the matter of intellectuality — his sister was left with no option but to set up *her* barricades in defence of conformity. In this, she was doing what the Clifts were so good at: turning values upside down. Thus

Shane rebelled against her left wing bookish family by making a point of saying that she read nothing but Agatha Christie, and by taking no interest in the political issues of her society (insofar as it was possible to be an ostrich in a household such as hers). Perhaps this lack of engagement also expressed an underlying feeling that the society surrounding Shane was not her own, for she was very much involved in the campaign against the Junta that had taken over the government of the country that she missed desperately and still regarded as home.[66] Overall, however, Shane's defiance was an adolescent's desperate attempt to be normal in a family that was decidedly abnormal.

And because the Johnston parents were at odds with the Australian norm, Shane's rebellion tended to lead to more arguments than Martin's rebellion. It really wasn't fair. In just about any other family at this time, the long-haired dirty pacifist layabout would be copping abuse from his parents on all fronts, and the girl who looked like all the other girls and dreamed of a white wedding would be regarded as the child who wasn't a problem. But in the Johnston family, it was Shane who could raise everyone's hackles by something as simple as singing along to an advertising jingle on commercial television. In particular, it was Charmian who became most affronted by what she saw as her daughter's support for crass consumerism. And as Shane was so similar to her mother in the matter of defiance, the conflict between these two could become at times 'ugly on both sides', Jason remembered.

> I suppose that, ultimately, there was a certain amount of what you might expect with a teenage girl — you know, clothes, and staying out till late, or whatever — but there was something which heightened it, so that [arguments about] those things got out of control a bit.
>
> But there were [also] a lot of fights about straightforwardly — you'd now call it ideology. And it spun from a million little things. Like, you know, singing along with a commercial [...] Or an argument over which television show to watch: 'Are we going to watch *The Man from Uncle* or something, or a *Four Corners* documentary?' It always started in little things like that. And got out of control.
>
> And on the one hand Charmian particularly — George a bit, but more Charmian — would find it hard to just let it be. You

know — just *let* her sing to the commercials or *let* her want the latest American pop music, or whatever.

And on the other hand, I remember Shane just wouldn't *be* told, either [...]

It worked both ways. I don't think Shane was particularly rebellious, but most children would not have to put up with a left-wing critique from their parents of them doing just the normal things that all their mates were doing. So that's one side. On the other hand, I suppose many other children would just have let it go, and not fought back as much as she did.

These conflicts between Charmian and Shane were sometimes witnessed by adult visitors to the household, and the memory of them has been incorporated into the public record. In *Searching for Charmian*, Suzanne Chick reports Toni Burgess as saying that Charmian 'put Shane down, you know. She was jealous of her youth'.[67] And in his biography of George Johnston, Garry Kinnane noted: 'Clift had, friends observed, a tendency towards jealousy of Shane now that her daughter was grown up and exceedingly attractive'.[68] These 'friends' are not named, but this view probably again came primarily from Burgess.

It is interesting that Jason — who tended to be Shane's supporter within the family — didn't see the situation as a matter of 'Charmian being jealous of *Shane's* youth, in particular'. In discussing the conflict between his mother and sister, he even repeated: 'As a particular thing about being jealous of Shane's youth — *no*, I don't think so'. He raised a more general matter of his mother's attitude to youth in the last months of her life, which we shall come to at the appropriate time. For the moment it is necessary to foreshadow this by noting that while the biographical record has focused exclusively on conflict between Charmian and Shane, by late 1967 there was also developing a certain degree of conflict between Charmian and Martin, and also between George and Martin.

Despite the fact that Martin and his parents were in agreement over issues such as censorship, conscription and the Vietnam War, this battle was typical of the confrontation going on in many Australian homes at this time. While conflict between parents and their adolescent children is as ancient as human society — or biology — there did seem something new in the 1960s in the way the generation of baby-boomers confronted their parents, who in turn were the generation who had suffered by growing up through the Great Depression and World War II. The phenomenon was so remarkable that the term 'generation gap' was coined. At the same time, a particular rhetoric developed which codified the two sides of this conflict as 'Youngies' and 'Oldies'. Naturally, the 'Oldies' found this labelling derogatory, particularly as many of them saw themselves as barely middle-aged.

For George and Charmian, the new politics of youth — which pushed them beyond the pale — were particularly hard to bear, because they themselves had always been on the side of youth. It was they who had organised the first public performance for the young folksinger Leonard Cohen, in the back room of Katsikas's grocery shop. But Martin and his friends gave no credit to these kinds of credentials. For the baby-boomers, age was the sole reference point: life was believed to stop at the age of thirty. Mick Jagger or someone had said so.

By at least the end of 1967, therefore, there was this increasing bone of contention between Martin and his parents. At the same time, Martin shared the fictional Julian's attitude of 'being sure of everything', coupled with the sanctimoniousness common to youth. Jason explained why this was particularly hard to bear:

> This is not to have a Martin-bash, but at this particular time he really was very unpleasant. This was *why* the sanctimoniousness was hard for all of us to take — [his] being on the side of the workers and the losers and all the rest — because on a personal level, in terms of things like consideration to his sick father, it just wasn't there.
>
> If he was being sanctimonious and priggish and at the same time in his own personal life he had the purity of Robespierre or something — well OK, that's a certain type of person; not very liked, but ...
>
> What made it so hard was that he'd bring over the friends, and the flagon of claret would come out, [there'd be] the incredibly loud Jimi Hendrix till all hours of the morning, when Dad is sick and has gone to bed, I have to get up for school in the morning ...
>
> And you'd wake up in the morning and there'd just be red wine — records stacked up everywhere — and you know, when you're experiencing *that,* you're not ready to be told by that person that

you're all bourgeois little shits, and that he's the only one that knows how to save the world.[69]

Naturally, Charmian 'didn't react well' to Martin claiming the moral high ground. In pointing out that this 'lack of manners and consideration [...] wasn't particularly *Martin*. It's just what up-themselves little adolescent intellectuals are like', Jason concluded that Charmian's conflict was as much with Martin as it was with Shane. 'The difference was that, whereas she didn't much agree with either what Shane said or what Shane did, she sort of agreed with a lot of what Martin said, but not what he did. Apart from going on marches, and all that good stuff.'

Jason is a very credible observer of all this, because at the age of eleven he was old enough to take things in, but not old enough to be a partisan in the generational battles. 'There's not much you can do at that age', he pointed out, in terms of getting into trouble with your parents. He remembered having 'no problems' or conflict with his mother at this particular time.

All in all, it seemed at times as if the household was engaged in the skirmishes of a long-running civil war. And yet Charmian Clift could allow none of this into the column. Obviously, she wouldn't embarrass her children by airing family arguments in the newspaper. But beyond this, she had to maintain the public image of the happy family that she had created. This column family and its life — especially the life of the mother and wife — was increasingly assuming an existence in a hypothetical or parallel universe to the one in which the writer was actually living.

22

PUBLIC PROPERTY

I feel so good that I would like to go on feeling good, and feeling private too, and not public property.[1]

This is an opportune time to interrupt the chronological narrative in order to assess the degree of strain caused by being 'public property', as Charmian called herself in her November 1967 letter to June Crooke. As it was the newspaper column which was primarily responsible for this, it is timely, too, to consider this work from a critical viewpoint.

From the time of its first publication in November 1964, Charmian Clift's column attracted a great popular following, with readers coming from a wide variety of socioeconomic, geographic, ethnic and age groups.[2] While perhaps the bulk of her readership was composed of middle-aged and middle class women of small 'l' liberal sympathies, Clift also had an enormous following among upper-class women whose lives centred around social events and charity 'dos'. At the same time, she had many devoted readers from the opposite end of the social scale.[3] Clift attracted a significant male readership as well, despite the fact that she argued for women's rights and occasionally even described herself as a feminist. There was further support for the Clift column from non-Anglo sections of society — especially from the Australian Greek community — for at a time when 'multiculturalism' was unheard of, Clift represented a 'migrant's' viewpoint. Last but not least, Clift had a following among young people, both the 'protestants' whose causes she so often espoused, and less radical teenagers, whose problems and rights she voiced.

Through the beauty of her prose style and her mastery of the essay form,

Charmian Clift was putting literature onto the breakfast tables of these thousands of very different Australians. Yet there has always been a kind of critical question mark over her place as a writer. She herself got to the heart of the matter when she told David Higham that she was 'writing essays for the weekly presses to be read by people who wouldn't know an essay from a form-guide, but absolutely love it'.[4] The problem, as far as her reputation is concerned, is that she was writing essays at the wrong time and in the wrong place.[5]

Out of fashion though it may have been, the essay form was perfect for Clift. Her highly individual and lyrical prose style, combined with her erudite and curious mind, found their true outlet in this genre, which projects the personality of the writer to develop a mood and point of view. There had always been something about Clift's writing which suggested that a process of distillation had gone on: as if the words had been refined and purified like a great wine or perfume, until the merest drop contained the essence. This quality, too, was eminently suited to the essay form, where compression is essential. Above all, however, the essay is a conversation, in which the writer addresses the reader directly and intimately, and draws the reader into her world. It was this conversational style which was the source of Clift's great appeal to readers — a style which she had developed in the travel books *Mermaid Singing* and *Peel Me a Lotus*. Indeed, it is possible to read the oeuvre of Clift's essays as a third travel book: as an account of a strange country and its people given by a traveller who, by virtue of her outsider status, is able to turn a clear eye on the customs, language, costume, lifestyle and general character of the inhabitants, and is also keen to report on interesting landmarks and geographical features.

Although Clift's starting point was the conversational mode of the classical essay, she contributed something of her own to the genre when she adapted this to the newspaper column. The hallmark of the Clift essay is the sense that the writer is conducting a two-way conversation — a *dialogue* — with the reader. Indeed, she created in her readers an almost uncanny feeling that they were part of a very special conversation with her. While Charmian Clift had the ability to reach all sorts of people simultaneously, the extraordinary thing is that Clift's fans all felt she was chatting privately with them.

The conversational mode of the column reflects the sheer importance which Charmian Clift and George Johnston assigned to the whole business of talking, conversation, thrashing out ideas. It was also heightened by the fact that many of the pieces had their starting point in talk — with family, friends, the children's friends, or with taxi drivers, shopkeepers, perfect strangers, from whom Clift would draw information as she did from the prawn sorters and fishermen of Karumba. And yet, as her rough notes to herself for one of the radio programs make clear, Charmian Clift actually preferred talking on paper:

> I love gossip, but I think ideas interest me more. Probably because I am a writer, and being a writer I think I probably regard conversation only as a sort of first draft — to be explored, worked on, polished, constructed, ordered. Conversation, the ideas that come out of it, are the raw materials for one's craft. As if, if one were a carpenter, one would assemble unplaned wood and nails and glue.[6]

The essays indeed reflect a very special sort of talking on paper which Clift's readers themselves did with her by way of the letters which every day Terry the postman would deliver in a huge bundle to 112 Raglan Street. The fact that Clift was that not-very-exalted figure, a woman columnist, made the writer herself seem accessible. And the context in which the column appeared — amidst ads for shoes and splayds, for wrinkle cream and wigs — was non-threatening. As a result, readers felt free to write to her about their own opinions and hobbyhorses, or even about their personal problems, in the same way that they might get in touch with a talkback radio host or an agony aunt. Although the prospect of answering all this correspondence made the columnist feel like Sisyphus rolling an enormous paper ball uphill,[7] she was in no doubt that her mail represented the other half of the dialogue:

> Sometimes a communication lands up on my desk that sings for me so sweet and clear, person to person as it were, that I turn giddy all over with enchantment [...]
>
> It's like an exciting conversation. I say this. You say, yes but. And ideally we should be off.[8]

Apart from bringing sheer pleasure to the writer, the letters were 'very important' to Clift because they 'gave [her] an indication of the thoughts and opinions and angers and philosophies of a very wide range of people'.[9] Clift sometimes opened up the dialogue even further by allowing readers to have their say in the column.[10] Finally, the letters could provide practical solutions to readers' problems.[11] This innovatory extension of the traditional conversational mode of the essay into a very real dialogue with readers was influenced, of course, by the nature of the publication outlet. Although the newspaper's cramped columns and weekly deadline exerted a certain pressure, Clift used the brevity of her space and the frequency of publication to give an even greater urgency and concision to her expression. The fact that a piece was published a few days after its writing meant that Clift could use current events, and the short time between the appearance of one piece and the next meant that the writer could refer back to an earlier opinion or incident with the reasonable expectation that a reader would know what she was talking about.

While it was Charmian Clift's personal style of conversing with her readers that was the great attraction and success of her column, this dialogue carried a terrible cost for the columnist herself. There were a number of different components of this cost.

For a start, the column functioned as a kind of serial story or soap opera, in which Charmian Clift shared intimate details of her domestic life with her readers. Although sometimes weeks could go by without any personal references, regular readers were familar with a cast of characters — the columnist's husband, her three children, even her cat Jeoffrey — who acted out the drama of family life. Readers would know when Charmian Clift moved house; when her husband was away in hospital; when she came down with flu; when her younger son began high school; when her elder son faced the call-up; when her daughter became engaged. The reader also knew about the columnist's mother, father, sister, brother; about friends such as Toni, Faith, Maisie, Cedric; about where she shopped, what she wore, how she spent her holidays. The reader even knew when the columnist's garbage collection was well overdue and the bottles were mounting up on the back deck.[12] And the reader knew what the columnist's own private room was like, could see the paintings on the walls and the books on the shelves and the stacks of letters on the desk.

While this revelation of the setting and characters of the drama worked towards a feeling of intimacy, Clift also increased the intimacy by involving — or seeming to involve — the reader in the immediacy of the writing of the column. For example, in an essay written during her time in the crowded Neutral Bay flat, she shared with her readers the interruptions to the writing process:

> Just a little while ago I overheard one of the chess players down at the other end of the room (that is to say about ten feet away

from where I am working) ask of my son, with a quite interested
glance in my direction: 'What is your mother writing about?'

'I don't know,' said my son, and of course there was no earthly
reason why he should, because he is not a clairvoyant and in any
case his mother didn't either.[13]

From here the writer swung into a magnificent single sentence of over 250
words as she described the hurly-burly that erupted around her as 'another
herd of young' arrived to collect her daughter; meanwhile the landlord
visited, the telephone rang, and a sudden rainstorm sent the columnist away
from her typewriter and down to the line, explaining that, if she hadn't
gone, 'there wouldn't have been any towels for anybody otherwise, or clean
shirts, or pyjamas for my hospital-incarcerated husband'.

Of course, there were limits. 'I don't tell all in these columns', warned Clift
on another occasion.[14] For a start, she was very careful to maintain her
children's privacy by never mentioning their names, and by not telling any of
their secrets.[15] She kept some of her own secrets too. Indeed, sometimes —
like a bird pretending to trail a wounded wing in order to lead the hunter
away from her nest — she deliberately drew readers away from any realisation
of the major pain by playing up the minor frustrations. This, indeed, was
what she was doing in the flat-life essay already quoted. She went on to
describe a conversation with a television producer friend (Storry Walton):

> [He] maintains that one should never permit the public to even
> peep behind the scenes of a performance. He says that mystery
> and illusion must be maintained. The curtain parts, the show is
> played, the curtain closes again, and that's all the audience
> should be allowed to know about it.

As opposed to this view, Clift claimed that she herself 'always thought the
show behind the show to be as interesting — if not more so — than the
show itself'. She explained: 'The show behind the show, as far as my own
little performance is concerned, is high comedy with Heath Robinson
devices in the way of stage machinery'.[16] This, of course, was Clift in her
Kate Perrin persona. But the very act of keeping a happy face all the time
was in itself a terrible pain, akin to the unhappiness during the early days of
her marriage, when she had to act the radiantly happy wife and mother.

However, within these certain limits that she set, Charmian Clift did tell a
very great deal in her column. It was as as if she were laying down the cards

of a Tarot pack, one at a time. Sometimes, a card would obviously seem to have a personal significance; often, though, there would seem to be no immediate relevance. Yet as more cards were laid down, as the pattern built up, certain readings would emerge as the links were made. The cumulative effect of all this — even though Clift herself had put the images on the cards, and laid them out — represented an extraordinary opening up of her private realm.

Another aspect of the cost of writing the column has already been touched upon. This was the business of creating a persona — an identity — which would be Charmian Clift the columnist. This persona was a composite, a blend of the 'real' person and certain aspects of personality and experience which were emphasised or exaggerated, together with other aspects which were diminished or completely self-censored. To a degree, the development of this character was a conscious construct; at the same time, once the character was up and running she did start to develop a life of her own, in the same way that a fictional character does. At the core of this Clift character was the voice that the writer adopted when speaking in her column. While again this was close to the voice which Clift would use in private letters, it was drafted, crafted, constructed, composed, polished. It was, as we have seen, a projection of the voice of her alter ego, Cressida Morley.

In many ways this whole business of the development of the persona and voice of the Clift columnist was very similar to what George Johnston was doing with his blend of fact and fiction in his alter ego character David Meredith. Years later, Martin Johnston would point out the similarity of this process, and explain something of how the public and private sides rubbed up against each other in his parents' work:

> I think that with any writer [...] public and private sides tend to get inextricably confused. A novelist, and particularly as overtly autobiographical a novelist as my father eventually became, is performing a paradoxical trick-cyclist act in the first place by making public at least one side of what is the fairly private side of his life, telling the world — publicly — that it *is* private.[17]

After explaining that 'David Meredith does not map, point by point, onto George Johnston, or vice versa', but that Meredith is 'a selective George Johnston, if you want', Martin went on to describe how this sort of fictional selective process worked for Clift:

My mother's situation was slightly different of course because most of her writing after we came back to Australia was in the column, [and] was not fiction at all — except of course it was. Any columnist of her kind adopts the persona of friend talking to friends — 'This is the real Charmian Clift having a chat to you over the back garden fence', and whatnot. In fact, it's nothing of the sort. Again it's a very artful, fictionalised, literary construct. So in a way public and private for her, in her aspect as an author, are just as confused as they are with George Johnston and David Meredith. Except she never went so far as to call the persona she adopted in her column, well, 'Cressida Morley' shall we say.

As time went on, this issue — of being Charmian Clift playing the role of Charmian Clift — became increasingly arduous, and even confusing. It is poignant to reflect that as a young woman it had been one of Charmian's great ambitions to be an actress on the stage — and, indeed, the kind of actress whose fame relies upon her image and style, as much as her ability to act. In many ways the column was Clift's stage, and the columnist was performing a one-woman show, week after week. Like many an actor, particularly those from soap opera, she found that the public expected her to *be* her character; and sometimes she found that even when she took the costume and greasepaint off, she stayed in role.

'There is this woman, Charmian Clift,' she confided in Toni Burgess. 'And I have to dress up as her and go out and be her'.[18] Burgess also remembered her friend 'saying that *that* Charmian Clift was a fraud'.[19] As the public persona increasingly seemed to become a mask or a disguise, it was now that Clift began to stress the importance of 'real people', such as the ones she had met in the Far North.[20]

The issue of style — of how Charmian looked, on stage and off stage — took on a particular significance because the column appeared in the Women's Section of the *Sydney Morning Herald*, which also featured society photographs and fashion advertisements. It was expected that the columnist would look like someone who attended posh weddings or race meetings, who would wear the kind of outfits that appeared in the advertisements run by Grace Bros or David Jones. It is in this context that we should consider the complicated issue of Charmian's attitude to her appearance and to the ageing process.

In *Searching for Charmian*, Suzanne Chick quotes Toni Burgess as saying that Charmian '*loathed* the idea of getting old. She hated being middle aged. She couldn't stand losing her beauty'.[21] Yet Anne Deveson argued emphatically against any link between Charmian's appearance and the unhappiness of her last years:

> I never had the sense that here was an immensely vain woman. She wasn't. She was aware of her beauty and she probably didn't like getting older, but I don't think she was someone who'd fuck up her whole life because that was happening. I just don't think it was about that.[22]

Certainly, the physical process of ageing was one of the things to which Charmian Clift had turned her mind. She had always examined her own body for outward signs of the inward journey. In *Peel Me a Lotus*, for example, she had recorded the changes wrought by wind and sun, by pregnancy and birth, by poverty and stress. In the drafts for the 1967 travel essays she had recorded the lacerations and bruises upon her legs.

The matter of being middle-aged also concerned Clift as an issue: it was central to the 'mandate' of her column, because the core readers of the women's pages of the *Herald* were women in that age group. Also, as pointed out in the previous chapter, the whole discussion of age and of generational differences was a hot media topic in the 1960s: as a public commentator, Charmian Clift could hardly avoid it. In January 1966, for example, the Clift column directly addressed the matter of 'Being Middle-Aged'. Although this essay begins with the writer remembering her fourteen year old self swearing that she would rather be dead, after seeing a naked middle-aged woman in the swimming pool changing room, the whole import of this essay is to turn this juvenile opinion around. By the second paragraph the writer uses the outward signs on the bodies of the female line of her own family as a shortcut to thinking about inward matters such as growth and experience:

> At about this same time too, I remember that one evening my mother put her hand — brown, blotched, swollen-knuckled, tobacco-stained and ripped and ragged at the nails (she worked hard in those Depression years — as a matter of fact she always worked hard)— beside the young firm smooth hand of my sister, who was polishing her nails with French chalk and a chamois pad. And my mother grinned a certain wry lop-sided grin I came

to know very well later when I was a little more perceptive and began to [...] recognise her as the incredible person she was.

The other day, scrabbling over the breakfast table in that early morning panic that always grips our lot, I saw my own hand next to the hand of my seventeen-year-old daughter. And I saw it in horror, outrage, and disbelief.[23]

As the writer moves on, it is clear that the outrage is not about having dishwasher hands, but about missed opportunities as evidenced by tiny matters of 'deterioration' which cannot be 'retrieved' — 'the torn nail, the grey hair, the loose tooth [...] the laughter lines and the worry lines'. The main thing, however, about this essay is that — with the typical twist of the essay form — it turns around on its tail. Ultimately, it is not even addressed to the middle-aged, but to the young. It is a plea, not for youth and beauty, but for greater tolerance from the young, and it reminds them — as Clift reminded them on other occasions — that 'They'll get there too one day'.

In another essay on the theme of ageing, written towards the end of 1968, Clift again makes a plea for tolerance, starting with the dropping of the labels of Young and Old. It is clear that the writer's greatest fear of ageing is that she might take on the social and political attitudes of those Olds who are 'the bigots, the moralists, the reactionaries, the disapprovers of the Youngs'.[24] From here it is only a small step to her conclusion — which is to champion the cause of the Young.

It is relevant to remember that these essays appeared amongst ads for lotions and potions promising to make women look and feel younger and thinner, wrinkle-free and magnificently coiffured. Just as the columnist subverted the message of the fashion pages by speculating about the anthropological role of fashion, so she gently discouraged women from 'spend[ing] hours of every week with masseuse, hairdresser, manicurist, skin specialist, dressmaker'.[25]

Of course, the public Charmian Clift was not contained within the medium of newsprint. There were also the regular radio broadcasts, and a certain number of television appearances. One of these was in early 1965, during her visit to Melbourne. Former television host Ray Taylor remembered Charmian coming onto his talk show; she was 'very nervous' and 'rather the worse for wear'. Taylor quickly added that 'she had every reason to be drunk', for she had been warned by a friend to 'watch out' for the other guest on the program. This was a former journalist colleague of

George Johnston and Charmian Clift, who proceeded on live-to-air television to humiliate Charmian by referring to the ancient scandal of her dismissal from the *Argus* and her elopement with George. He also showed a photo of her as a beautiful young woman, inviting the camera to contrast this with her middle-aged face. 'It was a cruel thing to do', Ray Taylor declared. She was 'very sensitive' about this part of her past, 'and she didn't want to go on television and be the Other Woman'. Yet although Charmian didn't handle the situation very well, Taylor insisted that it was still a 'beautiful interview', adding: 'There was contact'. Even under such pressure, Charmian's ability to listen, to respond, to communicate, shone out.[26]

For this woman who hated public exposure, there were also a great many live performances, for the columnist was regularly asked to speak at luncheons or to open festivals and fetes or to address meetings. These are the sorts of invitations to 'make speeches to bored ladies in floral hats' to which Charmian had referred in her November 1965 letter to her friend Jo.[27] Although at that time she had claimed she always replied 'Not on your life, mate', in fact the columnist would accept, more often than not. The variety of the events which she attended in an official capacity in these years is quite staggering, ranging from political rallies to the opening of a vintage car rally; from a tour of a new primary school in Sydney's west to the opening of a new art gallery; from a fete in aid of young female prisoners in Parramatta to a conference of Christian ladies or to a careers course for young country girls at the YMCA; from planning meetings of the Save the Children Fund and Freedom from Hunger Campaign to charity luncheons of upper-class matrons; from the launching of the books by young poets to gatherings of her professional colleagues in the Australian Writers' Guild. While most of this activity was in Sydney, there were a few occasions when she dashed down to Melbourne for a luncheon or meeting, for her audience in that city was just as clamorous to 'have' her.[28] In regard to this, Anne Deveson observed that people were 'constantly wanting bits of Charmian', and remembered how Charmian would sometimes talk about 'the sense that people wanted her to be there, to kind of wear on their arms as a handbag'.[29]

Given such comments — and given the further evidence of her hatred for all this toing and froing that is revealed in the letters to Jo Meyer and June Crooke — why did Charmian Clift accept so many invitations? The reason was partly that so many of the invitations were from causes which the columnist felt should be supported. Charmian Clift also often said yes because she was, in her own words, a yea-sayer: she found it hard to say no, either to people or to experiences — and besides, the column was like a greedy monster which needed to be fed a new experience every single week. And so, over the phone or by letter she would agree. As the event drew closer, however, she would regret her rashness. And when the time came to dress as people expected Charmian Clift to dress, and to go out and make a passionate and witty speech, she would increasingly panic at the thought of getting up on the platform and being herself — or not herself! — in public.

One such occasion was an International Students' Ball held at the Roundhouse of the University of New South Wales in early 1966, with the proceeds going towards housing for students from overseas; Charmian Clift was invited by her 'young Chinese friend, Peter'. This time, she gave the cause a plug before the event, mentioning that as she had 'a private niggle' that she was 'really past the age for that sort of romp', she had taken 'the practical step of inveigling a number of friends to support [her] in this venture', so that she would not be 'a lone Oldie sitting like a shag on the rock'.[30] Lightly phrased though all this is, it is possible to feel her already baulking and demurring.

On the night in question, Anne Deveson was in the group of Charmian's friends and supporters. She remembered that they sat at the main table and Charmian had to make a speech. By the time this was to happen, the stress had become unbearable, and Charmian 'had had too much to drink':

> Everybody was worried about her. She insisted on dancing — she got some Greek music put on — she danced fantastically. She then fell — Martin picked her up — she got to the rostrum, she managed her speech all right — and then she fell again.
>
> So it was this sense of somebody who was really on a tightrope — who kept falling off and people would haul her up, and she'd keep going another few steps, and then she'd fall again.
>
> But the thing that I was aware of was how everybody supported her. There wasn't a sense of 'That terrible woman — she's rotten drunk!' No, there was a sense that here was somebody who was suffering, and who was under enormous strain, and there was a great sense of admiration for her.[31]

On this occasion, there was support, and in any case students at a ball wouldn't particularly care if the speaker had drunk a bit too much. Other gatherings were less easy-going and understanding. The embarrassment Clift caused when she made a mess of a speech to an Architectural Society function would be remembered for a long time.[32]

Against this sort of thing must be set the record of her political appearances. Allan Ashbolt remembered a time in 1966 when he picked up Charmian and George and took them to a big anti-Vietnam meeting at the old stadium near Rushcutters Bay. Ashbolt talked in glowing terms about Charmian's performance that day as she spoke against the war she so hated:

> Charm was a good speaker, with prepared material. She really was [...] She was extremely nervous beforehand — extremely nervous — but she stood up there and carried the crowd.
>
> She held several thousand people spellbound, not by any political appraisal of the Vietnam conflict, but simply by speaking as a mother on behalf of her sons and of other mothers' sons everywhere. That was her style; she went straight to the human essence of any problem, straight to what a situation would mean in human happiness or human suffering.[33]

But it wasn't only on these sorts of occasions that Charmian Clift was expected to be the Clift of the column. Like other celebrities, she was recognisable in public — not least because the column each week had a thumbnail photograph of her. On one occasion, a ranger discovered her picking protected flannel flowers in Kuringai Chase. Although he 'went to jelly' when he realised she was 'the Charmian Clift',[34] a comparatively trivial infringement such as this was deeply embarrassing for the columnist. The problem was that she was known for taking a high moral stand, and she could not be seen letting her own standards slip. Ultimately the sense of being 'the Charmian Clift' would contribute to a fear of going out in public.

There were other costs, too, to the column. In December 1965 the writer shared with her readers something of the pain of the writing process which she experienced every week:

> It has been more than a year now that I have been writing these pieces every week. And this week, as every week, I have come smack bang up against crisis. Annihilation even. Because I know myself to be completely incapable of writing an article. This is the most terrible feeling, of panic and desolation, of terror, of the most awful loss.[35]

Although, as she went on to note, this 'chronic recurring paralysis of the talent' is 'common' among writers, most don't have to face it every single week of their lives. While her touch is light even in this description of her personal pain, these declarations of terror, panic, desolation and paralysis should not be taken as hyperbole. The column put Charmian Clift in the position of being 'annihilated' every week, until the 'piece' was produced.

Part of the paralysis was the problem of finding exactly the right topic. To get around this, Clift kept files of press-cuttings, recording both major events and odd things that took her interest.[36] After the topic was chosen, the column would occasionally come easily in a burst. There was many a week, however, when the process of producing the seemingly effortless prose would take three days of preparation. The writer would usually begin with a quick checklist, handwritten or typed. Next there was a search through reference books, or the questioning of family, friends, chance acquaintances. During this stage the columnist would make up to five pages of densely typed notes, listing bits of information drawn from historical, scientific and anthropological sources, as well as from her extensive and eccentric general knowledge. Yet if Charmian Clift had a talent for ordering and distilling information, her great strength was her lateral turn of mind, so as she jotted down facts and figures she would spin off into memories, anecdotes, quotations or word associations. And in the same way that she addressed her reader in the column, she talked to herself in her notes.

Finally, after the research and the speculation, there would come the writing. Or sometimes there wouldn't: Clift's papers contain drafts of at least twenty-five essays which she abandoned after making up to three typewritten pages of careful notes.[37] It is most likely that a great many more such rejects were not preserved. All being well, however, Clift would at this stage begin the laborious process of writing. In her 1965 interview for the National Library, she gave some insight into the benefits as well as the strain of regularly writing to meet the deadline:

> This involves even stronger disciplines that I've ever faced before. In a way I enjoy it, I find it terribly demanding [...] I know that I am writing faster and better than I ever did because of this. I think a great deal of writing is to do with the more one writes the better and faster one can write. That doesn't mean I believe in sloppy writing. I go over every draft, over and over, I sometimes make five drafts, six drafts, of everything I do before I'm satisfied.[38]

These comments were made only eight months after Clift started writing the column, when she was still feeling the pleasure of testing herself in the new medium. Although the satisfaction of this would considerably diminish, it is important to realise that the column gave the writer highs as well as lows. One of the highs was the adrenaline rush which the urgency of the Saturday deadline produced; this gave an emotional as well as creative focal point to the writer's week. Meeting the deadline also reassured Clift that, despite the level of her drinking and other elements of chaos, she was essentially in control of her life. Toni Burgess remembered:

> She was inordinately proud of her professionalism, proud as a kid with a lollipop of the fact that she never missed a deadline. She used that as the final word in arguments with George. She would look him straight in the eye and say very slowly and deliberately, 'In any case, I have *never* missed a deadline!'[39]

This is confirmed by the chronological record of the column,[40] and by Clift's editor, Margaret Vaile, who remembered that 'Charmian's copy was like the sunrise and the sunset. There was never a problem. Never!'

Once the article arrived on Vaile's desk, the title might be changed or added and sometimes Clift's long paragraphs were split to suit a newspaper column, but the pieces were not sub-edited in the normal sense after the columnist joined the *Sydney Morning Herald*. Margaret Vaile explained: 'I just thought that her work was so good, why wreck it? You might twist it, you might ruin its whole meaning. These were *essays!*'[41]

Charmian Clift was extremely lucky to have had the support of Margaret Vaile, and also that of John Douglas Pringle. However, even this did not make writing the column any less wearying, for on top of the pain of the actual production there was frequently the anguish of the subject matter. As each week Clift shuffled through her collection of press-cuttings, they often seemed to her to be more like 'desperate press-*fearings*': articles about Vietnam and conscription, the outpourings of right wing politicians and spokesmen from the RSL.[42]

As the sixties sped on — as more and more images of atrocities in Vietnam filled the nightly television screens and morning newspapers — the pain of all this became worse. Yet as the columnist's anguish increased, her opinions strengthened, and she would appeal to facts as well as to feelings, would use her head as well as her heart. A chronological reading of the column shows a development of political concern — both a radicalisation of the writer's declared opinions and a growing diversity of issues which provoked her outrage.

Over the first year — from late 1964 through 1965 — Clift tended overall to deal with domestic issues, with memories, and with her migrant-eye examination of the new world around her. Certainly, her opposition to conscription and the Vietnam War was evident, but her main political energy through this early period was devoted to probing and questioning Australian attitudes, Australian identity and Australian complacency.

Mention has already been made of the essay 'On a Lowering Sky in the East', with which Clift greeted the New Year in 1966. While she would still write a great many essays which did not touch upon political issues, from now, as the escalating commitment to Vietnam brought an escalating level of protest, the column would also deal more overtly with political issues. In late April 1966, 4500 additional troops, including the first overseas conscripts, were sent to Vietnam amid (a *Sydney Morning Herald* headline noted) 'mounting controversy'. A couple of weeks later, in 'Banners, Causes and Convictions', Charmian Clift recorded a change in attitude from the apathy and mental flabbiness of the society which she had first encountered in 1964:

> The list of Action Committees grows. The slogans multiply and surely beget their opposing slogans. More and more people are positively for or positively against bureaucratic policies. Students meet and march. Banners are snatched and torn like battle trophies. Political rallies are stormy and even physically violent. Mothers of sons march for one cause and outraged architects for another while another group vigorously demands racial equality. Dissension spreads. Hostility also. Vigils, protests, sit-ins, teach-ins and even freedom rides are becoming usual [...]
>
> Post-war apathy of the complacent affluent society has exploded into drama suddenly. Emotions run high, if not riot.[43]

That this change was healthy, Clift was certain, for she held that causes and beliefs were a necessary part of evolution. 'The lotus-eaters', she reminded her readers, 'dreamed their way into oblivion'. A few months later, when demonstrations disrupted the ceremonial motorcade intended to honour visiting US President Johnson and his First Lady, Clift again came down on 'The Right of Dissent', reminding her readers that this right was 'something that we Australian people used to hold dear, all the way back to the Eureka Stockade'.[44]

A is for the Atom Age

fairy story that is with us all the day long…

Charmian Clift expresses a very personal viewpoint

We're all vain and greedy

Talking in commercials

Mirror on the wall

TRAINS HER HUSBAND TO FIGHT

THE Mexican boxer, Roberto Perez, who arrived by Air New Zealand yesterday, has an unusual training routine.

The Shop Detective

New Boutique Opens

You're a Tree

Slim Your Figure Now

Fashion Winners

A club to beat the law

FROM A STAFF CORRESPONDENT

LONDON, Wednesday. — Britain's first controversial department store, operating from a converted warehouse near Manchester's Piccadilly, could revolutionise the entire retail business.

Continental Beauty

Unwanted Hair

Warehouse Price Pearls

Orphans

New Hair Beauty

No other spread at any price has more goodness for your family than ETA Table Margarine

Here's why

Energy — No other spread at any price is a better source of fuel for energy than ETA.

Nutrition — No other spread has more nutritive value than ETA — and its food value satisfies appetites, too.

Vitamins — ETA is a good source of Vitamins A and D.

Quality — ETA is a wholesome food made from carefully processed ingredients and is best wrapped to preserve its goodness.

It makes sense to buy ETA — and keep the change!

ETA
TABLE MARGARINE
SuperSpread
8 OZ. NET

Women's Section, *Sydney Morning Herald*, 21/10/65, p. 2. Note editorial warning that the columnist's attack on advertising is 'a very personal viewpoint'.

CHARMIAN ✳ CLIFT

There was a man called Martin Luther, once, a long time ago, and he protested. There was a man called Martin Luther King . . . and he protested.

On the right of dissent

Protested

Brave lunatics

I like Sydney BUT . . .

One of a series

By MARGARET VAILE

Not the rule of thumb

Women's Section, *Sydney Morning Herald*, 1/8/68, p. 3. By now the weekly Clift column appeared with the Grace Bros advertisement on p. 3.

Clift was writing this two years before the large student mobilisations against the war began to take off in 1968, and four years before the broad front of the Moratorium movement made anti-Vietnam protest almost respectable. Yet the conscription 'lucky dip' and the Vietnam War were not the only political issues to concern Charmian Clift. As a woman and a mother — and as a columnist in the women's pages — she took on the cause of starving children and hungry families. In particular, she 'endorsed' the Save the Children Fund, devoting three essays to advertising their appeals in the period 1967 to 1969; on two occasions she also backed the Freedom from Hunger Campaign.[45] While Clift personalised the issue of war orphans and starving children by making readers think of their own children, she also cut through the statistics by presenting the reader with the picture of an individual child: 'I know that if I saw one starving child my heart would turn over and I would do anything, anything, to nurse that child back to health and strength again. But all those millions are beyond me'.[46]

Throughout these appeals, Charmian Clift stressed the common humanity of people; indeed, one of these columns was titled 'Some Thoughts on a Large Family', the family in question being humankind. And although Clift gave 'reasons' for urging donations to causes such as Aboriginal preschools or orphanages in Vietnam, the bottom line of her argument was political rather than philanthropic. On Boxing Day 1968, she urged readers to give money to Save the Children and Freedom from Hunger 'not penitentially, or to compound for indulgence and gluttony, or even in the name of charity [...] but in common justice'. She added: 'If we believe in human existence, that is'.[47]

From this call for justice, it was a natural next step to question the division of the world's wealth. If more of the earth's resources were used properly, and shared properly, 'governments could, if they wished, put a meal into every hungry stomach in the world'.[48]

> Day after day I read in my newspaper of the increasing disparity between the Haves and the Have-nots of the world. Two-thirds of the world's population are suffering from under-nutrition or malnutrition or both. Since there are going to be more people tomorrow than there are today, it follows that there will be more hungry ones. Unless the Haves share out more evenly, and there is as yet not the slightest indication that they have any such intention.[49]

That piece was published in February 1968. Three weeks later, Clift returned to the problem of 'The Hungry Ones'. This time, as well as giving even more hard information, she attempted to express her 'own muddy, clouded, and terribly troubled thoughts on the subject, which might be put something like this': 'Yes indeed, I do like being a Have, and want to go on being a Have, but I wish every other human being in the world could be a Have too, so I can go on being one with a clear conscience'.[50]

While all of this was concerned with economic and social justice, Clift at the same time would challenge the political system and authority in general under the title of 'Big Daddy'. Thus in 'Report from a Migrant, Three Years After', the columnist declares her outrage against censorship, then notes: 'It is time Big Daddy treated us as grown-ups'. Later she complains that 'Massage parlours are more shocking' to the society's leaders 'than the insidious encroachment of foreign capital and foreign ownership; we've been told soothingly and smilingly not to worry about that, and Big Daddy knows best'.[51] A year after this, in mid 1968, Clift became angry when the New South Wales Chief Secretary banned the play *America Hurrah!*, declaring that 'only hippies and the lunatic fringe would object'. Around the same time, the state Premier advised his police that, when faced with protestors on the streets, they should 'Run over the bastards'. The essayist replied with a scathing attack on the 'paternalistic brand' of Australian 'authoritarianism' that could be epitomised by the name of the popular television sitcom *Father Knows Best*.

'But does Father know best, really?' she asked. 'Complacent Father, smug Father, slippers-and-pipe Father, well-fed Father, I-know-best Father, you-follow-in-my-footsteps-son-and-everything-will-be-all-right Father?' The rest of this piece addresses this figure directly and ironically as 'Dear Papa':

> As far as I know, no injustice has ever been overcome, no wrong ever righted, by putting up with it, or by meekly accepting the dictum that Father knows best [...]
> Oh, 'lunatic fringe' if you will. When you are counting the heads, Papa, count mine. Brown it is, and rather turbulent.[52]

Although the term 'Big Daddy' had a certain currency among the youth of the 1960s, it took on a special resonance when it was used by someone from the older generation. There is also a very personal ring to it. If Syd Clift shaped his daughter's politics with rhetoric, he also shaped Charmian's attitudes by providing her with the first authority figure that she would rebel against: the Big Daddy of Clift's column was an unlikely cross between Syd Clift and Sir Robert Menzies.[53]

All of this was strong stuff, not just for the women's pages but for the Australian press in general. It is clear, however, that when Clift wrote in these terms, the aim wasn't just to shock readers out of their apathy: these declarations were as personal to the writer as the accounts of moving house or missing her husband when he was in hospital. It was as if the famous slogan of that era that 'The personal is the political' had been reversed for Charmian Clift. She took the atrocities in the newspapers as if they involved her own babies, her own children, women and men she knew and loved.

All this was a far cry from the persona of the woman in the hat on the cover of *Images in Aspic*, the Kate Perrin character who lived in an atmosphere of 'high comedy', and couldn't change a light bulb. As time went on, the muddle-headed columnist disappeared. Meanwhile this new persona of Charmian Clift rode around tilting at windmills like the Don Quixote character she had played as a child, when she had galloped her wooden Rosinante through the paddocks of paspalum.

And yet, and yet ... Although this passionately caring Clift was closer to the model, it was still a created character, intended for public consumption. In Anne Deveson's words:

> I think the essayist's persona was a much more manageable persona — a more *managed* persona — than Charmian's interior persona, which I think was wilder and more troubled and darker than came through in the columns. Charmian probably had terrible black moments and if that had come through, [she] probably would have switched everyone off.

When asked if she thought there was a sense of discomfort for Clift with the essayist's persona, as if during the time of writing the column she had to adopt the role of a bright and sanitised version of herself, Deveson exclaimed:

> Oh yes! I mean, I very much relate to that, and again that might have been a bond between us, in that that was a period when I had a column in the *Sun* twice a week, I had a daily radio program, every three weeks I had a television documentary, and I was very much a public persona, and I found that an enormous

strain. I remember Charmian and I talking about that, because [in the column] you often switched onto automatic pilot, and although Charmian's column certainly was written in much more depth than mine, nevertheless it had an element of the charming and the colourful and the domestic about it that I think was not the whole of Charmian — and it is a very great strain, that.

For me, I actually remember waking up one morning, sitting bolt upright in bed and saying, 'I can't do this any longer!' Because the column had started to envelop my life and smother me.[54]

And so, forthwith, Anne Deveson stopped doing her column. For Charmian Clift, however, it was as if the whole thing had taken off in such a way that it could not be stopped.

While Deveson's comments have raised the 'black moments' which Charmian Clift had to hide from her 'Thursday ladies', there was of course one particular thing which the author had to obliterate, self-censor, keep silent about. This was the matter of Jennifer. Now the secret which Amy had insisted upon, more than twenty years before, assumed the dimensions of a big lie at the heart of the public Charmian Clift. The persona of the columnist was so much that of a super-mum — dealing brilliantly with her own kids and all their young friends, and extending her role to be a champion of the homeless and hungry children of the world — that her position may well have been compromised if it were discovered that this mother had once relinquished a baby.

It is difficult now to grasp the social context in which having had an illegitimate baby would be a cause of shame. If the swinging sixties promised sexual liberation, this was only for the young and for the present; it did not extend any remission to 'oldies' for past breaches of the moral code. Besides, the majority of Clift's readers were not part of this shift of moral values. Just as the Menzies era continued long after the man had retired, so the moral and social attitudes of the fifties continued through the sixties. If Clift's secret had got out, she would have lost a certain section of her readership. While many other readers would, no doubt, have been sympathetic to her plight, this would have been small consolation, for it was not really the content of the lie that mattered, but the fact that a lie had been perpetrated. The name of Charmian Clift and her integrity were so synonymous that any washing of her dirty linen in public would have ruined her. Or so it seemed. But how difficult it was for Charmian Clift to keep up this deception.

If this was all part of the past which the columnist had to keep hidden, another skeleton was starting to rattle in the closet. This was Cressida Morley — or, specifically, George Johnston's Cressida Morley. Although in her November 1967 letter to June Crooke Charmian declared that she liked what she had read so far of *Clean Straw for Nothing*,[55] this was a beginning of the defensive attitude of acquiescence which she would publicly adopt in regard to her husband's novel. Also, while the material which she had read at this stage contained nothing very alarming, Clift naturally suspected that, when the story got to the events in Greece, Johnston would go over the old matter of the infidelity with Jean-Claude Maurice.[56] While this had already appeared as Kate Meredith's adulterous love affair in *Closer to the Sun*, not many Australians had read that text, for few copies of the first Meredith novel had been distributed here. The success of *My Brother Jack* ensured that the second book of the trilogy would be widely distributed.

Fearing the worst, Clift did not read any more of her husband's work-in-progress after the material which she saw on her return from the trip north in November 1967. She was (as she would explain in an essay about the novel, written when it was due for publication) 'totally incapable' of helping George Johnston with this project:

> He needs a constant presence, an ear, a sounding board, an audience. Some writers are like that and it has been my peculiar pleasure to perform this function for him [...]
>
> But with *Clean Straw* I've had a complete emotional block, and not all my deep and genuine sympathy at the sight of him struggling and fighting with what was obviously proving to be recalcitrant (sometimes I thought intractable) could force me into the old familiar step-sitting role. Nor all my professionalism could lure me into listening dispassionately.[57]

Although Charmian disengaged herself from George's project, she could not help but be aware of the directions in which his thoughts were turning, for he started using his elder son to give him feedback on his fiction. In describing his role, Martin explained:

> I would come home from morning lectures at university and we'd discuss, over beer and pies, every phrase, every reference,

every implication: [my father] always needed what he called a 'sounding board', and my mother, who had functioned as such during *My Brother Jack,* found herself unable to do so — partly because she was herself, as Cressida Morley, so profoundly central a character, partly because she was also trying to write a novel — for either of the last two books.[58]

No doubt there is some exaggeration here of Martin's role: he wouldn't return home after morning lectures every day, and so wasn't vetting everything quite as it was written. But certainly, he had frequent discussions about the text with his father, and because of the way in which space was used in the house — George worked downstairs, often in the living room — these must have been to some extent public conversations, held when Charmian was around the kitchen or perhaps at the big refectory table. It is also significant that Martin saw Charmian's lack of ability to perform the sounding board role as specifically connected with her 'central' position as the character of Cressida. In her own account, cited above, Charmian hadn't spelled this out. Martin, however, didn't realise the connection between this and the other reason he gives — his mother's own novel-writing — because he wasn't aware that in her own text Clift was also writing about Cressida Morley.[59]

With Martin at university having the literary education which George idealised, the author enjoyed discussing with his elder son some of the classic texts of the English literature course, or old favourites of his own, or works by new authors which Martin would bring home. In his description of the change which ill-health had brought to his father's work rate, Martin noted that: 'He would do, on a good day, perhaps 600 words before lunch, and that might involve reading a dozen passages in other writers who seemed to him relevant — a practice he would have laughed at in earlier years'.[60]

George Johnston's reading of certain authors during the writing of *Clean Straw for Nothing* would have a direct bearing on the development of the character of Cressida Morley, as the author now began to interpret Meredith's wife as a kind of modern Australian version of a couple of classic literary female models. At this stage of Johnston's work on the novel — in late 1967 or early 1968 — three particular texts began to preoccupy the author so much that he made typed notes from them; at the same time he incorporated ideas from these notes and this reading directly into the two 'London, 1954' sections of his novel-in-progress. One of these texts was a curious book of pop psychology by Eric Hoffer, named *The Passionate State of Mind;* the notes show that Johnston was particularly interested in the passage entitled 'The Elements of Jealousy'. Another text was a selection of stories and essays by F Scott Fitzgerald, collected by the critic Arthur Mizener in an anthology entitled *Afternoon of an Author.* The third was Flaubert's classic novel, *Madame Bovary.*[61] Johnston had, of course, long been mulling upon the emotions of jealousy and possessiveness; now the Hoffer passage provided him with an interpretation of the workings of 'the suspicious mind'. This went together with the author's particular interpretation of two problematic literary heroines who awaken the jealousy of their long-suffering husbands.

It has already been noted that George Johnston was an admirer of the work of F Scott Fitzgerald, for the American author represented many of the between-wars attitudes which Johnston himself held. Fitzgerald's long-term illness and his European exile increased Johnston's sense of affinity with this other writer. Now another similarity which Johnston found was between Fitzgerald's fictionalised character Nicole (derived from Fitzgerald's wife Zelda) and his own fictionalised Cressida. The particular Nicole whom Johnston discovered in Mizener's anthology was an early version of the character, who appeared in a short story written three years before the novel *Tender is the Night.* Here Nicole is beautiful, vain, idle and mentally unstable.[62]

Even more important than Nicole's beauty and neuroticism is the fact that she has no role in the world except to be her husband's wife. This, too, is the problem of Flaubert's heroine, Madame Bovary. With nothing to do but be the wife of weak Charles Bovary, it is no surprise that she turns to adultery. In his notes from this time, George Johnston has included a page typed out from *Madame Bovary;* this is concerned with the expectations of happiness which Charles Bovary imposed upon his wife.[63] In his novel, Johnston declares: 'Like Emma Bovary [Cressida] must still strive to keep up the appearance of happiness so that David could continue to believe in its reality'.[64]

Developing out of his thoughts on Flaubert, coupled with his reading of Eric Hoffer's psychology, Johnston asked in his notes to himself: 'Can the compatibility of a marriage be jeopardised, or even destroyed, by the incompatibility of two myths selfishly and separately harboured?' The author replied that 'in the final analysis [...] it is the possessed and possessive myth which in the end destroys the marriage, and Emma Bovary with it. She is destroyed by the romantic malady'. The author also applied this notion of the destructive force of the 'possessed and possessive myth' to the marriage of David and Cressida Meredith, referring in the second 'London, 1954' passage to David's 'possessive jealousies' and Cressida's 'possessiveness of that silent uncommunicated private world in which her own myths were harboured'.[65]

The two literary models of Emma Bovary and the early Nicole Diver had certain affinities with the character of 'the social woman' — the idle beauty with her ruined face and multiple ex-lovers — who had formed an important element of George Johnston's hallucinations when he was in the recovery room. Just as the social woman imperceptibly took over the character of Cressida Morley, turning her from the writer-wife of David Meredith into just the wife, now elements of Fitzgerald's Nicole and Flaubert's Emma merged into the fictional portrayal of David Meredith's wife.

While these two heroines are difficult women, their husbands are virtually destroyed by them. This fitted the fictional portrayal of the Meredith marriage which George Johnston was now developing. In the notes from Flaubert, it is clear that the author is seeing parallels between his alter ego narrator and Charles Bovary. In Johnston's notes from the Fitzgerald text, it is not Nicole's fictional husband with whom Johnston is identifying, but the American writer himself; the bulk of the quotations are from Mizener's introductory notes about the author.

At the same time as he read these three texts and made these notes, Johnston wrote a set of 'Notes for the Study of a Woman' which encapsulate this development of the author's thoughts about David Meredith's unfaithful wife and his destructive marriage.[66] Here parallels between Johnston's heroine and Emma Bovary are overtly drawn. These notes would also be incorporated into the 'London, 1954' sections of *Clean Straw for Nothing*. It is after this time that Cressida Morley takes on the role of the fickle jade.

For Charmian at this time, no doubt overhearing George and Martin talk about some of this reading matter, it would be little wonder if she were becoming concerned about how she would appear in her husband's novel. As well as being hurtful on a personal level, a portrayal of an adulterous Cressida Morley might compromise the public image of Charmian Clift the columnist. This was particularly distressing because Johnston was writing this character at a time when Clift could not write about her own Cressida; despite his Commonwealth Literary Fund fellowship grant, she felt she had to keep writing the column so that her husband could have the luxury of writing *his* novel. At the same time, Johnston's use of Clift's alter ego and experience was becoming increasingly troublesome. There were implications now for the alter ego identity which Clift expressed in her column, as well as for the autobiographical narrator of *The End of the Morning.*

Although Martin Johnston states that his mother 'never went so far as to call the persona she adopted in her column [...] "Cressida Morley"', surely the Charmian Clift that was the column persona was very much part of the character of Cressida that Clift had created in the drafts of *The End of the Morning.* This was exactly the kind of woman who would grow out of the wild-spirited child that was nine year old Cress. As we have seen, the fact that the author on occasion used the same passages of text in both the novel and the essays shows that she saw both voice and character to be interchangeable.

By 1968, it was as if there were a number of different Charmian-characters living side by side in the Raglan Street house. There was Charmian Clift the columnist (who was Clift's own version of an adult Cressida Morley). There was also Johnston's Cressida, and there was Clift's child-Cressida. And somewhere about, there was the real Charmian.

Reference has already been made to some notes regarding Cressida Morley which George Johnston had written in 1963, and in which he describes the character's fragmentation into three Cressidas.[67] Insofar as this attempts to use a psychoanalytical framework, it is naturally an amateur job. However, Johnston did get it right in pinpointing that a fragmentation was going on, even if he didn't realise that his work was part of the cause of this. By now, the whole issue of identity was becoming problematic. Who was Charmian Clift? Where was she?

Clift had herself imaginatively projected such a situation in *Walk to the Paradise Gardens*, in which Julia tries 'to break through out of the public image of Charles Cant's wife — to be herself, Julia, distinct, separate, acting independently' but finds that every such attempt ends in humiliation or disaster. 'And "Oh! Oh!" she [cries] to Charles Cant's wife in misery, "that is all very well, but where am *I*?"'[68] For Clift, there was the problem of breaking out of the public image of George Johnston's wife, an image which cast her as the junior partner in the Johnston literary team. There was the further problem of breaking out of the fictional image of the adulterous wife which Johnston was creating. And there was the problem of breaking out of the public image which surrounded the columnist.

Some of Charmian Clift's problem in handling the public and private sides would be directly addressed by Martin Johnston, in a discussion of the later years of his mother's life:

> I think she was a very private person, although there was more and more of a public side to her life in her later years. You know, she always seemed to be addressing things, or judging Rolls Royce shows, or that sort of nonsense. But there was a side to her, or I should say a core to her, which was so private that I don't think I ever really knew it, in all the years I knew her. And I'm not entirely sure that my father did, although I'm sure that he came much closer to it than anyone else. I always had the feeling that she had, and needed, a place deep inside herself, to which she could run, where she could hide. A place which when she talks about it at all explicitly she seems to identify with her childhood on the beach [...] Ah, [we're back to] freedom again — privacy and freedom go together for her.
>
> At the same time she was fond of quoting, as was my father, an aphorism of Kafka's, which goes something like: 'Narrow your circle by all means, but make sure you don't leave yourself outside it.' She needed people too. She needed my father above all. But I think she needed them on her terms. In fact, in a sense she wanted to cheat. She wanted to have it both ways. She wanted to be able at any instance to run into wherever that core was at the centre of herself, slam the door, pull up the drawbridge, bang down the portcullis, and come out again when she felt good and ready.[69]

Perhaps this matter of handling public and private roles is a kind of occupational hazard for essayists. Virginia Woolf, in her essay about the French master of the genre, Montaigne, notes: 'To tell the truth about oneself, to discover oneself near at hand, is not easy [...] For beyond the difficulty of communicating oneself, there is the supreme difficulty of being oneself'. And in her account of 'The Modern Essay', Woolf goes on to make a vital distinction between the public self and the private self of the essayist, declaring: 'Never to be yourself and yet always — that is the problem'.[70]

That was indeed one of the problems that Charmian Clift was desperately trying to solve.

23

THE MOST CURIOUS SENSE
OF EXPOSURE

I had the most curious sense of exposure, as though I was play-acting
at being myself and not doing it very well.[1]

On the global front, 1968 was a year of escalation and confrontation; it is the quintessential sixties year. In the lives of Charmian Clift and George Johnston also, these twelve months would bring a sudden quickening of the pace — as if events were gathering momentum, snowball-style. The year began in Australia with the inauguration of a new prime minister. The month before, the country had been incredulous when Menzies' successor, Harold Holt, had simply disappeared. In January the Liberal Party elected Senator John Grey Gorton to be leader of their party and the country. Charmian Clift's satirical response revealed her disillusionment with the political system.[2]

The leadership struggles of the Liberal Party seemed particularly trivial to Clift at this time, for her political concern was focused on Greece. In April the previous year a military junta had seized power from the democratically elected government. Despite a major press crackdown, there were stories of people being jailed without trial and tortured without mercy. Towards the end of 1967, members of Sydney's Greek community had set up the Committee for the Restoration of Democracy in Greece. This aimed to make Australian citizens aware of the Junta's activities, and to lobby the Australian government to break off diplomatic relations with the illegal government of Greece. The day-to-day work of this group was done by left wing Greek

Australians led by the committee's president, James (Jim) Calomeras, but the committee was made up of fourteen Anglo-Australian vice-presidents. Amongst these people who lent their names to the cause were church leaders, academics, trade union leaders and three authors — Charmian Clift, George Johnston and Kylie Tennant. The Johnston family was further connected to the committee through Shane, who became Jim Calomeras's secretary at the Greek-language newspaper, the *Hellenic Herald*.[3]

In her Christmas essay for 1967, Charmian Clift alerted readers to the Greek situation after leading them through a tour of the imported goods on offer in the back room of her local Greek delicatessen:

> All this makes me think, inevitably, of other Greek grocers' back rooms, and other Christmases, and my heart is so torn and hurt for Greece and my Greek friends at this moment that if I could help them I would willingly transpose myself to the other back room I know best.[4]

The particular back room in her mind was, of course, the one behind the Katsikas brothers' grocery shop on Hydra, and Clift went on to 'wonder what goes on [there] these days'.

> One thing I do know is that Melina Mercouri won't be gracing the back room, this Christmas, as she did so often, or Theodorakis, or many many others who seem to have disappeared without trace, many many friends of whom we hear nothing any more.

This concern about Greece together with the involvement with the Sydney Greek community brought to the surface the homesickness which Charmian had managed to keep at bay during the first three years in Australia. From now her disenchantment with aspects of Australian political and social life would run hand in hand with longing for Greece. When she had first returned, she had been happy to be out of the incestuous Hydra foreign colony. It was the Greek people and their cultural attitudes that she now missed. What she craved was *i zoe*, which while meaning 'the life' also carries the feeling of the spirit. This had been foreshadowed as early as May 1965 when the Johnston family, newly settled in Australia, was visited by Yanni, the Kalymnian carpenter whom they had sponsored to come to Australia ten years earlier. Now he was emigrating back to Greece. 'But why?' Charmian had asked. After all, he said he had done well here, made money ...

'Look!' he said, 'where is the life here? The life! *Then ekhei zoe etho.* There is no life here. Me, I understand the life. You, you understand the life. These people are dead. Where is the little taverna, drink some wine, eat some fish, sing some songs, sometimes break a glass or two? Everybody asleep nine o'clock. No singing, no dancing, no nothing.'[5]

'I feel like nothing here', Yanni had concluded. 'It isn't really living you see. Not living at all.'

Three years later, Yanni's complaint could have been Charmian's own, as she made clear when she returned to this theme in a February 1968 essay concerned with the issue of migrants returning. 'I always ask migrants what they miss most', the columnist noted before going on to give their answer:

'The life,' they have often said to me. 'I miss the life. There is no life here.' And I understand that very clearly, because I too miss the life, and it has often occurred to me in the last three years that I am infinitely more isolated and more completely marooned in an Australian suburb than I ever was on a poor and primitive Greek island. Materially I am much better off, but spiritually I sometimes feel impoverished of the gaiety and social ease of Mediterranean living.[6]

In other ways, too, Charmian was unhappy at this time. As Jason remembered the sequence of events, there was his mother's trip away, followed by the happy homecoming, and then 'the slide began soon after'. This 'slide' didn't seem to him to have a particular origin or cause; it was rather 'the beginnings of a sort of unhappy feel, that could have come from a lot of things'.[7]

George, on the other hand, was in fine spirits in the opening months of 1968. This is clear from the letter which he wrote to David Higham this March. Once again, he and Charmian had left their loyal literary agent without any news for a year; again, George cited past pressures and illnesses — which were now indeed a thing of the past, he insisted.

Dear David,

I feel thoroughly ashamed that it is so long since I have been in touch [...] but I must have been going through a bad spell of alienation or something — not feeling all that well in health and far away from the real world and trying, as well, to overcome what writers call 'a block' which seemed to persist for a long time. So I suppose one was rather deliberately keeping *out* of touch rather than in touch. However, I think you'll be pleased to know that I seem to have overcome the problem at last, feeling quite a lot better than at any time since the surgery was over, and back to writing again in a state of good spirits and confidence. I scrapped the first two drafts of CLEAN STRAW FOR NOTHING but am now rather more than half my way through a third version which I think I am happy with. I should have it finished about June, perhaps with a month or so on top of that for final polishing. We'll keep our fingers crossed but I think it's shaping up to a good novel. I don't know whether you know that I have been awarded a Commonwealth Government Writing Fellowship for this year; it's worth $6000 and enables me to go on with my writing for a year without any economic worries, which is vastly pleasing. Charmian is now well, although she, too, went through a long period of worrying illness, and has also re-embarked on a novel she began and put aside because of the various strains attached to my illness and the problems of readjustment (the kids as well as us) back in this country.[8]

At the bottom, after sending 'all our love', he scrawled in handwriting: 'Charmian says to tell you she's sorry for being so churlishly uncommunicative'.

It is not surprising that George's mood was high, now that the novel was flowing at last. But what should we make of Charmian's 'long period of worrying illness'? This can only have been a reference to what George saw as his wife's menopausal problems, including the unhappiness and anxiety as well as the physical symptoms, for Charmian had suffered no illness beyond periodic bouts of bronchitis and flu. And what is meant by the claim that she was 'now well'? It was perhaps around this time that she discontinued the visits to the psychiatrist; it is clear in any case that these consultations only went on for a few months.[9]

It is timely to reconsider the line in Clift's notebook, that 'As soon as one felt strong, the other felt ill. As soon as the ill one recovered strength, down went the one who had been well'.[10] George had not been in such an ebullient mood since the euphoria about the publication of *My Brother Jack*; whether or not it was part of the seesaw effect described in the notebook, it is the case that on this occasion George's upswing coincided with Charmian's downswing.

Finally, what of this news that Charmian had re-embarked on her novel? This was a good sign, but by now the author had picked up *The End of the Morning* and put it down so many times that the drafts had about as much attraction as a piece of old knitting that had unravelled and knotted in the cupboard. She may have felt spurred back into her book by George's progress, but this same progress made it harder for her to make headway.

Something of all this pain — plus the ongoing anguish of the violation of privacy — came out in a letter which Charmian wrote to June Crooke in April 1968. By now, as we shall see, George's situation had changed.

Dearest June,

Please forgive the long silence. It's always been my instinct to hole up when things go badly, and things have been going pretty badly for quite some time now. I think I am pulling out of it, but I still have relapses into panic and desolation and have to force myself to see people or go out at all. We've had a bitter blow in these last couple of weeks to find out that George is positive again. It's hard after nearly eleven years of sickness and brutal surgery to be back again at the beginning. Everyone is being very cheerful and reassuring, and they are doing everything they can to make it easier for him, even to the extent of letting him stay at home for treatment instead of hauling him in again, but the new drugs make him sick and depressed and he has to force himself to work, and this is so disappointing when the novel was going so well. Anyway, I suppose we'll get through this lot eventually. We've got through worse before [...] How are the girls? And how is the full family life? I often wonder if the time will ever come when all one's children are progressing full steam ahead at the same time. Shane and Jason are blasting away in fine style at the moment — Shane as circulation manager of the *Hellenic Herald* and Jason eating up his first term at high school, but poor old Martin is going through something or other that is making him evasive, dishonest, and really rather shoddy. I wish he could tell us. I wish he would go to the dentist and have his teeth scraped. I wish he would cut his hair. I wish I knew what he was up to. I feel ashamed of him and for him and ashamed of myself for feeling this. The only good thing he's done lately was to sell a poem to the book pages of the S.M.H. Oh well. I have taken up gardening as a serious pursuit and have long consultations with Mr Griffiths, the nursery gardener, on what to plant where. I enjoy this, and so does George, who finds a little gentle pottering very therapeutic. Further than this I am trying to locate a marmalade kitten to complete the household and my final surrender to absolute domesticity. Jason is too big to sit on my knee any more and I need someone to pat. I suppose I also need someone to pat me. Poof. Sorry about this dreary letter, dear June — this is why I haven't been writing.[11]

After a few detailed replies to inquiries from her friend's last letter, Charmian reverts to George's illness ('Poor man feels like a leper'), and concludes with the observation that 'Life is a bitch sometimes'.

This letter reveals the depth of Charmian's love and concern for her children, and her dependence on the kind of connectedness given by the family unit, even when there might be incidental annoyance with any particular individual. At the same time, it reveals her happiness in the everyday routine of companionship with her husband.

And yet this text is alarming in its insight into Charmian's ongoing mental state — a state in which the norm was desolation, loneliness for physical affection, panic, and fear of going out or seeing people.

Despite these fears, Charmian Clift went out and saw people in a very public way at this very time. In April 1968, on the first anniversary of the colonels' putsch, the Committee for the Restoration of Democracy in Greece held a protest meeting at an old cinema in Paddington. As this coincided with Easter Saturday it was a particularly moving event, with people in mourning for the death of Christ as well as the death of democracy. Yet it also had the eclectic spirit of celebration which no Greek gathering can avoid:

One Australian poet recited Cavafy's 'Waiting for the Barbarians' in English, another Australian poet said 'Aghia Sophia' in Greek, a Greek group sang Australian bush ballads, another group danced Zorba, a very well known folk singer belted out 'Freedom', another belted out Cuban folk, the lights dazzled, the mike went on the blink, a slide of Melina Mercouri flashed on the screen brought cheers, and one of King Constantine hisses and some cries of 'Pig!' There was bouzouki music (amplified to torture pitch), and sweetly harmonised songs sung cantata-style and unaccompanied. There were also speeches.[12]

And indeed, one of these speeches was given by Charmian Clift. Jim Calomeras remembered how well she spoke to this crowd of two or three thousand people. Although this solidarity was deeply appreciated by the Sydney Greek community, the really important work which Clift did for this cause was through her column, backing up her claims of the Junta's brutality and her questions as to the regime's supposed economic 'clean-up' by citing reports from European and American economists, academics and journalists. Titling her piece on this occasion 'Long Live Democracy!' she expected to win the support of Anglo-Australians. Instead, she received a torrent of 'attacks, rebukes, castigations and instructions' from Australians who claimed to be speaking in the name of democracy.[13] With hate mail being delivered into her home, Charmian Clift personally suffered for her anti-Junta stand in a way that the other vice presidents did not. She also sacrificed the chance of returning to Greece for a holiday, for there was believed to be a danger of retribution by the Greek government.[14] Certainly, Jim Calomeras was in no doubt that the importance of the support given to the cause by the Clift column was 'tremendous'.[15]

Anxiety, both personal and political, caused Charmian to be so rundown at this time that she succumbed to a bad bout of influenza,[16] and the doctor was called in. In an essay which she wrote 'In Praise of the GP', Clift noted that a good general practitioner is 'a *family* doctor. In every illness he considers the whole unit, and how one component of it might be abrading another. And why. And in treating one he actually treats all'.[17]

Although for the Johnstons' family doctor, it was obvious that George was 'the more central medical problem' in the family, he was also terribly aware of how George's illness abraded upon the whole family unit, and to what degree Charmian bore the burden of this. 'She needed a lot of support,' he felt, 'and so that's what I tried to give'. On his frequent visits to George at Raglan Street, he was always aware of Charmian 'orchestrating the care at home'. She 'always had some questions to ask about how George was going and what she should be doing', and he remembers that 'Charmian and I used to talk, because I think she needed somebody to talk to'. At the same time, he felt that 'Charmian, in George's presence, was always sort of around the edges'.

As to the centrality of George's problem in the household, the doctor also remembered how, by this time, 'even the domestic arrangements revolved around George':

> They'd moved George and the double bed down to the front room, which opened through double doors into the living room, and then they had a glassed-in area on the back verandah which was a sort of dining area — so that George had command of the whole function of the household, and the kids were just relegated upstairs.[18]

It was not George's health alone that was troublesome; the drugs and the difficulty of working tended to make him depressed and short-tempered. When things were bad, George would criticise his wife for various faults, either of the present or of the distant past. This would contribute to Charmian's loss of self-esteem. Of this period, Garry Kinnane notes: 'The public humiliations went on':

> At Toni Burgess's house Johnston said of Clift: 'Look at her standing there like a fucking great preying mantis', implying, says Burgess, that she had devoured her mate. Clift would simply weep quietly after such attacks. 'George had persuaded her that *she* was responsible for his tuberculosis,' says Burgess, who winced at the way he could torment her over her loss of her looks.[19]

Some of these allegations were the same old ones which George had been making since the diagnosis of his illness in 1959, but by now Charmian had evidently come to accept blame for her husband's disease — blame that George laid at the door of her past infidelity. Yet surely part of the implication of the 'preying mantis' comment is that the female of the species is bigger and stronger, as well as predatory. This was the kind of resentment that Clift described in her account of the effects of the illness on her husband: the way he sometimes seemed 'affronted and outraged by anybody who didn't have corruption working in his lungs'.[20] When George felt ill and close to death, Charmian's comparative youth and health could seem an affront. Perhaps this was why he sometimes drew other people's attention to the way the ageing process was affecting her appearance.

As far as Cedric Flower was concerned, the problem was 'sex and jealousy'. On occasions when the couple came to visit, he was reminded of the film of Edward Albee's play *Who's Afraid of Virginia Woolf?*, in which

Richard Burton and Elizabeth Taylor slugged it out. 'I was shocked out of my mind [...] George was accusing Charmian of all sorts of things'. Yet if George made accusations about Charmian's sexual conduct, it is true that in this period she was sometimes unfaithful. While Johnston's reaction was partly that of any husband of his generation, his distress was exacerbated by his physical condition, coupled with the worries about masculinity that he had had since his boyhood. In tracing the source of the conflict in the relationship, Cedric referred back to the London days, and in particular to the occasion of the party that Charmian had 'turned on' for George's fortieth birthday, at which George had 'behaved very badly'.

> His worry was his virility, I think, even as early as that. That played a large part in the conversation, [which] upset Charm enormously. You know, she went out to the kitchen and had a good cry. Kept saying, 'Why does he do it? Why does he do it?' But she was saying that to the day she died.[21]

As well as the old areas of jealousy, a new rivalry was developing in the working partnership. In the past, George had always been acknowledged as by far the more experienced journalist. Since returning to Australia, however, it was Charmian who made regular appearances in the newspaper. Allan Ashbolt observed:

> Charmian was leading her own life and starting to make a genuine journalistic career for herself, which I think worried George in one sense because he was getting sicker and sicker and he was not happy with his own working life, and Charmian was suddenly becoming a better-known journalist than George, and I think that worried him.[22]

Ashbolt emphasised the link between George's illness and his jealousy of his wife's career. In the past, he had been genuinely proud of Charmian's talent. Now, however, he feared he would die before completing the major work of his trilogy, and it was aggravating to see Charmian's success, when she had decades left in which to work.

Meanwhile, rivalry was still going on over the old subject of *My Brother Jack*. As George continued to glow in the outstanding popular and critical success of the book, Charmian began to feel resentful about how much of *her* time had gone into it — time that could have been spent on her own novel — and how much of her personal experience and her hoard of carefully remembered Depression material had gone into it too. Although the novel had from first publication received excellent reviews, she believed that it would not have reached nearly so far into Australian public knowledge if it were not for the television serial that she had scripted. Some friends witnessed rows in which the couple argued the toss as to exactly who was responsible for the book's popularity and almost legendary status.[23]

But if the relationship between the couple was under stress, part of the problem was more general. In ways that George and Charmian themselves could only glimpse, they were part of a much wider conflict that was going on in domestic and professional circles in the 1960s, a conflict to do with men's roles and women's roles, with issues that would soon be expressed in words such as patriarchy and women's liberation.[24] Patricia Lovell remembered a sort of epiphany that occurred at a dinner party given by Anne Deveson and her husband Ellis Blain, which was attended by Charmian and George as well as by Pat and her husband, actor Nigel Lovell. This was the first time that Pat had met the Johnstons, although she had read a number of their books, and she found the experience 'amazing': 'I had never met two people who were so much on edge with each other, so angry with each other, but so totally bound to one another. You could almost see the cord stretched between them'. By this time, Pat knew that her own marriage was under considerable strain, but this was not public knowledge. Suddenly, however, in front of Nigel and the others, Charmian said to Pat: 'If you don't leave him, you'll die'.

> And I thought: Good Lord! Because I had been feeling this —
> I had been feeling totally overwhelmed and I had no idea who I
> was at that stage — really no idea. I had *thought* I did, but
> I didn't. And I didn't feel that there was much of actual *me* left.
> [...] I guess I owe Charmian a great deal for being as
> straightforward as that. Because she could obviously see that here
> was a marriage that was trying very hard to be OK, but one
> member of that marriage was disappearing from sight very fast.[25]

Pat was a fair bit younger than Charmian, and by the end of 1968 was able to realise that 'there was no solution except a clean break'.[26] However, even on the first meeting with the Johnstons she was aware that this option was not available to Charmian and George.

Despite the shouting and the arguments, there was this absolutely palpable bond. And I felt: this is terrifying! Here are two people who have been absolutely passionate about one another and yet things have somehow gone rotten over a long time. And yet [...] they can't part. There's no way they can part [...] It seemed like destruction.[27]

While many of the arguments between the couple were triggered by alcohol, Jason pointed to a difference that was developing — not so much in the *level* of drinking, but in its effect. From about the time when he started high school, he observed a kind of change starting:

At the time that she went away on that Centre trip, and came back — to that time, I don't recall believing there was any huge problem in the house. I mean, there were fights with Martin and Shane, which I took for granted. There was always booze on the table, but I had been used to that all my life. There was — you know — the facade, if you like, hadn't broken [...]

But [after she came back from that trip], the interesting but time-consuming Greek cuisine and unusual things gradually gave way to just chops. And the dinner time began to get later. And I mean you'd begin to notice how absolutely fucked some of the drinking was, as opposed to just [noticing that] there was a lot of drinking going on.[28]

Jason emphasised that this change was a gradual and even intermittent process, developing through 1968 and into the next year. He was also careful to try to disengage the wisdom of experience and hindsight from what he was aware of at this time, when he was twelve. He added that, despite this sort of change, he still 'didn't really think there was anything *strange* about it'. At no time — not even towards the end — did his parents hold heated personal arguments in his presence. All in all, 'life and whatever was going on seemed reasonably normal'. Dinner might sometimes be late and not wonderfully creative, but it was always eventually on the table. 'The household did function reasonably well'. Food shopping had always been difficult, because the family didn't have a car and the shops were not in walking distance. But from about this time Charmian began ringing up and ordering food from the Greek grocery shop, which offered a home delivery service.

In regard to the general level of drinking that was going on in the house at this time, the family doctor insisted that alcohol 'was not a significant health problem for either Charmian or George'. He added that he 'would think that Charmian was drinking more than George in the last few years', because of George's illness and the side effects of his drugs, but pointed out that Charmian was in 'good general health' and was 'well nourished'. To some extent, alcohol for her was a form of self-medication; her doctor remarked that 'she was using it as a prop of some sort'. He was also aware of its role in facilitating the flow of ideas. 'In the Johnston menage, alcohol was an important catalyst — something that they'd used for years'.[29]

Charmian herself was not uninformed about the medical effects of alcohol. Newspaper clippings and a draft essay on this subject in her files reveal that she had turned her mind to this matter.

> What is an alcoholic? It seems to demand a physiological *dependence* upon alcohol, a state of addiction, but not all people who drink regularly or even excessively can be considered alcoholics. To *not* be an alcoholic, however heavily you drink, you must not have to actually *need* it [...]
>
> People take alcohol for many reasons — to find stupor and forgetfulness, to ease strains and subdue anxieties, to promote social ease, to overcome inhibitions [...] One is no longer self-critical or self doubting and inhibitions are stilled. Carried too far, of course, this begins to exclude the more realistic means of meeting life's situations and this is the lead on to chronic alcoholism where the craving can result not only in social collapse but in very serious physical deterioration.[30]

While Clift used alcohol 'to ease strain and anxiety', this did not prevent her from meeting the commitments of her professional life and her home life. Overall, while by 1968 there was a problem developing with Charmian's drinking, it was both symptom and effect of the other anxieties, rather than being the major problem in itself.

For the moment — in April 1968 — there was the new worry of Martin's unfathomable behaviour, as well as the relapse in George's health. The mystery of Martin's evasiveness was finally solved when he told his parents that he had decided to drop out of university. To Charmian and George, who had themselves missed the opportunity of a tertiary education and who had invested so many academic hopes in Martin since his youngest days, this was very disappointing. Adding insult to injury, Martin took up a cadetship in journalism at the *Sydney Morning Herald*. Writing for the newspaper represented the life from which George and Charmian had escaped to Greece, in order to be real writers. And now their poet son was wilfully going off to be a hack. It seemed incomprehensible. At the same time, Martin moved out of home to live in a sleazy flat in Kings Cross.[31] At least Charmian could understand the need to leave home, and Martin went off 'to pig it alone' with her 'cheers and blessings'.[32] Indeed, life on the home front might be rather more peaceful.

By the time the problem with Martin was sorted out, the much greater worry was George's health. When the tuberculosis was found to be active again in April, the specialists had initially thought that they could treat the patient at home. Within a couple of weeks, however, he came down with a severe bout of bronchial pneumonia and it was decided that he needed full-time care. In late May he returned to Royal North Shore Hospital, where he would remain until early October.[33]

Immediately after her husband's hospitalisation, Charmian took her three weeks annual leave from the column,[34] to recover from these recent strains. So bonded were the couple, however, that it was no relief, to have George away from home — because the moment he was gone, Charmian missed him, as she had missed him during his last time in hospital, when she was living in the flat. And she missed the pattern of life which she and George had established together over twenty-five years. In her first essay after her break, she lamented that all her habits had been 'smashed up overnight'.

It wasn't just the habit of life with George that was 'unset': the whole system of family life which had developed over the last two decades was in the process of breaking. Not only had Martin left home but Shane, too, was moving out to live with friends. Moreover, she had just announced that she was going to marry her boyfriend Robert (Bob) O'Connor, and her mind was centred around 'wedding plans and the bells of St Pauls (recorded) and choristers at ten cents a head and whatever extra extras are offering'. So in the big house in Raglan Street there was only Charmian and Jason 'rattling around like the last two peas in the pod'.[35]

'Oh dear I do wish my kids were all at home', Charmian lamented. And in a later essay on 'Flying the Coop' she would express rather more of her feeling of loss:

It's a queer business, coop-flying. You know that it is coming up one day, but the day is always unexpected, and shattering somehow. For nineteen or twenty years the pattern of your life has been dictated by the needs and desires and whims and temperaments and triumphs and tragedies of these creatures you so recklessly brought into the world. Laboriously, creatively, with hope and love and pain and sacrifice and much joy and some bitter disappointment, you have spent nineteen or twenty years building a complicated edifice called Family. Not perhaps an entirely satisfactory edifice, not perhaps entirely as perfect as planned, a rather surprising edifice really, but your own, and therefore the most interesting edifice in the world. And just when you might sit back and contemplate it and enjoy it with just and happy pride, its very cornerstones casually remove themselves and the whole crazy structure lurches and topples and falls about your ears. It was, after all, never more than temporary.[36]

This toppling of the whole 'crazy structure' of family was a blow to Charmian's own sense of security. As Martin and Shane disengaged themselves, Charmian's own commitment would be subtly undermined.

Despite his illness, George continued through these months to forge ahead with *Clean Straw for Nothing*. By March 1968, as he revealed in his letter to David Higham, he believed himself to be rather more than halfway. And in a report to the Commonwealth Literary Fund in early April, Johnston declared that progress on the novel was continuing 'steadily and, I think, satisfactorily', and he was 'personally pleased by the way the book [was] shaping'. There were some 70 000 words written, 'although some of this, of course, may still be subject to final revision'.[37] There could be no setbacks now.

Even after his return to hospital towards the end of May, the author was able to keep working. This time, there was no violent surgery — just drug treatment, rest and care. Indeed, sometimes there was only the latter. Cedric Flower remembered that George 'took pills and things and [would] flush them down the toilet. It was a hopeless situation'.[38] The patient's concern was that the side effects of the medicine would interfere with his writing. In regard to work, the atmosphere during this stay in hospital was ideal. Thanks to the CLF money, George was able to afford a private room, leading onto a balcony. Soon this room took on 'much of the appearance of a writer's study: innumerable books scattered about; a transistor radio; papers; a typewriter'. Here George was able to follow his lifetime working routine of writing in the morning. Charmian and other visitors would come in the afternoons and evenings, to stimulate and amuse him. Indeed, so many 'hordes of people' came that Mary Andrews felt that Charmian felt: 'But what about *me*? Why doesn't anyone want to talk to *me*, fuss about *me*?'[39] Again we see how the sense of playing second fiddle that Charmian had grown up with was reinforced by her relationship with a man who was so magnetic that, even when he was sick, people were drawn to him.

Because of his celebrity status, the medical staff treated George as a special patient; he could have a cigarette or even a drink, and he was 'allowed to go out for brief, necessary conferences relating to his work'.[40] It was an added advantage that Charmian was at a distance from the writing of the novel during this stage, because this meant that the author was able to develop the portrait of Cressida without immediately worrying about how his wife might feel about it.

At the end of June, George Johnston wrote to David Higham noting that, since his arrival in hospital, the book had been 'making steady progress'. The author now estimated that he was 'a bit past the three-quarter mark'. He added: 'I still expect to finish within three months, September at the outside'.[41] In a report to the CLF made the same day, the author repeated that he had 'got about three-quarters of the way, or roughly 90 000 words'.[42]

While George was setting this cracking pace with *Clean Straw for Nothing*, Charmian was still feeling her way back into her own autobiographical novel. Towards the end of August, she applied to the Commonwealth Literary Fund for a fellowship for 1969, to write *The End of the Morning*. In her covering letter, we see the finicky standards of integrity which the author set herself, as well as her underlying feeling that she came second to George. Immediately after noting that she was making her application 'with much diffidence', she repeated:

> It is really with much diffidence, because my husband had a Fellowship for this year, and I am not quite sure of the ethics of the situation. Good friends have assured me that we are regarded as being quite separate identities — as indeed we are — but I still submit this with a slight uneasiness. Even though I want it and need it very much.[43]

The same tone imbues the 'Details of Proposed Project' in her application. After opening with the statement quoted in chapter 17 that the project is 'a novel of a semi-autobiographical nature [...] begun six years ago, before my husband started *My Brother Jack*, and set aside so that he would be free to complete his own project', the applicant moved on to list a series of domestic and economic reasons explaining why she was not further advanced with her work:

> Since my return to Australia, four years ago, [the novel] has been set aside again and again because of my husband's illness and the necessity for me to contribute to family income by working in journalism, radio and television [...]
>
> I do realise that everybody from George Johnston to Donald Horne has written his semi-autobiographical novel already, and that (through no fault of my own, but dreary economics) I'm a late starter in this field. I can only plead that mine is different.
>
> I will, of course, write it anyway — somehow, some time — but a Fellowship would enable me to employ the domestic and secretarial help I so desperately need (I have hundreds of letters every week to answer) and free me to get on with my business. Which is writing words on paper. I would not want to give up my weekly column, which I enjoy, and which, apart from anything else, keeps my name in the public eye and is good for the sale of my books.[44]

Clift went on to give a synopsis of the prospective novel's aims and themes; this indicates the idealistic way in which she was regarding her own childhood and family life at this time:

> *The End of the Morning* is about a girl called Cressida Morley, who has appeared already in *My Brother Jack* but I invented her first, and her eccentric family who live in a weatherboard cottage on the edge of a beach. They are liars and self-deluders all, but vibrant and very much people rather than non-people, and as out of place in a small sleepy Australian country town as six fresh oysters in Alice Springs. They rant and argue and read books and play music and are arrogant and superior and poverty-stricken (although not one of the children realise, until adolescence, that they are poor: they've always felt themselves to be rich). It is a

book about young love and young dreams and young longings, and (I hope and will try) filled with sand and sea and sun and wind and seaweed draped on the front picket fence after a storm. It is also bawdy (I can't help that: since that's the way it was).

I don't know what else I can say. The morning ends, and that's the end of the book. There are one hundred and fifty pages done, but might be re-done. And I know the last sentence.

The timing of this application is crucial in regard to Clift's emphatic declaration that she had begun her novel before Johnston started his autobiographical work, and that she had 'invented' Cressida first. In August 1968 she knew that George was only a month or so away from completing his novel, in which the character of Cressida Morley would play a leading role. Clift was therefore putting it on record that this was *her* character, and that it had been *her* idea to write a semi-autobiographical novel about the childhood and dreams of a young Australian in the Depression. The timing is also crucial in regard to Clift starting back on this work: while she feared that there would be no market left for yet another account of growing up in Australia, she was determined that *her* Cressida would have her say at last.

As Charmian Clift sifted through old drafts and tried to feel her way back into the novel, sudden new demands on her domestic routine were made by Shane, who at this time decided that she wanted to have a big party at home to announce her engagement. Four years earlier, on Hydra, Shane had found her engagement plans opposed by her mother. This time her brothers and both her parents disapproved of her fiancé. Jason reflected that: 'We were a little bit unkind to Bob, I think [...] He was just a normal sort of surfie guy [who] stumbled onto a situation that was just way beyond his control'.[45]

Charmian confided some of her concerns about the marriage to Anne Deveson — her feeling that Shane's choice was 'bizarre' and the whole thing was 'extraordinary'. Charmian also expressed her worries about seeing such a young woman tied to marriage and maybe trapped with children.[46] After all, Shane was still only nineteen years old, the age that Charmian had been when she had damaged her own life by becoming pregnant with her first child. In her August 1968 essay on Shane's betrothal, the writer states:

> I find myself walking around her warily and looking at her sideways and blinking suddenly to try to surprise the image of this young woman who is my only daughter. And sometimes she looks about fourteen and sometimes she looks about ten and I

find myself thinking wildly that this contract is quite impossible — child-brides are out in this family — but then I realise I am getting her mixed up with that incorrigible little barefooted kid who sat on the rafters in slaughter-houses, chased funerals, jumped from the masts of sponge boats, played five-stones, disappeared down trapdoors, I think, whenever she knew there was a possibility of being carpeted for misdemeanours.

Was this Shane at whom Charmian Clift was looking? Or was not the novelist looking through the female line into the young Cressida Morley? What was fascinating Clift here was the Shane-chrysalis, poised between childhood and adulthood. The writer continued: 'And when I blink back into focus again she looks so adult that I feel like asking her for advice on some of my own problems.'

Shane's desire for marriage also seemed peculiar to Charmian in the context of the 1960s. Other young women were defying society's values by living in sin. Why couldn't her own daughter do the same? Or at least just elope, and get married without fuss and bother. And yet Charmian was perceptive enough to see that this marriage was Shane's form of rebellion:

I am wondering now, with all this formality facing me, whether this generation of our children are not perhaps rebelling against their non-conformist parents as their parents rebelled against their own conformist ones [...] Perhaps the wheel has turned full circle and the conventional has now become the unconventional.[47]

As well as her concern about the marriage, Charmian found it hard to get into the role of mother-of-the-bride-to-be, as set out in the magazines which her daughter pored over. Proud as Charmian was of the way her own mother had got married in a sensible skirt and blouse, and proud of her own five minute ceremony at the registry office, she simply could not get into the swing of all the shopping and planning, the miles of tulle and scores of champagne glasses, which Shane wanted. The whole thing seemed so consumerist and commercial. Jason explained that the difference in attitude turned into conflict because of 'this strange relationship' whereby both Charmian and Shane 'couldn't help goading each other':

With two other individuals, it might just have been a case of: 'Oh well, I just don't approve of all this fuss but anyway, let's get on with it' — and that was to some extent [Charmian's] public face, in the [column] — but privately there was a lot of goading about: 'Why do you want this?'[48]

Charmian was determined to fix up the house for the at-home reception, but was not prepared for a succession of events that would have to be planned and paid for before the wedding took place. For the moment — in August 1968 — she faced the propect of organising the engagement party. With George still in hospital, and with Charmian's recurrent fears of seeing people, it was all very daunting. It is little wonder that she was happy to take Toni Burgess up on her offer to go shopping with Shane.

By September 1968, George's time in hospital was drawing towards its end. So was his novel. An interesting picture of the Johnstons at this time was given by the journalist Clifford Tolchard.[49] He interviewed Charmian first, by herself at Raglan Street. Whatever her fear of seeing people, she was still able to be the easy-going gregarious person who opened her house and her heart to strangers. Or at least, she was able to assume the role, at whatever private cost. Certainly, her act was convincing to an outsider. Tolchard wrote: 'I found in Charmian Clift a warm, uninhibited, hospitable person. She allowed me to wander from room to room, absorbing the atmosphere of their home'.

She told the journalist that her life was 'divided into two compartments, the housewife and the writer'. Tolchard continued: 'Unselfconsciously, she offers stories of her childhood in Kiama'. In fact, so deeply had the writer steeped herself in the early life of her alter ego that these 'stories' which flowed so spontaneously were descriptions of family life lifted from *The End of the Morning*. While Clift talked to Tolchard, the photographer snapped a series of pictures of someone who exemplified the warm, uninhibited person of the article. Here Charmian Clift is unselfconsciously at home in her pleasantly plump forty-five year old body. In the style she had favoured since her days as a garage attendant in Kiama, she wears a man's cotton shirt over trousers. Her face is healthy and alert. She smiles broadly, brimming with happiness.

Later that day, Tolchard accompanied Charmian Clift on her afternoon visit to the hospital. She carried an armful of flowers ('I like a man who likes flowers', she declared) and also took in the day's mail for her husband. Speaking together to the journalist, the couple revealed that they were at one in their attitude to the Australian political situation. Johnston expressed himself as being 'a bit at odds with the present climate of Australia which is unadventurous and conformist and, I think, veering towards a fascist style of authoritarianism'. Yet he had no real wish to be elsewhere, given his age and condition of health; besides, to this man whose pessimism had merged with a fatalistic sense of acceptance, it seemed 'that wherever you're living you really only live in a little enclave in an alien territory'.

Clift expressed a similar disillusionment with Australia, but through *her* criticism we feel that she really would have preferred to be elsewhere. Her comments show the terrible disappointment she had experienced since arriving:

> When I came back I was terribly enthusiastic. I wanted to love it. I wanted to believe in it, and I kept on saying there is a sense of imminence in this country, not that anything has happened yet, but I feel something is on the verge of happening. And I got very excited about this [...] But three and a half years later I am still saying, oh, there is an imminence here, and this sort of worries me. There is a complacency, an apathy. It is very bland living in Australia; you have no sense of hazard whatever. In Europe you're living with this sense of hazard that has gone on for centuries [...] and there's so much more liveliness. There's so much more agony too. There's no real agony here.

It may seem ironic that someone who was experiencing personal agony should wish for agony in the culture and way of life. For Clift, however, agony and hazard went together with *i zoe*, with that thing which she could only express in English as 'liveliness'. It was not just that Charmian Clift was bored by the suburban and conventional: she felt conformity as a matter of claustrophobia, of stiflement of the soul, just as George Johnston saw it as a political threat.

In this article, Tolchard refers to the 'almost-completed sequel to *My Brother Jack*' on the author's bedside table. On 2 October, Johnston sent the CLF his third report on the novel's progress:

> Hospital routine, drugs etc. haven't made a sustained creative effort all that easy, and there has been a slowing down of tempo, but I have been able to make some progress most days and the ms has now reached the point where 114,000 words of the book have been written to a finished final draft stage, which leaves only 20 to 30 pages still to be written. I intend now to send the ms as it stands out for re-typing while completing the balance.[50]

After being discharged from hospital a few days later,[51] the author proceeded to write the concluding passages at home, and the novel was completed within a couple of weeks of George's return to Raglan Street.

For over a month, however, the finished typescript sat on the author's desk in the living room, between the typewriter and a bowl in which a single goldfish circled and goggled. Meanwhile, George Johnston lay on the couch and worried; this time his normal state of post-book limbo felt like despair.[52] His wife would later note that 'He wouldn't — or couldn't — give it up. For weeks he tinkered and polished and fiddled and re-wrote'.[53] This nervous revising was driving her crazy.

On 8 November Charmian received a telegram announcing that the Commonwealth Literary Fund had awarded her a six-month fellowship, valued at $3000, to work on her novel. In her letter of acceptance — itself not written until a week after the CLF's confirmatory letter — the writer is somewhat less than exuberant, although twice politely expressing her gratitude:

> I accept most gratefully the Fellowship under the terms stated in your letter, although to complete a novel in only six months seems at the moment to be a formidable undertaking. Still, I can only try, I suppose. It is a most welcome breathing space anyway and I will use it for all I am worth [...]
>
> I am most grateful to the Commonwealth Literary Fund for this opportunity to get back to creative writing, and hope that the result will justify the award.[54]

Charmian Clift's tetchiness was reasonable. After all, George Johnston had been given $6000 and twelve months to write *his* novel: why was she expected to do hers for half the money and in half the time? Was it that they thought her a lesser writer? Or was her project considered only half as important? Gratifying though it was to get the fellowship, the terms unfortunately seemed to underline the writer's second class status.

The tone of anxiety was picked up by the Secretary of the Commonwealth Literary Fund, WR Cumming, who wrote back to assure the recipient that:

> Although the last instalment of the award is not paid until the receipt of the Fellowship work, I should like to make it clear that there would be no pressure from the Fund if you were unable to complete the work during the currency of the award.[55]

Cumming could hardly have known that, given Charmian Clift's attitude to deadlines, this was not much consolation. And in regard to deadlines, it was most unfortunate that Clift had recently accepted an invitation from Richard Walsh to write a series of a dozen or more long essays for the new monthly magazine *Pol,* of which he was the editor.[56] Obviously she wouldn't break her word about this, although the need for money was no longer so pressing.

The only solution was to increase her rate of work. When the journalist James Hall, from the *Australian*, visited the couple at Raglan Street towards the end of November, he found Charmian Clift to be 'busier than her husband, turning out a weekly column and preparing a novel' which she tellingly described to the journalist as having been 'like an owl on my shoulder for years'. Despite this pressure, the picture of Charmian given in both text and photographs was once again relaxed and hospitable. Again she played the combined roles of hostess and writer's wife as well as co-writer: 'A warm breeze brushe[d] at the drawn curtains and Charmian — still a pretty woman, and gay in red slacks and striped shirt — [kept] everyone supplied with cold beer'.

George Johnston, meanwhile, 'wheez[ed] with cheerful defiance through a discussion of the novelist's problems, despite his usual post-book depression'. Indicating the unsubmitted typescript of *Clean Straw for Nothing* on his desk, he told Hall: 'At the end it seems stinking to me', and added that this was 'the first book that Charm [...] has not been able to read for [me]'. She in turn explained: 'I'm too involved, I couldn't'.

Later, talking again of her work-in-progress, Clift made it clear just how important it was to her, describing it as 'the novel that every writer wants to do'. She also declared that through the 'strange success' of her column, writing had become easier for her. 'I'm faster now and I think I know better what I'm at. Anyway, this novel — about Australia — is bugging me'.[57]

Not surprisingly, the other novel — the one next to the goldfish bowl — was bugging her too, as was its author and his anxiety. He still wouldn't leave the text alone. This increased Charmian's own anxiety about the content of the novel. And so, after about five weeks, she told George: 'Send the blasted thing away to your publisher'.[58] This gave the author the permission he needed. 'I think he was relieved by this action,' Clift would later note, 'but nervous too, more nervous than I have ever seen him'.[59]

It was in late November that George Johnston sent the typescript to the Collins office in Sydney, where photocopies were made. By 28 November, one of these copies of the typescript was posted on to Sir William Collins in London, and another to the Commonwealth Literary Fund in Canberra.[60] In the early hours of 5 December, Billy Collins rang George from London to say that 'he had read the novel with great excitement, [and] thought it was "superb"' (the author later informed the secretary of the CLF). The publisher immediately followed this phone call with a letter noting that he regarded the book as a 'major work' and promising that his company 'intended to throw all its weight behind its publication next year'. Collins added: 'I have enjoyed it quite immensely and surely it must be the best writing you have ever done. I do think it is really miraculous how you have managed this with all the difficulties of stops with your illnesses'.[61]

On receiving this exuberant reader's report from the head of the publishing company, George Johnston immediately started planning the third book of his trilogy.

By the beginning of 1969, the cloud of unhappiness which had begun to engulf Charmian the previous year was becoming more evident to family members and a very small circle of friends. One person who was able to see the exent and some of the effects of the pain was June Crooke, who at this time moved with her husband and three children from Cairns to Mosman. Expecting to pick up the friendship which had been formed during the two women's magical escape to Thursday Island, June was 'confronted with a rather unpredictable, even prickly stranger':

> I was quite shattered, but of course before long could appreciate
> that, under the urbane exterior she was still trying to maintain,
> Charmian was now suffering the desperation of a cornered
> animal. So many consequences from the past, and of her present-
> making, were closing in on her. And the tragic thing was there
> was so little I could do about it, or anyone could, for that
> matter.[62]

Most people, however, were not aware how dark things were becoming, for still the cloud could suddenly seem to clear, particularly when Charmian had to become the public Charmian Clift, either in person or in writing. She had been role-playing for so long that even now, when most visitors came to the house, she could slip into character. She could do the same when she needed to enter the increasingly fictional life that she was portraying in the column.

Paradoxically, the real job of fictionalising seemed to get harder and harder. The most urgent issue confronting the author was the resumption of her novel. In the first week of the New Year, the first monthly cheque from the Commonwealth Literary Fund arrived. Now that she had to complete the book to fulfil her fellowship obligations, the author was worried. Although she had stated in her application that 150 pages were already done, this was a decidedly generous estimate, including all the old drafts of *Greener Grows the Grass*. In fact, the actual size of the working draft of *The End of the Morning* was around forty pages. What if she couldn't finish it? What if she had lost her powers of fictional storytelling? Had she 'sold out' to the column? Had George's writing sapped her creative energy? How could she write *her* Cressida, with George's Cressida soon to be let loose upon the public? And if George's fiction crossed the boundary into her private world, how was the author going to handle her own secrets? Most pertinently — would Cressida Morley give birth to a child at the age of nineteen? And how was the author going to solve all these problems in the mere six months that the fellowship allowed her? With her scrupulous attitude to meeting deadlines, the pressure was on. Yet this same pressure was likely to cause a paralysis of this author's ability to write.

In the same week that the fellowship deadline started ticking, Charmian spent a night of 'unburdening' (she told her readers) at her friend Toni's place.[63] It seems that these long hours of talking were initially prompted by *The End of the Morning*, for Toni has related that on one occasion around this time, Charmian rang full of excitement because she had made a start on her book, then came around to her friend's place to talk about it. Within a couple of hours, however, this celebration at breaking the block changed to anguish and anxiety.[64]

On this occasion, no doubt, there was also talk about Charmian's relationship with her husband, for this was a discussion which the two women had been having since the friendship began back at the Bondi flats. Toni was still the only person whom Charmian relied upon to take her side. A newer link between the two women was a mutual friend, Wally Summons. Described by Joan Flanagan as 'an interesting and intelligent and good-looking man', Summons was a successful stockbroker who had recently purchased an inner-city bookshop, where he employed Toni. It was common knowledge that Wally and Charmian had some sort of relationship, for he would escort her to parties at the Collins office, and people could see that he was very fond of Charmian.[65] For Charmian, however, it was impossible to contemplate leaving George.

Within a day or so of the unburdening at Toni's place, Charmian began yet another intensive exploration of herself and aspects of her past. Quite likely part of this particular examination — which involved going through old notebooks and drafts and photographs — was an attempt to connect with the character of Cressida Morley, and with the personal experience which would be transmuted into the autobiographical novel. Yet once again the column gobbled up the columnist's experience. The result was an extraordinary essay, 'On Being Alone with Oneself', which represents the writer at the height of her powers. The very title captures the paradox of Clift's column-writing, whereby the writer would reveal something of the private life while proclaiming publicly that it is private. Even alone with herself, Charmian Clift was not alone and arguably not her real self, for both the public persona and the audience were always present.

The starting point for this piece is the information that the family has all happened to go away ('quite fortuitously and separately'), and for a week Charmian Clift is 'for the first time in exactly half [her] life [...] quite quite alone, as [she] had so often longed to be'. It is the dream of any busy wife and mother:

> My plans were not dependent upon the plans of anybody else, my meals were not dependent upon other people's appetites, preferences, appointments or comings and goings, and my moods were not dependent upon other people's uncertain temperaments.[66]

She proceeds to explore the house, the silence and herself alone — watching herself, listening to herself . At first, as silence rushes into 'the vacuum' of the family's absence, she dabbles in it 'quite cautiously and tentatively'.

> My heartbeats were audible and even my thoughts too loud. I felt guilty and furtive and slightly out of control. Nefarious even. As though I had no right to ... to what? ... to be alone in my own house? Or just to be alone? I felt apprehensive, in imminent danger of discovery, but by whom or what I couldn't have said.

Though this is so lightly phrased, there is such a sense of vulnerability ringing through it. The writer goes on to make it clear that she is 'not in any way cut off from human contact':

But the normal and familiar human contacts seemed in some peculiar way to have changed subtly — almost to have become artificial — and in them I had the most curious sense of exposure, as though I was play-acting at being myself and not doing it very well.

Often in the column the writer pretended to be a little naive in order to make the reader take the next step along the line of the argument. Here, however, Clift truly seems not to realise the implication of what she is saying: once the family has gone, taking with it her role as wife and mother, she is not fully herself. At the same time, it does not appear to occur to her that this sense of exposure is connected with the column itself.

As the writer at last relaxes into the silence, the essay moves into one of the most sensuous passages of Clift's writing:

> I thought, I am myself alone at last, and I can do anything I please. What pleased me was evidently quite childish. Like making my breakfast on hock and iced peaches, served to myself quite ceremoniously with flowers and Beethoven quartets and nobody except Jeoffrey the cat to see, and he wouldn't tell. And lying in the bath for an hour, trickling in fresh supplies of hot water and extravagant quantities of cologne, and then going back to my great brass bed in the middle of the morning (the brass bed spread with the best lace-trimmed sheets) with a novel and a plate of fruit too beautifully arranged to be eaten, just as the novel was not actually to be read, because I was too intent discovering the scene to myself in the mirror. With satisfaction.

Did the person who was Charmian Clift really do this, or were these the fantasies of Charmian Clift the columnist and fiction writer? Whatever the answer to that, we can be sure that the night-time activities of the essay really happened, for these were the kind of nightly explorations — inner and outer — to which Clift had always been prone:

> What was more to my taste was spending the middle hours of the night, the really nefarious hours that are always potent with limitless possibility, in my study, going through old manuscripts and notebooks and letters and photographs, or just sitting in the dramatic shadow outside the exciting circle of the work lamp, listening to my own thoughts with astonishment and sometimes

dismay: it didn't seem to be myself thinking at all, but somebody else entirely. You just wait, I thought, until *she* hears what you've been up to. You'll cop it. And heard myself giggling defiantly.

Of course, this is part of a game which Clift is having with her readers; and yet in the line 'You just wait, I thought, until *she* hears what you've been up to' it is impossible not to wonder which of the three pronouns — I, you, she — is the real Charmian Clift.

More than just a holiday at home, this week was an opportunity for a kind of spiritual retreat and audit. Perhaps, if she did it right, there would be some kind of revelation. And so she turned her back on the telephone and radio and television, knowing that 'these ordinary little props to the lonely' were definitely not allowed. 'Not this time, anyway. Not if I was to discover whatever it was'.

Whatever meaning Charmian was seeking, again this time it was not revealed to her. She herself put the loss down to her giving in to temptation and making a phone call. 'The house turned against me after that'. But surely it was the public nature of the writing process which interrupted the search. Little wonder that the revelation for which she had hoped did not happen. At the end of this piece, when the family has returned 'clattering and chattering and demanding and interrupting and involving me', the writer poignantly inquires: 'Why do I feel so strangely that there was some marvellous mysterious opportunity in all that silence? That I missed'.

While Clift's sense of urgency about her own novel was causing her anxiety, her concern about her husband's novel was also becoming more pressing. In the second week of the New Year, George Johnston's publishers advised him that advance copies of *Clean Straw for Nothing* would arrive around July, for release in August or September.[67] As soon as the publication date was set, the Collins publicity machine began shifting into gear. According to Joan Flanagan, the people in the Sydney office were worried that the author might not live to see the book come out. At the same time, they were aware that this novel 'was very different from the other one [*My Brother Jack*], to say the least'. *Clean Straw* was being edited in the UK, but the local Collins people had read it; they were concerned about how reviewers and readers would react to the novel's unusual structure. In order to cover the joint possibilities of the novelist's death and reviewers' incomprehension, it was decided to get Joan Flanagan to interview George Johnston well in advance of publication, and prepare an explanatory article which could accompany review copies of the book.

And so one night in January, Joan arrived to interview George over dinner at his home. When Ken Wilder, the manager of Collins Australia, dropped her off at Raglan Street, he warned: 'You know, Charmian hasn't read the book. So if you're going to try to get the story — remember, she hasn't read it'. Joan already knew this, for it was common knowledge around the office. Indeed, she remembers that 'We were all sort of saying, "What the hell's she going to say when she *does* read it?"' Anticipating that Charmian would be present when the interview took place, Joan had prepared questions which did not engage with the issue of the depiction of Cressida Morley.

> Now, when I got there, George had cooked the dinner — he called it 'my stew', but it was a great casserole — and we sat in that big back room where the refectory table was, and Charmian was extremely welcoming, and the red wine flowed [...]
>
> And George talked about writing the book — don't forget, he could sit down and just turn it on — and I was thinking, 'Charmian hasn't read this,' so I wasn't asking how true it was or anything like that — because Cressida was never actually Charmian, though it was very close to her.[68]

As they sat and ate and talked and drank, George told Joan the story of the writing of *My Brother Jack* (quoted in chapter 18) and the account of his experience of pain in the recovery room (discussed in chapter 20). He also came out with a rather unusual literary theory which he had developed. The author maintained that, in the relatively short time that had elapsed since he had written the first book of the trilogy, 'tremendous changes [had] taken place in the character of the novel — "Probably more changes in that particular six years than in the previous sixty"'. Joan Flanagan's record of the interview goes on to report:

> He feels that people no longer look to the novelist to provide the entertainment narrative which they once demanded [...]
>
> 'I believe that the serious novel must more and more become a question of self-examination because your self-examination becomes the only thing which you can give to someone which is not seen on the television screen night after night. It is a form of

confession. I believe that it is only in the form of autobiography, of one kind or another, that the novel can survive.'[69]

Soon after dinner finished, George went to bed, as he could no longer cope with late nights. Joan and Charmian, however, remained talking and drinking red wine until about 2.00 a.m. The two women used to meet quite often at the numerous parties which Collins held, but Joan remembered this as the only time she ever 'really talked' to Charmian. She was always somewhat in awe of the older woman, although Charmian was always 'very nice' and 'went out of her way to help' Joan. Indeed, it was thanks to Charmian that Joan had a humorous column called 'Cassidy's Mob' in the *Sydney Morning Herald*. When George had been ill in hospital, Joan had written him some funny letters to cheer him up. Impressed with Joan's writing, Charmian had suggested to John Douglas Pringle that he give the young woman an opportunity.

Naturally, on this occasion, the two columnists talked about their newspaper work. Joan remembered Charmian commenting: 'Of course, I'm in the Women's Section, and *you* came along just fractionally behind me and you are not in the Women's Section'. It seemed to Joan that Charmian was concerned about being dismissed as only a women's writer.[70] At the same time, 'she didn't seem very confident about the essays'. She also spoke about the dread that filled her for days before she produced the column, of how she had to steel herself to do it.

Late in the night, after a considerable amount of red wine, something happened to come up about *Clean Straw for Nothing*. Suddenly Joan found the conversation shift in an astonishing direction:

> She turned around to me and said, 'Well, how would *you* like to have things like that said about *you*?'
> I think I said to her, 'You haven't read it, have you?'
> And she said, 'Yes, I *have* read it.' That was it: 'I *have* read it.' But she didn't expand hugely. She just said: 'How would *you* like it?'
> And of course I couldn't answer that.[71]

This evidence must be believed, despite Charmian's public declarations that she hadn't read *Clean Straw*. Joan Flanagan has no axe to grind in this matter. She was very fond of George, as well as admiring Charmian, and as someone from a younger generation who was not part of the immediate Johnston circle, she did not take sides in the relationship.

It is not clear at what stage Charmian had read the completed novel. Had she done so when she told George to send the 'blasted thing' off? Or had she read the copy of the typescript which the author retained? Had she read all the text, or just sneaked a look at some of it? Because the sections were headed with places and dates, it would have been easy to check the potential trouble spots, such as the passages set on 'The Island' in the summer of 1959. The real question is not when but how Charmian read the character of Cressida Morley.

Garry Kinnane, who believed that Clift was ignorant of the contents of *Clean Straw for Nothing*, asks:

> Is it true that Johnston was using the novel to malign [Clift]? My answer is an emphatic No. There can be no doubt that if he had chosen to give a full account of her affairs and the consequences, the picture could have been one of squalid drunkenness, public love-making, violent quarrels, beatings, all of which are still the subject of gossip among people who were on Hydra in those days. The novel depicts nothing of the kind. On the contrary, Cressida emerges from it with considerable dignity and with her sexual powers fully within her own control. How bitterly ironic it is, therefore, that Clift would not read the typescript. She continued in ignorance of the truth of Johnston's generous treatment of those bad times, totally convinced that it was a vengeful attack on her.[72]

Kinnane's defence — that the fiction could not be hurtful because the facts were far worse — had been taken by George Johnston himself. Maisie Drysdale was given the book to read in typescript, because the author wished to dedicate it to her and Tass. After finishing it, Maisie said to George: 'But you can't publish a portrayal like that of Charmian'. George replied: 'It's not nearly as bad as what really went on'.[73]

However, the truth or falsehood of the portrayal is not the issue. The problem was the way in which private matters were being made public property. Given the complex intertwining of fiction and life, this carried implications for the reputation not only of Charmian Clift, but also of Cressida Morley.

Since the invention of an alter ego, back in her childhood imaginings, Charmian had seen this character as an exemplary version of herself. Certainly, this was the way that Cressida was developing in *The End of the*

Morning. But how could Clift develop her fictional character through the early years of her life in a certain way when she knew that by the time her novel was published, the reading public would already be familiar with what was effectively the sequel? Could readers believe in the candour and integrity of Clift's Cressida, when they had already encountered her as the unfaithful wife in *Clean Straw for Nothing?* There hadn't been a problem with the portrait of Cress in *My Brother Jack,* because this was completely in key with Charmian's own Cressida. But this new portrayal threw a very different light on Charmian's fictional self.

Another part of the problem was the limitation of Cressida's characterisation to matters of the body, whether that of idle beauty, or of rampant sexuality. David Meredith's wife is either the goddess on the pedestal, or the fallen woman in the dust. By losing the vocation to be a writer, the character became the sort of woman who appears as 'the social woman' in the recovery room hallucinations. This portrayal also reflects the influence of George Johnston's two literary models, Emma Bovary and Nicole Diver. If, in developing this kind of composite, the author was trying to distance the character from his wife, the intention didn't come off.

Overall, no matter what George Johnston's intentions, the problem remained that he and Charmian Clift were drawing from a shared stockpile of experience. As Clift herself would point out:

> Everybody's experience is made up of unique particulars, and nobody can say for anybody else. I know this to be so because I have shared a great deal of [George's] experience, and I know too that we both remember the experience differently. It affected us differently. We write about it differently [...]
>
> I do believe that novelists must be free to write what they like, in any way they like to write it (and after all who but myself had urged and nagged him into it?), but the stuff of which *Clean Straw for Nothing* is made is largely experience in which I too have shared and — as I said earlier — have felt differently because I am a different person.[74]

Clift's generous public defence of a writer's right to his material was at the same time a kind of plea that the novel be seen as only one side of the story.

The issue of the use of shared experience would be raised in a rather different way by George Johnston's incorporation of material from Charmian Clift's travel diary from the couple's European trip of 1952 (described in chapter 11) into the section entitled 'From an Expatriate's Journal'.[75] This is presented as being David Meredith's diary of this journey, with some of Meredith's later-gained wisdom interspersed. With the incorporation of the travel diary, the real Charmian's memories — including her memories of the Lerici incident — became the fictional memories not of Cressida Morley, but of David Meredith.

If the use of a common fictional character and of shared material were problematic, perhaps the most crucial issue for Charmian was the particular nature of the fiction of *Clean Straw for Nothing*, which appeared to present itself as *non*-fiction. From her question to Joan Flanagan ('How would *you* like to have things like that said about *you*?') it is clear that Clift believed that people would read the book as an autobiographical memoir, and would identify her with the character of Cressida Morley. Given what George had said, earlier that night, about the development of the literary novel as a 'form of confession' and 'form of autobiography', this concern is understandable. The additional irony was that, if Clift were to publish her own account of Cressida Morley's early life, this would increase people's belief that Charmian Clift really *was* Cressida Morley, and it would also appear as if she were endorsing Johnston's character. It must sometimes have seemed as if the only solution would be to abandon her own novel, and her own alter ego.

Anxiety about fiction was only part of Charmian's unhappiness. In February, her London friend Jo made an unexpected ten-day visit to Australia, using Sydney as her base between tourist jaunts. Although it was good to catch up, Jo's visit ultimately made Charmian feel that Australia was 'far. Very far. Tucked away under the curve of the earth'. The writer felt herself to be 'Cut off from a lot of places and people and possibilities that interest me. Away from where the action is. Even, in a guilty sort of way, deprived'.[76]

'Cut off'. 'Tucked away'. 'Deprived'. She could have added: Marooned. Looking in from the outside. Or trapped. Here, as in the essay about being alone, there is this underlying sense that the writer feels she is missing out on whatever it is that she is meant to be discovering.

While this feeling had, of course, occurred at other times in Charmian's life, now there seemed no way out of the trap. All her options appeared to be closed. No longer could she sustain the hope that, if she were just to go somewhere else, make a new start, she would find the 'Big Thing' that she had been seeking for so long. Now it seemed that she would never discover her personal wonder or sign, never hear the words of the mermaids' song. Her frustrations about all these missed opportunities tended more and more to focus on George. It seemed to be his fault that she could not take control of her own destiny, or even try to change her situation, because she couldn't leave him to die without her support. At the same time, the burden of caring for a sick spouse was in itself contributing to Charmian's depression and anxiety; it was now more than ten years that she had been looking after a chronically ill husband. As the cloud of unhappiness became darker through these early months of 1969, the thought must occasionally have started to occur to Charmian that there was a way to escape; or at least there was something she could do to make people realise how much pain she was carrying.

The extent of Charmian's unhappiness was still hidden from almost everyone. Jason, who was now turning thirteen, was one of the few people to witness what was going on, and to experience the odd ways in which Charmian's stress would sometimes manifest itself. As he remembered the situation, 'there were no problems, ever' between him and his mother, 'until right at the very end'. Now, however, there was 'the sort of snappiness, around a highly depressed person, when you just can't do anything right'.[77] Although both his siblings had moved out of home, Shane tended to stay around Mosman, whereas Martin's base was on the other side of the harbour. It was Shane, therefore, who was the more frequent visitor to Raglan Street, and Shane as well as Jason who suffered Charmian's apparently irrational behaviour. Jason described 'the constant nature of her depression in those last months':

> She could lash out viciously for absolutely no external reason, so that one ended up feeling like a dog which is sometimes praised and sometimes kicked for exactly the same behaviour [...] This could happen at any time, and did happen several times every week.
>
> She became incredibly resentful: the woman who had so admired the lithe young pagan things would brood and snarl and spit at beautiful young bodies on the TV screen.[78]

On this last point, Jason added that, 'There is absolutely no doubt that the attitude to youth, by the last months, had changed, in a way that was obvious to everyone'. The provocation would be the appearance of scantily clad young bodies, in television advertisements or popular shows. 'It really would send her off into paroxysms of rage: [...] "Look at how she's flaunting herself, and how they're encouraging this!"' Jason explained that his mother's reaction was to young men as well as to young women, but in those days 'it wasn't like now, when there's male flesh everywhere', so that it could appear as if Charmian were particularly objecting to young women displaying themselves, or being displayed. 'The excuse' for Charmian's outbursts was 'that this was all commercialised [...] as opposed to just running around being natural and expressing natural youth and sexuality'.[79]

What was going on here? Over the previous eighteen months or so, there had been occasional hints in the column that Charmian Clift was becoming disillusioned with young people.[80] Her horror at the debasement of values in consumerist society had been building since she had arrived in Australia. So, taken separately, both these attitudes had elements of consistency. As an ideological issue, Clift's response can be seen as akin to that part of the feminist movement which objects to the exploitation of women's bodies on billboard advertising and magazine covers. Yet clearly Charmian's reaction was personal as well as political. It was as if the old Kiama attitudes were revealing themselves; or perhaps these were the particular attitudes of Charmian's mother Amy, who had been so prudish that she had not hung her undergarments on the washing line. At the same time, there is a kind of connection between these wowserish attacks on exposed bodies and the way in which Clift had punished her female characters for sexual misconduct. Again, we see how the small town girl was just underneath the skin of the cosmopolitan sophisticate.

Whatever was behind Charmian's attitudes, her outbursts were very disturbing for the other family members watching television with her. Jason remembered, 'It was very strange for us to hear'. Overall, Charmian's behaviour was puzzling for the children, both because it was erratic, and because they weren't aware of any reason for it.

> In a way — because we weren't exposed that much to the fights — because they did those in private — in a way that made it worse. Because, you know, we all knew that Mother's mood was very black — it wasn't always that she was nasty and vicious. Sometimes she was just — crying. And you know, you just felt ...[81]

This crying could occur when Charmian had been drinking, or it could start when she was sober. 'There began to be less and less of a distinction'.

In his account of this situation, Jason reverted to the subject of the lack of apparent cause for the unhappiness, given that his parents did not argue in front of him and Shane:

> So, in a way that made it more mysterious. Because we didn't even know that there was — *what* the cause was — or the fact that there had been these arguments.
>
> It just seemed even more — you know — *endogenous.*
>
> As if — you know — 'Mum has nothing, really, to be sad about, but there is just this huge sadness has come over her'.

By this time, the children were aware how ill their father was, but to them — as to everyone — George was the person who deserved sympathy.

Despite this growing burden of depression and anxiety, Charmian still had to keep the household running, and she had to keep writing the column: no matter how desperate things became, she still always met the Saturday deadline. Even with the addition of her fellowship money, the household expenditure continued to push the budget beyond the limit. The greatest expense was George's illness: hospital bills, medication, and fees to doctors and specialists cost a fortune. In her application to the Commonwealth Literary Fund, Charmian had noted that she would use the money to employ domestic and secretarial help which would free her to write, but this didn't work out in practice. No secretary could help with the column correspondence, because what the fans wanted was an intimate and individual reply from Charmian Clift herself. And although a cleaning lady came a couple of times each week, and George sometimes cooked the dinner, it was still Charmian who did the bulk of the household organisation. Jason made it clear that, even at this time, his mother was keeping the household going: 'It's not as if floors weren't cleaned and — I mean, obviously some of that more menial stuff was Mrs Dunger [the cleaning lady], but the laundry got done and shopping got done and food did arrive and I did have pressed uniforms'.[82]

Clearly the situation wasn't ideal, but the domestic routine hadn't collapsed completely, and nor had Charmian. There might be outbursts of anger or weeping, but there were still ups as well as downs, and most visitors continued to get the impression that everything was as good as it could be, given the strain and uncertainty of living with a dying husband.

Even the family doctor had no idea how vulnerable Charmian was. One Sunday afternoon around Easter of this year, Charmian rang the GP and asked him to come and see her husband. He remembered:

George was very sick. At that stage the question of going back to hospital was not on the agenda. [The specialist] had said, 'There's really nothing more we can do for him except to rest him in bed, and he can do that at home.'

And [Charmian] dragged me into the kitchen after I had seen George and she said, 'What's going to happen? How much longer is this going on?'

And I said to her, 'Charmian, I don't think he'll last until Christmas. I think he'll go before then.'

And she flew out of the kitchen and disappeared — she just left me. And I said goodbye to George and went out.[83]

Many years later, the doctor would feel that 'I think perhaps I made it worse for her on that Sunday'. At the time, however, although the medical practitioner was aware of the burden Charmian was carrying, he felt that she was very strong and capable, and was also an honest person who required an honest answer to her question. He was not to know that when she was younger and heard tales of George being beaten by his father, she would fly out of the room and burst into tears. She could not bear the thought of pain happening to George.

A month or two after this, Charmian came to see her GP at his surgery, concerned that George not be exposed to any additional respiratory infection that she might pass on if she were to catch influenza this winter. After some discussion, the doctor gave Charmian the first injection of a two-dose flu vaccine; she would need to make an appointment to come back for the second one.

Given the writer's ongoing burden of distress, how was *The End of the Morning* proceeding? By April 1969, Clift was three months down the track of her fellowship. In those days, it was a requirement of the Commonwealth Literary Fund that the recipient file quarterly progress reports. In early April, Clift wrote to the Secretary of the CLF:

Dear Mr Cumming,

This report isn't as exciting as I would have liked it to be. But then I never really did believe that I had a hope of finishing this novel within six months [...] It's going to take a year at least. Still, in this first three months I have 25,000 words down, and it is progressing quite steadily — if painfully — in the direction I want it to go, and on the whole I think I am more pleased than frustrated. It has been — and is being — a fabulous opportunity for me to get down a whole slab of writing that would have remained imprisoned in my head without the Fellowship.

George's *Clean Straw for Nothing*, written with the aid of a Fellowship last year, will be coming out in September. Everybody is very pleased with it.

Yours sincerely,
Charmian Clift[84]

This 25 000 word text is the one referred to in this biography as the second long draft of the novel. Although there was some new material and some polishing, it is essentially the same as the first draft, written back in 1962. If the tone of this letter is flat in relation to the writer's own project, the comment about *Clean Straw for Nothing* reflects the note of guarded approbation which Clift had decided would be her own public attitude to the book.

This tone also imbues the long essay which Clift wrote for *Pol* magazine, placing *Clean Straw for Nothing* in the context of George Johnston's oeuvre.[85] Written in May, during the author's three-week annual break from the *Herald* column,[86] this was scheduled to come out in August, just before the novel itself. It was here that Clift went on the public record to announce that she had not read the novel, but wished it and its author well. This was a smart move, to avoid the possibility either of professions of pity or of questions as to the book's veracity.

Charmian had intended to spend this annual leave at home, catching up on:

A few things I've been wanting to do for ages, like cleaning out my clothes cupboard and going into town for a day's shopping and meeting friends for luncheon and asking friends for dinner and doing the marketing in a leisurely, choosy sort of way, and indulging in hours of conversation with people I like and arranging flowers and new curtains and pages of manuscript and notebooks and wallowing in reading.[87]

Some of this arranging of 'pages of manuscript' involved going through the typescripts of the column pieces and selecting a new anthology collection. The author chose over two hundred pages of material, before putting this job aside. This selection would eventually form the basis of the collection, *The World of Charmian Clift*.[88] In the rest of this passage we see the home-loving Charmian, curled like a cat in the sun of the back yard, rereading Joyce Cary's *A Prisoner of Grace*, in which she came upon these words of the character Nina:

> 'I felt an immense calm gaiety, as if, so to speak, I had just inherited such an immense wealth of delights that I did not need to be extravagant; I could afford simply to feel the comfort of being so rich without the trouble of spending.'

'And I read this with such a stinging sense of recognition', the columnist remarks, 'Because of course that's exactly the way I was feeling too'. Clift goes on to tell how she 'felt like laughing out of sheer pleasure'.[89]

Given the unhappiness that the writer was suffering at this time, how 'true' or 'real' was this sort of expression of feeling? In a sense it was completely real, because the alter ego of Clift the columnist was by now such a developed role that *that* Charmian Clift could feel happy when she sat at her typewriter and communicated with her 'Thursday ladies'. The escape into the hypothetical or parallel life that she lived in the column was often a relief and release from the unhappiness that Charmian mostly lived in her other life. Yet as more of her self was poured into the column persona, her other or 'real' self seemed to become emptier. The lessening of self-esteem went hand in hand with a diminishing of self. The paradox of these two parallel realities is demonstrated by the fact that the writer was obviously *not* on holiday while she was writing about 'The Joys of Holidays'.

Charmian went on to declare herself pleased to be at home for her 'holiday' because there was 'a wedding anniversary coming up'. The couple had always celebrated this in May, as a reminder of their meeting at the Australia Hotel in May 1945 and their second meeting in the *Argus* lift in the May of 1946; the actual anniversary of their August 1947 marriage ceremony passed without notice. Extraordinarily — and even a little coyly — the writer reveals at the end of the piece that she has just been given a 'surprising and delightful' anniversary present in the form of an invitation from her husband to go away on holiday. Just the two of them, together. The way Clift deals with this 'invitation' is a classic example of how she would embroider the truth in her column. In fact, the trip was a 'freebie' provided by Qantas, which was trying at this time to boost travel to Norfolk Island.[90] Charmian was given the tickets in the hope that she would write about the island in her column. It was natural that a journalist would not mention a sponsorship deal of this kind. It was pure Charmian, however, to rearrange the story in a way that would reinforce the idea that she and George were a normal sort of happily married couple. And no matter who was responsible for the tickets, Charmian was truly ecstatic about the prospect of the trip. She spent the rest of her three week 'break' writing three long *Pol* essays[91] as well as the piece for the *Sydney Morning Herald*, in order to be able to go away.

This was the first holiday the couple had taken together since the island-hunting trip to Hydra in 1955, when Cedric and Pat Flower had looked after the children on Kalymnos. By an odd coincidence, Cedric and Pat were part of a National Trust tour that was inspecting heritage sites on Norfolk Island at the same time. Cedric Flower remembered this 'last pleasant time' with George and Charmian:

> It was delightful, like old times. George was very sick then, and he didn't move out of the hotel very much but Charmian came everywhere with us, and there were lots of laughs — it was just like old times, before all the traumas, and it was a nice time.
>
> She was the old Charm, you know, full of jokes and enjoying every minute, and crying in the graveyard about all the young convicts who were hanged. She was a very emotional person.[92]

This sense of enjoyment fills the pages of the three travel essays which Clift wrote while she was away. With its colourful history — from convict settlement to refuge of the *Bounty* mutineers — this place was guaranteed to appeal to Charmian Clift's romantic sentiments. She declared Norfolk to be 'one of the most beautiful [...] islands' that she had seen.[93] This was high praise indeed.

24

AN EVENT IN LIFE

See, it is death, nothing more — an event in life — as significant
or unsignificant as being born.[1]

Charmian and George arrived home from Norfolk Island around the
end of the third week of June. For Charmian, the brief holiday had not
been long enough to give the respite which she needed. After all, she had
produced three essays about the island while she was there. For George,
however, the break away had provided a nice finish to the gestation period
for the third book of his trilogy, *A Cartload of Clay*. Over the last few
months he had chosen the title with its classical reference to Prometheus
fashioning humankind out of clay, and in his writing journal he had
started to make notes about the material and themes which the book
would cover.

In keeping with Johnston's belief that the only valid subject matter of
the contemporary novel was autobiographical confession, this would be
an introspective examination of the life of David Meredith — 'A kind of
Walden Pond in an Australian suburban back yard — [...] the quiet
retreat — memories and intrusions'.[2] Fiction would be required, however,
for the ending, in which David Meredith was to die in an attack by young
thugs during a Hiroshima Day demonstration.[3] While the anti-war march
would provide a counterpoint to the exodus of the refugees in war-torn
China — the epiphany which had set David Meredith on his personal
journey — the author's sense of the futility of searching for meaning in
experience would be underlined by the irony of death coming not from
the hero's protracted illness, but as an arbitrary act of violence. Unlike the

second book of the trilogy with its fragmentary structure, this final text was to follow a traditional form, and would be narrated in the third person. Now, in the last week of June, the author began writing his two or three pages each morning, carefully correcting and retyping the previous day's work as he went.[4] Once again, Charmian did not feel able to be his sounding board.

From the moment George started this new novel, it flowed easily. This time there would be no block, no anguished puzzling over mode and structure. For Charmian, it was particularly difficult to witness George's progress at this time, as the Commonwealth Literary Fund had just withheld her sixth and final fellowship payment, because her project was not completed.[5] Although this was standard practice on the part of the Fund, it increased the author's sense of lost time, lost opportunity, of her failure to do the thing she most wanted to do and needed to do, for the sake of her career and as a way of sorting out her self and her experience.

If the trip away failed to relieve the stress on Charmian, it also made no change to the unpredictability of the relationship between her and George. Two incidents that Jason remembered from this particular period give some idea of how complex the situation was. On one occasion, as he was returning from school, 'Charmian was literally *through* the gate and running down the street in tears, just as I got off the bus'. He intercepted his mother, and comforted her, and persuaded her to come home with him. Although at the time he had no idea what the matter could be, with hindsight he assumed that some sort of argument between his parents 'must have gone on just a little too long'.[6]

Overall, Jason pointed out, while there was an 'element of mutual destructiveness in their relationship, [...] it does take two to keep that kind of thing going'. He added that 'There was also an enormous element of camaraderie, support, mutual loyalty and love — and that too goes for both sides'.[7] 'Even right towards the end, they still had an amazing loyalty towards each other'. To demonstrate this, he told 'a tale against [himself]':

> I remember one awful argument that happened, but that was in fact between me and Dad. And it was all about the issue of plastic versus metal garbage bins.
>
> Modern Jason of course wanted the most modern of everything. By that stage [...] it was my job to take out the garbage. And I had to lug these two enormous garbage bins.

Anyway, I insisted, 'Why don't we get the plastic ones?' and [Dad] wouldn't [agree], and it ended up [with] me *screaming* at him, that 'You're just doing this deliberately to make it hard for me!'

[...] It all got a bit ugly and he went off to bed. And it was Mum who took me and calmed me down and explained how sick he was. And it all ended up with me going in and apologising to him and kissing him goodnight, and all the rest.

And that was *really* near the end. So even in these —

The huge loyalties —

Whatever they might have said to each other, the criticism of either of them by anyone else was not [to be tolerated]. She was fiercely protective of his health.[8]

After agreeing that this was an example of how Charmian could not bear the thought of pain happening to George, Jason concluded:

This particular episode was handled particularly well. I mean, especially considering that this *was* in the period when she was so bleakly unhappy. And would just lash out at me verbally over the tiniest little things. And here there was something serious — you know, really serious — I think this was my first *serious* fight with Dad about something. And she could easily have just slapped me. And — well, it was a very calm, rational explaining of how sick he was.

This story is a powerful expression of Charmian's love, not just for her husband, but for her youngest child.

On Saturday 5 July, the columnist completed a lament about one of her pet grievances — Australia's lack of civilised outdoor eating places. She had made essentially the same complaint in 'Social Drinking', which was the second column piece she ever wrote.[9] Nothing about this society seemed to be improving. Would she be forced to go on repeating herself, like a cracked record?

Although a great deal of Charmian's political optimism had been vanquished, she could still manage to renew her energy in order to try to make some change to society. Thus Jason remembered that while 'the depression was constant and palpable', it could be 'relieved, if that's the word, by bouts of manic enthusiasm for causes'.[10] On this particular weekend, Charmian was full of plans for a walkathon which was due to take place the following Sunday, to raise money for an Aboriginal cause. The route was to go from Australia Square to the Aboriginal settlement at La Perouse. Allan Ashbolt would note that 'with typical generosity' Charmian 'had agreed to take part [...] and the *Sydney Morning Herald* was sponsoring her'. He added that 'Nobody who knew her had any doubt that she could and would do it'.[11] Jason vividly remembered his mother's excitement about this project: 'She was all bubbling with this Walk Against Want (from the City to Kurnell or something like that), and getting us all involved in it, with instructions for me and Shane to sign up sponsors at my school and her work'.[12] He added that 'We were plotting it endlessly, and there were maps of the route. And she was really bubbly and excited about it'. To Jason — caught up in Charmian's enthusiasm — it 'seemed like maybe we'd turned some corner'.[13]

On Monday 7 July, Charmian went to see her GP in order to have her second flu injection. Because of the patient's ongoing history of menopausal problems, the doctor automatically inquired about her periods. On this occasion Charmian 'complained of hot flushes and sweats which had made her miserable for many months', adding that 'another period had begun the day before'. The doctor prescribed Premarin, an estrogen formula commonly used to counteract hot flushes. He also took the opportunity to nag his patient a little about another outstanding medical matter. In January he had advised her to have a pap smear examination, and on a few occasions when he had visited George at home he had reminded Charmian to pop in to the surgery and have this test done. This was simply in line with his advice to all his female patients. On this particular Monday, it was impossible to do the procedure because Charmian was menstruating, and so she made an appointment to come in and have the test on the following Monday.[14] As the doctor remembered it, this wasn't a particular issue, and he and his patient didn't talk about it in any detail. 'What was more important was that she was depressed, and so was I — it just so happened that it was a time when I was feeling a bit depressed too. So we sat and talked about depression'.

Years later, the conscientious family doctor would blame himself for 'failing' Charmian that day — for not realising that she needed help, and for not 'mustering help'. But at the time he did not see any cause for alarm in the way Charmian was talking about her depression. 'There weren't any things on that day that didn't indicate some continuity'.[15] And surely the doctor was right to feel that someone who bothers to immunise herself against flu, and who makes an appointment for a standard medical procedure the following Monday, is conducting her life from day to day in a normal fashion.

There were more immediate appointments in Charmian's diary for this week. On the Tuesday night there was to be an opening at the Bonython Gallery of Charles Blackman's special exhibition to mark his fortieth year; Charmian had told Barbara Blackman that she didn't want to come in the crush, but would view the paintings on the Wednesday morning and would see the Blackmans then.[16] There was also to be a small luncheon party on the Wednesday, hosted by the Drysdales. The Duttons were to be in Sydney, and Tass wanted George to meet Geoffrey Dutton.[17] And of course there was to be the Aboriginal fundraising walkathon on Sunday.

Not surprisingly, Charmian was still depressed when she returned home from her doctor's appointment. George seems to have assumed that this depression occurred as the result of something discussed during the consultation. It is clear that Charmian mentioned the matter of the pap smear examination which she was planning to have on the following Monday. Later a story would circulate to the effect that she either had cancer and was facing an operation, or that she was afraid that she had cancer.[18] Certainly, some little while before this, Charmian had talked to family members about reading Solzhenitsyn's novel *Cancer Ward,* and about how depressed that novel made her.[19] However, it is hard to believe that the suggestion of a routine pap smear would cause Charmian to think that the test result would prove positive or, if it did, that cervical cancer would be fatal. Her doctor did not think that she had any particular worry about cancer, or about this particular examination. He pointed out that 'At this time, in the late 1960s, the campaign to encourage women to have pap smears was running full bore, and I don't remember it as being a particularly significant issue, as far as Charmian was concerned'.[20] It is clear that Charmian was not uninformed about the issue, for in her file of press clippings there were a couple of medical articles about cancer in women.[21] This was the sort of material that the columnist would collect, because it was part of the 'mandate' of the women's pages to inform women about such matters. And anyway, Charmian had clearly been depressed when she arrived at the doctor's surgery.

What else did Charmian and George talk about on this Monday? The files of the Commonwealth Literary Fund provide a fragment of information which is part of the jigsaw puzzle. On 7 July, George Johnston wrote to the secretary of the CLF, reporting that *Clean Straw for Nothing* was to be published on 23 August in both Australia and the UK, and noting that advance copies would be available in about ten days. Johnston concluded by asking to be sent an application form for the forthcoming round of Commonwealth Literary Fund grants.[22]

When George told Charmian that he was making this request, it no doubt reinforced her feeling that her own fellowship had run out, and she had made no headway with her novel. Yet here was George applying for funding again, as he forged ahead with the third book of his autobiographical trilogy. More pressing was the news that copies of *Clean Straw* would be arriving in little over a week.

That Monday night, Charmian went to Toni's place. According to an account which Toni gave to Garry Kinnane, she was 'deeply depressed and weeping incessantly'.

> She wanted Burgess to go away with her, to Fiji, or New Guinea, or Thursday Island, just the two of them, to leave everything in Sydney behind immediately. Of course, Burgess, who had her own commitments, could hardly agree to go like that. 'She cried all night,' said Burgess, 'and said nobody loved her except me.' She left early in the morning in despair.[23]

When talking about this night to Suzanne Chick, Toni phrased her friend's desperate statement as 'Everyone loves Charmian Clift. You're the only one who loves *me*!'[24] This poignantly brings out the sense that the public persona was eclipsing the real person.

Although Charmian had been sober when she arrived at Toni's on the Monday night, she drank a lot during the course of this unburdening. When Charmian returned home on the morning of Tuesday 8 July, she was exhausted and hungover. At midday she started drinking, as part of her regular lunchtime session with George. Three months later, in a statement to the Coroner's Court, he would be recorded as saying that 'In the middle of the day, we had a discussion about her drinking, she had been upset about this thing, and had been drinking heavily, I told her to pull herself together and stop the drinking, the argument was in no way heated'.[25]

What was 'this thing' which Charmian was so upset about? Whatever it was, the discussion about the drinking was clearly in addition to this other topic. Despite George's comment, the argument must have been 'heated', for that was the way in which these two passionate people argued. More credible is George's account — given the next morning, to Toni — that they had had a terrible fight, which had gone on for most of the afternoon.[26]

When Jason came home from school, there was a lull. The couple had dinner, together with Jason, and watched television in the kitchen/dining area. George later stated that during the evening Charmian 'had taken a glass or two of wine, whilst in my company'. When he retired to bed at about 9.30 p.m. 'she didn't seem to be affected by liquor. At that time she seemed rather quiet and subdued, but not affected'.[27]

Although in fact she had had a great deal to drink over the previous twenty-four hours,[28] this account of Charmian's subdued mood rings true. After two days and a night of hectic emotion, she was withdrawing into herself. She withdrew, too, to her room, her private place and space.

At some time she went into George's room to get the phenobarbitone sleeping tablets which her husband kept on his bedside table. The prescription had been renewed a few days earlier, and George had only taken one out of the bottle of thirty. Charmian went back into her study, and wrote a note to George. 'Darling,' she began. 'Sorry about this. I can't stand being hated — and you hated me so much today — I am opting out and you can play it any way you choose from now on. I am sure you will have a distinguished and successful career'. After boldly signing her name, 'Charmian', she scrawled on the bottom of the piece of paper: 'I would quite like some flowers'. And at the top she added the line 'I will cease upon the midnight and no pain — isn't that something?'[29] She took the tablets, and went to sleep in the bed in her study, lying on her right side with her hands together beside her head on the pillow.[30]

George found the note the next morning at about 8 a.m., when he took Charmian in a cup of coffee. He rang the family doctor, who came to the house immediately, and who in turn rang the police. Although versions of this wording have been given over the years, the only people actually to see the note were George, the doctor, the police and the Coroner.[31] All accounts of the note's contents include the phrase, or paraphrase, from Keats' 'Ode to a Nightingale', which was the part of the note that George himself included in *A Cartload of Clay*, when writing about the suicide of Cressida Morley. While quoting a Romantic poet was exactly the sort of gesture that people associated with the character of Charmian or Cressida, the full stanza provides a context for what Charmian perhaps had in mind as she referred to the line:

Darkling I listen; and for many a time
    I have been half in love with easeful Death.
Call'd him soft names in many a musèd rhyme,
      To take into the air my quiet breath;
Now more than ever it seems rich to die,
        To cease upon the midnight with no pain,
          While thou art pouring forth thy soul abroad
            In such an ecstasy!
        Still wouldst thou sing, and I have ears in vain —
          To thy high requiem become a sod.[32]

Overall, while it is possible to read a number of meanings into Charmian's short text, this was not the sort of letter that this careful writer would leave if she had been planning her death, and wishing to put on the record some sort of memorable testimony. Her handwriting is large, hasty — the sort of scrawl that would appear sometimes in her notebooks, when she was sitting alone late at night, having a few drinks and jotting down ideas, quotations and even phrases of dialogue as they came to her at random. Even the reference to feeling that George had 'hated' her 'today' underlines that this was a spur-of-the-moment response.

The view that this was an unplanned death is furthered by the set-up of the household. Although Charmian took the entire bottle of pills, she made no effort not to be interrupted in her sleep. It was quite possible that someone might come into her room in the night — Martin or Shane, maybe, making a late night visit home, or George himself — for this was a house in which people used to roam around at night, and Charmian's room was the common territory, where family members would go to borrow a book or have a chat. In many ways, the circumstances of Charmian Clift's death point to something which could be described as a suicide attempt, which accidentally turned into the real thing.

As always with this profoundly autobiographical writer, it is illuminating to check the fictional record. While in the work of George Johnston there is a recurring contemplation of suicide, including a number of successful attempts,[33] in Clift's solo writing there is only Kathy in *Honour's Mimic*, who is recuperating after attempting to kill herself by putting her foot on the car's accelerator and driving into a tree. It is relevant that this attempt was unpremeditated — a spontaneous action done on the spur of the moment at a time when Kathy had drunk too much and was feeling trapped by her loveless marriage and her claustrophobic existence. Later, she herself cannot remember exactly why she had tried to kill herself. The reader feels that, for Kathy, such an action is out of character. Ultimately, she will endure her fate rather than escaping it.

After a suicide, family members and friends often feel guilty, and blame themselves for failing to foresee and forestall the event. Certainly, with hindsight, it was possible for some people to see that Charmian had hinted at this course of action in conversations of the last few months. It is clear, for example, that Charmian had made some sort of threat to her daughter, for when Shane — at work on the Wednesday morning — was told of her mother's death, she immediately exclaimed to her colleagues at the *Hellenic Herald: 'To eipe kai to ekhomai!'* ('She said it and she's done it!') [34]

Against such warnings must be set Charmian's recent happiness, evident both in the holiday at Norfolk and in the planning of the walkathon. There was the sense of continuity revealed by the engagements Clift had in her diary. There was what seemed to be the ongoing affirmation of life evinced by someone who, only three months previously, had publicly declared: 'I have never worn a watch in my life, because that has always seemed to me like wearing your death on your wrist'. [35] Above all, there was Charmian's habit of coping cheerfully, no matter what crisis occurred. Her doctor would later remember: 'I felt that I had failed her completely because I had had no inkling that this was on the cards. I thought she was too sensible a person — that was my estimate of her — and too strong a person'. [36] This reading of Charmian's character was shared by just about everyone.

A large part of the problem was that Charmian Clift's public persona was so strong that most people could not see how vulnerable she was, and how far her self-esteem had slipped. Moreover, the couple's friends did not give much attention to any pain of Charmian's, because George's obvious suffering was the main focus. It seemed that, in the matter of sympathy, as in every other matter that had occurred during the marriage, Charmian played second fiddle to her husband. As George himself would say with astonishment to his old friend Elizabeth Riddell: '*I* was the one who was dying'. [37] And yet Charmian had threatened to Toni: 'I'll die before he does'. [38]

In his novel *A Cartload of Clay*, Johnston describes how his terminally ill alter ego, David Meredith, keeps a 'small brown vial' of barbiturate tablets on his bedside table as a kind of insurance policy 'held in reserve for that always looming moment when it became too much to be borne any longer'. Meredith, however, out of 'a kind of pig-headedness', leaves the vial unopened, for he comes to 'believe (with Camus) [...] that if existence was, in the final result, without meaning, the true revolt against its absurdity was not in suicide but in continuing to live'.[39]

By using an escape route that George had considered, Charmian's death was a way of calling her husband's bluff about the whole business of dying, as if to demonstrate what it was about. ('See, it is death — an event in life — as significant or unsignificant as being born'.[40]) It was also part of the mutuality of this couple, who may not have been able to live together peaceably, but who could not live apart. Like the characters Veshti and Salom in the collaborative novel which the couple wrote when they were deeply in love, they were 'locked together',[41] even in death.

And yet if Charmian's dying was part of George's death, it was also as if she suddenly asserted control over the character of Cressida Morley in the only way open to her: by writing herself out of the plot. She was 'opting out', not just of her life, but of the fiction that surrounded and ultimately stifled her.

Overall, as we try to determine 'reasons' for Charmian's death, we should avoid the temptation to look for a list, with factors neatly separated and numbered in order of importance. We must see the interlinking of diverse causes, the way one cause could add to the weight of another, and the way that the order or pattern could fluctuate in a general situation where self-esteem had diminished to the point at which self-survival was no longer operating. This terribly complex system of shifting but intertwining causes and effects of anguish was the ongoing situation when, on Tuesday 8 July 1969, the balance tipped. Insofar as Charmian Clift may have been considering suicide as a possible course of escape from the trap that seemed to enclose her, there had clearly been no plan for doing it on this particular night.

And yet even in this impulsive action, the main feeling is of a cry for help, a shout for rescue — which implies, of course, a strong sense of looking to life and the future, rather than a commitment to death as the only possible solution. While the note highlights the impulsiveness of the action by its lack of writerly craft, its terrible self-consciousness is surely the message of someone who is trying to make people realise how desperately she needs some attention and some care. This is the plea which Clift the novelist had analysed as the meaning of Cressida Morley's stormy adolescent behaviour: *Love me Love me. Help me someone.* Perhaps by now the boundary between fiction and life had been breached so many times that even an action such as this could seem not quite real.

One of the recurring reference points in Charmian Clift's writing is the song of the sea. We hear it first in the very early fragment of text about the stormy night, where the narrator listens to 'the surf crashing its entreaty: "Get out. Get out."'[42] This calling merged for the author with the Eliotic notion of the mermaids' singing. Like the songs of the sirens and the lotus-eaters, this was a dangerous melody. And yet it was so seductive, sometimes, this notion of escape. Even if the only way was easeful death.

Writing in *Peel Me a Lotus* of swimming in the pool beneath the cave during the height of summer, at a time when a certain smell lingers — the 'oozy, sweet, briny smell of black sponges dying' — the writer expresses something of the attraction of the idea:

> Sometimes, for a mad moment, when my hand slips on the ladder and the iron rungs suddenly leap above my head and the weeds pour down, or I feel myself being hurled forward towards those jagged, streaming rocks, the smell rises as though my mouth was stuffed with oozy sponges, and I am filled with something that is terror and desire both [...] to ride on with the wild horses to the waiting cliff, or to curl up small, close against the scaly rocks, to curl up small and let the wild horses ride over me.[43]

Mostly, Charmian recognised this moment for the madness that it was. She climbed up, and out, and high onto the rock above the cave, and then she dived in again. And even if on this particular night, when her hand slipped on the ladder, she did just 'curl up small', there is still, by Clift's way of reckoning, a sense of triumph rather than defeat to this deed. At the very least, she had been 'lifted from the ordinary and the dull into the romantic climate of high tragedy'. As one of her female characters reflects longingly about another:

> Things had happened to her. Unforgettable things. She would never have to rest dry and lonely outside the stream of life. Even if she could not keep her head above the water, even if she was bruised on the rocks, or caught at last in the whirlpools, she was part of it, for ever and ever.[44]

EPILOGUE

Myths arise in obscure places, in unknown or anonymous
circumstances, but people pour passion into it, storytelling,
it gets round like a pebble, and ultimately it comes to represent
something basic in the community, and it's called a myth.[1]

When Charmian Clift died, her autobiographical novel was still unfinished. With the death of George Johnston a year later,[2] it might be expected that the story of Cressida Morley and David Meredith would also be laid to rest. Yet the novel of Charmian's life was still being written. In this fictionalisation, there would continue to be a blurring of boundaries between private and public areas, and between the stories of Charmian and Cressida. Over the succeeding years, it would become harder and harder to untangle the 'real' identity from the myth of Charmian Clift.

In the second last essay that she would write, Clift returned to one of her favourite folk heroes — Ned Kelly — and to one of her main sources of inspiration — Sidney Nolan. Working from the transcript of the 1967 ABC documentary, Clift used some comments by the painter as a way of raising a topic which had run through the conversations which the Johnstons and Nolan had been having since the wild Hydra winter of 1955–56. This concerned the nature of myth, and the reasons why a myth should spring up and develop and come to mean something universal. On this occasion, Clift quoted the painter as saying:

Myths arise in obscure places, in unknown or anonymous
circumstances, but people pour passion into it, storytelling, it

gets round like a pebble, and ultimately it comes to represent something basic in the community, and it's called a myth.

When asked if he would do his own mythic Kelly series any differently, if he were to paint it now, Nolan replied:

> I think now that I would treat it more on the brevity of his life, the transitory nature of his life. This being his real destiny. And the mask — although in some way it must be there — is more the covering for this other shell that took this very brief life through this particular existence in this particular place.[3]

This could be a fitting description of Charmian Clift herself, and of her mythic portrayal. When we think of her, it is the mask which instantly appears in our minds, in the same way that the name 'Ned Kelly' summons up the armoured headpiece. In the case of Clift, the mask takes different forms. It can be the persona of the columnist, or the fictional construct of George Johnston's Cressida, or Clift's own Cressida, or simply a photographic image of Charmian's appearance (whether in the guise of Young Beauty or Ageing Crone). Charmian Clift's mask prevents us from thinking not just about the person inside the headpiece, but how that person felt when she was looking out through the eye slit. Ultimately, for Clift as for Ned Kelly, the mask became a trap, a physical liability which impeded her freedom.

The essential elements of Charmian's myth have all surfaced at some stage in the course of this biography. As the pebble of story starts rolling, there is the free child, the pagan sprite of the Australian beach, the wild little barefoot girl who played by day with her gang of friends and lay starbaking alone in her rockpool at night. It was Clift herself who not only started this myth, but was its most ardent believer. The appropriate background for this idealised alter ego was provided by the portrayal of the eccentric but perfect family, with the father a cross between Mr Shandy and Tom o'Bedlam and the mother epitomising both Poetry and Grace. Even the Ugly Sister was beautiful and talented. While this myth of the exceptional family was actually started by Charmian's parents, Charmian fell under its spell. From a very early time her security became so vested in it that she was completely incapable of coming to terms with the legacy of pain that she carried from her childhood, for to begin to do so would have meant acknowledging that the happy family was a fabrication.

The next phase of Charmian's myth began when she won the Beach Girl competition in 1941. After being applauded as a child for being clever rather than pretty, it was an extraordinary experience for the 'little speckled thrush' (as she identified herself)[4] to be acknowledged as a swan overnight. Charmian quickly adapted herself to the role of beauty queen, little realising that the trade-off would be the devaluation of her intelligence. From now on, many people would regard her solely for her outward self. Within a year of using her body as a way of personal advancement, this same body caught her out when the young woman suffered the misery of unplanned pregnancy. As the Clift family could not include a nineteen year old unmarried mother, that particular fact of Charmian's life had be written out of the story. The young mother had to lose, not just the child, but even the sense of loss. This would add a burden of unresolved grief to the other pains that Charmian carried from her childhood.

With her enlistment in the army would come that part of the myth which is epitomised in the portrayal of the pagan girl with sand between her toes, the green-eyed larrikin who reads *Tristram Shandy* in the gun-pit. When she began a career in journalism, it seemed only natural that she instantly won the heart of a man who had created his own legend as the Golden Boy of the Melbourne newspaper world, the working class lad who was pushing his way fast to the top. In the myth's next stage, Charmian was portrayed as the femme fatale of the *Argus* scandal, the young girl who stole the older man away from his wife and home. The scarlet woman. Started by journalist colleagues, this was never a myth which Charmian fancied. Indeed, she spent a lot of her life running from it.

More perilous to her, however, was the next movement of the mythic process, which began when Charmian Clift and George Johnston won the 1948 *Sydney Morning Herald* prize for *High Valley*. From this beginning of her career as a writer, she was portrayed as the junior partner in the collaborative writing team. Simultaneously, another fiction was starting. This was the myth of the Johnston marriage as the ideal partnership. Charmian now had to act the role of the beautiful young wife and mother. She had to keep smiling, look happy, to fulfil the fantasy that she felt was required not just by her husband, but also by the outside world. While Charmian had too much pride to admit that her marriage might be a mistake — or perhaps just as mundane as other people's relationships — she herself also desperately needed to believe in the myth of the happy family she was creating, just as she believed in the family her parents had created.

This role of ideal wife and mother would travel with Charmian from Sydney to London, with only a change to the style of beauty as she transformed herself into an urban sophisticate. By now, Charmian would feel that she was losing her own identity completely. While part of the problem was that the outward side eclipsed the inward, the professional collaboration with her husband was increasingly preventing her from expressing herself.

The escape to Greece in 1954 seemed a chance to revert to the state of happy freedom which Charmian had idealised in her myth of childhood paradise. And at first this new place appeared to be the Promised Land which she was seeking. When this promise was not fulfilled, however, both she and George mythologised their own happiness and good fortune in a desperate need to reassure themselves about the value of what they were doing. As travellers' tales about the couple filtered back to Australia, the audience reaction was not quite what the two expatriates might have hoped. At this time (Peter Coleman would note), 'the legends thickened — with tales of drunkenness, brawls, promiscuity, poverty and tuberculosis. There was no secrecy about it. Each new book they wrote added to the picture and each new visitor brought back further spectacular details'.[5] For many back home, the Johnstons' chosen life of exile seemed an insult or a criticism, and descriptions of the Johnstons' lifestyle confirmed the belief that writers were wealthy idlers. It was welcome news when stories started to circulate to the effect that there were worms in the lotus.

With the media campaign surrounding George Johnston's return to Australia in 1964, the wheels were set in motion for a whole new movement of the myth. This comprised a couple of different factors. Firstly, the obvious ill-health of the returning exile together with evidence of the years of poverty and hard living, allowed some people to congratulate themselves that they had had the good sense to stay home. Secondly, Johnston's new novel both recorded and extolled a particular Australian legend precious to the generation who had grown up through the hardship of the Great Depression, fought in the war, and then been left feeling anticlimactic through the dreary certainty of the Menzies era.[6] This book affirmed their experience as being valid and important, and it affirmed the values of a particular type of Australia which was just in the process of disappearing. While the story of *My Brother Jack* would penetrate the national psyche, this impact would be reinforced at a popular level through Clift's television version of the story. The legendary status of the whole *Jack* phenomenon would rub off on its creators.

It was most unfortunate that Charmian Clift's own return occurred in the wake of the media hype about her husband. With the earlier myth of the young beauty revived through photographs, no forty year old woman could have fulfilled the expectations put upon Charmian. And while the literary limelight shone upon her husband, she was relegated to the second division — namely, journalism in the women's pages, where her presence among advertisements for clothing and beauty aids added to the expectation that she would epitomise glamour and style. Increasingly, it was as if the outward persona was all that mattered.

Meanwhile, there was also a resurgence of the myth of the perfect marriage partners, as the couple did media interviews together to sell their work. Clift's column reinforced this idealised picture of the Johnston family life, and seemed to welcome the world into her home. At the same time, the continuing deterioration of George's health was reassuring for the audience, for it counteracted any idea that this lucky couple were having it too easy.

While by the latter part of the 1960s there was a growing disjunction between the public version of the couple's life and the private reality, it was at this time that both writers were engaged on major new developments in the fictional telling of their autobiographical stories. If in the work-in-progress there were two versions of Cressida Morley, in the life-in-progress there were also parallel versions of Charmian Clift.

Although the difficulty of sustaining the myth and living with the myth was a major factor in Charmian Clift's death, the death itself caused a reappraisal of the Johnston story. Given the columnist's public profile, it was inevitable that the media would report the event. At first, however, an extraordinary level of discretion was observed; the actual cause of death was not mentioned in print. As well as showing kindness to George, this silence was a mark of respect for Charmian.

On the afternoon of Wednesday 9 July, page 11 of the Sydney *Sun* carried the news that Miss Charmian Clift had 'died suddenly'. The small news item added that she had 'died in her sleep at midnight, after no hint of illness', and went on to mention her 'career in journalism'.[7] A similar article made the front page of that evening's Melbourne *Herald*.[8] Both there and in the Sydney paper, the news was completely eclipsed by the suicide attempt of popular singer Marianne Faithfull, who was visiting Australia to take part in the Ned Kelly film, which was starring her boyfriend, Mick Jagger.

On Thursday 10 July, the *Australian* ran a piece headed 'Sudden Death of Charmian Clift Ends a Literary Partnership'. After stating that 'she is believed to have had a heart attack in her sleep', this report added that the next month would see the publication of *Clean Straw for Nothing* in which Charmian was 'clearly identifiable, according to those who have known the Johnstons'.[9] In the report of the death in that day's Melbourne *Age*, readers were informed that 'Charmian Clift's romance with George Johnston and their married life together are the subject of the novel *Clean Straw for Nothing*'.[10]

Thursday, of course, was the day for the Clift column in the Women's Section of the *Sydney Morning Herald*. The columnist's piece about outdoor restaurants appeared in the usual place, followed by a 'tribute' by Maggie Vaile. The women's editor described Clift as 'the champion of the underdog and the little people', as well as praising her 'love of Australia'.[11] A couple of days later, the *Herald* published a moving obituary by Allan Ashbolt, titled 'Charmian Clift — A Writer who Believed in Human Dignity'. This referred to 'her own sense of moral values, her passion for social justice, and above all her own lyrical delight in being alive and belonging to the human race'.[12]

From the first announcement that Charmian had died, a large number of fans had started ringing the switchboard of the *Sydney Morning Herald*.[13] The death seemed like the loss of a personal friend or even family member to many readers. On Saturday 12 July, the *Sydney Morning Herald* published a small selection of letters from readers expressing their love for the Clift column and its writer, and their sympathy for the family. 'Charmian Clift's death has created a void', wrote one woman, and another said: 'Thursday won't be Thursday any more for a long time'. One of the Greek-Australian members of the Committee for the Restoration of Democracy in Greece declared: 'Every Greek democrat is mourning her premature death and is inspired by her example and her struggle for the dignity of man'.[14]

Despite the tact of the media, many people quickly realised that Clift's death was a suicide. Because of the intimacy of the column, many readers felt that they actually knew the columnist, and knew the family too. How could it be, that such a thing could be done by the happy, passionate, wise, committed, caring woman with whom so many people were familiar? Was that whole portrayal untrue? As rumours started to spread, there would quickly develop a series of myths about the reasons for Charmian Clift's death. It was at this time, and in this context, that once again the boundary blurred between fiction and fact, and between Cressida and Charmian, when *Clean Straw for Nothing* hit the bookstalls on 22 August.

If Charmian Clift had intended to do something to beat up publicity for her husband's novel, she could not have succeeded better.[15] Anything to do with the Johnstons was even more newsworthy than usual. As Sandra Hall commented in the *Bulletin*, Clift's death 'imbue[d] the publication of [*Clean Straw for Nothing*] with the kind of ironic poignancy at which life so often outdoes art'.[16] At the same time, the sympathy which Charmian might have won for her portrayal in the novel was destroyed by her committing a taboo action: this was not so much the suicide in itself, but the fact that she had left behind a mortally ill husband and three children. This created a great deal of public sympathy for George, who was depicted in press interviews as the grieving widower, struggling to look after the kids and run the household while he attempted to finish his life's work in the short time left to him.[17]

As the reviews started to come in, it was clear that Johnston's ill-health and his recent bereavement made some critics feel awkward.[18] Overall, whether commentators liked or disliked the novel, they made it clear that they read the text as thinly veiled autobiography. The author appeared to offer encouragement for this interpretation. Thus Elizabeth Riddell reported that 'Johnston says Davy Meredith is himself but not quite; Cressida is Charmian, but not quite'. And the author told Sandra Hall: 'The Cressida character, Meredith's wife, is in many ways different from Charm, but she was based on her'.[19]

This non-fictional reading of *Clean Straw for Nothing* was exactly what Charmian Clift had expressed her fear about in her late night conversation with Joan Flanagan. In which ways was the model 'different' from the character, or 'not quite' like her? Nobody asked this pertinent question. Meanwhile, sales for the book soared. It would always have done well, in the wake of the earlier novel and television serial, but Clift's death coming at this particular time gave added impetus, as readers sought in the text something which might explain why David Meredith's wife had found it impossible to bear her life.

In October, as publicity for George Johnston's new novel began to subside, the Coroner's Inquest into Charmian Clift's death was held. The Coroner found that the deceased 'died from the effects of poisoning by pentobarbitone self administered whilst in a state of severe mental depression and whilst considerably affected by alcohol'. Under Section 42 (b) of the relevant act, he prohibited publication of the contents of Charmian Clift's note.[20]

The media reports of the inquest were again comparatively discreet. For many of Clift's fans and even for some friends, it was the *Sydney Morning Herald* account which was the primary source of information. After reporting the Coroner's finding that 'Charmian Clift committed suicide whilst in a state of depression' it moved on to George Johnston's account of 'watching television with his wife on the night before her death', at which time ' "She appeared normal and gave me no cause for concern"'. George Johnston was also quoted as saying: 'After she saw her doctor on July 7 she became very depressed and concerned that she would have to have a major operation'.[21]

Melbourne readers received more information. On the evening of the inquest, the Melbourne *Herald* headed its report 'Charmian's Death: Depression' and twice repeated the Coroner's reference to the deceased's 'state of severe mental depression'. It went on to report George Johnston saying that 'In the two years before her death she had suffered fits of depression. She had mentioned a fear of cancer on the day before she died'.[22] The next morning's *Age* noted that 'after seeing the doctor on the Monday before her death, she had become very depressed and was very concerned that she would have to have a major operation'. This report attributed a final remark to George Johnston. ' "On the day before her death she said she had a fear of cancer," he said'.[23]

Within a few months of her death, the polite fiction of Charmian Clift's 'illness' was so accepted that it could be referred to without even naming the precise nature of it. In his Introduction to *The World of Charmian Clift*, George Johnston explained how it was that people had not known that Charmian was ill:

> It was one of her great professional prides that she never missed a deadline, even though she was often sick and desperately worried; indeed in the last few months of her life nobody was allowed to know how very sick she was — she went on being cheerful, helping others, and meeting her deadlines.[24]

This collection of essays was essentially the anthology which Clift herself had been compiling in May during her leave from the column. The cover featured an oil portrait of Charmian which Ray Crooke had painted a month or so after her death. It was an uncharacteristically sombre version of the subject: brown and brooding, with face half-turned and eyes seeming to look at something a long way out of the frame.

* * *

As the years went on, the tale of Charmian's death would 'get round like a pebble' as people poured more passion — and less fact — into the storytelling. When memory of the cancer story and the official verdict of 'depression' faded, for many people the most significant issue about Charmian's life became the question: why did she kill herself? Eventually her death had to be 'explained' by creating a new myth of a tortured woman, bent on self-destruction. This was part of a portrayal of the whole Johnston story as a Greek tragedy, in which hubris brought the revenge of the gods. Every so often, the media would add to the myth.

A classic example is an article which appeared in the *Age* in October 1977. Titled 'Island Legend for Sale', it began: 'A legend — and a genuine Aussie one at that — is for sale'. The Johnstons' Hydra house was on the market, and an Australian journalist visiting the island used this as his lead into a piece which started the myth ball rolling again.

> The stories which contribute to the Johnston legend are legion: tales of rowdy parties and brawls, jealous scenes and the like, that gossip has built up about the raffish life of the writers. How much of that is true? What kind of life did the Johnstons actually live in those idyllic days when you could live, so they say, as you pleased on practically nothing in the dreamy time before tourism was invented and Greece became expensive?[25]

If this reinforced the false impression of the ease of the Johnstons' economic circumstances, the rest of the article sifted through ancient gossip as the journalist interviewed members of the island's foreign colony who were hostile to the Johnstons. One such witness was described as 'a former CIA official, now a painter of Greek primitives'. Another observer, described as 'an American anthropologist who knew the two very well', reminisced about how he was initially 'enthralled' by this 'very theatrical pair'. But later he saw 'the dark side'. The article continued: 'The dark side? The public image the Johnstons fostered — deliberately? — was in the old-fashioned Hemingway tradition: heavy drinking, chain smoking, vociferous confrontations, jealous fights and rows'. This piece was also one of the early proponents of the myth of Charmian as a neglectful mother. This was demonstrated by the anecdote of a German tourist guide who remembered: 'Once I saw Charmian and little Jason strolling along, and the little boy, with a shout of glee pounced on an abandoned pair of sandals. "Look Mummy!" he cried, "now I've got shoes to wear"'.

The journalist revealed the source of his preconceived ideas about the 'legend' when he noted that *Clean Straw for Nothing* 'really took the lid off the writers' private lives'. Making no distinction between the fictional portrait and the model, he went on to ask: 'Was Charmian so heartless, so unfaithful, as the book clearly hints at?' Of course he found a female member of 'the inner circle' to answer on cue: 'No man was safe if she set her sights on him'. Now all the stops were pulled out:

> When fame came tragedy was ironically waiting in the wings, Greek style. George's health was perilous [...] Charmian's beauty was on the wane, a thing she hated. Recklessly, it seems, she flung herself into a final love affair. George set off for Australia alone.

With this piece of misinformation, the article reverted to the real estate angle, and concluded: 'Anyone want to buy a legend?'

Three weeks later Rodney Hall would write to the *Age* to correct the facts regarding George's departure from the island and Charmian's final Hydra fling. A Letter to the Editor, however, cannot hope to turn around the impression given by a full-page feature. Indeed, the headline which the newspaper placed above Hall's letter — 'Greek-island affair' — confirmed the impression that sex was at the core of the Johnston/Clift story. Rodney Hall also noted:

> Anyone wishing to know what went on in [the Johnston] household would be ill-advised to accept *Clean Straw for Nothing* as evidence. Plenty of information is there, but you have to know how to read it — especially where the hero himself is concerned.[26]

As time went on, however, 'information' selectively gleaned from *Clean Straw* would become increasingly accepted as fact. In particular, Charmian would again and again be portrayed as being identical with Cressida. And as the story pebble became rounder and rounder, it became unnecessary for researchers even to read the second book of Johnston's trilogy, because once an article such as the 'Island Legend' was on file, it in itself would provide the evidence for the next piece of journalism.

In the media's development of the legend, a certain point of view must be taken into account. By leaving the newspaper world and going off to chance their fortunes writing books full-time, George Johnston and Charmian Clift did what so many journalists dream of doing, but are afraid to risk. It is not surprising that some colleagues found it comforting to portray the couple's escape as a miserable failure. Meanwhile, the Johnstons' old connections in the newspaper world meant that there were also some people with ancient scores to settle, once George and Charmian were no longer around to defend themselves.

Yet while the attitude of some of the media to the Johnston story reveals a combination of envy and resentment, this reflects the more general attitude of sections of the Australian public. If a story becomes a myth, it is because it serves a need. In Sidney Nolan's words, it 'represents something basic in the community'. Myths contain morals, warnings, pieces of folk law as well as folk lore. They are essentially a conservative force, binding people together by expressing and upholding safe social values. This doesn't mean that they have one simple meaning. The fact that myths have accreted different bits of story over time means that they are open to different interpretations. They serve different needs at different times in history.

Part of the appeal of the Clift and Johnston story stems from the national self-consciousness, whereby Australian culture is seen as being isolated from the ancient cultural sources of the northern hemisphere. The fact that Clift and Johnston lived and worked in Europe — and particularly Greece — gave Australians a feeling that their culture was involved on the world stage.

Yet if Australians want their artists to be seen as equal players in the outside world, they reveal their sense of inferiority again in the way they use figures from that world as their measuring sticks or benchmarks. Thus in the development of the myth of Charmian and George's life on Hydra, it would be described as 'what some people, including the Johnstons, saw as a sort of Hemingway or Zelda and Scott Fitzgerald gesture'.[27] Similarities would also be drawn with the Mailers. These parallels, however, had nothing to do with *writing*. The source of pride was that the Australian Johnstons drank and fought and made public nuisances of themselves in the manner of these American exiles. It was only a small step from this to the idea that the Johnstons had modelled themselves upon the Americans. Certainly, at the end of his life, George drew a certain strength from the idea that F Scott Fitzgerald had kept working through illness and domestic crisis;[28] he had not gone seeking pain, however, in order to emulate the writer he admired. Nor did George share any of the machismo of Ernest Hemingway or Norman Mailer. More importantly, although Johnston had drawn part of the Cressida character from Fitzgerald's Nicole, Charmian herself had nothing in common with Zelda Fitzgerald. The final step of this process of comparison reveals the Australian cultural cringe again, as the Johnstons were derided for not equalling their American 'models'. After visiting the couple on Hydra, Colin Simpson would tell friends that 'Maybe they were trying to be a koala version of the Mailers or the Fitzgeralds'.[29] In other words, an Australian version of a romantic exile reminds us of a cuddly animal — or a fluffy toy.

Overall, as soon as the mythical figures are built up, they must be pulled down again. As strong as is the Australian need to worship local heroes, equally strong is the national impulse to iconoclasm. Essentially a secular and republican people, we feel that we can do without gods, heroes, kings, queens and tall poppies.

At the same time, having made certain figures larger than life in the hope of magnifying our national culture, we resent the fact that we still feel small — and we blame them for it. By emphasising the difference between heroes and ourselves, we go on to infer a criticism of our ordinariness, because the large figures seem to imply that there is something wrong with our way of life. Never is this clearer than in the complicated public attitude to the Johnstons' exile. While it initially made people feel that they were not isolated in their antipodeanism, ultimately it was threatening. What was wrong with Australia, after all, that these two people had to take their family and migrate somewhere else? It was this which lent a hostile attitude to the reception that the Johnstons tended to encounter from some quarters on their return. Clift summed this up brilliantly in her column when she commented:

> What I find is peculiar is the attitude of some people when you come back [...] who say, like patriot vigilantes: 'You were a traitor for leaving. But you are a coward for returning.'
> Personally I never know whether they are blaming me for failing, or blaming me for trying. Nobody ought to be blamed for trying.[30]

The same 'patriot vigilantes' also took exception to the Johnstons' social and political beliefs. What was wrong with Australian suburbia of the 1950s — or of the 1960s, for that matter? What was wrong with the safe, secure, small existence with which most Australians were content? By living outside these norms, by striving for something different, the Johnstons made people uncomfortable with their own lives. But it was Charmian Clift who was the more troubling figure, because it was more confronting when a woman defied the social norms. This was the same old double standard that Charmian had suffered since her girlhood. Her downfall — her death — made some feel secure in the thought that their small safe lives were ultimately preferable to the high life. Her suicide seemed proof positive that it was better to dwell on the earth than fly towards the sun. But again paradox asserted itself. Again she was blamed for failing, regarded as a traitor and a coward. Her death made people uncomfortable all over again. What was wrong with the life of a suburban mother and housewife, that she had to do that, to escape it?

And so the myth ball rolled, and became rounder. Sometimes the story would seem to slip out of the public memory for a few years. It would appear that at last people had forgotten about these two writers whose books were mostly out of print. And then something would start the stories rolling again.

Biographers create the lives of their subjects at the same time as they record them. Never is this clearer than in the telling of the Clift and Johnston story. The point at issue is not the biographical works in themselves, but the spate of feature articles and anecdotal book reviews which erupts in the wake of publication. As the readership of these journalistic pieces is considerably greater than the readership of the whole biographical texts, it is the media story that becomes the myth.

Interest in the Johnston/Clift story was awakened once again when Garry Kinnane's biography of George Johnston was released in October 1986, and both the *Age* and the *Sydney Morning Herald* published a two page extract. Jumping into the story in the difficult summer of 1958, this began with Clift's affair with Jean-Claude Maurice and the 'numerous public rows' which this occasioned.[31] Of course, Kinnane's biography of Johnston presents these passages in the context of less sensational material, but this two-page appetiser would be the full meal for many readers.

The version in the *Sydney Morning Herald* ran in large type a description of Charmian Clift as sexual aggressor. Her sister, Margaret Backhouse, was moved to protest to the Letters column, asking: 'Why did the biography of George Johnston present Charmian Clift, in large letters, as some kind of scarlet woman?'[32] But such objections incline to make people think that there is no smoke without fire.

A tendency to retell the myth would emerge in reviews of Kinnane's book, in which the subject under review would by and large be the life of Johnston and Clift, rather than an assessment of the biographer's presentation of it. While John Douglas Pringle in the *Sydney Morning Herald* provided a measured view of Charmian as being 'not notably unfaithful — certainly not more than George himself — until their marriage had already been destroyed by jealousy and alcohol', Pringle's moderate tone was completely undone by the headline assigned to the piece: 'Pushing Anarchic Life to the Edge of Disaster'.[33] This heading sums up the conservative social and political moral that was to be drawn the Johnston/Clift myth: anarchy leads to disaster.

Nearly a decade later, in the early months of 1994, it was the solo version of the Charmian myth which took off again at a great rate. Although Kinnane's biography had recorded the information that Clift as a young woman had given birth to an illegitimate daughter who had been relinquished for adoption, this fact suddenly became news with the publication of Charmian's first daughter's book about her discovery of her own identity. A great deal of media attention was given to Suzanne Chick's *Searching for Charmian*, with its poignant subtitle *The Daughter Charmian Clift Gave Away Discovers the Mother She Never Knew*. Certainly, adoption stories were newsworthy around that time, in the wake of legislation which allowed adopted children to access their family records. Even Robert Dessaix's unsensational and elegantly written memoir of adoption[34] — which came out around the same time — spent weeks on the bestseller list. The telling of the Chick story, however, had a multi-layered appeal for many people, irrespective of whether they were interested in adoption or whether they had ever read a word written by Charmian Clift, because it promulgated a new myth which was very reassuring in the prevailing political climate.

The story broke in a five page feature article about 'Charmian Clift's Lost Child' which appeared on Saturday 19 February 1994 in the *Good Weekend* magazine of the *Sydney Morning Herald* and the *Age*. The story opened with reference to 'the tangled, exotic, passionate life' of a woman 'whose writing, drinking, love affairs and marriage still burn in the memories of Australian literary circles'.[35] This introduced some of the elements which would be repeated — and sometimes amplified — in a number of succeeding articles and reviews.

Most accounts were quick to mention the suicide, and a number quoted the suitably romantic Keats line from the note.[36] In canvassing the reason why Charmian killed herself, most of the articles raised the notion of the middle-aged woman's distress at her lost beauty. A couple of writers nibbled at the idea of Clift's concern at her portrayal in *Clean Straw for Nothing*. But the vital addition to the myth fabric was the emergence of a new reason for the suicide: now it was seen as having been primarily caused by Charmian's guilt at the abandonment of her first child. One writer described Clift's life as 'a quagmire of drama, alcoholism and remorse'.[37] Such a message, of course, powerfully reinforces the values of mainstream society, for it shows the woman being punished (or — better still — punishing herself) for her infringement of the sexual and social code.

Overall, this new version of the Charmian myth was 'the stuff of fairytales'.[38] Many children dream that they are really the offspring of a beautiful princess who one day will come to rescue them from the nagging drudge who pretends to be their mother. This sort of belief is particularly prevalent among adopted children. Suzanne Chick appeared to fulfil this fantasy in her discovery that, while the mother who had raised her was the epitome of suburban ordinariness, her biological mother was beautiful and talented and famous and charismatic. Yet in the very moment of wish fulfilment, the dream mother turned out to be, not just dead, but a suicide. This reinforced the rejection implied by the initial relinquishment of the child. Moreover, the fact that this figure had died a taboo death completed the transformation of the princess into a witch. As Charmian was obviously not the beautiful perfect mother, she had to be an ugly old harridan, a drunk, a sexually loose woman, and — most importantly — a bad mother to the 'lost child's' half-siblings. Four separate writers would pick up a comment by Toni Burgess that Suzanne was 'very lucky that [Charmian] didn't choose to keep' her.[39] All of this strengthened the image of Charmian as a woman who had neglected and abandoned her children.

While it drew upon these archetypal elements, the story of the 'Daughter of a Legend' (as one piece was titled[40]) again reinforced conservative mainstream values. The moral to be drawn from a comparison of the life of Charmian and the life of her first daughter was that flying close to the sun will bring certain downfall.[41] Thus the media would pick up a reference by Suzanne Chick to her own 'small' life, and contrast this with Charmian's 'big life' — to Charmian's discredit. Newspaper readers could feel reassured about their own existence through the story of 'this ordinary middle class Australian woman [...] who by her own admission has lived a "small" life'.[42] Small was beautiful, after all. In the 1990s political climate of backlash against feminism, there were many who were keen to buy this particular telling of the myth.

In her essay entitled 'What Are You Doing It For?', Clift foreshadowed something of the process which has occurred to her reputation since her death. Asking herself this vital question, the writer went on to observe:

It is the most pretentious nonsense to believe that the work you do will live after you. It might, but then again it might not, and history will be the judge of that, not you. What most of us leave to posterity are only a few memories of ourselves, really, and possibly a few enemies. A whole human life of struggle, bravery, defeat, triumph, hope, despair, might be remembered, finally, for one drunken escapade.[43]

This epitomises the problem with the various stories which make up the Charmian myth: she becomes known as someone who drank too much, or someone who 'gave away' her daughter, or someone who killed herself. A bad mother. The wife of George Johnston. The scarlet woman. Or the girl with sand between her toes. In these 'few memories', the 'whole human life' becomes lost. Yet the worst loss is the way in which the work becomes subsumed, obliterated, as the myth of Charmian becomes increasingly alienated from the words she wrote, the convictions she fought for.

While the Charmian Clift myth is a highly political construct which reinforces conservative social values, this can only work if the written message left by Clift herself is depoliticised. This depoliticisation is evident in the way in which the writer's essays are generally acknowledged for their form rather than their content. The essayist is praised for her limpid and lyrical prose style, and not for the strenuous mind that crafted these pieces which, in the context of the women's pages of the Australian press of the 1960s, made up a highly subversive oeuvre — as the author herself knew. Once again, Clift is acknowledged for beauty, but not for her brains.

Yet the politics which Clift avowed were expressed not just in her writing, but through the autobiographical novel of her life. She turned her back on the Cold War attitudes of the Menzies era. She went into exile rather than live in a society which stifled her. She sacrificed security for art. She embraced openness, freedom and social justice. This whole outward and liberating statement is obliterated by the myth of the selfish and self-destructive hedonist. But of course the myth had to try to destroy Clift's message, because it was dangerous.

Bloody well fly, why don't you? This is the message that rings through everything Charmian Clift wrote and did. It doesn't matter if you fail. It doesn't matter if you fall. *Nobody ought to be blamed for trying.*

Ultimately it is this that is the cause of Charmian Clift's appeal: she did what so many of us would like to have done, but were not brave enough to dare. Through her ability to communicate, she allowed people to share for a moment in her escape. And escape she finally did.

Some have found it sad that Charmian Clift's ashes disappeared after her cremation — mislaid apparently, amongst everything else that was going on in family life — so that there is no physical resting place, marked by a headstone or a brass plaque. While this is symbolically wonderful, it is also just the sort of irony that Charmian herself would have loved. This woman, who was so burdened by her body, finally got rid of it. If for a while she has become Ned Kelly, dragged down by her mask, it is in her death that she reasserts herself as Icarus — aspiring, questing, flying. It is far better to celebrate her life through the only memorial that matters: a body of readers, new and old, who are as committed as ever to the writing and ideals of Charmian Clift.

BIBLIOGRAPHY

PRIMARY SOURCES

PUBLISHED WORKS
Published Works by Charmian Clift
First publication date in the UK, the USA and Australia (if relevant) is given for works by Charmian Clift. These publications are not necessarily the imprints used for page references. For these, and for abbreviations of titles, see 'A Note on the Endnotes'.

'Awakening, The', *The Australasian Post*, 11/7/46

Being Alone with Oneself, Essays 1968–1969, edited by Nadia Wheatley, Collins/Angus & Robertson, Sydney,1991

'Even the Thrush Has Wings', in Garry Kinnane (ed.), *Strong-man from Piraeus and Other Stories*, Nelson, Melbourne, 1983

Honour's Mimic, Hutchinson, London,1964

Images in Aspic, edited by George Johnston, Horwitz, Sydney, 1965

Mermaid Singing, Bobbs-Merrill, Indianapolis, 1956; Michael Joseph, London, 1958

'Other Woman', *Australia National Journal*, vol. 6, no. 6, May 1945

Peel Me a Lotus, Hutchinson, London, 1959

Selected Essays of Charmian Clift, The, edited by Nadia Wheatley, HarperCollins, Sydney, 2001

'Small Animus, The', in Garry Kinnane (ed.), *Strong-man from Piraeus and Other Stories*, Nelson, Melbourne, 1983

'Three Old Men of Lerici', in Garry Kinnane (ed.), *Strong-man from Piraeus and Other Stories*, Nelson, Melbourne, 1983

Trouble in Lotus Land, Essays 1964–1967, edited by Nadia Wheatley, Collins/Angus & Robertson, Sydney, 1990

Walk to the Paradise Gardens, Hutchinson, London, 1960; Harper,
 New York, 1960

'Wild Emperor', in Garry Kinnane (ed.), *Strong-man from Piraeus and Other
 Stories,* Nelson, Melbourne, 1983

World of Charmian Clift, The, edited by George Johnston, Ure Smith,
 Sydney, 1970

Published Works Written in Collaboration by Charmian Clift and George Johnston

Big Chariot, The, Angus & Robertson, Sydney,1953; Faber and Faber,
 London, 1953; Bobbs-Merrill, Indianapolis, 1953

High Valley, Angus & Robertson, Sydney, 1949; Faber and Faber, London,
 1950; Bobbs-Merrill, Indianapolis, 1950

Sponge Divers, The, Collins, London,1956; published as *The Sea and the
 Stone,* Bobbs-Merrill, Indianapolis,1956

Published Works by George Johnston

First publication date in the UK and Australia (if relevant) is given for
works by George Johnston. These publications are not necessarily the
imprints used for page references. For these, and for abbreviations of titles,
see 'A Note on the Endnotes'.

'Astypalaian Knife, The', *Cosmopolitan,* December 1955

Australia at War, Angus & Robertson, Sydney, 1942

Australians, The, Rigby, Sydney, 1966

Battle of the Seaways, Angus & Robertson, Sydney, 1941

Cartload of Clay, A, Collins, London, 1971

Clean Straw for Nothing, Collins, London, 1969

Closer to the Sun, Collins, London, 1960

Cyprian Woman, The, Collins, London, 1955

Darkness Outside, The, Collins, London, 1959

Death Takes Small Bites, Dodd, Mead & Co., New York, 1948

'Dying Day of Francis Bainbridge, The', in Garry Kinnane (ed.), *Strong-man
 from Piraeus and Other Stories,* Nelson, Melbourne, 1983

Far Face of the Moon,The, Collins, London, 1965

Far Road,The, Collins, London, 1962

'Gallipoli Paintings', *Art and Australia,* September 1967

Grey Gladiator, Angus & Robertson, Sydney, 1941

Journey Through Tomorrow, Cheshire, Melbourne, 1947

Moon at Perigee, Angus & Robertson, Sydney, 1948

My Brother Jack, Collins, London, 1964

New Guinea Diary, Angus & Robertson, Sydney, 1943

Pacific Partner, World Book Co., New York, 1944

'Requiem Mass', in Garry Kinnane (ed.), *Strong-man from Piraeus and Other Stories*, Nelson, Melbourne, 1983

Skyscrapers in the Mist, Angus & Robertson, Sydney, 1946

'Sponge Boat', in Garry Kinnane (ed.), *Strong-man from Piraeus and Other Stories*, Nelson, Melbourne, 1983

'Strong-man from Piraeus', *Argosy*, October 1956

'Terra Incognita Revisited', *Age Literary Supplement*, 25/4/64

'Vale, Pollini!', in Michael Radcliff (ed.), *Voices II*, Michael Joseph, London, 1965

'Verdict, The', in Garry Kinnane (ed.), *Strong-man from Piraeus and Other Stories*, Nelson, Melbourne, 1983

By 'Shane Martin' (pseudonym of George Johnston)

Man Made of Tin, The, Collins, London, 1958

Myth is Murder, The, Collins, London, 1959

Saracen Shadow, The, Collins, London, 1957

Twelve Girls in the Garden, Collins, London, 1957

Wake for Mourning, A, Collins, London, 1962

TYPESCRIPTS, DRAFTS, ETC BY CHARMIAN CLIFT AND GEORGE JOHNSTON AND LETTERS TO AND FROM CHARMIAN CLIFT AND GEORGE JOHNSTON IN THE FOLLOWING LIBRARY COLLECTIONS

Angus & Robertson Collection, Mitchell Library, State Library of New South Wales

Bobbs-Merrill Collection, Manuscripts Department, Lilly Library, Indiana University

Charmian Clift Collection, National Library of Australia

Commonwealth Literary Fund Records, Australian Archives

David Higham Archives, Harry Ransom Humanities Research Center, The University of Texas at Austin

George Johnston Collection, National Library of Australia

CERTIFICATES, REPORTS, ETC REGARDING CHARMIAN CLIFT AND GEORGE JOHNSTON (AND FAMILY MEMBERS) IN THE FOLLOWING PUBLIC RECORDS

Australian Army Records
Department of Births, Deaths and Marriages
Royal North Shore Hospital Records
State Coroner's Office, New South Wales Attorney General's Department

ORAL HISTORY

Recorded by Nadia Wheatley

Most of the oral history used for this biography consists of interviews recorded on audiotape, and transcribed. These are indicated, here and on first usage in the Endnotes for each chapter, by the term 'interview', and all instances are dated. Four interviews were recorded in handwritten notes, rather than on tape. These are indicated by the term 'interview (notes only)'.

Another form of oral history has been designated 'oral testimony'. This refers to situations in which I had not formally arranged an interview, but just had a short conversation with an informant. For these accounts, a tape recorder was not used. However, notes were taken at the time and, in most cases, were written up again shortly afterwards. These occasions are also dated.

A third form of oral history has been designated 'information'. This term is essentially used for information which came to me, often over a long period of time, from people with whom I had a personal relationship. In the case of some informants, such as Martin Johnston or Grace Edwards, the information came before I contemplated writing a biography of Charmian Clift. In the case of a couple of other people, including Charmian's sister, Margaret Backhouse, the information was given in an informal situation, or was volunteered without being prompted by a question. I will not list these informants (although a number of them occur anyway), but will specify this information, where appropriate, in the Endnotes. If I have a date on which the information was given, I will give it, but usually no date can be assigned.

Andrews, Mary, interview (notes only), 24/7/89
Ashbolt, Allan, interview, 3/11/95
Backhouse, Margaret, interview, October 1982; interview, June 1983;
    interview (notes only), January 1984; interview, 31/11/84
Brown, Jean, oral testimony (telephone), 13/3/83
Burgess, Toni, interview (notes only), October 1984
Calomeras, James, interview, 25/7/91
Davies, Mrs, oral testimony (telephone), 13/3/83

Deveson, Anne, interview, 7/11/95

Dow, Hume, interview (notes only), 27/4/83

Flanagan, Joan, interview, 6/4/93

Flower, Cedric, interview,17/9/89

Hall, Bet, interview,10/7/95

Hall, Rodney, interview,10/7/95

Heffernan, Edward, interview, 30/9/84

James, Maisie, oral testimony (telephone), 13/3/83

Jamison, Greeba, interview, 2/3/83

Jefferis, Barbara, interview, 26/2/92

Johnston, Jason, interview, 5/4/98

Johnston, Martin, interview, October 1984

Keavis, Mavis, oral testimony, 12/3/83

King, Joan, oral testimony, 8/2/83; interview, 12/3/83

Kneale, Bruce, interview, 2/3/85

Leatham, Cecily, oral testimony, 8/2/83

Lovell, Patricia, interview, 8/8/96

MacCallum, Mungo, telephone interview (notes only), 21/4/95

Mallos, Tessa, interview,12/10/84

Phillis, Roy, interview, 12/3/83

Pike, Harry, interview, 21/9/90

Pringle, John Douglas, interview, 10/3/90

Richardson, Mrs, interview, 14/3/83

Simmons, Neil, oral testimony, 13/3/83

Sweet, Cliff, interview, 12/3/83

Taylor, Ray, interview, 2/3/90

Vaile, Margaret, interview, 28/8/89

Walton, Storry, interview, 19/3/90

Weston, Marg, oral testimony, 8/2/83

Wood, Nona, interview, 29/8/96

Recorded by Other People

Charmian Clift, interview with Hazel de Berg, National Library of Australia, 8/6/65

Charmian Clift, interview with Ellis Blain, *Away From it All*, Australian Broadcasting Commission, 21/7/65

George Johnston, interview with Hazel de Berg, 13/3/64, National Library of Australia

George Johnston, interview with Tony Morphett, *The Lively Arts*, Australian Broadcasting Commission, 12/4/65

George Johnston, interview with Tony Morphett, *The Lively Arts*, Australian Broadcasting Commission, 19/4/70

Martin Johnston, interview with Hazel de Berg, 23/6/80, National Library of Australia

SECONDARY SOURCES

Adams, Brian, *Sidney Nolan — Such is Life*, Hutchinson, Melbourne, 1987

Armanno, Venero, 'Tragic Find', *Courier Mail*, 26/3/94

Ashbolt, Allan, 'A Writer who Believed in Human Dignity', *Sydney Morning Herald*, 12/7/69

Ayling, Jack, 'This Week with Jack Ayling', *TV Week*, 21/8/65; 28/8/65

Barrowclough, Nikki, 'Charmian Clift's Lost Child', *Sydney Morning Herald* and *Age Good Weekend*, 19/2/94

Beaumont, Janise, 'Daughter of a Legend', *Sunday Telegraph*, 13/3/94

Boston Women's Health Collective, The, *The New Our Bodies, Ourselves*, Penguin Books, Ringwood, Australia, 1985

Bouras, Gillian, *A Foreign Wife*, McPhee Gribble, Melbourne, 1986

Chick, Suzanne, *Searching for Charmian: The Daughter Charmian Clift Gave Away Discovers the Mother She Never Knew*, Macmillan, Sydney, 1994

Coleman, Peter, 'To Charmian, a Daughter', *The Weekend Review*, 5–6/3/94

Doherty, Frank, 'Frank Doherty's View', *TV Times*, 15/9/65; 22/9/65

Dundy, Elaine, *Finch, Bloody Finch*, Michael Joseph, London, 1980

Durrell, Gerald, *My Family and Other Animals*, Penguin, Middlesex, 1974

Durrell, Lawrence, *Bitter Lemons*, Faber and Faber, London, 1957

Eagle, Chester, 'Links with Greatness', *Age*, 11/10/86

Elliot, Helen, 'The Charm of a Daughter's Desire', *Australian Book Review*, May, 1994

Faulkner, Trader, *Peter Finch: A Biography*, Angus & Robertson, London, 1979

Fitzgerald, F Scott, *Afternoon of an Author, A Selection of Uncollected Stories and Essays with an Introduction and Notes by Arthur Mizener*, The Bodley Head, London, 1958

Flanagan, Joan, 'His Novels Were Born out of Pain', *Advertiser*, 12/7/69

Forster, E M, 'The Story of a Panic', in *Collected Short Stories*, Penguin, Middlesex, 1947

Gardner, Helen (ed.), *The Metaphysical Poets*, Penguin Books, Middlesex, 1966

Gleam, The, Wollongong School Magazine, 1939

Graves, Robert, *The Greek Myths,* vol. 1, vol. 2, Pelican, Middlesex, 1983

Greer, Patrick, 'George Johnston in Hydra', *London Magazine,*
    November/December 1980

Hall, James, 'And Now It's Two for the Load', *Australian,* 23/11/68

Hall, Sandra, 'Time to Face a Modern Australia', *Bulletin,* 23/8/69

Hancock, WK, *Australia,* Jacaranda Press, Brisbane, 1961

Harkness, Libby, *Looking for Lisa,* Random House, Sydney, 1991

Hetherington, John, 'An Australian Author Returns to his Native Land',
    Age, 8/2/64

Hoffer, Eric, *The Passionate State of Mind and Other Aphorisms,* Harpers,
    New York, 1955

Hutton, Geoffrey, 'He Died Alive', *Age,* 23/7/70

Hutton, Nan, 'Dipping into the World of Charmian', *Age,* 16/8/73

Inglis, Kate, *Living Mistakes: Mothers who Consented to Adoption,* George
    Allen & Unwin, Sydney, 1984

Jefferis, Barbara, 'Deep Feeling in Australian Novel of Depression Era',
    Sydney Morning Herald, 7/3/64

Johnston, Doug, *Kiama Through the Years,* Kiama Museum and Craft
    Centre, Kiama, 1973

Johnston, Martin, 'A Cartload of Clay', *Age,* 2/10/71

Keavney, Kay, 'From George with Sadness', *Australian Women's Weekly,*
    3/9/69

Kiama Information Booklet, (anon.), Kiama Municipal Tourism and
    Commerce Committee, Kiama, 1982

Kinnane, Garry, *George Johnston: A Biography,* Nelson, Melbourne, 1986

Kinnane, Garry, 'A Writer's Marriage' (extract from *George Johnston:
    A Biography*), *Age Saturday Extra,* 4/10/86

Knuckey, Marie, 'In Search of Charmian's Island', *Sydney Morning Herald,*
    1/6/72

Lawrence, D H, *Lady Chatterley's Lover,* Penguin Books, Middlesex, 1961

Liddell, Robert, *Aegean Greece,* Jonathan Cape, London, 1954

Loane, Sally, 'New Identity Calls for a "Big" Life', *Sydney Morning Herald,*
    5/3/94

Love, Harold (ed.), *The Australian Stage, A Documentary History,* New
    South Wales University Press, Sydney, 1984

Lovell, Patricia, *No Picnic: An Autobiography,* Macmillan, Sydney, 1995

McQueen, Humphrey, *Gallipoli to Petrov,* George Allen & Unwin, Sydney, 1984

Marr, David (ed.), *Patrick White Letters,* Random House, Sydney, 1994

Miller, Henry, *The Colossus of Marousi,* Penguin, Middlesex, 1950

Mills, Claire, 'Forecasts', *Australian Bookseller and Publisher,* February 1994

Mitchell, Adrian, 'Inside Jack's Famous Brother', *Weekend Australian,*
    4–5/10/86

Nadel, Ira Bruce, *Various Positions: A Life of Leonard Cohen,* Pantheon
    Books, New York, 1996

'New Novel from Ancient Island', (anon.), *Woman,* 13/8/56

Ollif, Lorna, *Women in Khaki,* Australian Women's Services Association of
    New South Wales, Sydney, 1981

Ovid, *Metamorphoses* (Mary M. Innes trans.), Penguin Classics, London, 1955

Park, Ruth, *Fishing in the Styx,* Viking, Melbourne, 1993

Park, Ruth, 'Nothing but Writers', *Independent Monthly,* September 1989

Pearce, Jan, 'On Reflecting the Spirit of her Times', *Age,* 1/2/91

Pringle, John Douglas, 'Clift: The Abandoned Daughter's Perspective',
    Sydney Morning Herald, 5/3/94

Pringle, John Douglas, *Have Pen Will Travel,* Chatto & Windus, London,
    1973

Pringle, John Douglas, 'Pushing Anarchic Life to the Edge of Disaster',
    Sydney Morning Herald, 18/10/86

Quiller-Couch, Sir Arthur (ed.), *The Oxford Book of English Verse,* Oxford
    University Press, Oxford, 1943

Raemaeker, Louis, *Kultur in Cartoons,* New York, The Century Company,
    1917

Racmaeker, Louis, *Raemaeker's Cartoons,* Land & Water, Kingsway, London,
    1916

Riddell, Elizabeth, 'George, for Whom Working is Therapy', *Australian,*
    16/8/69

Riddell, Elizabeth, 'Writing Near the Brink', *Australian,* 23/7/70

Rolfe, Patricia, 'The Charm of Clift', *Bulletin,* 16/10/90

Rolfe, Patricia, 'Child is Mother to the Woman', *Bulletin,* 22/2/94

Rothfield, Tom, 'Island Legend for Sale', *Age,* 1/10/77

Ruskin, John, *Sesame and Lilies,* George Allen, London, 1916

'"Sentimental" Visit by Famous Author', (anon.), *Kiama Independent,*
    24/11/64

Simpson, Colin, *Greece — The Unclouded Eye,* Angus & Robertson, Sydney,
    1968

Sriber, Charles, 'It's All Greek to Them', *People,* 14/5/58

Sriber, Charles, 'We'll Never Go Back', *Bulletin,* 20/10/62

Sriber, Ruth, 'Australians Find a Dream Life on the Isles of Greece', *Australian Women's Weekly*, 20/7/60

Sterne, Laurence, *The Life and Opinions of Tristram Shandy*, Penguin Books, Middlesex, 1977

Stratton, Jon, *Race Daze*, Pluto Press, Sydney, 1999

Thomas, Alan G and Brigham, James A, *Lawrence Durrell, An Illustrated Checklist*, Southern Illinois University Press, Carbondale and Edwardsville, 1983

Tolchard, Clifford, 'My Husband George: My Wife Charmian', *Walkabout*, January 1969

Tranter, John (ed.), *Martin Johnston, Selected Poems and Prose*, University of Queensland Press, St Lucia, 1993

Trengrove, Alan, 'Partners — It's in Writing', *Sun*, 6/7/66

Vaile, Margaret, 'Charmian Clift — a Tribute', *Sydney Morning Herald*, 10/7/69

Walter, W Grey, *The Living Brain*, Gerald Duckworth & Co Ltd., London, 1953

Webster, Owen, 'Straw that Broke the Critic's Back', *Age*, 23/8/69

West, Rebecca, *The Fountain Overflows*, Macmillan, London, 1977

Westwood, H R, 'Louis Raemaeker', *Modern Caricaturists*, London, Lovat Dickson Ltd, 1932

Williams, Sue, 'Searching for Charmian', *Mode*, April/May, 1994

Wollongong High School, A History of Fifty Years 1916–1966, (anon.)

Woolf, Virginia, 'Montaigne' and 'The Modern Essay', in *The Common Reader*, First Series, The Hogarth Press, London, 1984

A NOTE ON THE ENDNOTES

CHARMIAN CLIFT MATERIAL

When the National Library of Australia was given the papers of Charmian Clift and George Johnston by the Clift Johnston Estate in 1975, an unfortunate mistake was made. The library named the collection the George Johnston Collection, despite the fact that about half the material was comprised of the papers of Charmian Clift. In these endnotes, therefore, most of Clift's material is taken from the George Johnston Collection. This includes (in Box 3, Folder 11, item 13), seventy-seven pages of typescript of what Clift called her 'semi-autobiographical novel', *The End of the Morning* — a text narrated in the first person by an alter ego character named Cressida Morley, whose parents are named Grace and Tom and whose siblings are Cordelia and Ben (short for Benedick).

In 1989, the National Library acquired a small collection of typescript drafts of Clift's autobiographical work-in-progress, which the author had given to her friend June Crooke. The library named this the Charmian Clift Collection. This includes a forty-seven page typescript draft of *The End of the Morning*. The opening section is a revised version of the draft of this novel in the George Johnston Collection. After page 29, the text in the Charmian Clift Collection moves into new draft material, mostly fragmentary; similarly, after page 31, the text in the Johnston collection shifts into unnumbered pages of material, which falls into a number of distinct sections.

Overall, as I explain within the text of the biography, I believe that the draft in the George Johnston Collection (or at least the long opening section of numbered pages) was written in Greece in 1962. I believe that the version of *The End of the Morning* in the Clift Collection was written back in Australia, particularly after the author was awarded a Commonwealth Literary Fund grant for this novel in 1968.

In referring to material from *The End of the Morning*, I sometimes move between the two versions. I will indicate this by noting which collection the text comes from. When I reach the unnumbered pages (indicated by n.p.n.) in the text in the George Johnston Collection, I will add a page reference of my own (eg 39th page, or whatever), in case future researchers want to find the source.

Other fragments of material from *The End of the Morning* are located in the George Johnston Collection, in Box 5, Folder 4 (no item number). These loose pages of typescript are scattered among other pages which include bits and pieces of short stories written by Clift in London in the 1950s. One fragment of four numbered pages, which starts at page 48, is a revised version of text that also appears on the 38th page of the text at Box 3, Folder 11, item 13. Obviously, revised text from pages 39–47 has been lost.

More interestingly, in this same bundle of material there are also seventeen scattered pages of an earlier version of the novel. These fragments include an opening section, entitled *The End of the Morning* and consisting of five typed, numbered pages. These are virtually identical to both the other versions of the opening of the novel, except that the young alter ego heroine is named Miranda Morley and the text is narrated in the third person. (The siblings are named Cordelia and Ben and the parents are Grace and Tom Morley.) There are three additional pages of typescript (numbered 4, 8 and 9, though pages 8 and 9 are not sequential) of third-person Miranda material, plus six pages (pages 8–11 plus two unnumbered pages) in which a first-person narrator writes *about* Miranda Morley and her family. These pages all contain phrases or whole passages which reappear in the two later texts of *The End of the Morning*. Finally, there are three pages (20, 27 and n.p.n.) which are first-person text. While the latter two pages are tiny fragments, page 20 is a draft version of a crucial passage about Tom Morley, which appears in revised form in both the later versions. Although the narrator does not mention her name, I believe that with this shift into first person, we see the shift from an alter ego named Miranda Morley to an alter ego named Cressida Morley.

All in all, these 'Miranda narratives' (as I will refer to them in the endnotes) represent a crucial stage of development in Clift's many attempts to write her autobiographical novel.

As well as containing the latest extant revised text of *The End of the Morning*, the Clift collection also includes another bundle of typescript, consisting of sixty pages of autobiographical fiction. Although this includes half a dozen separate fragments, this material can be sorted into three distinct drafts of material. While these were written at somewhat different times, all three bear the title *Greener Grows the Grass* on at least one of the openings of typescript.

The earliest of these is what I call, for convenience, the 'Alma narrative'. This is comprised of material narrated primarily in the first person (with occasional jumps to third person) by a middle-aged woman named Alma Morley, who reflects on her life either in the early period of her marriage to her husband Tom, or during the time when her younger daughter Christine is about fourteen. (Her other children are named John and Judith.) This 'Alma narrative' can be further organised into four sections:

'Alma narrative (a)': ten pages, n.p.n., no title, starts with a one-page prologue, then moves into chapter 1. Alma is remembering her arrival at the quarry settlement.

'Alma narrative (b)': eleven pages, numbered (by hand) 21–31 (numbers probably added at a later date). Alma reflects on problems with fourteen year old Chris, compared with her beautiful elder daughter Judith. The quality of the typewriter ribbon shows this to have been written at the same time as Alma narrative (a).

'Alma narrative (c)': four pages, numbered 1–4, entitled *Greener Grows the Grass,* starts with a two-page prologue, then moves into chapter 1. This is a revised typescript of the opening of 'Alma narrative (a)'.

'Alma narrative (d)': three pages, n.p.n., no title. On a stormy night, Alma reflects on her difficult marriage with Tom.

In addition to these 'Alma narratives', this bundle of typescript contains three third-person narratives concerning the character Christine Morley. For convenience, these can be categorised as:

'Christine (Martin) narrative': nine pages, numbered 1–9, handwritten title *Greener Grows the Grass.* This text is set in a newspaper office, and describes the meeting between Christine Morley (a journalist in her early twenties) and an ex-war correspondent named Martin Smith.

'Christine (Justin) narrative (a)': nineteen pages, numbered 1–18 plus draft for page 17, entitled *Greener Grows the Grass,* starts with a six-page prologue in which a young woman writer named Christine Morley brings her cosmopolitan lover Justin to her home town. Chapter 1 jumps back to the time when Christine was fourteen, living with her parents (Tom and Alma) and siblings (Judith and John). By page 16, the text is drifting into Alma's memories of her arrival at the quarry settlement. The text breaks off mid-sentence on page 18. Then the author has bundled in 'Alma narrative (b)', continuing Alma's thoughts regarding fourteen year old Chris.

'Christine (Justin) narrative (b)': four pages, first page numbered 32, following n.p.n., entitled 'Chapter Three'. This picks up the story of Christine as a young woman, and deals with the episode when she returns from nursing. It is clear that this was to follow on from the rest of the 'Christine (Justin) narrative' material.

In the George Johnston Collection, Box 5, Folder 22, item 46, there are an additional two pages of untitled typescript from *Greener Grows the Grass*. One of these, a third-person account of Christine Morley at fourteen, would seem to be part of the same version of the story as we find in the 'Christine (Justin) narratives'. The other page runs straight on from the third page of 'Alma narrative (d)' (about the stormy night). (Interestingly, together with these two pages we find a one-page fragment of a very early, first-person version of *Walk to the Paradise Gardens*.)

As to the relationship between the *Greener Grows the Grass* material and the *End of the Morning* material, the quality of writing makes it clear that *Greener Grows the Grass* was very much the earlier work. Any doubt is dispelled by a comparative textual analysis of the description of the author's home town in a number of texts. This shows 'Alma narrative (a)' and 'Alma narrative (c)' to have been written before 'Christine (Justin) narrative (a)', which in turn was written before *Walk to the Paradise Gardens* (published in 1960). It is just as clear that the description of the town in *The End of the Morning* was written after the description of Lebanon Bay that appears in *Walk to the Paradise Gardens*.

GEORGE JOHNSTON MATERIAL

In the George Johnston Collection, Box 3, Folder 7, item 7, there are fragments from five separate drafts of *Clean Straw for Nothing*, none of which bears dates or draft numbers. A careful comparison of texts shows that they can be sorted and dated in the following way:

'CSFN draft (i)': pp. 1–28; 32–4. Written in Greece in mid to late 1963.

'CSFN draft (ii)': pp. 1–14. Written soon after GJ returned to Australia.

'CSFN draft (iii)': pp. 1–6: Written close to the time of (ii).

'CSFN draft (iv)': pp. 1–3: 'Recovery room revelations' written in hospital 1966.

'CSFN draft (v)': pp. 119–120; 122–130. Virtually final draft: 1968

ABBREVIATIONS FOR ENDNOTES

Libraries and Collections

CC Coll.: Charmian Clift Collection, National Library of Australia
GJ Coll.: George Johnston Collection, National Library of Australia

Books (including editions cited for page numbers)

ACOC: *A Cartload of Clay*, Collins, Sydney, 1971
BAWO: *Being Alone with Oneself*, Collins, Angus & Robertson, Sydney, 1991
CSFN: *Clean Straw for Nothing*, Collins, Sydney, 1969
EM: *The End of the Morning*, unfinished and unpublished novel
GGTG: *Greener Grows the Grass*, unfinished and unpublished novel
HM: *Honour's Mimic*, Collins Publishers Australia, Sydney, 1989
HV: *High Valley*, Collins/Angus & Robertson, Sydney, 1990
IA: *Images in Aspic*, Collins Publishers Australia, Sydney, 1989
MBJ: *My Brother Jack*, Collins/Angus & Robertson, Sydney 1988
MS: *Mermaid Singing* Collins Publishers Australia, Sydney, 1988
MS (B-M): American edition *Mermaid Singing*, Bobbs-Merrill, Indianapolis, 1956
PMAL: *Peel Me a Lotus*, Angus & Robertson, Sydney, 1989
TILL: *Trouble in Lotus Land*, Collins, Angus & Robertson, Sydney, 1990
WCC: T*he World of Charmian Clift*, Collins Publishers Australia, Sydney, 1989
WTTPG: *Walk to the Paradise Gardens*, Collins Publishers Australia, Sydney, 1989

People

CC: Charmian Clift
GJ: George Johnston
DH: David Higham (from David Higham Associates Ltd.)
IVA: Ivan von Auw (from Harold Ober Associates Inc.)
NW: Nadia Wheatley

The David Higham Archives (Harry Ransom Humanities Research Center, The University of Texas at Austin) contain copies of material from the American associates of the David Higham literary agency (initially called Pearn, Pollinger and Higham) as well as the British agency's own correspondence. During the period under review, three different American agencies were associated with David Higham. These were Ann Watkins Inc., followed by William Morris Agency, and then (from about mid 1955) Harold Ober Associates Inc. These American agents automatically represented Clift and Johnston. In the endnotes, I cite the name of the correspondent, but I do not name the American agency unless it seems necessary.

ENDNOTES

Epigraph

1 Laurence Sterne, *The Life and Opinions of Tristram Shandy*, Penguin, Middlesex, 1977, p. 96. Momus (the god of fault-finding) blamed Vulcan because, when he had made the human form out of clay, he had neglected to place in the breast a window through which the secrets of the soul could be seen. A dioptrical beehive had glass windows on opposite sides.

Prologue

1 CC, PMAL, p. 193.
2 GJ, note headed 'Elements of Jealousy (extracted from Eric Hoffer's *The Passionate State of Mind*)', GJ Coll., Box 1, Folder 4, item 7. This is half a page of typed notes from Eric Hoffer, *The Passionate State of Mind and Other Aphorisms*, Harpers, New York, 1955, reprinted 1968. Johnston refers to this reading of Hoffer's popular psychology in CSFN, p. 159.
3 See 'A Note on the Endnotes' for a description of this draft material, and an explanation of the dates I assign to it.

PART I — SMALL TOWN GIRL

Chapter 1 — The Centre of the World

1 CC, EM, CC Coll., p. 3.
2 Information re place name from *Kiama Information Booklet*, (anon.), Kiama Municipal Tourism and Commerce Committee, Kiama, June 1982, p. 2.
3 Some old residents remember this name. CC used it in 1960 in her novel *Walk to the Paradise Gardens*, and in 1962 in the drafts of *The End of the Morning*. This name for Kiama was later used by GJ in CSFN.
4 Doug Johnston, *Kiama Through the Years*, Kiama Museum and Craft Centre, Kiama, 1973, p. 13.
5 Doug Johnston, *Kiama Through the Years*, p. 8.
6 CC, EM, CC Coll., p. 3; CC, EM, GJ Coll., Box 3, Folder 11, item 13, p. 3. In quoting this text, I have followed the slightly revised version from CC Coll., but have kept the place names as they are in the earlier GJ Coll. version, as these are the same as the real names. In the revised text, the author slightly fictionalised some of the names (eg 'Bombo' to 'Bong-Bong').

7   However, there were in fact six, not five, cottages in the row. When counting them, the young Charmian obviously did not count her own cottage, because she was so firmly 'inside' it — just as it is easy to forget to count oneself when setting the table. This slip recurs in the *Greener Grows the Grass* description of the arrival of Alma Morley at the quarry settlement. While the architectural evidence of the six original cottages was still obvious when I began research in Kiama in 1982, this was confirmed by Joan King née McAuliffe (interview with NW, 12/3/83), who grew up in the quarry terrace at the same time as Charmian. Joan even named the six families. Working back from the creek there were the Clifts, the Drennans, the McAuliffes, the Corsos, then two households of Blairs. Further up the hill there was the Hayes family, and then the Davies' shop.

8   CC, EM, CC Coll., p. 1. As we see later in this chapter, the author had earlier used this image in WTTPG, pp. 3–4, in a description of this same landscape.

9   GJ, MBJ, p. 39. GJ mentions 'the army biscuit from Cairo' and 'the decorations from various wedding cakes and other things like that'. This was written after CC had published her description of the glass dome (including the list of items inside the dome) in WTTPG. It was as if the two authors saw these different domes as ways of differentiating their family circumstances.

10 CC, EM, CC Coll., pp. 1–2; CC, EM, GJ Coll., pp. 1–2. See note above re place names.

11 See, for example, CC, 'Winter Solstice', WCC, pp. 57–61.

12 CC, WTTPG, p. 74.

13 CC, WTTPG, pp. 2–3.

14 Originally these papers were rivals, but in about 1925 the Weston family, who owned the *Kiama Independent*, bought out the *Kiama Reporter*. The paper continued to come out under both names — one on Wednesday, the other on Saturday — but was produced by the same editorial and printing staff. In the 1940s the *Reporter* was officially amalgamated into the *Independent*. Marg Weston, oral testimony, 8/2/83.

15 For example, in the month of August 1923, when CC was born, amusements included a Grand Concert with minstrels in aid of the Jamberoo Methodist Church, the Kiama Oddfellows Ball with a popular dance program and Miss Prott's Orchestra, the Jamberoo School of Arts Annual Picnic and Sports, the Gerringong Catholic Picnic Sports Day and Ball, the Kiama Municipal Band Concert and Dance, and the Annual Dance of the Loyal Star of the South Lodge, with Miss Prott's Orchestra (Gentlemen three shillings plus tax, Ladies cater). The list of coming events for August/September/October 1935 included the Kiama School of Arts Ball, the Albion Park Footballers Ball, the Kiama Methodist Concert, the Jamberoo Silver Jubilee Ball, the Catholic Ball at Gerringong, the Kiama Parents and Citizens Ball, the Scots Fair at Kiama, the Rifle Club Ball at Jamberoo, the Kiama Show Ball, the Congregational Concert, the Kiama Church of England Tea and Concert, the Kiama Catholic Ball, the Methodist Flower Show at Kiama, the Ambulance and Hospital Sports at Albion Park, the Church of England Flower Shows at Shellharbour and Gerringong, the Presbyterian Fete at Jamberoo, the Convent Euchre Party and Dance at Shellharbour, the Hospital and Red Cross Ball at Jamberoo, and the Rover Scouts Euchre Party and 50–50 Old Time and Jazz Dance at the Kiama Oddfellows Hall.

16 Cliff Sweet and Roy Phillis, interview with NW, 12/3/83.

17 CC, GGTG, CC Coll., 'Christine (Justin) narrative (a)', pp. 4–6.

18 Cedric Flower, interview with NW, 17/9/89.

19 Interview with NW, 5/8/91.

Chapter 2 — Liars and Embroiderers

1 CC, 'Things that Go Boomp in the Night', IA, p. 133; CC, EM, GJ Coll., Box 3, Folder 11, item 13, n.p.n. (62nd page).
2 CC, 'A Portrait of My Mother', WCC, p. 80.
3 CC, EM, CC Coll., p. 6.
4 CC, EM, CC Coll., p. 14.
5 Birth certificate, Sarah Jane Carson, born 3 January 1866, birth registered 12 February 1866. The birthplace of her mother, Caroline née Day, is hard to read (possibly Wylies Flat), but the words 'near Singleton NSW' are clear.
6 CC, MS, p. 153.
7 CC, 'What Price Rubies?' TILL, p. 42.
8 CC, EM, GJ Coll., Box 3, Folder 11, item 13, n.p.n. (62nd page). The evidence of this 'fiery' nature was that this grandfather was described as 'holding up a stage coach at Inverell to read a political exhortation in verse (good verse too, my mother said)'.
9 See CC, 'What Price Rubies?' TILL, pp. 41–2.
10 Margaret Backhouse, interview with NW, June 1983.
11 Margaret Backhouse, June 1983.
12 CC, EM, CC Coll., p. 47.
13 CC, 'A Portrait of My Mother', WCC, p. 80.
14 Death certificate, Sarah Currie, 8 June 1898. This gives the cause of death as heart disease, and under 'Duration of last illness' notes 'Years'. The age of the youngest child, Robert, is given as one year. There were no children deceased.
15 CC, 'A Portrait of My Mother', WCC, p. 80.
16 CC, EM, CC Coll., p. 25; CC, 'A Portrait of My Mother', WCC, p. 81.
17 CC, 'A Portrait of My Mother', WCC, p. 81. The location of this boarding house is variously given as Kings Cross and the neighbouring suburb of Woolloomooloo.
18 CC, 'The Time of Your Life', WCC, p. 23.
19 CC, EM, CC Coll., p. 26.
20 Record of baptism, William Clift, St Mary's, Benares, 9 July 1865, British Library, India Office Library and Records.
21 CC, EM, GJ Coll., Box 3, Folder 11, item 13, n.p.n. (62nd page); CC, 'On England, My England', BAWO, p. 29.
22 CC, 'Things that Go Boomp in the Night', IA, p. 133.
23 Marriage certificate, William Clift and Emma Sharman, 7 September 1886.
24 Birth certificate, Emma Sharman, 2 February 1862. The maiden surname of Emma's mother is handwritten and very difficult to read.
25 Birth certificate, Sydney Clift, 20 August 1887.
26 CC, EM, GJ Coll., Box 3, Folder 11, item 13, n.p.n. (64th page).
27 CC, GGTG, CC Coll., 'Alma narrative (a)', n.p.n.
28 CC, EM, GJ Coll., Box 3, Folder 11, item 13, p. 24.
29 Margaret Backhouse, interview with NW, October 1982.
30 CC, 'The Pleasure of Leisure', BAWO, p. 146.
31 CC, 'On England, My England', BAWO, p. 29.
32 CC, EM, GJ Coll., Box 3, Folder 11, item 13, p. 22.
33 CC, 'The Pleasure of Leisure', BAWO, p. 146.
34 WK Hancock, *Australia*, Jacaranda Press, Brisbane, 1961, p. 181.
35 CC, GGTG, CC Coll., 'Alma narrative (a)', n.p.n.

36 CC, EM, CC Coll., p. 27.
37 CC, EM, CC Coll., pp. 24–7.
38 CC, 'A Portrait of My Mother', WCC, p. 81. Reference to marrying 'in a coat and skirt' from same source.
39 Marriage certificate, Sydney Clift and Amy Currie, 2 October 1916.
40 CC, 'Things that Go Boomp in the Night', IA, p. 133.
41 CC, EM, GJ Coll., Box 3, Folder 11, item 13, n.p.n. (62nd page).
42 CC, 'On England, My England', BAWO, p. 29.
43 Maisie James, oral testimony (telephone), 12/3/83.
44 CC, 'The Albatross Colony', TILL, p. 152. The following quotation is also from this source.
45 CC, EM, CC Coll., p. 46.
46 CC, EM, CC Coll., p. 24.
47 Margaret Backhouse, October 1982.

Chapter 3 — Rather an Alien Family

1 CC, interview with Hazel de Berg, National Library of Australia, 8/6/65.
2 CC, interview with Hazel de Berg, 8/6/65; CC, application to Commonwealth Literary Fund, Commonwealth Literary Fund Records, Australian Archives, 19/8/68.
3 CC, EM, GJ Coll., Box 3, Folder 11, item 13, p. 13.
4 CC, GGTG, CC Coll., 'Alma narrative (a)', n.p.n.
5 Joan King, interview with NW, 12/3/83. Joan's family lived two doors up the row from the Clifts.
6 Margaret Backhouse confirmed that this was what her father always used to say when her mother tried to persuade him to move to town, interview with NW, October 1982.
7 CC, GGTG, CC Coll., 'Alma narrative (a)', n.p.n.
8 The mother's bitterness about living in the quarry cottage is presented as still going on when Alma's daughter Christine Morley is fourteen — ie about twenty years after the marriage. See CC, GGTG, CC Coll., 'Christine (Justin) narrative (a)', p. 17.
9 CC, 'The Awakening', Australasian Post, 11/7/46. The following quotation is also from this source.
10 CC, GGTG, CC Coll., 'Alma narrative (d)', n.p.n.
11 CC, one page unnamed typescript (a direct continuation of 'Alma narrative (d)'), GJ Coll., Box 5, Folder 22, item 46.
12 CC, 'A Portrait of My Mother', WCC, p. 82.
13 Margaret Backhouse, October 1982.
14 The original edition (1871) consisted of three lectures, but although this remained in print, Ruskin soon put out a small edition comprised of only the first two lectures, for he saw the third as 'following the subject too far'. It was this that became a keepsake for so many liberal middle class families; by the 1906 edition, 110 000 copies had been sold. It was this edition that Syd would have given to Amy. Passages quoted here are from John Ruskin, Sesame and Lilies, George Allen, London, 1906, pp. 150–3.
15 CC, EM, CC Coll., p. 40.
16 Margaret Backhouse, interview with NW, June 1983. Also CC, EM, CC Coll., p. 47.
17 Margaret Backhouse, October 1982.
18 CC, 'A Death in the Family', IA, p. 103.
19 Margaret Backhouse, October 1982.

20 CC, EM, CC Coll., p.11.
21 Margaret Backhouse, October 1982.
22 CC, EM, CC Coll., p.12.
23 Mrs Richardson, interview with NW, 14/3/83.
24 Roy Phillis, interview with NW, 12/3/83.
25 Roy Phillis and Cliff Sweet, interview with NW, 12/3/83.
26 Mrs Richardson, 14/3/83; Joan King, 12/3/83.
27 Roy Phillis and Cliff Sweet, 12/3/83.
28 CC, EM, CC Coll., p. 21.
29 Roy Phillis, 12/3/83.
30 CC, EM, CC Coll., pp. 15, 22.
31 Roy Phillis and Cliff Sweet, 12/3/83. When asked if their old workmate had got his
   nickname 'because of his views and his manner', the answer was vague, and it wasn't
   at all clear that the original Chidley was even remembered.
32 Laurence Sterne, *The Life and Opinions of Tristram Shandy*, Penguin Books,
   Middlesex, 1977, pp. 79, 120, 160, 347, 243.
33 CC, GGTG, CC Coll., 'Christine (Justin) narrative(a)', pp. 15–16.
34 CC, EM, CC Coll., p. 45.
35 CC, 'The Pleasure of Leisure', BAWO, pp. 145–8.
36 CC, EM, GJ Coll., Box 3, Folder 11, item 13, n.p.n. (41st page).
37 CC, 'Banners, Causes and Convictions', WCC, p. 25.
38 CC, EM, CC Coll., p. 21.
39 NW, 'The Unemployed Who Kicked', MA, Macquarie University, 1975, pp. 355–67.
40 CC, EM, CC Coll., pp. 30–1.
41 CB MacPherson, *Democracy in Alberta: The Theory and Practice of a Quasi-Party
   System*, University of Toronto Press, Toronto, 1953, p. 108, cited by Jon Stratton, *Race
   Daze*, Pluto Press, Annandale, 1999, p. 26. Although MacPherson writes about the
   situation in Canada, his study is apposite because it deals with the appeal of the
   theory in the 1930s, and in an area which relied on primary as well as secondary
   industry. In the province of Alberta, the Social Credit League took 53 out of 65 seats
   in the election of 1935 — and continued to rule until 1971.
42 The ideological connection between Social Credit and One Nation (and, earlier,
   between Social Credit and Eric Butler's Australian League of Rights) is pointed out by
   Jon Stratton, pp. 25–7.
43 CC, 'The Pleasure of Leisure', BAWO, p. 145.
44 CC, EM, CC Coll., pp. 21, 32.
45 CC, EM, CC Coll., p. 24.
46 CC, 'A Rift in My Lute', BAWO, p. 23.
47 Laurence Sterne, p. 333.
48 Mrs Richardson, 14/3/83.
49 CC, EM, GJ Coll., p. 49; confirmed by Margaret Backhouse, October 1982.
50 Syd's workmates, Roy Phillis and Cliff Sweet, commented on this, 12/3/83.
51 Roy Phillis and Cliff Sweet, 12/3/83.
52 Mrs Richardson, 14/3/83. Mrs Richardson lived next door to *Hilldrop*, the house the
   Clifts bought in about 1935, and was still there when I interviewed her. She had also
   known the Clifts when they lived down beside the creek.
53 The description of Amy and Syd's drinking was given by Mrs Davies, former
   proprietor of the North Kiama shop. This account was not actually given to me, but

to my godmother, Bertha Knight, who was matron of Kiama Hospital for many years. In March 1983, when I was due to come to Kiama to do interviews, Bertha rang Mrs Davies to arrange a time for me to speak to her, and — as often happens — the informant's memory was instantly prompted to recollection. In evaluating this evidence, I believe that its credibility is increased by the fact that Mrs Davies was — of all the women of North Kiama — the closest to Amy Clift, in terms of interests and class. I also believe that it is relevant that she told this to a highly respected woman, who was closer to her age than I was. It was not said as something salacious or shocking, but simply as a piece of information. As to the men's memories, it was Cliff Sweet and Roy Phillis who remembered having a beer with Syd Clift after work — sometimes at the 'Parliament', outside the Davies' shop.

54 CC, EM, GJ Coll., Box 3, Folder 11, item 13, n.p.n. (33rd page).
55 CC, EM, CC Coll., pp. 6, 14; CC, 'A Portrait of My Mother', WCC, pp. 80–3.
56 CC, 'Don't Fence Me In', BAWO, p. 46.
57 CC, 'Don't Fence Me In', BAWO, p. 46; CC, 'Soldiering On', TILL, p. 181.
58 Mrs Davies, oral testimony (telephone), 13/3/83.
59 Joan King, 12/3/83.
60 Mrs Richardson, 14/3/83.
61 CC, EM, CC Coll., p. 44.
62 CC, EM, GJ Coll., Box 3, Folder 11, item 13, n.p.n. (66th page); Margaret Backhouse confirmed that her mother was indeed given this name.
63 CC, EM, CC Coll., p. 46 re High Priestess; p. 5 re wifely service.
64 Mrs Richardson remarked upon the way none of the family helped Mrs Clift. Margaret Backhouse (June 1983) also stated that she and her brother and sister were not expected to help around the house. This is also made clear in CC, EM, CC Coll., p. 44; CC, EM, GJ Coll., Box 3, Folder 11, item 13, n.p.n. (39th page).
65 CC, 'On Being a Private Ham', TILL, p.132.
66 CC, EM, CC Coll., p. 5.
67 Mrs Richardson, 14/3/83.
68 CC, EM, CC Coll., pp. 42–6.
69 CC, interview with Hazel de Berg, 8/6/65, re mother writing poetry and burning it.
70 CC, EM, CC Coll., pp. 46–7.
71 CC, 'The Magic Carpet of Learning', BAWO, p. 180.
72 DH Lawrence, *Sons and Lovers*, Penguin, Middlesex, 1966, p. 56.
73 CC, EM, GJ Coll., Box 3, Folder 11, item 13, n.p.n. (62nd page to 68th page). The subsequent quotations and descriptions of visits to grandparents are from this source also.
74 Marg Weston, oral testimony, 8/2/83. Neil Simmons (oral testimony, 13/3/83) remarked upon Will Clift's clipped moustache and summed up: 'He was an English gentleman'.
75 Mrs Richardson, 14/3/83. Joan King (12/3/83) remembered that, as a child, she was very frightened of Emma, whom she would see walk through the Cutting to North Kiama every week, with two or three library books held in a leather strap and her back like a ramrod.
76 Mrs Richardson, 14/3/83. This kind of remark was also made by Cliff Sweet and Roy Phillis, 12/3/83.
77 CC, 'On Being a Kangaroo', TILL, p. 266.
78 Mrs Richardson, 14/3/83.

79 Cedric Flower, whose own voice was beautifully modulated, commented on this, adding that 'Charm would sometimes put on what I used to call her "poetry-speaking voice". "Come off it, Charm!" I used to say, and she would burst out laughing'. Cedric Flower, interview with NW, 17/9/89.

80 CC, 'On Losing One's Good Name', IA, p. 19.

81 Mrs Richardson, 14/3/83.

82 CC, interview with Hazel de Berg, 8/6/65.

83 Margaret Backhouse, October 1982.

84 According to Margaret Backhouse (June 1983), James Currie lived with his sons on soldier settler farms in the Griffith area, and on a couple of occasions came to visit the family in Kiama, at which time Margaret would play up to his Scottish sympathies by dancing a highland fling. A photograph shows that there was also at least one visit in the other direction: Margaret is one of a number of children with Grandpa on a cart on the farm. It seems this was before Charmian was born. Charmian never mentions any memories of this grandparent.

85 Joan King, 12/3/83.

86 CC, 'Other People's Houses', WCC, p. 33.

Chapter 4 — A Free Child

1 CC, MS, p. 75.

2 CC, EM, CC Coll., pp. 30–1; CC, 'A Rift in My Lute', BAWO, p. 23.

3 CC, EM, GJ Coll., Box 3, Folder 11, item 13, p. 16. In the later version of this text, the word 'formally' has been changed to 'cheerfully every day'. CC, EM, CC Coll., p. 15.

4 CC, 'Goodbye Mr Chips', TILL, p. 298.

5 CC, EM, 'Miranda narrative', GJ Coll., Box 5, Folder 4, no item number, n.p.n. (following p. 11).

6 In GGTG, 'Alma narrative (b)', p. 36, Christine Morley, reaching adolescence, announces that she doesn't want to be a schoolteacher 'any more'. In a similar scene in EM, Cressida's mother is 'amazed' at the teenage girl's desire to go to art school and protests: 'But you used to always say that you wanted to be a schoolteacher'. CC, EM, GJ Coll., Box 3, Folder 11, item 13, n.p.n. (48th page).

7 CC, 'Winter Solstice', WCC, p. 60.

8 CC, interview with Hazel de Berg, National Library of Australia, 8/6/65.

9 CC, GGTG, CC Coll., 'Christine (Justin) narrative(a)', p.8.

10 CC, MS, p. 75.

11 CC, EM, GJ Coll., Box 5, Folder 4, no item number, three loose pages of first-person narrative, p. 20.

12 CC, EM, GJ Coll., Box 3, Folder 11, item 13, p. 25.

13 CC, EM, CC Coll., p. 24.

14 CC, EM, CC Coll., p. 19.

15 Margaret Backhouse, interview with NW, October 1982.

16 CC, EM, CC Coll., p. 23.

17 CC, EM, CC Coll., pp. 9–11.

18 CC, GGTG, 'Christine (Justin) narrative (a)', p. 9.

19 CC, 'On Losing One's Good Name', IA, p. 20.

20 CC, EM, GJ Coll., Box 3, Folder 11, item 13, p. 19.

21 CC, EM, CC Coll., p. 18; Margaret Backhouse (October 1982) confirmed that the Clift children were the only ones to surf Bombo beach.

22 Roy Phillis and Cliff Sweet marvelled about Charmian as a young girl surfing the back line of breakers at Bombo beach. Interview with NW, 12/3/83.

23 CC, 'A Death in the Family', IA, p. 102. Most of this description was lifted straight from the text of EM.

24 CC, EM, CC Coll., p. 16.

25 CC, WTTPG, pp. 21, 195. Selina also appears in the one page of typescript which is perhaps a very early draft for this novel. Here the unnamed girl narrator, her brother Tammy and the other kids go and spy on the old woman. GJ Coll., Box 5, Folder 22, item 46.

26 Margaret Backhouse could remember the Selina story, and the younger children giving themselves a thrill by creeping up to look at the woman.

27 CC, GGTG, 'Christine (Justin) narrative (a)', pp. 8, 10–12.

28 Roy Phillis and Cliff Sweet, 12/3/83.

29 Roy Phillis and Cliff Sweet, 12/3/83.

30 Mrs Richardson, interview with NW, 14/3/83.

31 Margaret Backhouse, October 1982.

32 CC, 'A Death in the Family', IA, p. 101.

33 Margaret Backhouse, October 1982. Same source for earlier reference to Charmian and Barré as 'mates'.

34 CC, EM, CC Coll., p. 47.

35 CC, GGTG, CC Coll., 'Christine (Justin) narrative (a)', p. 15.

36 CC, EM, GJ Coll., Box 3, Folder 11, item 13, n.p.n. (42nd and 43rd pages).

37 CC, EM, 'Miranda material', GJ Coll., Box 5, Folder 4, no item number, three loose pages: pp. 4, 9, n.p.n. (following p. 11).

38 CC, 'The End of the Morning', GJ Coll., Box 5, Folder 3, item 3. Subsequent quotations are also from this text.

39 CC, interview with Hazel de Berg, 8/6/65.

40 CC, 'On Little Noddy, Christopher Robin, Gargantua, Don Quixote, and All That Lot', BAWO, p. 94. This is described in almost identical words in 'The Magic Carpet of Learning', BAWO, p. 180. In the 'Little Noddy' essay, the author actually gives her age as seven. In the other version, she is eight — which is also the age she gives for this event in the National Library interview. I have changed the age in the passage quoted, because Charmian also gave eight as the age she was when she made her discovery of poetry (see note 48). However, readers should be aware that Clift used certain key ages — eight, nine, fourteen — for events, and there was obviously a bit of flexibility.

41 CC, interview with Hazel de Berg, 8/6/65.

42 CC, 'Read Any Good Books Lately?', TILL, p. 146.

43 In contrast to this, Margaret (October 1982) commented that she herself 'never questioned' her father 'at all', but that Charmian 'did start to query and to question and she found out he was wrong'. Margaret added: 'But I never thought he ever would be. That's just the difference'.

44 CC, 'Read Any Good Books Lately?', TILL, p. 146.

45 CC, EM, CC Coll., p. 22. In the essays 'Read Any Good Books Lately?' and 'On Little Noddy [...]', the author repeats phrases from this description.

46 CC, GGTG, CC Coll., 'Christine (Justin) narrative(a)', p. 10.

47 CC, 'On Little Noddy [...]', BAWO, p. 94; 'The Magic Carpet of Learning', BAWO, p. 180.

48 CC, 'On Being a Private Ham', TILL, p.133. The description here of the author's experience of sitting on the woodblock on laundry day and discovering poetry when hearing her mother start declaiming Byron is almost identical to the earlier description regarding the discovery of the novel.

49 CC, 'On Little Noddy [...]', BAWO, p. 94.

50 CC, 'On Being a Private Ham', TILL, p.133.

51 CC, interview with Hazel de Berg, 8/6/65.

52 Mrs Richardson, 14/3/83.

53 Cecily Leatham, oral testimony, 8/2/83.

54 Mrs Telfer (sister of Miss Vi Turner), letter to NW, 10/4/83. Mrs Telfer described her sister's pride in Charmian, and the way she would show the exercise book years later. Miss Turner kept her interest in her former pupil to the end, and purchased a copy of *Images in Aspic*, which Mrs Telfer kindly gave me.

55 Joan Fraser, a long-term Kiama resident, sent me photocopies of eight pages of Charmian's exercise book. These had been given to her mother by her friend, Miss Edna Turner, another sister of Miss Vi Turner. These bear the inscription 'Work done by Charmian Clift when in 4th class. V Turner's'. Joan Fraser, letter to NW, 10/1/96.

56 CC, 'Even the Thrush Has Wings', GJ Coll., Box 5, Folder 4, item 5. It is clear that this was submitted for publication before the author went overseas in 1951, because the author used her husband's address at the Sydney *Sun* office. The story was published in 1983 in Garry Kinnane (ed.), *Strong-man from Piraeus and Other Stories*, Nelson, Melbourne, pp. 1–9. Quotations cited can all be found in the published story.

57 He also has a turn of phrase that sounds like Syd's English dialect, rather than working class Australian speech. ' "Chin up, lass," he bellow[s] with awkward cheerfulness' when Tina sobs for sympathy.

58 The incident of dancing at the showground is based on a real event. Margaret Backhouse remembered that she was chosen to be May Queen. This incident recurs in CC, EM, Box 5, Folder 4, no item number, p. 48. Here, Cordelia is the Queen, but Cressida is chosen to be one of the dancers.

59 CC, 'Feeling Slightly Tilted?', WCC, p. 200.

Chapter 5 — The Dragging Years of Dependence

1 CC, EM, GJ Coll., Box 3, Folder 11, item 13, n.p.n. (45th page).

2 Through the even earlier drafts, Miranda is nine. CC, EM, 'Miranda narrative', GJ Coll., Box 5, Folder 4, no item number.

3 CC, EM, GJ Coll., Box 3, Folder 11, item 13, n.p.n. (38th page).

4 CC, EM, GJ Coll., Box 5, Folder 4, no item number, p. 48. This fragment starts at page 48, with text revised from that on the 38th page of the main section of text (at Box 3, Folder 11, item 13) re Cordelia's remoteness in her final year of school.

5 Margaret Backhouse agreed with this version of events, interview with NW, October 1982.

6 CC, EM, GJ Coll., Box 3, Folder 11, item 13, n.p.n. (45th and 46th pages).

7 CC, EM, GJ Coll., Box 3, Folder 11, item 13, n.p.n. (41st to 45th pages).

8 CC, EM, GJ Coll., Box 3, Folder 11, item 13, n.p.n. (45th page).

9 In the fictional account, the length and loneliness of these two successive summers are strengthened because the author remembers them together as one summer when the young narrator is left out by both sister and brother.

10 CC, EM, GJ Coll., Box 5, Folder 4, no item number, p. 48. For this incident, see also CC, 'A Pride of Lions', BAWO, p. 170. There is no doubt that this anecdote has at least some basis in fact. Without any prompting, Joan King volunteered the information that a twelve year old boy from the Drennan family died of tetanus that he developed after climbing through a wire fence. Oral testimony, 8/2/83.

11 CC, EM, GJ Coll., Box 3, Folder 11, item 13, n.p.n. (46th and 47th page).

12 CC, EM, GJ Coll., Box 3, Folder 11, item 13, n.p.n. (47th page).

13 CC, EM, GJ Coll., Box 3, Folder 11, item 13, n.p.n. (47th page).

14 CC, EM, GJ Coll., Box 3, Folder 11, item 13, n.p.n. (51st page).

15 CC, EM, GJ Coll., Box 3, Folder 11, item 13, n.p.n. (48th page).

16 CC, 'Goodbye Mr Chips', TILL, p. 298.

17 CC, 'Goodbye Mr Chips', TILL, pp. 298–9.

18 CC, EM, GJ Coll., Box 3, Folder 11, item 13, n.p.n. (54th page).

19 CC, EM, GJ Coll., Box 3, Folder 11, item 13, n.p.n. (55th and 56th pages).

20 CC, EM, GJ Coll., Box 3, Folder 11, item 13, n.p.n. (51st and 52nd pages). In writing her friend's name, Clift varies between 'Thelly' and 'Thellie'. I have standardised these to 'Thellie'.

21 CC, EM, GJ Coll., Box 3, Folder 11, item 13, n.p.n. (60th page).

22 CC, EM, GJ Coll., Box 3, Folder 11, item 13, n.p.n. (54th page).

23 CC, EM, GJ Coll., Box 3, Folder 11, item 13, n.p.n. (49th page).

24 CC, EM, GJ Coll., Box 3, Folder 11, item 13, n.p.n. (51st page).

25 CC, EM, GJ Coll., Box 3, Folder 11, item 13, n.p.n. (57th to 59th pages). CC wrote this first draft passage in one long paragraph. I have broken it into paragraphs and have added the quotation marks for direct speech, but I have not otherwise edited the prose. My only other change has been to include the phrase '[from my parents' bottom drawer]'. In a slightly earlier passage, the author referred to sneaking in and looking at this text by Havelock Ellis which her parents kept hidden away.

26 For example, see Garry Kinnane's summary of this, *George Johnston: A Biography*, Nelson, Melbourne, 1986, p. 73: 'Her impatience for experience got her into some risky situations, such as hitching rides on the highway with travelling salesmen and taxi drivers, and having to battle her way out of trouble'.

27 Clifford Meredith, letter to NW, n.d. This letter arrived in May 1983 in response to a general request for information about CC which I had sent to the newspapers. I wrote back (1/6/83) requesting more information, and a second letter arrived in June 1983. Meredith was a subaltern in whom Charmian confided when she was in the army in Sydney in 1943. For a long time I was not sure about this particular account of Clift's 'revelation', but as Meredith also cited Charmian Clift's confession about the birth of her daughter, Jennifer — a good fifteen years before this information, and especially the name of the child, was publicly known — I accept his account. He also included a little memo that Charmian had written to him on Australian Military Forces paper.

28 See Garry Kinnane, p. 172 . 'In her cups and in tears she confessed to [Charles] Sriber: "I have always been a bad girl, since I was thirteen and went with taxi-drivers." '

29 Maisie James, oral testimony (telephone), 14/3/83; Marg Weston, oral testimony, 8/2/83.

30 CC, GGTG, CC Coll., 'Christine (Justin) narrative (a)', p. 5.

31 CC, 'A Pride of Lions?', BAWO, p.171.

32 CC, EM, GJ Coll., Box 3, Folder 11, item 13, n.p.n. (47th page).

33 CC, GGTG, CC Coll., 'Alma narrative (c)', p.4.

34 CC, two loose pages of typescript re Christine Morley, GJ Coll., Box 5, Folder 22, item 46, n.p.n. Reference to Syd's comments also from this source.

35 CC, GGTG, CC Coll., 'Alma narrative (b)', p. 21.

36 CC, GGTG, CC Coll., 'Alma narrative (b)', p. 30. Subsequent quotation pp. 30–1. This is the end of this fragment of draft.

37 By this time, I had visited Margaret a number of times, and we no longer used the tape recorder. From the time of the first interview, I had mentioned the text of EM. Although I had warned Margaret that she would probably find it painful, she was naturally very keen to read it. I posted her a photocopy of the typescript, and a couple of months later, when I was next in Sydney, I went to visit her. Her pain about the subject matter was still very fresh.

38 After excerpts from Garry Kinnane's biography were published in the *Sydney Morning Herald,* Margaret wrote a letter of protest to the Editor, asking why her 'beloved sister' had been presented 'in large letters, as some kind of scarlet woman'. (Letter dated 4/10/86; published 16/10/86).

39 CC, EM, GJ Coll., Box 3, Folder 11, item 13, n.p.n. (50th page).

40 CC, GGTG, CC Coll., 'Alma narrative (b)', pp. 26–7.

41 Marg Weston, 8/2/83.

42 *The Gleam* (Wollongong school magazine), 1939, pp. 18–19; *Wollongong High School, A History of Fifty Years 1916–1966.* (Copies viewed at Wollongong High School, 1983.)

43 Allan Brownlee, letter to NW, 12/3/85.

44 *The Gleam,* 1939 (records Intermediate results for 1938).

45 CC, interview with Hazel de Berg, National Library of Australia, 8/6/65; CC, 'Preserver with a Book', WCC, p. 248.

46 For example, in CC, 'Goodbye Mr Chips', TILL, p. 298.

47 This was one of the sketches referred to in endnote 39. It was given to me by Margaret Backhouse. I subsequently gave it to Suzanne Chick. Another is among the family photos in Jason Johnston's possession and is reproduced here in the first collection of images.

48 CC, EM, GJ Coll., Box 5, Folder 4, no item number, p. 49; Box 3, Folder 11, item 13, n.p.n. (52nd page).

49 Mrs Richardson (14/3/83), Cliff Sweet (12/3/83), Roy Phillips (12/3/83) and Neil Simmons (13/3/83) all denied that Charmian had been beautiful. Indeed, when I even asked the question, they seemed to think that I had confused the two sisters.

50 Mrs Davies, oral testimony (telephone), 13/3/83.

51 CC, interview with Hazel de Berg, 8/6/65. Subsequent quotations are from the same source.

52 Information from Graham Tucker, who was told this by a Mrs Delaney, a judge in the competition.

53 Cecily Leatham, oral testimony, 8/2/83. Clift herself wrote about meeting up with old associates (including Thellie) on her return to Kiama in late 1964. ' "Do you remember," they said, "how you always swore you'd get out of this town and go and see the world?" ', CC, 'Youth Revisited', IA, p. 25.

54 CC, interview with Hazel de Berg, 8/6/65.

55 Clifford Tolchard, 'My Husband George: My Wife Charmian', *Walkabout,* January 1969.

56 CC, interview with Hazel be Berg, 8/6/65.

57 Jean Brown, oral testimony (telephone), 12/3/83.

58 CC, GGTG, 'Christine (Justin) narrative (b)', n.p.n.

59 Roy Phillis and Cliff Sweet, interview with NW, 12/3/83.

60 Roy Phillis and Cliff Sweet, 12/3/83.

Chapter 6 — A Country Girl's Search

1   CC, interview with Hazel de Berg, National Library of Australia, 8/6/65.

2   CC, interview with Hazel de Berg, 8/6/65.

3   CC, GGTG, CC Coll., 'Christine (Justin) narrative(b)', n.p.n.

4   Nona Wood, interview with NW, 29/8/96. The particular pine trees growing at
    Manly, which prompted this conversation, were Norfolk pines. This distinctive pine
    also grew at Kiama, around the harbour and on the headland near the showground.
    The clear reference to Kiama's Norfolk pine trees in this anecdote would seem to
    clear up a small mystery. In the essay 'The Wrong Road' (WCC, p. 20), Clift wrote:
    'When I was eighteen I took a wrong road through great Norfolk pines, that led me
    to disaster'. Both Garry Kinnane, *George Johnston: A Biography*, Nelson, Melbourne,
    1986, p. 305, endnote 9, and Suzanne Chick, *Searching for Charmian*, Pan
    Macmillan, Sydney, 1994, p. 22, assume that the disaster referred to here was the
    author's first pregnancy. I believe this is unlikely, because Clift in her column never
    flirted with the revelation of that particular secret. It is more likely that the author
    was thinking of this Kiama scandal, and misremembered her age at the time of this
    event. Clift wasn't very good at remembering ages and dates, and would often
    combine two events together. I believe she has confused the age of eighteen —
    which she was when she left Kiama for Sydney in 1941 — with her age when she left
    home for Lithgow in 1939.

5   CC, GGTG, CC Coll., 'Christine (Justin) narrative (b)', n.p.n.

6   Clifford Tolchard, 'My Husband George: My Wife Charmian', *Walkabout*, January
    1969; CC, interview with Hazel de Berg, 8/6/65.

7   Lithgow Hospital has no records from this period. In the GGTG passage cited, which
    was written much closer to the time than the 1965 interview, Clift put the time at six
    months. This would fit the time frame better than six weeks.

8   CC, GGTG, CC Coll., 'Christine (Justin) narrative (b)', n.p.n.

9   CC, interview with Hazel de Berg, 8/6/65.

10 CC, GGTG, CC Coll., 'Christine (Justin) narrative (b)', n.p.n.

11 Margaret Backhouse, interview with NW, October 1982.

12 CC, EM, GJ Coll., Box 3, Folder 11, item 13, n.p.n. (69th page).

13 CC, 'On Gothic Tales', TILL, pp. 80–1.

14 CC, 'On Being a Private Ham', TILL, p. 134.

15 CC, 'On Gothic Tales', TILL, p. 81.

16 CC, GGTG, CC Coll., 'Christine (Justin) narrative (b)', n.p.n.

17 Margaret Backhouse, October 1982.

18 *Pix*, 17/5/41.

19 CC, interview with Hazel de Berg, 8/6/65, said the prize was £20–25. In the interview
    with Clifford Tolchard for *Walkabout*, Clift gave the sum as £50.

20 CC, interview with Hazel de Berg, 8/6/65.

21 Margaret Backhouse, interview with NW, January 1984. Margaret was at that time
    working for Noel Ruby.

22 *The Film Weekly*, 25/5/39, 15/6/39. Copies in possession of Harry Pike.

23 Harry Pike, interview with NW, 21/9/90. Pike continued working as chief electrician at the Minerva for a number of years after David Martin's involvement ended. He did not remember Charmian Clift, as technical staff did not usually mix with front-of-house staff.

24 CC, interview with Hazel de Berg, 8/6/65.

25 *Mr Smart Guy* program, Whitehall Productions, 18/5/41 (in possession of Harry Pike); *Encyclopedia of Australian Art.*

26 Information re affair, Suzanne Chick, oral testimony (telephone), 20/8/91; the information came from Cedric Flower. In *Searching for Charmian*, p. 98, this appears as a reference to an unnamed 'notable stage designer'. Constable was later also to become a friend of George Johnston. In 1953, during discussions with Angus & Robertson over the collaborative novel *The Big Chariot*, Johnston pleaded with his publishers to commission Constable to do the jacket. GJ added that he would 'write separately' to Constable, as he 'owed him a couple of letters'. This dispels any notion that Constable may have been the father of Clift's child. GJ to Beatrice Davis, 17/2/53. Angus & Robertson Collection, Mitchell Library, State Library of NSW.

27 CC, GGTG, CC Coll., 'Christine (Justin) narrative (b)', n.p.n.

28 Clifford Tolchard, 'My Husband George: My Wife Charmian'.

29 CC, interview with Hazel de Berg, 8/6/65.

30 See chapter 7.

31 Suzanne Chick (p. 98), quotes Cedric Flower as saying 'What I can't understand is why you are here at all. There was a place up at Redfern that performed abortions'.

32 CC, 'Death by Misadventure', BAWO, pp. 190–2. As I state in the Notes to that collection (p. 325), the typescript for this essay appears among Clift's other essay typescripts in the GJ Coll., but I have not found it in published form. There is no way of determining whether this was because it was rejected, or because the author never submitted it.

33 CC, EM, CC Coll., p. 31.

34 I asked Margaret this before Garry Kinnane raised the matter either privately with Margaret or publicly in his biography. By this time, Margaret and I had become friendly, and the question was not asked during a taped interview, but over a cup of coffee in the kitchen. At the time, I believed that Margaret's ignorance of the matter was genuine. However, I have come to revise that opinion.

35 Toni Burgess, interview with NW (notes only), October 1984.

36 Margaret Backhouse, October 1982.

37 Suzanne Chick, pp. 243, 287.

38 CC, 'Death by Misadventure', BAWO, p. 192.

39 Information from Barbara Jefferis, interview with NW, 26/2/92. In 1950 Jefferis interviewed Matron Shaw about the procedure followed by unmarried mothers at Crown Street. See chapter 10.

40 See Suzanne Chick, p. 312, quoting from Matron Shaw, 'Women's Move on Adoption Laws', *Women's Weekly*, 7/10/53.

41 There are two different versions of Matron Shaw's regulations re relinquishing mothers' seeing and feeding of their children. Suzanne Chick (p. 308) quotes a recollection of a former Crown Street nurse (from Patricia Hayes (ed.), *Some Recollections of Working at Crown Street, The Women's Hospital*, March 1990) who remembered that Matron Shaw 'maintained that all babies are entitled to be cuddled by their mothers and to be breastfed for at least their first couple of weeks'. On the other hand, Barbara Jefferis (26/2/92) remembered that when, in her 1950 research interview with the Matron, she asked Miss

Shaw if the mothers saw their babies, Matron replied: 'Some do, but very much against our advice. We strongly advise the girls never to see the baby. However, if they want to see it, they're allowed to'. Jefferis's account seems more likely, because it reflects standard practice at the time. As Matron did not want the adoption process to 'come unstuck', she would obviously not encourage the mothers to bond with their babies.

42 Janise Beaumont, 'Daughter of a Legend', *Sunday Telegraph*, 13/3/94. Suzanne Chick noted in this interview that a former secretary of Crown Street Hospital and close friend of Edna Shaw — now a '92-year-old lady' with 'a wonderful memory' — had got in touch. 'She said, "Edna told me all about you. I knew about Charmian. I knew about you being born."'

43 Birth certificate, Jennifer Clift.

44 Barbara Jefferis, 26/2/92.

45 Suzanne Chick in the *Sunday Telegraph* interview with Janise Beaumont stated that the former secretary of Crown Street told her that her mother nursed her.

46 Kate Inglis, *Living Mistakes: Mothers who Consented to Adoption*, George Allen & Unwin, Sydney, 1984; Libby Harkness, *Looking for Lisa*, Random House, Sydney, 1991.

47 Garry Kinnane, p. 305.

48 Information, Martin Johnston.

49 CC, GGTG, CC Coll., 'Christine (Martin) narrative', pp. 4, 9.

50 CC, 'On Coming to a Bad End', WCC, p. 242.

51 Clifford Meredith, letter to NW, n.d. (received May 1983); Bruce Kneale, interview with NW, 2/3/85.

52 Suzanne Chick (p. 229) relates that 'Charles [Sriber] told the story of Charmian, in her cups, weeping and weeping in her kitchen and telling him how she'd been a bad girl and had a baby long before she met George'. Chick (p. 216) quotes Barbara Blackman as saying that 'Apparently Charmian had rambled on in her cups' to Maisie Drysdale 'but Maisie hadn't taken much notice. Thought she'd made it up. "She always was a drama queen." That's how she put it'.

53 CC, GGTG, CC Coll., 'Christine (Martin) narrative', p. 4.

54 CC, WTTPG, p. 102.

55 Nona Wood, 29/8/96.

56 The name 'Porters Garden' appears on some old maps as the name for Bombo beach. Just as the author borrowed the old name 'Lebanon Bay', she may have been led by this name to borrow the title of Delius's music.

57 CC, application to Commonwealth Literary Fund, Commonwealth Literary Fund Records, Australian Archives, 19/8/68.

PART II — THE BIG ADVENTURE

Chapter 7 — The Terms of a Novel

1 CC, interview with Hazel de Berg, National Library of Australia, 8/6/65.

2 Margaret Backhouse, interview with NW, October 1982.

3 Central Army Records Office, St Kilda Road, Melbourne, letter to NW, 26/10/84, CC's service record; Australian Army, Soldier Career Management Agency, letter to NW, 13/12/96, Margaret Backhouse's service record.

4 Information on AWAS from Lorna Ollif, *Women in Khaki*, Australian Women's Services Association of New South Wales, Sydney 1981. In April 1943 the Australian Women's

Recruiting Depot was established, and a new recruitment drive started. By the end of this peak year the AWAS was to double from 11 000 to 22 000 servicewomen.

5 CC, interview with Hazel de Berg, 8/6/65.

6 CC, 'Soldiering On', TILL, pp. 182–3.

7 Margaret Backhouse, Service and Casualty Form.

8 Nona Wood, interview with NW, 29/8/96. Subsequent quotation also from this source.

9 Margaret Backhouse, October 1982.

10 Nona Wood, 29/8/96.

11 Barbara Jefferis, interview with NW, 26/2/92. Charmian told this story to her friend Toni Hazelwood — later Burgess — around Christmas 1949. Toni in turn told it to her friend Barbara Jefferis a few months later. In the interview, Barbara Jefferis was very clear in her memories of Toni's account — down to the fact that they were sitting in a coffee shop at the time. The story of Charmian taking the present to Crown Street is confirmed by the memories of the former hospital secretary whom Suzanne Chick cites in her interview with Janise Beaumont, 'Daughter of a Legend', *Sunday Telegraph*, 13/3/94. Here Charmian's return with presents is described as occurring on a number of Christmases following the birth. However, Charmian was in Melbourne for Christmas 1944 and 1945, and in Kiama for Christmas 1946, so it probably only occurred once.

12 CC, 'A Pride of Lions', BAWO, pp. 172–3.

13 Nona Wood, 29/8/96.

14 CC, 'Soldiering On', TILL, p. 181.

15 Nona Wood, 29/8/96.

16 There is a reference to this in 'Soldiering On', p. 182. Gerry brings along a copy to the 25th AWAS reunion which CC attends in 1966.

17 Nona Wood, 29/8/96.

18 CC, 'Soldiering On', TILL, p. 182.

19 It is relocated onto the suburban golf links where the novel's narrator and his brother Jack had played as children — which in turn was borrowed from the golf course where George Johnston and his brother Jack had played.

20 GJ, MBJ, pp. 325–6. The two subsequent quotations are also from these pages.

21 GJ, MBJ, pp. 354–5.

22 'Practising' is another characteristic phrase of Clift's which appears in this section of MBJ. She uses it in the essay about wartime romance — 'A Pride of Lions', BAWO, pp. 169–73.

23 Clifford Meredith, letter to NW, n.d. (received May 1983). See endnote 27, chapter 5.

24 Margaret Backhouse, Particulars of Discharge Proceedings, 5/6/44. Margaret Backhouse, October 1982.

25 Central Army Records Office, 26/10/84, CC's service record; Alan Trengrove, 'Partners — It's in Writing', *Sun*, 6/7/66.

26 Douglas M Barrie, letters to NW, 16/10/90, 25/10/90.

27 Central Army Records Office, 26/10/84, CC's service record.

28 Clifford Tolchard, 'My Husband George: My Wife Charmian', *Walkabout*, January 1969.

29 CC, interview with Hazel de Berg, 8/6/65.

30 CC, 'Other Woman', *Australia National Journal*, vol. 6, no 6, May 1945. This was also included in the journal's annual anthology, *Australia Week-end Book* 4, Ure Smith Pty Ltd, 1945; republished in Connie Burns and Marygai McNamara (ed.), *Feeling Restless: Australian Women's Short Stories 1940–1969*, Collins, Sydney, 1989.

31 CC, interview with Hazel de Berg, 8/6/65.

32 Bruce Kneale, interview with NW, 2/3/85.

33 CC, interview with Hazel de Berg, 8/6/65.

34 Clifford Tolchard, 'My Husband George: My Wife Charmian'.

35 Bruce Kneale, 2/3/85.

36 James Hall, 'And Now It's Two for the Load', *Australian,* 23/11/68.

37 This is based on accounts by GJ and CC, in Alan Trengrove, 'Partners — It's in Writing'; James Hall, 'And Now It's Two for the Load'. Bruce Kneale remembered that, after the cocktail party, he was going to meet GJ, and CC asked what was happening, so spontaneously he invited her to come along. However, CC and GJ obviously remembered the details more clearly because the meeting proved to be so important for them.

38 Alan Trengrove, 'Partners — It's in Writing'; James Hall, 'And Now it's Two for the Load'. This incident — along with the phrase 'I'm as tight as a sonofabitch'— recurs as part of the tale of the first meeting between Christine Morley and the journalist Martin Smith in GGTG, 'Christine (Martin) narrative'.

39 CC, 'A Pride of Lions', BAWO, pp. 172–3.

40 CC, 'Betrothing a Daughter', WCC, p.78.

41 Information about Leo Kenny from Edward Heffernan, interview with NW, 30/9/84. In 1983 I rang the Kenny family, and was told that they did not want to speak about the matter. Leo Kenny had already died. As to his service rank, Heffernan stated he was a flight lieutenant. Clift described him as a squadron leader in her interview with Clifford Tolchard.

42 Clifford Tolchard, 'My Husband George: My Wife Charmian'.

43 Edward Heffernan, 30/9/84.

44 No year is given with the 'March 22nd' date, but it had to be 1946. Book in my possession.

45 Edward Heffernan, 30/9/84.

46 Clifford Tolchard, 'My Husband George: My Wife Charmian'.

47 Central Army Records Office, 26/10/84, CC's service record.

48 A couple of people remembered her as being in uniform when she was first at the *Argus,* and Cressida is in uniform in the early draft CSFN quoted later in this chapter.

49 Leo Kenny to Edward Heffernan, 26/5/46. Letter in possession of Edward Heffernan.

50 Leo M Kenny, 'Singapore and the Man in the Street', *Argus Week-end Magazine,* 1/7/46.

51 CC, GGTG, 'Christine (Martin) narrative', p. 8.

52 James Hall, 'And Now It's Two for the Load'.

53 GJ, 'CSFN draft (i)', p. 3, GJ Coll., Box 3, Folder 7, item 7. Interestingly, in GGTG it is Christine Morley who says 'Welcome home' and who then thinks that Martin Smith will think her 'a complete moron'. GJ's line about the 'invincible calm quality of a woman sure of her beauty' appears in the published version of CSFN at the opening of the Lebanon Bay passage — considerably after the first meeting.

54 GJ, 'CSFN draft (i)', p. 23, GJ Coll., Box 3, Folder 7, item 7.

55 While the initial lift encounter with Cressida Morley has been dropped in the published version of the novel, the morning visit to Turley is retained. (CSFN, pp. 24–8). This section even opens with Meredith thinking (as he does in the draft, on the morning after the lift scene, and after a subsequent final row with his wife Helen): 'Gavin Turley was the shot. He would know'. In the draft, it is clear that Meredith

means that Turley would know how to contact the beautiful young lieutenant. In the published version, the reader could be entitled to wonder: 'Know what?' In this text, as Meredith is leaving, Turley just happens to remind Meredith of his former meeting with Cressida by saying that *she* has been talking about *him*.

56 Edward Heffernan, 30/9/84. Shortly after this, Leo Kenny's sister sent Heffernan the full payment for the commission, but told the painter that her brother no longer wanted the portrait. Four decades later, it was still in the artist's studio: no one had ever bothered to collect it.

Chapter 8 — A Benevolent Steamroller

1   CC, 'On *Clean Straw for Nothing*', BAWO, p. 310.
2   CC, 'On *Clean Straw for Nothing*', BAWO, p. 310.
3   GJ, MBJ, pp. 10–11.
4   GJ, 'Childhood — "The Dollikos"', GJ Coll., Box 1, Folder 4, item 7. In this, the vine is spelled 'Dollikos'. In the novel, it is spelled 'Dollicus'. I will follow the spelling of whichever text I am citing. In the novel (pp. 10–11) it is the grandmother who has a 'rare malapropism with botanical names', and is credited with giving the strange name of 'Dollicus' to the vine, whereas in the note it is the mother who supposedly misnames the plant. This change was necessary because in the novel the mother is away, so the child could not know what she called the vine. In fact, there is a vine called 'Dollicus'.
5   John Hetherington, 'An Australian Author Returns to His Native Land', *Age*, 8/2/64.
6   GJ, MBJ, p. 29.
7   GJ, 'Childhood — "The Dollikos"', GJ Coll., Box 1, Folder 4, item 7.
8   GJ, MBJ, p. 35.
9   GJ, MBJ, pp. 21–2.
10 GJ, MBJ, pp. 2–3.
11 GJ, MBJ, p. 10.
12 Garry Kinnane, *George Johnston: A Biography*, Nelson, Melbourne, 1986, p. 7, citing Chester Eagle interview with Jack and Pat Johnston, 1980.
13 GJ, MBJ, p. 90.
14 GJ, 'Childhood — "The Dollikos"', GJ Coll., Box 1, Folder 4, item 7. In the novel, the grandmother is crying when she kisses Davy, but the author avoids the declaration of the meaning of love contained in the draft version of the little scene.
15 In the novel, because Davy's mother is away nursing at the Front, she does not start bringing soldiers home until she returns in 1919 and resumes work at the nearby convalescent hospital. In life, the house became a kind of hospital outstation during the war as well. Thus from a very young age George was surrounded by talk and evidence of war, whereas in the novel (p. 11) it is from the age of seven that Davy finds his home 'inhabited' by the 'jetsom' of the war.
16 GJ, MBJ, pp. 2, 11.
17 GJ, MBJ, pp. 2, 7.
18 GJ, MBJ, p. 13. It was not only a child who could have this response to Raemaeker. A reviewer for *Philadelphia America* described the cartoonist's work as 'pitilessly true as a photograph' and *Vanity Fair* noted: 'That each cartoon is a grim, merciless portrayal of the truth will be apparent to even the meanest intelligence'. (Louis Raemaeker, *Kultur in Cartoons,* The Century Company, New York, 1917).

Art historian H R Westwood quotes the war correspondent for the London *Times* as saying that the cartoonist was 'among the half dozen men — not excluding its famous statesmen and comrades in the field — whose influence had been most decisive on the conflict as a whole'. Westwood himself declares that 'The strength of Raemaeker's cartoons was their naked realism'. (H R Westwood, 'Louis Raemaeker', *Modern Caricaturists,* Lovat Dickson Ltd, London, 1932, pp. 55–64).

19 GJ, MBJ, pp. 12–13. Johnston misspells the cartoonist's name as 'Raemaker'. This indicates that he did not have access to any of the cartoonist's work when he was writing the text, but was drawing solely on memory. In the novel, the young Davy makes his visits to the drawer to see this material after the return of his father. I have placed this information before dealing with Pop Johnston's return, because it is likely that George saw this material while the war was on. Surely current issues of the *Illustrated War News* came into the house — purchased by the invalids — and were then stored as part of the memorabilia. The three volumes of Raemaeker cartoons were available in England in 1916, and were shipped forthwith to Australia (Louis Raemaeker, *Raemaeker's Cartoons,* Land & Water, Kingsway, London, 1916).

20 GJ, MBJ, pp. 4–5.

21 GJ, MBJ, pp. 37–9.

22 GJ, MBJ, p. 42.

23 Garry Kinnane, p. 1.

24 GJ, MBJ (Angus & Robertson Imprint Classics edition), n.p.n. (following p. 367). Curiously, although this and the other notes to the novel are taken almost verbatim from Garry Kinnane's biography, neither that text nor the author of these notes is acknowledged.

25 Garry Kinnane, p. 3.

26 Indeed, the author notes: 'Because of the differences in our ages, the impression of all these excitements on us four children could not expectably have been the same'. GJ, MBJ, p. 5. It was not just age, however, which led to a difference in experiencing and remembering.

27 As to George speaking of this, see CC, PMAL, p. 61. Cedric Flower remembered Charmian's distress when George would tell this story. Interview with NW, 17/9/89.

28 Garry Kinnane, pp. 2–6.

29 Garry Kinnane, p. 21.

30 Clifford Tolchard, 'My Husband George: My Wife Charmian', *Walkabout,* January 1969.

31 Eric Partridge lists the adjective 'sonkey' or 'sonky' as meaning 'silly, stupid; idiotic' ('Australian low: C 20'). However, from the way the word was used in the Johnston family, it was clearly more like 'sook', which Partridge glosses as 'a coward; a timorous person' ('Australian: since ca 1920'). Eric Partridge, *A Dictionary of Slang and Unconventional English,* Mary Martin Books, Adelaide, 1982, Supplement, pp.1420, 1421.

32 GJ, MBJ, pp. 56–7.

33 GJ, MBJ, pp. 58, 99.

34 Garry Kinnane, pp. 12–14.

35 Garry Kinnane, p. 20.

36 John Hetherington, 'An Australian Author Returns to His Native Land': 'Johnston has never been one for philosophising [...] but will sometimes expound [...] his players-and-spectators theory. "There might be a hundred thousand spectators," he explains,

"but the players are only a handful, and some of them will play badly, some good average, some well, some will chicken out, some will disgrace themselves. The spectators have the right to cheer or boo, be thrilled, disappointed, bored, ecstatic, but at the end of the game nobody is going to remember who the spectators were — it's only the players that really matter" '.

37 GJ, MBJ, p. 57.

38 Garry Kinnane, p. 15.

39 GJ, MBJ, p. 152.

40 See GJ, MBJ, p. 112. In David's first interview with the newspaper editor, when a cadetship is offered, he is told: 'We like to take [our cadet reporters] from one of the public schools, or the University'.

41 Garry Kinnane, p. 20.

42 These three books were *Grey Gladiator, Battle of the Seaways* and *Australia at War*.

43 Garry Kinnane, p. 37.

44 Information re GJ's relationship with Elsie and the basic timetable of his travels from Garry Kinnane, pp. 43–70.

45 GJ, 'Battle Looms in Kwangsi Province', *Argus*, 23/9/44. The figure of 'a hundred thousand' is the one that Johnston would always give. See GJ, CSFN, p. 43.

46 GJ, CSFN, p. 43.

47 GJ, *Journey Through Tomorrow*, Cheshire, Melbourne, 1947, p. 271.

48 GJ often told this story. It appears in ACOC, pp. 96–9.

49 Martin Johnston used to speak of an incident which his father used to relate, about how he had been in a military aeroplane in which a fireball had calmly rolled up the aisle, and down again, then out the open doorway. Also, flying the Hump out of Burma (which Johnston did a number of times) was notoriously dangerous.

50 GJ, CSFN, pp. 21–2. This account appeared in exactly this form through all the drafts of this novel.

51 Martin Johnston, 'A Cartload of Clay', *Age*, 2/10/71. This was expressed by GJ himself in one of the drafts of CSFN: 'The only important thing about everything that had happened was that it *had*, and did not have to be done again'. GJ, 'CSFN draft (iv)', p. 1, GJ Coll., Box 3, Folder 7, item 7.

52 GJ, 'CSFN draft (i)', p. 6, GJ Coll., Box 3, Folder 7, item 7.

53 GJ, CSFN, p. 21. This crucial statement also appeared in the first draft of the novel ('CSFN draft (i)', p. 4, GJ Coll., Box 3, Folder 7, item 7).

54 GJ, *Journey Through Tomorrow*, p. 399.

55 Clifford Tolchard, 'My Husband George: My Wife Charmian'.

56 GJ, 'CSFN draft (i)', pp. 3, 5, GJ Coll., Box 3, Folder 7, item 7.

57 GJ, 'CSFN draft (i)', pp. 3, 12, GJ Coll., Box 3, Folder 7, item 7.

58 GJ, 'CSFN draft (ii)', p.7, GJ Coll., Box 3, Folder 7, item 7.

59 GJ, 'CSFN draft (i)' p. 13, GJ Coll., Box 3, Folder 7, item 7.

60 GJ, CSFN, p. 15.

61 GJ, 'CSFN draft (i)', p. 9, GJ Coll., Box 3, Folder 7, item 7.

62 GJ, CSFN, p. 13.

63 GJ, 'CSFN draft (i)', GJ Coll., Box 3, Folder 7, item 7: 'Three weeks after his return to Melbourne he met Cressida Morley again' (p. 3); the time is 'autumn, in that year of 1946' (p. 7); in the row with Helen, she reminds David that he has only been back 'a few short weeks' (p. 13). In 'CSFN draft (ii)' and 'CSFN draft (iii)', GJ Coll., Box 3,

Folder 7, item 7, it is 'now autumn' (p. 1) and David has been back a 'few weeks' (p. 2). These drafts include the final row with Helen. In what remains of 'CSFN draft (ii)', David goes to Gavin Turley's place early the next morning. We can be sure that, in the missing material, Turley would be the link, providing David Meredith with a way of contacting Cressida Morley — as he does in 'CSFN draft (i)', p. 22, and in the published version of the novel, pp. 24–8.

64 In the first draft of the novel, this springtime is symbolised by having David and Cressida meet by accident in a flower shop, on the day after the lift meeting, and after David has asked Gavin Turley how to find the young woman. This verdant setting is the perfect backdrop for the romantic moment. GJ, 'CSFN draft (i)', pp. 24–27, GJ Coll., Box 3, Folder 7, item 7.

Chapter 9 — Setting Out Together

1   CC and GJ, HV, p. 259. Veshti is speaking to Salom.
2   Greeba Jamison, interview with NW, 2/3/83.
3   John Donne, 'The Sunne Rising', Helen Gardner (ed.), *The Metaphysical Poets*, Penguin Books, Middlesex, 1966, p. 60.
4   John Donne, 'A Valediction: Forbidding Mourning', Helen Gardner (ed.), p. 74.
5   Margaret Backhouse, interview with NW, October 1982.
6   Re George: CC, 'On *Clean Straw for Nothing*', BAWO, p. 310; re Syd: 'He probably never had a conversation in his life: at least I never heard anybody else get a word in'. CC, 'The Pleasure of Leisure', BAWO, p. 145.
7   Greeba Jamison, quoted by Garry Kinnane, *George Johnston: A Biography*, Nelson, Melbourne, 1986, p. 48.
8   Geoffrey Hutton, 'He Died Alive', *Age*, 23/11/70.
9   CC, 'On *Clean Straw for Nothing*', BAWO, p. 311.
10 GJ, 'CSFN draft (i)', p. 3, GJ Coll., Box 3, Folder 7, item 7.
11 GJ, 'Childhood — "The Dollikos"', GJ Coll., Box 1, Folder 4, item 7.
12 Although the author would later identify himself with Ulysses, the romantic story of CFSN has a more direct parallel with the eternal triangle of Arthur, with his faithless wife Guinevere and his disloyal friend Lancelot. Perhaps George's tragedy was that he never realised that he himself was the Lancelot in Charmian's life.
13 GJ, '*Clean Straw for Nothing* General Notes', pp. 4–5, GJ Coll., Box 1, Folder 4, item 7.
14 Greeba Jamison, 2/3/83.
15 GJ, CSFN, p. 28. Interestingly, in the first draft of this novel, Turley adds the proviso: 'Or perhaps you will last a long time and finally each of you will destroy the other' (GJ, 'CSFN draft (i)', p. 2, GJ Coll., Box 3, Folder 7, item 7). This, of course, was well and truly the view of hindsight.
16 Indeed, Greeba Jamison (2/3/83) stated that, on a number of past occasions, Elsie had appealed to her husband's colleagues and even to his employers for help and loyalty.
17 Bruce Kneale, interview with NW, 2/3/85.
18 Garry Kinnane, p. 85.
19 At Christmas 1942, Elsie had confronted her husband's current *Argus* girlfriend, and her rival had backed off. (Garry Kinnane, p. 45.)
20 Bruce Kneale, 2/3/85.
21 CC, 'Smile Sweetly, Your Highness', *Argus Week-end Magazine*, 22/6/46; 'Be an Original Not a Forgery', *Argus Woman's Magazine*, 26/6/46. This interview has no

byline, but Edward Heffernan spoke of Charmian interviewing him. The cover picture was of Heffernan's wife.

22 Greeba Jamison, 2/3/83.

23 Bruce Kneale, 2/3/85.

24 Bruce Kneale (2/3/85) maintained that it was not so much Knox himself as Rasmussen, the Chief of Staff, who initiated the sacking. According to Kneale, Rasmussen was a devout Catholic who hated adultery. Greeba Jamison (2/3/83) stated that while Knox was not a prude, he felt that Clift was a disturbing element.

25 GJ, 'China Looks Two Ways Into Tomorrow', *Argus Week-end Magazine*, 8/6/46.

26 CC, untitled speech re Australia's view of America, GJ Coll., Box 6, Folder 9, item 16.

27 Hume Dow, interview with NW (notes only), 27/4/83.

28 GJ, CSFN, pp. 40–5.

29 GJ, CSFN, p. 49.

30 GJ, CSFN, p. 55.

31 Bruce Kneale, 2/3/85.

32 Greeba Jamison, 2/3/83.

33 GJ, CSFN, p. 55.

34 GJ, '*Clean Straw for Nothing* General Notes', GJ Coll., Box 1, Folder 4, item 7, pp. 5, 4 (emphasis in original).

35 GJ, *Moon at Perigee*, Angus & Robertson, Sydney, 1948. This was published under the title *Monsoon* in Britain and America.

36 Kay Keavney, 'From George with Sadness', *Australian Women's Weekly*, 3/9/69.

37 Ruth Park, *Fishing in the Styx*, Viking, Melbourne, 1993, p. 142.

38 James Hall, 'And Now It's Two for the Load', *Australian*, 23/11/68.

39 Geoffrey Hutton, 'He Died Alive'.

40 Elizabeth Riddell, 'George, for Whom Working Is Therapy', *Australian*, 16/8/69.

41 GJ, Biographical Questionnaire, n.d. (early 1950), Bobbs-Merrill Collection, Manuscripts Department, Lilly Library, Indiana University.

42 GJ, MBJ, pp. 210–33. In chapters 17 and 18 I will discuss Charmian's input into the writing of this novel. This included the characterisation of the Helen Midgeley character. The text of this particular passage frequently rings with attitudes and descriptive phrases which are typical of Clift. For example, in Jack's criticism to David about Helen's political attitudes, he twice refers to her 'strong opinions' (p. 225) — a phrase which Clift would often use about her father's political attitudes.

43 GJ, CSFN, p. 57.

44 GJ, 'CSFN draft (i)', p. 25, GJ Coll., Box 3, Folder 7, item 7. Here Meredith encounters Cressida Morley in a florist shop, where she is sending flowers to her sick father.

45 Information, Margaret Backhouse.

46 See Suzanne Chick, *Searching for Charmian*, Macmillan, Sydney, 1994, p. 354, note 2.

47 Mrs Richardson spoke highly of George, interview with NW, 14/3/83. So did Roy Phillis and Cliff Sweet, interview with NW, 12/3/83.

48 GJ, CSFN, p. 60.

49 GJ, CSFN, pp. 58–60.

50 George Johnston had attacked the government for this housing crisis in the *Australasian Post*, 23/5/46, 13/6/46, 20/6/46.

51 Mrs Richardson, 14/3/83; Roy Phillis and Cliff Sweet, 12/3/83.

52 GJ, CSFN, p. 66.

53 Mary Andrews, interview with NW (notes only), 24/7/89.

54 Garry Kinnane, p. 92, re date of divorce.

55 Alan Trengrove, 'Partners — It's in Writing', *Sun*, 6/7/66.

56 It is hard to date exactly when GJ got this job. Garry Kinnane (p. 94) puts this event towards the end of 1947, when *High Valley* was finished and the child was due to be born. But if this was the case — what was George doing up in Sydney, while Charmian was in Kiama? He would have had the novel done in three months if he were working full-time on it. It is better here to follow the chronology of CSFN, p. 68: when pregnant Cressida suggests that David get a job, he rings the editor at the *Globe* and is employed immediately.

57 James Hall, 'And Now It's Two for the Load'.

58 GJ, *Journey Through Tomorrow*, Cheshire, Melbourne, 1947, pp. 217–355.

59 CC and GJ, HV, p. 9.

60 CC and GJ, HV, p. 266.

61 James Hall, 'And Now It's Two for the Load'; ' "Herald" Novel Prizes', *Sydney Morning Herald*, 8/5/48, p. 1.

62 Margaret Backhouse, October 1982.

63 John Hetherington, 'An Australian Author Returns to His Native Land', *Age*, 8/2/64.

64 Margaret Backhouse, October 1982.

65 ' "Herald" ' Novel Prizes', *Sydney Morning Herald*, 8/5/48, p. 1.

66 GJ, Biographical Questionnaire.

67 Her address is given as 'c/- Mrs S Clift, North Kiama', on the birth certificate of Martin Clift Johnston.

68 Allan Ashbolt, interview with NW, 3/11/95.

69 The suggestion has been made that Charmian Clift met Peter Finch while working at the Minerva Theatre. However, Trader Faulkner, *Peter Finch: A Biography*, Angus & Robertson, London, 1979, p.99, states that Finch made his first appearance at that theatre in June 1944. By this time Clift was in the army and in Victoria.

70 For example, in John Hetherington, 'An Australian Author Returns to his Native Land'; Clifford Tolchard, 'My Husband George: My Wife Charmian', *Walkabout*, January 1969. In May 1969, the couple would go away for a trip to Norfolk Island as a kind of celebration of their wedding anniversary (see chapter 23). Clift in her interview with Hazel de Berg, National Library of Australia, 8/6/65, pushes the date even further back — to 1946, before the couple 'left the *Argus* and came up to Sydney'.

71 Arthur Polkinghorne, quoted by Garry Kinnane, p. 92.

72 Mary Andrews, 24/7/89.

73 Jean Skea, letter to NW, n.d. (received July 1990).

74 Information, Martin Johnston.

75 Birth certificate, Martin Clift Johnston. Suzanne Chick (p. 59) incorrectly states that Martin 'was born at Crown Street Women's Hospital'.

76 CC, 'In Praise of the GP', BAWO, p. 134.

77 Jean Skea, n.d. A copy of the letter from 'Martin Johnston' was enclosed.

78 Indeed, in his first column he even wrote an account of an anonymous 'young couple', in an emergency, trying to persuade a surly taxi-driver to take them to King George V Maternity Hospital, *Sun*, 17/11/47.

79 Garry Kinnane, p. 96.

80 Mrs Richardson, 14/3/83; GJ, CSFN, p. 72.

81 Toni Burgess, interview (notes only), October 1984.

Chapter 10 — Terribly Difficult Years for a Young Woman

1 CC, interview with Hazel de Berg, National Library of Australia, 8/6/65.
2 CC, 'A Rift in My Lute', BAWO, p. 23.
3 Emma Clift, death certificate, 4/6/48; Margaret Backhouse, interview with NW, June 1983.
4 Ruth Park, 'Nothing but Writers', *Independent Monthly,* September 1989.
5 Clifford Tolchard, 'My Husband George: My Wife Charmian', *Walkabout,* January 1969.
6 CC, 'Monday. On Talking and Writing', GJ Coll., Box 5, Folder 6, item 13, n.p.n. This was a one-page typed note which Clift made for herself before going on a particular radio program.
7 Cedric Flower, interview with NW, 17/9/89.
8 Toni Burgess, interview with NW (notes only), October 1984. She remembered that Martin was about six months old at the time she met Charmian.
9 Toni Burgess (October 1984) talked about her early aspirations. In fact, she did have at least one success. *ABC Weekly,* 15 April 1950, lists a radio program by Antonia Hazelwood on Anna Pavlova, in the 'Famous Women' series.
10 Suzanne Chick, *Searching for Charmian,* Macmillan, Sydney, 1994, p. 240.
11 WB Yeats, 'For Anne Gregory', Michael Roberts (ed.), *The Faber Book of Modern Verse,* London, 1965, p. 61.
12 Suzanne Chick, pp. 241, 261.
13 It is difficult to date the completion of this work. While Jean Skea was given a typescript in late August (see chapter 9), the authors themselves commented (*Sydney Morning Herald,* 8/5/48) that 'a son was born during the writing of the novel, and that slowed its progress'. This suggests that the work wasn't fully revised until after Martin's birth in mid November.
14 In her memoirs, Ruth Park describes her own elation when told of her win, likening the experience to that of 'people who win large lottery prizes'. Ruth Park, *Fishing in the Styx,* Viking, Melbourne, 1993, p. 145.
15 ' "Herald" Novel Prizes', *Sydney Morning Herald,* 8/5/48, p. 1; 'Results of the "Herald" Novel Competition', p. 6; 'Journalist, Wife, Win Novel Prize', *Sun,* 8/5/48, p. 2.
16 James Hall, 'And Now It's Two for the Load', *Australian,* 23/11/68.
17 'Results of the "Herald" Novel Competition'.
18 GJ, 'Sydney Diary', *Sun,* 28/11/48.
19 The Bobbs-Merrill file on CC and GJ has copies of glowing British reviews from February and March 1950. Bobbs-Merrill Collection, Manuscripts Department, Lilly Library, Indiana University.
20 Garry Kinnane, *George Johnston: A Biography,* Nelson, Melbourne, 1986, p. 103.
21 Information, Martin Johnston. George Johnston also believed this. See GJ, CSFN, p. 54. This notion becomes part of David Meredith's musings regarding winning the 'prize' of Cressida at the beginning of the Lebanon Bay passage.
22 CC, interview with Hazel de Berg, 8/6/65.
23 CC, 'A Rift in My Lute', BAWO, p. 23.
24 Ruth Park, 'Nothing but Writers'. Park actually describes this as the first time she met Charmian, but this can't have been the case. The farewell party which Ruth Park gave for Peter Finch — to which she invited Charmian — must have occurred in October 1948. Park also describes how, by the time of the wisteria party, the Johnstons had already won the *Sydney Morning Herald* prize and were living in

Bondi, so she can't be confusing Charmian's pregnancy with Shane with her 1947 pregnancy with Martin.

25 Information, Martin Johnston.

26 GJ, Biographical Questionnaire; CC, Biographical Questionnaire, n.d. (early 1950), Bobbs-Merrill Collection.

27 Garry Kinnane, p. 100.

28 GJ, CSFN, p. 87.

29 In 1948 the potboiler *Moon at Perigee* had been published by Angus & Robertson, and the thriller *Death Takes Small Bites* by Dodd, Mead & Co in the United States.

30 Garry Kinnane, pp. 92, 96.

31 ' "Herald" Novel Prizes'. By early 1950, GJ would tell Bobbs-Merrill that 'we are collaborating on a second and more ambitious novel, *The Piping Cry*', GJ, Biographical Questionnaire.

32 CC, 'Even the Thrush Has Wings', GJ Coll., Box 5, Folder 4, item 5. On this typescript the author used her husband's address at the Sydney *Sun* office.

33 Barbara Jefferis, interview with NW, 26/2/92.

34 Garry Kinnane (p.101) states that 'So good were their ideas and scripts that Hutchison was able to build a whole ABC production team around them'.

35 The programs were: 29/5/49: *Quality Street:* 'I Want to be Alone', GJ; 2/8/49: *Radio Diary* series: 'Diary of a Cad', GJ; 14/8/49: *Quality Street:* 'The Edge [or Age] of Darkness', Charmian Johnston; 27/12/49: *Radio Diary* series: 'Diary of a Modern Woman', Charmian Clift; 28/2/50: *Radio Diary* series: 'Diary of an Unhappy Marriage', CC and GJ; 19/3/50: *Famous Women* series: 'Nofretete' (sic), GJ; 26/3/50: *Famous Women* series: 'Sappho of Lesbos', CC and GJ; 2/5/50: Dramatised Feature: 'The Lady Bright', CC; 27/6/50: Feature: 'Change Another Pound', CC; 29/8/50: Feature: 'The Sage's Return', GJ; 17/10/50: Feature: 'The Social Animal', GJ; 28/11/50: *Radio Diary* series: 'Diary of a Modern Woman' (repeat), CC.

36 Ruth Park, *Fishing in the Styx,* p. 163.

37 *ABC Weekly,* 29/4/50, p. 4.

38 *ABC Weekly,* 13/8/49, p. 24. Other photographs from this series in the family collection show Martin on the beach with Charmian.

39 *ABC Weekly,* 24/12/49, p. 25.

40 *ABC Weekly,* 29/4/50, cover, p. 4.

41 *ABC Weekly,* 18/3/50, p. 3.

42 CC, interview with Hazel de Berg, 8/6/65; CC, 'News of Earls Court — Fifteen Years Ago', WCC, p. 56.

43 Kate Cumming, Access Services, Australian Archives, letter to NW, 23/4/96, advising that 'ASIO [...] have been unable to locate any records in the open period relating to either Clift or Johnston'.

44 GJ, CSFN, pp. 90–7.

45 GJ, CSFN, p. 80.

46 Humphrey McQueen, *Gallipoli to Petrov,* George, Allen & Unwin, Sydney, 1984, p. 171.

47 The poet and journalist Elizabeth Riddell, looking back on this period, refers to 'that beckoning "overseas" to which we were all committed'. Elizabeth Riddell, 'Writing Near the Brink', *Australian,* 23/7/70.

48 Trader Faulkner (*Peter Finch: A Biography,* Angus & Robertson, London, 1979, p. 129) implies Finch and his wife left in September 1948. Elaine Dundy in *Finch, Bloody*

Finch (Michael Joseph, London, 1980, p. 130) has them leave in late October 1948. They evidently arrived in London on 17 November 1948 (Trader Faulkner, p. 132).

49 Ruth Park, 'Nothing but Writers'.

50 Ruth Park, *Fishing in the Styx,* pp. 161–4: Park and Niland set off for England via New Zealand at the close of 1949; however, they didn't get to England, as they ended up spending a year in New Zealand.

51 CC, 'On the Right of Dissent', BAWO, p. 106.

52 In early 1950 Johnston told the couple's American publishers that they were leaving for England at the end of the year. GJ, Biographical Questionnaire.

53 Bet Hall, interview with NW, 10/7/95.

54 I have checked Hansard for the relevant period, and can't find any reference to this program.

55 CC, 'We Three Kings of Orient Aren't', TILL, pp. 97–8; CC, 'The Party', WCC, p. 182.

56 Suzanne Chick, pp. 241–2, 308. In this account, Martin 'was just a baby, asleep in his bassinette'. This can't have been so. From Toni Burgess's October 1984 interview with me, Martin was about six months old when Toni met Charmian, the two women having first met in about May 1948. By Christmas 1948, Toni was living at the block of flats, but Charmian was not yet writing for ABC radio. The date would have to be Christmas 1949, when Shane was a ten month old baby. There is no record in the *ABC Weekly* of any Christmas program by CC, but of course it may have been a short Christmas 'filler'.

57 Toni Burgess, October 1984.

58 *ABC Weekly,* 18/3/50, p. 3; Barbara Jefferis, 'Problem of an Adopted Child', p. 16. Script in possession of Barbara Jefferis.

59 Barbara Jefferis, 26/2/92.

60 Suzanne Chick, pp. 7–9.

61 Barbara Jefferis, 26/2/92.

62 *ABC Weekly,* 25/2/50, p. 17.

63 Toni Burgess, October 1984.

64 Barbara Jefferis, 26/2/92.

65 GJ, '*Clean Straw for Nothing* General Notes', GJ Coll., Box 1, Folder 4, item 7.

66 'Notes of a talk with George Johnston on his new book, *Clean Straw for Nothing,* to be published in September 1969', a four-page typescript in Greeba Jamison's collection. (See the discussion of this interview, chapter 23.)

67 GJ, CSFN, pp. 92–3.

68 GJ, '*Clean Straw for Nothing* General Notes', GJ Coll., Box 1, Folder 4, item 7 (emphasis in original).

69 Allan Ashbolt, interview with NW, 3/11/95.

70 See also Allan Ashbolt, 'Charmian Clift — A Writer who Believed in Human Dignity', *Sydney Morning Herald,* 12/7/69.

71 GJ, '*Clean Straw for Nothing* General Notes', GJ Coll., Box 1, Folder 4, item 7 (emphasis in original). The subsequent quotation is also from this source.

72 Barbara Jefferis, 26/2/92.

73 GJ, '*Clean Straw for Nothing* General Notes', GJ Coll., Box 1, Folder 4, item 7. The following three quotations are also from this source (emphasis in original).

74 A production tape of this program was provided by Garry Kinnane, who in turn received it from Bettina Dixon (who played one of the roles). I have transcribed this tape for quotations given here; the punctuation is mine.

75 Garry Kinnane, p. 100, citing interview with Neil Hutchison, 1982.

76 GJ, 'Clean Straw for Nothing General Notes', GJ Coll., Box 1, Folder 4, item 7.
77 CC, HM, p. 41.

Chapter 11 — An Outsider Looking In

1 CC, interview with Hazel de Berg, National Library of Australia, 8/6/65.
2 CC, HM, p. 71.
3 CC, interview with Hazel de Berg, 8/6/65.
4 CC, interview with Hazel de Berg, 8/6/65.
5 Garry Kinnane, George Johnston: A Biography, Nelson, Melbourne, 1986, p. 109.
6 GJ, interview with Tony Morphett, 'The Lively Arts', ABC, 12/4/65.
7 Greeba Jamison, interview with NW, 2/3/83. The following quotation is from the same source.
8 Photo in collection of Margaret Backhouse, seen by NW, October 1982.
9 Greeba Jamison, 2/3/83.
10 Memo, David Higham (hereafter DH), 3/4/51, David Higham Archives, Harry Ransom Humanities Research Center, The University of Texas at Austin: 'They will have a permanent address presently'; but a memo dated 4 April notes 'George Johnston Esq, 25 Cliveden Place SW1'. Letters from the agency went to this address until 11 June 1951. After this, DH wrote to GJ at the Fleet Street address of Associated Newspaper Services — from which all GJ's letters were sent on newspaper letterhead. It is not clear when the Johnstons moved to 4 Palace Court, Bayswater Road, but this was their address for most of their time in London.
11 CC, 'On England, My England', BAWO, p. 30.
12 CC, 'The Man in the Corner', unpublished draft, n.d. (c. 1953–4), GJ Coll., Box 5, Folder 4, item 8.
13 CC, 'News of Earls Court — Fifteen Years Ago', WCC, p. 54.
14 Leter from DH to Mike, Ann Watkins Inc., 3/4/51. Also at this meeting, Higham raised a matter which was to be confirmed by the American agency within the fortnight: Pocket Books had bought the paperback reprint rights to High Valley with a minimum guaranteed advance of $3500 to be split fifty-fifty between the American publishers, Bobbs-Merrill, and the authors. Good though this news was, this 'advance' was not due till six months after publication, and in fact the writers were not to receive their $1750 until the middle of the next year. See Sheila St Lawrence, Ann Watkins Inc., to GJ, 13/10/51; Sheila St Lawrence to GJ, 16/10/51, David Higham Archives.
15 See chapter 6.
16 DH memo, 13/4/51; Mary Andrews, interview with NW (notes only), 24/7/89.
17 CC, 'News of Earls Court — Fifteen Years Ago', WCC, pp. 55–6.
18 See Martin Johnston, interview with Hazel de Berg, National Library of Australia, 23/6/80.
19 CC, 'News of Earls Court — Fifteen Years Ago', WCC, p. 54.
20 GJ, 'London Diary', Sun, 20/6/51.
21 CC, 'On England, My England', BAWO, p. 30.
22 CC, 'On England, My England', BAWO, p. 31.
23 GJ, 'London Diary', Sun, 16/5/51, 15/7/51, 14/11/51, 28/11/51.
24 GJ, 'London Diary', Sun, 6/2/52.
25 These photographs are in the collection of Jason Johnston.

26 Nan Hutton, 'Dipping into the World of Charmian', *Age*, 16/8/73.

27 GJ, CSFN, p. 160 (emphasis in original). The following quotation is from p. 159.

28 GJ, CSFN, pp. 156–7. The following quotation is also from p. 157.

29 GJ, CSFN p. 158.

30 CC, 'News of Earls Court — Fifteen Years Ago', WCC, p. 55.

31 GJ, 'Requiem Mass', in Garry Kinnane (ed.), *Strong-man from Piraeus and Other Stories*, Thomas Nelson, Melbourne, 1983, pp. 62–84.

32 DH to Mr and Mrs GJ, 24/4/51; GJ to DH, 8/5/51; Sheila St Lawrence to GJ, 11/5/51.

33 DH to GJ, 24/7/51.

34 GJ to DH, 1/8/51.

35 GJ to George Ferguson, 21/8/51, Angus & Robertson Collection, Mitchell Library, State Library of NSW.

36 Sheila St Lawrence to GJ, 24/10/51.

37 DH memo, 5/11/51; DH memo, 6/11/51.

38 CC, 'On Being Unable to Write an Article', TILL, p. 84.

39 Certainly A & R's publisher George Ferguson and the redoubtable editor Beatrice Davis would later have no memory of ever seeing the typescript for this novel. George Ferguson, letter to NW, 15/5/92. Beatrice Davis, phone call to NW, 16/5/92, in response to NW, letter to Beatrice Davis, 12/5/92.

40 In the Bobbs-Merrill Collection, Manuscripts Department, Lilly Library, Indiana University, there are three readers' reports: one signed by Herman Ziegner, one signed by Harry Sterk, and another unsigned report which is clearly also by Harry Sterk. All subsequent descriptions of *The Piping Cry* are taken from these sources. In regard to material from Sterk (including the summary of the novel's plot), I have drawn from both his reports. Sterk jumps back and forth between present and past tense, but I have changed all tenses to the present, for clarity.

41 Indeed, even the title seems to have relied upon a certain literary knowledge. Reflecting Clift's passion both for Shakespeare and for poetically resonant titles, this was clearly taken from Gloucester's opening speech in *Richard III*. As the deformed hero expresses his cynicism at the value of victory in his post-war world, he asks 'Why, I, in this weak piping time of peace,/Have no delight to pass away the time'.

42 James Hall, 'And Now It's Two for the Load', *Australian*, 23/11/68.

43 Under the colonial publishing practices of that era, Faber and Faber had the rights on the next two collaborative novels in regard to British and Empire territory, exclusive of Australia and New Zealand, for which the rights were held by Angus & Robertson. Faber and Faber was also trying to claim Australasian rights, but George Johnston was adamant that these remain with A & R, with whom he dealt personally.

44 Greeba Jamison, 2/3/83.

45 GJ, CTTS, p. 296.

46 GJ, CSFN, p. 161. Mary Andrews (24/7/89) also remembered this doctor.

47 CC, interview with Hazel de Berg, 8/6/65.

48 CC, 'The Man in the Corner', GJ Coll., Box 5, Folder 4, item 8.

49 Greeba Jamison, 2/3/83.

50 GJ, 'London Diary', *Sun*, 26/12/51.

51 GJ, 'London Diary', *Sun*, 7/2/52, 13/2/52.

52 CC, 'On England, My England', BAWO, p. 31. Clift always muddled the dates of the February 1952 accession and the mid 1953 coronation. This means that a little care has to be exercised when dating events from the essays. In this essay, the accession

and coronation are placed together after Clift's mid 1952 Europe trip. In 'Royal Jelly' (BAWO, p. 277), Clift transposes the dates, and puts the coronation at 6/2/52 instead of 2/6/53.

53 Re date of this trip: GJ's last 'London Diary' piece is 23/4/52. Confirmation that the trip occurred in May is provided by CC's references to gathering cultural 'nuts in May' in an unpublished essay about this European journey. Untitled typescript (opens 'Looking through the sailing lists'), GJ Coll., Box 6, Folder 8, item 15. Re the holiday establishment, see CC, 'The Joys of Holidays', BAWO, p. 275.

54 Unless otherwise stated, information here regarding this journey is taken from these notes. The reference to scraps of notes is an assumption, because this is how Clift regularly collected information. The typed-up notes can be found at GJ Coll., Box 1, Folder 2, black loose-leaf notebook, first seven pages. This consists of six sequential pages. Then the first page about Lerici is missing, and another page begins mid-sentence in the middle of the Lerici experience. Although the pages are numbered from 1 to 7, this has been done in two sets of handwriting — one for pages 1–6 and another starting at page 7. This numbering ignores the missing Lerici page. The extant Lerici page also has on it a draft for one of Clift's texts about her alter ego named Sarah.

55 CC, 'A Taxi Journey', WCC, pp. 84–5.

56 CC, Untitled typescript (opens 'Looking through the sailing lists'), GJ Coll., Box 6, Folder 8, item 15, p. 5.

57 Martin Johnston frequently mentioned his parents' anecdotes of this incident. It features in his elegy for his father, 'The Sea Cucumber', where Martin refers to 'three old men he'd seen/At Lerici, playing pipes and a drum under an orange sky'. John Tranter (ed.), Martin Johnston, *Selected Poems and Prose*, University of Queensland Press, St Lucia, 1993, p. 12.

58 CC, Travel notes, GJ Coll., Box 1, Folder 2, item 2, black loose-leaf notebook, p. 7 (emphasis in original).

59 CC, Travel notes, GJ Coll., Box 1, Folder 2, item 2, black loose-leaf notebook, p. 3.

60 CC, Untitled transcript (opens 'Looking through the sailing lists'), GJ Coll., Box 6, Folder 8, item 15, p. 5.

61 CC, Travel notes, GJ Coll., Box 1, Folder 2, item 2, black loose-leaf notebook, p. 1.

62 CC, Travel notes, GJ Coll., Box 1, Folder 2, item 2, black loose-leaf notebook, pp. 3, 6.

63 CC, 'Wild Emperor', in Garry Kinnane (ed.), *Strong-man*, pp. 43–61.

64 CC, 'Three Old Men of Lerici', in Garry Kinnane (ed.), *Strong-man*, pp. 10–25.

65 The heroine's name is borrowed from Ursula Colahan, with whom the Johnstons would travel to France in 1953. The author would later use it for the unflattering portrait of the Cynthia Nolan character in *Peel Me a Lotus*.

66 This character is named after the German town — literally 'Free Town' — where the couple had spent a romantic night in an inn where Goethe had once lived. See CC, 'Taking the Wrong Road', WCC, p. 19.

67 CC, 'Three Old Men of Lerici', Garry Kinnane (ed.), *Strong-Man*, p. 22. The subsequent quotation is from the same page.

68 In this connection between the Pan pipes and the revelation, it seems likely that Clift was drawing — whether consciously or subconsciously — on two other literary texts. The first reference point is E M Forster's 'The Story of a Panic', which had been republished in Forster's *Collected Short Stories* in 1947. Here also it is May in Italy, and when the boy Eustace/Eustazio (a link with Ursula?) plays upon a whistle, he is in

some way possessed by Pan, and comes to 'understand almost everything'. The boy is on the verge of another revelation but is interrupted, and weeps, 'I nearly saw everything, and now I can see nothing at all'.

If Forster's story suggests that, by properly hearing the music of Pan's pipes, one will gain some sort of key to the meaning of the universe, this is also a vital element to *The Wind in the Willows* by Kenneth Grahame, a book which Charmian knew well from her own childhood and which, during these London years, she often read to her two children. Martin would pick up from his mother a lifelong admiration for the 'Piper at the Gates of Dawn' chapter, in which Rat and Mole row up the river on a moonlit midsummer night and hear the music of Pan, which leads them to a small secret island. 'This is the place of my song-dream', Rat whispers, 'the place the music played to me'.

69 CC, 'Three Old Men of Lerici', Garry Kinnane (ed.), *Strong-man,* p. 24.

70 Never one to waste a good image, Clift used this again in WTTPG (p. 78) as the conclusion to the chapter in which sadistic Roy boils some lobsters and eventually sobs upon the maternal breast of his wife. 'Roy's tears soaked through her thin cotton shirt and spread hot and wet across her bosom, as though her heart had burst'.

71 Garry Kinnane, *George Johnston,* p. 123.

72 As far as the actual Lerici passage of Johnston's novel is concerned, the first part seems to be drawn from Clift's story, and it is the latter part that reflects the travel note passage included earlier in this chapter. As mentioned, the first page of Lerici notes — which may have provided the source for both story and novel — is missing.

73 Transposing these numbers, Johnston gives the time on this clock at the start of the passage as seven minutes past nine.

74 GJ, CSFN, p. 110.

Chapter 12 — Losing Identity

1 CC, interview with Hazel de Berg, National Library of Australia, 8/6/65.

2 CC, 'On England, My England', BAWO, p. 31.

3 CC, 'The Household Treasure', WCC, p. 86; GJ, CSFN, p.132.

4 Jo Meyer, letter to NW, September 1989.

5 Information, Martin Johnston.

6 Garry Kinnane, *George Johnston: A Biography,* Nelson, Melbourne, 1986 p. 133, citing interview with Neil Whitlock, 1982.

7 Jo Meyer, September 1989.

8 CC, MS, p. 75.

9 Cedric Flower, interview with NW, 17/9/89.

10 James Hall, 'And Now It's Two for the Load', *Australian,* 23/11/68.

11 CC and GJ, *The Big Chariot,* Angus & Robertson, Sydney, 1953, p. v.

12 Garry Kinnane, p. 119, citing GJ to Albert Arlen, 17/9/52.

13 In America the book quickly went into a second impression but the publisher had overspent on promotion; the publisher's profit from the book was only $400. Herman Ziegner to Ross Baker, 22/3/55, Bobbs-Merrill Collection, Manuscripts Department, Lilly Library, Indiana University.

14 CC, 'The Joy of a Good Old Cuppa', TILL, p. 130.

15 GJ to Aubrey Cousins, 8/4/53, Angus & Robertson Collection, Mitchell Library, State Library of NSW.

16 CC's notes for this novel can be found in GJ Coll., Box 1, Folder 2, item 2; 20 page typescript of *Barbarian* in Box 5, Folder 22, item 45.

17 This textual evidence can be found by tracking various names and incidents through fragments of drafts, and cross-referencing dates where possible. Thus a half-page description of a sixteen year old character called Sarah is on the bottom of the Lerici notes from the 1952 trip. This connects with a draft of a story about an adolescent alter ego named Sarah, who falls in love with a criminal whom she has rescued from drowning (GJ Coll., Box 5, Folder 22, no item number — attached to item 40.) The author had already used Sarah Clint as the child in the graveyard story 'The End of the Morning', and of course 'Sarah' was a family name, borrowed from grandmother Sarah Carson. In the cast list of the projected girl-and-criminal story Sarah's sister was to be named Judith — borrowed from Christine Morley's sister Judith in GGTG. This same list proposes 'Tam' as the name for Sarah's brother.

   This name provides a link with another set of material which Clift was trying to work on at this time. Among the author's papers there is also a page of first-person narrative in which an adult returns to the quarry settlement, sees a mad old woman called Selina, and remembers how she and her brother Tammy used to spy on the old woman (GJ Coll., Box 5, Folder 22, item 46). This is clearly an early draft of WTTPG, because the Selina story is a central theme of the published novel of this name, in which Julia's brother is called Tammy. It is possible that this unnamed narrator was Christine Morley — to be renamed and reshaped as Julia Cant after George Johnston used Christine as the name for the adulterous wife in *The Cyprian Woman*.

   Another link which suggests that a part or version of GGTG may have spun into WTTPG is the fact that both texts include the dramatic opening scene on the promontory, in which the heroines (either Christine Morley or Julia Cant) show off their home town to their lover or husband. And, as I explain in the Note to these Endnotes, Clift would use the description of the town in the GGTG material as a draft for the description in WTTPG.

18 GJ, CTTS, p. 60.

19 GJ, CTTS, p. 69.

20 CC, MS, p. 126.

21 GJ, CSFN, p. 135–6.

22 Garry Kinnane, p. 127, citing interview with Sidney Nolan, 1982. Kinnane uses this anecdote to suggest that 'the idea of going to Greece might well have come indirectly through Nolan'. However, as we have seen, the Johnstons were thinking about Greece as early as the winter of 1951. It is more likely that Nolan, knowing of his friends' interest in living in Greece, took them to meet someone who could give them an up-to-date account of what it was like.

23 Re date, see GJ to Aubrey Cousins, 8/4/53; GJ's article produced as a result of this trip, 'The Last Magic', GJ Coll., Box 5, Folder 22, item 28, also makes it clear that the year was 1953. CC's long essay on 'Wine Country' was published in *Pol*, September 1969.

24 Garry Kinnane p.127, quoting GJ to Morley Kennerley, 19/5/53, Faber and Faber files.

25 GJ, CSFN, pp. 136–8; CC, MS, p. 9.

26 CC, 'Royal Jelly?', BAWO, pp. 277–9; CC, 'On Choosing a National Costume', TILL, p. 117.

27 GJ to Aubrey Cousins, 8/1/53.

28 GJ to Aubrey Cousins, 17/9/53.
29 GJ, *Bed of Thorns*, television play script, GJ Coll., Box 4, Folder 14, items 20–22.
30 Garry Kinnane, p. 128, citing Royal North Shore Hospital Records.
31 CC, MS (B-M), p. 18.
32 GJ, CSFN, p. 135. Martin would retain a lifelong loathing for fish, which he attributed to the fish he was forced to eat at this establishment.
33 GJ to David Higham (hereafter DH), 25/4/54, David Higham Archives, Harry Ransom Humanities Research Center, The University of Texas at Austin.
34 GJ, 'The Orient Express', GJ Coll., Box 5, Folder 22, item 41, p. 8.
35 GJ, 'Holiday with Homer', GJ Coll., Box 5, Folder 22, item 39. Subsequent quotations in this paragraph and the one following are also from this source.
36 Martin Johnston used to say that his parents had initially planned to live in Nauplion.
37 GJ, 'Holiday with Homer', GJ Coll., Box 5, Folder 22, item 39.
38 CC, MS (B-M), p. 18.
39 Cedric Flower, 17/9/89.
40 Jo Meyer, September 1989.
41 DH memo, 17/6/54.
42 GJ to DH, 14/9/54.
43 CC attempted one story set in Zennor, at the time of the 1954 summer holiday there. Some pages of typescript remain in GJ Coll., Box 5, Folder 4, no item number.
44 CC, MS, p. 210.
45 CC, 'The Wreck of the Traute Sano', TILL, pp. 221–4. This summer of 1954 in Cornwall was a particularly memorable one because the German freighter the *Traute Sanow* ran aground on Gurnards Head. There are numerous photographs in the family collection showing Shane and Martin excitedly exploring the shipwreck. Martin's memories of these Cornwall holidays were so happy that we went to Zennor in 1978 and stayed in the Bed & Breakfast where he and Charmian and Shane had stayed.
46 Garry Kinnane, p. 130.
47 GJ, CTTS, p. 296. Curiously, as his fictional name for this particular London girlfriend, the author chooses 'Sara' — which of course was another name which Clift herself used for her fictional alter ego.
48 GJ, CSFN pp. 159–68.
49 GJ, CSFN, p. 130.
50 GJ, CSFN, p. 134.
51 GJ, CSFN, p. 154.
52 CC, interview with Hazel de Berg, 8/6/65.
53 GJ, '*Clean Straw For Nothing* General Notes', GJ Coll., Box 1, Folder 4, item 7.
54 CC, MS, p. 9
55 Garry Kinnane, p. 135, citing interview with Anthony Whitlock, 1982.
56 Garry Kinnane ,p. 137. Again, Kinnane refers to his interview with Whitlock, but clearly Whitlock did not put an exact date to this rumour. Kinnane actually puts this hearing of the rumour closer to the September date, when GJ listened to the Thomas program. However, given that the decision to go to Greece was made earlier, I think this rumour was earlier too.
57 This version of the story is derived from the account given by Garry Kinnane, p. 137, citing his interview with Wilfred Thomas, 1983.

58 CC, MS, pp. 10, 14.

59 Garry Kinnane, p. 136.

60 CC, MS (B-M), pp. 34–6.

61 CC, MS (B-M), p. 42.

62 This foggy London night — 'the colour of a Guernsey cow' — was described so wonderfully that the author transplanted the description into the short version of the text, and changed it into the night after the couple heard the BBC program.

63 CC, MS (B-M), pp. 15–16.

64 Garry Kinnane, p. 139.

65 CC, MS (B-M), p. 17.

66 Garry Kinnane, p. 138. Kinnane notes that Johnston was given cash equivalent to the return ticket to Australia. To this they added the proceeds from selling the car.

67 CC, MS, pp. 10–11.

68 DH memo, 11/11/54.

69 GJ, CSFN, p. 124. Garry Kinnane p.140 cites Wilfred Thomas as remembering Clift saying this on this occasion.

70 Jo Meyer, September 1989. Guy also appears in CC, MS (B-M) pp. 26–27.

71 CC, HM, pp. 71–2.

72 CC, MS (B-M), p. 20.

PART III — THE PROMISED LAND

Chapter 13 — Another World

1 CC, MS (B-M), p. 25.

2 Ovid, *Metamorphoses*, Mary M Innes (trans.), Penguin Classics, London, 1955, p. 185.

3 CC, MS (B-M), p. 31.

4 GJ to Jo Meyer, 30/11/54.

5 David Higham (hereafter DH) to GJ, 26/11/54 (with news of offers); GJ to DH, 30/11/54 (referring to sending cable on 29th), David Higham Archives, Harry Ransom Humanities Research Center, The University of Texas at Austin.

6 GJ to Jo Meyer, 30/11/54. Date of travel to Kos foreshadowed in this letter.

7 CC, MS (B-M), pp. 43–53.

8 'My strongest memory of the first few weeks in Greece is the fact that it was impossible to get peanut butter there'. Martin Johnston, interview with Hazel de Berg, National Library of Australia, 23/6/80.

9 CC, MS, pp. 1–2. This passage — which occurred in chapter 6 in the original American text of *Mermaid Singing* — was moved to the opening of the revised British text (published by Michael Joseph), which this Australian edition follows.

10 CC, MS, p. 11.

11 CC, MS, pp. 6–7.

12 CC to Jo Meyer, 13/12/54.

13 CC, MS, pp. 122–3. The subsequent quotation is from the same source.

14 GJ to DH, 29/12/54.

15 This Manolis was not at all like the lounge lizard Manolis of the opening passage of *Mermaid Singing*.

16 CC, MS, pp. 75–6.

17 CC, MS, p. 39.

18 CC to Jo Meyer, 2/2/55. Subsequent reference to 'writing to Jo' and 'Charmian's February letter' are from the same source.

19 CC, MS, p. 124.

20 Clift and Johnston were eventually to sponsor their Kalymnian friend Yanni as a migrant to Australia. See CC, 'An Exile's Return', IA, pp. 93–6.

21 CC, MS, pp. 126–7.

22 CC, MS, p. 160.

23 GJ, '*Clean Straw for Nothing* General Notes', p. 6, GJ Coll., Box 1, Folder 4, item 7.

24 CC to Jo Meyer, 2/2/55; CC, MS, pp. 95, 154.

25 CC, MS, p. 167.

26 Clifford Tolchard, 'My Husband George: My Wife Charmian', *Walkabout*, January 1969.

27 CC, MS, p. 85.

28 GJ to DH, 29/3/55. It is clear from unsigned readers' reports on *The Sea and the Stone*, 9/5/55 (Bobbs-Merrill Collection, Manuscripts Department, Lilly Library, Indiana University), that the typescript had arrived at the American publishers around the same time.

29 GJ to DH, 29/3/55.

30 GJ to George Ferguson, 29/3/55, Angus & Robertson Collection, Mitchell Library, State Library of NSW.

31 GJ referred to it as 'the new novel by the two of us' (GJ to DH, 29/3/55) and on the same date he told George Ferguson that 'Charmian and I have completed the novel we came down here to write. It's another collaboration'. Charmian Clift's references to the novel in *Mermaid Singing* make it clear that she, too, was happy at this time for it to be seen as a combined effort.

32 GJ to Gae Johnston, 16/2/60, quoted by Garry Kinnane, *George Johnston: A Biography*, Nelson, Melbourne, 1986, p. 143.

33 CC, interview with Hazel de Berg, National Library of Australia, 8/6/65.

34 James Hall, 'And Now It's Two for the Load', *Australian*, 23/11/68.

35 Alan Trengrove, 'Partners — It's in Writing', *Sun*, 6/7/66.

36 GJ to DH, 26/3/55, 29/3/55.

37 CC, MS, p. 167.

38 CC, MS, p. 167.

39 GJ to George Ferguson, 29/3/55.

40 CC, MS, p. 168.

41 GJ to DH, 19/5/55, re acceptance and Bobbs-Merrill's high praise. Ivan von Auw (hereafter IVA) from the American literary agency wrote to DH, 27/5/55, re terms of the advance; in fact, by the end of June the advance money still had not arrived. GJ to DH (27/6/55) complained that they had been seven months in Greece with no income. It seems the money still hadn't arrived by the end of July. Re cutting out 'dirty words', see GJ to DH, 6/7/55. Johnston made no objection to this in regard to the American edition, but was keen that these words (whatever they were) be retained in the British edition. They weren't.

42 CC, MS, pp. 197–8.

43 CC, MS, p. 206.

44 Clift was still so invisible in the business correspondence that courtly George Ferguson, when replying to George Johnston's March letter, began: 'My dear George — and may I also include Charmian?' George Ferguson to GJ, 13/4/55.

45 GJ to DH, 19/5/55.

46 These treatments were sent out by mid July. GJ to Lawrence Pollinger (at the British literary agency), 2/9/55. There actually was some encouragement of these film dreams, initially from the American side. By August a film agent called Swanie had written to Ivan von Auw that 'I think we can sell this to Paramount, if not another of the majors, for a good price'. IVA to Lawrence Pollinger, n.d. (received 22/8/55). This information was passed on to GJ: Lawrence Pollinger to GJ, 24/8/55. But like all the subsequent film nibbles, it came to nothing.

47 GJ to DH, 19/5/55. The first three were 'The Good Gorgona', 'The Anatolian Turk', 'Strong-man from Piraeus'; the fourth was 'The Astypalaian Knife'.

48 GJ to DH, 27/6/55.

49 On 4/7/55, DH cabled GJ: 'KALYMNIAN FABER OFFER SAME TERMS AS FOR BIG CHARIOT COLLINS WOULD PAY SAME TERMS AS FOR CYPRIAN WOMAN SUGGEST WE ACCEPT COLLINS'. GJ to DH, 6/7/55, instructed his agent to accept Collins' offer. Further discussion in DH to GJ, 8/7/55, 12/7/55. In the letter of 8/7/55 some doubts were expressed as to the saleability of the short stories on the British market. GJ responded 'with mixed feelings' to this on 28/7/55.

50 Cedric Flower, interview with NW, 17/9/89.

51 Harrison Platt to IVA, 31/5/56.

52 CC, MS, p. 70.

53 This had been first published in 1941 by a small San Francisco firm, but the British paperback edition made it widely available.

54 In its year of publication *Bitter Lemons* was chosen as the Book Society Choice for July, and the next year an edition was published in conjunction with The Readers' Union. In 1958 the book was published in America, and in 1959 Faber brought out a paperback edition. At a somewhat later stage, the Schweppes soft drink company circulated copies of the paperback as an advertisement for their Bitter Lemon drink! See Alan G Thomas and James A Brigham, *Lawrence Durrell, An Illustrated Checklist*, Southern Illinois University Press, Carbondale and Edwardsville, 1983.

55 DH to CC, 17/3/58.

56 IVA to CC, 28/5/57.

57 In late 1956 when Sidney Nolan briefly visited Hydra, GJ wrote to A&R on Clift's behalf, noting that Sid Nolan would bring them a copy of the newly published US edition of *Mermaid Singing*. However, A&R could not have accepted the book without jeopardising its possibility of gaining a UK publisher. GJ to A&R, 3/12/56; Beatrice Davis to GJ (6/2/57), noted that A&R would wait to hear what Michael Joseph did with the book. There is no more correspondence between A&R and CC and GJ until 1959.

58 GJ to DH (15/6/56) noted that the typescript of MS was being posted to the agency that day, and asked that it be sent on to Collins without delay. GJ wrote to William Collins (15/6/56) 'to flag the fact' that MS was coming. Files of the Higham agency are missing for July–December 1956, so there is no record as to why Collins rejected it.

59 Lawrence Durrell, *Bitter Lemons*, Faber and Faber, London, 1957, pp. 136, 140.

60 Robert Liddell, *Aegean Greece*, Jonathan Cape, London, 1954, p. 58.

61 CC, MS, pp. 16–17.

62 For example, this is how the taxi driver introduces himself to the Durrell family: 'Spiro's my name, Spiro Hakiapulos ... they alls calls me Spiro Americano on accounts of I lives in America [...] That's where I learnt my goods English ... Wents there to makes moneys'. Gerald Durrell, *My Family and Other Animals*, Penguin, Middlesex, 1974, p. 29.

63 CC, MS, p. 35.
64 Years later, considering again her relationship with Sevasti, Clift noted: 'I think we loved each other in our separate ways'. (CC, 'The Household Treasure', WCC, p. 88.)
65 CC, MS, p. 34.
66 Robert Graves, 'Introduction', *The Greek Myths,* vol. 1, Pelican, Middlesex, 1983.
67 Compare CC, MS, p. 51, with Robert Graves, *The Greek Myths,* vol. 1, p. 17.
68 CC, MS, pp. 50, 41, 46.
69 CC, MS, p. 98.
70 Cedric Flower, 17/9/89.
71 GJ, CSFN, p. 171.

Chapter 14 — The Commitment

1 CC, PMAL, p. 24.
2 CC, PMAL, pp. 25–6.
3 Cedric Flower, interview with NW, 17/9/89.
4 Garry Kinnane, *George Johnston: A Biography*, Nelson, Melbourne, 1986, p. 115.
5 Information, Martin Johnston.
6 CC, PMAL, p. 40.
7 CC, interview with Hazel de Berg, National Library of Australia, 8/6/65.
8 Clifford Tolchard, 'My Husband George: My Wife Charmian', *Walkabout,* January 1969. For George's plan to return, see chapter 12.
9 There are no records of agency and publishing correspondence between August 1955 and February 1956, so it is impossible to tell when the typescript of *Mermaid Singing* was posted. However, it had been accepted by early February (GJ to DH, 12/2/56), so it must have been posted before Christmas.
10 CC, Hydra notes, GJ Coll., Box 1, Folder 2, item 2, black loose-leaf notebook, n.p.n. These observations were done in beautiful handwriting — as if copied from drafts — and were put into the loose-leaf binder that CC had used for her 1952 Europe trip.
11 CC, Hydra notes, GJ Coll., Box 1, Folder 2, item 2, black loose-leaf notebook, n.p.n.
12 Brian Adams, *Sidney Nolan — Such is Life*, Hutchinson, Melbourne, 1987, p. 131: 'There would be conversations [...] long into the night when the two men discussed their boyhoods in Melbourne and planned books and paintings, while Cynthia and Charmian often talked guardedly about their current work'. This unfootnoted biography relies very heavily on Nolan's telling of the tale.
13 Cynthia Nolan to Pat Flower, n.d. (April 1956). Mitchell Library, State Library of New South Wales.
14 CC, PMAL, pp. 15–21.
15 Cynthia Nolan to Pat Flower, n.d. (April 1956).
16 CC, PMAL, p. 40.
17 W Grey Walter, *The Living Brain*, Gerald Duckworth & Co Ltd., London, 1953.
18 CC, 'The Rare Art of Inspiring Others', IA, p. 62.
19 GJ, 'Gallipoli Paintings', *Art and Australia,* September 1967. Subsequent quotations are also from this source.
20 CC, PMAL, p. 64.
21 CC, PMAL, p. 42.

22 John Hetherington, 'An Australian Author Returns to His Native Land', *Age*, 8/2/64. This article was based on the press kit of information which GJ sent back to Australia as publicity before his return in 1964.
23 Charles Sriber, 'It's All Greek to Them', *People*, 14/5/58.
24 CC, PMAL, pp. 10, 25.
25 CC, PMAL, pp. 31–2.
26 John Hetherington, 'An Australian Author Returns to His Native Land'.
27 CC, PMAL, p. 11.
28 GJ to David Higham (hereafter DH), 13/3/56: 'baby due yesterday', David Higham Archives, Harry Ransom Humanities Research Center, The University of Texas at Austin.
29 GJ to DH, 12/2/56.
30 GJ to DH, 24/4/56.
31 CC, PMAL, p. 47.
32 CC, PMAL, p. 37.
33 GJ, CSFN p. 123; also GJ, CTTS, p. 172.
34 CC, PMAL, p. 52
35 Cynthia Nolan to Pat Flower, n.d. (April 1956).
36 Cynthia Nolan to Pat Flower, n.d. (April 1956).
37 Jason Johnston, interview with NW, 5/4/98.
38 CC, PMAL, p. 60.
39 CC, PMAL, p. 64.
40 CC, PMAL, p. 91.
41 CC, PMAL, p. 148 (also p. 135).
42 Clifford Tolchard, 'My Husband George: My Wife Charmian'.
43 A French potter named Christian Heidsieck, with his Russian wife Lily Mack, owned the house which the Greers were living in. Information, Martin Johnston.
44 GJ to DH, 24/4/56, 15/5/56.
45 Harrison Platt to Ivan von Auw, 31/5/56, David Higham Archives.
46 GJ to DH, 15/6/56; GJ to William Collins, 15/6/56, David Higham Archives.
47 GJ to DH, 13/3/56, 15/6/56.
48 DH to GJ, 23/5/56 re publication date 11 June; DH to GJ, 1/6/56 re sending authors' copies; GJ to DH, 15/6/56 re William Collins' personal intervention.
49 As contracts for *Mermaid Singing* were not signed until 25 June, even the $US250 advance on that would not have come in until the latter half of the year. Agency correspondence is missing from 1/7/56 to 1/1/57, so it is not clear quite when it arrived.
50 GJ to DH, 24/4/56.
51 DH to GJ, 9/5/56.
52 GJ to DH, 15/5/56, 15/6/56.
53 CC, PMAL, p. 125.
54 CC, PMAL, pp. 125–6. The following two quotations are from the same source.
55 CC, PMAL, p. 131.
56 CC, PMAL p. 121.
57 CC, PMAL, pp. 79–80.
58 CC, PMAL, pp 110–11.
59 CC, PMAL, p. 120.
60 CC, PMAL, pp. 80–1.
61 CC, PMAL, p. 83.

62 CC, PMAL, p. 131. Zoe is named 'Cassandra' in this text.

63 CC, PMAL, p. 82.

64 CC, PMAL, p. 163.

65 CC, PMAL, p. 163.

66 See views expressed in Johnston's short story 'Vale, Pollini!', Garry Kinnane (ed.), *Strong-man from Piraeus and Other Stories*, pp. 173–92.

67 CC, PMAL, pp. 158–9, 128.

68 CC, PMAL, pp. 169–82.

69 GJ to George Ferguson, 3/12/56, Angus & Robertson Collection, Mitchell Library, State Library of NSW. Brian Adams, *Sidney Nolan — Such is Life*, also notes this brief return visit.

70 Because correspondence is missing, there is no date for acceptance of the manuscript. From CC to Mr Scott (at the David Higham agency), 5/1/57, it is clear acceptance has occurred; actual terms in DH to CC and GJ, 28/1/57. The comment from Platt at Bobbs-Merrill re reviews is quoted by CC to Mr Scott, 5/1/57. Gant's comment was made when he compared her subsequent book with 'that delightful *Mermaid Singing*', DH to CC, 17/3/58.

71 CC to DH, 5/1/57.

72 CC, PMAL, pp. 130–1.

73 CC, PMAL, p. 163.

74 See GJ, CTTS, p. 311. Mark Meredith accuses his brother, David Meredith, of frightening the wits out of his wife, and trying to break her heart, by his threat to sell the house as punishment for her affair with Achille Mouliet.

75 CC, PMAL, p. 112.

76 CC, PMAL, p. 144.

77 CC, PMAL, p. 191.

Chapter 15 — A Life for Ourselves

1 CC, interview with Hazel de Berg, National Library of Australia, 8/6/65.

2 CC, interview with Hazel de Berg, 8/6/65.

3 Jason Johnston, interview with NW, 5/4/98.

4 CC, PMAL, p. 110.

5 David Higham (hereafter DH) to CC, 28/3/57, David Higham Archives, Harry Ransom Humanities Research Center, The University of Texas at Austin.

6 CC to DH, 13/4/57.

7 It had arrived in London by 26 April (memo to DH, 26/4/57); it seems to have been posted to the US on 13/4/57. (Ivan von Auw, hereafter IVA, to CC, 29/5/57, David Higham Archives.)

8 James Hall, 'And Now It's Two for the Load', *Australian*, 23/11/68.

9 GJ to George Ferguson, 3/12/56, Angus & Robertson Collection, Mitchell Library, State Library of NSW.

10 GJ to DH, 1/5/57.

11 Charles Sriber, 'It's All Greek to Them', *People*, 14/5/58.

12 CC, radio interview with Ellis Blain, 'Away From It All', ABC, 21/7/65. She said they had only £6 in the bank.

13 GJ to DH, 1/5/57.

14 DH to GJ, 6/5/57.

15 See IVA to GJ, 14/8/58, re American tax requirements. At the beginning of their time in Greece, the couple had avoided the 30% American withholding tax because they were still supposedly residents of Britain. In order to escape the American tax, they needed proof of Greek residency and tax responsibilities — which they were unable to obtain.

16 GJ to DH, 1/5/57.

17 GJ to DH, 1/5/57.

18 IVA to CC, 28/5/57. As he also pointed out, 'sold' really only meant distributed, because booksellers 'enjoy a return privilege'.

19 IVA to CC, 4/6/57, quoting letter from Harrison Platt.

20 I met Grace Edwards, through Martin Johnston, in early 1976, staying with her in Athens for a fortnight and travelling with her to Skyros for the *apokreas* festivities. Through the next year I saw her frequently, both in Athens and at the seaside village of Paralion Astros, where Martin and I lived full-time and Grace had a weekend house. Grace would often talk of George and Charmian, both when Martin was present and — in a rather different way — when she and I were alone. As I was not even considering a biography of Clift at that time, I naturally did not document our conversations; however, I clearly remember certain anecdotes and attitudes that Grace would repeat.

21 Story related in Garry Kinnane, *George Johnston: A Biography*, Nelson, Melbourne, 1986, p. 172, citing interview with Grace Edwards, 1983.

22 CC, interview with Hazel de Berg, 8/6/65.

23 On a couple of occasions when I lived in Greece I heard vitriolic attacks on Clift from people who had felt excluded from her circle.

24 Mary Andrews, interview (notes only), 24/7/89. The *agora* is the marketplace — which, in the case of Hydra, is also the waterfront.

25 CC to DH, 1/7/57.

26 CC to DH, 22/7/57. A handwritten memo from someone at the literary agency notes: 'Her letter was 2nd May to R.G.; R.G. wrote her 15 May'.

27 DH to CC (16/7/57) noted there was 'no record that it passed through here (though there might well not be)'. There was a flurry of correspondence in the course of which the agency even asked Ivan von Auw for a copy of the American proofs — but nothing turned up.

28 PMS (for DH) to CC, 23/8/57: 'book ready for production'; but GJ to DH (29/11/57) notes CC has recently done the proofs; DH to CC, 20/1/58 — a note on publication day.

29 IVA to CC, 24/9/57.

30 GJ, CSFN, p. 171: 'I still do get my books published [...] and the more intellectual of the foreigners here seem to find this unforgiveable; they, being avant garde and unpublished, consider me a "commercial" writer and therefore contemptible'. This attitude of the avant garde is also a complaint of the Johnston character in Charles Sriber's 'We'll Never Go Back', *Bulletin*, 20/10/62 (a fictionalised version of the Johnstons' island life).

31 Lawrence Pollinger (an associate of DH) to GJ, 9/10/58. This does not make clear how much money Johnston was after.

32 Harrison Platt to IVA, 2/10/57 (David Higham Archives).

33 GJ to DH, 14/5/58.

34 George Johnston, *The Darkness Outside*, Collins, London, 1959, p. 191.

35 GJ, *The Darkness Outside*, p. 221.

36 GJ, *The Darkness Outside*, p. 80.

37 GJ, *The Darkness Outside*, p. 187.
38 CC, PMAL, p. 74.
39 CC, PMAL, p. 127.
40 GJ, CTTS, p. 214.
41 GJ, CTTS, p. 214.
42 GJ, '*Clean Straw for Nothing* General Notes', GJ Coll., Box 1, Folder 4, item 7.
43 Cynthia Nolan to Pat Flower, n.d. (April 1956), Mitchell Library, State Library of New South Wales.
44 Account by Carolyn Ross, previously Gassoumis, in Tom Rothfield, 'Island Legend for Sale', *Age*, 1/10/77.
45 Patrick Greer, 'George Johnston in Hydra', *London Magazine*, November/December 1980. The following quotation is also from this source.
46 In *The Darkness Outside* the repressed young German archaeologist Steindorf suicides after the object of his homosexual passion dies in an accident. And in *Closer to the Sun*, the little Czech potter, Conrad Fegel, throws himself off the cliff, unable to bear his memories of the past. Later the same day, Kate Meredith — recoiling from her husband's anger at her infidelity — contemplates suicide when she goes to sit alone at that very place on the cliff-top. Yet, as her lover points out to her, Kate is not the sort of person for whom suicide is 'the answer'. GJ, CTTS, p. 304.
47 GJ, CSFN, pp. 290–1. Although this passage is set in 1959, it has as much bearing on 1958.
48 DH to CC, 17/3/58.
49 DH to CC, 10/7/58.
50 CC, PMAL, p. 111.
51 DH to CC, 10/7/58.
52 DH to CC, 17/3/58.
53 IVA to GJ, 19/12/57; IVA to CC, 2/1/58; IVA to DH, 18/3/58; IVA to GJ, 14/8/58; IVA to DH, 8/1/59; DH to GJ, 21/9/59.
54 CC, WTTPG, p. 7.
55 CC, WTTPG, pp. 87–8.
56 CC, WTTPG, pp. 120–1.
57 CC, WTTPG, p. 176.
58 CC, WTTPG, p. 31.
59 CC, WTTPG, p. 154.
60 CC, WTTPG, p. 194.
61 DH to GJ, 28/7/58; GJ to DH, 28/7/58.
62 GJ to DH, 10/9/58.
63 DH to GJ, 30/10/58; GJ to DH, 10/11/58.
64 CC to DH, 14/12/58.

Chapter 16 — Almost Foundering

1 CC, 'On *Clean Straw for Nothing*', BAWO, pp. 311–12.
2 GJ, CSFN, p. 168.
3 GJ to David Higham (hereafter DH), 3/1/59, David Higham Archives, Harry Ransom Humanities Research Center, The University of Texas at Austin, 20/1/59.
4 CC to DH, 29/1/59.
5 CC to DH, 27/1/59.

6   To avoid confusion, the published title will be used throughout this discussion despite the fact that, at the time of writing, the author was not thinking in terms of this title. Indeed, the reference to the Icarus myth implied by this title does not connect with the novel's theme. In the text there are no references to the Icarus story, or even to the notion of reckless daring that the myth raises; the new title was simply a last minute choice when the publishers did not like the original one that the author provided.

7   GJ, CTTS, p. 273.

8   GJ, CTTS, p. 319.

9   GJ, CTTS, pp. 38–9.

10   GJ, CTTS, pp. 210–11.

11   CC, 'On *Clean Straw for Nothing*', BAWO, p. 312.

12   Sandra Hall, 'Time to Face a Modern Australia', *Bulletin*, 23/8/69; Elizabeth Riddell, 'George, for Whom Writing Is Therapy', *Australian*, 16/8/69.

13   Ivan von Auw (hereafter IVA) to CC, 26/5/59, David Higham Archives.

14   CC to DH, 30/5/59.

15   CC to DH, n.d., but attached to it is a letter from GJ to DH, received 23/7/59. After Clift's complaint, Higham managed to get the terms of the contract revised, so that the advance equalled that given for the earlier book. DH to CC, 23/7/59.

16   GJ to DH, n.d. (received 23/7/59).

17   GJ to DH, n.d. (received 23/7/59).

18   These excerpts from reviews of *The Darkness Outside* appear on the back jacket of *Closer to the Sun*, Collins, London, 1960. There are also comments from the *Scotsman* ('so good a novel') and the *Spectator* (again referring to Johnston's 'Conradian knack'). The *Yorkshire Evening Post* was rather closer to the mark, declaring: 'Here is one of the century's finest story-tellers, with the same skill in plot-weaving as Nevil Shute, but with a richer prose'.

19   GJ to DH, n.d. (received 23/7/59).

20   GJ to DH, 23/3/59.

21   In CSFN (p. 194), in a passage set in the summer of 1959, Calverton tells Meredith that he is looking like 'a bloody Belsen victim'. This description was applied by Sid Nolan to the whole family. See David Marr (ed.), *Patrick White Letters*, Random House, Sydney, 1994, p. 278, PW to Frederick Glover, 8/4/65: '[The Nolans] visited [the Johnstons] once when they were living on Hydra, and there was a kind of Belsen atmosphere, with the whole family more or less starving, and George in a state of TB'.

22   At this time he told Grace Edwards he was 'convinced' he had cancer. See Garry Kinnane, *George Johnston: a Biography*, Nelson, Melbourne, 1986, p. 186. See also John Hetherington, 'An Australian Author Returns to His Native Land', *Age*, 8/2/64.

23   See Elizabeth Riddell, 'George, for Whom Writing Is Therapy', GJ noted he had been 'goaded by Charmian and friends' to see a doctor.

24   Garry Kinnane, p. 188.

25   This is a common effect of tuberculosis — which, of course, George did not know that he had.

26   In *Closer to the Sun*, David Meredith sleeps upstairs on the divan in the study while Kate sleeps alone in the bedroom (CTTS, p. 137). In the extant fragment of Clift's play of *Walk to the Paradise Gardens* (probably written at this time), Julia and Charles sleep in single beds in separate rooms. GJ Coll., Box 6, Folder 1, item 5.

27 GJ, CTTS, p. 68.

28 GJ, CTTS, p. 166.

29 GJ, CTTS, p. 60: 'Women with their husbands at home could still feel lonely, neglected, left to their own devices'.

30 Garry Kinnane, p. 184. The internal quotation is from Charles Sriber.

31 GJ to Monica Preston, 26/10/59, David Higham Archives.

32 Jason Johnston, interview with NW, 5/4/98.

33 GJ to Monica Preston, 26/10/59.

34 Garry Kinnane, p. 188, citing interview with Grace Edwards, 1983. I also remember the line 'He said he wasn't going to let her bug him any more' from Grace telling me about this time. An odd thing was that Grace rarely said Charmian's name. It was always 'she' or 'her'.

35 GJ to DH, 8/12/59. As Johnston explained in this letter, although the novel was to be by Shane Martin, it was 'not [. . .] a suspense story, nor does it concern Professor Challis, but there seems no reason to me why an author has to stick to one genre'. He added that Ivan von Auw was submitting it to Morrow as a Shane Martin.

36 Garry Kinnane (p. 188) notes: 'Clift visited Johnston at the Edwards flat, and seems even to have displayed a little jealousy herself that Johnston's recuperation was taking place outside her sphere of influence'.

37 This offer of a long-term living arrangement appears in *Clean Straw for Nothing*, pp. 220–1. Grace often said how upset she was on reading this, because she felt that the author had made her seem to be trying to have an affair with him, whereas what she had been offering George was a relationship of two friends sharing company together.

38 When Martin and I stayed with Grace at her flat in 1976, we would always sit and have a drink on the balcony at midday, and she would frequently reminisce about the pattern of this time when George stayed with her. The only critical comment I ever heard her make about George was when she said that she was shocked to find that he got his ancient history from William Durant.

39 On one occasion, when Grace and I were lunching alone together, she told me of a night when she and Charmian went out by themselves to a Piraeus taverna. The point of this story was that this was the only occasion on which Grace had felt at all close to Charmian. Grace attributed this to the fact that there were no men present. As part of the same conversation, I asked: 'Do you think Charmian was jealous of you?' Grace replied in a self-deprecatory fashion: 'Look at me! I was never beautiful!' However, I think Grace completely misunderstood the sort of thing that would provoke Charmian's jealousy. From this discussion of jealousy, Grace went on to talk about Charmian leaving notes (presumably from or to her lover) in her pockets for George to find. Then she talked about Charmian making the infidelity known because she needed reassurance.

40 CC, 'In Praise of the GP', BAWO, p. 135; GJ, CSFN, p. 143.

41 GJ to DH, 8/12/59.

42 GJ, 'The Verdict', GJ Coll., Box 3, Folder 7, item 7. This 15-page typescript is obviously what was written in 1959. Meredith's wife is named 'Kate', but in handwriting over this the author has later written 'Cressida'. Similarly, there is reference to 'the journey he and Al had made from Kweilin to Liuchow'. Over the name 'Al', the author has handwritten 'Conover', which is the name of Meredith's companion in the novel *The Far Road*, written in 1960. Quotations up to 'afraid to touch her' are from this version of the text.

43 GJ, 'The Verdict', GJ Coll., Box 3, Folder 11, item 12. This 20-page typescript is the same as the 1959 version up to page 15, but incorporates the handwritten substitution of the names 'Cressida' and 'Conover', and a couple of minor additions or changes. Then after page 15, there are an extra five pages. This is the version published in Garry Kinnane (ed.), *Strong-man from Piraeus and Other Stories*, Nelson, Melbourne, 1983, pp. 156–72. (The 1959 version ends with the passage that apppears on p. 169 of the Kinnane edition, with the words 'something putrescent'.) As to the dating of the author's two periods of writing this story, we know from Grace Edwards' testimony that the author wrote what he regarded as a completed version of this story at her place in 1959. Mungo MacCallum remembered George Johnston writing this story — and showing it to him — on Hydra in the summer of 1963. Mungo MacCallum, telephone interview (notes only) with NW, 21/4/95.

44 GJ, CSFN, p. 34. Subsequent quotation pp. 35–6.

45 Although in some places the novel's timeframe does not correspond to factual time, the author in his basic dating framework of island events follows the real chronology; however, as Kalymnos and Hydra are conflated into one place, the second year on the island means the second year in Greece — 1956.

46 GJ, CSFN, pp. 180–1.

47 Information, Martin Johnston.

48 This would later be acknowledged by the Australian Government, which would award him a repatriation pension.

49 GJ, CSFN, pp. 214, 220.

50 Garry Kinnane, *George Johnston*, p. 189.

51 John Hetherington, 'An Australian Author Returns to His Native Land'. (Article based on written information supplied by GJ.)

52 Tom Rothfield, 'Island Legend for Sale', *Age*, 1/10/77. The Hydra resident quoted is Carolyn Ross (previously Gassoumis).

53 Garry Kinnane, *George Johnston*, p. 189.

54 GJ to Gae Johnston, 16/2/60.

55 CC, 'On *Clean Straw for Nothing*', BAWO, pp. 312–13.

56 CC, 'On *Clean Straw for Nothing*', BAWO, pp. 311–12.

57 Alan Trengrove, 'Partners — It's In Writing', *Sun*, 6/7/66.

58 Ira Bruce Nadel, *Various Positions: A Life of Leonard Cohen*, Pantheon Books, New York, 1996, p. 77; Marie Knuckey, 'In Search of Charmian's Island', *Sydney Morning Herald*, 1/6/72.

59 Garry Kinnane, *George Johnston*, p. 191.

Chapter 17 — Playing the Role Assigned

1 CC, PMAL, p. 179.

2 CC, 'Social Drinking', IA, p. 7.

3 CC, 'On Debits and Credits', TILL, p. 19.

4 Jason Johnston, interview with NW, 5/4/98.

5 See CC, 'On Junior Thespians', TILL, pp. 251–52.

6 Martin Johnston, interview with Hazel de Berg, National Library of Australia, 23/6/80.

7 CC, 'Social Drinking', IA, p. 7.

8 CC, 'An Old Address Book', WCC, pp. 51–2.

9   CC, 'An Old Address Book, WCC, p. 51.

10 As the Higham agency's correspondence for 1960 is missing, we cannot be sure of the reasons for the novel's rejection. It was accepted in America, but with no immediate publication schedule. In May 1961 Morrow still had made no publication date for it; at this stage, Johnston suggested that they should look at publishing *The Far Road* first. Ivan von Auw (hereafter IVA) to GJ, 4/5/61; CMS (for IVA) to David Higham (hereafter DH), 10/5/61, David Highan Archives, Harry Ransom Humanities Center, The University of Texas at Austin.

11 GJ to DH, 1/5/61.

12 Colin Simpson, *Greece — The Unclouded Eye,* Angus & Robertson, Sydney, 1968, p. 105.

13 CC, 'On *Clean Straw for Nothing*', BAWO, pp. 312–313.

14 As the 1960 correspondence is missing, there is no record of submission, but by the beginning of January 1961 the contractual agreements were being drawn up. Jacqueline Kern (DH's assistant) to GJ, 4/1/61. Agreement returned, GJ to Jacqueline Kern, 7/2/61. DH to GJ, 28/12/61 quotes from letter from George Hardinge (at Collins) saying that £300 advance for *The Far Road* had been paid in December 1960.

15 CC, 'Other People's Houses', WCC, p. 34.

16 CC, 'The Magic of Mornings', WCC, p. 17.

17 CC, 'Things that Go Boomp in the Night', IA, p. 136.

18 Clift would lament that the ending of post-war austerity seemed a change for the worse. CC, 'On England, My England', BAWO, p. 32.

19 When David Higham heard of this 'SOS' second-hand, he tactfully pointed out to his client that 'questions of tax as well as of commission arise'. DH to GJ, 10/2/61.

20 Later, when the issue of this £300 started to become complicated, Johnston was to tell Higham that Collins had loaned him £300 for fares back to Greece. GJ to DH, 3/2/62.

21 DH to GJ, 10/2/61.

22 DH to GJ, 14/4/61. It is clear, however, that by mid to late March Johnston already knew the publisher's position on this.

23 CC, radio interview with Ellis Blain, *Away From it All*, ABC, 21/7/65.

24 CC, 'The Rare Art of Inspiring Others', IA, p. 64.

25 The gift was confirmed by Sidney Nolan. See Garry Kinnane, *George Johnston: A Biography,* Nelson, Melbourne, 1986, p. 20, citing interview with Nolan, 1982. This incident appears in CSFN, when Kiernan sends the Merediths an art book containing forty £5 notes. (CSFN, pp. 241–242). The timing of this in the novel is straight after David Meredith's attempt to find work in Fleet Street. In regard to the real gift, there is no record of when it actually happened, or how much money was involved.

26 GJ to DH, 1/4/61.

27 Johnston later told Colin Simpson that 'Vic Valentine lent us the fare to come back'. (Colin Simpson, p. 106.)

28 CSFN, pp. 248–250. This passage concludes: 'It was Calverton once again who came to the rescue'. This character's other rescues included convincing Meredith to see a doctor in 1959, and forcing Meredith to return to Cressida after the affair with Galloway. This fictional gift from Finch ended up in the biographical record. One of Finch's biographers refers to it, quoting the Johnston novel as proof. (Elaine Dundy, *Finch, Bloody Finch,* Michael Joseph, London, 1980, pp. 274–5.) And John Tranter in his introduction to *Martin Johnston: Selected Poems and Prose,* University of Queensland Press, St Lucia, 1993, p. xvii, notes that when the family was in England

at this time, 'a notable benefactor, according to Martin, was the actor Peter Finch'. This was a case where Martin also had come to believe the novel.

29 CC, 'An Old Address Book', WCC, pp. 51–52.

30 Colin Simpson, p. 106. Same source for description of the welcome home party at Katsikas's.

31 GJ to DH, 1/5/61.

32 Martin Johnston, interview with Hazel de Berg, 23/6/80.

33 Jason Johnston, 5/4/98.

34 CC, 'On Debits and Credits', TILL, p. 19.

35 Jason Johnston, 5/4/98.

36 CC to Jo Meyer, n.d. (23/8/61). This letter is clearly from 1961, but it is dated only '23rd (I think)'. A reference in it to George receiving a cable 'yesterday' regarding a film offer for *The Sponge Divers* correlates with a letter in the agency files from Richard Gregson to GJ, 23/8/61, confirming his telegram re this film offer.

37 IVA to GJ, 26/4/61.

38 GJ to DH, 1/5/61.

39 DH memo, 14/4/61.

40 This script, *Beachhead*, was done for the London production firm Re-Diffusion. GJ to DH, 1/5/61.

41 IVA to GJ, 22/5/61.

42 Garry Kinnane, p. 203, quotes GJ to Elsie, 5/10/61, to the effect that Johnston had returned 'in debt to the extent of £1500'.

43 IVA to GJ, 27/7/61.

44 CC to DH, 9/6/61.

45 DH to CC, 15/6/61; undated memo with sales figures in file with this letter.

46 Jacqueline Kern to CC, 4/7/61.

47 John Hetherington, 'An Australian Author Returns to his Native Land', *Age*, 8/2/64.

48 Clifford Tolchard, 'My Husband George: My Wife Charmian', *Walkabout*, January 1969.

49 James Hall, 'And Now It's Two for the Load', *Australian*, 23/11/68.

50 CC, 'An Old Address Book', WCC, pp. 52–3.

51 GJ to John Ulm, 19/11/63, GJ Coll., Box 1, Folder 4, Item 6.

52 Geoffrey Hutton, 'He Died Alive', *Age*, 23/7/70, p. 6.

53 CC, 'An Old Address Book, WCC, pp. 52–3.

54 Marie Knuckey, 'In Search of Charmian's Island', *Sydney Morning Herald*, 1/6/72.

55 CC to Jo Meyer, n.d. (23/8/61).

56 Garry Kinnane, p. 208, paraphrasing and quoting GJ to Elsie, 5/10/61.

57 DH to GJ, 16/10/61: Hardinge (at Collins) had told DH that GJ had been ill; GJ to DH, 4/12/61.

58 CC to Jo Meyer, n.d. (23/8/61).

59 IVA to GJ, 5/12/61.

60 CC to Jo Meyer, n.d. (24/3/62). It is clear the book was begun around January.

61 GJ to IVA, 28/5/62.

62 Information, Martin Johnston.

63 GJ to DH, 3/2/62.

64 DH to GJ, 24/1/62.

65 GJ to William Collins, 19/2/62.

66 CC, 'On CSFN', BAWO, p. 312.

67 GJ to DH, 3/2/62.

68 See GJ letter to Elsie, cited next chapter. In chapter 16 I discussed Clift's reference to how the relationship 'almost foundered'. This can be found in passage cited next note.

69 CC, 'On *Clean Straw for Nothing*', BAWO, p. 311.

70 Jason Johnston, 5/4/98

71 Amy's death certificate gives her usual address as 4 Lang Street Woonona; this is also given as Barré's address. Information re Amy's last years from Margaret Backhouse, interview with NW, June 1983. In Charles Sriber's fictionalised account of the Johnstons' life, the Charmian character, when asked if there isn't anybody she would want to go back and see in Australia, replies, 'Oh, Mother perhaps. But we've been away too long to ever go back'. Charles Sriber, 'We'll Never Go Back', *Bulletin*, 20/10/62.

72 IVA to GJ, 5/12/61.

73 IVA to GJ, 5/3/62.

74 GJ to IVA, 14/3/62.

75 IVA to GJ, 21/3/62; IVA to DH, 21/3/62; DH memo to IVA, n.d.

76 GJ to DH, 30/5/62.

77 GJ to DH, 24/6/62.

78 CC, HM, p. 112. Re being outside society, see p. 57 (Fotis); p. 86 (Kathy).

79 CC, HM, p. 108.

80 DH Lawrence, *Lady Chatterley's Lover*, Penguin Books, Middlesex, 1961, pp. 48–9, 70–1.

81 CC, HM, p. 203.

82 Richard Lovelace, 'To Lucasta, Going to the Wars', Helen Gardner (ed.), *The Metaphysical Poets*, Penguin Books, Middlesex, 1966, p. 232.

83 Such speculation was perhaps fuelled by the Author's Note to the novel, which as well as declaring that 'The characters do not exist, nor did the incidents occur, except in my imagination' adds: 'although the book was occasioned by the actual face of a sponge diver which has haunted me for eight years'.

84 GJ to DH, 24/5/62; 10/7/62.

85 GJ to IVA, 28/5/62.

86 CC, PMAL, pp. 178–9. In the 1962 Warner Bros movie shot on Hydra, *Island of Love* (concerning an American conman who discovers a Greek island named Paradiso and decides to exploit its tourist potential), a glimpse is sometimes to be had of a stylish woman in a large-brimmed hat, sitting at a harbour cafe. She is Charmian, acting herself.

87 Martin Johnston, interview with Hazel de Berg, 23/6/80.

88 In the *Island of Love* film, Shane and Martin can be seen running down a cobbled lane, followed by Jason and his little friend Ellenitza.

89 Jason Johnson, 5/4/98.

90 Jacqueline Kern to CC & GJ, 8/8/62.

91 IVA to GJ, 20/8/62.

92 DH to GJ, 5/9/62. He proposed offering it to James Michie at The Bodley Head.

93 Alan Williams to IVA, 25/9/62; IVA to GJ, 13/11/62.

94 Over the next twelve months it would be refused in Britain by Collins, Batsford and Murray. DH to GJ 5/2/64; Jacqueline Kern to GJ, 19/2/64.

95 Amy Clift, death certificate. Date of death 29/9/62. Unlike Syd Clift and his parents, who were buried at the cemetery at Bombo, Amy Clift was cremated at Wollongong Crematorium, 2/10/62.

96 Cordelia's name was also perhaps derived from the unflatteringly portrayed elder sister in Rebecca West's novel *The Fountain Overflows*, Macmillan, London, 1977. According to Martin Johnston, Clift was an avid reader of West.

97 CC, assorted pages of typescript, GJ Coll., Box 5, Folder 4 (no item number). See A Note on the Endnotes. A late-draft page of *Honour's Mimic* mixed in with these drafts is further evidence for dating this work as occurring during this time. Also, in one of the Miranda pages, the author writes: 'And now, so far away, let me try to remember it clearly'. Clift would not have written this if she were writing the text in Australia.

98 Johnston's biographer — who assigns a date as late as 1969 to the typescript of *Greener Grows the Grass* — believes that Clift chose at this late stage to use the name *Christine* Morley, thereby 'totally shunning all the literary and moral connotations of the name Cressida', which he believes Johnston had chosen alone. Garry Kinnane, pp. 77, 79, 267. However, all the evidence — including CC's 1968 application to the Commonwealth Literary Fund — is weighed against Kinnane on this.

99 Rodney Hall, interview with NW, 10/7/95. Some years later Rodney and his wife Bet named one of their daughters 'Cressida' as a kind of tribute to Charmian. When they told her, she was delighted, and repeated her love for the name.

100 The first five pages of Miranda text entitled *The End of the Morning* were reproduced almost verbatim — except for the change to first person narrative and the change of heroine's name — as the opening section of the novel-in-progress. This suggests that the author was happy with this Miranda opening, but shortly after writing it had the bright idea of changing narrative mode and the narrator's name. Four pages (numbered pp. 48–51) of the first person text narrated by Cressida Morley are in the the same bundle of the author's typescripts as the Miranda material cited above. GJ Coll., Box 5, Folder 4 (no item number).

101 CC, application to Commonwealth Literary Fund, Commonwealth Literary Fund Records, Australian Archives, 19/8/68.

102 Johnston later declared that he had thought about the story that would become *My Brother Jack* for 17 years before writing it. (John Hetherington, 'An Australian Author Returns to his Native Land'.) This takes the time back from 1962 to 1945. In a taped interview with Russell Drysdale in March 1967, he repeated that he had thought about the story for 17 or 18 years before he started writing it. Transcript, *Russell Drysdale* television documentary, 21/3/67, GJ Coll., Box 4, Folder 20, item 31.

103 In a letter written to his ex-wife early the following year, Johnston would pose this sort of question. After noting that 'Charmian and I have been grappling with a domestic and emotional crisis for some little time' he adds: '(Maybe it's just me who can't make these things work out!)', GJ to Elsie Johnston, 15/1/63.

104 GJ, 'Childhood — "The Dollikos"', GJ Coll., Box 1, Folder 4, item 7.

105 CC, PMAL, p. 61.

106 GJ, 'The Meredith Papers', GJ Coll., Box 1, Folder 4, item 8. As to the dating of this work, it must have been done on Hydra and before MBJ. The 'editor' refers to 'the island where [Meredith] finally came to rest', and also notes that 'Of the numerous books he wrote I doubt if one was remembered a year after its publication'. Once the persona of David Meredith had 'written' the first person narrative of MBJ, then such a statement could not be made in regard to Meredith.

107 Moreover, in the collaborative China novel, *The Big Chariot,* Clift and Johnston had written of the parallel fates of two warlord brothers.

108 See Garry Kinnane, p. 215.

109 GJ, red-bound notebook, 11th page, GJ Coll., Box 1, Folder 1, item 1. George Johnston would later note that one of his 'objects' had been 'to attempt to analyse the growth and development of two very different types of Australian out of an identical

suburban environment; in other words, to examine the social, moral, economic and emotional forces that shape human character'. GJ, 'English for School Certificate', Transcript, ABC, 12/6/70, GJ Coll., Box 5, Folder 23, item 47.
110 CC, 'On Being Unable to Write an Article', TILL, p. 86.

Chapter 18 — Some Inscrutable Bond

1 CC, notes in CC's handwriting, slipped into back of GJ's red-bound notebook, GJ Coll., Box 1, Folder 1, item 1.
2 Joan Flanagan, 'His Novels Were Born Out of Pain', *Advertiser*, 12/7/69; unsigned four-page press release, 'George Johnston — Notes of a talk with George Johnston on his new book: *Clean Straw for Nothing*'. See chapter 23 for dating of this interview.
3 GJ, 'English for School Certificate', Transcript, ABC, 12/6/70, GJ Coll., Box 5, Folder 23, item 47.
4 Kay Keavney, 'From George, with Sadness' *Australian Women's Weekly*, 3/9/69.
5 Storry Walton would comment on CC's amazing recall of 1930s period detail, in regard to the input Clift gave to the set design for the television series of *My Brother Jack*. He remembered that she produced pages of notes about furniture and furnishings, labels on jars, costumes. Storry Walton, interview with NW, 19/3/90.
6 GJ, red-bound notebook, GJ Coll, Box 1, Folder 1, item 1.
7 GJ to David Higham (hereafter DH), 11/11/62. David Higham Archives, Harry Ransom Humanities Center, The University of Texas at Austin.
8 Information, Martin Johnston. So much did Martin see the daily production of three pages as the kind of standard authorial practice that he would himself adopt this 'target' when he was writing his own first novel, *Cicada Gambit*, in 1974.
9 GJ to Elsie, 15/1/63.
10 Joan Flanagan, 'George Johnston — Notes of a talk with George Johnston on his new book: *Clean Straw for Nothing*', p. 2. In this interview the author actually referred to keeping the fire going and the couple working together in 'the bedroom'. However, in the interview with Alan Trengrove he specifically refers to 'the sunken living room'. ('Partners — It's In Writing', *Sun*, 6/7/66.) The living room with the open fire was functioning as bedroom, living room and study.
11 James Hall, 'And Now It's Two for the Load', *Australian*, 23/11/68. The couple may have been remembering the initial story session, which CC describes as taking 13 hours. (CC, 'On Being Unable to Write an Article', TILL, p. 86.) Or this may have been another occasion, later in the writing process.
12 GJ, red-bound notebook, GJ Coll., Box 1, Folder 1, item 1.
13 Rodney Hall, interview with NW, 10/7/95. This explanation was given when Rodney had 'really objected to the first wife, the Communist first wife [...] I said to George, "I honestly have to say I don't believe in this woman" [...] And Charmian said, "Well, she was a concoction of ours"'.
14 Rodney Hall, 10/7/95.
15 Kay Keavney, 'From George, with Sadness'.
16 Alan Trengrove, 'Partners — It's in Writing'.
17 Ivan von Auw (hereafter IVA) to GJ, 13/11/62 (David Higham Archives).
18 GJ to Robert Knittel, 3/12/62.
19 CC, notes in CC's handwriting, slipped into back of GJ's red-bound notebook, GJ Coll., Box 1, Folder 1, item 1. These particular notes constitute nine unnumbered

pages of material, clearly written in one session. The phrase 'My hot, pained, confused self' recurs in the midst of the notes on the character of Jack which Clift wrote in Johnston's red-bound notebook. There are also a few phrases which recur in *Honour's Mimic*: 'another world' (p. 155); 'courage of an inherited despair' (p. 155); 'She had longed to die, positively' (p. 112); 'time of dark, palpable joy' (p. 110); 'another, denser element' (p. 143); 'rough as a cat's tongue' (p. 45). These confirm the dating of this passage as occurring at this time.

20 Breaking off abruptly at the end of an eight-page book section, it forms the last part of 38 pages of handwritten notes ripped from a notebook and slipped into the back of the red-bound journal in which George Johnston made notes for all three books of his trilogy. In *A Cartload of Clay* (pp. 109–10) David Meredith, after the death of Cressida, discovers amongst his wife's papers in her desk drawer a white notebook with a leather cover. As Meredith 'fingers through the pages' he sees it is 'a documentation of private thoughts and anxieties jotted down at intervals over a period of quite a few years, part-confessional, part self-examination'. Later in this part of the novel, Meredith shows the journal to his son Julian. Martin Johnston — the model for Julian — always said that this scene was lifted directly from life. Although Julian (and Martin) only saw the outside of the journal, it was intact in the drawer after Clift's death. No such journal remains among her papers.

21 GJ to Elsie, 15/1/63.

22 Elizabeth Riddell, 'George, for Whom Working is Therapy', *Australian*, 16/8/69.

23 John Hetherington, 'An Australian Author Returns to his Native Land', *Age*, 8/2/84.

24 Clifford Tolchard, 'My Husband George: My Wife Charmian', *Walkabout*, January 1969.

25 Martin Johnston, interview with Hazel de Berg, National Library of Australia, 23/6/80.

26 CC, interview with Hazel de Berg, National Library of Australia, 8/6/65.

27 John Hetherington, 'An Australian Author Returns to his Native Land'.

28 Mungo MacCallum, who was on Hydra during the summer of 1963, could not remember hearing discussion of the return. After he had moved on to London — ie after September 1963 — he received a letter from George, telling him about the decision to go back to Australia. Mungo MacCallum, telephone interview with NW (notes only), 21/4/95.

29 In the 1964 publicity information sent to John Hetherington ('An Australian Author Returns to his Native Land'), GJ said MBJ 'took him six months to write, working seven days a week'. In the 'English for School Certificate' talk given on the ABC in 1970, he put the novel's writing time at seven months. It is more reasonable to accept the earlier version, especially as this would fit the period from early October 1962 (the starting time provided by Johnston's correspondence) to late March. Mungo MacCallum arrived on Hydra in late March or early April 1963, and he remembered that the typescript was already sent off. (Interview, 21/4/95.) Garry Kinnane, *George Johnston: A Biography*, Nelson, Melbourne, 1986, p. 223, gives the time for the completion of MBJ as June 1963, but this is too late.

30 Mungo MacCallum, 21/4/95.

31 In his 'English for School Certificate' radio talk, George Johnston stated that after finishing the novel he 'went to hospital for six weeks'. (Transcript, GJ Coll., Box 5, Folder 23, item 47, p. 9.) This cannot be true. There was no hospital on Hydra, and Mungo MacCallum is sure that George was never gone from Hydra for as long as six weeks, though he 'did go back and forth to doctors in Athens'.

32 Elizabeth Riddell, 'George, for Whom Working is Therapy'.

33 Mungo MacCallum remembered Johnston showing him this story, which Mungo thought to be new. As we know, it was originally written in Athens in 1959. (The 15 page version in GJ Coll., Box 3, Folder 7, item 7.) The 'new' story was the second version. (The 20 page version in GJ Coll., Box 3, Folder 11, item 12.) In early February 1964, Johnston offered Higham a number of stories for submission, including 'The Verdict'. GJ to DH, 5/2/64.

34 GJ, 'Clean Straw for Nothing General Notes', GJ Coll., Box 1, Folder 4, item 7; GJ, 'CSFN draft (i)', GJ Coll., Box 3, Folder 7, pp. 1–28 plus pp. 32–34.

35 CC, interview with Hazel de Berg, 8/6/65.

36 In April 1964 it was still being rejected. Blanche Knopf declined it but said that, if the agency didn't sell it, she would like to see Clift's next book. Jacqueline Kern (DH's assistant) to CMS (at Harold Ober Associates), 21/4/64.

37 Mungo MacCallum, 21/4/95. Subsequent quotation same source.

38 GJ, 'Clean Straw for Nothing General Notes', GJ Coll., Box 1, Folder 4, item 7. References to Meredith's need to 'save himself so that he could get back to Australia' make it clear these notes were written in the months before the author left Hydra.

39 Jason Johnston, interview with NW, 5/4/98.

40 At a somewhat younger age, Martin had awarded marks out of 10 to a number of the poems in Australian Bush Ballads, Douglas Stewart and Nancy Keesing (eds), Angus & Robertson, Sydney, 1955. Copy in my possession.

41 GJ to George Ferguson, 11/9/63, Angus & Robertson Collection, Mitchell Library, State Library of New South Wales.

42 GJ to Elsie, 7/11/63, quoted by Garry Kinnane, p. 224.

43 Rodney Hall, 10/7/95.

44 GJ to John Ulm, 19/11/63. GJ Coll., Box 1, Folder 4, item 6. GJ's initial letter and Ulm's reply are not extant, but the gist of them is clear in this long third item of correspondence.

45 GJ to DH, 25/1/64.

46 GJ to Gae Johnston, 12/12/63.

47 Martin Johnston, interview with Hazel de Berg, 23/6/80.

48 See CC, 'The Charm of Old Houses', BAWO, p. 132.

49 Rodney Hall, 'Introduction', The World of Charmian Clift, Collins Publishers Australia, Sydney, 1989, pp. 9–12.

50 Rodney Hall, 10/7/95.

51 Rodney Hall, 'Introduction', WCC.

52 Bet Hall, interview with NW, 10/7/95.

53 DH to GJ, 9/1/64. In April Collins printed an extra 3000 copies for the Australian market. DH to GJ, 8/4/64.

54 GJ to DH, 25/1/64.

55 GJ to DH, 25/1/64.

56 GJ to Elsie, 5/2/64, quoted in Garry Kinnane, p. 233.

57 Bet Hall, interview with NW, 10/7/95.

58 Rodney Hall, 10/7/95. See also Epilogue.

59 GJ to DH, 25/3/64.

60 Joan Flanagan, interview with NW, 6/4/93; email to NW 23/1/01. Next quotation and description of welcome party and TV interview from Joan Flanagan, 6/4/93.

61 Adrian Mitchell, 'Inside Jack's Famous Brother', Weekend Australian, 4–5 October 1986; Chester Eagle, 'Links with Greatness', Age, 11/10/86.

62 Martin Johnston, interview with Hazel de Berg, 23/6/80.

63 GJ, 'Terra Incognita Revisited', *Age Literary Supplement*, 25/4/64.

64 Rodney Hall, 10/7/95.

65 Bet Hall, 10/7/95.

66 Rodney Hall, 'Introduction', WCC, pp. 10–11.

67 Rodney Hall, 10/7/95. Subsequent quotation same source.

68 Bet Hall (10/7/95) described how very distressed Charmian was when she returned from this experience, and how she wrote a letter to the Australian Ambassador protesting at the treatment of Greek women. Martin Johnston (interview with Hazel de Berg, 23/6/80) referred to 'very humiliating preliminaries which make me sorry for every other migrant'.

69 Bet Hall, 10/7/95, spoke of Zoe's situation, and how there was sometimes a very uneasy atmosphere in the house when Zoe was present.

70 GJ to Elsie re 19 March wedding anniversary noted by Garry Kinnane, p. 237.

71 GJ to Elsie, 30/4/64. GJ wrote again to his ex-wife from the Carroll's property at Coolah on 7/6/64.

72 See Garry Kinnane, p. 234, citing interview with Anthony Kingsmill, 1983. Kingsmill remembered the initial meeting as being the day after Johnston left. It is clear from Rodney Hall's account that he and Charmian returned to Hydra the same day. The initial introduction at the Athens cafe by Jean-Claude Maurice can only have happened in the few minutes when Rodney Hall went out into the street, for he is sure that he met only the strange man who had been staring at him so piercingly. Rodney Hall, 10/7/95.

73 Ira Bruce Nadel, *Various Positions: A Life of Leonard Cohen*, Pantheon Books, New York, 1996, p. 80.

74 Information, Martin Johnston.

75 Ira Bruce Nadel, p. 80

76 Garry Kinnane, p. 238, states that Charmian Clift 'angered [George] with the suggestion that she bring Anthony Kingsmill with her' to Australia. No footnote is given for this assertion, and I have not been able to find any evidence that Clift wanted Kingsmill to accompany her — let alone that she told this to her husband.

77 George pressed Higham to get £500 from Collins as an immediate advance on CSFN and put it in the London account for Charmian to draw on. GJ to DH, 26/6/64.

78 Re publication: DH to CC, 23/3/64; re reviews: GJ to DH, 30/7/64; sales: Jacqueline Kern to GJ, 12/8/64; payment: DH to GJ, 7/7/64.

79 Information, Martin Johnston.

80 CC, 'Coming Home', IA, p. 2.

81 CC, 'On Being a Home Grown Migrant', TILL, p. 100.

PART IV — RETURN TO ITHACA

Chapter 19 — An Odd Sort of Migrant

1 CC, 'Report from a Migrant, Three Years After', TILL, p. 246.

2 Garry Kinnane, *George Johnston: A Biography*, Nelson, Melbourne, 1986, p. 244. For the 'quivering' comment, Kinnane cites interview with Mungo MacCallum (Snr), 1982. As to the list of 'old friends', the Nolans were not there; the Drysdales were new friends of George's.

3 Suzanne Chick, *Searching for Charmian*, Pan Macmillan, Sydney, 1994, p. 275.

4   Joan Flanagan, interview with NW, 6/4/93; email to NW 23/1/01; oral testimony (telephone), 24/1/01.
5   See CC, 'A Birthday in Kelly Country', IA, p. 145; CC, 'On Being a Home-Grown Migrant', TILL, p. 100.
6   CC, 'Coming Home', IA, p. 3.
7   CC, 'Fig Leaves and Fish Tails', IA, p. 30.
8   CC, 'The Joys of a City', IA, pp. 71–2.
9   Joan Flanagan, 6/4/93.
10 CC, 'The Joys of a City', pp. 69–70.
11 Jason Johnston, interview with NW, 5/4/98.
12 Martin and Shane arrived back just as the NSW secondary syllabus was in the process of a radical change. Martin joined the last group of students doing the five year Leaving Certificate course. Shane joined the first group of 'Wyndham Scheme' students, who would do a six year secondary course. Thus in the new year of 1965, Martin faced only one more year of school, and his sister faced the prospect of another three.
13 Jason Johnston, 5/4/98.
14 CC, 'On Lucky Dips', TILL, pp. 22–4.
15 Jason Johnston, 5/4/98.
16 Interview with NW, 5/8/91. This first appointment occurred in September 1964.
17 GJ to David Higham (hereafter DH), 25/3/64, David Higham Archives, Harry Ransom Humanities Research Center, The University of Texas at Austin.
18 GJ to DH, 1/5/64.
19 DH to GJ, 12/5/64.
20 GJ to DH, 25/5/64.
21 Garry Kinnane, p. 239, dates the 'General Notes on *Clean Straw for Nothing*' including the 'Particular Notes on Cressida' at being written while Johnston was at Coolah in mid 1964. From their tenor, however, it is clear that these notes date from the Hydra period. (eg Johnston notes in regard to Meredith that 'The one certain thing was that he had to save himself so that he could get back to Australia'). On p. 241 Kinnane himself describes these as 'the notes typed out on Hydra'.
22 GJ to Elsie, 7/6/64, cited by Garry Kinnane, p. 239.
23 GJ to DH, 28/9/64.
24 GJ, 'Introduction', *Images in Aspic*, Horwitz, Sydney, 1965, pp. 11–12.
25 John Douglas Pringle denies any part in initially engaging Clift, and states that he did not meet the Johnstons until the latter months of 1964. (John Douglas Pringle, letter to NW, 13/8/89, and interview with NW, 10/3/90.) As we shall see, John Douglas Pringle was not editor of either the *Sydney Morning Herald* or the Melbourne *Herald* in 1964, so he could not have engaged her.
26 There is quite a difference between the version of the first essay, 'Coming Home', as published in *Images in Aspic* (presumably from CC's original typescript) and the version published in the Melbourne *Herald*.
27 Margaret Vaile, interview with NW, 28/8/89. Vaile stated: 'The interesting thing about Charm was that she was basically engaged by the Melbourne *Herald* and we bought from the Melbourne *Herald*'.
28 CC, 'Report from a Migrant, Three Years After', TILL, p. 246.
29 CC, 'Coming Home', IA, p. 1.
30 CC, 'On Being a Home-Grown Migrant', TILL, p. 101. Although this was written after 16 months in Australia, it repeated these initial statements.

31 CC, 'Coming Home', IA, p. 4.
32 See CC, 'Joys of a City', IA. p. 69: first paralysis of terror at the size of the place; CC, 'On Painting Bricks White', IA, pp. 33–6: 'Australian suburban architecture is without doubt or question the ugliest in the world'; CC, 'The Sounds of Summer', IA, pp. 41–4 : re noise of lawnmowers, televisions, pneumatic drills, car engines, speedboats, planes, transistors, ice cream van, etc.
33 See CC, 'On Waste Not Want Not', TILL, pp. 44–7; CC, 'Hallelujah for a Good Pick-up!', BAWO, pp. 269–72.
34 CC, 'Coming Home', IA, p. 6.
35 CC, 'Social Drinking', IA, p. 11.
36 CC, 'Second Class Citizens', IA, p. 14.
37 CC, 'The Law of the Stranger, IA, pp. 81–4.
38 CC, 'On Lucky Dips', TILL, pp 22–24. The timing of this essay is clear, because the author refers to discussion of the issue at her elder son's recent seventeenth birthday party. Although the typescript is among the author's papers in the National Library, I have not been able to find it among Clift's newspaper publications.
39 CC, 'On Letting Asia In', WCC, p. 124.
40 Storry Walton, interview with NW, 19/3/90.
41 CC, untitled speech on problems of adapting MBJ to television, n.d. (internal dating shows it to be just before the serial went to air), GJ Coll., Box 6, Folder 9, item 17.
42 This is clear from the scripts. GJ Coll., Box 2, Folder 3, item 3. I also viewed a tape of Episode 1.
43 Storry Walton, 19/3/90.
44 This schedule was scribbled inside a manilla folder, later recycled to contain other material. GJ Coll., Box 2, Folder 2, item 2.
45 Storry Walton, 19/3/90.
46 Tessa Mallos, interview with NW, 12/10/84. Mallos played Jessica Wray, the artist's model.
47 CC 'Youth Revisted', IA, pp. 22–5.
48 Oral testimony, various Kiama residents, March 1983.
49 *Kiama Independent*, 24/11/64.
50 GJ to Elsie Johnston, 1/4/65.
51 DH to GJ, 27/4/64.
52 Garry Kinnane p. 247, citing interview Chester Eagle with Jack Johnston, 29/7/80.
53 Anne Deveson, interview with NW, 7/11/95. Subsequent quotations same source.
54 CC, 'A is for the Atom Age', TILL, pp. 65–6, *Sydney Morning Herald*, 21/10/65.
55 GJ to DH, 20/5/65.
56 CC, 'A Death in the Family', IA, pp. 101–4.
57 GJ to Jack and Pat Johnston, 22/7/65.
58 John Douglas Pringle, *Have Pen Will Travel*, Chatto & Windus, London, 1973, pp. 161–8.
59 John Douglas Pringle, 10/3/90.
60 Margaret Vaile, 28/8/89.
61 CC, 'Leaving for What?', IA, pp. 113–6, SMH 8/7/65. Incidentally, Pringle himself notes that his editorship was 'clouded by the Vietnam War', for he had problems with the *Sydney Morning Herald*'s commitment 'to supporting Australia's intervention'. John Douglas Pringle, p. 170.
62 Margaret Vaile, 28/8/89, raised this matter of the Grace Bros advertising. The Clift column moved to page 2 in September 1965.

63 It is hard to date this radio work precisely, but the ABC Archives contain a tape of a program which Clift did with Ellis Blain in the series 'Away From it All', 21/7/65. From the way Blain asked Clift to describe her life in Greece etc, it seems as if this was the first time she appeared with him on radio. It would make sense if his invitation to her came after this successful program. It is clear from CC to Jo Meyer, 10/11/65, that she was doing the program by November.

64 Anne Deveson, 7/11/95. Deveson quite often collected Clift from the Ben Boyd Road flat (into which she would soon move) and took her to the studio.

65 GJ to Joy and Felix Russo, 3/8/65.

66 CC to Jack and Pat Johnston, 17/8/65.

67 Jason Johnston, 5/4/98.

68 CC, 'A Birthday in Kelly Country', IA, pp. 145–8.

Chapter 20 — A Lone Woman

1 CC, *Kate Perrin's Life*, GJ Coll., Box 5, Folder 2, item 5.

2 Frank Doherty, 'Frank Doherty's View', *TV Times*, 15/9/65.

3 Jack Ayling, 'This Week with Jack Ayling', *TV Week*, 28/8/65.

4 Re ratings and popularity, see *TV Times*, 8/9/65, p. 6; 22/9/65, p. 5.

5 Jack and Pat Johnston, letter to the ABC, 2/10/65, shown to me by Storry Walton, interview with NW, 19/3/90.

6 Jack Ayling, 'This Week with Jack Ayling', *TV Week*, 21/8/65.

7 Frank Doherty, 'Frank Doherty's View', *TV Times*, 15/9/65.

8 Frank Doherty, 'Frank Doherty's View', *TV Times*, 22/9/65.

9 Storry Walton, 19/3/90.

10 Albie Thoms, letter to NW, 8/1/90.

11 GJ and CC, *Coastline*, GJ Coll., Box 6, Folder 1, item 3.

12 CC to David Higham (hereafter DH), 10/9/65, David Higham Archives, Harry Ransom Research Center, The University of Texas at Austin.

13 CC, 'Getting with the Forward-Lookers', TILL, pp. 56–9.

14 CC, 'On Waiting for Things to Turn Up,' TILL, p. 76.

15 Jason Johnston, interview with NW, 5/4/98.

16 CC, 'Living in a Neighbourhood', WCC, p. 108.

17 CC, 'On Waiting for Things to Turn Up', TILL, p. 76; *Sydney Morning Herald*, 18/11/66.

18 CC to Jo Meyer, 10/11/65. Re CC's claim that the flat was close to the hospital, it was more the case that it was close to public transport so that she could get there.

19 DH to GJ, 17/11/65.

20 GJ to DH, 27/11/65. Subsequent quotations same source.

21 DH to GJ, 17/12/65; 28/12/65 refers to the letter from Sir William Collins to GJ, 13/12/65.

22 GJ, application to the Commonwealth Literary Fund (hereafter CLF), CLF Records, Australian Archives, 19/8/67; CC, application to the CLF, 19/8/68.

23 Anne Deveson, interview with NW, 7/11/95.

24 GJ refers to CC 'giving radio talks' in his interview with Alan Trengrove, 'Partners — It's in Writing', *Sun*, 6/7/66.

25 CC, 'On Being Unable to Write an Article', TILL, pp. 86–7.

26 Royal North Shore Hospital Records: GJ out of hospital 18/12/65 to 05/01/66.

27 CC, 'We Three Kings of Orient Aren't', TILL, p. 99.

28 Jason explained that the Russos' 'real eldest son', Michael, had recently gone to boarding school, so 'in the family demographics' Jason was taking his place. He was only a few months younger than the oldest girl, Jenny. Jason Johnston, 5/4/98.

29 Royal North Shore Hospital Records; confirmed in a letter from Chris Bell, Medical Records Department, to NW, 1/3/96. The information that the tracheotomy was an emergency from GJ's first draft description of the post-operative period, written shortly after the event. GJ, 'CSFN draft iv', GJ Coll, Box 3, Folder 7, item 7.

30 Elizabeth Riddell, 'George, for Whom Working is Therapy', *Australian*, 16/8/69, p. 18.

31 Joan Flanagan, 'His Novels Were Born out of Pain', *Advertiser*, 12/7/69. This was the interview which Flanagan conducted in January 1969 (see chapter 23). Here the operation and post-operative experience is stated as occurring in Johnston's second period in hospital. This is a mistake. The author foreshortened the timescale by putting the insight into the most recent hospital experience, when indeed the bulk of the work on the novel was done. The draft fragments cited in the next footnote make it clear beyond any doubt that the hallucinations and revelations happened during the post-operative period in early 1966. Indeed, in his later hospital visit he did not have surgery.

32 GJ, 'CSFN, draft iv', GJ Coll., Box 3, Folder 7, item 7, 3 pages (two versions of p. 1, plus p. 2). On the first version of p. 1 the author has typed the novel's title neatly at the top.

33 GJ, CSFN, p. 29.

34 GJ, CSFN, p. 31. Subsequent quotation (re 'Jack Tars') same source. The 'social woman' also appears in the original draft, written in 1966.

35 Kay Keavney, 'From George with Sadness', *Australian Women's Weekly*, 3/9/69.

36 Kay Keavney, 'From George with Sadness'.

37 The fragment of the next draft (which exists in two slightly different versions) ends before David Meredith meets Cressida Morley, so her occupation isn't clear. However, as this opening follows the flow both of the first draft and of life, it is probable that Cressida remained a writer through these versions. See GJ, 'CSFN draft ii' and 'CSFN draft iii', GJ Coll., Box 3, Folder 7, item 7.

38 Martin Johnston, 'A Cartload of Clay', *Age*, 2/10/71.

39 Kay Keavney, 'From George with Sadness'.

40 CC, 'On a Lowering Sky in the East', TILL, pp. 111–14. Published *Sydney Morning Herald*, 6/1/66.

41 GJ Coll., Box 5, Folder 2, item 5, *Kate Perrin's Life*, material includes: Proposal for an ABC-TV Series, Draft Submission No 1, by CC ('or CC and GJ'), 30 May 1966 (five pages); attached to this is a later character description (2 pages); rough and completed drafts of Episode 1 ('The Wide Brown Land'); treatments of certain other episodes (e.g. 'The Suitor') and drafts of other episodes (e.g. 'The Demo'). Apart from the first draft submission, nothing is dated, but references to monetary pounds change to dollars as drafts go by, so it is clear writing went on into 1967. (This fits with Storry Walton's memory.) Footnotes will not be given for specific references to this material.

42 Storry Walton, 19/3/90.

43 *Kate Perrin's Life*, Draft Submission No. 1, p. 1, GJ Coll., Box 5, Folder 2, item 5.

44 This break occurred between 17/3/66 and 28/4/66.

45 Interview with NW, 5/8/91.

46 Royal North Shore Hospital Records.

47 GJ to DH, 25/2/67.

48 By the 1967 treatments of *Kate Perrin's Life*, the accreditation is 'CC and GJ', but it is clear that most of the writing is hers alone, and the stories are still the ones developed during the time when he was in hospital.

49 Johnston's earlier efforts at 'tele-plays' while in Greece were mostly unsuccessful. (eg GJ Coll., Box 4, Folder 13: GJ, *The Albatross Colony*, 1964; Box 4, Folder 14, items 20–22: GJ, *Bed of Thorns*, 1963; Box 4, Folder 15: GJ, *Clean Straw for Nothing*, 1963.) The only drama ever to be produced — *Beachhead* (Box 4, Folder 16) — drew on Johnston's experience as a war correspondent. During the early months of 1964 Johnston wrote the script for a drama called *The Party Next Door* (Box 4, Folder 12, item 17.) This, too, was never produced. Now, in a projected series called *Holus Bolus*, he turned his hand to the genre of situation comedy. GJ Coll., Box 6, Folder 3, item 6. Synopses for this sound pretty wooden.

50 CC, Speech on Adapting MBJ for Television, GJ Coll., Box 6, Folder 9, item 17.

51 Alan Trengrove, 'Partners — It's in Writing'. This was the conclusion of a series of features on 'Partners'.

52 David Marr (ed.), *Patrick White Letters*, Random House, Sydney, 1994, p. 278: Patrick White to Frederick Glover, 8/4/65.

53 Kate Perrin is driven crazy by relatives Valma and Ted Armstrong nagging her to move up the North Shore — where they live in dreary suburbia.

54 CC, 'A Sense of Property', TILL, p. 150.

55 CC, 'Goodbye to a Skyline', WCC, pp. 95–7.

56 CC, 'The Jungle at the Bottom of the Street', WCC, pp. 98–101; *Sydney Morning Herald*, 22/9/66.

Chapter 21 — Finding Australia

1 CC, 'The Cadences of the Bush', TILL, p. 241.

2 CC, 'Resolutions', TILL, pp. 202–3.

3 CC to Joy and Felix Russo, 1/1/67.

4 CC, 'A Room of Your Own', WCC, pp. 161–3.

5 CC, 'A Room of One's Own', TILL, pp. 213–6.

6 David Higham (hereafter DH) to GJ, 28/9/66. The other three letters along these lines were dated 3/3/66, 5/4/66, 7/6/66. Meanwhile, the authors had not even bothered to tell their representatives in America that they had moved from Kirkoswald Avenue. On 6/11/66 a letter from the Harold Ober agency to David Higham asked for the Johnstons' current address, as mail sent to Kirkoswald Avenue had been returned. David Higham Archives, Harry Ransom Humanities Research Center, The University of Texas at Austin.

7 DH to CC & GJ, 7/2/67.

8 GJ to DH, 25/2/67.

9 GJ Coll., Box 4, Folder 20, item 31: transcript of interview between GJ and Russell Drysdale, 21/3/67.

10 *Russell Drysdale*, written and narrated GJ, produced and directed Gil Brealey, ABC, 1967.

11 CC, 'The Cadences of the Bush', TILL, pp. 238–41.

12 CC, 'Report from a Migrant, Three Years After', TILL, pp. 246–9.

13 Anne Deveson, interview with NW, 7/11/95.

14 CC, 'Report from a Migrant, Three Years After', TILL, pp. 246–9.

15 The documentary was originally to be titled *The Seven Day Bicycle Rider*, as an obscure tribute to the painter's youthful habit of riding around the countryside seeking landscapes to paint. It would later be retitled *This Dreaming, Spinning Thing*. GJ Coll., Box 6, Folder 4, item 7, ABC letter of agreement (3/8/67) with GJ re documentary *The Seven Day Bicycle Rider*: fee of $2000; Box 4, Folders 17, 18, 19 (items 28, 29 and 30) contain some working drafts and transcripts of this documentary. For date of Nolan's arrival, see Folder 18, item 29.

16 The Johnstons had last seen Nolan for dinner in Sydney in April 1965. During this visit the painter denigrated his old friends, particularly George, to Patrick White. See David Marr (ed.), *Patrick White, Letters*, Random House, Sydney, 1994, p. 278: PW to Frederick Glover, 8/4/65.

17 Allan Ashbolt, interview with NW, 3/11/95. According to Nolan's version of this meeting in his biography, Storry and the crew were also present when he 'declined to support [Ashbolt] by agreeing to speak at a rally to protest against Australian and American involvement in the Vietnam conflict'. The painter added that Allan Ashbolt initially 'shocked them all by announcing that the film would have to be cancelled through lack of funds'; Nolan then 'offered to pay his own fares around Australia' as long as the film went ahead, and Ashbolt agreed 'to let the production proceed on a reduced budget and with an attenuated script'. Brian Adams, *Sidney Nolan, Such Is Life*, Hutchinson, Melbourne, 1987, pp. 194–5. This doesn't hold water, because shooting had started the minute Nolan arrived at the airport, and Ashbolt would not have let the cameras roll if he were going to cancel the project. I contacted Nolan in 1984 and asked to interview him, but he declined.

18 CC, 'Uncrating Mr Nolan', WCC, pp. 74–6.

19 GJ Coll., Box 4, Folder 18, item 29: *The Seven Day Bicycle Rider*, transcript of audiotape, 'Location: Lord Mayor's Reception', 7/9/67.

20 Allan Ashbolt, 3/11/95.

21 In a passage of *Clean Straw for Nothing* relating to this period, Johnston refers to the 'intense humility' of the Nolan-figure, Tom Kiernan, p. 63.

22 Storry Walton, interview with NW, 19/3/90

23 CC, 'Monday. On Talking and Writing', GJ Coll., Box 6, Folder 7, item 14.

24 In regard to timing, the retrospective opened to the public on 13 September, and Walton interviewed Nolan in Sydney on this day. There is no date on the transcript of the interview at the Olgas but 'Location: Waterhole & Budgies, Centre' is dated 26/9/67. Storry Walton remembered that they were in the Centre for about two weeks.

25 CC, 'The Great South Land', TILL, p. 288.

26 CC, 'The Centre', WCC, pp. 203–6.

27 CC, 'The Olgas', WCC, pp. 210–12.

28 GJ Coll., Box 4, Folder 18, item 29: *The Seven Day Bicycle Rider*, 'Location: Near Alice Springs'. This conversation reappears as a conversation between Cressida Morley, David Meredith and Tom Kiernan in *Clean Straw for Nothing*, in the 'Central Australia, 1965' section, pp. 62–5.

29 CC, 'The Olgas', WCC, p. 212.

30 GJ Coll., Box 4, Folder 18, item 29: ABC Radio Studio, Melbourne, Transcript of interview between Storry Walton and Sidney Nolan, 2/10/67.

31 This account of how the trip came about is from Garry Kinnane, interview with Ray and June Crooke, 1982, cited in *George Johnston: A Biography*, Nelson, Melbourne, 1986, p. 265. Kinnane seems to date the trip as occuring earlier in the year, and does

not connect it with the documentary filming. Clift's essays, however, make it clear that her trip north immediately followed her trip to the Centre.

32 June Crooke to NW, 3/4/85.

33 It is not quite clear how it came about that Clift went to Karumba. I initially assumed that June had also accompanied her there, but June Crooke (letter to NW, 30/1/01) insisted that 'we did not BOTH go to Karumba'. From the dating of the essays in the SMH, it is clear that the writer went to Karumba before Thursday Island. It seems that Clift went initially to Cairns, because regular flights from Alice Springs went to Cairns but not to the tiny settlement of Karumba. From Cairns she would have caught a small plane to Karumba and back, before teaming up with June and going to Thursday Island.

34 CC, 'The Gulf', WCC, p. 213.

35 CC, 'Karumba Observed', TILL, p. 280.

36 CC, 'Karumba Observed', TILL, p. 283.

37 CC, 'The Gulf', WCC, p. 217.

38 CC, 'The Island', WCC, p. 218.

39 GJ Coll., Box 1, Folder 3, item 4: CC's notebook includes a number of tombstone jottings from Thursday Island. CC, 'The Hippy Warriors', WCC. pp. 226–9 describes exploring the cemetery with June.

40 June Crooke to NW, 3/4/85.

41 CC, 'The Great South Land', TILL, p. 286.

42 June Crooke to NW, 3/4/85.

43 June Crooke to Suzanne Chick, August 1991. Part of 4 pages photocopied by Suzanne Chick and sent to NW, 29/8/91. Quoted with permission of June Crooke (30/1/01).

44 CC, 'On Coming Home', TILL, p. 290.

45 GJ, application to Commonwealth Literary Fund (hereafter CLF), CLF Records, Australian Archives, 19/8/67. GJ had written requesting an application form on 21/4/67.

46 This was in line with the way he had outlined his plan for the novel four years earlier, when writing to Qantas executive, John Ulm, whom he hoped would supply an air ticket to Australia. GJ to John Ulm, 19/11/63. GJ Coll., Box 1, Folder 4, item 6.

47 Kay Keavney, 'From George with Sadness', *Australian Women's Weekly*, 3/9/69.

48 GJ, CSFN, pp. 9–12.

49 GJ, CSFN, pp. 12–13.

50 The second 'Melbourne, 1945' passages opens with the line 'Gavin Turley was the shot — he would know' (CSFN, p. 24). This is from 'CSFN draft (i)', GJ Coll., Box 3, Folder 7, item 7. In the first draft, this thought occurs after David Meredith meets Cressida Morley in the lift of the newspaper office. David wants to find out how to get in touch with Cressida, and realises that their mutual friend, Turley, would know. But in the published version, Cressida is not working in the newspaper office and David has not met up with her again, and thus the plot does not have this 'trigger' that makes David want to know Cressida's whereabouts. The reader is left wondering what it is that Turley would know. Later Turley happens to mention Cressida Morley; only then does David even remember her. This changes the emphasis of the plot from the hero pursuing the woman he loves to a much more casual matter of happenstance.

51 Kay Keavney, 'From George with Sadness'. It is clear, however, that the kaleidoscope image could not have occured to the author at this earlier time, because even in this

interview the story leads on from the account of the Nolan retrospective — which was over eighteen months after Johnston's operation.

52 GJ, CSFN, p. 39.
53 The fact that it is really 1967 and not 1968 is confirmed by this detail: in 1968, Martin left university to take up a job at the *Sydney Morning Herald*. He also left home, so was not bringing friends around in the daytime in this fashion.
54 GJ, CSFN, p. 100.
55 WR Cumming, Secretary CLF, to GJ, 1/11/67, confirming telegram of 27/10/67; GJ to WR Cumming, 1/11/67, 6/11/67; payment statements (various dates). CLF Records.
56 GJ to June Crooke, 6/11/67.
57 CC to June Crooke, letter commenced 8/11/67, continued 9/11/67. Subsequent quotation same source.
58 CC to June Crooke, 18/11/67.
59 Interview with NW, 5/8/91.
60 Letter to City Coroner, 9/7/69 (Exhibit 2, Inquest held at City Coroner's Court, Sydney, 8/10/69).
61 I wrote to the psychiatrist on 5/8/96, asking if he felt he were able to tell me anything about Charmian Clift's consultations with him. He kindly wrote back (9/8/96), but noted that, after taking advice, he felt it best that he 'remain silent'. He added: 'I can say that I have no blockbusters up my sleeve, but I think I should leave it at that'.
62 Interview, 5/8/91.
63 The Boston Women's Health Collective, *The New Our Bodies, Ourselves*, Penguin Books, Ringwood, Australia, 1985, p. 444.
64 Interview, 5/8/91.
65 Jason Johnston, 5/4/98. Subsequent quotations are also from this interview.
66 Jason Johnston (5/4/98) noted that Shane's homesickness for Greece 'got worse' over time.
67 Suzanne Chick, *Searching for Charmian*, Macmillan, Sydney, 1994, p. 329.
68 Garry Kinnane, p. 278.
69 Jason Johnston, 5/4/98.

Chapter 22 — Public Property

1 CC to June Crooke, 18/11/67.
2 For example, the letters from women readers published in the *Sydney Morning Herald* after Clift's death range right across the city, from the posh northern suburb of Wahroongah to lower middle class Miranda in the south, and from the harbourside suburb of Neutral Bay to Blacktown in the outer west. Meanwhile, of the two male contributors to the valedictory letters, one, from the affluent eastern suburb of Double Bay, had become 'an inveterate reader of the Women's Section', thanks to Clift; the other correspondent was L. Paschalides for the Committee for the Restoration of Democracy in Greece, recording that Clift had 'endeared herself to the Greek people of this country'. *Sydney Morning Herald*, Letters to the Editor, 12/7/69; reproduced in BAWO, pp. 214–15.
3 *Sydney Morning Herald* Women's Editor Margaret Vaile remembered how one woman from the working class suburb of Padstow used to ring her (Vaile) every Thursday morning at her home in order to quote and praise that week's Clift column. Margaret Vaile, interview with NW, 28/8/89.

4 CC to DH, 10/9/65.

5 See NW, 'Introduction', BAWO, for a discussion of the classical traditions of the essay and Clift's place in the genre.

6 CC, 'Monday. On Talking and Writing', GJ Coll., Box 6, Folder 7, item 14.

7 CC, 'On Not Answering Letters', BAWO, p. 140.

8 CC, 'Feeling Slightly Tilted', WCC, p. 198.

9 CC, 'The Hungry Ones', BAWO, p. 49.

10 Sometimes there was even a dialectic of essay-response-essay, eg CC, 'Notes from Underground', BAWO, pp. 161–4; 'On Student Demonstrations', BAWO, pp. 245–8; CC, 'Requiem for a Spinster', WCC, p. 89; 'On Black and White Balls, BAWO, p.102.

11 For example, a flood of suggestions, offers of help and even sums of money poured in after Clift wrote about the plight of a widow who was tangled up in the bureaucracy of the Means Test. CC, 'A Home of Your Own', BAWO, p. 228; 'In Response to Letters', BAWO, p. 236.

12 CC, 'Hallelujah for a Good Pick-up!', BAWO, p. 269.

13 CC, 'A Room of Your Own', WCC, pp. 161–2.

14 CC, 'The Habitual Way', BAWO, p. 91.

15 For example, on one occasion, writing about the choice some of Martin's friends faced over whether or not to register for National Service, Clift made sure that all had decided to do so before telling the story, and she specifically declared: 'No, I'm not pimping'. CC, 'A Matter of Conscience', BAWO, pp. 85–86.

16 CC, 'A Room of Your Own', WCC, p. 162. The reference to these views of the 'television producer friend' appear in almost identical words in the notes titled 'Monday. On Talking and Writing', GJ Coll., Box 6, Folder 7, item 14.

17 Martin Johnston, interview with NW, October 1984.

18 Toni Burgess, quoted by Suzanne Chick, Searching for Charmian, Macmillan, Sydney, 1994, p. 285.

19 Suzanne Chick, p. 304. Burgess quickly added: 'It wasn't [a fraud]. It was real and it was true'.

20 CC, 'Karumba Observed', TILL, p. 283; 'The Great South Land', TILL, p. 286.

21 Suzanne Chick, p. 297.

22 Anne Deveson, interview with NW, 7/11/95.

23 CC, 'On Being Middle-Aged', TILL, p. 119.

24 CC, 'The Rule of the Olds', WCC, p. 194.

25 CC, 'On Being Middle-Aged', TILL, p. 121.

26 Ray Taylor, interview with NW, 2/3/90.

27 CC to Jo Meyer, 10/11/65. See chapter 20.

28 Vintage car rally: CC, 'Horseless Carriages', WCC, pp. 24–7; primary school: CC, 'The Magic Carpet of Learning', BAWO, pp. 178–81; new art gallery: CC, 'The Modern Artist: Pro or Con', BAWO, pp. 240–4; Fete for prisoners: CC, 'Victims of our Society', TILL, pp. 269–73; Christian ladies: CC, 'On Black and White Balls', BAWO, pp. 102–5; YWCA careers course: essay draft 'Women in the Future', GJ Coll., Box 6, Folder 7, item 14; planning meetings for Save the Children Fund, CC, 'Let's Save Some Children', TILL, pp. 217–20; charity luncheons: 'Kate Perrin's Life', GJ Coll., Box 6, Folder 2, item 5; young poets: CC, 'On Plugging Poetry', BAWO, pp. 61–4; Australian Writers' Guild: speech on Adapting MBJ for Television, GJ Coll., Box 6, Folder 9, item 17; Melbourne: CC, 'A Tale of Two Cities', BAWO, pp. 120–3.

29 Anne Deveson, 7/11/95.

30 CC, 'On Choosing a National Costume', TILL, pp. 115–8.

31 Anne Deveson, 7/11/95.

32 Cedric Flower, interview with NW, 17/9/89.

33 Allan Ashbolt, interview with NW 3/11/95; Allan Ashbolt, 'Charmian Clift — A Writer who Believed in Human Dignity', SMH, 12/7/69.

34 Patricia Rolfe, 'The Charm of Clift', *Bulletin*, 16/10/90.

35 CC, 'On Being Unable to Write an Article', TILL, pp. 84–7.

36 GJ Coll., Box 5, Folder 5, item 12. Some clippings are bundled in with essay typescripts, eg an article by Lilian Roxon on 'Rebellion in American Kitchens'; a bundle of items concerned with a widening range of cancers among women; a number of items about living conditions of Aborigines.

37 GJ Coll., Box 6, Folder 7, item 14. The topics for these include 'Phobias', 'Women in the Future', 'Cliches', 'Superstition', 'Sport', 'Parties', 'Television Ten Years Out', 'Civilians and War', 'Keeping Up Traditions', 'Charles Perkins', 'Weekends', 'Slang', and 'Alcoholism'.

38 CC, interview with Hazel de Berg, National Library Australia, 8/6/65.

39 Suzanne Chick, p. 305.

40 This matter of the deadlines would seem to require verification, because Garry Kinnane, p.278, notes that 'She frequently phoned her editor excusing her failure to get [the column] done because of "pneumonia" or "flu". Sometimes she did have such ailments, but that was often itself a consequence of prolonged drinking bouts, insufficient sleep and poor diet'. These remarks have been picked up by journalists such as Jan Pearce, 'On Reflecting the Spirit of Her Times', *Age*, 1/2/91. Therefore it should be put on record that Clift had two weeks holiday in September 1965, after eleven months straight on the column. In March–April 1966 she had five consecutive weeks off, officially because of her own illness but also in preparation for her husband's return from hospital. At Christmas that year she had one week off. In 1967 she had three weeks holiday in May–June and one week in August. In the twenty-three months between this August week and her death in July 1969, Charmian Clift had three weeks annual holiday in June 1968 and again in May 1969 — and not a single extra or unscheduled week off, despite the fact that in the last nine or so months she was also publishing a long essay in *Pol* magazine every four weeks.

41 Margaret Vaile, 28/8/89.

42 CC, 'On Being Unable to Write an Article', TILL, pp. 84–5.

43 CC, 'Banners, Causes and Convictions', WCC, pp. 253–5.

44 CC, 'The Right of Dissent', TILL, p. 179.

45 CC, 'Let's Save Some Children', TILL, pp. 217–20; 'On a Second Chance', TILL, pp. 258–61; 'Lamentable Brothers', BAWO, pp. 141–4; 'I Shall Not Want', BAWO, pp. 186–9; 'Some Thoughts on a Large Family', BAWO, pp. 261–4.

46 CC, 'Lamentable Brothers', BAWO, p. 142.

47 CC, 'I Shall Not Want', BAWO, p. 189.

48 CC, 'Lamentable Brothers', BAWO, pp. 143–4.

49 CC, 'Tomorrow is Another Day', BAWO, p. 43.

50 CC, 'The Hungry Ones', BAWO, p. 50.

51 CC, 'Report from a Migrant, Three Years After', TILL, pp 247–8.

52 CC, 'On the Right of Dissent', BAWO, pp. 106–9.

53 Clift's use of the term 'Big Daddy' also awakens echoes of Sylvia Plath's poem 'Daddy' written in the poet's last winter of 1962–63 and published in *Ariel* (1965).

This poem, in which the poet brings together her love/hatred for her dead father and, by association, her father-figure husband from whom she was recently separated, seems apposite to Clift's personal circumstances as well as those of Plath herself. It is likely that Clift knew Plath's work through her elder son, who was passionate about Plath.

54 Anne Deveson, 7/11/95.

55 CC to June Crooke, letter commenced 8/11/67, continued 9/11/67.

56 In her essay 'On *Clean Straw for Nothing*', she notes 'I've been living with *Clean Straw for Nothing* for all those years since *Closer to the Sun*' (BAWO, p. 312). This demonstrates the way she always knew that *Clean Straw* would return to the material of the first Meredith novel.

57 CC, 'On *Clean Straw for Nothing*', BAWO, pp. 314–15.

58 Martin Johnston, 'A Cartload of Clay', *The Age*, 2/10/71. This discussion of conversations when Martin came home from university lectures must refer to the writing of *Clean Straw* over the latter part of 1967 and into the first term of 1968, because after this Martin left university.

59 When I first read the typescript of *The End of the Morning* at the National Library in 1980, and came back to Sydney and told Martin about it, it was clear that he was completely unfamiliar with the subject matter of the novel that his mother had been working on. Even after this, he never read the typescript.

60 Martin Johnston, 'A Cartload of Clay'. Among the 'other writers' whom his father was reading at this time, Martin Johnston specifically mentioned Flaubert.

61 These notes are in GJ Coll., Box 1, Folder 4, Item 7: 'From Flaubert's *Madame Bovary*'; 'From Arthur Mizener's introduction to Scott Fitzgerald's *Afternoon of an Author*'; 'Elements of Jealousy (extracted from Eric Hoffer's *The Passionate State of Mind*)'. Reference to these texts and these notes crop up in the two 'London, 1954' sections of CSFN, pp. 130–40 and 154–68. In particular, quotations from notes which GJ made from the Hoffer text recur on pp. 154, 159, 162. On p. 159, the author states: 'I have been reading up a bit lately on the elements of jealousy'. References to the notes from *Madame Bovary* occur on p. 134; there is a further reference to Emma Bovary on p. 156. The notes from the Fitzgerald anthology don't specifically crop up in GJ's text, but Cressida's way of speaking in these London sections is similar to GJ's transcription of a bit of Nicole's dialogue taken from the story 'One Trip Abroad'. 'Why did we lose peace and love and health, one after another? If we knew, if there was anybody to tell us, I believe we could try. I'd try so hard.' It could be Cressida Morley speaking: 'I do think we have to try', Cressida says to David when the marriage looks at its worst. 'I'd try so hard'. CSFN, p. 287.

62 See F Scott Fitzgerald, 'One Trip Abroad', *Afternoon of an Author, A Selection of Uncollected Stories and Essays with an Introduction and Notes by Arthur Mizener*, The Bodley Head, London, 1958.

63 GJ Coll., Box 1, Folder 4, item 7: 'From Flaubert's *Madame Bovary*'.

64 GJ CSFN, p. 134.

65 GJ CSFN, p. 154. This paragraph goes on to include material from GJ's 'Notes for the Study of a Woman', and from the second page of his notes 'From Flaubert's *Madame Bovary*'.

66 GJ Coll., Box 1, Folder 4, item 7: 'Notes for the Study of a Woman'. For a long time the dating of this document puzzled me, because in the opening words Meredith's wife is called 'Kate'. I wondered why, after changing the name from Kate to Cressida,

the author had slipped back into the old name. Internal evidence makes it absolutely clear that these notes were written at the same time as the notes on Flaubert, and as the London section of *Clean Straw*. The slip in regard to the name is less puzzling when it is realised that the name 'Kate' was being used againat this time for the character of Kate Perrin.

67 GJ, '*Clean Straw for Nothing* General Notes', GJ Coll., Box 1, Folder 4, item 7.
68 CC, WTTPG, pp. 120–1.
69 Martin Johnston, interview, October 1984.
70 Virginia Woolf, 'Montaigne' and 'The Modern Essay', *The Common Reader*, First Series, The Hogarth Press, London, 1984, pp. 59, 217.

Chapter 23 — The Most Curious Sense of Exposure

1 CC, 'On Being Alone with Oneself', BAWO, p. 201.
2 CC, 'Concerning the Hippopotamus', BAWO, p. 25.
3 James Calomeras, interview with NW, 25/7/91.
4 CC, 'What'll the Boys in the Back Room Have?', TILL, pp. 294-5. In early February 1968, Clift let her readers know where these old habitués of the back room had got to: Mercouri in fact was safe in America, but stripped of her property and citizenship; Theodorakis was in prison. CC, 'The Voices of Greece', BAWO, p. 36.
5 CC, 'An Exile's Return', IA, pp. 95-6.
6 CC, 'On Gathering No Moss', WCC, p. 118.
7 Jason Johnston, interview with NW, 5/4/98. The dating of this 'slide' is confirmed by his memory that he was now in first year at North Sydney Boys' High.
8 GJ to DH, 3/3/68.
9 Letter to City Coroner, 9/7/69 (Exhibit 2, Inquest held at City Coroner's Court, Sydney, 8/10/69).
10 See discussion chapter 18.
11 CC to June Crooke, n.d. (clearly April 1968).
12 CC, 'Long Live Democracy!', BAWO, p. 65.
13 CC, 'Democracy Laid Low', BAWO, p. 78.
14 The virulence of the pro-Junta forces in this country should not be underestimated. Although the majority of the Greek community opposed the illegal regime, of course the consular officials supported the Junta. James Calomeras related that these officials tried to break the *Hellenic Herald* by threatening the travel agents (who provided a major part of the newspaper's revenue) that if they advertised in this anti-Junta paper their clients would not receive visas to visit Greece.
15 James Calomeras, interview with NW, 25/7/91.
16 'Democracy Laid Low' was written from her sick-bed. It was published in the *Sydney Morning Herald* on 16/5/68.
17 CC, 'In Praise of the GP', BAWO, p. 133.
18 Interview with NW, 5/8/91. It is clear from other sources that George's bed had been moved to the downstairs front room by November 1967. In one of her letters to June Crooke just after her return, Charmian referred to coming out of the bedroom into the living room to see the painting which Ray had sent her.
19 Garry Kinnane, *George Johnston: A Biography*, Nelson, Melbourne, 1986, p. 259. See also Suzanne Chick, *Searching for Charmian*, Macmillan, Sydney, 1994, p. 262.
20 CC, 'On *Clean Straw for Nothing*', BAWO, p. 311.

21 Cedric Flower, interview with NW, 17/9/89.
22 Allan Ashbolt, interview with NW, 3/11/95.
23 Mary Andrews, interview with NW (notes only), 24/7/89.
24 Among Clift's press clippings was an article by Lilian Roxon alerting readers to 'Rebellion in American Kitchens'. GJ Coll., Box 6, folder 7, item 14.
25 Patricia Lovell, interview with NW, 8/8/96.
26 Patricia Lovell, *No Picnic: An Autobiography,* Macmillan, Sydney, 1995, pp. 107-8.
27 Patricia Lovell, 8/8/96.
28 Jason Johnston, 5/4/98.
29 Interview, 5/8/91.
30 CC, 'Alcoholism', GJ Coll., Box 6, Folder 7, item 14.
31 Martin Johnston, interview with Hazel de Berg, National Library of Australia, 23/6/80.
32 CC, 'The Habitual Way', BAWO pp. 89-92.
33 Royal North Shore Hospital Records: GJ admitted 28/5/68; discharged 6/10/68. Re pneumonia see GJ letter to WR Cumming, Secretary Commonwealth Literary Fund (hereafter CLF), 29/6/68, CLF Records, Australian Archives.
34 There was no Clift column in the *Sydney Morning Herald* on 6/6/68; 13/6/68; 20/6/68.
35 CC, 'The Habitual Way', BAWO, pp. 89-92.
36 CC, 'On Flying the Coop', BAWO, pp. 249-50.
37 GJ to WR Cumming, 9/4/68.
38 Cedric Flower, 17/9/89.
39 Mary Andrews, 24/7/89.
40 Clifford Tolchard, 'My Husband George: My Wife Charmian', *Walkabout,* January 1969.
41 GJ to David Higham (hereafter DH), 29/6/68 David Higham Archives, Harry Ransom Humanities Research Center, The University of Texas at Austin.
42 GJ to WR Cumming, 29/6/68.
43 CC to WR Cumming, 20/8/68.
44 CC, application to the CLF, 19/8/68.
45 Jason Johnston, 5/4/98.
46 Anne Deveson, interview with NW, 7/11/95.
47 CC, 'Betrothing a Daughter', WCC pp. 77–80.
48 Jason Johnston, 5/4/98.
49 Clifford Tolchard, 'My Husband George: My Wife Charmian'.
50 GJ to WR Cumming, 2/10/68.
51 Royal North Shore Hospital Records: GJ discharged 6/10/68.
52 Kay Keavney, 'From George with Sadness', *Australian Women's Weekly,* 3/9/69.
53 CC, 'On *Clean Straw for Nothing*', BAWO, p. 315.
54 WR Cumming to CC, 19/11/68 (confirming telegram of 8 November, and setting out the terms of the award); CC to WR Cumming, 25/11/68.
55 WR Cumming to CC, 6/12/68.
56 CC's first *Pol* essay was in the first issue of the magazine, December 1968. She had an essay in each of the first ten issues, and was clearly writing the pieces two months ahead. (Essays appeared for two months after her death.)
57 James Hall, 'And Now It's Two for the Load', *Australian,* 23/11/68.
58 This is how George reported the conversation to Kay Keavney, in the interview for *Australian Women's Weekly,* 3/9/69. In CC's own account (BAWO, p. 315), she also makes it clear that it was she who pushed him to 'get rid of the damn thing. For better or worse'.

59 CC, 'On *Clean Straw for Nothing*', BAWO, p. 315.
60 GJ to WR Cumming, 28/11/68; Joan Flanagan to WR Cumming, 28/11/68.
61 GJ to WR Cumming, 14/12/68.
62 June Crooke, letter to NW, 3/4/85.
63 CC, 'A Sense of Ease', BAWO, pp. 196-9. Toni is not actually named in this essay.
64 Toni Burgess, interview with NW (notes only), October 1984.
65 Joan Flanagan, interview with NW, 6/4/93; James Calomeras, interview with NW, 25/7/91.
66 CC, 'On Being Alone with Oneself', BAWO, pp. 200-203.
67 GJ to WR Cumming, 10/1/69.
68 Joan Flanagan, 6/4/93.
69 'Notes of a talk with George Johnston on his new book: *Clean Straw for Nothing*, to be published in September 1969', 4 page typescript from Greeba Jamison's collection of press clippings. There is no author's name on this, but it is identical — apart from a couple of omitted paragraphs, such as this one — with the article by Joan Flanagan that was published in the *Advertiser*, 12/7/69. Greeba assumed that this typescript was sent to her with a review copy of the novel.
70 On this point, Flanagan stressed: 'You've got to think back to the time, what it was like in the papers. I can actually remember Alec Chisolm saying to me: "I read the *Herald* this morning and it was disgusting — there were 17 women's bylines in there, including yours." As if to say: "It wouldn't have happened in my time!" He was an old editor of the *Argus*'.
71 Joan Flanagan, interview with NW, 6/4/93.
72 Garry Kinnane, p. 273.
73 Maisie Drysdale, oral testimony, 18/3/94.
74 CC, 'On *Clean Straw for Nothing*', BAWO, p. 310, p. 315.
75 CSFN, pp 101–16. The travel diary can be found in GJ Coll., Box 1, Folder 2, item 2, black loose-leaf notebook, pp. 1–7. GJ has moved the date of the couple's first year in London back to 1950, and has therefore backdated this journey to 1951. The relevant passages are those headed 'France', 'Germany', 'Orvieto', 'The Loire Valley', 'Brittany' and 'Lerici'. Re Lerici see discussion chapter 11.
76 CC, 'As Others See Us', BAWO, pp. 224–7.
77 Jason Johnston, 5/4/98.
78 Jason Johnson, letter to NW, 28/3/98
79 Jason Johnston, 5/4/98.
80 For example, 'Come Off It, Kids',WCC, pp. 236-8, *Sydney Morning Herald*, 21/3/68: published around the time of annoyance and puzzlement with Martin.
81 Jason Johnston, 5/4/98.
82 Jason Johnston, 5/4/98.
83 Interview, 5/8/91.
84 CC to WR Cumming, 8/4/69.
85 CC, 'On *Clean Straw for Nothing*', BAWO, pp. 312-6. CC's typescript for this essay bore no title. It was titled by Pol 'My Husband, George', and was published posthumously. I gave it the current title when preparing CC's essays for BAWO.
86 There was no column in the *Sydney Morning Herald* on 1/5/69; 8/5/69; 15/5/69. This was in keeping with the annual break that she had around this time of the year.
87 CC, 'The Joys of Holidays', BAWO, p. 273.

88 Ten of Clift's typescripts in the National Library (GJ Coll., Box 5, Folder 6, item 13 and Box 6, Folder 7, item 14) bear either essay numbers (up to number 42) or page numbers (up to pp. 225-8). The other numbered essays must be the ones which ended up in *The World of Charmian Clift*, which Johnston edited after Clift died. The WCC essay typescripts are not in the National Library collection. Presumably they did not come back from the publisher after typesetting.

89 CC, 'The Joys of Holidays', BAWO, pp. 273-276.

90 Cedric Flower, 17/9/89.

91 It is obvious that it was during this period that she wrote the last three *Pol* essays — 'Winter Solstice', published in July; 'My Husband, George', published in August; and 'Wine Country', published in September.

92 Cedric Flower, 17/9/89

93 CC, 'Norfolk Island (1)', BAWO, p. 290.

24 — An Event In Life

1 CC, PMAL, p. 91.

2 GJ Coll., Box 1, Folder 1, item 1. GJ's red-bound journal, in which he had made notes for MBJ and CSFN, also contains 15 pages of notes for the third book of the trilogy.

3 The account of the projected end of this novel was given by Martin Johnston, 'A Cartload of Clay', *Age*, 2/10/71.

4 Sandra Hall, 'Time to Face a Modern Australia', *Bulletin*, 23/8/69. GJ told Hall that he had begun writing *Cartload* 'about two weeks before' his wife's death; he also told her the title and explained the classical reference.

5 Commonwealth Literary Fund (hereafter CLF) Records, Australian Archives. Fifth instalment has handwritten note: 'Hold final payment 26/5'. This sixth payment would have been due in June.

6 Jason Johnston, interview with NW, 5/4/98.

7 Jason Johnston, letter to NW, 28/3/98.

8 Jason Johnston, 5/4/98.

9 CC, 'Anyone for Fish and Chips?', BAWO, pp. 306–9; CC, 'Social Drinking', IA pp. 7–12.

10 Jason Johnston 23/3/98.

11 Allan Ashbolt, 'Charmian Clift — A Writer who Believed in Human Dignity', *Sydney Morning Herald*, 12/7/69.

12 Jason Johnston, 28/3/98.

13 Jason Johnston, 5/4/98.

14 Letter to City Coroner, 9/7/69 (Exhibit 2, Inquest held at the City Coroner's Court, Sydney, 8/10/69).

15 Interview with NW 5/8/91.

16 See Suzanne Chick, *Searching for Charmian*, Macmillan, Sydney, 1994, p. 176.

17 Maisie Drysdale, letter to NW, 2/4/00.

18 See Epilogue.

19 Jason Johnston, 28/3/98.

20 Interview, 5/8/91.

21 Clippings are among CC's notes and drafts for essays in GJ Coll., Box 6, Folder 7, item 14.

22 GJ to WR Cumming, Secretary CLF, 7/7/69.

23 Garry Kinnane, *George Johnston: A Biography*, Nelson, Melbourne, 1986, p. 280.

24 Suzanne Chick, p. 245.

25 Inquest held at the City Coroner's Court, Sydney, 8/10/69, p. 5, Information and Deposition of Witnesses, Deposition by George Johnston.

26 See Garry Kinnane, p. 281, citing his interview with Toni Burgess, 1982. Toni also told me this. Toni Burgess, interview (notes only), October 1984.

27 Inquest held at the City Coroner's Court, Sydney, 8 October 1969, p. 5, Deposition by George Johnston.

28 Her blood sample contained 260 mg of alcohol per 100 ml blood (equivalent to 0.26%). Inquest held at the City Coroner's Court, Medical Report — analyst's certificate.

29 Exhibit 3, Inquest held at the City Coroner's Court, Sydney, 8/10/69.

30 Letter to City Coroner, 9/7/69 (Exhibit 2, Inquest held at the City Coroner's Court, Sydney, 8/10/69).

31 George showed the note to the doctor, then put the note back where it had been, beside Charmian's bed. The doctor rang Mosman Police Station, and when Constable Parry arrived shortly afterwards, he took possession of the note. This is confirmed by Constable Parry's written Statement (21/9/69) and his Deposition to the Coroner's Court (8/10/69). The doctor remained in the house until after the constable left with the note. No one else had yet arrived, and indeed George did not start ringing people until after the doctor had gone.

32 John Keats, 'Ode to a Nightingale', *The Oxford Book of English Verse,* Sir Arthur Quiller-Couch (ed.), Oxford University Press, Oxford, 1939. p. 744.

33 For example, after confessing her adultery to her husband, Kate Meredith contemplates suicide while sitting on the cliff above the sea-cave in *Closer to the Sun* (p. 304), but agrees with her lover Achille Mouliet that it cannot be 'the answer' for her. In *Clean Straw for Nothing* (pp. 290–1), David Meredith stands on the same cliff and thinks about suicide after the confirmation of his wife's adultery, but finds the idea 'too terrifying [...] too cold and sinister and lonely'. Only minor characters, such as the potter Conrad Fegel (in CTTS) and Ernst Steindorf (in *The Darkness Outside*), carry out the action.

34 James Calomeras, interview with NW, 25/7/91. His wife Sylvia, who also worked at the newspaper office at this time, confirmed that these words were Shane's reaction immediately after she heard the news on the phone.

35 CC, 'On Tick and Tock', BAWO, p. 268. The author also attributed this idea to the character Ursula in 'Three Old Men of Lerici'. Garry Kinnane (ed.), *Strong-man from Piraeus and Other Stories,* Nelson, Melbourne, 1983, p. 19.

36 Interview, 5/8/91.

37 Elizabeth Riddell, 'George for Whom Working is Therapy', *The Australian,* 16/8/69.

38 Suzanne Chick, p. 302.

39 GJ, *A Cartload of Clay,* pp. 123–4. The notes in GJ's journal (GJ Coll., Box 1, Folder 1, item 1) include a passage to this effect, copied out from Camus' *Le Mythe de Sisyphe*. It is interesting to see George Johnston realising, at last, that his personal philosophy has elements in common with the existentialism which he used to loathe.

40 CC, PMAL, p. 91.

41 CC and GJ, HV, p. 266.

42 Half page untitled typescript, GJ Coll., Box 5, folder 22, item 46. (A continuation of GGTG, 'Alma narrative (d)'.)

43 CC, PMAL, p. 158.

44 CC, WTTPG, p. 194.

Epilogue

1 CC, 'The Kelly Saga Begins Again', BAWO, p. 302.

2 George Johnston died at home on 22/7/70, two days after his 58th birthday.

3 CC, 'The Kelly Saga Begins Again', BAWO, p. 302.

4 CC, 'Even the Thrush Has Wings', in Garry Kinnane (ed.), *Strong-man from Piraeus and Other Stories*, Nelson, Melbourne, 1983, p. 1.

5 Peter Coleman, 'To Charmian, a Daughter', *Australian Weekend Review*, 5–6/3/94.

6 For a penetrating analysis of Johnston's exploration of the Australian myth, written at the time of first publication of MBJ, see Barbara Jefferis's book review, 'Deep Feeling in Australian Novel of Depression Era', *Sydney Morning Herald*, 7/3/64.

7 *Sun*, 9/7/69, p. 11.

8 *Herald*, 9/7/69, p. 1.

9 *Australian*, 10 July 1969, p. 3.

10 *Age*, 10/7/69, p. 2.

11 Margaret Vaile, 'Charmian Clift — a Tribute', *Sydney Morning Herald*, 10/7/69. Reproduced BAWO, p. 213.

12 Allan Ashbolt, *Sydney Morning Herald*, 12/7/69.

13 Margaret Vaile, interview with NW, 28/8/89.

14 *Sydney Morning Herald*, Letters to the Editor, 12/7/69; reproduced BAWO, pp. 214–5.

15 As early as Saturday 12 July, the Adelaide *Advertiser* published the article Joan Flanagan had filed in advance to be part of the publicity for Johnston's novel. Now entitled 'His Novels Were Born Out of Pain', it was introduced with the note that it had been written 'before the death occurred suddenly in Sydney this week of George Johnston's wife, Charmian Clift'.

16 Sandra Hall, 'Time to Face a Modern Australia', *Bulletin*, 23/8/69, p. 56.

17 See Kay Keavney, 'From George with Sadness', *Australian Women's Weekly*, September 1969: Elizabeth Riddell, 'George for Whom Working is Therapy', *Australian*, 16/8/69; Sandra Hall, 'Time to Face a Modern Australia'.

18 See Owen Webster, 'Straw that Broke the Critic's Back', *Age*, 23/8/69.

19 Elizabeth Riddell, 'George for Whom Working is Therapy'; Sandra Hall, 'Time to Face a Modern Australia'.

20 Inquest held at the City Coroner's Court, Sydney, 8/10/69, p. 1. This suppression order was lifted, with certain conditions, in regard to publication of the note in this biography. Graham O'Rourke (Executive Officer to State Coroner) to Messrs Phillips Fox, 2/3/01.

21 'Suicide Finding on Author', *Sydney Morning Herald*, 9/10/69, p. 14. The same day's *Australian* was even more subdued, simply reporting the Coroner's finding and the events of the Wednesday morning. 'Author "Killed Herself"', *Australian*, 9/10/69, p. 3.

22 'Charmian's Death: Depression', *Herald*, 8/10/69, p. 9.

23 'Depressed Writer Took Life', *Age*, 9/10/69. This was a misquotation. At the end of George Johnston's Deposition, the Coroner had asked him: 'Had she ever expressed a fear of cancer?' and George replied: 'Yes, and in fact only the other day she had mentioned the fear of cancer'. Inquest held at the City Coroner's Court, Sydney, 8/1069, p. 5.

24 GJ, 'Introduction', WCC, Ure Smith, Sydney, 1970, p. 11.

25 Tom Rothfield, 'Island Legend for Sale', *Age*, 1/10/77.

26 Rodney Hall, letter to the Editor, *Age*, 20/10/77.

27 Patricia Rolfe, 'Child is Mother to the Woman', *Bulletin*, 22/2/94. Sue Williams, 'Searching for Charmian', *Mode,* April/May 1994, referred to them as 'Australia's golden couple, the dynamic and daring, though dangerously volatile, Scott and Zelda Fitzgerald of their age'. Adrian Mitchell, 'Inside Jack's Famous Brother', *Weekend Australian,* 4–5/10/86, also drew the parallel with Fitzgerald.

28 When interviewed shortly after Charmian's death, George quoted Fitzgerald: 'When in the lowest depths — Work, boy, work. It's therapy'. Elizabeth Riddell, 'George for whom Work is Therapy'.

29 Ruth Park, 'Nothing but Writers', *The Independent Monthly,* September 1989.

30 CC, 'On Being a Culture Vulture', WCC, p. 141.

31 *Age* Saturday Extra, 4/10/86; *Sydney Morning Herald,* Saturday Review 4/10/86; continued *Sydney Morning Herald,* Agenda, 6/10/86.

32 Margaret Backhouse, letter to the Editor *Sydney Morning Herald,* 16/10/86, letter dated 4/10/86.

33 John Douglas Pringle, 'Pushing Anarchic Life to the Edge of Disaster', *Sydney Morning Herald,* 18/10/86.

34 Robert Dessaix, *A Mother's Disgrace,* Angus & Robertson, Sydney, 1994.

35 Nikki Barrowclough, 'Charmian Clift's Lost Child', *SMH* and *Age* Good Weekend, 19/2/94.

36 See Claire Mills, 'Forecasts', *Australian Bookseller and Publisher,* February 1994; Peter Coleman, 'To Charmian, a Daughter'; Venero Armanno, 'Tragic Find', *Courier Mail,* 26/3/94.

37 Janise Beaumont, 'Daughter of a Legend', *Sunday Telegraph,* 13/3/94.

38 Helen Elliot, 'The Charm of a Daughter's Desire', *Australian Book Review,* May 1994.

39 See Peter Coleman, 'To Charmian, a Daughter'; John Douglas Pringle 'Clift: the Abandoned Daughter's Perspective', *Sydney Morning Herald,* 5/3/94; Nikki Barrowclough, 'Charmian Clift's Lost Child'; Sue Williams, 'Searching for Charmian'.

40 Janise Beaumont, 'Daughter of a Legend'.

41 For example, Claire Mills, 'Forecasts', referred to Clift as 'the celebrity who "tried too hard, drank too much"' and 'found peace in a Keatsian "easeful death" by barbiturate overdose'.

42 For example, Sally Loane, 'New Identity Calls for a "Big" Life', *Sydney Morning Herald,* 5/3/94.

43 CC, 'What Are You Doing It For?', BAWO, p. 40.

INDEX